ULTIMATE STAR WARS™

NEW EDITION

ULTIMATE STAR WARS™ NEW EDITION

Written by

Adam Bray Cole Horton

Patricia Barr Daniel Wallace Ryder Windham Matt Jones

CONTENTS

INTRODUCTION

If you're familiar with Ric Olié, the sando aqua monster, *Slave I,* Varykino, IG-88, Lobot, and Ewoks, you must be a fan of *Star Wars*. But if you recognize any of those names, that's remarkable because none are mentioned in the *Star Wars* movies themselves, so you must have gained that knowledge elsewhere, possibly from toy packages, comics, books, or pure osmosis.

Because numerous aliens, droids, starships, weapons, and locations are never identified on screen, it can be quite a challenge for fans to learn more about specific subjects. How does one go about looking up a subject in an encyclopedia if one doesn't know the name of the subject? That's almost as difficult as trying to pinpoint the origin of an unusual lethal dart for which no records exist in the Jedi Archives.

Fortunately, the editors, designers, and authors of *Ultimate Star Wars* are here to help. Unlike any previously published *Star Wars* reference books, this unique compendium features a wealth of images and information about many characters, creatures, vehicles, devices, and locations, each one presented in chronological order according to its first appearance in the *Star Wars* movies, *The Clone Wars*, *Rebels*, *Resistance*, and other official lore.

So if you're familiar with the *Star Wars* saga, you should have little difficulty finding what you're looking for. And if you're new to the *Star Wars* galaxy, I encourage you to keep *Ultimate Star Wars* handy as you watch the movies and TV episodes. Soon, you'll be a *Star Wars* expert, too!

RYDER WINDHAM

FOREWORD BY ANTHONY DANIELS

"Hello, I am See-Threepio, human-cyborg relations. How might I serve you?"

EPISODE I: *THE PHANTOM MENACE*

I didn't want to be in a film called *Star Wars*. Seeing Ralph McQuarrie's concept painting changed my mind. Instantly. That portrait, of a quirky metal figure staring bleakly from an inhospitable planet, sealed my fate. For the next four decades I would be doomed to wander strange planets like Tatooine, chill on the planet Hoth and party on the Moon of Endor. I would tread the halls of Cloud City and fear for my very survival in the Death Star's labyrinths and the burrows of Crait—all seen through the tunnel vision peepholes of C-3PO's eyes, so watching the finished films was always a revelation.

Another surprise, in spite of my initial reluctance, I'm the only actor to work on all nine episodes of the saga, as well as *Rogue One* and *Solo*. I've had the luck and the joy of being C-3PO—with or without the red arm—in lots of spin-offs too; in the animated series of *The Clone Wars* and *Rebels* and the ever-hilarious LEGO *Yoda Chronicles*. I even made the pages of this book, not just as the golden droid but as the seminal character, Tak, in *Solo*. Then there's my involvement in so many exhibitions and events and radio serials and concerts and Disney's *Star Tours* ride and… so, I should know every fact about *Star Wars*. I don't.

The saga overflows with such an abundance of exciting details that I really can't keep up. This book is a bit of a life saver for things I've forgotten, didn't know, or never understood and was too afraid to ask. It's a hugely significant and entertaining resource—an essential guide for anyone who wants to explore the details of that far away galaxy; particularly for younger fans, desperate to explain it all to their parents and grandparents—or the other way round. Because there are now three generations who love to share those enthralling worlds, at the movies and beyond.

The saga is unlike any other story in popular culture. From the moment, in 1977, when audiences ducked down as that Star Destroyer roared overhead, it has enchanted fans around the planet. Children and parents have been absorbed into a global family for whom the saga has become part of their own history and tradition. *Star Wars* is a truly international language and in these pages there's something for everyone. And everyone who studies them is keeping the story alive. It's a story that came from the inspired and inspiring mind of George Lucas. A story that became a reality through the work of exceptionally talented artists and craftsmen, for whom these pages are a terrific testament.

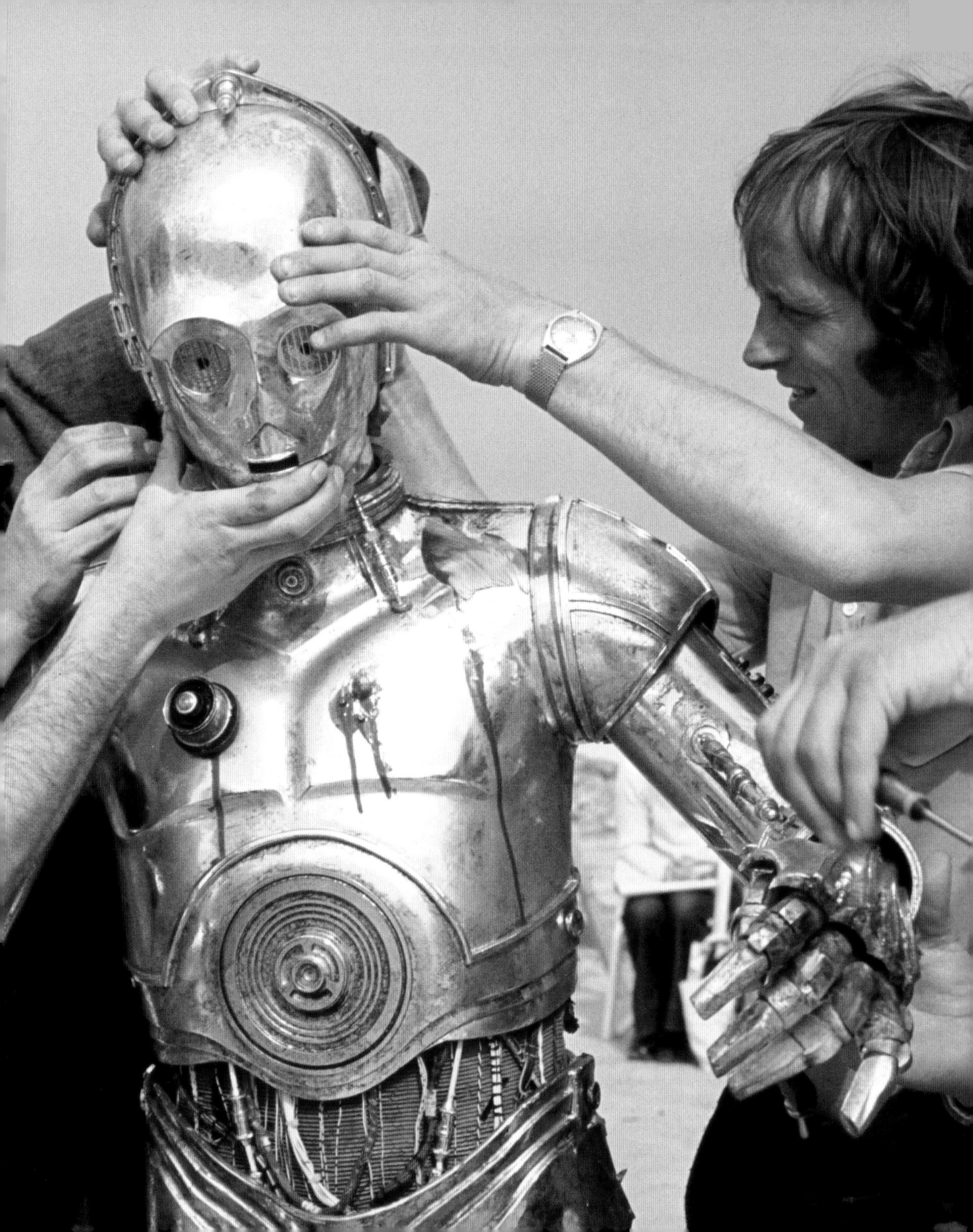

GALACTIC CONFLICT

The galaxy has been locked in a seemingly endless cycle of war. While the factions may change over the decades, there are always groups who want to enforce their will upon others, and those who rise up to resist them to fight for freedom and democracy.

CRISIS IN THE REPUBLIC

BATTLE OF NABOO
When the greedy Trade Federation invades Naboo, the planet's leader, Padmé Amidala, allies with the Gungans and the Jedi Qui-Gon Jinn and Obi-Wan Kenobi to resist. Together, they initiate a successful three-pronged counter-attack.

THE EMPIRE ERA

BATTLE OF ATOLLON
The Empire's Grand Admiral Thrawn tracks a large portion of the Rebel Alliance to Atollon and oversees a devastating assault. Thanks to Alliance leader Jun Sato's sacrifice and Hera Syndulla's tenacity, a small number of rebels flee to safety.

DUEL ON MALACHOR
Ahsoka, Kanan, and Padawan Ezra Bridger travel to the Sith temple on Malachor to find a way to defeat the Sith. While Kanan and Ezra escape, Ahsoka duels her former master, Darth Vader, at the temple's pinnacle.

MISSION TO MUSTAFAR
Surviving Jedi and rebel Kanan Jarrus is captured by the Empire and taken to Mustafar, so his friends embark upon a rescue mission. Kanan defeats the Grand Inquisitor and, thanks to the intervention of a larger rebel cell, he and his allies escape.

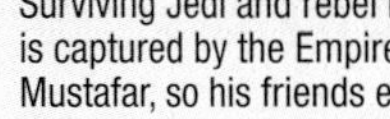

SHOWDOWN ON SAVAREEN
Alongside their allies, smugglers Han Solo and Chewbacca bring coaxium to Savareen to be given to criminal Dryden Vos. Following a sword fight and a shoot-out, Chewbacca and Han are betrayed twice and leave to start new adventures.

THE EMPIRE ERA

LIBERATION OF LOTHAL
Ezra and his allies commence a campaign to free his homeworld, Lothal, from the Empire. Although Kanan falls in an early battle, the rebels ultimately succeed. However, Ezra and his enemy Thrawn are transported by purrgil to an unknown place.

BATTLE OF SCARIF
Rebel Jyn Erso leads a rogue team to retrieve the plans for the Empire's Death Star, a weapon that can destroy planets, from Scarif. The Alliance fleet reinforces Jyn's forces and she manages to transmit the plans to the fleet, scoring a key victory.

BATTLE OF YAVIN
Having discovered a fatal flaw built into the Death Star, the Alliance attacks the battle station before it can obliterate their base. Anakin's secret son, Luke Skywalker, fires the critical shot, freeing the galaxy of this terror.

BATTLE OF HOTH
Following the Battle of Yavin, the Alliance eventually relocates to Hoth. It is, however, discovered there by the Empire. The Empire deploys AT-ATs to attack from the ground but the Alliance manages to flee with its fleet.

THE NEW REPUBLIC ERA

BATTLE OF CRAIT
The Resistance lands on Crait, hoping to hole up in an old Alliance base until its allies arrive. The First Order orders a ground assault, and Luke sacrifices his life to buy the Resistance time to escape aboard the *Millennium Falcon*.

DUEL ABOARD THE SUPREMACY
Rey travels to the First Order's *Supremacy* to try to redeem Kylo. However, Kylo kills the First Order's commander, Supreme Leader Snoke, forcing Rey to fight against Snoke's Praetorian Guard. Kylo takes over the First Order, but Rey escapes.

EVACUATION FROM D'QAR
The First Order sends a force to D'Qar to destroy the Resistance, which promptly evacuates. Disobeying direct orders, Poe leads an assault on the First Order's siege dreadnought. While Poe destroys the ship, the Resistance suffers heavy losses.

DUEL ON STARKILLER BASE
After Finn is struck down by Kylo, Rey summons her lightsaber with the Force to duel the villain. Kylo is surprised by Rey's power, and she defeats him. Rey escapes with Finn before Resistance pilot Poe Dameron destroys the base.

THE CLONE WARS

BATTLE OF GEONOSIS
On Geonosis, Obi-Wan, Anakin Skywalker, and Padmé are about to be executed, so the Republic launches a rescue mission. The situation escalates into the first battle of the Clone Wars between the Republic's clone army and the Separatist droid army.

THE SECOND BATTLE OF GEONOSIS
When the Republic learns that the Separatists have built powerful new factories on Geonosis, they decide to attack. Two Jedi Padawans, Ahsoka Tano and Barriss Offee, are instrumental in achieving a Republic victory.

BATTLE OF KAMINO
The Separatists initiate a sneaky attack on Tipoca City on Kamino. Using debris from Separatist ships destroyed in space, aqua droids on Kamino build crafts to launch a planetary attack but are repelled by the Republic.

THE CLONE WARS

DUEL ON MUSTAFAR
Palpatine ends the Republic, declaring that he will preside over the Galactic Empire. Obi-Wan travels to Mustafar and duels his former Padawan, Darth Vader. Obi-Wan leaves Vader grievously wounded and takes his lightsaber.

ORDER 66
The Jedi discover that Palpatine is a Sith, so they try to arrest him. Palpatine persuades Anakin to join the dark side, naming him Darth Vader. Then, Palpatine invokes Order 66, requiring Vader and the clones to annihilate the Jedi Order.

BATTLE OF CORUSCANT
The Separatists boldly kidnap the Republic's leader, Supreme Chancellor Palpatine, from Coruscant. Anakin and Obi-Wan Kenobi rescue the chancellor from the Separatist flagship and safely land the ship on the planet.

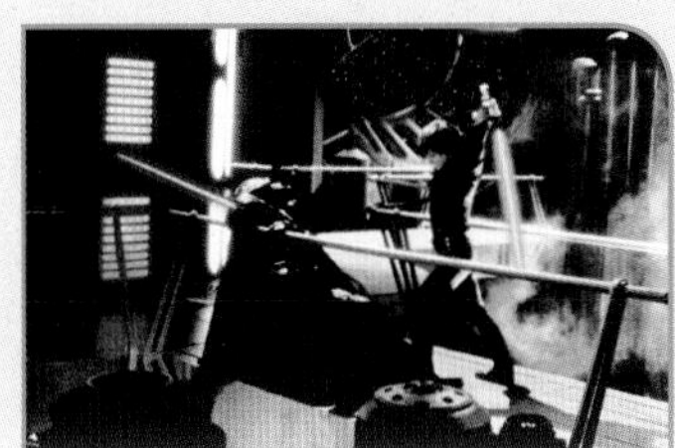

THE EMPIRE ERA

DUEL ON CLOUD CITY
While training to be a Jedi with Yoda, Luke senses his friends are in danger, so travels to Cloud City on Bespin. Here, he duels Vader and discovers that the Sith is his father. Luke loses a hand in the battle but escapes with his friends.

BATTLE OF ENDOR
The Alliance discovers that the Empire is building a second Death Star in orbit of Endor. While Alliance troops destroy the shield generator on the forest moon of Endor, the rebel ships attack the Imperial fleet and the station itself.

DUEL ON DEATH STAR II
Luke is brought in front of the Emperor on Death Star II. There, Luke duels his father once more and persuades him to turn against the Emperor. Now redeemed, Anakin kills his master. Luke escapes the battle station before the rebels destroy it.

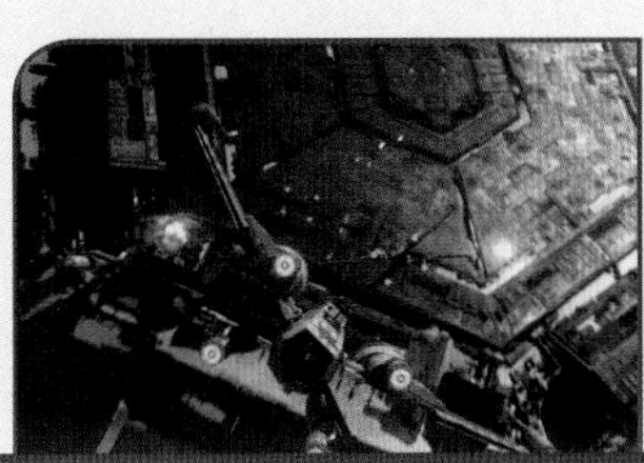

THE NEW REPUBLIC ERA

ASSAULT ON STARKILLER BASE
The Resistance witnesses the terrifying power of the First Order's Starkiller Base, so decides to attack it. Rey escapes the First Order and reunites with her friends. Together, they deactivate the base's shield, but Han Solo is killed by his son, Kylo Ren.

THE COLOSSUS RISES
Resistance agent Kazuda Xiono and his allies on the *Colossus* refueling station rebel against the First Order's occupation. Kaz and his friends activate the *Colossus*' hyperdrive and escape to an unknown location.

BATTLE ON TAKODANA
Both the First Order and the Resistance send forces to Takodana when they learn that BB-8, a droid who possesses part of the map to the missing Luke Skywalker, is there. While the First Order captures Rey, the Resistance recovers BB-8.

CHARACTERS AND CREATURES

Remarkable individuals, incredible life-forms, and sentient droids coexist throughout the galaxy. Space travel brings them together in fascinating, and at times combustible, combinations.

From the smallest scavengers and largest monsters on the desert planet Tatooine to the impoverished denizens, cultured aristocrats, and droid servants on the metropolitan city-planet Coruscant, the galaxy is populated by innumerable beings. Although not every civilization has achieved or acquired the appropriate technology, and some remain isolationists, space travel has led to commercial trade and cultural exchanges between thousands of worlds and cultures. It is not unusual to find literally dozens of alien species in any given spaceport.

For millennia, many planets have been protected by the Jedi, an ancient order of peacekeepers with seemingly supernatural powers. The Jedi maintain that all life-forms in the galaxy, as well as the universe itself, are bound together and connected by an energy field called the Force. The Jedi's battles with evil, power-hungry Sith and dark side Force-users leaves a significant impact on many worlds, affecting lives and the course of galactic history.

"The Force will be with you... always!" OBI-WAN KENOBI

OBI-WAN KENOBI

A Jedi and veteran of the Clone Wars, Obi-Wan Kenobi's achievements include surviving duels with three Sith Lords and training two generations of Skywalkers before he becomes one with the Force.

APPEARANCES I, II, CW, III, Reb, IV, V, VI **SPECIES** Human **HOMEWORLD** Stewjon **AFFILIATION** Jedi

GALACTIC PEACEKEEPERS

As members of the Jedi Order, Jedi Master Qui-Gon Jinn and his Padawan, Obi-Wan Kenobi, use their Force powers and training in service to the Galactic Republic. Like most Jedi, Obi-Wan is identified within six months of his birth and begins his training immediately so that he can learn to control emotions of fear and anger at an early age. For the first few years, Obi-Wan and Qui-Gon struggle to understand each other, until their Mission to Pijal, where they overcome their differences to stop a war. Afterward they become good friends and capable partners. Their final mission together is to Naboo, where they help free the planet from the Trade Federation. However, Qui-Gon falls in battle to a Sith, who Obi-Wan then defeats. Qui-Gon's dying wish is that Anakin Skywalker is trained as a Jedi, so Obi-Wan—who has just been knighted—takes Anakin as his Padawan.

Jedi Master and apprentice
Attacked on a Trade Federation battleship, Qui-Gon and Obi-Wan defend themselves.

Clone Wars heroes
Commander Cody and General Kenobi watch for enemies during the Clone Wars.

REPUBLIC ARMY GENERAL

Following ten years of training Anakin as his apprentice, Obi-Wan finds himself and his Padawan at the epicenter of the first battle of the Clone Wars. They are some of the few Jedi to survive the Battle of Geonosis, and both of them are promoted within the Order soon after. They are also conscripted as officers of the rapidly formed Grand Army of the Republic. As Jedi generals, Obi-Wan and Anakin Skywalker participate in many battles against the Confederacy and confront its armies or agents on many worlds—including Christophsis, Orto Plutonia, Felucia, Mandalore, and Utapau. Obi-Wan's diplomatic skills, specifically his reputation for preventing and stopping battles without using a single weapon, earn him the appellation "The Negotiator."

FRIENDS BECOME ENEMIES

Obi-Wan loves Anakin like a brother. However, after he learns that Anakin has become the Sith Lord Darth Vader and is responsible for destroying the Jedi Order, he attempts to bring his former friend to justice. Vader is unwilling to surrender, and they duel with lightsabers on the volcano planet Mustafar. Obi-Wan cuts down Vader and takes his lightsaber before leaving him seriously wounded on the shore of a lava river.

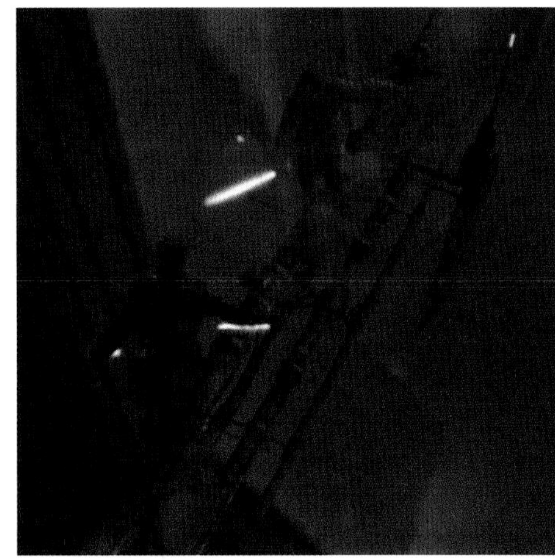

Heated duel
Anakin and Obi-Wan trade blows as the mining facility collapses around them on Mustafar.

Anakin's lightsaber
When Obi-Wan gives Anakin's lightsaber to Luke, he believes that Luke may be the galaxy's only hope for defeating Darth Vader and the Emperor.

SECRET GUARDIAN

After the Clone Wars, Obi-Wan delivers the infant Luke Skywalker to Anakin's relatives Owen and Beru Lars on Tatooine. Obi-Wan assumes the name "Ben" Kenobi and lives as a hermit in an abandoned hut while discreetly watching over Luke, protecting him from harm, even killing Maul when he tracks Obi-Wan to Tatooine and realizes who Luke is. Unknown to Darth Vader, Luke is his son. Obi-Wan knows that if Vader or the Emperor ever learn of Luke's existence, they will try to capture him and make him join the dark side. He also knows that if they fail, Luke could be killed.

From hero to exile
Throughout his entire life, Obi-Wan honors the ways of the Jedi Order by using his powers to help those in need. After the fall of the Republic, he assumes the persona of a hermit on Tatooine while secretly safeguarding Luke Skywalker and his family.

timeline

CRISIS IN THE REPUBLIC

Jedi training
Raised at the Jedi Temple on Coruscant, Obi-Wan is a rebellious youngling until he becomes Qui-Gon's Padawan.

Mission to Pijal
Obi-Wan accompanies his master to Pijal. Following disagreements, they work together to uncover a conspiracy and a strong bond is forged between them.

▲ Mission to Coruscant
While escorting Queen Amidala to Coruscant with Qui-Gon, Obi-Wan meets R2-D2 and Anakin.

▲ Battle of Naboo
Obi-Wan defeats the Sith Lord who killed Qui-Gon and promises to train Anakin to become a Jedi.

▲ Battle of Geonosis
Obi-Wan duels Count Dooku, a renegade Jedi who helps lead the galaxy into civil war.

Order 66
Obi-Wan survives Order 66, but learns that Anakin has become a Sith Lord.

Secret transmission
Obi-Wan's message warns surviving Jedi not to return to the Jedi Temple.

Duel on Mustafar
Obi-Wan defeats Anakin and takes Luke to the desert planet Tatooine.

THE EMPIRE ERA

Ending Maul
To protect Luke Skywalker from being discovered, Obi-Wan slays Maul in their final encounter.

Years in hiding
"Ben" Kenobi protects Luke from harm, including an attack by Tusken Raiders.

▲ Death Star rescue
Obi-Wan duels Darth Vader for the last time and becomes one with the Force.

Battle of Hoth
On the ice planet, Obi-Wan's spirit sends Luke to Jedi Master Yoda on Dagobah.

▲ Battle of Endor
Obi-Wan's and Yoda's spirits smile as Anakin's spirit returns to the Jedi fold.

timeline

CRISIS IN THE REPUBLIC

Jedi training
Raised in the Jedi Temple, Qui-Gon becomes the Padawan of Jedi Master Dooku when he is 12 years old and becomes obsessed with the prophecies of ancient Jedi mystics.

Mission to Numidian Prime
Dooku and Qui-Gon hunt down sadistic bounty hunter Shenda Mol, and Dooku uses Force lightning to save Qui-Gon's life.

Trials on Felucia
Qui-Gon's commitment to the Jedi Order is severely tested, but he remains loyal.

Taking an apprentice
Yoda asks Qui-Gon Jinn to take Obi-Wan Kenobi as his apprentice. However, Qui-Gon struggles to connect with Obi-Wan.

Mission to Teth
Qui-Gon and Obi-Wan stop the Hutts from stealing food shipments. Afterward, Qui-Gon is offered a seat on the Jedi Council.

Mission to Pijal
Qui-Gon and his apprentice are sent to protect the Pijali Princess. They uncover a conspiracy and prevent a war. Qui-Gon believes the time of prophecies is at hand.

Turning down the Council
Qui-Gon rejects the Council's offer to join it, as he has decided to dedicate himself to the Force. He later learns how to retain his consciousness after death through the Force.

Mission to Naboo
Investigating the Neimoidian Trade Federation's blockade of Naboo, Qui-Gon discovers that the Federation is determined to invade the planet.

▲ Mission to Coruscant
While escorting Queen Amidala to Coruscant, an emergency detour to Tatooine leads Qui-Gon to discover Anakin Skywalker.

▲ Battle of Naboo
Mortally wounded by Darth Maul, Qui-Gon Jinn instructs Obi-Wan to train Anakin to become a Jedi.

THE CLONE WARS

▲ Communion with Yoda
By the will of the Force, Qui-Gon's spirit survives, and Yoda eventually hears Qui-Gon's disembodied voice.

Communion with Obi-Wan
After Order 66, Yoda informs Obi-Wan that Qui-Gon's spirit lives, and that he will resume communication with Obi-Wan, teaching him to become one with the Force.

"Feel, don't think. Use your instincts." QUI-GON JINN

QUI-GON JINN

Unlike many Jedi, Qui-Gon Jinn is willing to bend the rules to achieve his objectives. His maverick tendencies and belief in ancient Jedi prophecies often clash with colleagues, including those on the Council.

APPEARANCES I, II, CW **SPECIES** Human **HOMEWORLD** Coruscant **AFFILIATION** Jedi

EMPATHETIC NATURE

Soon after arriving on the swamplands of Naboo, Qui-Gon rescues the Gungan outcast Jar Jar Binks from a stampede of creatures fleeing from the Trade Federation's invading warships. Jar Jar swears a life-debt to Qui-Gon, whose compassionate nature is such that he takes the hapless Gungan under his protection, much to the consternation of his Jedi apprentice, Obi-Wan Kenobi. With Jar Jar's help, the Jedi journey to the city of Otoh Gunga and obtain a submersible that allows them to proceed through Naboo's core to Theed. Noble, patient, wise, and closely attuned to the Force, Qui-Gon is also a cunning warrior whose greatest strength is perhaps his empathy for other life-forms, including the most unfortunate.

Deep trouble
Inside a Gungan submersible, Jar Jar, Qui-Gon, and Obi-Wan travel through Naboo's hazardous underwater passages.

THE CHOSEN ONE?

While escorting Queen Amidala to Coruscant, Qui-Gon and his allies make an unscheduled stop on the Outer Rim world of Tatooine, where he discovers a young slave boy named Anakin Skywalker. Qui-Gon senses that Anakin is strong in the Force and soon has reason to believe that Anakin is the Chosen One of an ancient prophecy, and is destined to become a Jedi, destroy the Sith, and bring balance to the Force. Qui-Gon helps liberate Anakin from slavery and resolves that Anakin will be trained as a Jedi on Coruscant.

Escape plan
Stranded on Tatooine, Anakin and Shmi welcome Qui-Gon, Jar Jar, and Padmé Naberrie to their home, where they plot to repair the latter's damaged ship.

THE DARK WARRIOR

On Tatooine, a black-cloaked warrior wielding a lightsaber attacks Qui-Gon. Qui-Gon escapes with his allies and tells the Jedi Council that he believes his opponent is a Sith Lord strong in the Jedi arts. At the Battle of Naboo, the dark warrior attacks again, mortally wounding Qui-Gon. With his dying breath, Qui-Gon makes Obi-Wan promise to train Anakin to become a Jedi.

Duel in the desert
Qui-Gon's clash with Darth Maul is perhaps the first battle between a Jedi and a Sith in a thousand years.

FROM THE NETHERWORLD OF THE FORCE

More than a decade after Qui-Gon's death, Obi-Wan and Anakin travel to the mysterious planet Mortis, where they are astonished to encounter a ghostly apparition of the slain Jedi. Qui-Gon's spirit tells Obi-Wan that the planet is a conduit through which the Force flows and that it presents great dangers for the Chosen One. He tells Anakin to remember his training and trust his instincts.

Jedi spirit
On Mortis, Qui-Gon's spirit maintains his belief that Anakin is fated to bring balance to the Force.

Jedi maverick
A highly trained Jedi Master, Qui-Gon Jinn is nonetheless an instinctive, restless soul who steadfastly follows his own path in bringing balance to the Force.

NUTE GUNRAY

APPEARANCES I, II, CW, III **SPECIES** Neimoidian **HOMEWORLD** Neimoidia **AFFILIATION** Trade Federation, Separatists, Confederacy of Independent Systems

Neimoidians are well known for their exceptional organizational and business skills, but Nute Gunray, Viceroy of the Trade Federation, is more unscrupulous and cutthroat than most. The assurances of his shadowy Sith benefactor, Darth Sidious, prompt Gunray to take the ambitious and blatantly illegal path to power as he oversees the blockade and subsequent invasion of Naboo. But Gunray's true, cowardly nature is revealed when Queen Amidala and her Naboo freedom fighters blast his droid protectors, reclaim their planet, and declare the Trade Federation's occupation is over. Thanks to his organization's resources, Gunray is found not guilty during the fourth Republic trial on the invasion of Naboo. During the Clone Wars, Nute Gunray continues to obey the Sith Lords. While hiding on the planet Mustafar, he is unprepared when Darth Vader arrives to kill him.

Separatist ally
When Count Dooku invites the Trade Federation to join the Separatists, Gunray insists that Dooku first disposes of Padmé Amidala, against whom he holds a personal grudge.

"Your feeble skills are no match for the power of the dark side."

EMPEROR PALPATINE

SHEEV PALPATINE

A seemingly unassuming representative of the peaceful planet Naboo, Palpatine is in fact the Sith Lord Darth Sidious, who schemes to destroy the Jedi Order and rule the galaxy as Emperor.

APPEARANCES I, II, CW, III, Reb, V, VI **SPECIES** Human **HOMEWORLD** Naboo **AFFILIATION** Republic, Sith, Empire

SENATOR OF NABOO

When the Trade Federation invades Naboo, Queen Amidala seeks advice from Palpatine, who serves as Naboo's representative in the Galactic Senate. Palpatine confides that the Republic's leader, Supreme Chancellor Valorum, has little power in the Senate and that bureaucrats are in charge. Palpatine adds that if Amidala wants the Trade Federation brought to justice, her best course of action is to call for a vote of no confidence in Valorum and then push for the election of a stronger leader. At Palpatine's urging, Amidala follows his advice, and Valorum is forced to leave office. To Amidala's surprise, the Senate elects Palpatine as Supreme Chancellor.

Meeting Anakin
After the Battle of Naboo, Palpatine meets the young pilot who helped defeat the Trade Federation's invasion force.

POLITICAL MANEUVERING

After the Senate learns that the Separatists are using Geonosian foundries to manufacture a massive droid army, the senators vote to grant emergency powers to Supreme Chancellor Palpatine. This vote enables Palpatine to immediately activate an army of clones to fight the Separatists, even though the Jedi Order is baffled by the clones' dubious origins. Palpatine professes his regret that the civil war requires him to take emergency powers, and claims that he looks forward to relinquishing those powers when the war is over. During the ensuing Clone Wars, Palpatine assumes even more responsibilities; his many duties include working with the Senate to pass laws to fund the war and to prevent bureaucracy from interfering with programs that the Jedi Council considers vital to the war effort.

Supreme leader
Palpatine addresses the Senate at the height of the Clone Wars, convincing it to grant him full autonomy to successfully prosecute the war.

SITH LORD REVEALED!

In the last days of the Clone Wars, Palpatine tells Anakin a story about the Sith Lord Darth Plagueis, who used the Force to create life and prevent death. According to Palpatine, only the dark side of the Force offers a route to Plagueis' secrets. Palpatine later reveals that he himself is a Sith—Darth Sidious—and promises to teach Anakin his dark side knowledge if Anakin allies with him. As a Jedi, Anakin knows it is his duty to stop Palpatine. However, nightmarish visions of his beloved Padmé dying in childbirth convince him that only Palpatine's Sith powers can save her. Anakin agrees to become Sidious' apprentice, Darth Vader, and to crush the Jedi Order. Palpatine then declares himself Galactic Emperor.

Sith secrets
In his chambers, Palpatine draws Anakin into his confidence by revealing his true identity and suspicions about the Jedi's seditious activities.

IMPERIAL EXPANSION

Throughout his reign, Palpatine expands his dictatorship's reach across the galaxy by bringing more systems under Imperial control. Nineteen years into his rule, Palpatine dissolves the Galactic Senate and places governing power in the hands of regional Moffs. While the Empire promises order and justice to far-flung worlds, their citizens pay a heavy price as the Empire presses them into service and exploits their systems' resources. This Imperial expansion is necessary to successfully sustain myriad secret projects, including the Death Star battle station, a growing fleet of Super Star Destroyer Dreadnoughts, and the advanced weapons research program known as the Tarkin Initiative.

The World between Worlds
One of Palpatine's aims is to control the World between Worlds, presumably so he can have dominion over all time and space. When Ezra Bridger visits the place and saves Ahsoka Tano from death, Palpatine attempts to capture them, but they escape his clutches.

THE EMPEROR'S DOWNFALL

Palpatine meets his fate at the hands of his apprentice, Darth Vader. In a bid to protect his son, Luke Skywalker, Vader hurls his master down the second Death Star's core to a fiery death. The Emperor's defeat puts into motion his final secret plan known as the Contingency. Upon his death, select Imperial leaders are instructed to carry out Operation: Cinder, a plot devised by Palpatine to punish many of the worlds that he deemed had failed him. In the ensuing chaos, select Imperials are under instruction to flee to the Unknown Regions of the galaxy and rebuild—in the hope that they can return someday and rule once more.

Before the fall
Having lured Luke to the Death Star, Palpatine manipulates the young Jedi into a fight with his father, Darth Vader.

The phantom menace
Palpatine's true goals are known only to himself, but to achieve them he uses a terrifying combination of political intrigue, deception, ruthlessness, and raw dark side power.

timeline

CRISIS IN THE REPUBLIC

Path to the dark side
A native of Naboo, Palpatine secretly becomes Darth Sidious, apprentice to the Sith Lord Darth Plagueis. He eventually kills Plagueis and assumes the mantle of Sith Master.

Mission to Dathomir
Darth Sidious takes a male Zabrak infant named Maul from Dathomir and raises him as his apprentice.

▲ Galactic Senate
Keeping his Sith Lord identity secret, Palpatine becomes a senator of Naboo.

▲ Battle of Naboo
Palpatine manipulates events to become Supreme Chancellor. Darth Sidious instructs Darth Maul to kill Queen Amidala, but Maul fails. Palpatine then meets Anakin Skywalker.

THE CLONE WARS

Secret machinations
After Darth Sidious takes Count Dooku as his new apprentice, they conspire to conquer the galaxy.

The apprentice returns
Having survived the Battle of Naboo, Maul tries, but fails, to take revenge on Darth Sidious.

Battle of Coruscant
Captured by General Grievous, Palpatine manipulates Anakin Skywalker to kill Count Dooku and lures him to the dark side. Anakin becomes the Sith apprentice Darth Vader.

▲ Order 66
A Jedi task force learns that Palpatine is a Sith Lord and tries to capture him. Palpatine kills them, but his own Force lightning leaves him disfigured.

THE EMPIRE ERA

Galactic Empire
After destroying the Jedi Order, Palpatine seizes power and declares himself Emperor. He recovers the wounded Darth Vader from Mustafar and transforms him into a cybernetic nightmare.

The Death Star
The Emperor directs Vader to oversee the construction of the enormous Imperial battle station.

Dangerous enemies
Palpatine survives an assassination attempt organized by the freedom fighter Cham Syndulla in the Ryloth system.

Tempting Ezra Bridger
Palpatine tries to persuade Ezra Bridger to open a portal to the World between Worlds so he can spend time with his dead parents, but he refuses.

Battle of Endor
On the second Death Star, the Emperor fails to lure Luke Skywalker to the dark side and also does not anticipate Darth Vader's fatal attack.

"I will not condone a course of action that will lead us to war." QUEEN AMIDALA

PADMÉ AMIDALA

A representative of her idyllic homeworld, and an idealist during a time of corruption and war, Padmé Amidala is determined to do what she can to right wrongs in the ailing Republic.

APPEARANCES I, II, CW, III, FoD **SPECIES** Human **HOMEWORLD** Naboo **AFFILIATION** Royal House of Naboo, Galactic Senate

ROYAL SERVICE

Born to humble parents on Naboo, Padmé Naberrie dedicates herself to public service, joining the Apprentice Legislature at the age of eight. She is elected Queen of Naboo at the age of 14, adopting the formal name Queen Amidala, and her loyal staff includes five handmaidens. When the Trade Federation invades Naboo, Amidala and one of her handmaidens, Sabé, disguise themselves as each other. While pretending to be a handmaiden, Padmé makes an emergency detour to Tatooine and there meets the slave boy Anakin Skywalker, who joins her on her trip to Coruscant. When she arrives on the planet, the Galactic Senate fails to help her, so she upends the Senate by triggering a new election for its leader. With no help forthcoming, Padmé returns to her home, where she allies with the Gungans to free her planet. Padmé is so beloved by her people that some attempt to change Naboo's constitution so she can serve longer, but she refuses.

Retaking the palace
Padmé is trained for combat extensively by Captain Panaka. She puts her skills to use during the assault on the Royal Palace.

SENATORIAL LIFE

Padmé is surprised when her successor, Queen Réillata, asks her to serve as the senator of Naboo. While Padmé had planned to spend her time freeing slaves on Tatooine (including Anakin's mother, Shmi), she accepts the new job and Sabé covertly assists her. Padmé excels as a senator, and her first major piece of legislation, the Mid Rim Cooperation Motion, saves millions on Bromlarch from starvation. Years later, Padmé is nearly assassinated on Coruscant, so retreats in secret to Naboo with Anakin as her Jedi protector. When Anakin senses Shmi is in danger they both travel to Tatooine, but cannot save Shmi from death. They then head to Geonosis to help Obi-Wan Kenobi and survive the first battle of the Clone Wars. Having fallen in love during their reunion, Padmé and Anakin marry in secret.

Aggressive negotiaions
While Padmé would rather not resort to violence, she is more than prepared to defend herself if the need arises. Padmé survives the Battle of Geonosis, even though more than 100 Jedi do not.

Secret trip
Padmé arrives on Raxus, alongside Anakin's Jedi Padawan, Ahsoka Tano, to meet with Mina Bonteri.

During the Clone Wars, the galaxy becomes a dangerous place for a loyalist senator, but Padmé journeys to many trouble spots—including Rodia, Mandalore, Batuu, and Scipio—in her efforts to use diplomacy to resolve problems. She tries to reconnect with her old friend Mina Bonteri—a former Republic senator who is now part of the Separatist Senate. They work together to achieve a peaceful solution to the Clone Wars. While their motion passes in the Separatist Senate, General Grievous attacks Coruscant's power supply as the Republic vote is taking place. The terrorist attack strikes fear into the Republic's senators and stops the motion passing. Count Dooku also orders Bonteri to be killed, publically claiming that she died in a Republic attack. Thanks to Dooku and Grievous, peace talks on both sides are abandoned.

THE TWILIGHT OF THE REPUBLIC

When Anakin returns from the Battle of Coruscant, Padmé reveals that she is pregnant. Like the rest of the Republic, Padmé is unaware that Chancellor Palpatine is actually a Sith Lord. When Anakin learns of Palpatine's identity, he tells Jedi Master Windu, who leads a team to arrest Palpatine. While Palpatine easily kills most of the team, he can only defeat Windu after he persuades Anakin to turn on his fellow Jedi. Unaware of Anakin's involvement, Padmé is shocked when Windu's actions are used by the chancellor as pretext to declare the founding of the Galactic Empire and to annihilate the whole Jedi Order. Obi-Wan then tells Padmé that Anakin has turned to evil and become Palpatine's Sith apprentice. She travels to the planet Mustafar to confront Anakin, but he becomes enraged and nearly kills her. Obi-Wan defeats Anakin in a terrible duel, before rushing Padmé to a medical facility, where she gives birth to twins. Tragically, she dies afterward, leaving behind her children, who will go on to liberate the galaxy from the Empire and restore democracy.

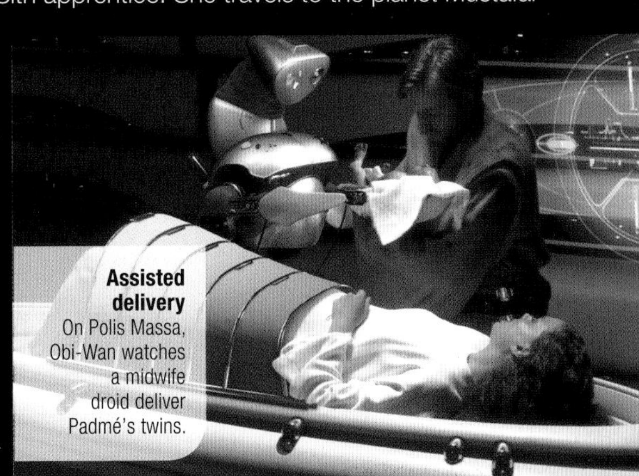

Assisted delivery
On Polis Massa, Obi-Wan watches a midwife droid deliver Padmé's twins.

Crafted couture
Queen Amidala's gown is covered with historic symbols that express the majesty of the free people of Naboo. Her elaborate gown also serves to protect her, as it is blaster resistant and can be easily shed if required. Much of her jewelry conceals useful, hidden gadgets.

timeline

CRISIS IN THE REPUBLIC

Early life
At age 8, Padmé Naberrie joins the Apprentice Legislators on Naboo and later becomes a Senatorial adviser.

Democratic queen
At age 14, Padmé is elected Queen of Naboo and adopts Amidala as her name of office.

Invasion of Naboo
Failing to prevent the Trade Federation's invasion, Padmé leaves Naboo to get help from the Republic.

▲ Tatooine detour
Briefly stranded on Tatooine, Padmé meets Anakin, C-3PO, and Anakin's mother, Shmi.

Battle of Naboo
With help from the Jedi and the Gungans, Padmé defeats the Federation's droid troops.

Senator of Naboo
After her term as queen ends, Padmé becomes the senator of Naboo, narrowly avoiding an attempt on her life in the first six weeks.

Saving Bromlarch
Padmé ingeniously constructs the Mid Rim Cooperation Motion, which saves the inhabitants of Bromlarch from devastation.

Assassination attempts
Anakin and Obi-Wan are assigned to protect Senator Amidala from an assassin on Coruscant. A further assassination attempt prompts Padmé to discreetly return to Naboo with Anakin.

THE CLONE WARS

Battle of Geonosis
Padmé attempts to prevent civil war, but the Senate conscripts an army of clones to fight the Separatists' droids.

▲ Secret wedding
After declaring their love for each other, Padmé and Anakin are married on Naboo. Because Jedi are forbidden to marry, they choose to keep their union a secret.

▲ The Clone Wars
Padmé fights a losing battle to maintain democracy among the worlds that have yet to defect to the Confederacy of Independent Systems.

THE EMPIRE ERA

Order 66
After the destruction of the Jedi Temple, a fugitive Obi-Wan informs Padmé that Anakin has turned to the dark side and is responsible for the deaths of many Jedi. Padmé leaves for Mustafar to help Anakin, but her husband attempts to kill her and Obi-Wan.

▲ Funeral on Naboo
After Padmé dies, her body is brought back to Naboo, where her people sadly mourn her passing.

SIO BIBBLE

APPEARANCES I, II, CW, III
SPECIES Human **HOMEWORLD** Naboo
AFFILIATION Royal House of Naboo

Sio Bibble is a noble philosopher and member of the Naboo Royal Advisory Council, elected Governor of Naboo during King Veruna's reign. Bibble serves many successive monarchs, aiding them in their regal duties, and deals directly with regional representatives. He remains on Naboo during the Trade Federation's occupation of the planet while Queen Amidala travels to Coruscant to secure aid. Years later, he attends former Queen Amidala's funeral and retires shortly after.

QUARSH PANAKA

APPEARANCES I **SPECIES** Human
HOMEWORLD Naboo
AFFILIATION Royal Naboo Security Forces, Empire

The brave and resourceful Quarsh Panaka first sees action fighting pirates in his homeworld's space sector. He goes on to become the captain of Queen Amidala's Security Forces. Although he trained his forces well, he knows that his world is vulnerable to a planetary assault and argues for stronger security measures, but his counsel is unheeded. After the Trade Federation's invasion begins, Panaka accompanies the queen to Coruscant so that she can submit an appeal to the Galactic Senate to bolster Naboo's defenses, and then participates in the battle to free Naboo. Panaka continues to serve Amidala throughout her reign, but their relationship becomes strained after they disagree again over the level of defenses for Naboo. He retires when Queen Amidala's sovereignty ends.

After Governor Bibble retires, the Empire makes Panaka a Moff, and he quickly implements change on Naboo. Years later, he hosts Princess Leia Organa and suspects she is related to Padmé Amidala. Before he can convey his theory to Palpatine, he is assassinated by rebel extremist Saw Gerrera—who unwittingly helps keep Leia's parentage secret.

Royal security
The highly capable Captain Panaka *(left)* leads the Naboo Royal Security Forces, the closest thing to a regular infantry on Naboo. Intensely loyal, Panaka fights alongside Padmé during the Battle of Naboo, as they face heavy fire in the halls of Theed Palace *(above)*.

OOM-9

APPEARANCES I **MODEL** OOM command battle droid **MANUFACTURER** Baktoid Combat Automata **AFFILIATION** Trade Federation

Like all B1 battle droids, OOM-9 is incapable of independent thinking, and receives instructions from a central source aboard a Trade Federation Droid Control Ship. However, OOM-9 was specially programmed to serve as a command droid for the Federation's invasion of Naboo, and to act as the primary contact for the Federation's leaders, the Neimoidians Nute Gunray and Rune Haako. On Naboo, OOM-9 directs droid ground troops and pilots to occupy settlements and destroy communication transmitters, preventing the planet's citizens from reporting the invasion or summoning help. OOM-9 leads the battle droids against Gungan warriors in the Battle of Naboo.

Receiving orders
Communicating via hologram, the Trade Federation leaders direct OOM-9 during the invasion of Naboo.

Leader in the field
OOM-9 signals Trade Federation Multi-Troop Transports and armored assault tanks to move into position as the Battle of Naboo commences.

KAADU

APPEARANCES I, CW **HOMEWORLD** Naboo
SIZE 2 m (7 ft) tall **HABITAT** Swamps

Kaadu are two-legged reptavians indigenous to Naboo. They are swift, agile creatures with sharp hearing and a keen sense of smell, and although primarily land-dwellers, they can also breathe underwater for extended periods. For generations, Gungans have used domesticated kaadu as steeds to travel through Naboo's swamps and forests, so much so that the Gungan Grand Army comes to rely on them as mounts for their patrols.

Battle steed
Decorated with giant feathers, kaadu carry Gungan warriors into battle. In return, Gungans respect kaadu for their strength, endurance, and loyalty.

Reluctant guide
Jar Jar is hesitant to bring Obi-Wan and Qui-Gon to Otoh Gunga because he fears Boss Nass may still be angry with him for destroying Nass' property.

JAR JAR BINKS

APPEARANCES I, II, CW, III **SPECIES** Gungan
HOMEWORLD Naboo **AFFILIATION** Gungan Grand Army, Galactic Senate

Banished from the underwater city Otoh Gunga after accidentally destroying Gungan leader Boss Nass' prized submersible, Jar Jar Binks is foraging for raw shellfish in the murky Naboo swampland when the Trade Federation's invasion force nearly crushes him. Fortunately, the Jedi Knight Qui-Gon Jinn rescues Jar Jar, who immediately declares himself the Jedi's humble servant. The hapless Gungan guides Qui-Gon and his apprentice, Obi-Wan Kenobi, to Otoh Gunga, where they obtain a bongo submarine that allows them to proceed to the Jedi's destination, the city of Theed. Once there, they warn Queen Amidala about the impending Trade Federation blockade.

After the Galactic Senate fails to help Amidala's people, she asks Jar Jar to contact his fellow Gungans. With Jar Jar's help, the Naboo and the Gungans forge an alliance to liberate their besieged world. Immediately prior to the ground battle against the Trade Federation's droid army, Boss Nass makes Jar Jar a general in the Gungan Grand Army. After the battle, Jar Jar continues to ascend in Gungan society, putting his awkward past as an outcast behind him.

Eventually elected as a senior representative for Naboo, Jar Jar serves alongside Padmé Amidala in the Galactic Senate. While his compassion speaks volumes for the quality of his character, his inherent gullibility and trusting nature are easily exploited by the less scrupulous in the field of politics. Although Jar Jar is opposed to the Military Creation Act, he unwittingly enables Supreme Chancellor Palpatine to conscript an army of clones to fight Separatist forces. Still, in the corrupt inner confines of the Senate, he stands as a rare example of a virtuous politician, interested only in the greater good of the Republic and his people.

During the Clone Wars, Jar Jar takes on an active role for the Republic, accompaning more experienced Senators to Toydaria, Rodia, and Florrum. He also helps stop a lethal virus escaping from a secret laboratory on Naboo. When the Separatists incite a civil war on Mon Cala, Jar Jar convinces the Gungans to send their army to help the Republic and joins the fight himself. After relations between the Gungans and the humans on Naboo break down, Jar Jar, Padmé, and Anakin Skywalker return to the planet and stop the Separatist Gungan minister who is behind it. At the request of Queen Julia of Bardotta, Jar Jar, with Jedi Master Mace Windu, investigates the disappearance of the planet's Dagoyan masters. They rescue the queen when she herself is taken and prevent Mother Talzin from gaining even more power. At the end of the Clone Wars, Jar Jar remains a representative of Naboo and attends Padmé's funeral in Theed.

Years later, Jar Jar returns to Naboo and is banished once more by the Gungans for his role in the rise of Palpatine. Jar Jar now spends his days entertaining young refugees in Theed. While the children adore Jar Jar and affectionately call him the clown, the adults ignore him. Jar Jar meets a wounded refugee named Mapo, whom he takes as his clown apprentice.

Bold proposal
During a Senate meeting, Jar Jar takes the initiative and proposes the motion granting emergency powers to Supreme Chancellor Palpatine, a move that has profound impact on the Galactic Republic.

Affable companion
Although his bungling, erratic ways constantly land him in trouble, Jar Jar's innately good nature and loyalty somehow help him triumph in the end.

Gungan culture

The native inhabitants of the planet Naboo, Gungans are an amphibious species with hardy lungs, who are capable of holding their breath for extended periods. As such, they are as comfortable in water as they are on land. While they have great reverence for nature and balance, making every effort not to overburden their native ecosystem, the Gungans are suspicious of outsiders and maintain a large standing militia, the Gungan Grand Army.

"Yousa guys bombad!"
JAR JAR BINKS

CAPTAIN TARPALS

APPEARANCES I, CW
SPECIES Gungan **HOMEWORLD** Naboo
AFFILIATION Gungan Grand Army

A kaadu patrol chief in Otoh Gunga, Captain Tarpals watches out for thieves and dangerous creatures that threaten the underwater city. He blames the accident-prone Jar Jar Binks for numerous altercations before Jar Jar becomes a hero, whom Tarpal fights alongside in the Battle of Naboo. During the Clone Wars, the courageous Tarpals subdues and helps capture General Grievous on Naboo, but at the cost of his own life.

BOSS NASS

APPEARANCES I, III **SPECIES** Gungan
HOMEWORLD Naboo **AFFILIATION** Gungan Rep Council, Gungan Grand Army

As the ruler of Otoh Gunga, Boss Rugor Nass chairs the Rep Council, which is responsible for governing Naboo's Gungan inhabitants. He dislikes Naboo's human population because he believes they view the Gungans as a primitive species. However, after the Trade Federation invades Naboo, and Queen Amidala asks Nass for help, he realizes that the Gungans and the Naboo must join forces to defend their world. Nass eventually steps down from his role, but he still attends Amidala's funeral in Theed.

SANDO AQUA MONSTER

APPEARANCES I, FoD **LENGTH** 200 m (656 ft)
HOMEWORLD Naboo

A muscular monster with webbed hands and immense snapping jaws, the sando aqua monster is the largest predator in Naboo's oceans, and the only one able to bite through an opee sea killer's armored shell. The sando must constantly eat to maintain its enormous form, and easily devours entire schools of fish. Rarely seen by Gungan explorers and navigators, the sando is somehow capable of hiding in deep environments but is known to emerge should its progeny be threatened.

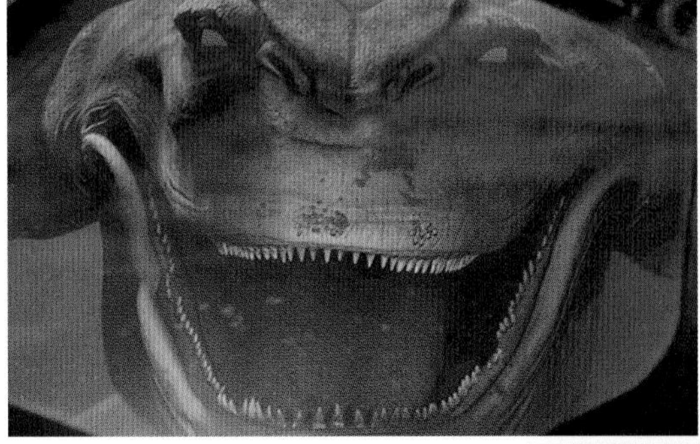

Killer instinct
The mysterious, gigantic, and always voracious sando aqua monster closes in for the kill *(above)*. Using its razor-sharp teeth, the sando easily dismembers a hapless opee sea killer that has strayed within its reach *(right)*.

OPEE SEA KILLER

APPEARANCES I **AVERAGE LENGTH** 20 m (65.5 ft)
HOMEWORLD Naboo, Strokill Prime

A vicious underwater predator, the opee sea killer lurks inside caves on the ocean planets of Naboo and Strokill Prime. Using a long lure to attract potential prey, the opee employs a combination of swimming and jet propulsion to pursue its target. Snagging victims with its adhesive tongue, the creature then draws its captured meal into its deadly maw. As aggressive as they are persistent, opees are unafraid of larger predators. Even the most experienced Gungan navigators avoid routes inhabited by these creatures, as they know opees regard the bongo's passengers as irresistible treats.

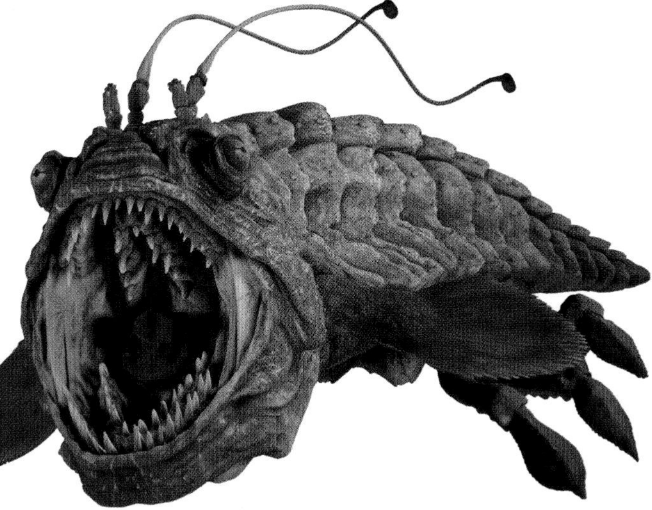

Tongue lashing
An opee sea killer's long, sticky tongue snares the Gungan bongo that carries Qui-Gon Jinn, Obi-Wan Kenobi, and Jar Jar Binks through the core of Naboo. Fortunately, a larger fish unwittingly intervenes, and they escape intact.

"Big gooberfish! Huge-a teeth!"

JAR JAR BINKS

COLO CLAW FISH

APPEARANCES I **AVERAGE LENGTH** 40 m (131 ft)
HOMEWORLD Naboo

Hidden in tunnels along Naboo's oceanic floor, the serpentine, spine-studded colo claw fish can lie still for hours waiting to capture its prey within the huge pectoral claws for which it is named. Before attacking, the colo emits a hydrosonic shriek to disorient its victim, which it stuns with its venomous fangs, distending its jaw so wide that it can swallow prey much larger than its own head. If the colo does not render its victim unconscious prior to swallowing, there is a big risk that the consumed creatures will attempt to chew their way out of its stomach. For the wealthy in the galaxy, colo flesh is a rare delicacy.

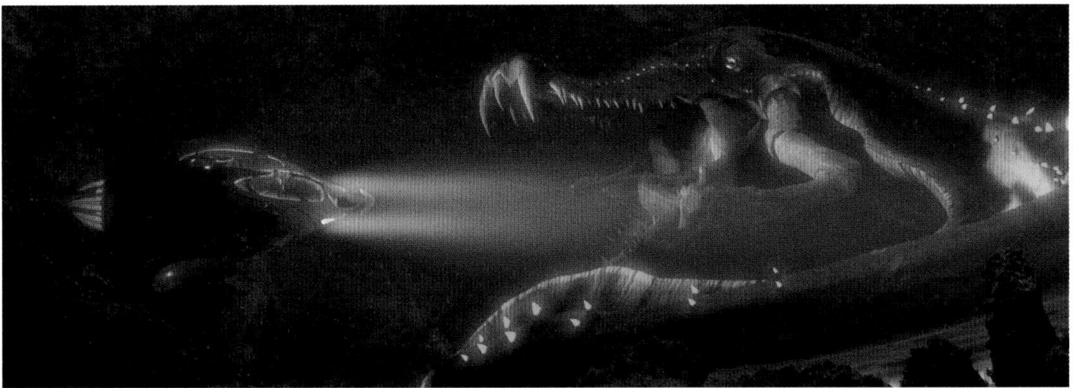

SABÉ

APPEARANCES I **SPECIES** Human **HOMEWORLD** Naboo **AFFILIATION** Royal House of Naboo

A highly trained and capable royal handmaiden, Sabé serves Queen Padmé Amidala, and is one of her most trusted friends. Sabé occasionally impersonates the queen to deceive Padmé's enemies, including during the Trade Federation's invasion of Naboo. Sabé and Padmé switch roles, successfully fooling the Neimoidians into believing that Sabé is the queen. When Padmé's reign ends and she becomes a senator, Sabé continues to serve her friend from the shadows—freeing 25 slaves on Tatooine and investigating who is trying to kill Padmé. Sabé is distraught when Padmé dies and attends her funeral. Alongside her partner, Tonra, Sabé resolves to look into her death, but is suddenly contacted by rebel leader Bail Organa.

RIC OLIÉ

APPEARANCES I **SPECIES** Human
HOMEWORLD Naboo **AFFILIATION** Naboo Royal Security Forces, Naboo Space Fighter Corps

A veteran flier and the top pilot in the Naboo Space Fighter Corps, Ric Olié is qualified to fly any craft in the Corps' fleet, and answers directly to Captain Panaka. It is his honor to captain the queen's royal starship, and soon after meeting nine-year-old Anakin Skywalker he shows the boy how to operate the starship's controls. During the Battle of Naboo, Olié pilots an N-1 starfighter, leading Bravo Squadron's assault on the Federation battleship. Sadly, he sustains an inner ear wound in the battle that afterward causes him pain whenever he leaves Naboo's atmosphere.

"Excuse me, sir, but that Artoo unit is in prime condition. A real bargain." C-3PO

R2-D2

Always willing to risk his own destruction to help his friends, R2-D2 has a close association with the protocol droid C-3PO, with whom he has participated in numerous historic battles.

APPEARANCES I, II, CW, III, Reb, RO, IV, V, VI, VII, VIII, IX, FoD **MANUFACTURER** Industrial Automaton **TYPE** R2 series astromech droid **AFFILIATION** Republic, Rebel Alliance, Resistance

BRAVE ASTROMECH

A versatile utility robot generally used for the maintenance and repair of starships and related technology, the astromech droid R2-D2 is equipped with a variety of tool-tipped appendages that are stowed in recessed compartments. As property of the Royal Security Forces of Naboo, R2-D2 is one of several droids who serve aboard Queen Padmé Amidala's Royal Starship. After the Trade Federation forces Padmé to flee Naboo and her ship has to thread its way through a blockade, R2-D2 is instrumental in helping Amidala and her Jedi allies escape across space. R2-D2 subsequently meets a young pilot, Anakin Skywalker, and inadvertently serves as Anakin's co-pilot during the Battle of Naboo.

Fearless mechanic
Ignoring enemy laserfire, R2-D2 quickly repairs Queen Amidala's starship to save the queen and her allies.

Reunion on Tatooine
Ten years after first meeting C-3PO, R2-D2 travels with Anakin and Padmé to the sand planet and reunites with the protocol droid.

SERVICE TO THE REPUBLIC

After Padmé's reign as queen ends, R2-D2 continues to serve her during her travels as a Republic senator. When an assassin attempts to kill Padmé on Coruscant, the Jedi Order assigns Anakin to be her bodyguard, and R2-D2 provides backup for Anakin. Along with C-3PO, R2-D2 is present for the secret wedding of Padmé and Anakin. During the Clone Wars, he serves as Anakin's astromech support in Jedi starfighters. He also witnesses Anakin's fall to the dark side of the Force and the birth of Padmé and Anakin's twins, Luke and Leia. Unlike C-3PO, R2-D2 is not subjected to a memory wipe. He remembers everything.

Secret plans
Princess Leia entrusts R2-D2 with the stolen plans for an Imperial superweapon, the Death Star battle station.

DETERMINED MESSENGER

Nearly two decades after the rise of the Empire, R2-D2 and C-3PO serve Princess Leia Organa of Alderaan, who is also an agent of the Rebellion. While attempting to deliver data about the Death Star to her allies, Leia's blockade runner is captured by Darth Vader. She hastily records a message and instructs R2-D2 to deliver it and its accompanying data to Obi-Wan Kenobi. Despite C-3PO's protests, the faithful astromech doggedly follows his orders and ultimately helps the rebels destroy the Death Star.

SECRET AGENT

Because astromech units are among the most ubiquitous droids, they attract relatively little attention or suspicion at Imperial spaceports and criminal outposts. R2-D2 becomes extremely skilled at covertly insinuating himself into enemy territory in order to help his friends.

Droid bartender
Apparently reduced to menial labor on Jabba the Hutt's sail barge, R2-D2 is actually concealing Luke's lightsaber and is part of a daring plan to rescue Han Solo.

Durable droid
Having survived countless battles and desperate situations, R2-D2 has developed a remarkably resilient attitude for a droid. He remains an endlessly reliable astromech and is never reluctant to put himself in danger to help his allies.

LOYAL DROID

After the Galactic Civil War, R2-D2 accompanies Luke Skywalker on his quest to uncover secrets of the Force and train the next generation of Jedi. The astromech bears witness to Kylo Ren's fall to the dark side and the ensuing destruction of Luke's temple. Having lost hope, Skywalker goes into hiding and leaves R2-D2 behind with Leia Organa. Deeply affected by his master's disappearance, the droid enters low power mode for many years. He only returns to full operation upon realizing that he has the missing map data indicating Luke's location on Ahch-To. Upon being reunited with Skywalker, R2-D2 convinces Luke to reconnect with the Force.

Plea from the past
While aboard the *Millennium Falcon* with Luke Skywalker, R2-D2 plays an archived hologram of Princess Leia's appeal to Obi-Wan Kenobi for help.

timeline

CRISIS IN THE REPUBLIC

Invasion of Naboo
When Federation droid starfighters attack Queen Amidala's starship, R2-D2 makes an emergency repair that allows Padmé and her allies to escape.

▲ Detour to Tatooine
R2-D2 ventures into Mos Espa and meets Anakin, who introduces the droid to C-3PO and his mother, Shmi. Anakin leaves Tatooine with R2-D2 on Queen Amidala's starship, but Shmi and C-3PO remain on the sand planet.

Battle of Naboo
After taking protective cover in a Naboo starfighter, Anakin and R2-D2 race into space to attack the Trade Federation Droid Control Ship.

Return to Tatooine
Following Shmi Skywalker's funeral on Tatooine, Anakin, Padmé, and R2-D2 leave the Lars family homestead with C-3PO.

THE CLONE WARS

Battle of Geonosis
R2-D2 and C-3PO infiltrate a Geonosian droid factory and help the Jedi fight the Separatist Droid Army.

The Clone Wars
Frequently serving as Anakin's co-pilot on dangerous assignments, R2-D2 also proves resourceful when confronted with deadly predators, including a gundark on Vanqor.

Order 66
After Anakin destroys the Jedi Order, R2-D2 helps Obi-Wan bring the injured Padmé to a medical center on Polis Massa.

THE EMPIRE ERA

Bail's droid
During the Galactic Empire's reign, R2-D2 enters the service of secret rebel leader Bail Organa.

Secret mission to Tatooine
After the Battle of Scarif, Princess Leia Organa entrusts R2-D2 to deliver the stolen plans for the Death Star to Obi-Wan on Tatooine.

Battle of Yavin
R2-D2 serves as Luke's droid co-pilot during the rebel assault on the Death Star. R2-D2 is damaged during the battle, but the rebels destroy the Death Star and soon repair R2-D2.

Solo mission
Using upgraded weapons systems, R2-D2 infiltrates an Imperial Star Destroyer to rescue C-3PO after his capture by the elite Scar Squadron.

Mission to Dagobah
Following the Battle of Hoth, R2-D2 travels with Luke to find the Jedi Master Yoda on the planet Dagobah. Neither Yoda nor R2-D2 acknowledge that they have met previously.

Escape from Cloud City
After Imperial forces surround the rebels on Cloud City, R2-D2 hastily repairs the *Millennium Falcon*'s hyperdrive.

Battle of the Great Pit of Carkoon
Infiltrating Jabba the Hutt's palace, R2-D2 helps the rebels rescue Han from Jabba.

Battle of Endor
R2-D2 befriends the Ewoks and helps them defeat Imperial ground troops.

THE NEW REPUBLIC ERA

Luke's companion
After the Battle of Endor, R2-D2 accompanies Luke on his adventures across the galaxy.

▲ R2 awakens
Now with the Resistance, R2-D2 wakes up from standby mode and announces that he is able to piece together the map to Luke Skywalker. Afterward, he accompanies Rey to Ahch-To.

A new master
R2-D2 stays by Rey's side as she returns to help rescue the Resistance at the Battle of Crait.

"At last we will reveal ourselves to the Jedi. At last we will have revenge."

DARTH MAUL

DARTH MAUL

Forged by Darth Sidious into a hate-fueled killing machine, Maul may be the first Sith to slay a Jedi in combat in more than 1,000 years, but is ultimately betrayed by his own master.

APPEARANCES I, CW, S, Reb **SPECIES** Zabrak **HOMEWORLD** Dathomir **AFFILIATION** Sith, Nightbrothers, Crimson Dawn

THE PATH TO EVIL

Born a Nightbrother on Dathomir, Maul is taken from his mother, Talzin, by Darth Sidious as his Sith apprentice, and learns the power of the dark side. Sidious trains Maul to wield a double-bladed lightsaber, with which Maul intends to exact vengeance upon the Jedi for the decimation of the Sith ranks. Dispatched by Sidious to kill the troublesome Queen Amidala, Maul tracks her to Tatooine, where he duels with one of her two Jedi protectors, Qui-Gon Jinn, who escapes with Amidala. When the two Jedi escort Queen Amidala back to Naboo, Maul sets out to finish them all. He confronts the Jedi, drawing them into Theed's generator complex. Maul manages to kill Qui-Gon Jinn, but Qui-Gon's apprentice, Obi-Wan Kenobi, strikes Maul down.

Generator duel
Maul slays a Jedi Master on Naboo, but underestimates the lightsaber skills of the Knight's apprentice, who cuts the murderous Sith in half.

SHATTERED CREATURE

For over a decade, the Jedi Order believes Darth Maul is dead. But during the Clone Wars, after Asajj Ventress betrays Savage Opress, Mother Talzin informs Savage that he has an exiled brother in the Outer Rim who can teach him to become more powerful. Opress goes to the planet Lotho Minor, where he finds Maul in a wretched state, his damaged torso grafted to spider-like droid legs. Opress helps Maul recover, and together they seek revenge against those who turned them into monsters.

Craving vengeance
The burning desire to kill the Jedi who crippled him is the only thing that keeps Maul alive.

New Sith Order?
With his Sith memories restored, and Savage Opress on his side, Maul believes they can take on Darth Sidious.

THE SHADOW COLLECTIVE

After Mother Talzin restores Maul's mind and gives him new cybernetic legs, Maul and Savage Opress lure Obi-Wan into a trap, so Maul may take his revenge. They fail to kill Obi-Wan, but cause death and destruction on several worlds, as Maul draws support from space pirates and the ranks of the Mandalorian Death Watch to build his own army, the Shadow Collective. Unwilling to allow Maul's influence to grow unchecked, Darth Sidious takes matters into his own hands. The Sith Lord duels Maul face to face, beating him easily. Maul is then incarcerated at the Separatist prison on Stygeon Prime. He is tortured, but left alive by Sidious, who believes Maul might still be of use. Maul's loyal Mandalorian allies rescue him, and he flees to Dathomir under the protection of Mother Talzin. Once again, Sidious is forced to act, this time utilizing the might of the Separatist army. Its droid fleets crush the Shadow Collective, Talzin is killed, and Maul retreats to Mandalore to make his last stand. At the close of the Clone Wars, Republic forces besiege Mandalore. Led by Captain Rex and Ahsoka Tano, Maul and his remaining Mandalorian supporters are defeated. The villain barely escapes with his life.

CRIMSON DAWN

Undeterred by his previous attempts to rule through the criminal underworld, Maul leads the shadowy mercenary group Crimson Dawn. Maul rules from the safety of his homeworld of Dathomir and allows his lieutenants to be the face of the organization. One such leader is Dryden Vos, whose ruthless tactics help Maul build Crimson Dawn into a formidable criminal enterprise in the early years of the Empire. Only upon Vos' death does Maul reveal himself to Qi'ra, Vos' top aide, who becomes the organization's figurehead.

Changing leaders
Maul contacts Qi'ra via hologram, revealing himself as the true leader of Crimson Dawn, and offering her the chance to succeed her recently deceased boss, Dryden Vos.

Vengeful warrior
One of the deadliest, most efficiently trained Sith in the Order's history, Darth Maul's tattooed face is as symbolic of his utter devotion to the dark side, as it is marking his hatred of the Jedi.

FINAL ACT

Maul's insatiable thirst for power leads him to Malachor in search of an ancient Sith superweapon that will allow him to take vengeance on all his enemies. He claims to have been stranded on Malachor for years when he is found by Ahsoka Tano, Kanan Jarrus, and Ezra Bridger, who arrive on the planet searching for ways to defeat the Sith. Their arrival provides Maul with an opportunity to manipulate young Ezra Bridger into becoming his "apprentice." Ezra unknowingly leads Maul to Tatooine in search of Jedi Master Obi-Wan Kenobi. The former Sith confronts his old adversary in the desert, sensing Kenobi's real reason for going into hiding: to protect Luke Skywalker. With the future of the Jedi at stake, Kenobi has no choice but to fight back. Maul is defeated with just three swift strokes of the Jedi's lightsaber. He dies in the arms of his greatest foe, bringing an end to a decades-long quest for revenge.

Fight to the finish
In their final showdown, Obi-Wan Kenobi feigns his old master Qui-Gon Jinn's fighting style to catch Maul off guard, before quickly ending the duel with lethal force.

timeline

CRISIS IN THE REPUBLIC

Witch's son
Mother Talzin of the Nightsister coven of witches on Dathomir, gives birth to a son, Maul.

Sith Apprentice
The Sith Lord Darth Sidious takes Maul from Dathomir, trains him to become a warrior and assassin, and eventually proclaims Darth Maul as his apprentice.

Test of might
Against his master's orders and risking their secrecy, Maul kills Jedi Padawan Eldra Kaitis on the Moon of Drazkel to test his skills.

Duel on Tatooine
Darth Maul fights Qui-Gon Jinn on Tatooine.

Battle of Naboo
Darth Maul slays Qui-Gon on Naboo, but is cut in half by Qui-Gon's Padawan, Obi-Wan Kenobi. However, Maul survives and escapes capture.

▼ The lost years
In hiding on Lotho Minor, Maul loses most of his memories, but remains consumed by desire for vengeance against Obi-Wan.

THE CLONE WARS

Recycled villain
Savage Opress recovers an amnesiac Maul on Lotho Minor and delivers him to Mother Talzin, who restores his memories and strength, and gives him cybernetic legs.

Second duel with Obi-Wan
Teamed with Savage Opress, Maul seeks revenge on Obi-Wan. He duels the Jedi on the planet Raydonia, but Obi-Wan escapes.

Shadow Collective
Maul organizes the Shadow Collective, an alliance of criminals and renegade bounty hunters, which briefly takes control of the planet Mandalore.

Splinter of the Sith Order
Although the Sith Order traditionally consists of only two members, and although Darth Sidious remains alive, Maul proclaims that he and Savage Opress are respectively the new Sith master and Sith apprentice.

▲ Showdown with Darth Sidious
On Mandalore, Darth Sidious kills Savage Opress and captures Maul, but Maul escapes.

Duel on Dathomir
On the planet Dathomir, Maul joins forces with Mother Talzin to fight Count Dooku and General Grievous, but Talzin sacrifices herself so Maul can escape.

THE EMPIRE ERA

Puppet master
Maul becomes the secret leader of the criminal organization Crimson Dawn.

Bitter end
Maul returns to Tatooine to take revenge on his old archenemy Obi-Wan Kenobi, but is swiftly dispatched by the Jedi Master.

"Someday I will be the most powerful Jedi ever." ANAKIN SKYWALKER

ANAKIN SKYWALKER

A child born of prophecy, possibly conceived by the will of the Force itself, Anakin Skywalker leaves an indelible mark on the history of the galaxy, leading it through periods of light and darkness.

APPEARANCES I, II, CW, III, Reb, RO, IV, V, VI, FoD **SPECIES** Human **HOMEWORLD** Tatooine **AFFILIATION** Jedi, Sith

PODRACE TO FREEDOM

When the Jedi Qui-Gon Jinn and his allies become stranded on Tatooine and require replacement parts for their starship, Anakin Skywalker, a young slave, endeavors to help them. He enters a podrace, hoping to win prize money to buy the necessary starship parts, but unknown to the boy, Qui-Gon makes a wager with Anakin's owner, Watto. When Anakin wins, he not only defeats the reigning podracer champion, Sebulba, and gains the prize money, but also gains his freedom. Anakin later becomes Obi-Wan Kenobi's Jedi apprentice.

Daring pilot
Anakin's heightened perception and quick reflexes make him a podracing legend and the only human ever to win the Boonta Eve Classic.

ROGUE APPRENTICE

While Anakin is supposed to be protecting Padmé Amidala, he senses that his mother is in trouble. He finds his dying mother in a Tusken Raider camp on Tatooine and slaughters the Tuskens without mercy. Shattered by his mother's death, he promises that he will learn how to stop people from dying. Prior to the Battle of Geonosis, Anakin and Padmé admit their love to each other. Following the battle, they get married in secret on Naboo, even though it is against the Jedi code.

Solemn vow
Although Anakin does all he can to rescue his mother from her captors, he blames himself for her death. At her graveside, he regrets not being strong enough to save her and vows he will not fail again.

DRAWN TO THE DARK SIDE

Supreme Chancellor Palpatine takes a strong interest in Anakin's career as a Jedi, and Anakin comes to regard Palpatine as a friend. Anakin even trusts him with his dark secret about how he killed the Tuskens on Tatooine. However, during the Clone Wars, Anakin learns that Palpatine and the Jedi Council don't trust each other and is torn between loyalty to Palpatine and his obligations to the Council. After Anakin learns Palpatine is a Sith Lord, he notifies the Council but then allies with Palpatine, who promises to give him life-prolonging powers.

Sith tales
During a performance at Galaxies Opera House, Anakin listens to Palpatine's tale of a powerful Sith Lord who used the Force to defeat death.

BECOMING DARTH VADER

Renamed Darth Vader, Anakin becomes Palpatine's Sith apprentice. He helps to destroy the Sith's enemies, including his former allies at the Jedi Temple, enabling Palpatine to declare himself Emperor. When a ferocious duel with Obi-Wan Kenobi on fiery Mustafar leaves Vader dismembered and near death, Palpatine retrieves Vader and transforms him into a cyborg. The rebuilt Vader undertakes a series of missions for Palpatine, starting with building a new lightsaber. He hunts down a Jedi survivor and repurposes their kyber crystal, turning it from green to red. He also builds a castle on Mustafar, a planet that not only holds painful memories for Vader but is also strongly connected to the dark side.

Armored warrior
After his near-fatal duel with Obi-Wan Kenobi, Anakin Skywalker is reborn as Darth Vader, a cyborg encased in life-sustaining armor.

CRUSHING REBELLION

Vader serves as the Emperor's enforcer as rebel cells rise up throughout the galaxy. When rebel activity on Lothal escalates, he confronts Jedi Kanan Jarrus and his Padawan Ezra Bridger and learns that they are working with his own former apprentice, Ahsoka Tano. After the Rebel Alliance steals the Death Star plans from the archive on Scarif, Vader tries to retrieve them, but fails. The Alliance uses the plans to discover a weakness in the Death Star and destroy it. The Emperor blames Vader for failing to stop the rebels, so Vader has to work hard to regain his master's favor. He teams up with Doctor Aphra to form his own secret army and to find the rebel pilot who destroyed the Death Star. After discovering the pilot is his own son, Luke Skywalker, Vader begins plotting to turn Luke to the dark side so they can rule the galaxy together.

Dueling the past
On Malachor, Vader faces his former Padawan, Ahsoka, in battle, but she mysteriously disappears before he can strike the final blow *(above)*. Years later, Vader encounters Obi-Wan aboard the Death Star *(right)*. Vader kills Obi-Wan, but the Jedi becomes one with the Force.

Father vs. son
The Emperor manipulates Vader into fighting Luke, but Luke's faith in his father's innate goodness ultimately restores Anakin Skywalker.

REDEMPTION

Vader lays a trap for Luke Skywalker on Cloud City, drawing him into a duel in order to reveal that he is the young Jedi's father. Failing to gain Luke's allegiance, he later helps the Emperor lure Luke and his rebel allies into a trap at the second Death Star in orbit around Endor. Luke enters the Emperor's throne room on the battle station, and the Emperor goads him into fighting his father. When Luke refuses to kill Vader, the Emperor unleashes a barrage of Force lightning on the young Jedi. Vader suddenly realizes that he wants to save his son, so has to destroy the Sith Lord. Although Vader manages to kill the Emperor, he does not survive the encounter. Thanks to his son Luke, Anakin Skywalker is redeemed and becomes one with the Force.

Darth Vader
Widely feared as Emperor Palpatine's deadliest enforcer, Darth Vader is, in reality, a tormented soul imprisoned inside life-supporting armor. His armor both sustains his damaged body and enhances it with advanced prostheses and augmented sensory, skeletal, and nervous systems.

timeline

CRISIS IN THE REPUBLIC

Tatooine slave
Anakin Skywalker and his mother, Shmi, are slaves owned by Gardulla the Hutt before she loses them in a podracing bet to Watto, a junk dealer on Tatooine.

Battle of Naboo
After winning his freedom, Anakin leaves Tatooine, destroys the Federation Droid Control Ship orbiting Naboo, and becomes Obi-Wan's Jedi apprentice.

Reunion on Coruscant
Ten years after the Battle of Naboo, Anakin and Obi-Wan serve as bodyguards for Padmé Amidala. Anakin and Padmé fall in love.

Return to Tatooine
Hunting the Tusken Raiders who abducted his mother, Anakin finds their camp but is too late to save her. He kills every Tusken in the camp.

THE CLONE WARS

Battle of Geonosis
Anakin and Obi-Wan duel with Count Dooku on Geonosis. Later, Anakin weds Padmé in a secret ceremony on Naboo.

The Clone Wars
Anakin serves the Republic as a Jedi general and takes an apprentice, Ahsoka Tano. At Palpatine's command, Anakin kills a defenseless Count Dooku.

Order 66
Seduced to the dark side by Palpatine's alter ego, Darth Sidious, Anakin becomes Darth Vader and helps destroy the Jedi Order.

THE EMPIRE ERA

Duel on Mustafar
Left mortally wounded by Obi-Wan, Vader is rescued by Sidious, who transforms him into an armored cyborg and convinces him that he is responsible for Padmé's death.

Fortress Vader
Vader builds an imposing castle on the planet Mustafar, selecting a site that once held a Sith temple.

Battle of Scarif
Vader boards the Alliance flagship, the *Profundity*, to try to recover the stolen Death Star plans. However, some rebels escape with the schematics just in time, aboard the *Tantive IV*.

Death Star duel
On the Death Star battle station, Darth Vader duels Obi-Wan for the last time.

Battle at Yavin
Vader senses that the rebel pilot (Luke) who destroys the Death Star is extremely strong with the Force.

Son of Skywalker
Vader learns from the bounty hunter Boba Fett the surname of the rebel pilot who destroyed the Death Star: Skywalker.

Playing favorites
Vader competes for the Emperor's favor with Grand General Tagge and a cyberneticist named Cylo. He outwits them both to win back his master's trust.

▲ Duel on Cloud City
Vader identifies himself as Luke's father, but fails to persuade Luke to join the dark side and help him defeat the Emperor.

▲ Battle of Endor
Vader duels Luke and learns that Princess Leia is also his daughter. Vader kills the Emperor and becomes one with the Force.

RONTO

APPEARANCES I, IV **HOMEWORLD** Tatooine
AVERAGE SIZE 5 m (16 ft) high
HABITAT Desert

Indigenous to Tatooine, the saurian ronto is a huge, four-legged herbivore. Jawas use these easily domesticated beasts as mounts and to haul cargo to and from trading posts. Despite their imposing size and appearance, rontos are skittish and easily startled, but also loyal to their masters. They require a great deal of water, but are well suited to the desert. Their skin sheds heat, as do the flaplike folds framing their faces, which can extend to cover their small eyes during sandstorms.

Dastardly Dug
Sebulba uses very shady tactics to win podraces.

SEBULBA

APPEARANCES I **SPECIES** Dug
HOMEWORLD Malastare **AFFILIATION** None

The reigning champion of the Outer Rim podrace circuit is Sebulba, who pilots a souped-up, overpowered orange racer. Although no one disputes that his expensive racer is fast, the shifty Dug's winning streak has less to do with his piloting skills and more to do with his refusal to let rules get in the way of victory. He is not above sabotaging a competitor's vehicle before a race and frequently uses illegal weaponry hidden aboard his own racer to distract or even bring down other pilots. On one occasion, he even uses his podracer to flash the podracer of a local slave boy, Anakin Skywalker, destroying it and stopping Anakin from completing the race.

Despite his unsportsmanlike conduct, Sebulba is popular with many race fans because he is an excellent showman, as podrace organizers are well aware. Whenever Sebulba competes, he guarantees large crowds and thus high profits.

At the Boonta Eve Classic, Sebulba wears a custom-made leather racing outfit that is decorated with coins, his victory prizes from previous races. Although Sebulba is the favorite to win the Boonta Eve Classic, Anakin evades the Dug's vicious tactics this time and is first to cross the finish line. As if losing the race isn't bad enough, Sebulba also loses control of his podracer and crashes into the desert sands. Luckily for him, he survives the crash and lives to race in many more competitions.

QUINLAN VOS

APPEARANCES I, CW **SPECIES** Kiffar
HOMEWORLD Kiffu **AFFILIATION** Jedi

Former Padawan to Master Tholme, Quinlan Vos is a Jedi Master with a sarcastic sense of humor and a reputation for not playing by the rules. Vos is an expert tracker, renowned for his psychometric ability to perceive the memories of others by touching objects that they handled. He often takes missions that deal with the galactic underworld, which is how he meets Aayla Secura, the Force-sensitive Twi'lek who becomes his Jedi apprentice. He is on a covert assignment in Mos Espa on Tatooine when Qui-Gon Jinn and Obi-Wan Kenobi arrive just before the Boonta Eve Classic.

During the Clone Wars, Vos is partnered with Obi-Wan to track the fugitive crime lord Ziro the Hutt. Thanks to his underworld connections, Vos believes that the Hutt Council hired bounty hunter Cad Bane to break Ziro out of prison. Vos and Obi-Wan travel to Nal Hutta and meet with the Hutt Council. The Hutts deny all knowledge of Ziro or Cad Bane's whereabouts. The Jedi eventually learn that Ziro has escaped to the planet Teth and that Cad Bane is also stalking Ziro. They proceed to Teth, where they find Cad Bane lurking near Ziro's corpse. Although Bane claims he isn't responsible for killing Ziro, the Jedi attempt to apprehend him for previous crimes, but he escapes.

Months later, Vos accepts a mission to assassinate Count Dooku. Vos pretends to be a bounty hunter and tracks down Asajj Ventress—Dooku's former apprentice who is now a bounty hunter. He joins her on a mission to Mustafar and goes on to reveal his real identity and mission. Asajj agrees to aid him as long as he accepts her tutelage in the dark side. While training, Vos and Asajj unexpectedly fall in love. They strike Dooku on Raxus, but they fail, and Vos is captured.

Soon after, Vos appears to be broken by Dooku's torture, but he is pretending in order to complete his mission. When Asajj tries to rescue Vos, he refuses her aid and becomes a Separatist agent known only as Admiral Enigma. Asajj and the Jedi attempt to capture Enigma, but instead find Vos in a cell. The Jedi welcome him back in spite of Asajj's protests that he is still on the dark side. When Asajj's fears are confirmed, the Jedi test Vos' loyalty by once again asking him to kill Dooku. Vos and Asajj travel together to Dooku's ship but, due to Jedi meddling, end up crash-landing with Dooku on Christophsis. Asajj sacrifices herself to save Vos from the Sith. Enraged, Vos defeats Dooku, but decides to spare him and the Sith escapes. Because of this display of mercy, Vos is allowed to rejoin the Order and eventually returns to active duty. He fights on Kashyyyk when Order 66 is activated and his fate is unknown.

Hunt for Ziro
Seeking Ziro the Hutt, Quinlan and Obi-Wan confront members of the Hutt Council in a club on Nal Hutta *(left)*.

BANTHA

APPEARANCES I, II, CW, IV, VI
HOMEWORLD Tatooine
AVERAGE SIZE 2 m (8 ft) tall **HABITAT** Desert

Large, shaggy-furred quadrupeds with bright, inquisitive eyes, banthas are easily domesticated, and are bred on many worlds throughout the galaxy. Male banthas are distinguished by a pair of long, spiraling horns. Bantha meat and milk are common food items, and bantha-hide boots, jackets, and other wares are quite popular. On Tatooine, banthas are used as beasts of burden by moisture farmers, and as loyal pack animals by the savage Tusken Raiders. Tuskens are known to ride their banthas in single file, thus leaving few tracks in the desert and effectively concealing their numbers.

DEWBACK

APPEARANCES I, CW, Reb, IV
HOMEWORLD Tatooine **AVERAGE SIZE** 9 m (6 ft) long **HABITAT** Desert

Dewbacks are large lizards used as mounts and beasts of burden on their native Tatooine, where they can be found hauling goods for merchants or moisture farmers, pulling podracer parts to starting grids, or serving stormtrooper patrols assigned to the planet's Imperial garrison. A dewback can withstand the heat and dust that often leads to mechanical breakdowns in high-tech conveyances. When the suns set and the temperatures plunge, dewbacks become lethargic and rarely move about.

WATTO

APPEARANCES I, II **SPECIES** Toydarian
HOMEWORLD Toydaria
AFFILIATION Watto's shop

An injured Toydarian veteran, Watto is the proprietor of a junk shop and scrapyard in Mos Espa, as well as an inveterate gambler and an avid fan of podracing. In a wager over a podrace with another gambler, Gardulla the Hutt, Watto wins two of Gardulla's slaves, Shmi Skywalker and her son Anakin, who happens to be a gifted mechanic. Some years later, after a tall, bearded stranger (Qui-Gon Jinn) tries to buy a used hyperdrive motivator from Watto, the latter is simultaneously intrigued and perturbed when the stranger proposes a wager that may result in Watto either losing Anakin or winning a starship. Watto loses the bet, and Anakin leaves Tatooine to become a Jedi.

Without Anakin's mechanical aptitude, Watto's business soon declines, and he sells Shmi to moisture farmer Cliegg Lars, who essentially buys her freedom and makes Shmi his wife. When Anakin returns to Mos Espa in search of his mother, Watto encounters his former slave and gives him a lead on Shmi's whereabouts.

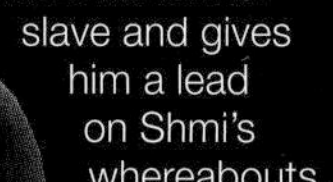

"No matter where you are, my love will be with you." SHMI SKYWALKER

SHMI SKYWALKER

APPEARANCES I, II, CW **SPECIES** Human
HOMEWORLD Tatooine
AFFILIATION Moisture farmer

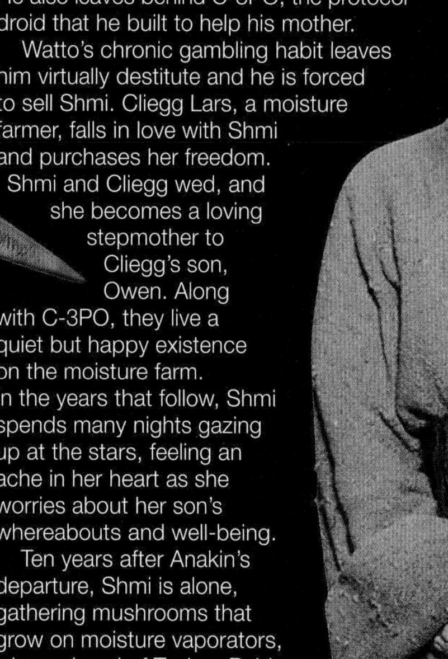

Anakin's mother, Shmi, is a loving, soft-spoken woman. Although they are both slaves of the junk dealer Watto, Shmi provides a good home for her son and is determined that he will have a better future. She is aware that Anakin has special powers—he can see things before they happen. But it is not until the Jedi Knight Qui-Gon arrives in Mos Espa that Shmi realizes her son has the potential and opportunity to become a Jedi. With Qui-Gon's help, Anakin wins his freedom by competing in a podrace, but Qui-Gon is unable to persuade Watto to release Shmi, too. Before Anakin departs with Qui-Gon, he promises he will return to free her. He also leaves behind C-3PO, the protocol droid that he built to help his mother.

Watto's chronic gambling habit leaves him virtually destitute and he is forced to sell Shmi. Cliegg Lars, a moisture farmer, falls in love with Shmi and purchases her freedom. Shmi and Cliegg wed, and she becomes a loving stepmother to Cliegg's son, Owen. Along with C-3PO, they live a quiet but happy existence on the moisture farm. In the years that follow, Shmi spends many nights gazing up at the stars, feeling an ache in her heart as she worries about her son's whereabouts and well-being.

Ten years after Anakin's departure, Shmi is alone, gathering mushrooms that grow on moisture vaporators, when a band of Tusken Raiders abducts her. Cliegg and a posse of moisture farmers attempt to rescue her, but the Tuskens ambush the farmers, maiming Cliegg and leaving most of his allies dead. A month later, Anakin—plagued by nightmares about Shmi being tortured—returns to Tatooine, determined to find his mother. Although Cliegg insists that Shmi must be dead, Anakin borrows a speeder bike and tracks the Tuskens across the desert. When he arrives at their camp, he finds his mother barely alive. She has just enough strength to tell him that she loves him before she dies. Enraged, Anakin gives in to the dark side and slaughters the Tuskens. He returns to the Lars homestead, where he buries Shmi. This traumatic experience makes Anakin desire the power to prevent his loved ones from dying.

JAWA

APPEARANCES I, II, CW, Reb, IV, VI
SPECIES Jawa **HOMEWORLD** Tatooine
AFFILIATION Desert scavengers

Combing the deserts in search of discarded scrap and wayward mechanicals, Jawas are meter-tall humanoids with small bodies completely hidden behind rough, hand-woven robes. Using cobbled-together weaponry, they incapacitate stray droids and haul them into their immense mobile fortress-homes, known as sandcrawlers. Because Tatooine moisture farmers live far from droid dealers and scrapyards, they routinely trade with Jawas, even though Jawas are notorious hucksters of hastily-refurbished junk.

"Don't call me a mindless philosopher, you overweight glob of grease!" C-3PO

C-3PO

Perpetually fussy, timid, and prone to worry, the human-cyborg relations protocol droid C-3PO is also a loyal friend who survives numerous adventures with his astromech counterpart, R2-D2.

APPEARANCES I, II, CW, III, Reb, RO, IV, V, VI, Res, VII, VIII, IX, FoD **MODEL** Protocol droid **HOMEWORLD** Tatooine
AFFILIATION Republic, Rebel Alliance, Resistance

"THANK THE MAKER"

Cobbled together from discarded scrap and salvaged parts from Watto's junkyard on Tatooine, C-3PO is created by 9-year-old Anakin Skywalker, who programs the droid to help his mother, Shmi. Initially lacking an outer shell, C-3PO endures the indignity of being "naked," with his parts and wiring showing. Shortly after activation, he meets R2-D2, Qui-Gon Jinn, Padmé Amidala, and Jar Jar Binks, who are en route to Coruscant. Anakin departs with his new allies, leaving C-3PO with Shmi. Eventually, Shmi and C-3PO move to the Lars moisture farm, and Shmi adds metal coverings to C-3PO's body.

Anxious friend
Though C-3PO is embarrassed when he realizes his unplated body leaves his framework exposed, he still manages to serve with R2-D2 as Anakin's podracer pit crew during the Boonta Eve Classic at Mos Espa Grand Arena.

Mission to Rodia
C-3PO serves Senator Padmé Amidala and Senator Jar Jar Binks during the Clone Wars.

SENATORIAL SERVICE

A decade after Anakin leaves C-3PO on Tatooine, the protocol droid reunites with his maker and is swept into the battle that begins the Clone Wars. Along with R2-D2, he witnesses the secret wedding of Anakin and Padmé and subsequently becomes a translator and personal assistant for senatorial meetings and diplomatic missions. After the Sith seize control of the Republic, C-3PO is present for the birth of Padmé's twins, Luke and Leia. To ensure that no one—especially the Sith—learns about the twins' existence, C-3PO is given a memory wipe, leaving him without any knowledge of his past.

Versatile translator
Owen Lars buys C-3PO because the droid understands the binary language of moisture vaporators.

DROID SALE

Almost 20 years after the Clone Wars, C-3PO is the property of Princess Leia Organa when he reluctantly joins R2-D2 on a mission to find Obi-Wan Kenobi on Tatooine. Both droids are captured by Jawas, who bring them to the Lars moisture farm and sell them to Owen Lars and his nephew, Luke Skywalker. Although Owen and C-3PO coexisted on the farm years earlier, Owen does not recognize C-3PO, and C-3PO's memories of Owen are long gone.

GOLDEN DEITY

Accompanying a rebel strike team to Endor's forest moon, C-3PO encounters the Ewoks, an indigenous species of primitive warriors who are wary of humans but regard the golden droid as a god. Although C-3PO does not consider himself a good storyteller, his retelling of key events of the Galactic Civil War encourages the Ewoks to ally with the rebels. By gaining their allegiance, C-3PO plays a crucial part in the Rebellion's victory at the Battle of Endor.

Elevated status
Discreetly levitated by Luke's Force powers, C-3PO appears to fly before the awed Ewoks.

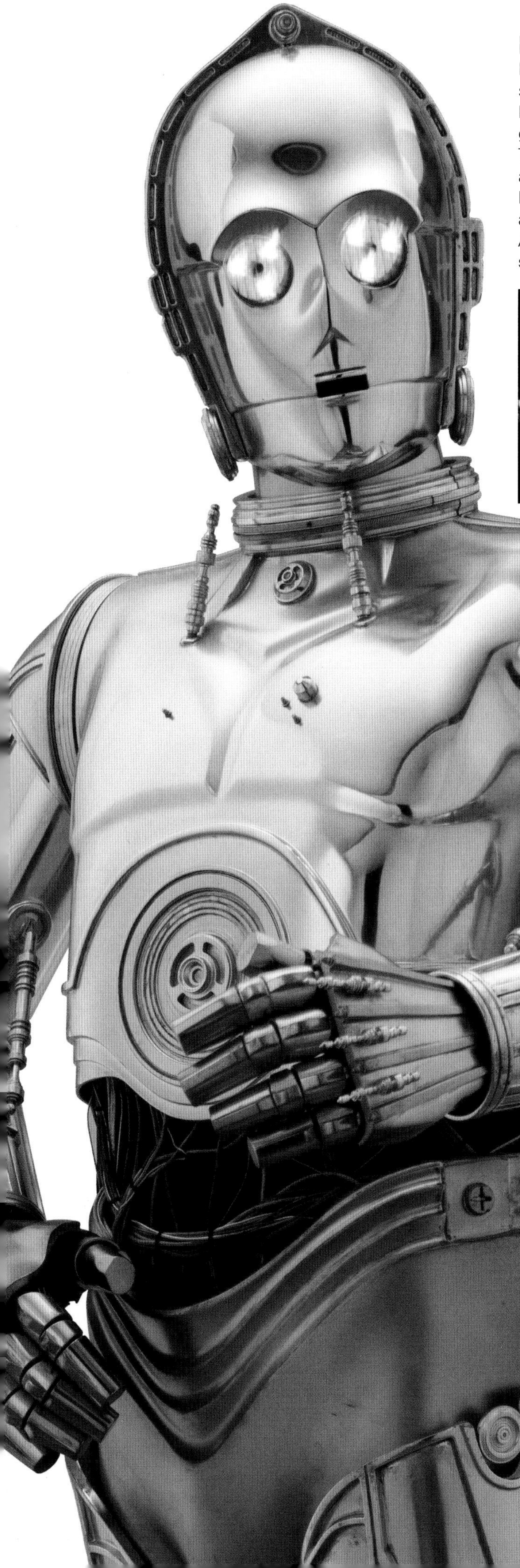

RESISTANCE SPYMASTER

Ever loyal to Leia Organa, C-3PO remains at her side as she leads the Resistance against the First Order. C-3PO serves the fledgling military group as leader of a droid intelligence network. Throughout the galaxy, C-3PO's agents secretively act as the mechanical eyes and ears of the Resistance, monitoring the Order's activities and reporting back to C-3PO for analysis. After the Battle of D'Qar, the droid spy ring suspends operations as the Resistance flees.

All-seeing C-3PO
Although he may often protest that nobody ever tells him anything, C-3PO is at the heart of the Resistance's intelligence services.

Expert translator
Like most protocol droids, C-3PO is fluent in more than seven million forms of communication. However, he is more talkative than typical protocol models, and some friends say he talks too much. Through his exploits, he has accumulated more than 30 secondary functions, including landspeeder piloting and programming binary loadlifters.

timeline

CRISIS IN THE REPUBLIC

Tatooine origins
Built by Anakin, C-3PO remains on Tatooine with Shmi after Anakin leaves to become a Jedi.

Lars family homestead
Shmi gains her freedom and marries Cliegg Lars, a moisture farmer. Shmi and C-3PO move to Cliegg's farm, where his son, Owen, also lives.

▲ Reunion with Anakin
A decade after leaving Tatooine, Anakin returns too late to save his mother. C-3PO leaves with Anakin and R2-D2 and participates in the Battle of Geonosis.

The Clone Wars
C-3PO serves as a translator for Senator Amidala and other Senate representatives.

Order 66
After learning of Anakin's role in the destruction of the Jedi Order, Alderaan Senator Bail Organa gives C-3PO a memory wipe for security reasons.

THE EMPIRE ERA

▲ Secret mission to Tatooine
After Darth Vader captures Princess Leia, C-3PO follows R2-D2 to Tatooine, where they meet Luke on their way to find Obi-Wan.

Escape from Mos Eisley
After stormtroopers kill Luke's aunt and uncle, C-3PO and his allies flee Tatooine aboard the *Millennium Falcon*.

Escape from the Death Star
C-3PO helps rescue Princess Leia from the Death Star and travels to the rebel base on Yavin 4.

▲ Cloud City capture
When a captive C-3PO comes in close proximity to Darth Vader on Cloud City, he remains unaware that Vader was once his own maker, Anakin Skywalker.

▲ Rescuing Han Solo
Accompanied by R2-D2, C-3PO infiltrates Jabba the Hutt's palace and helps rescue Han Solo.

Battle of Endor
C-3PO helps the Ewoks defeat Imperial ground forces on Endor.

THE NEW REPUBLIC ERA

Upgraded
C-3PO's TranLang communication module is upgraded. C-3PO is now fluent in over seven million forms of communication.

Phantom limb
C-3PO loses his left arm while stranded on the planet Taul. First Order protocol droid O-MR1 sacrifices himself to save him and C-3PO wears O-MR1's red arm to honor him.

Loyal servant
In the Resistance, C-3PO serves as a droid spymaster for General Organa, informing her of First Order activity across the galaxy.

EOPIE

APPEARANCES I, II, CW, III **HOMEWORLD** Tatooine **AVERAGE SIZE** 2 m (7 ft) high **HABITAT** Desert

A herbivore and a stubborn beast of burden on Tatooine, the eopie is renowned for its endurance and is often pushed to the limit by the denizens of the twin-sunned world. This sure-footed quadruped has pale skin, a flexible snout, and a grumpy temperament. Because their young are extremely vulnerable and often fall prey to predators, eopies instinctively travel in herds. Moisture farmers use older eopies to eat excess desert weeds that would otherwise sap crops of valuable moisture.

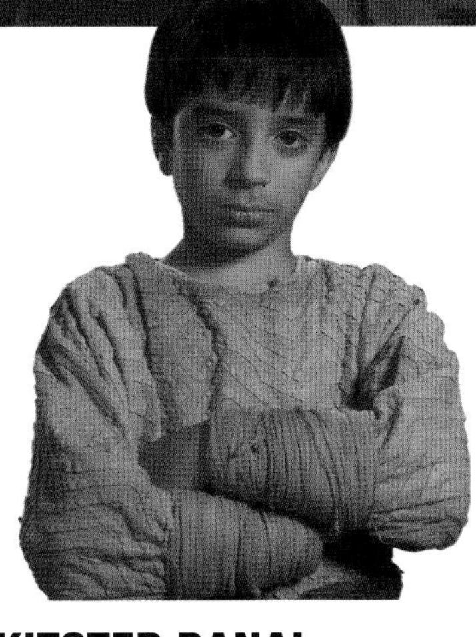

KITSTER BANAI

APPEARANCES I **SPECIES** Human **HOMEWORLD** Tatooine

An optimistic boy about the same age as Anakin, Kitster is one of Anakin's best childhood friends. When Anakin competes in the Boonta Eve Classic, Kitster serves as a member of his trusted pit team. After winning the Boonta, Anakin gives a few prize credits to Kitster, who uses the money to improve his livelihood.

BEN QUADINAROS

APPEARANCES I **SPECIES** Toong **HOMEWORLD** Tund **AFFILIATION** None

Short by Toong standards, Ben Quadinaros is the tallest entrant in the Boonta Eve Classic and also the least experienced. His hastily put-together podracer malfunctions, stalling on the starting grid before its four engines break loose and blast off in all directions. Quadinaros perseveres with the sport and is eventually billed as Sebulba's greatest rival.

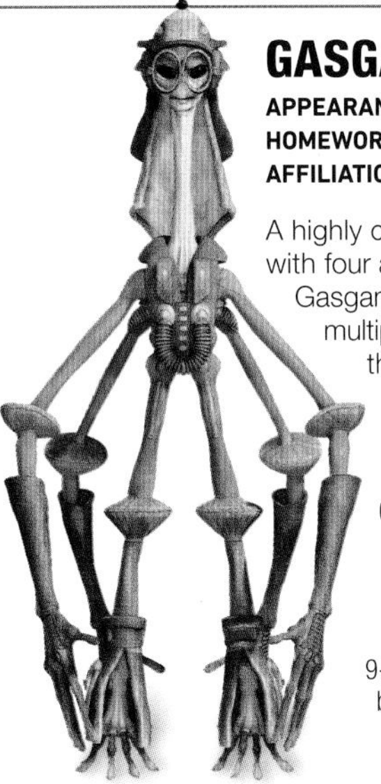

GASGANO

APPEARANCES I **SPECIES** Xexto **HOMEWORLD** Troiken **AFFILIATION** None

A highly competitive pilot with four arms and two legs, Gasgano can manipulate multiple controls at the same time. His predilection for high speed combines with a nasty temper that ignites when other pilots attempt to pass him. He races on behalf of Gardulla the Hutt in the Boonta Eve Classic, and is the object of intense betting between Gardulla and Jabba. Gasgano finishes in second place, after Anakin Skywalker.

Custom racer Gasgano pilots a custom Ord Pedrovia podracer with 9-meter (29-foot) bulbous engines that boast great acceleration.

CLEGG HOLDFAST

APPEARANCES I **SPECIES** Nosaurian **HOMEWORLD** New Plympto **AFFILIATION** None

A journalist for *Podracing Quarterly*, the arrogant Clegg Holdfast enters competitions to cover stories from the inside. Although his fellow racers maintain that he's a better writer than pilot, he proudly displays a set of decorative medals on his lapel as a testament to his racing prowess. In the second lap of the Boonta Eve Classic, Sebulba opens up his own podracer's flame-jets while next to Holdfast. The blaze cooks Holdfast's engines and forces him to crash into the desert.

TEEMTO PAGALIES

APPEARANCES I **SPECIES** Veknoid **HOMEWORLD** Moonus Mandel **AFFILIATION** None

An outcast from his homeworld, the flamboyant Teemto Pagalies pilots an IPG-X1131 LongTail podracer with 10.67-meter (35-foot) engines. During the second lap of the Boonta Eve Classic, Tusken Raiders snipe his podracer, causing him to crash. Fortunately, Pagalies survives.

Long engines Seated in the cockpit of his IPG-X1131 LongTail *(above)*, Pagalies boasts the longest pair of engines in the Boonta Eve Classic *(left)*.

ODY MANDRELL

APPEARANCES I **SPECIES** Er'Kit **HOMEWORLD** Tatooine **AFFILIATION** None

A foolhardy thrill-seeker with an insatiable appetite for high speeds, Ody Mandrell pilots his massive Exelbrok podracer with wild abandon and a blatant disregard for safety. During a pit stop in the Boonta Eve Classic, one of his pit droids is sucked into his podracer's engine intakes, crippling his vehicle and eliminating him from the race.

FODE AND BEED

APPEARANCES I **SPECIES** Troig **HOMEWORLD** Pollillus **AFFILIATION** None

Exuberant, colorful, and not always too accurate with facts, Fode and Beed are the popular announcers of the Boonta Eve Classic. Like all Troigs, Fode and Beed share a body with two heads, each with its own distinctive personality and speech patterns. Fode's red-mottled head provides commentary in Basic, while Beed's green-mottled head provides counterpoint in Huttese.

JABBA THE HUTT

APPEARANCES I, CW, IV, VI **SPECIES** Hutt **HOMEWORLD** Tatooine **AFFILIATION** Hutt Grand Council, Crymorah Syndicate

A loathsome slug and a vile gangster, Jabba the Hutt is the preeminent kingpin of crime in the Outer Rim Territories. Basing his operations out of an opulent palace on Tatooine, Jabba's lucrative and unsavory rackets include slavery, gunrunning, spice smuggling, gambling, and extortion. While Jabba attends the Boonta Eve Classic that Anakin Skywalker unexpectedly wins, he is actually bored by the races.

During the Clone Wars, Jabba's son Rotta is kidnapped. The Jedi rescue Rotta and uncover that the Separatists and Jabba's own uncle Ziro are behind the kidnapping, so Jabba pledges to help the Republic war effort. When Chairman Papanoida visits his palace, demanding a blood sample from Jabba's bounty hunter Greedo, Jabba grants his request after hearing that Papanoida is searching for his missing children. Fearing that Ziro will expose the Hutts' illegal activities, Jabba hires bounty hunter Cad Bane, who extracts Ziro from prison. Jabba then secretly pays Sy Snootles to locate Ziro's incriminating records, kill him, and then pass the documents to Jabba. When Maul forms his own criminal organization called the Shadow Collective, Jabba and the rest of the Hutt cartel are coerced into joining. They leave the group after Maul is imprisoned.

Jabba continues operating during the Imperial era. After a drought on Tatooine, he extracts a water tax from its residents, sending bounty hunters after anyone who resists. He also sends Greedo to capture Figrin D'an, leader of the band Figrin D'an and the Modal Nodes. Jabba agrees that D'an can pay off his debts by having the band play for him, and only releases them from servitude after they expose Greedo for conning Jabba. Han Solo, captain of the *Millennium Falcon*, is hired by Jabba as a smuggler, becoming the best on his payroll. At one point, Han has to jettison Jabba's cargo into space to escape arrest. The Hutt later demands compensation and sends bounty hunters after Han. Greedo attempts to gun down Han in the Mos Eisley Cantina, but fails. Afterward, Han confronts Jabba, who agrees to give him an extension on his repayment, but with the addition of a hefty percentage. Jabba places a large bounty on Han's head when he learns he has joined the Rebel Alliance instead of working to pay him back.

Bad business
Han assures Jabba inside Docking Bay 94 at Mos Eisley spaceport that he'll repay the Hutt for a lost shipment of valuable spice. Jabba reminds Han that failure to do so could cost the smuggler his life.

Following the Battle of Yavin, the Empire requires more weapons, so the Emperor sends Darth Vader to negotiate with Jabba. After Vader dispatches a few of the Hutt's guards and demands the personal use of two of his bounty hunters, they agree that Jabba will supply the Empire with weapons in exchange for credits. The Hutts can also continue to operate their criminal enterprises. On another occasion, smugglers Lando Calrissian and Sana Starros swindle Jabba, stealing weapons and 20,000 credits from him. Jabba shows leniency to Max Rebo's thieving brother Azool Phantelle. Instead of killing him, Jabba forces him to serve as a drinks trolley aboard his sail barge, the *Khetanna*. Eventually, the bounty hunter Boba Fett delivers a carbonite-frozen Han to Jabba's palace. Jabba anticipates that Han's friends will attempt to rescue him from the palace, but is confident that they will fail. Jabba's misplaced confidence leads to his death aboard the *Khetanna* at the hands of Leia Organa—who becomes known as the Huttslayer.

Podracing
Jabba presides over the Boonta Eve Classic from the royal box at Mos Espa Arena.

"There will be no bargain, young Jedi. I shall enjoy watching you die."

JABBA ***(translated from Huttese)***

GARDULLA THE HUTT

APPEARANCES I, CW **SPECIES** Hutt **HOMEWORLD** Nal Hutta
AFFILIATION Hutt Grand Council

The Hutts control the smuggling trade in the Outer Rim, earning their crooked profits far outside the watchful eyes of law and order. In the years leading up to the Battle of Naboo, Gardulla the Hutt is one of the most powerful Hutt crime lords on Tatooine, and, alongside Jabba the Hutt, wields control over the criminal underworld. Both Anakin Skywalker and his mother Shmi are Gardulla's slaves, but she loses them to Watto in a bet. During the Clone Wars, Gardulla imprisons the traitorous Ziro the Hutt in her palace on Nal Hutta, which brings the unwanted attention of Jedi investigators Obi-Wan Kenobi and Quinlan Vos.

BIB FORTUNA

APPEARANCES I, VI **SPECIES** Twi'lek
HOMEWORLD Ryloth
AFFILIATION Jabba's court

This sharp-toothed Twi'lek works for Jabba the Hutt as his chief aide and majordomo for over three decades. Fortuna demonstrates tremendous patience in dealing with his master's bad habits, including waking Jabba every time the Hutt dozes off during podraces. Originally from Ryloth, Fortuna controls most operations inside Jabba's Tatooine palace, including welcoming visitors who call at the remote stronghold. After Jabba displays a carbonized Han Solo on the wall of his throne room, Fortuna is the first of the Hutt's administrators to intercept Luke Skywalker when he arrives to rescue Han. Fortuna's weak will makes him particularly susceptible to Jedi mind tricks, which allows Luke to get to Jabba with little trouble.

RATTS TYERELL

APPEARANCES I **SPECIES** Aleena
HOMEWORLD Aleen
AFFILIATION None

Short in stature, but with lightning-fast reflexes, Ratts Tyerell rises through the ranks of the galaxy's best podracers to earn a starting place in Tatooine's Boonta Eve Classic, just prior to the Battle of Naboo. Tyerell's podracer is capable of tremendous thrust, but a jammed accelerator in the second lap of the race causes him to lose control. As his podracer roars through a cave, it smashes into a rocky stalactite, and Tyerell perishes in a fiery explosion.

AURRA SING

APPEARANCES I, CW **SPECIES** Palliduvan **HOMEWORLD** Nar Shaddaa
AFFILIATION Bounty hunter

One of the galaxy's most lethal killers, Aurra Sing earns her keep as a freelance assassin. The tell-tale antenna of a biocomputer protruding from her skull means that Sing receives extrasensory data, enabling her to track multiple threats simultaneously and line up distant shots with her long-barreled sniper rifle. Though Sing prefers to work solo, she finds a kindred spirit in space pirate Hondo Ohnaka, with whom she even shares a brief romance. Other associates occasionally recruited by Sing include the cowardly Klatooinian Castas and Bossk, the brutal Trandoshan bounty hunter.

Prior to the Naboo Blockade, Sing, Cad Bane, and two other bounty hunters are hired by Darth Maul to assist him with capturing and killing a Jedi Padawan. During the Clone Wars, Aurra Sing finds an unlikely partner in Boba Fett, a boy who inherits the ship *Slave I* from his bounty-hunting father, Jango Fett. Sing entices Boba with the promise of taking revenge on the Jedi who had executed his father, and then exploits the boy's resemblance to younger Republic clones to sabotage and destroy the Republic attack cruiser *Endurance*. Abducting survivors from the wreckage of the *Endurance*, Sing retreats to Hondo Ohnaka's outpost on Florrum, with Jedi investigators in hot pursuit. Sing tries to escape in *Slave I*, but Ahsoka Tano severely damages the ship, leaving Sing for dead. Unbeknownst to her pursuers, Sing survives and is freed from the crashed ship by Hondo. Disappearing offworld to lick her wounds, Sing later attempts to assassinate Senator Amidala at a refugee conference on Alderaan. Thwarted again by Ahsoka, Sing is taken prisoner, but escapes to find work with Cad Bane, where she serves as team sniper during Bane's bold mission to rescue Ziro the Hutt from a Coruscant prison. Sing later dies at the hands of Tobias Beckett, a smuggler working for Crimson Dawn.

Lethal weapon
Aurra Sing's legendary skills as an assassin keeps her employed for decades *(far right)*. During the Boonta Eve Classic podrace, an observant Sing watches in astonishment as the young Anakin Skywalker wins the race fairly *(right)*.

Nomadic warriors
Tusken tribesmen stand guard outside a robust—yet easily dismantled and transported—shelter, built to withstand the devastating sandstorms that plague their desert home.

Desert ambush
The Tusken leader URoRRuR'R'R attacks Luke Skywalker seconds before Obi-Wan Kenobi comes to his rescue.

TUSKEN RAIDERS

APPEARANCES I, II, Reb, IV **SPECIES** Tusken
HOMEWORLD Tatooine **AFFILIATION** None

Tusken Raiders, commonly called Sand People, are fierce desert nomads native to Tatooine. Unlike the Jawas, Tatooine's other intelligent species, Tusken Raiders are aggressive and easily drawn into conflict with moisture farmers and other settlers. Few have seen a Tusken's true face, as they cover their bodies with multiple layers of tight wrappings and wear masks with breathing filters to survive Tatooine's harsh desert environment. Tusken Raiders live in small clans within the rocky Jundland Wastes, moving around on the backs of shaggy banthas, and disguising their numbers by marching in single file. Tusken warriors carry stolen rifles and gaderffiis—metal weapons that function as both clubs and axes. A typical Tusken encampment consists of a small cluster of tents guarded by snarling massiffs.

Just before the Battle of Geonosis, Anakin Skywalker's mother, Shmi, is kidnapped by a Tusken raiding party. By the time Anakin arrives at their camp, the injured Shmi has been held captive for weeks, and dies before her son can rescue her. In retaliation, an enraged Anakin slaughters the entire Tusken tribe.

During the Imperial era, Tuskens ambush Ezra Bridger and rebel astromech Chopper, who are saved by the former Sith apprentice Maul. Years later, Anakin, now known as Darth Vader, returns to Tatooine following the Battle of Yavin and decimates another Tusken village. Fearing his wrath, the Tuskens erect a shrine to Vader and sacrifice some of their own to him in the hope this act will stop him from returning.

"I never ask for permission to do anything." **AURRA SING**

SUPREME CHANCELLOR VALORUM

APPEARANCES I, CW **SPECIES** Human
HOMEWORLD Coruscant
AFFILIATION Galactic Senate

Finis Valorum rules the Republic as Supreme Chancellor in the years leading up to the Battle of Naboo. He sends his political aide Silman and Jedi Master Sifo-Dyas on a secret mission to meet with the Pyke Syndicate, but they never return and are believed dead. Though he is well-intentioned, Valorum is unable to prevent the Trade Federation from blockading the planet Naboo. Valorum arranges for two Jedi, Qui-Gon Jinn and Obi-Wan Kenobi, to negotiate an end to the blockade, but instead the Trade Federation invades Naboo. Ultimately, Naboo's Queen Amidala calls for a vote of no confidence in Valorum, forcing him out of office. During the Clone Wars, Valorum is visited by his old friend Yoda, and Valorum informs him of the mission he sent Silman and Sifo-Dyas on.

"Choose what is right, not what is easy." YODA

YODA

The last Grand Master of the Jedi Order, Yoda is more than 900 years old. Forced into exile by the Empire, Yoda trains Luke Skywalker in the ways of the Jedi, then passes into the Force.

APPEARANCES I, II, CW, III, Reb, V, VI, VIII, FoD **SPECIES** Unknown **HOMEWORLD** Unknown **AFFILIATION** Jedi

ON THE COUNCIL

Though little is known of Yoda's early life, his influence within the Jedi Order is tremendous. As Grand Master, the oldest and wisest of the Order, he serves on the elite Jedi Council with other high-ranking masters and teaches young students in the Jedi Temple. When Qui-Gon Jinn brings Anakin Skywalker before the Council, Yoda argues that the boy is too dangerous to be trained. He later changes his mind after Qui-Gon is killed by a Sith on Naboo, but he never entirely conquers his feelings of unease. During the next few years, Yoda keeps watch over Padawan Skywalker and his master, Obi-Wan Kenobi.

Discussion among equals
Master Yoda shares his wisdom with Council members. When duty calls the Jedi to other parts of the galaxy, they report to Yoda in the form of a long-distance hologram.

THE RISING DARKNESS

Count Dooku, one of Yoda's former students, emerges as the leader of a Separatist movement. When Dooku becomes a threat to galactic peace, Yoda leads an army of clone troopers against Separatist forces on Geonosis and defeats Dooku in lightsaber combat. During the Clone Wars, Yoda strives to treat each clone soldier as an individual worthy of respect. Yet as the war drags on, Yoda and Mace Windu sense a gathering darkness that diminishes their ability to use the Force. Finally, Yoda is ambushed by his clone troopers on Kashyyyk and flees offworld with help from the Wookiee Chewbacca.

Duel with the dark side
Yoda fights Count Dooku on Geonosis, forcing his former student to flee.

Duel of masters
The full power of the light side and the dark side of the Force is on display during Yoda's clash with Emperor Palpatine. Outmatched, Yoda retreats and waits to train a new champion to lead the fight against evil.

INTO EXILE

Returning to Coruscant, Yoda fights Emperor Palpatine in a spectacular test of Force powers. Their showdown begins inside Palpatine's office and spills into the Galactic Senate Chamber. Though Yoda is a tough combatant, the Emperor uses his Sith powers to release lightning bolts and hurl floating platforms at his foe. Ultimately the battle proves too much for Yoda, who barely escapes and is whisked away to safety by Senator Bail Organa. After leaving Anakin and Padmé's twin children in the care of Obi-Wan and Bail Organa, Yoda travels to the swamps of Dagobah to begin a new life away from the Empire's hunters. The remote world gives Yoda the chance to meditate on the Force, and a dark-side cave serves as a place of spiritual trial.

A NEW HOPE

Luke comes to Dagobah after the Battle of Hoth to learn the ways of the Jedi. Throughout Luke's training, Yoda keeps the truth of his relationship to Vader a secret for fear it might trigger Luke's fall to the dark side. Luke loses his first fight with Vader on Cloud City, but Yoda declares him a true Jedi when he returns to Dagobah. Yoda then passes into the light of the Force.

Luminous being
Yoda gains strength from the living things in Dagobah's swamps and tries to teach Luke that the Force is everywhere.

MASTER TO MASTER

Decades later, Yoda appears to Luke, who has since grown disillusioned with the Jedi Order and is about to burn down the Jedi library on Ahch-To. Before Skywalker can act, Yoda destroys the library himself with a lightning strike. Rather than looking to the past, Master Yoda teaches Skywalker one more lesson: Failure is the greatest teacher. This insight helps Luke move past his failings and realize he must help the Resistance stand up to Kylo Ren.

Luke's final lesson
"We are what they grow beyond." Yoda explains to Luke that the true burden of all masters is that they will be surpassed by their students.

More than he seems
Both Count Dooku and Luke Skywalker seem to underestimate Yoda, thinking his small size and advanced age make him less formidable. But Yoda's true strength comes from within.

timeline

CRISIS IN THE REPUBLIC

Jedi Master
Yoda is centuries old and becomes a leading member of the Jedi Council long before the Battle of Naboo.

Rescue mission
Yoda rescues a Force-sensitive youth named Lo from pirates hoping to sell him to the Jedi.

Force calling
Yoda follows the Force to the Vagadarr system and discovers the last of a race of enormous stone creatures. There he pacifies a war between the local tribes that live in the shadow of these mountainous beings.

Evaluating Anakin
Yoda senses fear and attachment in young Anakin's heart, but eventually allows him to be trained as a Jedi.

Return of the Sith
Qui-Gon dies on Naboo at the hands of Darth Maul, a Sith. Yoda becomes gravely worried.

Separatist crisis
Count Dooku, Yoda's former Jedi student, forms a Separatist movement that threatens the Republic.

THE CLONE WARS

▲ Dueling Dooku
On Geonosis, war breaks out with the Separatists. Yoda and Dooku fight one-on-one.

▲ Clone Wars
As a Jedi general, Yoda leads the Republic's clone troopers into battles across the galaxy.

Order 66
Yoda's clone troopers turn against him on Kashyyyk. He slips away and meets up with other surviving Jedi.

THE EMPIRE ERA

Facing the Emperor
Yoda tries to stop Palpatine, the new Emperor, from taking control. He loses, and barely escapes with his life.

Dagobah
On a distant swamp planet, Yoda goes into exile and awaits the rise of one who can overthrow the Empire.

Ezra's guidance
Speaking through the Force, Yoda counsels Ezra Bridger to find Malachor, a planet that could hold answers to defeating Darth Vader and the Inquisitors.

▲ Training a Jedi
Luke, Anakin's son, becomes Yoda's final student.

One with the Force
After instructing Luke, the great Jedi Master passes on and is reborn as a Force spirit.

"I'm going to put an end to this, once and for all!" MACE WINDU

MACE WINDU

Second only to Master Yoda in reputation, Master Mace Windu leads the Jedi Council during the waning years of the Republic. Betrayal costs him his life, but he never relents in his fight against the dark side.

APPEARANCES I, II, CW, III **SPECIES** Human **HOMEWORLD** Haruun Kal **AFFILIATION** Jedi

SITH THREAT

A high-ranking member of the Jedi Council at the start of the Battle of Naboo, Mace Windu is troubled by signs indicating the return of the Sith. He investigates the growing influence of the dark side as Count Dooku's Separatist movement takes shape, and when Obi-Wan Kenobi discovers evidence that the Separatists are preparing to go to war against the Republic, Mace leads a task force of 200 Jedi to Geonosis to do battle. He faces off against Dooku's agent, Jango Fett, in the Geonosian execution arena and beheads the bounty hunter with one swipe of his lightsaber.

High standards
Mace Windu isn't impressed by young Anakin Skywalker and initially refuses his admittance to the Jedi Order.

Jedi authority
As a Jedi general during the Clone Wars, Mace is an elite military figure.

THE CLONE WARS

Mace Windu accepts the rank of general in the Grand Army of the Republic during the Clone Wars, and serves as both a strategist and a frontline combatant in numerous conflicts with the Separatists. On Ryloth, Mace leads the AT-RT drivers of Lightning Squadron to assist freedom fighter Cham Syndulla in the liberation of his world. He discovers the slumbering Zillo Beast on Malastare and escapes several attempts on his life from Boba Fett, the orphaned son of Jango Fett, who is out for revenge. Late in the war, Mace becomes alarmed by the rising threat of the dark side and steps up his efforts to unmask the suspected Sith manipulator behind it all.

Against the Separatists
Mace gives counsel to Anakin as the Clone Wars rage across the galaxy.

Final battle
The dark side power wielded by Palpatine is a shocking surprise for Mace.

CONFRONTING EVIL

Following the Battle of Coruscant, Mace receives news that Supreme Chancellor Palpatine is actually the Sith Lord behind the recent turmoil across the galaxy. Mace selects a small squad of Jedi—Agen Kolar, Kit Fisto, and Saesee Tiin—to arrest the chancellor, but they die when Palpatine fights back. Mace seems to be winning until Anakin suddenly intervenes and cuts off the Jedi Master's hand. Palpatine seals Mace's fate with a blast of Force lightning, sending him through the window to his death.

timeline

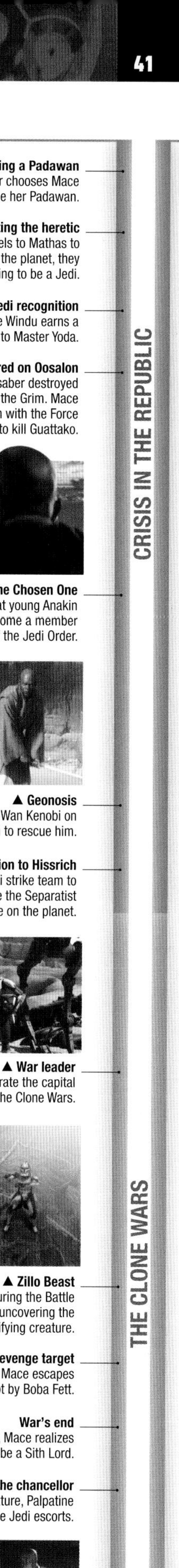

Becoming a Padawan
Jedi Master Cyslin Myr chooses Mace Windu to become her Padawan.

Hunting the heretic
Alongside Myr, Mace travels to Mathas to look into a rogue Jedi. On the planet, they uncover a swindler pretending to be a Jedi.

Jedi recognition
For his skill and wisdom, Mace Windu earns a place on the Jedi Council next to Master Yoda.

Captured on Oosalon
Mace is captured and his lightsaber destroyed by forces of warlord Guattako the Grim. Mace reconstructs his weapon with the Force and uses it to kill Guattako.

▲ The Chosen One
Mace believes that young Anakin should not be trained to become a member of the Jedi Order.

▲ Geonosis
When Count Dooku captures Obi-Wan Kenobi on Geonosis, Mace leads the team to rescue him.

Mission to Hissrich
Mace leads a small Jedi strike team to Hissrich to investigate the Separatist presence on the planet.

▲ War leader
On Ryloth, Mace helps liberate the capital from the Separatists during the Clone Wars.

▲ Zillo Beast
Mace's efforts during the Battle of Malastare lead to uncovering the gigantic, terrifying creature.

Revenge target
Aboard a Republic fleet carrier, Mace escapes an assassination attempt by Boba Fett.

War's end
As the Clone Wars wind down, Mace realizes that Chancellor Palpatine might be a Sith Lord.

Arresting the chancellor
Forced into revealing his true nature, Palpatine cuts down Mace's three Jedi escorts.

▲ Fatal battle
Desperate to preserve Palpatine's life, Anakin cuts off Mace's hand. A blast of lightning sends the Jedi Master through the window to his death.

Defender of the Force
Mace Windu is a formidable warrior and a stern judge of character. He believes in action, not words, and is the first Jedi to move against Count Dooku on Geonosis. He assembles a squad to arrest Chancellor Palpatine when he learns of Palpatine's Sith secret.

KI-ADI-MUNDI

APPEARANCES I, II, CW, III **SPECIES** Cerean
HOMEWORLD Cerea **AFFILIATION** Jedi

Ki-Adi-Mundi is a Cerean Jedi Master whose white beard and wise features attest to his years spent in the Jedi Order. He joins the Jedi Council prior to the Battle of Naboo and helps evaluate Anakin Skywalker's Force potential when Qui-Gon Jinn brings him to Coruscant. Qui-Gon's concerns that the Sith may have returned aren't enough to trouble Ki-Adi-Mundi, who reminds the Council that the Sith haven't been sighted for a millennium. Years later, Ki-Adi-Mundi is part of the Republic force that travels to Carnelion IV, where the group rescues Jedi Knight Obi-Wan Kenobi and his Padawan, Anakin, and stops a war raging between two groups on the planet. When Count Dooku later abandons the Jedi Order and emerges as the head of a Separatist movement, Ki-Adi-Mundi refuses to believe Dooku could be capable of orchestrating bombings, emphasizing to his colleagues that Dooku is a political idealist who seems incapable of murder.

Nevertheless, war soon breaks out between the Republic and Dooku's Separatists. Ki-Adi-Mundi is one of the Jedi who travels to Geonosis, where he infiltrates the execution arena. He survives the subsequent battle and receives the rank of general in the Grand Army of the Republic. Ki-Adi-Mundi leads the Galactic Marines, clone troopers captained by Commander Bacara, in engagements against the Separatist droid armies. As the war continues, Ki-Adi-Mundi sees how much Anakin has grown as a Jedi and a warrior, and during the Second Battle of Geonosis, he engages Anakin in a friendly wager over which of them can destroy the most battle droids.

With the Galactic Marines, Ki-Adi-Mundi scores a number of Republic victories and forms a close professional bond with Commander Bacara. During the late-stage Outer Rim Sieges, Ki-Adi-Mundi leads his clones to capture Mygeeto from the Separatists, which is where they are stationed when Darth Sidious issues Order 66. Commander Bacara orders his troopers to open fire on their Jedi general as he leads the charge across a bridge, and Ki-Adi-Mundi falls under the surprise onslaught.

Evaluating Anakin
With his fellow Council members, Ki-Adi-Mundi decides the fate of young Anakin.

Unprepared
Ki-Adi-Mundi's clone troopers betray him on Mygeeto.

PLO KOON

APPEARANCES I, II, CW, III **SPECIES** Kel Dor
HOMEWORLD Dorin **AFFILIATION** Jedi

Plo Koon is a Kel Dor who needs a mask to protect his eyes and lungs from oxygen-rich environments. Early in his Jedi career, Plo Koon discovers a young, Force-sensitive Togruta girl named Ahsoka Tano and brings her to Coruscant to become a Jedi. Plo Koon sits on the Jedi Council, where his guidance is always respected, but the outbreak of the Clone Wars allows him to demonstrate his battle skills as well. One early engagement pits Plo Koon's armada against the Separatist cruiser *Malevolence*, which ends in near-total defeat for the Republic. Plo Koon and a small number of clone troopers survive in an escape pod and evade battle droid clean-up squads until they are rescued.

Plo Koon quickly jumps back into the fight, helping Ahsoka navigate the Coruscant underworld to uncover the whereabouts of Aurra Sing. Plo Koon and Ahsoka travel to the headquarters of space pirate Hondo Ohnaka on Florrum and arrest a young Boba Fett. On a later mission, Plo Koon leads the Republic fleet to the prison planet of Lola Sayu to rescue Jedi Master Even Piell from the Citadel, and personally pilots the gunship that extracts the groundside rescue team.

At the end of the Clone Wars, Plo Koon flies his Jedi starfighter during the Republic's capture of Cato Neimoidia. During a post-battle patrol flight, his clone pilot escorts receive Order 66 and fire shots that cripple Plo Koon's ship. He dies when his starfighter crashes into one of Cato Neimoidia's bridge cities.

Meeting Ahsoka
Plo Koon senses the Force in a Togruta girl while visiting her planet. Impressed by her potential, he brings young Ahsoka Tano to the Jedi Temple for training.

SAESEE TIIN

APPEARANCES I, II, CW, III **SPECIES** Iktotchi
HOMEWORLD Iktotch **AFFILIATION** Jedi

Saesee Tiin is a Jedi Master and a member of the Jedi Council who belongs to the horned species known as the Iktotchi. One of the quieter members of the Council, Tiin is known more for his starfighter piloting skills than his Force teachings. During the Clone Wars, Tiin is among the Council members who receive the distressing news that their colleague Even Piell has been captured by the Separatists and imprisoned in the impenetrable Citadel on the planet Lola Sayu. While Obi-Wan Kenobi and Anakin lead the rescue mission, Tiin flies cover for Plo Koon's gunship during the dangerous extraction process and commands fellow pilots Adi Gallia and Kit Fisto in the fight against Lola Sayu's droid forces. The Battle of Umbara offers another opportunity for Tiin to provide air cover for Republic troops when he helps Obi-Wan, Anakin, and Jedi Master Pong Krell capture the shadowy world for the Republic.

At the end of the Clone Wars, Mace Windu entrusts Tiin with the news that Supreme Chancellor Palpatine is actually a powerful Sith Lord. Tiin follows Master Windu into the chancellor's office, backed up by fellow Jedi Agen Kolar and Kit Fisto. None of the Jedi expect resistance, but when Mace announces he is placing Palpatine under arrest, the chancellor suddenly springs into action. Agen Kolar is the first to fall. Tiin moves to strike, but Palpatine is faster and cuts down the Iktotchi Jedi Master.

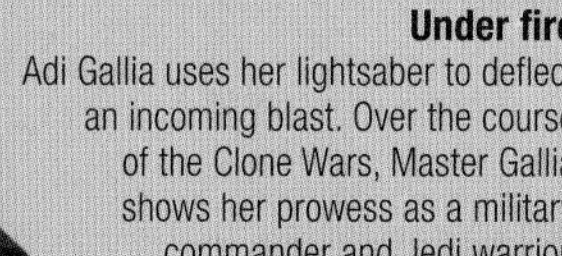

War veteran
A war weary General Saesee Tiin *(left)* has seen more than his fair share of combat during the Clone Wars, including the audacious rescue of Obi-Wan, Anakin, and Padmé during the Battle of Geonosis *(above)*.

Under fire
Adi Gallia uses her lightsaber to deflect an incoming blast. Over the course of the Clone Wars, Master Gallia shows her prowess as a military commander and Jedi warrior.

ADI GALLIA

APPEARANCES I, II, CW **SPECIES** Tholothian
HOMEWORLD Tholoth **AFFILIATION** Jedi

Both Adi Gallia and her cousin Stass Allie serve in the Jedi Order, but only Gallia sits on the Jedi Council prior to the Battle of Naboo. She serves in this elite role for years, observing with concern the rise of Count Dooku's Separatists. When armed conflict finally breaks out on Geonosis, she is on the frontlines and becomes a battlefield commander as the Clone Wars take hold of the galaxy. With Anakin Skywalker, Gallia leads the effort to rescue Jedi Master Eeth Koth from the flagship of General Grievous, and in a later engagement, she pilots a starfighter during a daring prison break from the Citadel of Lola Sayu. When General Grievous destroys her fleet, Gallia is taken captive. Plo Koon pursues Grievous, boarding his vessel with a contingent of clone troopers and rescuing Gallia. Along with Obi-Wan Kenobi, Gallia travels to the planet Bray to help its people. They discover Count Dooku is in league with Ravna, Lord of Shadows—a powerful individual whose blood can turn others into batlike beings like him. When Ravna turns on Dooku, the Jedi and Sith team up to defeat this dangerous threat.

Gallia meets her end when she and Obi-Wan hunt the dangerous team of Maul and Savage Opress, the vengeful dark-side Nightbrothers determined to destroy the Jedi. At the Cybloc transfer station, Gallia picks up their trail and follows the duo to Florrum. They arrive to find a battle raging between pirate leader Hondo Ohnaka and the two Nightbrothers, with many of Ohnaka's former crew members now working for the Sith. Obi-Wan and Gallia try to even the odds, but the power of their foes proves to be too great. Opress gravely injures Gallia by ramming her with his horns and then delivers a killing blow with his red-bladed lightsaber. Her cousin Allie takes her place on the Council.

EETH KOTH

APPEARANCES I, II, CW **SPECIES** Zabrak **HOMEWORLD** Iridonia
AFFILIATION Jedi, the Ganthic Enlightenment

An esteemed Zabrak Jedi Master who sits on the Jedi Council at the time of the Battle of Naboo, Eeth Koth is among the masters that evaluate Anakin Skywalker's fitness for Jedi training. Koth remains on the Council throughout the Separatist crisis and serves on the strike force that invades Geonosis at the beginning of the Clone Wars. He is believed to have been killed in battle when his gunship takes a direct hit, but Koth later returns to active duty, and is placed in command of the Republic Star Destroyer *Steadfast*. General Grievous attacks the ship and captures Koth, but the latter shrewdly reveals his location using a secret tap-code during a hologram transmission from Grievous. This enables the Council to track Koth and dispatch Anakin Skywalker and Adi Gallia to lead the mission to free him. Toward the end of the Clone Wars, Koth is kicked off the Council and leaves the Order. He becomes a priest of the Ganthic Enlightenment and marries a fellow Zabrak named Mira. Darth Vader and his Inquisitors track the couple down just after Mira has given birth to their child. Koth tries to offer them information on other Jedi survivors in exchange for his family's lives, but the villains refuse him. While Vader kills Koth in battle, Mira escapes, but their child is captured by an Inquisitor.

OPPO RANCISIS

APPEARANCES I, II, CW **SPECIES** Thisspiasian
HOMEWORLD Thisspias **AFFILIATION** Jedi

The long-lived Oppo Rancisis is a curious sight in the Jedi Council. A Thisspiasian, he has the lower body of a snake and often sits coiled in quiet contemplation. Master Rancisis has long, claw-like fingernails and a thick beard that masks his face. A skillful tactician, he gains a position on the Council prior to the Battle of Naboo, and is among the first Jedi to learn that the Sith have returned after the appearance of Darth Maul. Rancisis remains a high-ranking Jedi and a key military adviser throughout the Clone Wars, during which he becomes a Jedi general coordinating Republic forces across the galaxy. Rancisis is one of a handful of Jedi that survive Order 66.

"To walk the path of the Jedi, one's spirit must be strong. That requires discipline." **OPPO RANCISIS**

EVEN PIELL

APPEARANCES I, II, CW **SPECIES** Lannik
HOMEWORLD Lannik **AFFILIATION** Jedi

The battle-scarred Even Piell earns a place on the Jedi Council prior to the Battle of Naboo. Master Piell takes part in the Republic assault on Geonosis at the start of the Clone Wars, and later becomes a prisoner of war when Separatist forces capture him and Republic Navy Captain Wilhuff Tarkin. Incarcerated in the impregnable Citadel prison on Lola Sayu, Piell withstands torture to preserve the top-secret coordinates of the hyperlane known as the Nexus Route. Despite a rescue effort led by Anakin Skywalker and Ahsoka Tano, Piell is mortally wounded by a wild anooba hound as he escapes from the Citadel.

DEPA BILLABA

APPEARANCES I, II **SPECIES** Human **HOMEWORLD** Chalacta
AFFILIATION Jedi

Jedi Master Depa Billaba is a former Padawan of Mace Windu and is highly regarded for her wisdom. Billaba is a valued member of the Jedi Council during the final years of the Republic. She accompanies the senatorial mission to Bromlarch, which leads to its people being saved from famine. Her sister, Sar Labooda, also serves as a Jedi, but is killed in the Battle of Geonosis at the start of the Clone Wars. During the wars, Billaba suffers a devastating defeat at the hands of General Grievous' forces on Haruun Kaal and falls into a coma. Billaba eventually recovers and, with a youngling named Caleb Dume, stops a bombing of the Jedi Temple. She decides to take Caleb as her Padawan, and together they see action on Kardoa and face Grievous on Mygeeto. When the clone troopers attack the Jedi during Order 66, she dies protecting Caleb on Kaller. He adopts the name Kanan Jarrus, and later honors Billaba's memory by operating a rebel cell on Lothal and taking Ezra Bridger as a Padawan.

Elite company
Alongside Mace Windu and Saesee Tiin, Depa Billaba attends the ceremony marking the defeat of the Trade Federation in the Battle of Naboo.

YADDLE

APPEARANCES I **SPECIES** Unknown
HOMEWORLD Unknown **AFFILIATION** Jedi

Very little is known about Yaddle's species. Her short build, long ears, and extended lifespan mark her as a member of the same species as Jedi Master Yoda, and Yaddle also shares Yoda's remarkable affinity for the Force. After rising through the ranks of the Jedi Order, Yaddle achieves the highest possible reward for her contribution—a seat on the Jedi Council. She helps judge Anakin Skywalker's fitness for Jedi training and contributes to the Jedi efforts to resolve the Naboo blockade crisis and uncover clues about the return of the Sith. Following the Battle of Naboo, Yaddle takes a less active role in Jedi affairs.

YARAEL POOF

APPEARANCES I **SPECIES** Quermian **HOMEWORLD** Quermia
AFFILIATION Jedi

This famed Jedi hails from the planet Quermia, homeworld of a species known for their willowy appearance and craning necks. After being promoted to Jedi Master, Yarael Poof wins a place on the Jedi Council, where he serves alongside Yoda and Mace Windu. Blessed with two brains, Master Poof is an expert practitioner of Jedi mind control. He stands out among his fellow Council members thanks to his towering stature and possesses a second pair of arms that he hides beneath his robes. By the time of the Battle of Geonosis, Yarael Poof's spot on the Jedi Council has been filled by Jedi Master Coleman Trebor.

LOTT DOD

APPEARANCES I, CW **SPECIES** Neimoidian
HOMEWORLD Cato Neimoidia
AFFILIATION Trade Federation, Galactic Senate, Separatists

The Trade Federation controls most interstellar shipping in the Outer Rim, making it one of the most powerful entities in the galaxy. Its influence is evident when Lott Dod is appointed to the Galactic Senate, a post normally reserved for representatives of systems and sectors. As a senator, Dod thwarts the taxation of the Free Trade Zones and secretly helps organize the Trade Federation's invasion of Naboo. When Naboo's queen, Padmé Amidala, comes to Coruscant to plead for the liberation of her world, Dod claims that she has no proof of her accusations. Throughout the Clone Wars, Dod continues to advance the interests of the Separatists while claiming neutrality.

MAS AMEDDA

APPEARANCES I, II, CW, III **SPECIES** Chagrian
HOMEWORLD Champala **AFFILIATION** Republic, Galactic Senate, Empire

This politically savvy Chagrian is given an elite post in the Republic's government when he becomes vice chancellor during the tenure of Supreme Chancellor Valorum. The events surrounding the Battle of Naboo result in a vote of no confidence against Valorum and his removal from office, yet Amedda retains his position under Valorum's successor, Chancellor Palpatine. Power-hungry and pragmatic, Amedda advises Palpatine during the Separatist Crisis, and before the Clone Wars arranges the sudden Senate vote that grants the chancellor emergency war powers, allowing the Republic to seize control of the clone army discovered on Kamino. Following Order 66, Amedda proclaims that Palpatine will usher in a new age of freedom—and then throws Jedi Master Yoda's lightsaber into a furnace. His longstanding loyalty to Palpatine later earns him the position of Grand Vizier in the Galactic Empire, nominally second-in-command to Palpatine himself.

However, following Palpatine's death, Amedda lacks any real power, and the Empire shatters into multiple factions. Fleet Admiral Gallius Rax, who is in charge of much of the surviving fleet, does not assist Amedda on Coruscant. Amedda attempts to turn himself in to the New Republic, but their leaders refuse to accept his empty surrender. He is imprisoned in the Imperial Palace by Rax's forces until his rescue by a gang of children who deliver him to the New Republic. After the Battle of Jakku, most of the remaining Imperial forces are defeated, so Amedda represents the Empire at the signing of the Galactic Concordance. He then becomes the head of Coruscant's provisional government.

SENATOR TIKKES

APPEARANCES I, II, III **SPECIES** Quarren
HOMEWORLD Mon Cala **AFFILIATION** Republic, Galactic Senate, Separatists

Tikkes represents Mon Cala in the Galactic Senate. Sympathizing with Count Dooku's Separatist movement, he resigns from the Senate to support the Confederacy of Independent Systems, and is rewarded with a seat on the Separatist Council. At the end of the Clone Wars, Tikkes, along with the rest of the Council, is killed by Darth Vader on Mustafar.

SLY MOORE

APPEARANCES II, III **SPECIES** Umbaran
HOMEWORLD Umbara **AFFILIATION** Republic

A pale-skinned Umbaran, Sly Moore serves as the senior administrative aide to Supreme Chancellor Palpatine. Often at Palpatine's side—even when he addresses the galaxy from atop the chancellor's podium in the center of the Senate Chamber—Moore keeps silent in most situations and zealously guards her Master's secrets.

ORN FREE TAA

APPEARANCES I, II, CW, III **SPECIES** Twi'lek
HOMEWORLD Ryloth
AFFILIATION Galactic Senate, Imperial Senate

A larger-than-life senator who represents Ryloth in the Galactic Senate, Orn Free Taa is a symbol of greed and corruption. Senator Taa serves as the leader of Chancellor Palpatine's Loyalist Committee and pushes for the Military Creation Act, which results in the creation of the Republic's clone army. When the Separatists occupy Ryloth during the Clone Wars, Taa agrees to an alliance with his rival Cham Syndulla to help Mace Windu retake the planet. Taa later becomes a hostage during Cad Bane's strike on the Senate building. Following his release, Taa remains a senator throughout the Clone Wars and during the Imperial era, rarely returning to his homeworld. When Syndulla's Free Ryloth Movement disrupts the planet's spice productivity, the Emperor, Darth Vader, and Taa visit aboard the Star Destroyer *Perilous* and are soon attacked by the rebels. Out of anger, Vader nearly kills Taa, but the Emperor urges him to stop. Senator Taa escapes the *Perilous*' destruction by Syndulla's rebel forces.

Security duty
Captain Typho confers with Senator Amidala, disguised as a Naboo starfighter pilot, after landing on Coruscant.

GREGOR TYPHO

APPEARANCES II, CW, III **SPECIES** Human
HOMEWORLD Naboo **AFFILIATION** Royal House of Naboo

Gregor Typho bravely fights during the Battle of Naboo, losing his left eye. Queen Amidala later selects Typho as a sergeant, and he goes on to serve as Padmé's loyal bodyguard and security adviser during her senatorial career. He eventually succeeds Mariek Panaka as captain of Padmé's security detail. During the rise of the Separatist movement, Padmé faces an increased number of threats to her safety, including the bombing of her starship and the release of venomous kouhuns in her apartment. Typho endorses a plan to send Padmé back to Naboo in disguise with Anakin Skywalker. Meanwhile, Typho stays on Coruscant with Padmé's handmaiden Dormé acting as a decoy. During the Clone Wars, he continues to serve Padmé, and even sees action on Naboo. After Order 66, Padmé ignores Typho's advice not to travel to Mustafar, and he never sees her again.

Battle scarred
Though Captain Typho has lost his left eye, he continues to serve the Royal House of Naboo.

KIT FISTO

APPEARANCES II, CW, III **SPECIES** Nautolan
HOMEWORLD Glee Anselm **AFFILIATION** Jedi

As one of the only amphibious members to serve on the Jedi Council, Kit Fisto leads the Republic's armies to victory on strategic waterworlds across the galaxy. His Nautolan physiology makes him ideally suited to battle above and below the waves. During the Clone Wars, Master Fisto first sees action on Geonosis, serving as one of the Jedi who infiltrate the execution arena to battle Count Dooku's droid soldiers. Soon after this battle, Fisto joins Mace Windu and two other Jedi on a mission to the planet Hissrich. They stop the Separatists from stripping the planet of any more of its unique flora to use as an energy source. Later in the war, Fisto and his former Padawan Nahdar Vebb trail General Grievous to the third moon of Vassek, only to find themselves trapped inside Grievous' fortress, where Vebb is killed by Grievous during a lightsaber duel. Thanks to his astromech R6-H5, Fisto escapes Vassek alive. Fisto dives under the waves again to save Prince Lee-Char of Mon Cala from a Separatist insurrection led by Commander Riff Tamson and backed by the revolutionary forces of the Quarren Isolation League.

As the Clone Wars begin to draw to an end, Mace learns that Supreme Chancellor Palpatine has been successfully living a double life as a Sith Lord. Kit Fisto, along with Masters Agen Kolar and Saesee Tiin, accompanies Mace to the chancellor's office to confront him and make an arrest. Instead, Palpatine demonstrates his formidable fighting skills. He reveals a hidden lightsaber and explodes into lethal motion, cutting down Fisto before the shocked Nautolan can raise his own blade in defense and block the attack.

Battle tactics
Consulting with a medical officer clone, Fisto is trying to determine what to do with a medical frigate that is approaching a Republic outpost and is believed to be infected with contagion.

Leading the charge
Fisto commands a unit of clone troopers during the fierce fighting on Geonosis. Throughout the war, Master Fisto keeps his famously good humor intact.

LUMINARA UNDULI

APPEARANCES II, CW, III, Reb
SPECIES Mirialan **HOMEWORLD** Mirial
AFFILIATION Jedi

With their matching robes and facial tattoos, Jedi Master Luminara Unduli and her Padawan, Barriss Offee, are an unmistakable duo. Honoring the cultural traditions of the near-humans of Mirial, Unduli selected fellow Mirialan Offee as her apprentice.

By the time the Clone Wars break out, Offee's skills have grown enough for Unduli to trust Offee in combat, and both Jedi serve as members of the vanguard force that participates in the Battle of Geonosis. As the war takes shape, Unduli accepts a command rank and takes control of the 41st Elite Corps, working closely with Clone Commander Gree. She later helps escort high-ranking Trade Federation captive Nute Gunray, only to be surprised when Separatist commander Asajj Ventress boards the vessel to free its prisoner. Unduli rejects Padawan Ahsoka Tano's offer of help and loses the fight against Ventress, allowing Nute Gunray to escape Republic custody.

During the Second Battle of Geonosis, Master Unduli pursues Separatist leader Poggle the Lesser into a remote network of catacombs where insectoid matron Queen Karina keeps her nest. Overwhelmed by Queen Karina's drones, Unduli nearly becomes an unwilling host for mind-controlling brain worms, until Anakin Skywalker and Obi-Wan Kenobi free her.

As the Clone Wars draw to a close, Unduli participates in the series of battles known as the Outer Rim Sieges. She leads Commander Gree and the 41st Elite Corps to the contested planet of Kashyyyk, the Wookiee homeworld where Master Yoda is also stationed. Though the Republic forces win the day against the Separatist invaders, the Jedi generals do not foresee the shocking betrayal at the hands of their clone troops. When Darth Sidious transmits the top-secret Order 66 to all clone commanders, Gree and his clone troopers turn their weapons on the Jedi. Unlike Master Yoda, Unduli does not escape their ambush and is captured.

Unduli is imprisoned in the Spire on Stygeon Prime until she is executed. Some Jedi survivors believe a rumor that she is still alive and travel to the planet, but it is an Imperial trap. The Grand Inquisitor has kept her remains (which still possess a lingering Force presence) in a cell to attract the unwitting Jedi to their deaths—or worse, corruption to the dark side.

In hot pursuit
On Geonosis, Luminara pilots a speeder bike to chase down the fleeing Poggle the Lesser.

BARRISS OFFEE

APPEARANCES II, CW **SPECIES** Mirialan
HOMEWORLD Mirial **AFFILIATION** Jedi

Barriss Offee, the Padawan of revered Jedi Master Luminara Unduli, serves with distinction during the Clone Wars until she turns on the Republic in a shocking act of betrayal. Both Offee and Unduli share the heritage of the Mirialan people, though they share a much stronger bond as Jedi. When the Clone Wars break out, Master Unduli feels her student has earned the right to fight her own battles. Offee fights at Geonosis and later returns to the planet to target an advanced droid factory.

Teaming up with Padawan Ahsoka Tano, Offee damages the facility and helps bring about a Republic victory. On the way back from Geonosis, Offee and Ahsoka struggle to contain an outbreak of mind-controlling brain worms aboard their starship. Offee falls under the influence of the worms, but Ahsoka breaks their spell by exposing them to freezing temperatures.

Later in the war, following Offee's participation in the Battle of Umbara, a mysterious explosion at the Jedi Temple causes multiple deaths and prompts an investigation that names Ahsoka as the chief suspect. Placed on trial and forced to defend her loyalties, Ahsoka is exonerated only after Anakin's own investigation reveals Barriss Offee as the culprit. Offee makes a full confession, claiming that the Jedi had become the aggressors in the war and that her actions were a justifiable blow against a corrupt, misguided Order.

Clone Wars combatant
Barriss Offee struggles with her role as a warrior, eventually concluding that the Jedi have lost their way and falling to the dark side.

Quick pickup
Piloting an airspeeder, Bail Organa is on his way to pick up Yoda after his battle with Emperor Palpatine.

BAIL ORGANA

APPEARANCES II, CW, III, Reb, RO
SPECIES Human **HOMEWORLD** Alderaan
AFFILIATION Galactic Senate, Rebel Alliance

Though he never lives to see the end of the Empire, Bail Organa spends decades fighting its tyranny. A viceroy of the House Organa on Alderaan, Bail is elected to the Galactic Senate, where he befriends like-minded politicians such as Mon Mothma and Padmé Amidala. The Separatist Crisis sees Bail take up an advisory position to Supreme Chancellor Palpatine. Given Alderaan's pacifist history, Bail strives to halt the escalation of the Clone Wars and leads relief efforts on Christophsis. He is also instrumental in negotiating with King Katuunko of Toydaria to get vital aid to the suffering Twi'leks on Ryloth and hosts a refugee conference on his homeworld. Bail soon realizes that Palpatine's emergency powers threaten to give the chancellor the authority of a dictator. Speaking out against funding additional troops, Bail finds his suspicions of foul play growing as some of his colleagues die under strange circumstances.

As the Clone Wars draw to a close, Bail watches Jedi being killed at the Jedi Temple by Republic clone soldiers. He quickly moves to offer refuge to two of his closest allies: Yoda and Obi-Wan Kenobi. After Padmé's death, Bail and his wife Breha adopt Padmé's infant daughter, Leia. Continuing to serve on the Senate, Bail and Mon Mothma secretly plot an armed resistance against Emperor Palpatine.

Early in the Emperor's reign, Bail tracks down former Jedi Ahsoka Tano and helps her rescue persecuted farmers on Raada. Ahsoka goes on to head Bail's intelligence network. Years later, he sends R2-D2 and C-3PO to gather intel on the Spectre rebel cell, then, soon after, Ahsoka with a small rebel fleet to assist the Spectres on Mustafar. Bail is proud when Leia saves a rebel group from Imperial attack, proving herself to be a capable rebel operative. Following the Battle of Garel, Bail and Leia surreptitiously provide Phoenix Squadron with three ships to reinforce their fleet.

When the Rebel Alliance officially forms with Mothma as its public leader, Bail remains a secret member in order to protect Alderaan. After the Alliance learns of the Death Star, Bail advocates fighting the Empire. Mothma asks Bail to call his old ally Obi-Wan out of exile, so he sends his daughter Leia on this mission, although she is rerouted to Scarif, while he returns to Alderaan to prepare his pacifist people for war. Grand Moff Tarkin orders the Death Star to fire upon Alderaan, and a single blast kills Bail, Breha, and millions more. Bail is remembered as a rebel hero and a martyr for the New Republic.

ZAM WESELL

APPEARANCES II **SPECIES** Clawdite
HOMEWORLD Zolan **AFFILIATION** Bounty hunter

A Clawdite shape-shifter, this bounty hunter can assume the appearance of anyone she chooses. Zam Wesell prefers to hit her targets from afar, either with her long-range sniper rifle or her remote-operated probe droids. A frequent accomplice of Jango Fett's, she accepts a job from him to assassinate Senator Padmé Amidala of Naboo. But when her quarry's Jedi guardians corner Wesell and cut off her arm, Wesell becomes a liability, whom Fett silences forever with a poisoned Kamino saberdart.

Evasive measures
Jango Fett uses his Z-6 compact jetpack to allow him to rocket out of the reach of his enemies.

JANGO FETT

APPEARANCES II **SPECIES** Human
HOMEWORLD Unknown **AFFILIATION** Bounty hunter, Separatists (under contract)

Jango Fett is the prime clone in the creation of the Republic's clone army, becoming the template for millions of soldiers during the Clone Wars. He earns this role after years at the top of the bounty-hunting trade, where he has expertly used his twin blaster pistols and advanced Mandalorian armor.

On one of the Moons of Bogden, Count Dooku—calling himself Tyranus—approaches Fett with the lucrative prime clone offer shortly after the Battle of Naboo. Though it means relocating to the distant world of Kamino, Fett agrees, as long as the Kaminoan geneticists give him an unaltered clone to raise as his child.

Over the next decade, Jango Fett cares for his son, Boba, training him to follow in his footsteps, feeling no pride for the clone army created around him. Alongside three other bounty hunters, Jango takes Boba on a job to capture a Twi'lek on Ord Mantell. Jango is proud of how Boba kills two of the other bounty hunters when they betray them, letting the neutral third one survive to spread the story. With his sometime partner, Zam Wesell, Fett takes on a contract from the Trade Federation's Nute Gunray to kill Senator Padmé Amidala of Naboo. When Wesell bungles the job, Fett is forced to eliminate her before she can spill her secrets to Jedi investigators. But the dart he leaves behind provides the clue that leads Obi-Wan to Kamino. Jango and Boba Fett escape the planet in their ship, *Slave I*. Later, on the planet Geonosis, the conflict between the Republic's Jedi and Count Dooku's Separatists explodes into war. Fett squares off against Jedi Master Mace Windu, but loses his head to a swipe of his enemy's lightsaber. Boba Fett, who inherits the *Slave I*, continues his father's legacy.

Flying lessons
Jango teaches his son, Boba, how to fly his prized starship, *Slave I*.

Equipped to hunt
Fett carries a matching pair of blaster pistols. He locates his quarry using his helmet's built-in computer and wears energized armor designed with a durasteel alloy.

KOUHUN

APPEARANCES II **HOMEWORLD** Indoumodo
AVERAGE SIZE 30 cm (12 in) long
HABITAT Throughout the galaxy

The kouhun is a highly venomous, multilegged arthropod with a segmented carapace and stingers on the front and rear of its body. Most victims injected with kouhun venom die within minutes. Because kouhuns easily evade security, bounty hunter Wesell employs two of them in an attempt to kill Padmé in her Coruscant apartment. Anakin and Obi-Wan exterminate the creatures.

COLEMAN TREBOR

APPEARANCES II **SPECIES** Vurk
HOMEWORLD Sembla **AFFILIATION** Jedi

Coleman Trebor earns his place on the Jedi Council during the Separatist Crisis. When he and the other Council members learn of a Separatist force on Geonosis, Master Trebor joins the vanguard to stop Count Dooku before the situation explodes into all-out war. While ambushing Dooku in his viewing box at the execution arena, Trebor is shot and killed by Jango Fett.

"Adversity in war is a constant. The enemy won't play fair." SHAAK TI

SHAAK TI

APPEARANCES II, CW, III **SPECIES** Togruta
HOMEWORLD Shili **AFFILIATION** Jedi

Jedi Master Shaak Ti advances to the Jedi Council in the years leading up to the Clone Wars. Surviving the Battle of Geonosis, she assumes a leadership role among the Republic's newly activated clone troopers. During her deployment on Kamino, Ti leads a counterattack on the combined forces of General Grievous and Asajj Ventress. Joined by Obi-Wan and Anakin, she rallies the clones, ordering them to take on Separatist aqua droids and other robotic soldiers. Her heroic actions prevent Kamino's vital clone laboratories from falling into enemy hands. When clone trooper Tup mysteriously turns on his Jedi General Tiplar and kills her, Ti attempts to uncover the reason for his shocking act. Due to the interference of the Sith and the Kaminoans, the Jedi never discover that all clones have a bio chip in their brains containing orders that can be activated and carried out without question. At the end of the Clone Wars, Ti fails to prevent General Grievous from slipping onto Coruscant and kidnapping Supreme Chancellor Palpatine. During Order 66, Ti is at the Jedi Temple and records a holocron message pleading that whoever opens the holocron ensures the Jedi continue. While she is meditating, Ti is then killed by Darth Vader.

High-ranking Jedi
Jedi Master Shaak Ti is stationed on Kamino to keep an eye on the vital cloning operations during the war.

DEXTER JETTSTER

APPEARANCES II **SPECIES** Besalisk **HOMEWORLD** Ojom
AFFILIATION None

The four-armed proprietor and chef of Dex's Diner on Coruscant, Jettster is a brawny Besalisk with a colorful past who is an old friend of Obi-Wan Kenobi's. On one occasion, he enlists the Jedi to help him capture a thief operating in his diner. Before the Clone Wars, Obi-Wan shows Dex a strange object, which he identifies as a deadly Kamino saberdart, something he had encountered in his former life as a prospector on the planet Subterrel. Dex urges his old friend to continue his investigations on Kamino, which leads Obi-Wan to uncover a mysterious clone army that has been secretly constructed by the Republic. Meanwhile, Dex looks after his loyal customers, ignoring the galaxy-shaking events taking place beyond his humble diner.

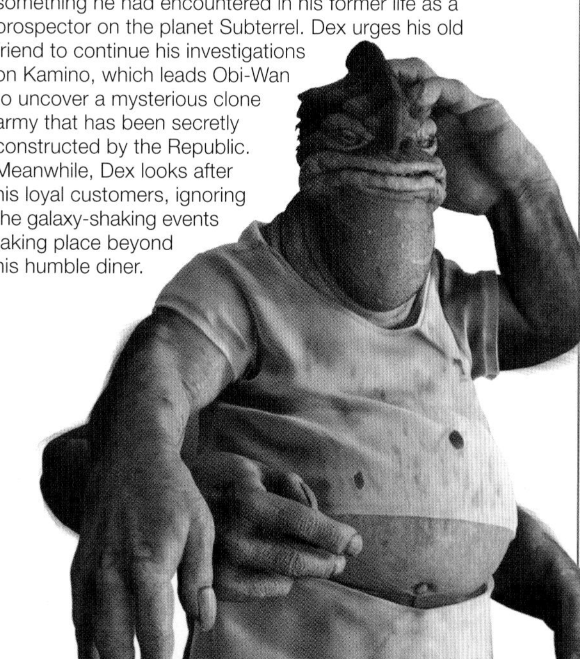

JOCASTA NU

APPEARANCES II, CW **SPECIES** Human **HOMEWORLD** Coruscant
AFFILIATION Jedi

As Chief Librarian of the Jedi Archives, Jocasta Nu has complete confidence in her records, until that confidence is shaken when she cannot help Obi-Wan Kenobi find Kamino's location. During the Clone Wars, Nu is knocked out by Cato Parasitti, a shape-shifter who takes her place until she is unmasked by Ahsoka Tano. Nu survives Order 66 and tries to resurrect the Jedi Order. Far from Coruscant, she builds a hidden base with a library of holocrons. Nu then returns to Coruscant to retrieve a holocron in the Archives containing a list of known Force-sensitive children. After stealthily grabbing her prize, she sees the Grand Inquisitor disrespectfully perusing the Archives and cannot resist dueling him. He nearly kills Nu, but Darth Vader arrives and stops him, which leads to a fight between them and gives Nu the chance to erase the Archives. Nu tries to escape but is captured by Vader. He realizes that the holocron could be used by Darth Sidious to replace him, so he destroys it and kills Nu as well. Years later, Nu's hidden base is found by Luke Skywalker, who is building his own Jedi Order.

Battle ready
Anakin, Ahsoka, and other Jedi shared Secura's role as battlefield commanders.

First warrior
At Geonosis, Aayla Secura fought in the earliest battle of the Clone Wars.

AAYLA SECURA

APPEARANCES II, CW, III **SPECIES** Twi'lek
HOMEWORLD Ryloth **AFFILIATION** Jedi

Aayla Secura's Force-sensitivity is discovered by Jedi Knight Quinlan Vos, who recruits her into the Order and takes her as his Padawan. As a Jedi Knight, Secura is among the rescuers sent to Geonosis to retrieve Obi-Wan Kenobi, Anakin Skywalker, and Padmé Amidala from the execution arena. She distinguishes herself in combat against the Separatist droid armies, and as the Clone Wars begin, she is in charge of a Republic fleet. An early engagement with a Separatist armada ends badly, with Secura's ship badly damaged by rocket droids. Anakin and Ahsoka Tano come to Secura's aid, but only escape the battle alive by making a highly dangerous blind hyperspace jump. Their vessel crash-lands on Maridun, where Secura seeks medical assistance from the native Lurmen tribe for the injured Anakin. Secura explains to the leader of the Lurmen that the Republic does not support violence, but despite her words, the actions of Separatist General Lok Durd soon bring the war to Maridun. Thankfully, Secura's heroism brings an end to Durd's deadly defoliator weapon.

Later in the war, Secura accepts a post on Coruscant alongside such high-ranking Jedi as Yoda and Mace Windu. When a strange Zillo Beast, brought to the capital for scientific study, escapes and rampages through the city, Secura and Yoda distract the titanic creature in order to give Supreme Chancellor Palpatine enough time to avert its attacks. Alongside Masters Windu, Kenobi, and Tiplee, Secura travels to Ord Mantell to investigate the scene of a battle between Count Dooku's Separatist forces and Maul's troops. The Jedi track down their now-allied enemies to Vizsla Keep 09 and fight them. Dooku kills Tiplee and then escapes with Maul.

Toward the end of the Clone Wars, Secura takes command of the 327th Star Corps, working closely with Commander Bly. The Outer Rim Sieges look as if they will be the final stage in the war. Secura, confident of the Republic's imminent triumph, accepts an assignment to Felucia. But as she leads the 327th Star Corps through the planet's jungles, Commander Bly receives the command to initiate Order 66. Bly's clone troopers open fire, shooting the unsuspecting Secura in the back.

Betrayed
Aayla Secura loses her life on Felucia when her clone troopers turn on her.

QUEEN JAMILLIA

APPEARANCES II **SPECIES** Human
HOMEWORLD Naboo
AFFILIATION Royal House of Naboo

Jamillia is a passionate proponent of democracy, who puts herself forward as a candidate when the vote takes place to elect the next royal to replace Queen Amidala. However, Jamillia loses to Réillata, who becomes the next monarch. Jamillia stands in a later election and wins, reigning during the height of the Separatist crisis.

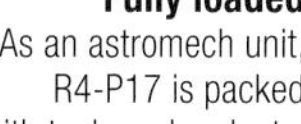

Fully loaded
As an astromech unit, R4-P17 is packed with tools and gadgets, including an arc welder and a fire extinguisher.

End of a droid
After R4 is attacked by buzz droids during the Battle of Coruscant, she is dismantled and there isn't enough time during the chaotic dogfight to repair her.

R4-P17

APPEARANCES II, CW, III **MANUFACTURER** Industrial Automaton **TYPE** Astromech droid **AFFILIATION** Republic

R4-P17, known familiarly as R4, is the astromech droid assigned to Obi-Wan's Jedi starfighter. R4 shows great bravery in the face of Separatist aggression. As a product of Industrial Automaton, R4 is designed to serve as a hyperspace navigator for calculating lightspeed jumps and also as a general-purpose repair and maintenance droid. Prior to the Clone Wars, R4-P17 joins up with Obi-Wan as the plug-in counterpart for his Delta-7 starfighter. When Obi-Wan's investigation into suspicious dealings on Coruscant leads him from Kamino to Geonosis, R4 accompanies her master through a hazardous asteroid field in pursuit of Jango Fett. She continues in this role throughout the Clone Wars, transferring from the Delta-7 to the new Eta-2 interceptor as Obi-Wan runs missions to Teth, Rodia, Mandalore, and other trouble spots across the galaxy. At the end of the Clone Wars, R4 and Obi-Wan team-up one last time during the Battle of Coruscant. As Obi-Wan pilots his interceptor through a cloud of enemies, a swarm of buzz droids attaches to his ship, bent on sabotage. The droids pull R4's dome loose from her head, ending her operational life. Obi-Wan replaces R4 with another droid, R4-G9, for his mission to Utapau.

TAUN WE

APPEARANCES II **SPECIES** Kaminoan
HOMEWORLD Kamino
AFFILIATION Cloners

This graceful Kaminoan is the project coordinator of the Republic's clone army and serves Lama Su as the administrative aide to the prime minister. When Obi-Wan arrives on Kamino, Taun We arranges for a meeting between the visitor and Prime Minister Lama Su to discuss the progress of the cloning project. She later brings Obi-Wan to visit the prime clone, Jango Fett, where she introduces the Jedi Master to Jango and his clone son, Boba.

PRIME MINISTER LAMA SU

APPEARANCES II, CW **SPECIES** Kaminoan
HOMEWORLD Kamino **AFFILIATION** Cloners

The prime minister of Kamino, Lama Su receives the order for the vast clone trooper army to be used by the Jedi on behalf of a buyer he knows as Sifo-Dyas. Su is also in league with the Sith and is given a bio chip by Darth Tyranus, to be copied and implanted into every clone. During the Clone Wars, one of the clones malfunctions and kills a Jedi. Tyranus orders Su and the Kaminoans to take control of the investigation. They prevent the Jedi from discovering the chip contains secret orders that can be activated to kill them.

"We're just clones, sir. We're meant to be expendable." CLONE SERGEANT

CLONE TROOPER

Lacking an army to fight Count Dooku's Separatists, the Republic took delivery of thousands of clone troopers. But the clones existed only to make Palpatine into the Emperor by eliminating the Jedi Knights.

APPEARANCES II, CW, III, Reb **SPECIES** Human **HOMEWORLD** Kamino **AFFILIATION** Republic

SECRET CREATION

Supreme Chancellor Palpatine and Count Dooku join forces to create a clone army in the genetics laboratories of Kamino. Each clone, an altered copy of bounty hunter Jango Fett, grows at an accelerated rate and receives extensive training in battlefield tactics. Some fill elite roles as Advanced Recon Commandos, while others study tactics to become officers. Yet none of the clones know the details of Palpatine's scheme, and when the order comes to go into action as the soldiers of the Grand Army of the Republic, the clones do their duty and fight with honor.

Programmed learning
Young clones receive educational instruction *(above)*. Obi-Wan Kenobi reviews the inner workings of the cloning facility on Kamino *(right)*.

General Yoda
The wise Jedi Master leads a squad of new clone troopers during the Battle of Geonosis.

FIRST GENERATION

After Master Yoda takes delivery of the first batch of clones, they quickly see action at the Battle of Geonosis. The earliest clone troopers wear all-white armor with fins on the top of their helmets. On Geonosis, they deploy their heavy equipment, including AT-TE walkers and LAAT/i gunships, and achieve a hard-fought victory against the Separatists.

Preparing a counterstrike
Three first-generation clones take the initiative against a wave of Separatist battle droids.

THE CLONE WARS

The Republic's clone troopers give the conflict between the Republic and the Separatists its name: the Clone Wars. Shipping out to every part of the galaxy on vast warships, the clones fight on Christophsis, Maridun, Ryloth, and elsewhere. With the Jedi as generals, clone troopers such as Captain Rex and Commander Cody work closely with Anakin Skywalker, Obi-Wan Kenobi, and others. The troopers' original armor is retired in favor of more advanced Phase 2 armor, more easily customized with patterns and colors.

Treachery
Jedi Knight Aayla Secura is shot in the back by the clone troopers she once commanded.

ORDER 66

Palpatine arranges for the Kaminoans to give each clone trooper an inhibitor chip implant. This ensures the clones will be unable to resist certain commands, in particular one designed to wipe out the Jedi, code-named Order 66. The conspiracy nearly comes to light when one clone's inhibitor chip malfunctions, but the evidence is suppressed by the Kaminoans. When the Clone Wars come to a close, Darth Sidious issues Order 66, causing the clone troopers to turn on the Jedi.

CLONES OF THE EMPIRE

In the years immediately following Order 66, the clone army remains in service of the Galactic Empire. With their DNA modified so that they age rapidly, the remaining clone troopers' service horizon is limited. Some are forced to retire, some find special positions in Palpatine's Royal Guard, and others serve behind the front lines as training officers. Clone production on Kamino quickly halts in favor of a volunteer stormtrooper corps recruited from loyal Imperial systems throughout the galaxy. The final batch of clones delivered from Kamino form a special death squad for the Inquisitorius, also known as purge troopers, who are equipped to help Darth Vader and the Inquisitors hunt down the last of the Jedi Order.

Long in the tooth
Wolffe, Gregor, and Rex escape their restrictive clone life by removing their data chips and living in an AT-TE on Seelos.

Perfect soldier
Clone troopers are bred to never question orders and are identical, so they can easily share armor and equipment.

timeline

CRISIS IN THE REPUBLIC

Commissioning the Kaminoans
Jedi Master Sifo-Dyas orders the Kaminoan cloners to grow an army for the Republic. After organizing the Jedi's death, Count Dooku takes over the project.

▲ Growing clones
Bounty hunter Jango Fett becomes the genetic donor for the clones, who receive advanced military training.

Ready for action
Soon after Obi-Wan discovers the clone army, it sees action against the Separatists in the Battle of Geonosis.

▲ Shipping out
With the Clone Wars in full swing, the Republic sends clone troopers into battlefields across the galaxy.

Further training
More clones continue to roll out from Kamino, leading to a Separatist attack on the cloning facility.

Serving with Jedi
With Jedi Knights as their commanders, clone troopers fight at Orto Plutonia, Ryloth, Lola Sayu, and elsewhere.

THE CLONE WARS

▲ Umbara
Clones show heroism on Umbara, where a duplicitous Jedi general tries to sabotage their efforts.

Coruscant and Utapau
Late in the war, clone troopers defend the capital and pursue General Grievous in the Outer Rim.

Order 66
After receiving orders from Palpatine, the clones turn on their Jedi commanders.

▲ Jedi Temple
Anakin leads clone troopers into the Jedi Temple to kill any Jedi who remain.

Final batch
Kamino produces the final batch of clones for the Empire using Jango Fett's DNA.

Mon Cala
A squad of purge troopers join the Inquisitorius on Mon Cala to hunt down a Jedi being sheltered by King Lee-Char. They are tricked into turning on their own leaders and are virtually wiped out in the ensuing battle.

"He's no good to me dead." **BOBA FETT**

BOBA FETT

A clone of Jango Fett who is raised as Jango's son, Boba Fett survives the Clone Wars to become a relentless and highly paid bounty hunter.

APPEARANCES II, CW, IV, V, VI **SPECIES** Human **HOMEWORLD** Kamino **AFFILIATION** Bounty hunter

CLONE ORIGINS

When Jango Fett agrees to become the genetic donor for a clone army being grown on Kamino, he requests an unaltered clone to raise as the heir to his legacy. For 10 years, Boba Fett grows up in the sterile environs of Kamino's Tipoca City, occasionally accompanying his father on the ship *Slave I* to track down bounties for money. Boba's first mission is to Ord Mantell, where he kills two fellow bounty hunters who try to betray him and his father. Obi-Wan Kenobi eventually uncovers the Kamino cloning operation, prompting Jango and Boba to flee to Geonosis. There, a Jedi strike force raids the execution arena and overwhelms the Separatist defenders. The leader of the Jedi, Mace Windu, uses his lightsaber to behead Jango Fett.

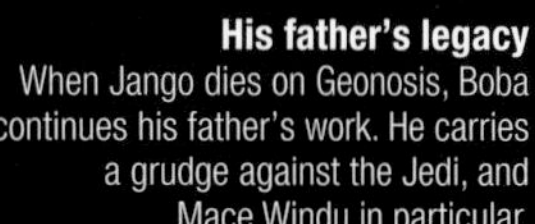

His father's legacy
When Jango dies on Geonosis, Boba continues his father's work. He carries a grudge against the Jedi, and Mace Windu in particular.

TRACKING DOWN HAN

Over the years, Boba uses the *Slave I* and a customized suit of Mandalorian armor to become the galaxy's most notorious bounty hunter. After the Battle of Hoth, Darth Vader assembles a group of top bounty hunters to find Han's *Millennium Falcon*. Boba arranges a trap for Han at Cloud City, which ends with Han being safely encased in a slab of carbonite. Boba delivers Han to Jabba the Hutt and is present at Jabba's palace when Luke Skywalker attempts a rescue. During a fight at the Great Pit of Carkoon, Boba's jetpack malfunctions and he falls into the mouth of the Sarlacc monster.

Rough crowd
The young Boba receives tips on the bounty-hunting trade from *(left to right)* Bossk, Castas, and Aurra Sing, among others.

LEARNING THE ROPES

The orphaned Boba finds guidance from assassin Aurra Sing. Joined by bounty hunters Bossk and Castas, Fett poses as a clone cadet and causes the crash of the Republic vessel *Endurance*. Fett is captured by the Republic on Florrum, but later pulls together a new team that he names Krayt's Claw. Together, they are hired to defend a hovertrain on Quarzite and later rescue a Jedi from Count Dooku's palace on Serenno.

The hunt for Han Solo
The Dark Lord hires only the best bounty hunters to track the *Millennium Falcon* and its passengers *(above top)*. With Han trapped in carbonite, Boba completes another successful hunt *(above)*.

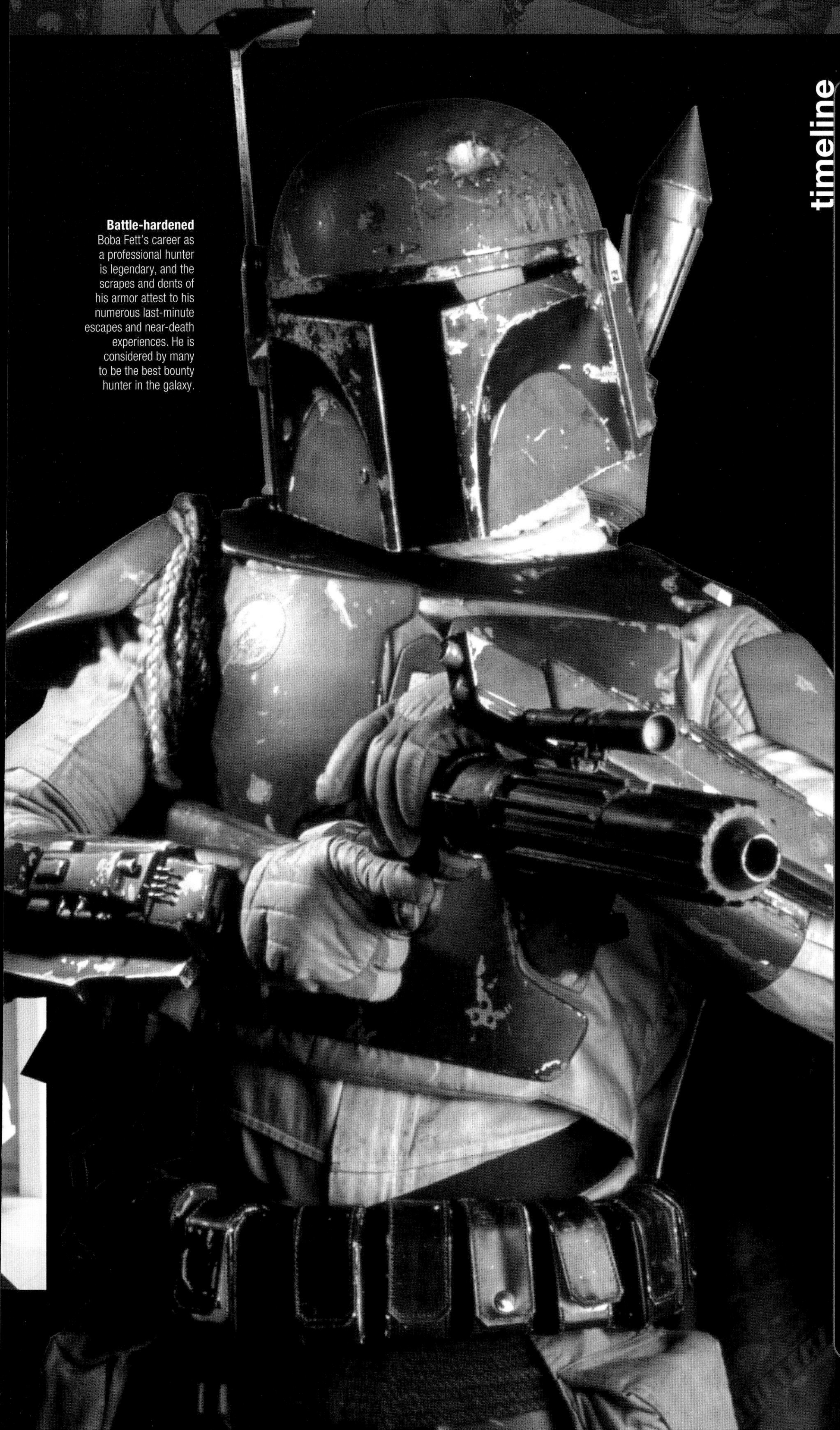

Battle-hardened
Boba Fett's career as a professional hunter is legendary, and the scrapes and dents of his armor attest to his numerous last-minute escapes and near-death experiences. He is considered by many to be the best bounty hunter in the galaxy.

timeline

CRISIS IN THE REPUBLIC

▲ Young clone
A cloned copy of his father, Jango, Boba grows up in the laboratories of Kamino.

Death of Jango
Boba's father dies while fighting Mace Windu on Geonosis, after which Boba inherits the starship *Slave I*.

THE CLONE WARS

Becoming a hunter
Boba joins Bossk, Aurra Sing, and others to learn the tricks of the bounty hunting trade.

▲ Looking for revenge
During the Clone Wars, Boba tries to kill Mace Windu in retaliation for his father's death.

THE EMPIRE ERA

Krayt's Claw
Boba forms his own team of bounty hunters, named Krayt's Claw. The group goes on missions to Quarzite and Serenno.

▲ Working for Jabba
Many jobs bring Boba into the employ of notorious gangster Jabba the Hutt on Tatooine.

In Vader's employ
Vader hires Boba to track down the rebel who destroyed the Death Star.

Showdown in Ben's hut
Boba finds the pilot in Old Ben's hut on Tatooine, but fails to apprehend him.

Delivering the news
While Boba doesn't bring the pilot to Vader aboard the *Devastator*, he does tell Vader the pilot's surname—Skywalker.

▲ Cloud City
Boba works with Vader to set a trap for Han and his friends. He leaves with his prize, Han frozen in carbonite, aboard the *Slave I*.

Jabba's palace
Boba delivers the carbonite slab containing Han's body to Jabba's palace, where it hangs on the wall.

Sarlacc
During Han's execution, Luke springs a surprise rescue, during which Boba falls into the mouth of the Sarlacc.

Fateful meeting
Owen and Beru meet Padmé Amidala and Anakin Skywalker, the couple whose son Luke they will later raise as their own *(right)*. By the time Luke becomes a teenager, time and Tatooine's harsh climate have left their marks on Owen's visage *(below)*.

"I guess I'm your stepbrother. I had a feeling you might show up someday."

OWEN LARS TO ANAKIN

OWEN LARS

APPEARANCES II, III, IV **SPECIES** Human **HOMEWORLD** Tatooine **AFFILIATION** None

A pragmatic and serious-minded Tatooine moisture farmer, Owen Lars has learned his strong work ethic from his father, Cliegg Lars. When his father marries Shmi Skywalker, a former slave, Owen is drawn into the complicated life of Shmi's son Anakin. Owen and Anakin meet for the first time following Shmi's kidnapping at the hands of Tusken Raiders. Anakin manages to retrieve Shmi's lifeless body and returns to the Lars' farm, while Cliegg dies not long after from wounds sustained in the search for his wife. Owen and his new wife Beru inherit the moisture farm and agree to Obi-Wan Kenobi's request that they raise Anakin's son Luke as their own. When Owen is taken by bounty hunter Black Krrsantan, Obi-Wan attempts a rescue, but Owen falls off a cliff. Luckily, Luke flies to the rescue in his T-16. He manages to maneuver the ship underneath Owen, so he lands on one of its blasters. Many years later, and despite Owen's best efforts to keep Luke safe from the Empire, stormtroopers arrive at the Lars homestead, and on orders from Darth Vader execute both Owen and Beru.

BERU WHITESUN LARS

APPEARANCES II, III, IV **SPECIES** Human **HOMEWORLD** Tatooine **AFFILIATION** None

Tatooine native Beru Whitesun falls in love with Owen Lars just prior to the Battle of Geonosis and is present at the Lars moisture farm when Anakin Skywalker arrives in search of his mother Shmi. Beru and Owen later marry, and Obi-Wan Kenobi places Anakin's infant son Luke in their care. Where Owen presents a gruff face to the boy, Beru shows a more caring side. Both of them keep his true parentage a secret. After a bounty hunter captures Owen, Beru bravely grabs a rifle to go after her husband, but Obi-Wan and Luke save him first. When Imperial stormtroopers arrive at the farm searching for the droids R2-D2 and C-3PO, Beru and Owen die under the blasters of a stormtrooper executioner squad.

Eyes on the future
Beru Lars plays a vital role in shaping the destiny of the galaxy when she agrees to raise Luke Skywalker. Her sensitive and nurturing nature instills in Luke a love of family and a strong moral sense *(above)*.

CLIEGG LARS

APPEARANCES II **SPECIES** Human **HOMEWORLD** Tatooine **AFFILIATION** None

The tough and strong-willed Cliegg Lars lives as a moisture farmer on Tatooine with his wife, former slave Shmi Skywalker. He loses his love—and his right leg—to a hunting party of Tusken Raiders. Anakin Skywalker retrieves his mother's body, but Cliegg dies shortly after, leaving the farm to his son Owen and Owen's wife, Beru.

POGGLE THE LESSER

APPEARANCES II, CW, III **SPECIES** Geonosian **HOMEWORLD** Geonosis
AFFILIATION Separatists

Archduke Poggle the Lesser controls the droid factories of Geonosis during the Clone Wars. Backed by Darth Sidious, Poggle manufactures millions of B1 battle droids for the Trade Federation and later produces the new super battle droid on behalf of Count Dooku's Separatists. When Poggle's warriors capture Obi-Wan Kenobi, Anakin Skywalker, and Padmé Amidala on Geonosis, Poggle orders their executions, and remains on the scene to fight the Republic's invading clone troopers. He passes on the Geonosian plans for a battle station to Dooku for safekeeping.

Later in the Clone Wars, Poggle destroys his droid factory to prevent it from falling into the hands of the Republic. He hopes to find refuge with the Geonosian Queen Karina, but instead becomes a prisoner of war. Poggle is interrogated by the Republic and is only released when he agrees with Lieutenant Commander Orson Krennic that the Geonosians will now build a battle station for the Republic. The Archduke has other plans though, and covertly begins an uprising on Geonosis that sabotages the construction and enables him to rejoin the Separatist Council. He dies with the rest of the Council on Mustafar.

Commanding presence
Poggle is in charge of all Geonosians and most of the robotic products produced in their factories, such as this T-series tactical droid.

WAT TAMBOR

APPEARANCES II, CW, III
SPECIES Skakoan
HOMEWORLD Skako Minor
AFFILIATION Separatists, Techno Union

As a Skakoan, Wat Tambor wears an elaborate pressure suit and speaks through an electronic loudspeaker. As lead engineer of the Techno Union, he controls the most advanced war assets in the galaxy. Tambor serves on the Separatist Council during the Clone Wars and briefly becomes a Republic prisoner following the Battle of Ryloth. Returning to Skako Minor, Tambor uses a captured clone trooper named Echo to access Republic military tactics in order to help the Separatists, until the clone is rescued. Tambor later perishes on Mustafar.

SHU MAI

APPEARANCES II, III **SPECIES** Gossam **HOMEWORLD** Castell
AFFILIATION Commerce Guild, Separatists

As Presidente of the Commerce Guild, Shu Mai controls the pooled financial resources of some of the galaxy's largest corporations. She uses her influence to gain a seat on the Separatist Council, but tells Count Dooku that the Guild will only covertly support his movement. It is a secret allegiance that leads to her death on Mustafar.

SAN HILL

APPEARANCES II, III **SPECIES** Muun **HOMEWORLD** Scipio
AFFILIATION InterGalactic Banking Clan, Separatists

As the Chairman of the InterGalactic Banking Clan, San Hill wields considerable influence. Just prior to the Battle of Geonosis, he meets in secret with Count Dooku and pledges the support of his financial cartel to the Separatists. Along with others in the Separatist Council, he is murdered by Darth Vader on Mustafar.

MASSIFF

APPEARANCES II, CW **HOMEWORLD** Various
AVERAGE SIZE 1 m (3 ft) high **HABITAT** Desert

Massiffs are snarling hunters found on both Tatooine and Geonosis. Though their powerful bites are dangerous, trained massiffs are employed by many, including Tusken Raider tribes, Weequay pirates, and clone troopers, as guard beasts. The spines on a massiff's back provide an extra level of defense, and the creature's large eyes allow it to see well in nighttime conditions.

PASSEL ARGENTE

APPEARANCES I, II, III **SPECIES** Koorivar
HOMEWORLD Kooriva **AFFILIATION** Corporate Alliance, Separatists

After winning the post of Magistrate of the Corporate Alliance, Passel Argente serves in the Galactic Senate and is among the senators who support Chancellor Valorum's removal from office. Argente resigns from office to become a member of the Separatist Council, and is among those killed on Mustafar.

"I have become more powerful than any Jedi. Even you." COUNT DOOKU

COUNT DOOKU

No one suspected that Count Dooku was a Sith. Yet the ex-Jedi worked as Darth Sidious' apprentice, secretly pulling the strings of a false war that tore the galaxy in two.

APPEARANCES II, CW, III **SPECIES** Human **HOMEWORLD** Serenno **AFFILIATION** Jedi, Sith, Separatists

FALLEN JEDI

Trained by Master Yoda himself, Dooku rises through the ranks to become one of the finest Jedi of his generation. Dooku's lightsaber skills are inspirational to many younglings, and he is a veteran of many conflicts. During his time with the Jedi Order, he takes two Padawans (Rael Avercross and Qui-Gon Jinn), forming strong attachments with them. Known only to Rael and Qui-Gon, Dooku becomes obsessed with the ancient prophecies of the Jedi mystics. These prophecies lead Dooku to secretly explore the dark side of the Force, even using Force lightning to protect Qui-Gon in battle. At one point, Dooku ascends to join the Jedi Council, but he leaves the Order so he can inherit the title of Count of Serenno. While Dooku claims his reason for leaving is that he disagrees with the Order's methods, he is secretly keen to further explore the dark side of the Force. Dooku joins the Sith as Darth Tyranus, and supervises the creation of a clone army on Kamino. He also emerges as the leader of a Separatist movement that persuades thousands of star systems to split away from the Republic. On Geonosis, war finally breaks out between the Separatists and the Republic. Dooku slips away safely after a lightsaber duel with Master Yoda. While the Jedi are aware he is a Sith, they are unsure if he is the master or the apprentice.

Geonosis escape
Pursued by a Republic gunship, Dooku flees on a speeder bike to a hangar so that he can abandon the Battle of Geonosis.

Sith master
While Count Dooku controls the Separatist forces, his master, Darth Sidious, rules over the Republic. Between them, they plot to bring the galaxy under Sith control.

CLONE WARS

Count Dooku leads the Separatists' battle droid armies, aided by his dark side apprentice Asajj Ventress and the cyborg General Grievous. After failing to pit the Hutts against the Republic by kidnapping Jabba's son, Rotta, Dooku briefly becomes a hostage of the pirate king Hondo Ohnaka. Later, when Darth Sidious orders Dooku to eliminate Ventress, he abandons his apprentice to her fate and obtains the Zabrak warrior Savage Opress as a replacement bodyguard from Mother Talzin's Nightsisters. Ventress and the Nightsisters try to assassinate Dooku, but he retaliates by obliterating their Dathomir stronghold. When the Separatists strike at Coruscant, Dooku obeys the orders of his Master Darth Sidious and waits aboard the flagship *Invisible Hand* to set a trap for Anakin Skywalker.

Playing his part
Dooku believes that his master will come to his aid if his duel with Anakin grows dangerous, but he is unprepared for Palpatine's duplicity.

THE ENDGAME

Despite his own machinations, Dooku never suspects that Sidious plans to remove him all along. Dooku defeats Obi-Wan Kenobi and challenges Anakin while Palpatine watches, pretending to be a helpless prisoner. Because Dooku has dueled Anakin multiple times before, he does not expect the Jedi Knight to put up much of a fight. Anakin, however, has gained considerable skill since their last encounter, and engages Dooku in an intense duel. After disarming his opponent, Anakin picks up Dooku's fallen lightsaber and holds both blades to Dooku's throat. Dooku hopes his master will intervene, but when Palpatine growls "Kill him," Dooku finally understands the inevitability of Sith betrayal.

From Jedi to Count
When Dooku grows disillusioned with the Jedi Order, no argument can convince him to remain. Dooku's former master, Yoda, is suspicious and believes his former Padawan has hidden motivations for leaving.

timeline

CRISIS IN THE REPUBLIC

Joining the Order
Dooku is taken as an infant by the Jedi and eventually chosen by Yoda to be his Padawan.

Meeting Qui-Gon
After his first Padawan, Rael, is knighted, Dooku becomes impressed by Qui-Gon and takes him as his second Padawan.

Leaving the Order
Dooku leaves the Jedi Order so he can inherit the title of Count of Serenno.

Rise of the Separatists
Count Dooku emerges as a political leader and encourages star systems to withdraw from the Republic.

Darth Tyranus
Count Dooku secretly joins the Sith, becoming Darth Sidious' second apprentice.

Hiring the Pykes
Dooku hires the Pyke Syndicate to kill Jedi Master Sifo-Dyas.

Clone army
As Darth Tyranus, Dooku co-opts the creation of the clone army on Kamino ordered by Sifo-Dyas. Dooku chooses Jango Fett as the genetic donor for the army and orders the Kaminoans to insert control chips into each clone.

▲ Separatist summit
Dooku holds a meeting on Geonosis to gain the support of the galaxy's most powerful corporations.

▲ Fighting Yoda
After the Republic attacks Dooku's operations on Geonosis, Dooku escapes, but only after facing Yoda, his former teacher.

THE CLONE WARS

False war
The Clone Wars begin, but the Republic does not know that Dooku has arranged the conflict on orders from Supreme Chancellor Palpatine.

▲ Hostage
During the war, Dooku briefly becomes the prisoner of the pirate king Hondo Ohnaka.

Savage Opress
Dooku dismisses his apprentice Asajj Ventress and recruits a tattooed Zabrak warrior in her place.

Nightsisters
To get revenge on Mother Talzin for arranging an attempt on his life, Dooku wipes out the Nightsisters in the Battle of Dathomir.

Tyranus unmasked
While investigating the Pyke Syndicate, Obi-Wan and Anakin learn that Count Dooku is Darth Tyranus.

Atrocity on Mahranee
Following Dooku's brutal attack on the Mahran people, the Jedi Council orders his assassination, asking Asajj Ventress and Jedi Master Quinlan Vos to carry it out.

Showdown on Christophsis
While Vos attempts to complete the mission, Asajj Ventress sacrifices her life to save Vos from Dooku, who escapes the planet.

Death
Above Coruscant, Dooku duels Anakin Skywalker but loses his life to the young Jedi.

ONACONDA FARR

APPEARANCES I, II, CW **SPECIES** Rodian
HOMEWORLD Rodia
AFFILIATION Galactic Senate

Republic Senator Onaconda Farr is a family friend of Senator Amidala. However, he still kidnaps her on behalf of the Separatists when she visits his homeworld, Rodia. Farr later delivers Trade Federation Viceroy Nute Gunray into custody and is welcomed back into the Senate. When Farr joins forces with Senator Organa to stop the deregulation of the banks in order to help the Republic finance the war, his aide poisons him for the benefit of the Separatists.

ORRAY

APPEARANCES II **HOMEWORLD** Geonosis
AVERAGE SIZE 2 m (7 ft) high, 3 m (10 ft) long **HABITAT** Desert

Orrays serve as mounts for picadors in the Geonosian execution arena. Due to their strength, Geonosians use orrays to haul heavy loads, including the carts that carry condemned prisoners into the arena. The tamed orrays in the arena have had their tails removed; metal caps cover their tail stumps.

REEK

APPEARANCES II, CW **HOMEWORLD** Geonosis (Codian Moon) **AVERAGE SIZE** 2 m (6 ft) high, 4 m (13 ft) long **HABITAT** Grasslands

Reeks are three-horned herbivores with stubborn attitudes and a dangerous headlong charge. In the execution arena on Geonosis, reeks are used to threaten prisoners, and these specimens have rings through their noses that their Geonosian handlers use to keep them under control. The animals are found on Ylesia and the Codian Moon but have been exported across the galaxy due to their strength and ability to resist injury. When Anakin faces a reek in the arena, he calms the creature by using the Force and then hitches a ride on its back. Sadly, the reek proves no match for a blaster pistol—bounty hunter Jango Fett takes it out with a single shot.

Warning signs
When a reek paws at the ground, it is preparing to charge at its target *(above)*. General Grievous rides a reek through the jungles of Felucia (*right*).

Predator and prey
An angry nexu bares its teeth at the Geonosian wrangler.

NEXU

APPEARANCES II **HOMEWORLD** Cholganna
AVERAGE SIZE 1 m (3 ft) high, 2 m (7 ft) long **HABITAT** Forests

The nexu is a feline-like predator with multiple eyes and a long, hairless tail. Nexu evolved on the forested planet Cholganna and have spread offworld, owing to their value as attack beasts. Once a nexu has pinned its prey beneath its sharp claws, it bites down and savagely shakes its victim to death. Padmé Amidala faces death in the Geonosis execution arena from a fierce nexu, which first kills one of the Geonosian guards before turning its attention to her. Padmé suffers a slash from one of the nexu's claws before the animal dies after being struck by a charging reek.

ACKLAY

APPEARANCES II **HOMEWORLD** Vendaxa
AVERAGE SIZE 3 m (10 ft) high
HABITAT Land and water

The acklay is a gigantic amphibious crustacean originally from Vendaxa. Protected by a hard carapace, it scuttles around on six pointed legs and uses its claws to spear prey. It has a mouth filled with sharp teeth and uses an organ beneath its chin to sense the body electricity of its prey. On Geonosis, acklays are used as killer beasts inside the execution arena. Geonosian picadors keep the larger creatures under control by jabbing at them with long-handled spears. Obi-Wan Kenobi nearly loses his life to an acklay inside the arena, avoiding the beast's claws until he retrieves his lightsaber and finishes off the acklay.

Deadly standoff
Armed with a spear, Obi-Wan faces off against an acklay in the execution arena.

STASS ALLIE

APPEARANCES II, III **SPECIES** Tholothian
HOMEWORLD Tholoth **AFFILIATION** Jedi

Stass Allie sits on the Jedi Council during the Clone Wars and fights bravely as a member of the Jedi strike team assigned to the First Battle of Geonosis. Stationed on Saleucami during the Outer Rim Sieges, Master Allie dies during the Jedi betrayal of Order 66. Her clone trooper escorts suddenly fire on her speeder bike, sending her into a fatal crash.

GENERAL WHORM LOATHSOM

APPEARANCES CW **SPECIES** Kerkoiden **HOMEWORLD** Kerkoidia **AFFILIATION** Separatists

After General Loathsom captures the planet Christophsis, the Republic invades to liberate it. Loathsom counters the attack, dispatching his battle droids, which are protected behind a powerful deflector shield. Unable to penetrate this barrier, Obi-Wan Kenobi discusses terms of surrender with Loathsom, allowing Anakin Skywalker and Ahsoka Tano time to destroy the shield generator. Loathsom is captured and taken to Coruscant, where he is imprisoned for treason.

ADMIRAL WULLF YULAREN

APPEARANCES CW, Reb, IV **SPECIES** Human
HOMEWORLD Coruscant **AFFILIATION** Republic Navy, Empire

Wullf Yularen is one of the Republic's most notable fleet commanders with a long history of involvement in naval conflicts, including a loss to Admiral Trench at the Battle of Malastare Narrows. During the Clone Wars, Yularen fights at Christophsis, Ryloth, Devaron, and Geonosis, working with high-ranking Jedi at nearly every engagement.

After the war, Yularen becomes a colonel in the Imperial Security Bureau (ISB), taking particular interest in the career of the capable ISB Agent Kallus. Yularen befriends the Chiss rising star Lieutenant Thrawn, and helps him build connections with high-ranking Imperials. Yularen also assists Thrawn's investigation into the criminal named Nightswan. During Thrawn's hunt for Phoenix Squadron, Thrawn calls on Yularen's aid to uncover the undercover rebel operative code named "Fulcrum" in the Imperial ranks. Yularen is shocked when Thrawn reveals that "Fulcrum" is Kallus, but they both decide to let Kallus continue to operate so they can pass misinformation to the rebels. Following the completion of the Death Star, Yularen is assigned to the station and perishes when it is destroyed.

ADMIRAL TRENCH

APPEARANCES CW **SPECIES** Harch
HOMEWORLD Secundus Ando **AFFILIATION** Separatists

Prior to the Clone Wars, the spider-faced Harch named Trench earns fame as a naval commander when he defeats Wulff Yularen in the Battle of Malastare Narrows. Named an admiral in the Separatist fleet, Trench blockades Christophsis but loses his cruiser to Anakin's stealth ship. He survives, and later assumes command of Separatist operations at Ringo Vinda. When Trench attempts to bomb the planet Anaxes, he is stopped by the Republic forces and is killed by Anakin Skywalker.

CLONE COMMANDER CODY

APPEARANCES CW, III **SPECIES** Human (clone)
HOMEWORLD Kamino **AFFILIATION** Republic

Given the designation CC-2224, this clone takes the name "Cody" and is assigned to General Kenobi's 212th Attack Battalion as his second-in-command. Commander Cody enjoys camaraderie with Captain Rex and fights alongside Obi-Wan Kenobi at Christophsis, Teth, and the Second Battle of Geonosis. He helps extract Jedi Master Even Piell from the Citadel prison on Lola Sayu and later captures Umbara's capital city, despite Master Pong Krell's treachery. Cody works with Kenobi, General Skywalker, and Ahsoka Tano to free slaves on Kadavo and participates in the Battle for Anaxes. On General Windu's orders, Cody and Rex form a team to discover how the Separatists have obtained Rex's strategy algorithm. Cody is injured early in the mission, but Rex and the others complete it, and Cody soon recovers. At the end of the Clone Wars, Cody accompanies Obi-Wan to Utapau, where he receives Order 66. At Cody's command, an AT-TE fires at Obi-Wan, knocking him into the water.

Under orders
Cody fights side by side with Obi-Wan Kenobi on Utapau *(left)*. The clone troopers and their Jedi generals intercept a communication between two Separatist generals planning an attack on Kamino *(below)*.

"You swore an oath to the Republic. You have a duty."

CAPTAIN REX

CAPTAIN REX

Assigned the designation CT-7567 on Kamino, this high-ranking clone chooses the name Rex and spends the Clone Wars working side by side with Jedi commanders.

APPEARANCES CW, Reb **SPECIES** Human **HOMEWORLD** Kamino **AFFILIATION** Republic

Commanding presence Identifiable by his blue-patterned armor, Rex is bred to lead clone troopers.

Fighting shadows Anakin and Captain Rex react to a threat from hidden attackers on the shadowy world of Umbara.

PARTNER OF THE JEDI

When the Clone Wars begin, Captain Rex is assigned command of Torrent Company in the 501st Legion and immediately ships out to handle Separatist trouble spots across the galaxy. On Christophsis, Rex serves under Anakin Skywalker and Anakin's new Padawan, Ahsoka Tano. This is the beginning of a partnership between Rex and a tightly knit group of Jedi, including Anakin, Ahsoka, and Obi-Wan Kenobi, through which Rex learns that his opinions are highly valued.

REPUBLIC VICTORIES

The trust between the Jedi and Captain Rex leads to Rex's participation in high-priority engagements, including the destruction of Skytop Station and the fight against General Lok Durd on Maridun. On the Rishi moon, Captain Rex and Commander Cody play vital roles in uncovering a Separatist takeover of a Republic listening post. Rex pushes for total success in every mission, despite the personal risk, even becoming infected with the Blue Shadow Virus in his zeal to destroy a Separatist laboratory on Naboo. When Captain Rex leads a squad into battle, the Republic usually wins the day.

Planning an attack Having received advanced tactical training on Kamino, Rex uses his knowledge to formulate and test new battle strategies.

GROWING DOUBTS

Not every mission is clear cut. On Saleucami, a blaster shot from a commando droid leaves Rex near death. He recovers in the care of a fellow clone who abandoned the Republic army to live the relatively quiet life of a farmer. Initially disgusted by this deserter, Rex learns to take a more nuanced view. In later engagements of the Clone Wars, Rex stands up for himself and his troopers when both are given foolish, overly risky orders. On Umbara, Rex refuses to obey reckless commands issued by Jedi Master Pong Krell, leading to Krell's exposure as a Separatist sympathizer. These experiences show Rex a different side of war. He begins to see that doing his duty involves more than just blind obedience.

REBEL OFFICER

Having removed his inhibitor chip prior to Order 66, Rex does not follow the command to betray the Jedi. He deserts the Empire and goes into hiding, living with two other clones on the remote planet Seelos. His old friend Ahsoka Tano sends the crew of the *Ghost* to Rex to gain information on abandoned Republic-era military bases. Kanan Jarrus is skeptical about working with a clone, but the two resolve their differences and Rex becomes a trusted ally of the Spectres. He is crucial to the success of key rebel missions, including the heist of Y-wing starfighters at Reklam Station, the liberation of Lothal from Imperial blockade, and the Battle of Endor to destroy the second Death Star.

Joining forces After years of solitary living, Rex teams up with fellow war veteran and former Jedi Ahsoka.

timeline

THE CLONE WARS

Kamino
After completing his training, Rex becomes a captain in Torrent Company of the 501st Battalion.

First action
On Geonosis, Captain Rex fights alongside his fellow clone troopers against the Separatists.

▲ Battle of Christophsis
Rex serves with Anakin and Ahsoka in many engagements, including an early battle to defeat General Loathsom.

Crash landing
Stranded on Maridun, Rex guards a wounded Anakin and frees the planet from invaders.

Blue Shadow Virus
While assaulting a bioweapons lab on Naboo, Rex becomes infected with the virus. Fortunately he receives the antidote in time.

▲ Another side to war
A clone trooper who abandoned the war to live in exile on Saleucami challenges Rex's views of honor and duty.

Battle-hardened
Heroism at Kamino and the Citadel demonstrates Captain Rex's value as an elite soldier.

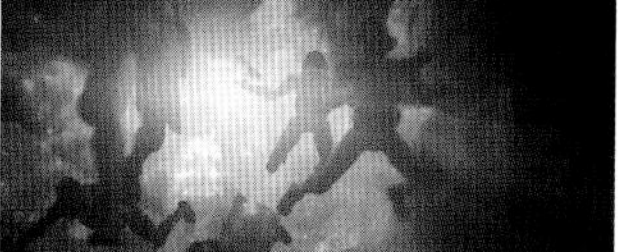

▲ Umbara
Jedi General Pong Krell makes things difficult for Rex during the campaign to seize Umbara's capital.

▲ War continued
Rex continues to do his duty, even when his orders force him into difficult situations. When Ahsoka falls under suspicion of being a traitor, Rex helps track her down on Coruscant.

THE EMPIRE ERA

Siege of Mandalore
Rex and the 501st Legion clones work with Ahsoka Tano to break Maul's rule on Mandalore. Ahsoka and Rex fake their deaths to escape the Empire and go their separate ways into exile.

Seelos
Clones Rex, Wolffe, and Gregor live in hiding on Seelos, hunting worm-like joopas from their modified AT-TE walker home.

Joining the Rebellion
Rex departs Seelos to join Ahsoka and the *Ghost* crew in their insurgence against the Empire.

Chopper Base
Rex leads the construction of Chopper Base on Atollon, the main base of operation for the Phoenix group of rebels.

Endor
Rex serves at the Battle of Endor as a Commander in the Rebel Alliance.

With the Jedi
Rex is one of the few clone troopers to spend extensive time with high-ranking Jedi commanders such as Anakin and Ahsoka. He has a high opinion of the Jedi, having seen their courage under fire.

"Now you fall... as all Jedi must." ASAJJ VENTRESS

ASAJJ VENTRESS

Her life marred by tragedy—from the death of a Jedi mentor to a Sith master who wants her dead—Asajj Ventress is a lethal assassin with her own agenda: to be seen as a true Sith.

APPEARANCES CW **SPECIES** Dathomirian **HOMEWORLD** Dathomir **AFFILIATION** Separatists, Nightsisters

DARK ASSASSIN

As Count Dooku's apprentice, Asajj Ventress is an agent for his machinations. On Tatooine, she kidnaps Jabba the Hutt's son Rotta for Dooku, who intends to frame the Republic to bring the Hutts into the Clone Wars on the Separatist side. However, the Jedi attack Ventress on Teth and return Rotta to his father. Later, Dooku sends Ventress to free Nute Gunray from a Republic cruiser and take him to Coruscant. There she duels Jedi Master Luminara Unduli, nearly defeating her until Ahsoka Tano joins the battle. Helped by a traitorous Senate Guard, Argyus, Ventress rescues Gunray, but then kills Argyus when he boasts of his role in the mission. On Kamino, Ventress tries to steal the clone DNA, but is foiled by Anakin Skywalker.

Showdown
In the B'omarr Order Monastery on Teth, Ventress prepares for battle with Jedi intent on rescuing Rotta the Huttlet.

NIGHTSISTER

Sensing Ventress growing more powerful in the Force, Sidious orders Dooku to kill his dark acolyte. When her command ship is destroyed at Sullust, Ventress flees to Dathomir, where Mother Talzin reveals the assassin's past as a Nightsister, leading Ventress to swear vengeance on Dooku. While she undergoes a Rebirth Ritual to signify her allegiance to the clan, Dooku sends General Grievous to Dathomir to annihilate the Nightsisters. At the urging of Talzin, Ventress flees the planet, believing she is the only remaining Nightsister.

Nightsister found
When Ventress arrives on Dathomir, the Nightsisters are prepared to kill her, until Mother Talzin reveals that Ventress is one of them.

BOUNTY HUNTER

After killing bounty hunter Oked, Ventress takes his place on a mission led by Boba Fett to protect a chest on a train which, when opened, reveals a young girl held captive inside. Ventress double-crosses Fett and frees the girl. Later, discovering a bounty on Savage Opress, Ventress hunts down the Nightbrother. Her search leads her to Opress and Maul, who are holding Obi-Wan Kenobi prisoner. Ventress and Obi-Wan join forces, barely escaping with their lives. Obi-Wan tries to enlist Ventress, but she refuses.

Catching a Jedi
Now a bounty hunter, Ventress pins down former Jedi Ahsoka Tano, who has a price on her head after escaping from a Republic prison.

DARK DISCIPLE

Ventress allies with Jedi Quinlan Vos in a plot to assassinate Count Dooku. To prepare for their mission, Ventress trains the Jedi in the darker aspects of the Force by taking him to her homeworld of Dathomir. The two form a romantic bond during their time together. Using her contacts in the Separatists, Ventress learns that Dooku will be attending a gala on the planet Raxus, giving Ventress and Vos an opportunity to strike. Their assassination attempt fails when Vos is captured by Dooku and fully turns to the dark side, believing that Ventress has set him up. Hoping to redeem her lover, Ventress partners with her former adversary Obi-Wan Kenobi to free Vos and return him to the Jedi. Still clinging to the dark side, Vos attempts once again to kill Dooku on the planet Christophsis, but Dooku gains the upper hand. Ventress gives her life to save Vos from the Sith Lord and her sacrifice inspires Vos to return to the light side.

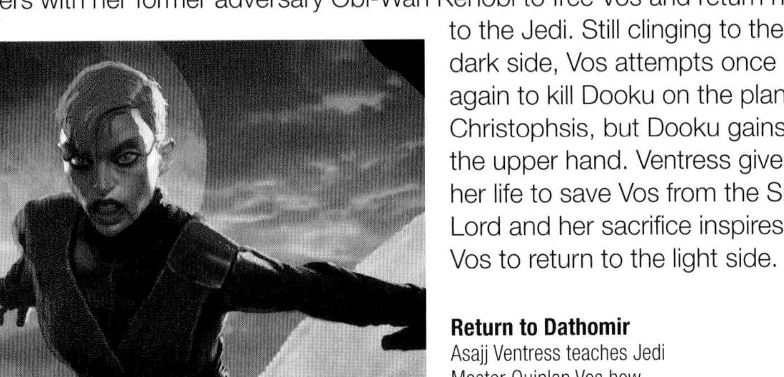

Return to Dathomir
Asajj Ventress teaches Jedi Master Quinlan Vos how to draw upon the dark side of the Force on her homeworld, Dathomir.

Dark side apprentice
A lethal assassin trained in the Force and ruthlessly tested by Count Dooku, Asajj Ventress burns to be accepted as a true Sith, and wields her unique twin lightsabers/saberstaff with deadly force.

timeline

CRISIS IN THE REPUBLIC

▲ Taken
Asajj's mother is forced to trade her to the criminal Hal'Sted to protect their clan.

▲ Jedi training
Jedi Ky Narec observes Ventress' Force sensitivity and trains her until he is murdered.

THE CLONE WARS

The bet
Ventress attempts to bring Toydaria into the Separatist fold, but loses both a bet to Yoda and the Toydarian king's allegiance.

Liberating Nute Gunray
Dooku dispatches Ventress to free Nute Gunray, who is being held for questioning by the Republic.

Dooku's betrayal
Sensing Ventress' growing strength in the Force, Sidious orders Count Dooku to kill his apprentice.

Making a monster
Ventress recruits Nightbrother Savage Opress, whom the Nightsisters offer to Count Dooku as a new apprentice.

▼ Nightsister massacre
General Grievous invades Dathomir and wipes out the Nightsister clan. Mother Talzin disappears, leaving Ventress alone.

Train heist
Ventress alters the deal when an unexpected twist arises in a bounty hunter team-up with Boba Fett.

▲ Unexpected rescuer
Seeking to collect the bounty for Savage, Ventress instead ends up rescuing Obi-Wan Kenobi from Opress and Maul.

Unlikely ally
Ventress helps Anakin Skywalker clear Ahsoka Tano of treason charges by providing clues to the real traitor's identity.

A pirate's life
Ventress partners with pirate Lassa Rhayme to pull a job on a competing pirate, Hondo Ohnaka.

Assassination attempt
Along with Jedi Quinlan Vos, Ventress attempts to assassinate her former master, Count Dooku. The unlikely pairing is motivated by her thirst for revenge and the Jedi's desperation to end the Clone Wars by any means necessary.

A heroic death
Ventress is laid to rest on Dathomir after sacrificing her life to save Quinlan Vos.

"I look forward to adding your lightsabers to my collection."

GENERAL GRIEVOUS

GENERAL GRIEVOUS

Commander of the Separatist military, General Grievous is feared throughout the Republic. The cyborg has a vengeful lust for slaying Jedi and keeps their lightsabers as trophies.

APPEARANCES CW, III **SPECIES** Kaleesh (cyborg) **HOMEWORLD** Kalee **AFFILIATION** Separatists

JEDI HUNTER

The leader of the Separatist army, General Grievous frequently clashes with the Republic's Jedi generals. Even members of the Jedi Council struggle to challenge him. Grievous annihilates a fleet commanded by Plo Koon, leaving only a handful of survivors. Soon afterward he almost adds apprentice Ahsoka Tano's lightsaber to his collection during a duel at Skytop Station. He flees when her powerful teacher, Anakin Skywalker, intervenes at the last second. Jedi Master Kit Fisto is then assigned to track down Grievous' lair, but he barely escapes with his life after his former Padawan Nahdar Vebb is slain by the cyborg. Grievous later kidnaps Master Eeth Koth and taunts the Jedi via a holographic transmission; the rescue mounted by Anakin, Obi-Wan Kenobi, and Adi Gallia nearly fails.

Mortal combat
Jedi General Obi-Wan Kenobi and Separatist General Grievous face off early in the Clone Wars aboard the *Malevolence*.

No surrender
Grievous refuses to surrender on Naboo and fights off the Gungans one by one. General Tarpals finally stuns him, but not before receiving a mortal wound.

SEPARATIST STRIKES

Attacking key targets, General Grievous' army wreaks havoc across the galaxy. At Kamino, his cautious tactics make Obi-Wan suspect a bigger plan, which is confirmed when Obi-Wan discovers aqua droids mounting underwater assaults. The droids are bent on destroying the cloning facility crucial to the Republic war effort, but the Jedi turn the tide and Grievous retreats. Count Dooku also dispatches the cyborg on missions to serve the Sith's vengeful ends: at Naboo, Senator Amidala is forced into a prisoner exchange with Grievous to save Anakin, and on Dathomir, Grievous wipes out an entire clan of Nightsisters witches.

Standoff
General Grievous assumes an aggressive stance before attacking Obi-Wan on Utapau.

SITH DISTRACTION

General Grievous' flagship, *Invisible Hand*, leads the Separatist assault on Coruscant that captures Supreme Chancellor Palpatine. Obi-Wan and Anakin board the vessel to rescue Palpatine, and Grievous flees, leaving his MagnaGuards to fend off the Jedi. While the Jedi Council focuses its attention on pursuing the cyborg across the galaxy, Palpatine—truly Darth Sidious hiding in plain sight—unfolds his nefarious plot to wipe out the Jedi and declare himself Emperor. He tips off the Jedi on Grievous' location on Utapau, and Obi-Wan is sent in pursuit. After Obi-Wan makes a sudden appearance during the Separatist gathering on Utapau, Grievous and Obi-Wan battle and the Jedi kills him.

Feared by Jedi

Once a feared Kaleesh warrior, General Grievous is now more cybernetic machine than living flesh. He believes his mechanical limbs have made him superior to all foes. Scientists implanted his brain and eyes into a duranium alloy body, and his remaining vital organs are protected by a synthskin gut-sack. Count Dooku trains Grievous in the art of lightsaber combat, for which his cyborg enhancements are well suited. Grievous lacks Force powers, instead relying on agility and strength when in combat with a Jedi. A master of many of the classic forms of Jedi arts, he is able to adapt quickly to an opponent's fighting style.

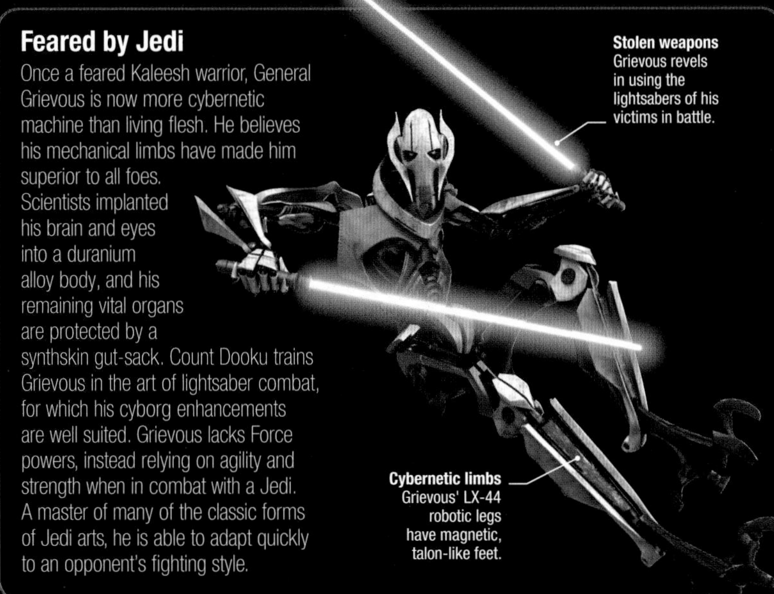

Stolen weapons
Grievous revels in using the lightsabers of his victims in battle.

Cybernetic limbs
Grievous' LX-44 robotic legs have magnetic, talon-like feet.

Beware of this mistake
While General Grievous' cybernetics enhance his fighting prowess, he reacts with rage when mistaken for a droid.

timeline

Cyborg implants
Following near-lethal injuries, the warrior who would become Grievous receives cyborg implants, which grant him fighting prowess equal to that of a Jedi.

The ship Malevolence
After Grievous uses *Malevolence* to destroy Plo Koon's fleet, Anakin's sabotage ultimately destroys the warship.

▲ Skytop Station
Grievous attacks Ahsoka, who accompanies her Master, Anakin, on a mission to rescue R2-D2. Ahsoka fends Grievous off and escapes.

Saleucami
During a duel with Obi-Wan, Grievous declares his desire to see a future where the Jedi are no more.

Raid on Kamino
When Grievous attacks Tipoca City, Obi-Wan again duels with the general. Grievous escapes when a Trident unit crushes the platform.

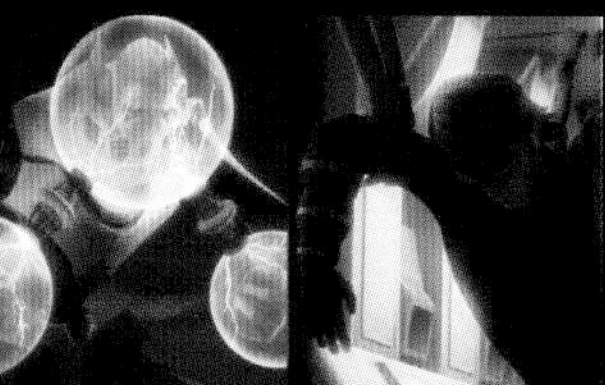

▲ Capture on Naboo
Captured by Gungans after he kills General Tarpals, the cyborg is traded for Anakin by Senator Amidala.

▲ Massacre on Dathomir
Despite Asajj Ventress' best efforts, Grievous kills the elder Daka, while his droids slaughter the Nightsisters.

Kyber demand
When Obi-Wan and Anakin stop the Separatists from buying a giant kyber crystal on Utapau, Grievous intervenes but cannot stop the Jedi blowing up the crystal.

Return to Dathomir
Alongside Darth Sidious, Grievous travels to Dathomir to rescue Count Dooku from Mother Talzin and Maul. Unlike on his last visit, Grievous manages to slay Talzin.

Duel on Invisible Hand
Jedi heroes Anakin and Obi-Wan battle General Grievous during the rescue of Chancellor Palpatine.

▲ Death on Utapau
Obi-Wan and Grievous engage in a brutal battle. The Jedi slays him with the cyborg's personal blaster.

"No one has her kind of determination." ANAKIN SKYWALKER

AHSOKA TANO

The apprentice Anakin Skywalker never expected, Ahsoka Tano is as headstrong as her master. She earns his respect and friendship, taking his Jedi lessons and passing them on. Ultimately, on her path to becoming a Jedi, she remains true to herself.

APPEARANCES CW, Reb, FoD **SPECIES** Togruta **HOMEWORLD** Shili **AFFILIATION** Jedi Order

ANAKIN SKYWALKER'S PADAWAN

When the Jedi Council assigns Ahsoka to train beside Anakin, they believe that the rule-following, optimistic new Padawan will be a good influence on her impulsive master. They also hope that mentoring the talented young Jedi will help Anakin learn to let go of his attachments. Her master's training quickly makes an impression: When she teams with Barriss Offee, apprentice of Luminara Unduli, during the second Battle of Geonosis, Ahsoka's bold style contrasts with the more reserved demeanor of her counterpart. Their partnership falters, however, on the mysterious monolith Mortis, where a Force vision of her older self warns Ahsoka that her future seems bleak if she remains with Anakin.

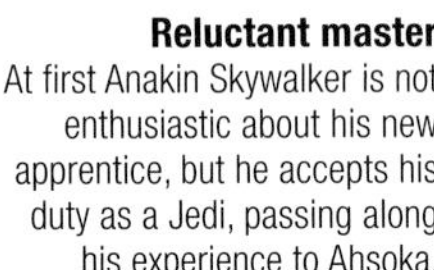

Reluctant master
At first Anakin Skywalker is not enthusiastic about his new apprentice, but he accepts his duty as a Jedi, passing along his experience to Ahsoka.

Important lessons
When Ahsoka is kidnapped during a mission, she must use all her Jedi training to escape her Trandoshan captors.

SOLO MISSIONS

Ahsoka's exceptional Jedi skills lead to missions away from her master early in her apprenticeship. When Pantoran Chairman Papanoida's daughters are kidnapped, she volunteers to help her friend Senator Riyo Chuchi investigate the crime, using Force levitation and her first Jedi mind tricks along the way. Soon after, she assists Duchess Satine Kryze in exposing corruption at the highest levels of Mandalore's government. Plagued by visions of Padmé Amidala's assassination, Ahsoka insists on joining the senator's security detail and thwarts the assassin Aurra Sing. By the time Ahsoka is captured by Trandoshan hunters and taken to Wasskah, she possesses the confidence to lead abducted Jedi younglings to fight back against their captors.

THE TEACHER

While working with Duchess Satine's nephew, Korkie, and his friends to root out traitors, Ahsoka exhibits a talent for leadership.

Rebel leader
Ahsoka fights alongside Onderon rebels during a battle against a Separatist droid army supporting King Rash.

When the Jedi Council agrees to Anakin's proposal to train Onderon insurgents striving to depose the Separatist-allied king, Ahsoka and Obi-Wan join him for the mission. Impressed by Ahsoka's development, the two senior Jedi have enough confidence to leave her behind as the sole Jedi adviser during the final stages of the successful Onderon uprising. Not long after, Yoda entrusts Ahsoka with safeguarding the travels of Jedi younglings venturing to Ilum, where they undergo rigorous tests of physical and inner strength before they can construct their own lightsabers.

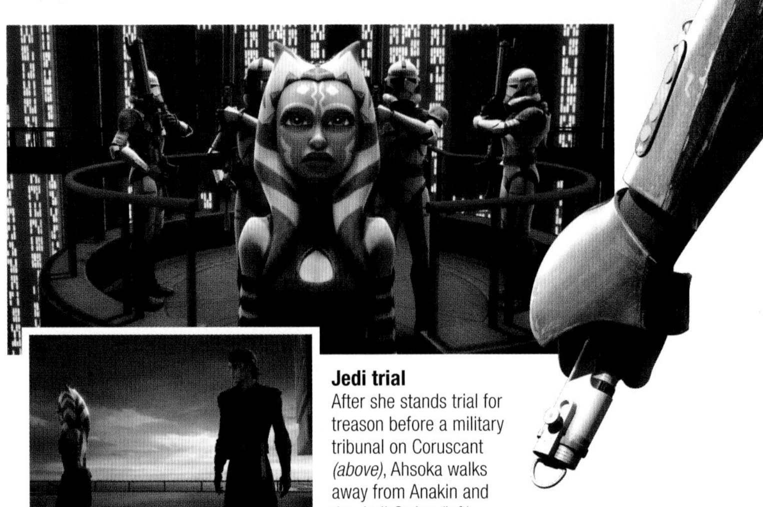

Jedi trial
After she stands trial for treason before a military tribunal on Coruscant *(above)*, Ahsoka walks away from Anakin and the Jedi Order *(left)*.

JEDI NO MORE

Following a bombing of the Jedi Temple, Ahsoka and Anakin are recalled to investigate. While Ahsoka interrogates the bomber, Letta Turmond, about her accomplice, the prisoner is Force choked by an unseen person. Despite protesting her innocence to Admiral Tarkin, Ahsoka is arrested for Turmond's murder. Mysterious assistance—a keycard outside her cell, incapacitated guards, and a comlink—aid Ahsoka's escape from prison, but also further incriminate her. Anakin finds her but cannot convince his Padawan to turn herself in. Ultimately, she finds an unlikely ally in Sith outcast Asajj Ventress, who leads Anakin to clues proving Barriss Offee is the true traitor. Her faith in the institution shaken, Ahsoka refuses the Jedi Council's offers of reinstatement.

Instinctive talent
While Ahsoka is gifted with raw Force talent, her tendency to follow her heart challenges her path to knighthood. As a young Jedi, emotions inhibit her ability to make wise decisions. Eventually, Ahsoka gains the confidence to make the right choice, even at great cost to her own feelings.

RE-EMERGENCE

After years of concealing her Force powers from those around her, Ahsoka leads a resistance group on Raada to fight back against Imperial farming techniques meant to leave the moon barren. Her activities attract the attention of the Inquisitorius, culminating in a confrontation with the Sixth Brother. Emerging victorious against this fellow Force user, Ahsoka takes the kyber crystals from his lightsaber. Freed of their dark corruption, the crystals turn from red to white and are forged into Ahsoka's new blades. She arranges for the refugees of Raada to be saved by Viceroy Bail Organa of Alderaan and, using the code name Fulcrum, joins his Rebellion.

Agent Fulcrum
Ahsoka is one of many who have used the code name Fulcrum, along with Alexsandr Kallus and Cassian Andor.

FACING VADER

Working with the crew of the *Ghost*, now part of the Phoenix rebel group, Ahsoka crosses paths with Darth Vader. Reaching out through the Force, she begins to suspect that he is Anakin Skywalker, her former master. Ahsoka travels to the planet Malachor with Ezra Bridger and Kanan Jarrus in search of answers about the Inquisitorius. There they find an ancient Sith temple and are cornered by Vader himself, at which point Ahsoka's fears about his identity are proved true. Unmoved when Ahsoka pleads to the Anakin she used to know, Vader attacks. Ahsoka appears doomed—until a hand pulls her into a portal. The hand belongs to Ezra Bridger, who has traveled through the mysterious World between Worlds and reached through time to save her. Ahsoka and Ezra must return to their own times, but she promises to meet him again one day.

Allies turned enemies
Ahsoka beseeches Vader to return to the light, promising not to leave him again, but he draws his lightsaber, engaging her in a fierce duel.

timeline

THE CLONE WARS

▼ Discovered
Plo Koon finds the three-year-old Force-sensitive child on the planet Shili and brings her to the Jedi Temple.

Battle of Christophsis
Ahsoka is sent by Yoda to train as Anakin's Padawan.

Battle of Ryloth
Ahsoka is forced to take command after Anakin makes a reckless solo assault on the Droid Control Ship.

Second Battle of Geonosis
Ahsoka and Barriss Offee infiltrate and destroy the Geonosian droid factory.

Death on Mortis
Anakin enlists the Father to use the remaining life force from the Daughter to resurrect Ahsoka.

Citadel rescue
Before his death, Even Piell entrusts Ahsoka with Nexus Route information she must deliver to the Jedi Council.

Trandoshan hunt
Hunted on a moon by Trandoshans, Ahsoka teams with Chewbacca to help a group of captive Jedi younglings escape.

Battle of Kadavo
Ahsoka and Anakin free Obi-Wan, Rex, and Togrutans held captive in a Zygerrian slaver facility.

Liberation of Onderon
Ahsoka, Anakin, and Obi-Wan assist Onderon rebels in liberating their planet from Separatist occupation.

Framed and betrayed
Framed by Barriss Offee for murder and treason, Ahsoka is expelled by the Jedi Order and made to stand trial.

▲ Ahsoka leaves Jedi Order
After she is cleared of wrongdoing, Ahsoka refuses the offer to rejoin the Jedi Order.

THE EMPIRE ERA

Exile
Ahsoka lives in exile on the Outer Rim planet of Thabeska. Fearing she has been exposed and unwilling to bring danger to the family sheltering her, she departs without notice to the moon of Raada.

Pivotal moment
Taking a stand at Raada brings Ahsoka to the attention of Bail Organa. Under the code name Fulcrum, she works with the senator as a messenger between disparate rebel cells.

Joining the Spectres
Ahsoka brings the crew of the *Ghost* into the Rebel Alliance, joining them for missions as they combat the Empire, the Inquisitorius, and come face to face with Darth Vader.

Mission to Malachor
Ahsoka stands up to Darth Vader, confronting her former master to allow Ezra and Kanan to escape.

The search for Ezra
After the fall of the Empire, Ahsoka leads Sabine Wren on a search to find Ezra Bridger, lost years before on an unknown course through hyperspace.

ROTTA THE HUTTLET

APPEARANCES CW **SPECIES** Hutt
HOMEWORLD Tatooine
AFFILIATION Hutts

Rotta is the son of Jabba the Hutt. After the Huttlet is kidnapped by Asajj Ventress, Jabba makes a deal with the Galactic Republic to rescue him. When Anakin Skywalker and Ahsoka Tano free Rotta on Teth, they realize that the Huttlet has fallen ill. Ahsoka finds the medicine that saves him.

ZIRO THE HUTT

APPEARANCES CW **SPECIES** Hutt
HOMEWORLD Sleheyron
AFFILIATION Hutts

Crime lord Ziro is Jabba the Hutt's uncle. Ziro conspires with Count Dooku and Asajj Ventress to kidnap Jabba's son, Rotta. Senator Padmé Amidala tries to open communications with the Hutts, who believe the Jedi abducted Rotta. After a failed assassination attempt on Padmé, Ziro is arrested. Via holocomm, Ziro confesses to Jabba his part in Rotta's kidnapping and is imprisoned on Coruscant. Cad Bane later frees Ziro and hands him over to the Hutt Council, which fears that Ziro might reveal its many dirty dealings to the Republic. With the help of Sy Snootles, Ziro escapes the Hutts. Snootles follows Ziro to Teth, retrieves a holopad filled with Hutt secrets, and then kills him.

KING KATUUNKO

APPEARANCES CW **SPECIES** Toydarian
HOMEWORLD Toydaria
AFFILIATION Republic

Due to his planet's reliance on the Trade Federation, King Katuunko could only secretly aid the planet Ryloth during the Clone Wars. When Chancellor Palpatine requests negotiations to use Toydaria as a base, he sends Yoda to Rugosa. Yoda impresses Katuunko with his Jedi character, and the king commits Toydaria to the Republic. Dooku's apprentice, Savage Opress, eventually kills the king for supporting the Jedi.

COMMANDER FOX

APPEARANCES CW **SPECIES** Human (clone)
HOMEWORLD Kamino **AFFILIATION** Republic

Fox, clone trooper commander CC-1010, leads the famed Coruscant Guard. He assists Padmé Amidala in the capture of Ziro the Hutt. Assigned to a Republic military base, he pursues the fugitive Ahsoka, who is blamed for the murder of Letta Turmond, but she evades capture. Fox later kills rogue trooper Fives before he can reveal a conspiracy within the Republic.

Fox participates in Order 66 on Coruscant. When Jedi survivor Jocasta Nu returns to the Jedi Temple, Fox surrounds the building with his forces. Nu escapes the Temple with Darth Vader in pursuit, but Fox's troops fire on both of them, since Fox hadn't informed them that the menacing figure was on their side. Vader kills Fox for his oversight.

CLONE TROOPER ECHO

APPEARANCES CW **SPECIES** Human (clone)
HOMEWORLD Kamino **AFFILIATION** Republic

CT-21-0408 is nicknamed "Echo" for constantly repeating rules. As a cadet, he is part of Domino Squad. Echo and other rookies thwart General Grievous' attempt to capture Rishi Station and are inducted into the 501st Legion. Echo works with Fives and Captain Rex on a strategy algorithm that identifies Republic weaknesses in order to overcome them. Echo obsessively checks the program before each battle.

Following their heroism during the Battle of Kamino, Echo and Fives are promoted to ARC troopers. Echo subsequently participates in the rescue of Jedi Master Even Piell from the Citadel, but ends up missing in action and is presumed dead. However, Echo survives and is captured by the enemy. Separatist leader Wat Tambor transforms Echo into a cyborg so he can interface with computers. Tambor then forcefully uses Echo's knowledge of the strategy algorithm to help the Separatists in battle. Suspecting Echo is alive, Rex leads Clone Force 99, a small team of unique clones, to rescue him. Echo uses his abilities to feed the Separatists misinformation to ensure a critical Republic victory on Anaxes. Now known as the Hero of Anaxes, Echo is promoted to corporal and joins Clone Force 99.

CLONE TROOPER FIVES

APPEARANCES CW **SPECIES** Human (clone)
HOMEWORLD Kamino **AFFILIATION** Republic

Fives' nickname comes from his clone designation, CT-27-5555. As a cadet, he trains with Domino Squad. After defending Rishi Station from General Grievous' attack, he is inducted into the 501st Legion. On Umbara, Fives is the loudest voice against Jedi General Krell, who is revealed to be a traitor. Fives also uncovers the truth about Chancellor Palpatine and Order 66, but is killed by Commander Fox before he can expose the conspiracy.

COMMANDER WOLFFE

APPEARANCES CW, Reb **SPECIES** Human (clone) **HOMEWORLD** Kamino
AFFILIATION Republic, Rebels

Commander Wolffe, also known as clone CC-3636, leads Wolf Pack Battalion, which serves under Jedi General Plo Koon. During a mission to eliminate the *Malevolence*, the entire Wolf Pack is killed, except for Wolffe, Sinker, and Boost. At the Battle of Khorm, Wolffe loses his right eye during a fight with Asajj Ventress. Despite this, Wolffe continues to serve, helping Plo to rescue Jedi from behind enemy lines. He also delivers aid to the Aleena. On Coruscant, Wolffe is knocked out when he fights fugitive Jedi Ahsoka Tano and Ventress. With Plo, he finds the deceased Jedi Sifo-Dyas' lightsaber.

Along with fellow clones Gregor and Rex, Wolffe removes his control chip. During the Imperial era, the three clones live in a modified AT-TE on the planet Seelos and meet the *Ghost* crew. Wishing to protect his brother clones, Wolffe tells the Empire about the visitors, but Rex convinces him that the *Ghost* crew aren't the enemy. After beating an Imperial force, Rex leaves Seelos and Gregor and Wolffe begin living in an AT-AT. Three years later, they join Rex to help liberate Lothal.

Brother clone
Wolffe fears the Jedi, so hides messages from Rex's old friend Ahsoka Tano to try and protect Rex.

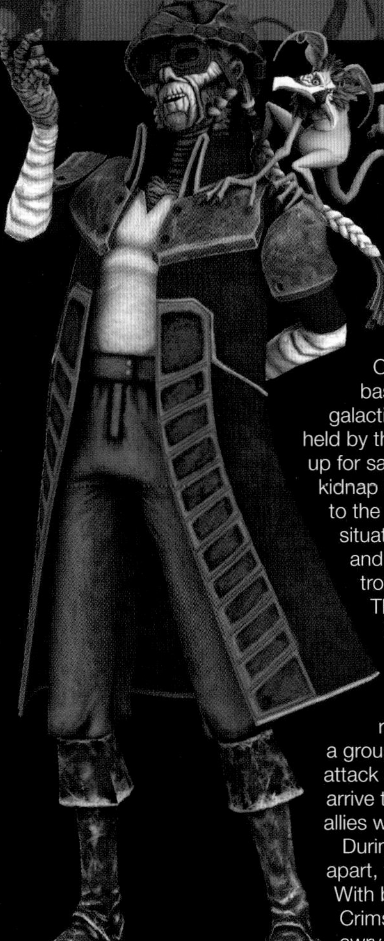

Monkey business
Hondo's pet Kowakian monkey-lizard, Pikk Mukmuk, helps him do the dirty work.

HONDO OHNAKA

APPEARANCES CW, Reb, FoD
SPECIES Weequay **HOMEWORLD** Florrum
AFFILIATION Ohnaka Gang, Ohnaka Solutions

Opportunistic and cunning, Hondo Ohnaka is the leader of the Ohnaka Gang based on the planet Florrum. Alongside other galactic criminals, Ohnaka attends an auction held by the Xrexus cartel where a Jedi Padawan is up for sale. During the Clone Wars, Hondo's pirates kidnap Count Dooku, and he attempts to sell him to the Republic for a hefty ransom. The hostage situation allows Hondo to also capture Obi-Wan and Anakin. With the assistance of clone troopers, Obi-Wan, Anakin, and Dooku escape. The Jedi later face Hondo's gang on the planet Felucia, where the Jedi help defend farms alongside hired bounty hunters.

Later in the war, Anakin pays Ohnaka to deliver missile launchers to the Onderon rebels. Ohnaka teams up with Ahsoka and a group of Jedi younglings to repel a Separatist attack on Florrum. When Maul and Savage Opress arrive to hire a gang of bounty hunters, Ohnaka allies with Obi-Wan to drive them off.

During the Imperial era, Hondo's pirate gang falls apart, forcing him to undertake smaller operations. With bounty hunter IG-88, he attempts to capture Crimson Dawn Lieutenant Qi'ra, but the plan goes awry, and she collects bounties on them instead. Hondo eventually escapes and joins Han Solo and Chewbacca in the *Millennium Falcon* on an adventure.

Years later, Hondo takes over criminal Cikatro Vizago's ship, the *Broken Horn*, locking up the former owner in a cell on his own ship. He encounters rebel Ezra Bridger, whom he lets in on his latest scheme. After lots of double-crossing, Hondo and Ezra part ways, striking up an unlikely friendship. Hondo runs into Ezra once more when he tips him, and the Empire, off to the location of two Lasat that survived the Siege of Lasan. The rebels rescue the Lasat, and Hondo ends up in Imperial captivity. He shares his cell with an Ugnaught named Melch who lets him know of a reclamation station with valuable starfighters that could be stolen for the Rebellion. Hondo contacts Ezra and secures his and Melch's release in exchange for the station's location. Hondo assists the rebels with the heist, taking a shuttle for himself and his new Ugnaught crew, which he modifies and names the *Last Chance*.

Later, Hondo begrudgingly helps the Spectres free a rare creature captured by the Empire and calls on their aid when a raid on an Imperial ship goes wrong above the planet Wynkahthu. Hondo responds to the call for help to free Ezra's homeworld. Decades later on Batuu, Hondo manages Ohnaka Transport Solutions and regales visitors of his many adventures.

Life of a leader
Hondo Ohnaka leads his fierce gang of Weequay pirates, who specialize in extortion and kidnapping, from a base on Florrum *(above)*. Melch is Hondo's latest accomplice, and soon wises up to his leader's lack of concern for his welfare *(below)*.

GUNDARK

APPEARANCES CW **HOMEWORLD** Vanqor
AVERAGE SIZE 2 m (7 ft) high
HABITAT Caves

Gundarks are fierce, aggressive creatures known for their overwhelming strength. After crash-landing on Vanqor, Anakin and Obi-Wan disturb a gundark in a cave. Using the Force to pelt the beast with rocks, the Jedi successfully repel it. When the *Endurance* crashes on Vanqor, R2-D2 faces off with a gundark. The droid ties the creature to Anakin's starfighter and sends it blasting off.

RIYO CHUCHI

APPEARANCES CW **SPECIES** Pantoran
HOMEWORLD Pantora
AFFILIATION Republic

When a Republic base falls silent, Senator Riyo Chuchi joins Chairman Chi Cho, Anakin, and Obi-Wan to investigate. After Cho is killed, Chuchi negotiates peace between the Pantorans and Talz. When the daughters of Baron Papanoida are kidnapped, she enlists Ahsoka Tano's help. Finding one daughter on a Trade Federation vessel, they overhear a conversation that confirms the Federation is working on behalf of the Separatists.

THI-SEN

APPEARANCES CW **SPECIES** Talz **HOMEWORLD** Orto Plutonia
AFFILIATION Talz village

Thi-Sen leads a peaceful tribe caught between the Galactic Republic and Separatist task forces. Protecting its territory, the tribe attacks the Republic outpost and the droid forces. A second Republic task force under the command of Anakin and Obi-Wan negotiates a cease-fire. Believing the Talz to be trespassers, Chairman Cho of the neighboring moon Pantora declares war on them. After the chairman dies, Senator Riyo Chuchi uses C-3PO to make peace with Thi-Sen.

NARGLATCH

APPEARANCES CW **HOMEWORLD** Orto Plutonia
AVERAGE SIZE 6 m (20 ft) long
HABITAT Adaptable

The narglatch is a stealthy predator that can live in a variety of climates. On the frozen world of Orto Plutonia, narglatch are used as mounts by the Talz. Narglatch hide is vulnerable to blaster fire and valued by some cultures as a trophy. Narglatch cubs are cute and often taken as pets, but become extremely dangerous when they mature. Escaped narglatch are a threat on Coruscant.

DR. NUVO VINDI

APPEARANCES CW **SPECIES** Faust
HOMEWORLD Adana
AFFILIATION Separatists

Nute Gunray sponsors Nuvo Vindi's work to re-create the Blue Shadow Virus in a Trade Federation laboratory built beneath Naboo's swamps. Padmé stumbles upon the lair while investigating the death of a shaak herd. Arriving on Naboo, her Jedi friends help to capture Vindi. He refuses to hand over the antidote to save Padmé and Ahsoka, but Obi-Wan and Anakin travel to Iego to find a cure.

CLONE TROOPER WAXER

APPEARANCES CW **SPECIES** Human (clone) **HOMEWORLD** Kamino **AFFILIATION** Republic

Waxer serves in the Ghost Company during campaigns to retake Ryloth and Geonosis. The recon team of Waxer and Boil scouts an abandoned Twi'lek village and finds a young girl, Numa, who reveals the underground passages the clone troopers use to free the Twi'leks. Waxer dies when General Krell deceives the clones on Umbara.

TODO 360

APPEARANCES CW **MANUFACTURER** Vertseth Automata **TYPE** Techno-service droid **AFFILIATION** Bounty hunter

Todo 360 is destroyed in a ventilation shaft as a distraction when Cad Bane steals a holocron from the Jedi Temple for Darth Sidious. Todo is rebuilt by Anakin Skywalker and escapes. He assists Bane in capturing C-3PO and R2-D2.

CATO PARASITTI

APPEARANCES CW, FoD **SPECIES** Clawdite **HOMEWORLD** Zolan **AFFILIATION** Bounty hunter

Posing as Ord Enisence and Chief Librarian Jocasta Nu, changeling Cato Parasitti neutralizes the Jedi Temple's security so that Cad Bane can reach the Holocron Vault. Ahsoka Tano later defeats Parasitti in a duel, and while she is in Jedi captivity, Parasitti offers information on Bane's next target: Bolla Ropal, the keeper of the kyber memory crystal. After leaving prison, Parasitti tries to kill some Arthurian delegates, but Ahsoka and Padmé stop her.

CAD BANE

APPEARANCES CW **SPECIES** Duros **HOMEWORLD** Duro **AFFILIATION** Bounty hunter

A legendary and ruthless bounty hunter, Cad Bane will take on any job as long as the amount of credits is right. Along with three other bounty hunters, Bane works for Maul when the former Sith wants to steal a captive Jedi Padawan from crime lord Xev Xrevus.

Following Jango Fett's death, Bane becomes the best bounty hunter in the galaxy. Working for Darth Sidious, Bane steals a holocron from the Jedi Temple that can unlock the kyber memory crystal, a list of the identities of all Force-sensitive infants. After taking the crystal from Jedi Bolla Ropal and forcing Anakin Skywalker to unlock it, Bane is sent to kidnap four of the infants. Foiled halfway through his job by Anakin and Ahsoka Tano, Bane escapes.

Jabba the Hutt hires Bane to break his uncle Ziro out of a Republic prison. Bane captures several prominent members of the Galactic Senate and uses them as hostages to compel Chancellor Palpatine to free Ziro, whom Bane delivers to the Hutt Council. When Ziro escapes from their custody, Bane is hired again to track him down. He fails to secure this bounty and has to evade Obi-Wan Kenobi and Quinlan Vos.

Mastermind Moralo Eval offers Bane a fortune to break him out of the Republic Judiciary Central Detention Center. Bane succeeds and enters Eval's competition, the Box, which is an event that will determine which five mercenaries will be hired in a plot to kidnap Palpatine. After passing the tournament test, Bane is personally selected by Count Dooku to lead the team of Embo, Derrown, Twazzi, and Rako Hardeen, who is really Obi-Wan undercover. They travel to Naboo to abduct Palpatine during the Festival of Light. The team succeeds, but Dooku betrays Bane. Having intended that the bounty hunters' operation should just be a diversion, Dooku misses his rendezvous with them. Bane is then defeated by Obi-Wan.

Tackling the Box
Cad Bane and his fellow contestants study the next phase of Moralo Eval's bounty hunter skills challenge, the Box.

SUGI

APPEARANCES CW **SPECIES** Zabrak **HOMEWORLD** Iridonia **AFFILIATION** Bounty hunter

Sugi owns the starship *Halo* and is guided by a strong sense of honor and duty. Along with fellow bounty hunters Rumi Paramita, Embo, and Seripas, Sugi is hired to defend a Felucian farming village plagued by the Ohnaka Gang. Sugi's team joins forces with three Jedi, Obi-Wan, Anakin, and Ahsoka, to fight off the pirate gang. Paramita dies in battle, but Sugi and her remaining allies chase off the pirates. They receive their payment, and Sugi offers the stranded Jedi a ride aboard her ship. Sugi is then hired by Wookiee chief Tarfful to help liberate the people that are being hunted by the Trandoshans on Wasskah. Sugi takes some Jedi survivors back to Coruscant. After this contract, Sugi, Embo and two other bounty hunters are employed by the Grand Hutt Council to protect them. However, they cannot stop Maul and the Shadow Collective, so run away. Sugi inspires her niece Jas Emari to follow in her footsteps, and Jas becomes the next owner of the *Halo*.

Taking aim
Sugi's weapon of choice is an EE-3 carbine rifle.

SERIPAS

APPEARANCES CW **SPECIES** Ssori **HOMEWORLD** Unknown **AFFILIATION** Bounty hunter

Diminutive bounty hunter Seripas wears a mechanical bodysuit to make up for his size. As part of Sugi's team, he protects a Felucian farm from a band of Weequay pirates led by Hondo Ohnaka. Alongside Ahsoka, Seripas trains the farmers to fight. Despite Seripas' suit being destroyed, he still manages to defeat a pirate during the farmers' successful defense of their homes. Later, Seripas and Sugi bring Wookiees in to help rescue Chewbacca and Ahsoka, who are being held captive by Trandoshans on Wasskah.

GWARM

APPEARANCES CW **SPECIES** Weequay **HOMEWORLD** Florrum **AFFILIATION** Ohnaka Gang

Gwarm serves as second-in-command of the Ohnaka Gang that extorts valuable Nysillin crops from Felucian farmers. The pirates are challenged by bounty hunters hired by the farmers and three Jedi. When the gang's captain, Hondo Ohnaka, is at the mercy of Anakin, Gwarm calls for retreat to rescue him, and the pirates leave the planet empty-handed.

EMBO

APPEARANCES CW
SPECIES Kyuzo
HOMEWORLD Phatrong
AFFILIATION Bounty hunter

Accompanied by his beloved anooba Marrok, Embo is deadly with a shot from his bowcaster or a decisive blow from his pan-shaped hat. He often works with Sugi and is hired as part of her team to defend farmers on Felucia. Embo is one of 11 bounty hunters, including Obi-Wan—disguised as Rako Hardeen—and Cad Bane, to fight in the Box competition. Embo is hired to target Rush Clovis, but fails when Anakin interrupts his plans. Later, he defends the Hutt Grand Council from Maul and Savage Opress. Afterward, Embo joins Boba Fett's crew of bounty hunters and participates in missions to Quarzite and Serenno.

Embo works throughout the Imperial era, but sadly, Marrok, dies. After the Battle of Endor, Embo works with Dengar and Jeeta to capture Sugi's niece and fellow bounty hunter Jas Emari for Mercurial Swift. They find Jas on Jakku, and they are ready to capture her until she persuades them to switch sides for full pardons. Following the Battle of Jakku, Embo joins Jas' new bounty hunter crew.

SIONVER BOLL

APPEARANCES CW **SPECIES** Bivall
HOMEWORLD Protobranch
AFFILIATION Republic

Sionver Boll designs the electro-proton bomb that is deployed during the Battle of Malastare to deactivate an entire Separatist droid invasion force. The bomb awakens the Zillo Beast. Despite Boll's protest, Chancellor Palpatine orders the beast killed. The beast escapes, rampaging on Coruscant before Boll creates enough toxin to kill it.

ZILLO BEAST

APPEARANCES CW **HOMEWORLD** Malastare
AVERAGE SIZE 97 m (318 ft) high
HABITAT Underground

The Zillo Beast is a legendary monster unearthed during the Battle of Malastare by an electro-proton bomb. The beast's armor proves nearly invulnerable to Republic weaponry, stirring the interest of Chancellor Palpatine. The creature is captured and transported to a research facility on Coruscant. The Zillo Beast breaks free from its restraints, wreaking havoc through the capital. It is killed by a toxin created by Sionver Boll, but its body is kept for possible cloning.

MON MOTHMA

APPEARANCES CW, III, Reb, RO, VI **SPECIES** Human **HOMEWORLD** Chandrila **AFFILIATION** Republic, Rebel Alliance, New Republic

An experienced and inspiring politician, Mon Mothma plays a crucial role in galactic history. Alongside fellow senators Padmé Amidala, Bail Organa, and Onaconda Farr, Mothma promotes a movement to put an end to the fighting and let diplomacy resume during the Clone Wars. Mothma, Organa, and Padmé oppose Chancellor Palpatine's abuse of wartime powers and worry that the chancellor will refuse to relinquish them after the war. Her fears are realized when Palpatine reorganizes the Galactic Republic into the First Galactic Empire. She loses her friend Padmé shortly after Palpatine's power grab.

During the Imperial era, Mothma and Organa remain in the Senate, but secretly form a network of independent rebel cells to oppose the Empire. Following the Ghorman Massacre, Mothma publicly rebels and is branded a traitor. While fleeing Coruscant with the rebel cell named Gold Squadron, Mothma's ship is attacked, but its crew are rescued by Phoenix Squadron—another rebel group. Mothma reaches Dantooine where she addresses the galaxy, announcing her resignation from the Senate and the formation of the Alliance to Restore the Republic. She becomes the group's leader and must make tough decisions. When a contingent of rebels is besieged on Atollon, Mothma refuses to send help in order to protect the rest of the Alliance. Much later, she sanctions the attack on Lothal that liberates the planet.

Soon after, the Alliance learns of the Death Star, and Mothma elicits Jyn Erso's help to track down Jyn's father—who helped design it. They learn that the plans for the Death Star are held at an Imperial base on Scarif. Lacking the Alliance council's full support, Mothma can't sanction a mission to retrieve them, so Jyn goes rogue. Mothma is glad when Admiral Raddus decides to reinforce her above Scarif. The mission results in the successful theft of the plans, albeit at the cost of many rebel lives. A year later, Mothma barely escapes the crushing rebel defeat at the Mako-Ta Space Docks and orders the survivors to disperse until the time is right to reunite. Two years later, the rebels learn that the Empire is building a second Death Star over Endor. Mothma approves the attack on it and personally briefs the rebel leaders.

Following the rebel victory over Endor, Mothma establishes the New Republic and its Galactic Senate on Chandrila. Mothma is elected its first chancellor, but she nearly dies when the Imperial Navy feigns peace talks in order to attempt to assassinate her and other New Republic leaders. She returns to office and, with the help of her allies, persuades the senators to sanction a battle with the Empire's forces above Jakku. After the New Republic victory at Jakku, Mothma signs the Galactic Concordance, a peace treaty between the New Republic and the Empire. Mothma continues to lead the New Republic until illness forces her to step down. Years later, Mothma contacts Leia Organa offering support to her friend when it is revealed to the galaxy that Leia's birth father is Darth Vader.

Champion of democracy
Senators Mon Mothma, Bail Organa, and Padmé Amidala discuss methods of countering the chancellor's increasing war powers *(left)*. Mon Mothma and Hera Syndulla discuss Hera's plan to destroy the TIE defender elite factory on Lothal *(below)*.

Rebel leader
Mon Mothma addresses the members of the Rebel Alliance strike team set to attack the second Death Star in the Endor system.

RUSH CLOVIS

APPEARANCES CW **SPECIES** Human **HOMEWORLD** Scipio **AFFILIATION** InterGalactic Banking Clan

Senator Rush Clovis works with fellow Senator Padmé Amidala to pass the Mid Rim Cooperation motion that saves the people of Bromlarch from a natural disaster. Years later, during the Clone Wars, the Jedi Order is suspicious of Clovis, so enlists Padmé to gather information about him. She is poisoned when she discovers he is allied to the Separatists, but Clovis, who harbors feelings for her, forces his co-conspirator, Lott Dod, to provide the antidote. Bitter about Clovis' affection for Padmé, Anakin Skywalker abandons Clovis. Hoping to atone for his wrongs, Clovis later pleads for Padmé's help in exposing corruption in the Banking Clan, but is killed during a battle on the planet Scipio when Anakin saves Padmé and Clovis falls to his death.

Intrigue on Scipio
On Cato Neimoidia, Rush Clovis conspires with Separatists to fund a droid factory *(above)*. Clovis and Padmé arrive on Scipio to investigate corruption in the Banking Clan *(right)*.

KARINA THE GREAT

APPEARANCES CW **SPECIES** Geonosian **HOMEWORLD** Geonosis **AFFILIATION** Separatists

Some believe the ruling queen on Geonosis is always called Karina the Great. Residing in the catacombs beneath the planet, each queen controls an army of Geonosian drones. During the Clone Wars, the ruling Karina gives orders through Poggle the Lesser. The Jedi discover her after she captures Luminara Unduli, who had followed Poggle to her location. This Karina is presumably killed when clone troopers destroy the temple while rescuing the Jedi.

TERA SINUBE

APPEARANCES CW **SPECIES** Cosian **HOMEWORLD** Cosia **AFFILIATION** Jedi

Jedi Master Tera Sinube is an expert on Coruscant's criminal underworld. When Ahsoka Tano's lightsaber is stolen, the Padawan enlists Sinube's help. They track prime suspect Nack Movers and find him dead in his apartment. With him are the bounty hunters Cassie Cryar and Ione Marcy. Ahsoka chases after the fleeing Cryar, while Sinube interrogates Marcy before she also flees. When the Jedi locate the fugitives on a train platform, Marcy is arrested by nearby police droids and Cryar is cornered on a train by Ahsoka. A desperate Cryar tries to exit the train with two hostages, but is foiled by Sinube, who disarms her before returning the stolen lightsaber to Ahsoka.

PRIME MINISTER ALMEC

APPEARANCES CW **SPECIES** Human **HOMEWORLD** Mandalore **AFFILIATION** Mandalorian ruling council, Shadow Collective

Almec is a member of the peaceful New Mandalorian faction. He serves in the New Mandalorian government as prime minister, taking up residence in the capital city of Sundari. When Mandalore is cut off from Republic aid, Almec establishes a black market to bring much-needed supplies to his people. But the smugglers poison the people of Sundari with slabin-tainted tea. Almec's crime is exposed and he is imprisoned for his crimes, though he remains unapologetic for helping his people. After Maul takes over Sundari, he reinstates Almec as a figurehead prime minister. When Maul is imprisoned by Darth Sidious on Stygeon Prime, Almec sends Death Watch to rescue him as recompense for Maul securing his own release.

DUCHESS SATINE KRYZE

APPEARANCES CW **SPECIES** Human **HOMEWORLD** Mandalore **AFFILIATION** Mandalorian ruling council

At the beginning of the Clone Wars, Duchess Satine Kryze advocates for peace. When rumors swirl that she is secretly creating an army for the Separatists, the Jedi High Council sends Obi-Wan Kenobi, whom Satine had befriended during the Mandalorian Civil War, to investigate. Satine and Obi-Wan travel to Mandalore's moon Concordia, where they are attacked by Governor Pre Vizsla and his Death Watch mercenaries. After they narrowly escape, Satine heads to Coruscant to warn the Galactic Senate about the danger Death Watch presents. Unfortunately, her ship is attacked by Separatist droids, and she is taken hostage by Senator Tal Merrik, a Separatist conspirator. When she is freed, with help from Obi-Wan and Anakin, Satine hurries to the Senate and proves that the evidence favoring a military intervention has been faked, resulting in the senators voting down the resolution to invade Mandalore.

As a black-market culture grows on Mandalore, Satine, with the help of the like-minded Senator Padmé Amidala, seeks to prevent the entire population from becoming implicated. She requests aid from the Jedi to expose the smugglers, and Padawan Ahsoka Tano arrives to work with cadets at the Mandalorian Royal Academy to combat them. Satine reveals Prime Minister Almec as the culprit behind the black market. He imprisons her, but she is eventually rescued by Ahsoka and the cadets.

When Maul and Savage Opress arrive on Mandalore, Viszla convinces the planet's people that only Death Watch is strong enough to stop Maul and Opress' Shadow Collective. Ousted from power, the duchess sends a distress signal to Obi-Wan, who attempts to rescue her, but they are both captured. Maul mortally wounds Satine before a helpless Obi-Wan, for whom she expresses her eternal love as she dies.

Duchess' allies
When she travels to Coruscant seeking a peaceful resolution to the conflict on Mandalore, Duchess Satine enlists the help of Senator Padmé Amidala *(right)*. Korkie Kryze and his friends from the Royal Academy free the imprisoned duchess *(below)*.

PRE VIZSLA

APPEARANCES CW **SPECIES** Human **HOMEWORLD** Mandalore **AFFILIATION** Death Watch, Shadow Collective

While governing Mandalore's moon Concordia, Pre Vizsla publicly maintains loyalty to pacifist Duchess Satine Kryze. Secretly he leads Death Watch, a society of commandos intent on returning the Mandalorians to their ancient roots as warriors. Terrorist attacks on Mandalore bring Obi-Wan and Duchess Kryze to Concordia, where they discover Death Watch's secret base and Vizsla reveals himself as its leader. After a short duel, Obi-Wan and Satine are forced to flee Concordia.

Vizsla dispatches a Death Watch assassin to Coruscant to kill the duchess and silence her opposition to the Senate's upcoming resolution to send Republic troops to occupy Mandalore. However, Vizsla hopes the Republic's occupation will convince Mandalore's people to support Death Watch. The assassination attempt is foiled and the Senate vote favors Satine, forcing Vizsla to postpone his attack on Mandalore. Harboring a common hatred of Obi-Wan, Maul and Vizsla gather an army of criminals called the Shadow Collective. The criminals attack Mandalore's capital Sundari, allowing Death Watch to be cast as heroes to a desperate population. Vizsla ousts Duchess Kryze and appoints himself prime minister, claiming the title of Mand'alor. Maul challenges Vizsla to a duel to determine the true ruler of the Mandalorians. Vizsla loses and is executed for his failure.

The toast
Pre Vizsla reveals himself as leader of Death Watch.

Claiming the title
Pre Vizsla addresses the people after Death Watch wrests control of the planet from Duchess Kryze.

BOSSK

APPEARANCES CW, V, VI **SPECIES** Trandoshan **HOMEWORLD** Trandosha **AFFILIATION** Bounty hunter, Krayt's Claw

Notorious bounty hunter Bossk teams up with Aurra Sing and Castas to mentor young Boba Fett, who has a vendetta against his father's killer, Jedi Mace Windu. Fett destroys the engines of a Republic attack cruiser carrying Windu, causing it to crash. The bounty hunters take hostages recovered from the wreck, but the Jedi eludes them. Unluckily for them, Jedi Ahsoka Tano rescues the prisoners and captures the bounty hunters. While imprisoned together on Coruscant for their crime, Bossk acts as Fett's bodyguard.

After they escape, Bossk continues working with Fett, joining his team of bounty hunters named Krayt's Claw. When Oked, a fellow team member, is killed by Asajj Ventress, Bossk and Latts Razzi blackmail Ventress into replacing Oked on their next job—they have been hired by Major Rigosso to protect a large chest. While on the job, the tram carrying the chest is attacked by Kage warriors. Bossk is blinded by one of the warriors and kicked off the tram. Fortunately, he still receives his payment for the assignment. Asajj leaves Krayt's Claw but hires the team to help her rescue Quinlan Vos from Count Dooku on Serenno.

During the Imperial era, Bossk brings down a corrupt Imperial officer on Lothal with the help of a young Ezra Bridger. He also captures a rogue Imperial astromech containing top-secret data. During the Galactic Civil War, Bossk is employed by amoral archaeologist Doctor Aphra to steal credits from the Empire. He is furious when he discovers she has double-crossed him and taken the credits for herself.

Following the Battle of Hoth, Bossk is one of six bounty hunters hired by Darth Vader to hunt down the *Millennium Falcon*, but his old partner Boba Fett beats him to the mark. Bossk meets up with Fett at Jabba the Hutt's palace, where the *Falcon*'s captain, Han Solo, is hanging on a wall, imprisoned in carbonite. Both bounty hunters accompany Jabba's retinue aboard a sail barge to witness the execution of Han and the team of rebels who have tried to rescue him. The barge is destroyed when Han and his friends fight back.

Working with Fett
Bossk teams up with young Boba Fett on Quarzite *(left)* and is assigned the same target as Fett years later on the *Executor (above)*.

KORKIE KRYZE

APPEARANCES CW **SPECIES** Human **HOMEWORLD** Mandalore **AFFILIATION** New Mandalorian

The nephew of Duchess Satine Kryze, Cadet Korkie attends the Royal Academy of Government on Mandalore. With his friends Soniee, Amis, and Lagos, Korkie exposes fabricated food shortages that strengthen the black market supported by Mandalorian Prime Minister Almec. With the help of his friends and Bo-Katan Kryze, the Duchess' sister, Korkie frees Satine from prison after Death Watch attacks Mandalore.

BARON PAPANOIDA

APPEARANCES CW, III **SPECIES** Pantoran **HOMEWORLD** Pantora **AFFILIATION** Republic

During their blockade of Pantora, the Trade Federation kidnaps Chairman Papanoida's two daughters, Chi Eekway and Che Amanwe, as extra leverage to convince the planet's leader to side with the Separatists. Papanoida tracks the kidnapper, the bounty hunter Greedo, to Jabba the Hutt's palace on Tatooine. When brought before Jabba by Papanoida, Greedo admits Chi Eekway is being held in Mos Eisley. Papanoida and his son Ion rescue Eekway, while Amanwe is recovered by Senator Riyo Chuchi and Ahsoka from a Droid Control Ship. Years later, following the Battle of Coruscant, Papanoida and Eekway visit the Coruscant opera house.

To the rescue
Baron Papanoida may lead a world, but he is not afraid to take matters into his own hands, firing on assailants in a daring rescue of his daughter Chi Eekway.

ROBONINO

APPEARANCES CW **SPECIES** Patrolian
HOMEWORLD Patrolia
AFFILIATION Bounty hunter

Bounty hunter Robonino is regarded for his computer-hacking skills and expertise with explosives. During the Senate hostage crisis led by Cad Bane, Robonino triggers the emergency lockdown in the Republic Executive Building. Later, he grabs and electroshocks Anakin Skywalker when the Jedi battles his partners Shahan Alama and Aurra Sing. Under the employ of Count Dooku, he roughs up Senators Onaconda Farr and Padmé Amidala, who oppose increased funding for the Republic's militarization.

SY SNOOTLES

APPEARANCES CW, VI **SPECIES** Pa'lowick
HOMEWORLD Lowick **AFFILIATION** Hutt cartel

A successful singer and part-time bounty hunter, Sy Snootles dates Ziro the Hutt. Ziro's nephew Jabba hires Sy to steal Ziro's holopad, which contains damaging information about the Hutt crime families. She rescues Ziro from Nal Hutta, then accompanies him to Teth to obtain the holopad. Once she has it, Sy turns on Ziro and shoots him. In the years that follow, she focuses on her singing career and helps form the Max Rebo Band. She stays with the group until its break-up after Jabba the Hutt's death.

Entertainer
Sy Snootles *(far right)* sings for Jabba, her performances accompanied by the Max Rebo Band and the Hutt's dancing trio *(right)*.

Solo bounty
When Rodian bounty hunter Greedo corners Han Solo in the Mos Eisley Cantina *(left)*, Han takes aim.

GREEDO

APPEARANCES CW, IV **SPECIES** Rodian
HOMEWORLD Rodia **AFFILIATION** Bounty hunter

During the Clone Wars, Greedo is hired by the Trade Federation to kidnap Pantoran Chairman Papanoida's daughters, Chi Eekway and Che Amanwe. A statue that Che defends herself with is discovered, and the blood on it identifies Greedo, a known criminal, as the kidnapper. Papanoida and his son, Ion, track the Rodian to Tatooine, where they take him to Jabba along with proof of his involvement in the kidnapping. Greedo admits to working for the Separatists. During the rescue of Che, Greedo escapes and continues his work as a bounty hunter.

Years later, Greedo nearly duels an opponent outside Chalmun's Cantina. The fight is stopped by Obi-Wan Kenobi, who subtly uses the Force to persuade Greedo's foe to buy him a drink instead. Later, Greedo captures Figrin D'an, leader of the Modal Nodes, and delivers him to Jabba. The Hutt gangster forces the band to play for him for a year to pay off their debts. Band member Ickabel G'ont notices that Greedo collects bounties from Jabba, then helps the targets escape, so he can capture them once more. When D'an informs Jabba of Greedo's acts, the crime lord is furious with Greedo. Soon after, the bounty hunter pursues Jabba's contract for the smuggler Han Solo, who shoots and kills him.

NIX CARD

APPEARANCES CW **SPECIES** Muun
HOMEWORLD Scipio
AFFILIATION InterGalactic Banking Clan

Nix Card represents the InterGalactic Banking Clan. He plots with Count Dooku to bomb power generators on Coruscant to prevent peace talks. When power is cut to the Senate District, many senators call for the deregulation of the banks to secure the money necessary to finance troop production.

LUX BONTERI

APPEARANCES CW **SPECIES** Human **HOMEWORLD** Onderon
AFFILIATION Onderon rebels, Rebel Alliance, Dreamers

Lux Bonteri's family sides with the Separatists when Onderon secedes at the beginning of the Clone Wars. Count Dooku orders the death of his mother, Mina Bonteri, to stop a peace proposal that she has introduced. Seeking justice after her assassination, Lux allies with Death Watch. His friend Ahsoka Tano helps him recognize the Mandalorian warriors' dishonorable goals. Returning to Onderon, he joins the rebel movement helping to liberate the planet alongside Saw and Steela Gerrera. Following in his mother's footsteps, Lux becomes Onderon's senator when the planet rejoins the Republic.

At some point during the Imperial era, Lux marries an Imperial woman, becoming close to her daughter, and then secretly joins the Rebel Alliance. When Lux learns of the deaths of Saw and many of his followers on Jedha, he decides to assist a group of Partisan survivors called the Dreamers. He pretends to offer Alliance intelligence to his wife's daughter, in exchange for amnesty, but it is a ruse to get the names of Imperial officers. Known as the Mentor, Lux provides these human targets to the Dreamers. Soon after, the Imperial Inferno Squad infiltrates the rebel group, uncovering Lux's role in the process, and destroys the Dreamers. It is unknown whether Lux survives a confrontation with the Squad's leader, Iden Versio.

MINA BONTERI

APPEARANCES CW **SPECIES** Human **HOMEWORLD** Onderon **AFFILIATION** Republic, Separatists

Mina Bonteri is a Republic senator, who mentors the young Senator Padmé Amidala from Naboo and leads the senatorial mission to Bromlarch. She admires Count Dooku for taking a stand against the Republic, and with her planet defects to the Separatists. Even though clone forces kill her husband, she advocates a peaceful resolution to the war. Padmé and Mina's work to broker peace ends when Mina is killed by Dooku's agents.

Peace talks
In the Separatist Senate, Mina Bonteri moves to open peace negotiations with the Republic.

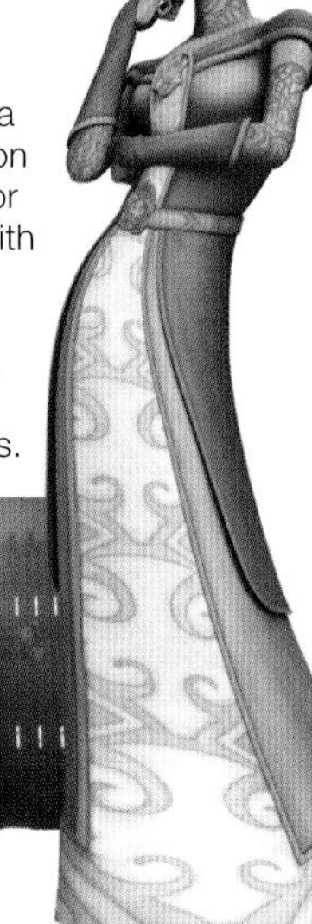

Duplicitous apprentice
Talzin presents Savage Opress to Count Dooku as his new apprentice. Opress' loyalties have been bound to Talzin by spells that provide his strength and power.

MOTHER TALZIN

APPEARANCES CW **SPECIES** Dathomirian **HOMEWORLD** Dathomir **AFFILIATION** Nightsisters

Both a clan mother and a shaman on Dathomir, Mother Talzin uses any means to protect the Nightsisters and also rules over the Nightbrothers. When Darth Sidious visits Dathomir, Talzin trusts his word that he will take her as his apprentice, but he betrays her and kidnaps her young son Maul to take Talzin's place. Talzin swears that she will get her revenge on Sidious.

To protect her sisters, Talzin has to give the infant Asajj Ventress to the criminal Hal'Sted. Ventress later trains with Dooku, but flees to Dathomir when he tries to kill her. Talzin reveals Ventress' true identity as a Nightsister and sends her and two other Nightsisters to assassinate Dooku, but they fail. When Dooku later requests a new apprentice from Talzin, she and Ventress select her second son Savage Opress. Before sending Opress, she casts a spell on him to make him stronger and ensure his ultimate loyalty to her.

On Talzin's orders, Opress tries and fails to defeat Dooku. Talzin then sends him on a quest to find his brother Maul, long believed dead. Dooku orders Grievous to attack the Nightsisters in retaliation for Talzin's strikes. Talzin uses her witchcraft to destroy numerous battle droids, then retreats to conjure dark magic to torture the Count. When Grievous reaches her, she vanishes into thin air. The Separatist assault wipes out the Nightsisters, leaving Ventress as the only other survivor.

After finding Maul, Opress brings him to Talzin, and she uses magic to restore Maul's memories and create a pair of cybernetic legs. The disorder strewn by Maul's newly formed criminal organization, named the Shadow Collective, ultimately draws the attention of Darth Sidious himself, allowing Talzin, Opress, and Maul to seek revenge. When Maul and Opress face Sidious, Opress is killed, and Maul is captured. Soon after, Talzin orders the Frangawl Cult, her followers on Bardotta, to capture the Force-sensitive Dayogan Mystics so she can absorb the living Force from them. Jedi Mace Windu engages her in battle, and, with Jar Jar Binks' help, stops Talzin.

When Maul escapes his incarceration he calls upon Talzin, who tells him to gather his forces to strike against the Sith, sending the Nightbrothers to aid him. Maul captures Dooku, taking him to Dathomir, where Talzin plans to drain the Sith Lord of energy to revive herself. Sidious and Grievous arrive on the planet and free Dooku from Talzin's control. Talzin sacrifices herself to ensure her son Maul can escape.

Nightsister returned
After Asajj Ventress' mentor Count Dooku tries to kill her, Mother Talzin welcomes her back into the Nightsister fold *(above)*.

SAVAGE OPRESS

APPEARANCES CW **SPECIES** Dathomirian Zabrak **HOMEWORLD** Dathomir **AFFILIATION** Nightbrothers, Shadow Collective

After Nightbrother Savage Opress is handpicked by Asajj Ventress to become her apprentice, Mother Talzin uses dark magic to grant him fearsome abilities and to ensure his loyalty. He kills his fellow Nightbrother Feral to prove his allegiance. Mother Talzin offers him to Count Dooku as a dark acolyte. Dispatched alone to the Devaron system, Opress slaughters Jedi Master Halsey and his apprentice Knox. Impressed, Dooku accepts Opress as his Sith apprentice, intending to use him to overthrow his own Sith master, Darth Sidious. However, Ventress subjects Opress to brutal training in order to pit him against Dooku. When Ventress and Opress battle Dooku on Toydaria, she cannot control his rage-filled impulses. Opress escapes to Dathomir, where he learns from Talzin about the fate that has befallen his brother Maul: he was cut in half by Jedi Knight Obi-Wan Kenobi. Opress rescues Maul from Lotho Minor and brings him to Talzin, who heals him.

Opress joins his brother in seeking vengeance on Kenobi, who pursues Opress and Maul across the galaxy. Ultimately the brothers ally with Death Watch and form the Shadow Collective to seize control of Mandalore. This attracts unwanted attention from Darth Sidious, who confronts the powerful brothers and strikes down Opress.

Deadly foe
Savage Opress is transformed by Nightsister magic into a terrifying opponent for the Jedi.

Duel to the death
Noting the growing power of the brothers, Sidious confronts Savage Opress and Maul on Mandalore *(left)*. As he dies, Opress expresses regret that he was never Maul's equal.

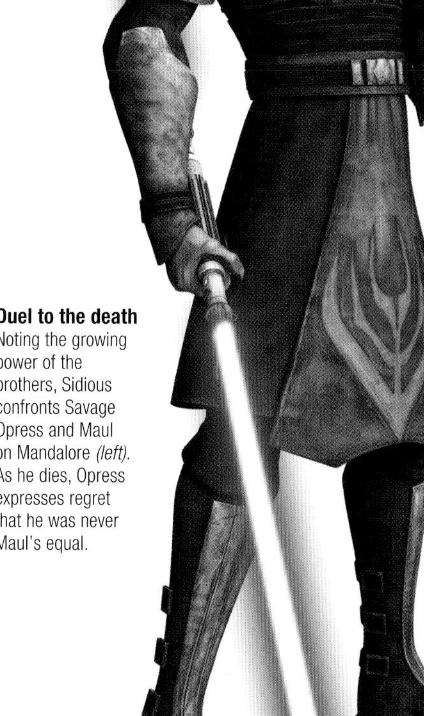

BROTHER VISCUS

APPEARANCES CW **SPECIES** Zabrak
HOMEWORLD Dathomir
AFFILIATION Nightbrothers

A leader of a Nightbrothers village on Dathomir, Viscus oversees the tournament used by Asajj Ventress to select Savage Opress as a worthy apprentice. Mother Talzin dispatches Viscus and a squad of Nightbrothers to aid Maul and the Shadow Collective in capturing Count Dooku and General Grievous in a clash at Ord Mantell.

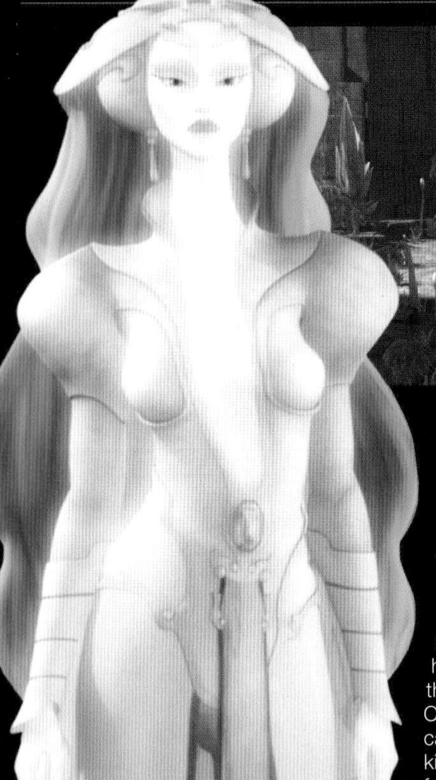

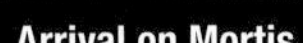

Arrival on Mortis
The landscape shifts seasons as the Jedi travel across Mortis, depending on whether the Daughter or the Son is influencing the area.

THE DAUGHTER

APPEARANCES CW **SPECIES** Force-wielder **HOMEWORLD** Mortis
AFFILIATION The Force

The Daughter is a Force-wielder aligned with the light side of the Force. A visit by Anakin Skywalker, Obi-Wan Kenobi, and Ahsoka Tano brings conflict between the Daughter and her brother, the Son, who is aligned with the dark side. When the Son attempts to murder their father, the Daughter takes Obi-Wan to retrieve the Dagger of Mortis, the only weapon that can stop him. The Son gains control of the dagger from the Jedi, kills Ahsoka, and strikes at the Father. The Daughter shields him from the blow and is mortally wounded. With the Father's help, Anakin uses the Daughter's remaining energy to resurrect Ahsoka.

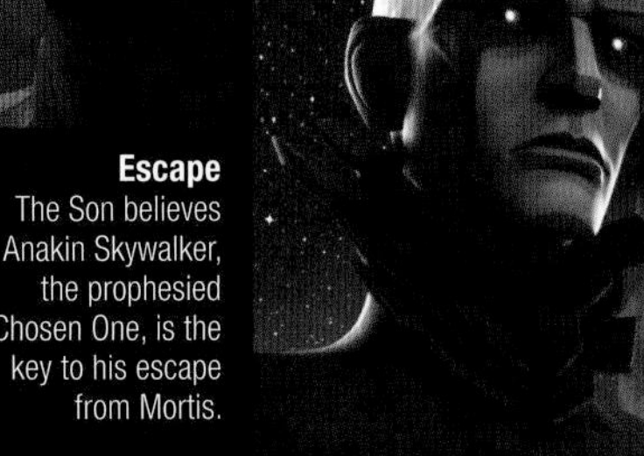

Escape
The Son believes Anakin Skywalker, the prophesied Chosen One, is the key to his escape from Mortis.

THE SON

APPEARANCES CW **SPECIES** Force-wielder
HOMEWORLD Mortis **AFFILIATION** The Force

The Son seeks to escape Mortis and wreak havoc in the galaxy. His ambitions are hindered by the Father, who has bound his children to Mortis, where he can maintain balance between the two. With the arrival of Anakin, the Son sees an opportunity to escape. He corrupts Ahsoka, but the Padawan's brief fall to the dark side fails to turn Anakin—he and Obi-Wan refuse to harm Ahsoka. The Son then tries to kill the Father, instead inadvertently slaying his sister, the Daughter. The Father forsakes his own life, thereby robbing the Son of his immortality and allowing the Chosen One, Anakin, to kill the dark one.

THE FATHER

APPEARANCES CW **SPECIES** Force-wielder **HOMEWORLD** Mortis
AFFILIATION The Force

A powerful family of Force-wielders, known as the Ones, resides in the mysterious realm of Mortis. There, the Father maintains balance between his daughter, who has an affinity for the light side of the Force, and his son, who aligns with the dark side. When Anakin, Obi-Wan, and Ahsoka arrive on Mortis, Anakin encounters the Father at his monastery and is given a test to determine if he truly is the prophesied Chosen One. When Anakin succeeds, the Father admits he is dying and asks Anakin to take his place on Mortis to maintain the balance of the Force.

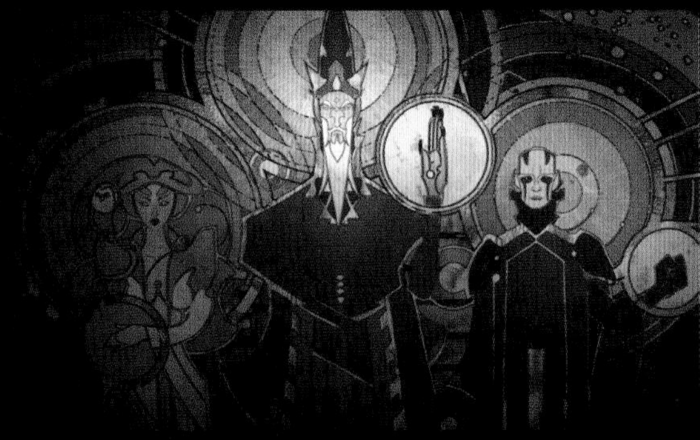

Interactive art
The Ones are depicted in a mural in an ancient Jedi temple on Lothal. Interacting with the painting can grant access to the World between Worlds, a place between space and time where visitors can influence past or future events.

OSI SOBECK

APPEARANCES CW **SPECIES** Phindian **HOMEWORLD** Lola Sayu
AFFILIATION Separatist

Osi Sobeck is the warden of the infamous Separatist prison known as the Citadel. He specializes in torturing and breaking Jedi prisoners of war. Count Dooku assigns Sobeck the responsibility of learning the coordinates of a well-hidden hyperspace lane, information Jedi Even Piell and Captain Wilhuff Tarkin had memorized prior to their capture.

GRAND MOFF TARKIN

APPEARANCES CW, III, Reb, RO, IV
SPECIES Human **HOMEWORLD** Eriadu
AFFILIATION Republic, Empire

Son of a rich family from Eriadu, Wilhuff Tarkin begins his military career in a local force that protect his homeworld's sector. Soon after, he trains to join the Republic's Judicial Department and meets Senator Palpatine. The senator suggests Tarkin move into politics, and Tarkin heeds his words, becoming Eriadu's governor.

When the Clone Wars begins, Tarkin becomes a captain in the Republic Navy, leading a successful assault on the planet Murkhana. He and the Jedi General Even Piell, serve alongside each other. Before they are captured by the Separatists, each of them memorizes a separate half of a critical hyperspace route. They are imprisoned at the Citadel, a facility on Lola Sayu. After General Piell is killed during a Jedi rescue operation, Tarkin learns that Piell shared his half of the route with Jedi Padawan Ahsoka Tano prior to his death. Tarkin passes his half of the route to Palpatine, whereas Ahsoka informs the Jedi Council of her part. Tarkin is promoted to admiral and joins the Special Weapons Group of the Strategic Advisory Cell, a team working toward building a battle station. When the Jedi Temple hangar is bombed, Tarkin believes Ahsoka is behind it, so prosecutes her at a military tribunal. Before the verdict can be read, however, Barriss Offee confesses to the crimes.

After Palpatine becomes Emperor, he makes Tarkin a Moff. Tarkin founds his own group called the Tarkin Initiative, which is given responsibility for the Death Star's construction. With Darth Vader, Tarkin travels to Mon Cala to quell a nascent rebellion. In order to end it quickly, Tarkin requests that Vader abandon the hunt for a Jedi survivor to focus on capturing King Lee-Char instead, promising that he would be in Vader's debt. Around this time, Tarkin is ordered to make an example out of Antar 4, a former Separatist world that had a Republic resistance movement. Tarkin sanctions a series of mass executions on the moon, paying no heed to whether the victims once held Separatist or Republic affiliations. Tarkin's atrocities cause a public outcry that leads to him being reassigned to overseeing pacification operations in the Western Reaches. When the Salient system in the region resists the Empire, Tarkin confronts the Salient Battle Group and Saw Gerrera's Partisans, who are in league with them. He quashes the Battle Group and takes over the system.

Following the escape of kyber scientist Galen Erso, Tarkin stops his own campaign in the Western Reaches to oversee Director Krennic's running of the Death Star Project from Sentinel Base. On one occasion, Tarkin successfully defends the base from a rebel attack. He returns to Murkhana with Vader on the trail of the attackers, where his personal ship, the *Carrion Spike*, is stolen by rebels led by former Republic agent Berch Teller. Working together, Vader and Tarkin dispatch an Imperial traitor, recover the *Spike*, and neutralize the rebel cell, even though Teller escapes. As a reward for his successes, the Emperor bestows upon Tarkin the title of Grand Moff. Returning to Eriadu, Tarkin encounters Teller in the wild, leaving the rebel with a broken ankle and the prospect of certain death. Vader, keen to test his own skills, calls in Tarkin's debt, requesting that Tarkin try to capture him. Tarkin is the only survivor out of 20 hunters. Soon after, Tarkin gives Arihnda Pryce the Governorship of Lothal in exchange for political information.

After the rebel *Ghost* crew interferes with Lothal's productivity, Tarkin decides to intervene himself. He orders the execution of two useless Imperial officers and leads the mission that captures the rebel Jedi Kanan Jarrus. When a rebel fleet rescues the Jedi, Tarkin and the Emperor come to suspect a larger rebellion is forming. Tarkin approves Governor Pyrce's request to use Grand Admiral Thrawn's fleet to hunt down the rebel group.

When the Death Star becomes fully operational, Tarkin orders a partial test of its capabilities on Jedha's Holy City. Tarkin takes control of the Death Star after the successful test, claiming that Krennic is inadequate. As the Rebel Alliance attacks Scarif to steal the Death Star plans, Tarkin arrives at the battle station, ordering it to fire upon the base where the plans are held. Later, he demonstrates the station's power to Princess Leia by destroying her homeworld of Alderaan. Tarkin dies soon afterward when the Death Star is destroyed by the Alliance during the Battle of Yavin.

Cunning opponent
Be it hunting quarry in the wilds or navigating the power hierarchy of the Empire (*left*), Tarkin is a ruthless, skilled, and cunning combatant.

"You may fire when ready." GRAND MOFF TARKIN

Empire's protector
Tarkin and Agent Kallus listen to a rebel message before the communications tower broadcasting it is destroyed *(top)*. Tarkin and his Imperial strategists meet aboard the original Death Star *(above)*. Princess Leia must reveal the location of the secret rebel base or watch Alderaan be destroyed *(left)*.

"Let the Wookiee win." C-3PO

CHEWBACCA

Co-pilot of the *Millennium Falcon*, Chewbacca follows his best friend Han Solo until the very end. Together they take up the fight against the Empire and join the battle against the First Order.

APPEARANCES CW, III, IV, V, VI, VII, VIII, IX, FoD **SPECIES** Wookiee **HOMEWORLD** Kashyyyk **AFFILIATION** Rebel Alliance, Resistance

THE CLONE WARS

Chewbacca is captured by Trandoshan trophy hunters and taken to Wasskah, where Ahsoka Tano and Jedi younglings O-Mer and Jinx are already held as prey. In hopes of commandeering a flight off the moon, the Jedi attack the dropship delivering Chewbacca. Though the vessel crashes, they find a powerful ally in the mighty Wookiee, who cobbles together a transmitter from the crashed ship's remains and sends a distress call. When things look their bleakest, Chief Tarfful and a team of Wookiees arrive to rescue Chewbacca and his new friends. At the conclusion of the Clone Wars, Chewbacca fights by Tarfful's side during the Battle of Kashyyyk and aids Jedi Master Yoda's escape after Order 66.

Wookiee intimidation
Chewbacca helps the Jedi convince Trandoshan hunter Smug to call the main lodge for help.

KESSEL RUN

Chewbacca is once again held captive, this time by Imperial forces on Mimban. There he meets Han Solo for the first time, and they devise a plan to escape their shared prison. Together, they flee the planet as part of Tobias Beckett's criminal crew. Their exploits send them to a hyperfuel mine on Kessel, where Chewie discovers that his fellow Wookiees are being used there as slave labor by the Pyke Syndicate. After freeing the slaves and stealing unrefined coaxium, the crew flees the planet aboard the *Millennium Falcon*, currently under the ownership of Lando Calrissian. With limited time and the Empire not far behind, Chewbacca takes the co-pilot seat next to Han for their record-setting Kessel Run through the heart of the Akkadese Maelstrom. The duo survives the dangerous maneuver, dodging planet-sized carbonbergs and the colossal summa-verminoth creature. It is the beginning of a long-standing partnership.

Shaky start
Chewbacca is shocked when his new human cellmate can speak the Wookiee language Shyriiwook—albeit stiltingly. It is just enough for Han Solo to communicate an escape plan.

SMUGGLING PARTNERSHIP

Chewbacca remains the loyal co-pilot of the *Millennium Falcon* well into the reign of the Empire. On one fateful spice run, he and Han are forced to dump their cargo to escape Imperial pursuit. This puts them into debt with Jabba the Hutt, who seeks retribution for his lost contraband. Tempted by the sizable payment for delivering Obi-Wan and his protégé plus two droids to Alderaan, Han and Chewbacca accept the job, unwittingly taking the first step toward new friendships with Luke Skywalker and Princess Leia Organa and a life with the Rebel Alliance.

Longtime partners
After learning Obi-Wan Kenobi is willing to pay for a fast ride, Chewbacca introduces the Jedi to his partner, Han Solo.

REBEL WARRIOR

When Han Solo wants to leave with their reward for delivering Princess Leia to the rebel base on Yavin 4, Chewbacca provokes his friend's conscience, convincing him to turn around. The *Millennium Falcon*'s shot at Darth Vader's TIE fighter buys Luke Skywalker the time to fire the torpedo that destroys the Death Star. Despite Han's reservations, the duo continues to aid the Alliance after the Death Star's destruction. Chewbacca assaults the Imperial Weapons Factory Alpha on Cymoon 1, freeing slave laborers. He later commandeers the Star Destroyer *Harbinger* alongside his rebel allies.
When the second Death Star threatens the galaxy, Chewbacca joins the strike force that destroys its shield generator.

Two against the Empire
On Hoth, Han and Chewbacca scout for Imperial threats outside Echo Base.

Chewie, we're home
Han and Chewbacca are delighted to be back with the *Falcon*. They investigate the ship to discover who is piloting it.

BACK AT IT AGAIN

Three decades after the Battle of Endor, Chewbacca and Han Solo take to smuggling again. Their beloved *Millennium Falcon* has been stolen by Ducain, so they operate a large bulk freighter—the *Eravana*. While transporting lethal rathtars to King Prana, Han and Chewbacca intercept the *Falcon* with Rey, Finn, and BB-8 onboard. Kanjiklub and the Guavian Death Gang board the *Eravana* demanding payment from Han and Chewbacca, and Rey accidentally releases the rathtars. Chewbacca is wounded during the ensuing chaos, but the heroes escape aboard the *Falcon* and eventually join Leia and the Resistance. During the mission to Starkiller Base, Chewbacca helplessly witnesses Han fall to Kylo Ren's lightsaber. Roaring with rage, Chewbacca wounds Kylo—his friend's son—with a retaliatory bowcaster blast. Chewbacca accompanies Rey to the planet Ahch-To to deliver the news of Han's demise to Luke Skywalker, before they depart to help the Resistance at the Battle of Crait. There, Chewie uses the *Millennium Falcon* to rescue survivors and shuttle them offplanet.

Loyal friend
Typical of many Wookiees, Chewbacca values honor and friendship above all else. He does not hesitate to put his life on the line for his smuggler partner Han Solo.

timeline

THE CLONE WARS

Helpful friend
Chewbacca's repair skills assist Anakin Skywalker's apprentice, Ahsoka Tano, in escaping Trandoshan captivity.

▲ Jedi ally
When Yoda is betrayed after Order 66, Chewbacca delivers the Jedi Master to an escape pod.

THE EMPIRE ERA

Fast friends
After escaping Imperial imprisonment on Mimban, new friends Chewie and Han Solo complete the Kessel Run in the *Millennium Falcon* in a record-breaking time.

▼ First mate
Obi-Wan Kenobi consults Chewbacca before hiring Han Solo for passage from Tatooine to Alderaan.

Solo's conscience
Han wants to take the rebels' reward payment and leave, but Chewbacca openly questions him.

▲ Repairing "Goldenrod"
Han may think C-3PO is obnoxious, but Chewbacca gently rebuilds the de-limbed protocol droid.

Loyalty honored
Chewbacca submits to temporary imprisonment by Jabba the Hutt as part of the plan to rescue Han.

Hungry Wookiee
A slab of meat gets the rebels' Endor strike team captured when Chewbacca cannot resist the bait.

Big and small
Chewbacca teams with the diminutive Ewoks to capture an Imperial AT-ST walker.

Homecoming
Chewbacca returns to Kashyyyk to liberate his homeworld from the Empire. He leads an uprising against Grand Moff Lozen Tolruck.

THE NEW REPUBLIC ERA

▲ Wounded warrior
Chewbacca is wounded in a fight with Kanjiklub and the Guavian Death Gang. Finn does his best to attend to his wounds.

Honoring Han
After witnessing Han Solo's death, Chewbacca rescues Rey and Finn from the planet's surface, delivering them to D'Qar and accompanying Rey to Ahch-To.

Continuing the fight
After rescuing the remnants of the Resistance from Crait, Chewbacca assists in the hunt for allies to fight back against the First Order. On Batuu, he leaves the *Falcon* in the care of former pirate Hondo Ohnaka, who promises to repair the ship.

Adaptable An aquatic species, Mon Calamari can breathe and work both underwater and on land.

ADMIRAL ACKBAR

APPEARANCES CW, VI, VII, VIII **SPECIES** Mon Calamari **HOMEWORLD** Mon Cala **AFFILIATION** Republic, Rebel Alliance, Resistance

Admiral Ackbar's esteemed military career spans decades. During the Clone Wars, he holds the rank of captain of the Mon Calamari Guard. He protects Prince Lee-Char during the Mon Cala Civil War, which is instigated by the Quarren with support from the Separatists. The Separatist leader Riff Tamson betrays the Quarren, leading them to reunite with the Mon Calamari, and Ackbar helps lead the counterassault to drive out the invaders.

A year into the Emperor's reign, Lee-Char incites a war on Mon Cala between its people and the Empire. Ackbar follows his king's orders and defends Mon Cala's northern hemisphere, while his comrade Raddus protects the other half. The Empire quashes the rebellion and captures the king, but Raddus and a small force escape and go on to join the Rebel Alliance.

Ackbar follows his compatriots at a later stage and becomes a key Alliance leader. Following the Death Star's destruction, Ackbar helps lead the evacuation of the rebel base on Yavin 4 and offers Princess Leia his sympathies for Alderaan's destruction. Soon after, Ackbar accompanies the rebel team that travels to Mon Cala to meet with his old friend Regent Urtya. They unsuccessfully try to persuade Urtya to hand over the Mon Cala Mercantile fleet to their cause. Princess Leia tries to rescue Lee-Char from Imperial custody. He dies in the attempt, but Leia records his inspirational last words. She passes the recording to Urtya, who decides to transmit them across Mon Cala, encouraging the Mon Calamari crew to mutiny and regain control of the fleet. The Empire sends Star Destroyers to Mon Cala to destroy the mutineers, but Ackbar arrives with a small rebel fleet to save them. Most of the Mercantile fleet escapes to the Mako-Ta Space Docks. Thanks to Queen Trios of the Shu-Torun, the ships are refitted with Shu-Torun tech to become Alliance warships. After the retrofit, Trios, who is secretly in league with Darth Vader, uses a code to render the fleet inoperable. Vader's Death Squadron arrives and begins annihilating the ships. After Leia recovers the code to regain control of the cruisers, she conveys them to the remaining ships, including Ackbar's vessel, and the survivors escape.

By the time of the Battle of Endor, Ackbar is the leader of the Rebel Alliance fleet and commands the attack on the second Death Star. Seeing the size of the Imperial fleet massed to protect the space station, which is still under construction, Ackbar realizes the rebels have been led into a trap and prepares to order a retreat. At the last moment, Lando Calrissian convinces him to give Han Solo and Leia more time. Their mission to take down the Death Star's shields succeeds, and Ackbar leads his fleet in routing the Imperials.

Following the victory, Ackbar becomes the Fleet Admiral of the New Republic fleet and battles the surviving Imperial forces, leading his forces to a critical victory at Kuat. When the Empire prepares to bombard the planet Kashyyyk from orbit, Ackbar leads a fleet to save it. He personally commands the New Republic attack on Jakku, where most of the remaining Imperial fleet has gathered, and ensures the New Republic is victorious.

After the Battle of Jakku, the Empire and New Republic sign a peace treaty. Ackbar eventually retires from the New Republic military, spending his time on Mon Cala, but he joins Leia's Resistance movement to protect the New Republic and galactic peace.

During the assault on Starkiller Base, Ackbar is stationed on D'Qar and, after the battle, attends Han Solo's funeral. Following the Resistance's evacuation of the planet, Ackbar is on the *Raddus*' command bridge and is killed when a First Order TIE fighter fires upon it.

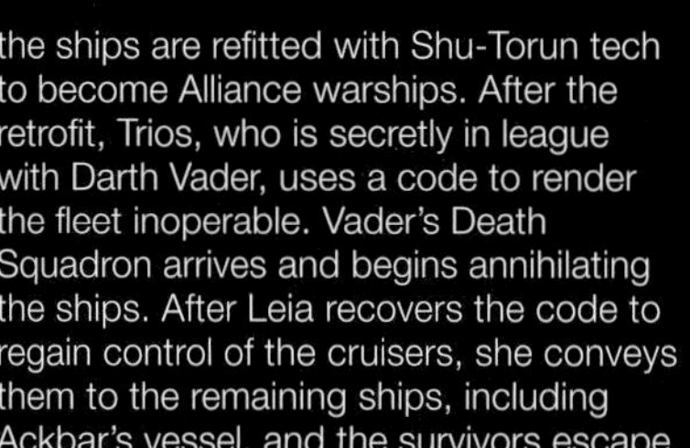

War veteran Ackbar has served with distinction on the front lines, be they from the command bridge of a capital cruiser *(left)* or in the depths of the ocean *(below)*.

SENATOR MEENA TILLS

APPEARANCES CW, III **SPECIES** Mon Calamari **HOMEWORLD** Mon Cala **AFFILIATION** Republic

A female Mon Calamari, Meena Tills is a Galactic senator during the Clone Wars. When Quarren insurgents on Mon Cala threaten to ally with the Separatists, Tills returns to her homeworld to assist the Jedi and clone army intervention that ultimately defeats the Separatist uprising. Tills joins the delegation of senators who oppose Chancellor Palpatine's continuation of his emergency powers, which later puts her at risk.

HYDROID MEDUSA

APPEARANCES CW **HOMEWORLD** Karkaris **AVERAGE SIZE** 22 m (72 ft) long **AFFILIATION** Separatists

Hydroid medusas are gargantuan jellyfish weaponized with cybernetic enhancements. Impervious to blasters and lightsabers, they wreak havoc on underwater battlefields with their electrified tentacles. In the Battle of Mon Cala, the Gungan Grand Army uses boomas to short-circuit the hydroid medusas.

BOSS LYONIE

APPEARANCES CW **SPECIES** Gungan **HOMEWORLD** Naboo **AFFILIATION** Gungan High Council

Boss Lyonie bears an uncanny resemblance to Jar Jar Binks. He is hypnotically controlled briefly by an aide, Rish Loo, who is in league with Count Dooku to start a civil war. When Lyonie is gravely injured, Jar Jar poses as him to restore trust between the Gungans and the Naboo.

PONG KRELL

APPEARANCES CW **SPECIES** Besalisk **HOMEWORLD** Ojom **AFFILIATION** Jedi

The only thing more imposing than Pong Krell's Besalisk physique is his reputation as a Jedi general in the Clone Wars. Renowned for his ruthlessness on the battlefield and intolerance of insubordination, he wields two double-bladed lightsabers but rarely chooses to fight alongside his troops. With war dragging on, Krell foresees the demise of the Jedi Order and the Republic and chooses the dark side of the Force in self-preservation. On Umbara, Krell tricks two legions of clone troopers into attacking each other. After his treason is discovered by Captain Rex, Krell is killed by a devoted trooper named Dogma.

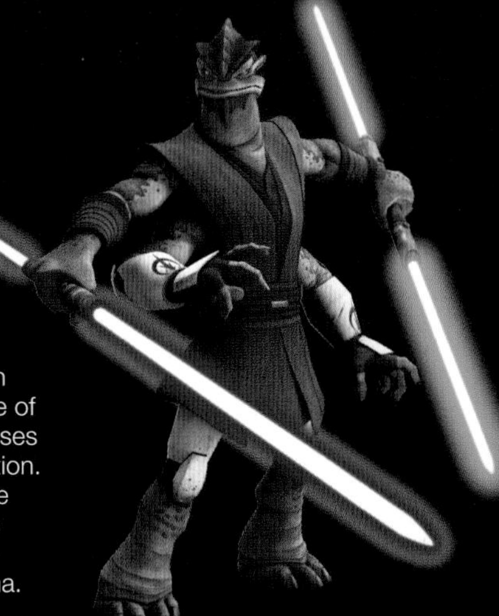

MIRAJ SCINTEL

APPEARANCES CW **SPECIES** Zygerrian **HOMEWORLD** Zygerria **AFFILIATION** Separatists

Queen of Zygerria Miraj Scintel seeks to restore her planet's former glory as the center of a slave-trading empire. She allies with the Separatists in the Clone Wars, leading the Jedi to intervene. Scintel attempts to romance Anakin Skywalker but is rebuffed. Later, when she turns against Count Dooku, he kills her.

C-21 HIGHSINGER

APPEARANCES CW **MODEL** Unknown
MANUFACTURER Unknown
AFFILIATION Bounty hunter

A heavily modified assassin droid of unknown origin, C-21 Highsinger is presumably the only one of his kind. Serving no master, his autonomous programming is well suited to a bounty-hunting career. Most vicious among his capabilities is a rotator assembly that spins his upper torso at high speed, allowing him to unleash his blasters in a devastating circle of laser fire. His servomotors are optimized for swift reflexes, giving him proficiency in movement and hand-to-hand combat. C-21 joins Boba Fett's team of bounty hunters, named Krayt's Claw, during the Clone Wars. On the planet Quarzite, C-21 dispatches many Kage Warriors in combat on a subtram; he is only stopped when they propel him overboard. With the rest of Krayt's Claw, C-21 joins former member Asajj Ventress to rescue Jedi Quinlan Vos from Count Dooku on Serenno, but they are unsuccessful. During the Galactic Civil War, C-21 is hired by Darth Vader to track down the Sith Lord's former acquaintance, Doctor Aphra, but she evades him and his competition.

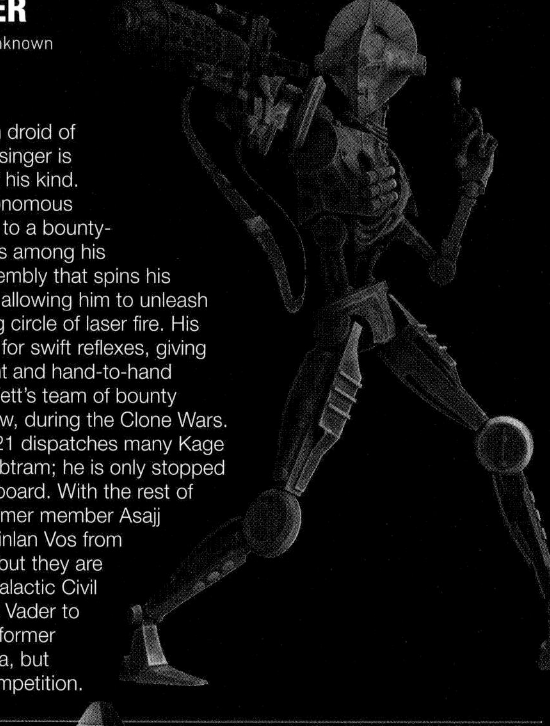

MORALO EVAL

APPEARANCES CW **SPECIES** Phindian
HOMEWORLD Phindar
AFFILIATION Separatists

A heartless and deranged criminal, Moralo Eval brags that he killed his mother because he got bored. He escapes Republic prison alongside Cad Bane and Rako Hardeen, who is actually Obi-Wan Kenobi undercover. Bane and Hardeen compete in Eval's skill challenge, the Box, earning spots on a team that will attempt to kidnap Chancellor Palpatine.

OLD DAKA

APPEARANCES CW **SPECIES** Dathomirian
HOMEWORLD Dathomir
AFFILIATION Nightsisters

Old Daka is the oldest and wisest of the elders in Mother Talzin's Nightsisters clan, and her mastery of ancient magic is unparalleled. When General Grievous' forces attack the clan, Daka's incantation conjures an undead horde of Nightsister zombies to fight the battle droids. Grievous personally tracks down Daka in her hidden cave and slays her.

LATTS RAZZI

APPEARANCES CW **SPECIES** Theelin
HOMEWORLD Unknown
AFFILIATION Bounty hunter

Even more distinctive than Latts Razzi's bright red hair is her primary weapon of choice, the grappling boa. Razzi spars with opponents by either cracking the green, scaled boa like a whip or using it as a lasso to ensnare them. Razzi joins Boba Fett's bounty hunter syndicate, named Krayt's Claw, and accepts a delivery job on the planet Quarzite, where she fends off attacking Kage Warriors. Later, Razzi takes work from the Hutts and goes on a mission with the rest of Krayt's Claw to rescue captured Jedi Quinlan Vos from Count Dooku.

BO-KATAN KRYZE

APPEARANCES CW, Reb **SPECIES** Human
HOMEWORLD Mandalore **AFFILIATION** Death Watch, Mandalorian rebels

Like her sister, Duchess Satine, Bo-Katan Kryze is faithfully devoted to her homeworld of Mandalore. Rejecting Satine's commitment to pacifism, Bo-Katan joins Death Watch, an outlawed warrior sect that seeks to return Mandalore to its glorious past. However, she is skeptical of Death Watch leader Pre Vizsla's alliance with Darth Maul to depose Satine. When the Sith Lord slays Vizsla, Bo-Katan sees her worst fears for her planet come true. She frees captured Jedi Obi-Wan Kenobi, and they try to save Satine from Maul, but he kills her. Bo-Katan ensures that Obi-Wan escapes to get Republic help to liberate Mandalore. When the Republic forces arrive, Bo-Katan and her troops fight alongside former Jedi Ahsoka Tano during the Siege of Mandalore. The Republic name Bo-Katan regent after their victory.

Following the Empire's formation, Bo-Katan refuses to work for them, and she is deposed by Clan Saxon, a group loyal to the Emperor. Years later, she works with Mandalorian rebel operative Sabine Wren and the Wren clan to retake Mandalore from the Empire. Together, they stop an experimental weapon designed to obliterate Mandalorian armor. Sabine recognizes that Bo-Katan can unite the clans to achieve their aim, so bestows upon her the legendary Darksaber. With the clans' support, Bo-Katan becomes the honored leader of the Mandalorians.

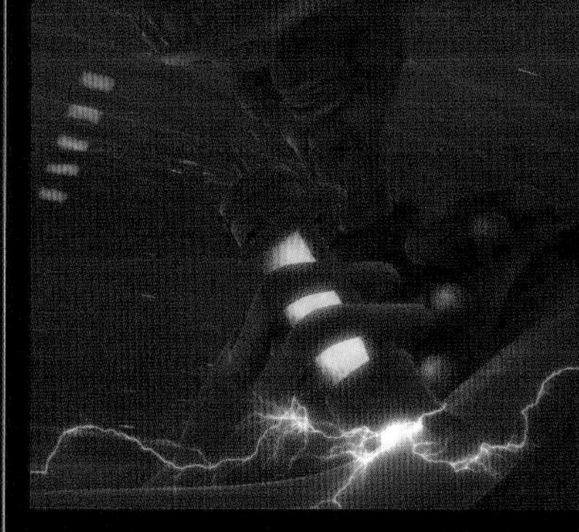

DERROWN

APPEARANCES CW **SPECIES** Parwan
HOMEWORLD Parwa
AFFILIATION Bounty hunter

Derrown is a ruthless bounty hunter who has earned the nickname "The Exterminator." He has the innate ability to electrify his body with crackling energy, and his tentacled physiology, containing lighter-than-air gasses, enables him to float to positions others would struggle to reach. These advantages help him successfully pass the Box, Count Dooku's bounty-hunter challenge.

DENGAR

APPEARANCES CW, V, VI **SPECIES** Human
HOMEWORLD Corellia **AFFILIATION** Bounty hunter

Dengar is one of the most dangerous bounty hunters in the galaxy. Wearing plated battle armor and a turban, he pursues targets with his blaster rifle and mini grenades. During the Clone Wars, he becomes a part of Krayt's Claw—a bounty hunter team led by Boba Fett. The team takes on a mission to safeguard a locked chest being shipped by tram on the planet Quarzite. When Kage Warriors attack, Dengar fights off as many as he can until he is thrown from the tram. Another time, while in the service of the Hutts, Dengar and three other bounty hunters are attacked by forces commanded by Darth Maul and Pre Vizsla. Dengar flees with his fellow mercenaries when it becomes clear defeat is inevitable.

Years later, Dengar encounters wanted smuggler Han Solo on Nar Shaddaa. Dengar tries to capture Han but is thrown off the roof of a building instead! Following the Battle of Hoth, Dengar is one of the bounty hunters summoned by Darth Vader to hunt for the *Millennium Falcon*. After the Battle of Endor, Dengar works with new bounty hunter Mercurial Swift to capture Jas Emari, the niece of his old colleague Sugi, but betrays Swift when Emari offers a better deal. Dengar joins Emari's new bounty hunter crew, declaring that they need to stick together as times are changing.

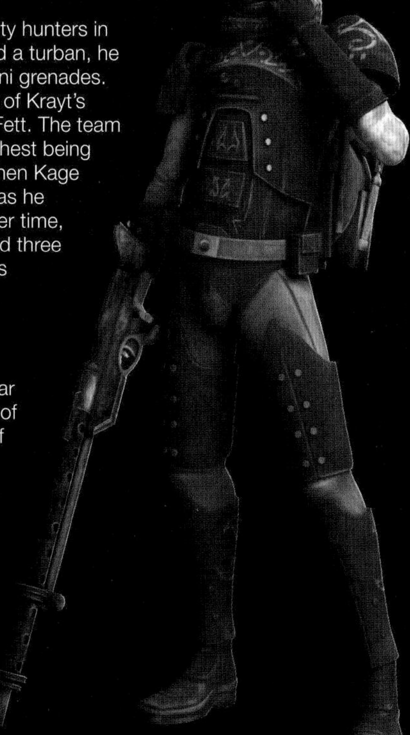

KING SANJAY RASH

APPEARANCES CW **SPECIES** Human **HOMEWORLD** Onderon **AFFILIATION** Separatists

After King Ramsis Dendup refuses to commit Onderon to the Clone Wars, Sanjay Rash deposes him, assuming the crown. Some Onderon citizens successfully rebel against the Separatist droid army occupation requested by Rash. Before the Separatists' retreat, however, Rash is killed by super tactical droid Kalani on Count Dooku's command.

STEELA GERRERA

APPEARANCES CW **SPECIES** Human **HOMEWORLD** Onderon **AFFILIATION** Onderon rebels

After the Onderon rebels destroy a key power generator, Steela is elected their leader. Her courageous speech to the people of Onderon prompts Sanjay Rash and his Separatist allies to set a trap during former King Dendup's public execution. With the help of Steela's brother Saw, the rebels succeed in rescuing Dendup and restoring him to power, but Steela falls in battle.

GREGOR

APPEARANCES CW, Reb **SPECIES** Human (clone) **HOMEWORLD** Kamino **AFFILIATION** Republic

Designated CC-5576-39, Gregor is a clone commando and a captain in the Republic Army. He suffers amnesia following a Republic defeat on the planet Sarrish and ends up on Abafar, where he is employed as a dishwasher. When D-Squad runs into Gregor, they help him recover his memory and enlist his help. At the local Separatist mining facility, Gregor dispatches battle droids and provides cover for D-Squad. After Gascon and M5-BZ get separated from the group, Gregor retrieves them. When D-Squad escapes aboard the shuttle, Gregor is overrun by the droid forces as the facility is destroyed. Somehow, Gregor survives and is promoted to the rank of Commander.

Much like Captain Rex and Commander Wolffe, Gregor removes his control chip, a procedure that adversely affects him. The three clones end up living in a customized AT-TE on Seelos. Years later, a rebel team named the Spectres visits the clones. Together, the rebels and clones defeat an Imperial force. While Rex joins the rebels, Gregor and Wolffe stay on Seelos in a commandeered AT-AT. Two years later, they answer Rex and the Spectres' call for help to free Lothal. Sadly, Gregor is fatally wounded, but he dies feeling honored to have fought for something he chose to fight for.

Selfless hero
On the planet Sarrish and again on Abafar, Gregor acts bravely, putting the lives of others before his own.

GENERAL TANDIN

APPEARANCES CW **SPECIES** Human **HOMEWORLD** Onderon **AFFILIATION** Royal Onderon Militia

Although General Tandin initially supports King Rash, he disagrees with super tactical droid Kalani on how to deal with the Onderon rebels, and a conversation with captured rebel Saw Gerrera reinforces his doubts. The general leads the palace guard to stop Dendup's execution and pledges his support to the rightful king.

WAC-47

APPEARANCES CW **SPECIES** DUM-series pit droid **HOMEWORLD** Unknown **AFFILIATION** Republic

WAC-47 serves as D-Squad's pilot when the team infiltrates a Separatist dreadnought to steal an encryption module. After crash-landing on Abafar, D-Squad uncovers a plot to blow up a space station using a stolen Republic cruiser. To foil the plan, WAC-47 has to leave R2-D2 behind to destroy the cruiser.

MEEBUR GASCON

APPEARANCES CW **SPECIES** Zilkin **HOMEWORLD** Unknown **AFFILIATION** Republic

Meebur Gascon is a tactical adviser during the First Battle of Geonosis. Later, he leads a D-Squad mission to steal an encryption module. Diminutive in stature, he often rides inside the droid M5-BZ. Gascon devises the daring plan to stop the Separatists from destroying a space station.

ZITON MOJ

APPEARANCES CW **SPECIES** Falleen **HOMEWORLD** Falleen **AFFILIATION** Shadow Collective, Black Sun

Ziton Moj is Captain of the Guard for the Black Sun crime syndicate during the Clone Wars. After Savage Opress kills Black Sun leader Xomit Grunseit, Moj joins Maul's Shadow Collective and helps their takeover of Sundari. Moj leads disruptions throughout the city, before his staged capture by Bo-Katan Kryze, a member of Death Watch—a Mandalorian group that is secretly in league with Maul. When Moj kidnaps the Pyke Syndicate leader's family, Moj loses in battle to bounty hunter Asajj Ventress who rescues the family. Moj stays loyal to Maul until the Separatists begin attacking Moj's forces.

LOM PYKE

APPEARANCES CW **SPECIES** Pyke **HOMEWORLD** Oba Diah **AFFILIATION** Shadow Collective, Pyke Syndicate

Lom Pyke is the leader of the Pyke Syndicate, a criminal group known for dealing in illicit spices. He attends Xev Xrevus' criminal auction. Later, Pyke is hired by Darth Tyranus to kill Jedi Master Sifo-Dyas. Pyke also covertly captures the Jedi's companion, Silman, who is Chancellor Valorum's aide. During the Clone Wars, Pyke joins the Shadow Collective. When Obi-Wan Kenobi and Anakin Skywalker confront Pyke during their investigation of Sifo-Dyas' death, Pyke reveals that Dooku is Tyranus. He is then killed by Dooku.

QUEEN JULIA

APPEARANCES CW **SPECIES** Bardottan
HOMEWORLD Bardotta
AFFILIATION Dagoyan Masters

Queen Julia rules over the peaceful planet Bardotta. After the Dagoyan Masters mysteriously vanish, she requests help from her old friend Jar Jar Binks. When Julia also is kidnapped by the Frangawl Cult, Jar Jar and Mace Windu track down and rescue her before Mother Talzin can steal her life essence.

DARTH BANE

APPEARANCES CW **SPECIES** Human
HOMEWORLD Unknown **AFFILIATION** Sith

Darth Bane is the sole survivor when the Jedi Order destroys the Sith a thousand years before the Clone Wars. Recognizing that infighting has weakened the Sith, Bane creates the Rule of Two when he reforms the order, mandating that there can be only a master and an apprentice.

SIFO-DYAS

APPEARANCES II, CW **SPECIES** Human
HOMEWORLD Cassandran Worlds
AFFILIATION Jedi

Some time prior to the invasion of Naboo, Master Sifo-Dyas takes a seat on the Jedi Council. Foreseeing a coming galactic war, he advocates for the creation of an army for the Republic. He is removed from the Council because his ideas are considered too extreme. Sifo-Dyas nevertheless proceeds with his plan, secretly commissioning the clone army from the Kaminoans while pretending to act with authorization from the Galactic Senate and the Jedi Council. Under this subterfuge, Chancellor Valorum covertly dispatches Sifo-Dyas to negotiate with the Pyke Syndicate. However, after initially mediating a tribal dispute on Felucia, Sifo-Dyas is killed when the Pykes are paid by the Sith to shoot down his shuttle.

FORCE PRIESTESSES

APPEARANCES CW **SPECIES** Unknown
HOMEWORLD Unknown **AFFILIATION** Force

These mysterious Force-entities represent five emotions: serenity, joy, anger, confusion, and sadness. They test Yoda with daunting trials as a Jedi Master, including visiting the Sith homeworld. When the trials are complete, the priestesses deem Yoda worthy of retaining his identity in the Force beyond death, thus granting him immortality.

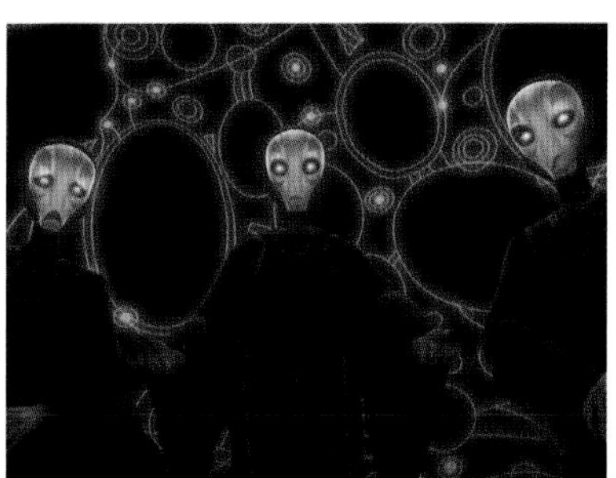

VARACTYL

APPEARANCES III **HOMEWORLD** Utapau **SIZE** 15 m (49 ft) long **HABITAT** Arid scrubland, Utapauan sinkholes

A reptavian species native to Utapau, varactyls are known to be loyal and obedient steeds. To track down General Grievous in Pau City, Obi-Wan Kenobi rides a particularly swift varactyl named Boga. They quickly reach the tenth level and chase General Grievous on his wheel bike through the city. Along the way, Boga smashes several battle droids before the Jedi Master fights and kills Grievous. After Palpatine gives the command for Order 66, the clone troopers turn against Obi-Wan. Boga and her Jedi rider are caught in an AT-TE cannon blast that strikes a nearby wall, forcing the pair to plummet into the water at the bottom of the sinkhole.

GAR SAXON

APPEARANCES Reb **SPECIES** Human
HOMEWORLD Mandalore
AFFILIATION Shadow Collective, Empire

Gar Saxon is a Mandalorian supercommando in the Shadow Collective. Gar and Rook Kast liberate Maul from the Spire prison. He leads Maul's ground forces during General Grievous' attack on the Shadow Collective base at Ord Mantell. Gar stays loyal to the Collective until its dissolution.

During the Imperial era, Gar and the rest of the Saxon clan align with the Empire and betray Bo-Katan Kryze, the regent of Mandalore. Gar is put in charge of Mandalore by the Emperor for his loyalty, and attacks any Mandalorians who don't pledge allegiance to him, including the Journeyman Protectors. After destroying a Protectors' camp, Gar encounters their leader Fenn Rau and three rebel agents: Mandalorian Sabine Wren, Jedi Ezra Bridger, and an astromech named Chopper. Gar captures Ezra and Chopper, but Sabine and Rau mount a rescue and they escape. Saxon encounters the rebels once more when they visit Sabine's family on Krownest, and her mother Ursa Wren contacts Gar to try and trade Sabine's friends for her daughter's safety. When Gar arrives to capture them, the Wren clan has a change of heart and turns on him. Sabine and Gar duel with lightsabers and Sabine emerges victorious. Gar attempts to shoot her in the back, but Ursa fires at him first.

"There is no war here unless you've brought it with you." TION MEDON

TION MEDON

APPEARANCES III **SPECIES** Pau'an
HOMEWORLD Utapau
AFFILIATION Republic

As Port Administrator of Pau City, Tion Medon welcomes and offers his services to guests. When Obi-Wan Kenobi arrives at the sinkhole spaceport in search of General Grievous, Medon discreetly divulges helpful information about the Separatist presence on Utapau. Obi-Wan suggests that Medon gather the planet's warriors for the coming battle.

GOBI GLIE

APPEARANCES CW, Reb **SPECIES** Twi'lek **HOMEWORLD** Ryloth **AFFILIATION** Twi'lek Resistance, Free Ryloth Movement

During the Clone Wars, Gobi Glie is a member of Cham Syndulla's Twi'lek Resistance against the Separatist occupiers of Ryloth. When Palpatine's Empire rises from the Republic to take their place, he continues the fight as part of the Free Ryloth Movement.

NUMA

APPEARANCES CW, Reb **SPECIES** Twi'lek **HOMEWORLD** Ryloth **AFFILIATION** Free Ryloth Movement

As a child growing up under Separatist occupation, Numa befriends two clone troopers named Waxer and Boil, both of whom make a lasting impression. Later in life, she joins Cham Syndulla's rebel Free Ryloth Movement, and works with Hera Syndulla and Kanan Jarrus' rebel cell.

CLONE PILOT

APPEARANCES II, CW, III **SPECIES** Human (clone) **HOMEWORLD** Kamino **AFFILIATION** Republic

The Grand Army of the Republic's pilots are a special class of clone troopers. They start out as regular clones who are randomly chosen and trained as pilots. Their flight academy training is run by expert pilots such as Mandalorian Fenn Rau, giving them an edge with unconventional but proven flight maneuvers. They sit at the helm of battle vehicles designed for air, land, sea, and space battles. Their uniforms vary according to their assigned units, vehicles, and time period in service. Notable clone pilots toward the end of the Clone Wars include Odd Ball and Jag.

CLONE SCUBA TROOPER

APPEARANCES CW **SPECIES** Human (clone) **HOMEWORLD** Kamino **AFFILIATION** Republic

Clone scuba troopers are an elite division of the Grand Army of the Republic during the Clone Wars, though at times standard clone troopers may also be fitted with their specialized gear. Scuba troopers are trained in the seas of Kamino for battle in aquatic environments. They are equipped with flippers, oxygen tanks, underwater propulsion systems, specialized blasters, and OMS Devilfish subs. Among their ranks is Commander Monnk, a brave scuba trooper who serves under Jedi Master Kit Fisto during the Battle of Mon Cala.

CLONE TUP

APPEARANCES CW **SPECIES** Human (clone) **HOMEWORLD** Kamino **AFFILIATION** Republic

CT-5385, known as Tup, is a rookie clone trooper and member of the 501st Legion. He mutinies against the fallen Jedi Pong Krell during the Battle of Umbara. During the Battle of Ringo Vinda, the bio chip in his brain malfunctions. He becomes unstable and executes Order 66 early by killing Jedi Tiplar. Tup is taken into custody and sent to a medical facility on Kamino for tests. He dies in the hands of the Kaminoans, who attempt to cover up the truth behind the bio chips.

ARC TROOPER

APPEARANCES CW **SPECIES** Human (clone) **HOMEWORLD** Kamino **AFFILIATION** Republic

Advanced Recon Commandos (ARC) are the elite troopers of the Grand Army of the Republic. ARC troopers are selected as cadets for their exemplary performance and given advanced training and gear. They can be identified by the pauldrons on their shoulders, the kamas wrapped round their waists, and their dual use of DC-17 blaster pistols. They wear an experimental version of Phase II clone trooper armor. Notable ARC troopers include Colt, Echo, Fives, Havoc, and Jesse.

CLONE KIX

APPEARANCES CW **SPECIES** Human (clone) **HOMEWORLD** Kamino **AFFILIATION** Republic, 501st Legion, Sidon Ithano's crew

CT-6116, otherwise known as Kix, is a clone medic in the 501st Legion. He fights at the Battle of Saleucami, where Captain Rex is seriously injured. There Kix and fellow troopers Jesse and Hardcase must leave Rex at Cut Lawquane's farm. Kix fights in the Battle of Umbara and arrests the fallen Jedi Pong Krell. He uncovers the conspiracy to implant chips in clone brains, but he is kidnapped by Separatists and frozen in stasis. Almost half a century later, Kix is discovered by the pirate crew of Sidon Ithano. Kix joins their company after they awaken him.

CONVOR

APPEARANCES CW, Reb
HOMEWORLD Wasskah
AVERAGE SIZE 0.2 m (8 in) high
HABITAT Jungle canopies

Convorees are intelligent birds with prehensile tails, native to the Wasskah moon orbiting Trandosha. They are closely related to purple Kiros Birds, sold in the pet trade. Convorees have also been seen on Takodana. The birds appear to have a strong connection to the Force—and to Ahsoka Tano.

SENATE GUARD

APPEARANCES I, II, CW, III **SPECIES** Human **HOMEWORLD** Various **AFFILIATION** Galactic Senate

Senate Guards are the security force of the Galactic Senate, guarding the Senate facilities and traveling with senators and Chancellor Palpatine. Elite Senate Guards are promoted to the Senate Commandos and take part in secret missions. Chancellor Palpatine forms his own red-robed security detail, which becomes his Royal Guards when he appoints himself Emperor. Notable Senate Guards include Captain Taggart, who accompanies Ahsoka Tano and Senators Padmé Amidala, Bail Organa, and Mon Mothma to Mandalore, as well as the traitor Captain Argyus, who is killed by Asajj Ventress.

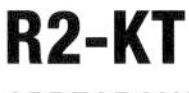

BARC TROOPER

APPEARANCES CW, III **SPECIES** Human (clone)
HOMEWORLD Kamino **AFFILIATION** Republic

Biker Advanced Recon Commandos (BARC) are specialized ARC troopers trained to ride high-speed BARC speeder bikes in combat. Their helmets are usually fitted with blinders to direct attention forward and minimize distractions. BARC troopers tend to get impatient riding in slow, conventional clone trooper craft because they are trained to think and move quickly. BARC troopers are in prominent use on Christophsis, Orto Plutonia, Kashyyyk, and Saleucami during the Clone Wars. Commander Neyo of the 91st Reconnaissance Corps notably leads a squad of BARC troopers to assassinate Jedi General Stass Allie upon receiving Order 66.

R2-KT

APPEARANCES CW, VII **MANUFACTURER** Industrial Automaton **TYPE** R-series astromech
AFFILIATION Republic, 501st Legion, Resistance

R2-KT is a loyal and kindly droid with feminine programming who agelessly serves the heroes of the galaxy as empires rise and fall. She is stationed on the Republic ship *Resolute* (under the command of Anakin Skywalker) and serves during the Battle of Teth, the Battle of Quell, and at the destruction of the Separatist blockade prior to the Battle of Ryloth. During the Resistance era, she serves on D'Qar as a starfighter astromech and leaves the planet before the First Order attacks.

SHOCK TROOPER

APPEARANCES CW, III **SPECIES** Human (clone)
HOMEWORLD Kamino **AFFILIATION** Republic

Shock troopers are a special division of clone troopers bred to replace the Senate Guard and Coruscant police force. They patrol government facilities and act as security guards for senators and dignitaries friendly to Chancellor Palpatine. Shock troopers are more militaristic and aggressive than Senate Guards. They carry out the search for rogue Jedi Ahsoka Tano prior to the fall of the Jedi Order. In the time of the Empire, their division evolves into shock stormtroopers. Fox, Jek, Rys, Stone, Thire, and Thorn are well-known shock troopers during the Clone Wars.

HEVY

APPEARANCES CW **SPECIES** Human (clone)
HOMEWORLD Kamino **AFFILIATION** Republic

Hevy (CT-782) gets his nickname from the heavy weapons he carries, such as his Z-6 rotary blaster. He is a member of Domino Squad and assigned to Rishi Outpost, where he sacrifices his own life in a battle with Separatist battle droids.

JESSE

APPEARANCES CW **SPECIES** Human (clone)
HOMEWORLD Kamino **AFFILIATION** Republic

Jesse (CT-5597) is a member of the 501st Legion who is promoted to an ARC trooper. He fights at the battles of Saleucami, Umbara, Ringo Vinda, and Anaxes. Jesse works with the Bad Batch to recover Captain Rex's algorithm when it is used by the Separatists.

99

APPEARANCES CW **SPECIES** Human (clone)
HOMEWORLD Kamino **AFFILIATION** Republic

Clone 99 is deemed physically unfit for battle due to a cloning error that also renders him unique. He is assigned janitorial work on Kamino. 99 befriends Domino Squad and assists them during a Separatist attack, but is killed in his efforts. Clone Force 99 (the "Bad Batch") is named in his honor.

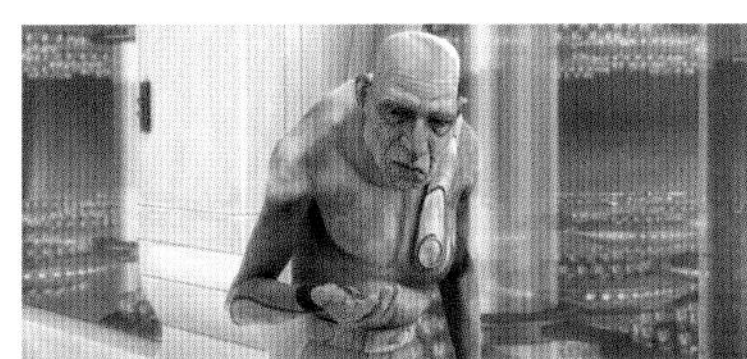

DOGMA

APPEARANCES CW **SPECIES** Human (clone)
HOMEWORLD Kamino **AFFILIATION** Republic

The clone trooper known as Dogma is a member of the 501st Legion who fights at the Battle of Umbara. He is fiercely loyal and rigid in his approach to following orders. Dogma defends his commander, Jedi General Pong Krell, until Krell admits to treason. Dogma then executes him.

COLD ASSAULT CLONE TROOPERS

APPEARANCES CW **SPECIES** Human (clone)
HOMEWORLD Kamino **AFFILIATION** Republic

Cold assault clone troopers wear suits for low-temperature environments with high winds, deep snow, and ice cliffs. They fight on worlds such as Orto, Orto Plutonia, Rhen Var, and Toola.

41ST ELITE CORPS TROOPER

APPEARANCES III
SPECIES Human (clone)
HOMEWORLD Kamino
AFFILIATION Republic

41st Elite Corps troopers patrol difficult environments such as the jungles of Kashyyyk. They typically ride AT-APs, AT-RTs, and speeder bikes. Commander Gree and one of his troopers attempt to assassinate Yoda after they receive Order 66.

HUNTER

APPEARANCES CW **SPECIES** Human (clone)
HOMEWORLD Kamino **AFFILIATION** Republic

Hunter is the leader of Clone Force 99, otherwise known as the "Bad Batch." This specialist unit is comprised of clone commandos, each with beneficial mutations. Hunter has enhanced senses, making him a superb tracker. His team includes Crosshair, Tech, and Wrecker. They are called by Commander Cody to assist on a mission to recover Captain Rex's battle strategy algorithm from the Separatists. Echo (a clone with cyborg enhancements) joins the team after they rescue him from a secret Separatist facility on Skako Minor.

JEDI TEMPLE GUARD

APPEARANCES CW, Reb **SPECIES** Various
HOMEWORLD Various **AFFILIATION** Jedi

Jedi Knights take turns serving as guards at the Jedi Temple on Coruscant under the leadership of Jedi Master Cin Drallig. During the Clone Wars, the guards accompany Ahsoka Tano and Bariss Offee to hearings. They wield double-bladed yellow lightsabers and wear standardized uniforms with masks that keep their identities anonymous. Their attire dates back to ancient times. Kanan Jarrus dons a Temple guard mask for a brief time when he is blinded by Maul on Malachor. During a Force vision at the Jedi temple on Lothal, the Grand Inquisitor appears to Kanan as a Jedi Temple guard, revealing his mysterious origins.

SAW GERRERA

APPEARANCES CW, Reb, RO **SPECIES** Human **HOMEWORLD** Onderon
AFFILIATION Onderon rebels, Partisans, Rebel Alliance

Saw Gerrera is a notorious figure in the galaxy, known for his extreme methods of fighting oppression. During the Clone Wars, Saw and his sister Steela lead the Onderon rebels, receiving training from the Jedi. During the rebel victory, Saw shoots down a Separatist gunship that crashes near Steela, causing her to fall off a cliff to her death. Saw feels guilty for this and is haunted by her passing.

During the Imperial era, the Empire imposes its rule on Onderon, so Saw reforms his rebels to fight back, renaming them the Partisans. While his operations begin on Onderon, Saw's forces go on to strike across the galaxy, including the Salient system. Soon after, Saw smuggles Imperial scientist Galen Erso, his wife Lyra, and their child Jyn away from Coruscant, helping them to live in hiding on Lah'mu. When the Imperials find them, Galen is taken, Lyra is killed, and Jyn hides in a cave and is later taken in by Saw. Saw later receives a large amount of coaxium from fellow rebel Enfys Nest, which he uses in his attacks. Saw continues his vicious campaign, ordering the death of a scientist on Tamsye Prime, and killing Imperials and innocents alike at a festival on Inusagi.

Over the years, Saw becomes paranoid that Jyn's real identity might be discovered by his troops, so he tortures some of them to see if they know. When Jyn is 16 years old, Saw abandons her, giving in to his paranoia. Soon after, Saw allies himself with Bail Organa and the other rebel cells, but his extreme tactics, including the Partisans' assassination of Moff Quarsh Panaka, concern them. Regardless, Saw accepts a mission from them to look into Geonosis. The *Ghost* crew are sent in when they don't hear back from Saw—they proceed to save him from attack by battle droids and discover that the Empire has wiped out most of the Geonosians with poison. Saw is irritated that they don't find out what the Empire is constructing and becomes obsessed with uncovering it.

Over time, the extreme actions of Saw and his Partisans estrange them from the rest of the Rebel Alliance, leaving them as rogue operatives. When Alliance members Ezra Bridger and Sabine Wren hack an Imperial relay on Jalindi, they are discovered by the Empire and are rescued by Saw, who bombs the relay. He recruits them on a mission to infiltrate a civilian transport carrying secret cargo for the Empire. They discover a contingent of captured technicians, one of whom mentions that they heard talk from their captors of the Jedha system. They also find a giant kyber crystal. While Saw turns the crystal into a bomb, the other rebels rescue the technicians and escape.

After this, Saw focuses his attention on Jedha, believing he will find the answer there. He bases his forces in the Catacombs of Cadera near Jedha's Holy City, and recruits local rebels, including, temporarily, Guardians of the Whills Chirrut Îmwe and Baze Malbus, to his cause. Caring little for civilian casualties, his forces try to stop the Empire stealing kyber crystals. Soon after, Saw's forces bring him Bodhi Rook, a former Imperial pilot who claims to have an urgent message from Galen Erso. Saw refuses to believe him, so uses a mind-reading Mairan to determine the veracity of his claims. His troops also capture Jyn, Alliance member Cassian Andor, and their new acquaintances Chirrut and Baze. Saw is at first pleased to see Jyn, but then believes she might have been sent to kill him. She reveals that she is actually on an Alliance mission. Saw plays Galen's message to Jyn just as the Death Star is preparing to fire upon Jedha's Holy City. Saw lets Jyn leave with the message to save herself, the Rebellion, and the dream, while he decides he will run no longer and dies in the catacombs.

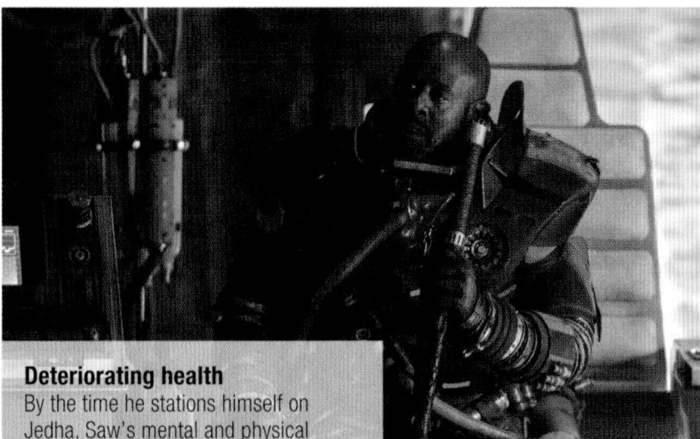

Deteriorating health
By the time he stations himself on Jedha, Saw's mental and physical health are both deteriorating.

Proof of poison
During their investigation on Geonosis, Saw and the *Ghost* crew recover some poison canisters that prove the Empire wiped out the Geonosians. Unfortunately, they lose them during their escape from the planet.

CHAM SYNDULLA

APPEARANCES CW, Reb **SPECIES** Twi'lek **HOMEWORLD** Ryloth
AFFILIATION Twi'lek Resistance, Free Ryloth Movement

After the Separatists invade Ryloth, political leader Cham Syndulla forms the freedom fighters who oppose them, while his family hide underground. Eventually, a small Republic force led by Jedi Ima-Gun Di arrives to help Cham's forces. Thanks to Di's sacrifice during a Separatist attack, the Twi'lek Resistance lives to fight another day. Later, General Mace Windu arrives with more forces, and Cham resolves his issues with Ryloth's senator, Orn Free Taa. He then leads the combined army and liberates his home.

During the Imperial era, Cham forms the Free Ryloth Movement to resist the Imperial occupation. Tragedy strikes when Cham's wife is killed, which leads him to focus fully on Ryloth's liberation. He is upset when his daughter Hera leaves Ryloth to pursue her dream of freedom for the whole galaxy. Cham later learns that Darth Vader and the Emperor are traveling in a Star Destroyer to Ryloth, so he launches an attack. Cham's forces destroy the ship and force the Sith to crash-land on the planet, but sustain heavy losses in doing so. Cham fails to defeat them on the ground, and the Sith kill even more of his troops before leaving Ryloth.

Years later, Hera requests his help to steal an Imperial ship orbiting Ryloth. Sensing an opportunity, Cham agrees to lend his aid, secretly hoping to destroy it to inspire his people. Cham helps Hera's rebels, befriending them and even reconciling with Hera. When his plan is revealed, Hera persuades him to abandon it, and they complete her mission. Later, Cham tells Hera that their family home on Ryloth is occupied by the Empire and that their Kalikori—an important Twi'lek family heirloom—has been taken. Hera is captured when she tries to retrieve the Kalikori, so Cham offers to hand himself in to save her. In the end, Hera blows up their old home, allowing them to escape.

Fleeing the Empire
Riding atop blurrgs, Cham and fellow rebel Numa flee an Imperial patrol.

RIFF TAMSON

APPEARANCES CW **SPECIES** Karkarodon
HOMEWORLD Karkaris **AFFILIATION** Separatists

One of Count Dooku's vicious Separatist warlords, Riff Tamson's Karkarodon physiology makes him the perfect choice to lead military operations on aquatic worlds. He secretly assassinates the king of Mon Cala, then openly leads agitators, urging a civil war between its Quarren and Mon Calamari populations. He hunts the rightful heir, Prince Lee-Char, who ultimately kills Tamson with one of his own exploding knives.

CHIEF TARFFUL

APPEARANCES CW, III **SPECIES** Wookiee **HOMEWORLD** Kashyyyk **AFFILIATION** Republic

Tarfful is a Wookiee chieftain and general. During the Clone Wars, he leads the rescue of his friend Chewbacca, held captive with Ahsoka and other young Jedi by Trandoshan hunters. In the Battle of Kashyyyk, the two Wookiees serve alongside Jedi Generals Yoda and Luminara Unduli and help Yoda escape the Order 66 massacre.

NOSSOR RI

APPEARANCES CW **SPECIES** Quarren **HOMEWORLD** Mon Cala **AFFILIATION** Separatists, Republic

The Quarren chieftain on Mon Cala, Nossor Ri plots to switch the planet's allegiance to the Separatist side of the Clone Wars. When he realizes Count Dooku is merely exploiting the situation for his own ends, however, he leads his people to rejoin the Mon Calamari, and expel the Separatists.

GENERAL KALANI

APPEARANCES CW, Reb **MANUFACTURER** Baktoid Combat Automata **TYPE** Super tactical droid **AFFILIATION** Separatists

Kalani fights for the Separatists during the Clone Wars. He is sent by Count Dooku to assist Dooku's ally, King Sanjay Rash, on Onderon against the rebels there. When the rebels are victorious, Dooku orders Kalani and his remaining forces to retreat to Agamar. After Order 66, Kalani believes the code to shut down the droid forces is a Republic trick, so he and his troops ignore it. Years later, he encounters clone Captain Rex and the *Ghost* crew. Kalani seeks to finish the Clone Wars on his own terms, so forces them to participate in one final battle. When the Empire attacks, he allies with his opponents, escaping Agamar with some of his troops. He refuses to join the rebels stating that they only have a one per cent chance of beating the Empire.

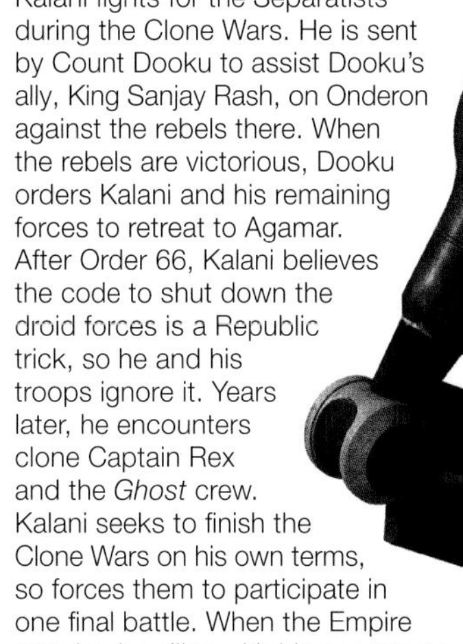

LEE-CHAR

APPEARANCES CW **SPECIES** Mon Calamari **HOMEWORLD** Mon Cala **AFFILIATION** Republic

Prince Lee-Char is the rightful heir to the throne of Mon Cala after his father's assassination, but he faces opposition from the Separatists who wish to see a Quarren king instead. Lee-Char faces a violent uprising led by Riff Tamson. With Captain Ackbar and the Republic's aid, Lee-Char leads his warriors to victory. Afterward, he is crowned king.

During the Imperial era, Lee-Char falls under the influence of Jedi Purge survivor Ferren Barr, who has a vision that the Mon Cala will save the galaxy. After the Imperial envoy, Telvar, is killed, Lee-Char decides to fight the Empire, leading to heavy casualties on the planet. Lee-Char is captured by Darth Vader, and only orders his forces to cease fire when Barr reveals that he is behind Telvar's death. Lee-Char is imprisoned on Strokill Prime, leaving a regent named Urtya to rule Mon Cala in his place.

Years later, Princess Leia Organa attempts to liberate Lee-Char in order to inspire more of Mon Cala's people to join the Rebel Alliance. She finds Lee-Char on life support and records his dying message. Leia passes the recording to Urtya who transmits it all over Mon Cala. The crews of 12 Mon Cala cruisers join the Rebel Alliance.

BREHA ORGANA

APPEARANCES III **SPECIES** Human **HOMEWORLD** Alderaan **AFFILIATION** House Organa, Rebel Alliance

Wise and compassionate, Breha Organa is the Queen of Alderaan. After nearly dying during her scaling of Alderaan's Appenza Peak, she requires replacement mechanical organs to live. Breha and her husband, Senator Bail Organa, adopt Leia when her mother, and the Organas' friend, Padmé Amidala, dies in childbirth. Breha decides a large-scale rebellion against the Empire is the only option and helps unite the various rebel cells. She also secretly siphons off some of Alderaan's riches to fund them. When Grand Moff Tarkin interrupts an Alderaanian banquet full of rebel sympathizers, she skillfully deals with him, feigning a marital dispute to embarrass Tarkin into leaving without any suspicions. Breha is proud that Leia becomes a rebel operative and that she passes her Day of Demand challenges. Breha and Bail are both killed when Alderaan is blown up by the Death Star.

ROYAL GUARD

APPEARANCES II, CW, III, Reb, RO, VI **SPECIES** Human **HOMEWORLD** Various **AFFILIATION** Empire

Emperor Palpatine's Royal Guards are an elite group of sentries trained in martial arts like Teräs Käsi. They are originally selected from the Senate Guard or clone trooper ranks, but are all anonymous under their red armor. They wield powerful force pikes capable of restraining a Jedi, or worse. The Royal Guard only follow the Emperor's orders without question and are among the few trusted with witnessing his full power. They accompany him on virtually all trips and stand as sentries in his quarters. The Royal Guards may be dispatched on secret missions or assigned to guard other dignitaries at the Emperor's sole discretion. For example, some are assigned to Darth Vader's castle on Mustafar.

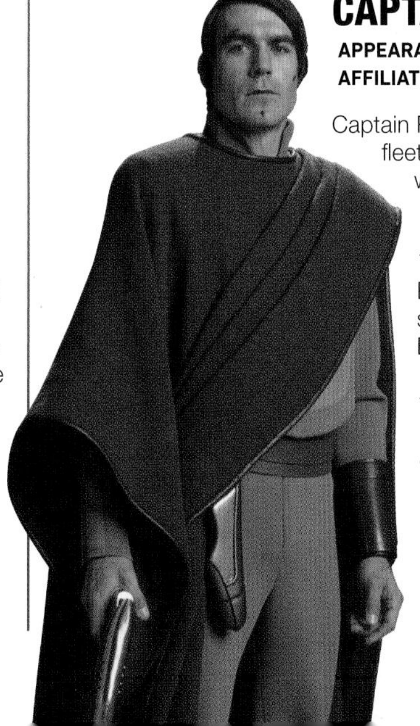

CAPTAIN ANTILLES

APPEARANCES III, RO, IV **SPECIES** Human **HOMEWORLD** Alderaan **AFFILIATION** House Organa, Republic, Rebel Alliance

Captain Raymus Antilles is commander of Bail Organa's fleet of diplomatic cruisers. Antilles joins the rebels, wanting to secure a better life for his daughters. A year after Emperor Palpatine's ascension, Antilles works with Bail and former Jedi Ahsoka Tano to rescue the farmers on Raada from the Empire. Over the years, Antilles becomes very skilled at getting past Imperial blockades. When Bail's daughter Leia is old enough to request the use of the *Tantive IV* herself, she orders Antilles and the ship to accompany her to Wobani. After many missions together, Antilles and Leia come to trust and rely upon each other completely. During the Battle of Scarif, they are aboard *Tantive IV*, and Antilles delivers the Death Star plans to Leia before they jump to hyperspace. In the ensuing battle over Tatooine, Darth Vader boards the ship and demands the stolen Death Star plans. When Antilles refuses, Vader kills him.

"I am a Jedi, like my father before me." LUKE SKYWALKER

LUKE SKYWALKER

Hidden on Tatooine, Luke emerges as a rebel hero and redeems his father on the way to becoming a Jedi. Sadly, his attempt to train a new generation of Jedi fails.

APPEARANCES III, Reb, IV, V, VI, VII, VIII, FoD **SPECIES** Human **HOMEWORLD** Tatooine **AFFILIATION** Jedi

CALL TO ADVENTURE

In need of new droids to work on his moisture farm, Luke's uncle, Owen Lars, purchases R2-D2 and C-3PO from Jawa traders. Little does Owen know that the Empire is scouring Tatooine for the two missing droids. When R2-D2 takes off in search of Jedi Knight Obi-Wan Kenobi, C-3PO accompanies Luke to chase down the determined astromech. R2-D2 delivers Princess Leia's message to an old hermit named Ben, who reveals his Jedi past as Obi-Wan and gives Luke the lightsaber that belonged to Luke's father, Anakin.

Wistful dreamer
Bored with the humdrum life of a moisture farmer, Luke dreams of unknown adventures awaiting him across the galaxy.

REBEL HERO

Luke joins Obi-Wan on his mission to deliver the stolen Death Star plans to rebels on Alderaan. After the *Millennium Falcon* is trapped in the Death Star's tractor beam, Luke teams up with the freighter's captain, Han Solo, and first mate, Chewbacca, to free Princess Leia, who is imprisoned on the space station. After sabotaging the tractor beam, Obi-Wan sacrifices his life to let Luke and the others escape with the Death Star plans. Luke joins the rebel fleet and makes a daring X-wing run through the superweapon's trench, torpedoing the exhaust shaft and triggering a chain reaction that destroys the Death Star.

JEDI APPRENTICE

A spectral Obi-Wan appears to Luke, instructing him to journey to Dagobah and train with Jedi Master Yoda. After crashing his X-wing in a Dagobah swamp and being harassed by a mischievous creature, Luke despairs until his tormentor reveals his true identity—he is Yoda. The Jedi Master expresses doubt as to whether Luke is ready for Jedi training, but Luke persists, and Yoda accepts him as his new apprentice. As Luke's powers grow, he sees a vision of his friends in peril and abandons his training to mount a rescue.

Unexpected tutor
Luke arrives at Dagobah seeking to train with a legendary Jedi Master. The being he finds isn't quite what he expects.

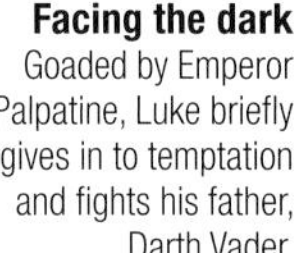

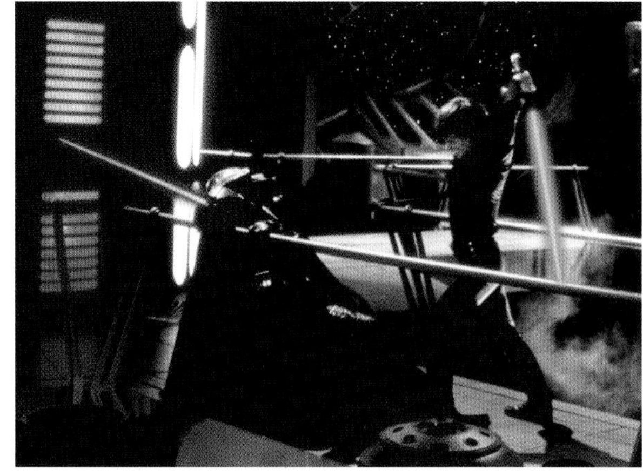

Facing the dark
Goaded by Emperor Palpatine, Luke briefly gives in to temptation and fights his father, Darth Vader.

REDEEMING ANAKIN SKYWALKER

On Cloud City, Luke learns the truth about his father. Darth Vader had not betrayed and murdered Anakin Skywalker; Darth Vader *is* Anakin Skywalker. When Luke next crosses paths with Vader on the Endor moon, the Jedi surrenders peacefully. Although the temptation of the dark side is great, Luke resists Emperor Palpatine's overtures. In response, the vengeful Emperor attacks Luke with Force lightning, inciting Vader to kill his Sith Master and save his son. With that act, Anakin is redeemed.

DISILLUSIONED

Following Yoda's command to pass on what he has learned, Luke Skywalker sets out to train a new generation of Jedi. Among them is his nephew, Ben Solo, whose potential to use the Force is unmatched by the other students. Luke grows suspicious that Ben might be falling to the dark side; tragically, Luke's distrust only serves to push Ben over the edge. The young apprentice lashes out against his Jedi Master, destroying Luke's new temple and most of the other students with it. Overcome by this disaster, Luke withdraws from galactic events, going into hiding and cutting himself off from the Force. He seeks out the first-ever Jedi temple and settles on the world of Ahch-To. Knowing that Supreme Leader Snoke wants to eliminate her brother, General Leia Organa sends her best pilot, Poe Dameron, to find the one man she believes can locate Luke: the explorer Lor San Tekka. He gives Poe part of a map which, when combined with R2-D2's portion of the same map, pinpoints Luke's location. Leia then sends Rey there to meet him—and hopefully receive training as a Jedi.

Mysterious visitor
Luke harbors suspicions about Rey, who has arrived on Ahch-To with his father's lightsaber.

Force fighter
Meditating from the Jedi temple on Ahch-To, Luke harnesses all of his strength to project an image of himself on Crait.

RECONNECTING WITH THE FORCE

When Rey arrives, Luke is not ready to take on a student and has shut down his connection to the Force. However, Luke agrees to teach Rey three lessons to show her why the Jedi were wrong and to explain his choice to let the Order die with him.

During Rey's time with Luke, his previous failings with Ben Solo are revealed, and Rey leaves to carry on the legacy of the Jedi alone. Seemingly at his lowest point, Luke is visited by Master Yoda. In his wisdom, Yoda shows Luke that learning from failure is part of a master's duty. Luke lets go of the past and steps in to help the Resistance. The effort succeeds in allowing his allies to escape the First Order, but he does not survive this excruciating feat. Luke Skywalker, hero of the Rebellion, becomes one with the Force.

Redeeming hero
With the rise of the Empire, Luke is one of the last hopes of the Jedi Order. Raised in secret on remote Tatooine, he must face his destiny: to redeem his father, Anakin Skywalker, and restore balance to the Force.

timeline

THE EMPIRE ERA

Luke's birth
When Padmé Amidala dies after childbirth, Obi-Wan delivers Luke to Owen and Beru Lars on Tatooine.

Message from a princess
Luke follows R2-D2 to the home of Ben (Obi-Wan) Kenobi, where they hear a desperate plea from Princess Leia.

Death of Owen and Beru
Orphaned again, Luke heads for Alderaan with Obi-Wan and the droids on board the *Millennium Falcon*.

Inside the planet killer
Luke and his new friends free Leia from her cell, then escape from the Death Star.

Battle of Yavin
Luke's torpedoes hit the Death Star exhaust port, which destroys the superweapon.

Jedi journal
Luke discovers Obi-Wan Kenobi's journal inside the old master's hut on Tatooine. It contains valuable stories about the history of the Jedi and the time Obi-Wan was watching over Luke.

Retracing history
Luke discovers a ruined Jedi temple on Vrogas Vas, sparking his interest in finding other such places around the galaxy.

Voice from the past
A vision of Obi-Wan impels Luke to seek out Yoda on Dagobah.

Yoda trains Luke
Luke learns the ways of the Force from the wise Jedi Master, Yoda.

▲ Luke discovers the truth
After an intense lightsaber duel, Darth Vader reveals that he is Luke's father.

Rescue of Han Solo
Jedi Luke Skywalker demands Jabba release Han Solo. The Hutt and his minions are defeated by the reunited friends.

▲ Another Skywalker
Before leaving to confront his father, Luke reveals to Leia that she is his sister.

Anakin redeemed
Luke lays down his weapon, refusing to fight his father. Darth Vader turns on the Emperor as he attempts to kill Luke.

THE NEW REPUBLIC ERA

Pointing the way
Luke travels to Pillio and discovers a mysterious compass, just one of many relics he collects on his personal journey to learn about the Force.

New Jedi
Luke begins training new Jedi, but they are destroyed by his nephew and former student—Ben Solo.

Exile
Luke goes into exile. A race between the Resistance and the First Order to find Skywalker begins.

Battle of Crait
Having been located on Ahch-To, Luke eventually agrees to aid the Resistance. In the course of joining the fight on Crait, he passes into the Force.

"Somebody has to save our skins. Into the garbage chute, flyboy."

LEIA ORGANA TO HAN SOLO

LEIA ORGANA

A leader in the Rebel Alliance, New Republic, and Resistance, Leia Organa follows in her adoptive father's footsteps and is dedicated to protecting democracy and peace in the galaxy.

APPEARANCES III, Reb, RO, IV, V, VI, Res, VII, VIII, IX, FoD **SPECIES** Human **HOMEWORLD** Alderaan **AFFILIATION** Rebel Alliance, New Republic, Resistance

Fixing things
Repairs on the *Millennium Falcon* put Han and Leia in tight quarters, where they share their first kiss.

PRINCESS OF THE PEOPLE

With Princess Leia aboard, the *Tantive IV* flees the Battle of Scarif, but is captured by an Imperial Star Destroyer. As her mission to deliver the stolen Death Star plans to the rebels is in jeopardy, Leia records a holographic message and tasks R2-D2 with seeking out Jedi Master Obi-Wan Kenobi on the nearby planet Tatooine. She distracts stormtroopers searching her ship while R2-D2 and his companion C-3PO jettison in an escape pod. Her brave refusal to reveal the rebels' location marks Alderaan as the Death Star's first target. With the planet's destruction, Leia becomes a princess without a home. Her duty to the peoples oppressed by the Empire carries on despite her loss. Escaping Imperial custody, Leia helps deliver the stolen plans, and the Death Star is eventually destroyed.

Critical mission
By way of a recorded message in R2-D2, Princess Leia delivers a desperate plea for help to her father's old ally, Obi-Wan Kenobi.

REBEL LEADER

Although Leia is a senator and diplomat, she is also a warrior. An excellent markswoman, she assumes command during her rescue from the Death Star. As the *Millennium Falcon* rockets away from the space station, Leia assists Chewbacca in flying the freighter while Luke and Han operate the quad lasers to fend off TIE fighters. On Hoth, Leia briefs the pilots as the Empire closes on Echo Base. She remains in the command center overseeing the evacuation until Han Solo insists it is time to go.

Hoth briefing
In Echo Base's icy hangar, Princess Leia briefs rebel pilots on their roles in the impending emergency evacuation.

MATTERS OF THE HEART

Unable to reach her rebel transport off Hoth, Princess Leia escapes on the *Millennium Falcon*. Eluding Imperial Star Destroyers, Han Solo decides the best option for needed repairs is the planet Bespin. During the journey, Leia and Han confess their feelings for each other. They are soon captured by Darth Vader, who uses them as bait to lure Luke Skywalker into a trap. Leia admits she loves Han just before he is frozen in carbonite. She later frees him at the palace of Jabba the Hutt.

GALACTIC DIPLOMAT

Dinner surprise
Leia discovers her Ewok hosts have brought home new captives for dinner. They happen to be Luke, Han, and Chewbacca.

Serving on General Solo's command squad for the rebel strike team planning to destroy the second Death Star's shield generator on the Endor moon, Leia is separated from the others after she pursues biker scouts who might report their presence. Leia encounters Wicket, a short, furry native, in the forest and is kind and patient with him despite her predicament. She and her unlikely ally take out a pair of biker scouts together. Wicket and the other Ewoks of Bright Tree Village agree to help the strike team against Imperial forces and later even help the team escape when they are captured.

RISE OF THE RESISTANCE

Following the rebel victory on Endor, Leia and Han Solo marry and have a child, whom they name Ben. Leia is integral to the formation of the New Republic and serves as senator for the Alderaan sector. During her campaign for the powerful position of First Senator, the truth about her parentage—that her father is Darth Vader—is leaked to the public. The scandal ends her political career, but her concerns about the First Order lead her to form the Resistance to keep them in check. Leia recruits a young New Republic pilot, Poe Dameron, to lead a squadron on a series of secret missions to collect valuable intelligence and interfere with the First Order's growing influence. Though unable to wage open warfare, Leia does everything she can to undermine the Empire's successors, including uncovering a corrupt New Republic senator who secretly supports them. The struggle against the First Order is personal for Leia, as she and Han separate after their son Ben falls to the dark side and joins their new enemy.

Resistance-base reunion
In their final meeting, Leia begs Han to bring their son home.

Unassuming aristocrat
The simple white robes of a princess help to keep Leia's enemies off guard. She is just as handy with a blaster or at piloting as she is versed in royal protocol.

ON THE RUN

The First Order wipes out the New Republic fleet and its capital on Hosnian Prime using the devastating superweapon Starkiller Base. Although Leia's Resistance forces manage to destroy it, a small Resistance fleet is now all that remains to oppose Supreme Leader Snoke's military might. Fleeing from the planet D'Qar, the fleet is running out of fuel as the First Order bears down upon it. Leia herself is nearly killed during a starfighter strike on her command ship, *Raddus*. The fleet sends out a distress call throughout the galaxy, hoping that Leia's old allies will come to its aid. The Resistance makes its last stand at the planet Crait, only to realize that no one has answered the call. Leia, Rey, and a handful of others flee aboard the *Millennium Falcon,* hoping to rekindle the Rebellion and fight another day.

Resistance general
General Leia Organa watches, helpless, as the Resistance fleet dwindles ship by ship.

timeline

▲ Leia's birth
When Padmé Amidala dies after childbirth, Senator Bail Organa of Alderaan adopts Leia.

Heir apparent
In line with Alderaanian tradition, Leia must earn her right to inherit the crown of Alderaan by taking on challenges of mind, body, and heart.

Mercy missions
Though she is an aide in the Imperial Senate, Leia conducts missions to secretly aid rebel factions, including delivering Hammerhead corvettes to Lothal.

Buying time
After entrusting R2-D2 with the stolen Death Star plans, Leia distracts stormtroopers while the droid escapes with C-3PO.

Destruction of Alderaan
While a captive Leia watches in horror, Tarkin destroys her homeworld, Alderaan, to display the Death Star's might.

Escape from the Death Star
Luke, Han, and Chewbacca free Leia and dodge stormtroopers to escape the space station.

THE EMPIRE ERA

Princess of Alderaan
Leia rallies survivors of her destroyed homeworld and protects them from Imperial retaliations.

Battle of Hoth
With the Empire closing in, Leia escapes on the *Millennium Falcon* and is separated from the rebel fleet.

▲ Cloud City
Instead of refuge, Leia, Han, and Chewbacca find a trap set by Darth Vader on Cloud City.

Declaration of love
Before Han is encased in carbonite by Darth Vader, Leia admits she loves him.

To the rescue
Disguised as a bounty hunter named Boushh, Leia joins her friends at Jabba's Palace to rescue Han Solo.

▲ Slaying Jabba
Captured by Jabba, Leia strangles the criminal with the chains of her captivity.

Mission to Endor
Leia volunteers for General Solo's strike team to destroy the Endor moon's shield generator.

Death to the Death Star
The strike team blows up the shield generator, allowing the rebels to destroy Death Star II.

THE NEW REPUBLIC ERA

New mother
Leia and Han's son Ben Solo is born on Chandrila, a rotating capital seat of the New Republic.

New Republic senator
The New Republic Senate is restored and Leia becomes a senator once again. Her opposition to disarmament gets her branded as a warmonger.

General Organa
From D'Qar, Leia leads the Resistance in its battle against the First Order.

"Chewie, we're home." HAN SOLO TO CHEWBACCA

HAN SOLO

At times a smuggler, gambler, racer, general, lover, husband, and father… Han Solo is transformed from scoundrel to hero by the love of a woman whose stubborn independence is matched only by his own.

APPEARANCES S, IV, V, VI, VII, FoD **SPECIES** Human **HOMEWORLD** Corellia **AFFILIATION** Rebel Alliance, Resistance

Mimban days
Han serves as a mudtrooper on Mimban. A tour of duty on this muddy planet is often given as a form of Imperial punishment.

THE SCOUNDREL

Orphaned at a young age, Han grows up on the streets of Corellia, and his tough upbringing shapes who he becomes as an adult. Han's time among the White Worms gang teaches him how to run scams and talk his way out of trouble. He falls in love with fellow scrumrat, Qi'ra, with whom he tries to escape Corellia. When he and Qi'ra are separated, Han is forced to join the Imperial Academy to make it off the planet. Han's free spirit and disregard for authority make for a tough time as an Imperial cadet. Despite his innate ability, he fails as a pilot, and is reassigned to the infantry on Mimban. There, questioning orders leads to Han facing execution at the hands of "the Beast," a Wookiee named Chewbacca. Instead, Han convinces Chewie that they can escape together.

BECKETT'S CREW

Solo and Chewbacca flee Mimban as part of smuggler Tobias Beckett's crew. The gang's first job is a failed attempt to steal coaxium—a valuable hyperfuel. Now in debt to criminal syndicate Crimson Dawn, Han and Beckett negotiate to complete the job. Han is surprised to find his old friend Qi'ra working for Crimson Dawn, but is pleased to have her accompany the crew on its journey to Kessel to secure more coaxium. The crew also adds Lando Calrissian and his ship, the *Millennium Falcon*, to its ranks, but soon fall into trouble and are forced to take a shortcut through the dangerous Maelstrom around Kessel. With Han in the pilot's seat the crew completes the maneuver in record time, but Lando's pristine starship receives substantial damage. At the end of the job, Han is betrayed by Lando, Beckett, and Qi'ra. Han and Chewie leave with just enough money to wager in a card game to win the *Millennium Falcon* from Calrissian. Han also learns to be careful who he trusts.

Cocky kid
Young Han has faith in his piloting skills, but his crewmates are less certain about his odds when they must complete the notorious Kessel Run.

IMPRISONED IN CARBONITE

When Han finally comes to care deeply for Leia Organa, his world is turned upside down. On Cloud City, he is captured by Darth Vader and used as a test subject in a carbon-freezing chamber. Incapacitated and frozen in carbonite, he is handed over to Boba Fett and finally delivered to Jabba the Hutt on Tatooine. As a trophy hanging on the gangster's palace wall, Solo's plight seems hopeless until Leia and Han's friends orchestrate a successful rescue attempt. The former rogue is now helpless and temporarily blinded by hibernation sickness. Han becomes dependent on his compatriots, and through this humbling experience learns to trust others.

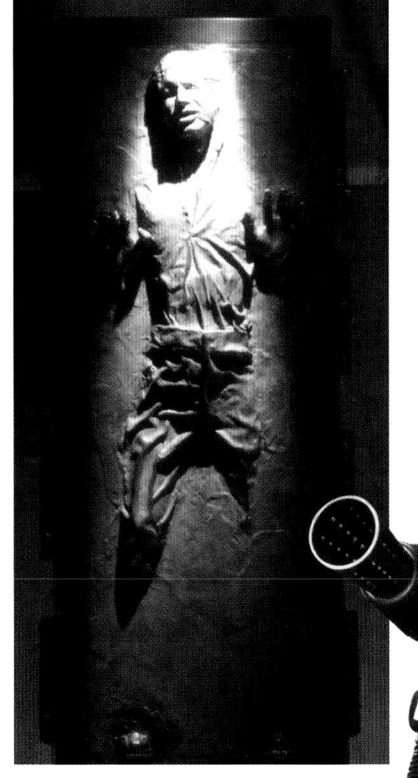

Frozen solid
Darth Vader uses Han to test whether a human would survive Cloud City's carbonite-freezing process before attempting it with Luke Skywalker.

GENERAL SOLO

After his rescue on Tatooine, Han fully embraces his place in the Rebel Alliance. Now a general, he leads a team to destroy the second Death Star's shield generator on the moon of Endor. Meanwhile, he reluctantly loans the *Millennium Falcon* to its previous owner, Lando Calrissian, to spearhead the attack on the Death Star. During the mission on Endor, Han becomes a prisoner of the Ewoks and once again must place his faith in others to survive. When the shield generator is destroyed and the Empire overthrown, Leia breaks the news that Luke is actually her brother. Han is delighted to discover that Luke is not a rival for Leia's affections.

Love and war
Despite his mercenary, cynical approach to life, Han falls for Princess Leia and, ultimately, the rebel cause.

THE RELUCTANT REBEL

Han Solo agrees to transport Luke, Obi-Wan, and their droids purely as a business deal; he has no interest in their rebel mission. When plans change, Han only agrees to rescue Princess Leia because of the promise of a big financial reward. When they reach Yavin 4, he intends to leave before the impending battle so he can pay off Jabba the Hutt. At the last moment, however, he has a change of heart and returns to help his newfound friends. On Hoth, Han tries to leave the rebels once again, but changes his mind to get Leia safely off the planet. Until now, the quest for money and saving his own skin were his primary motivations, but everything changes when he falls in love.

Guns and confidence
Han Solo believes that he doesn't need much more than a good blaster at his side, especially his trusty, customized DL-44 pistol.

Solo and son
Han attempts to reason with his son on Starkiller Base. Han hopes there is still enough light in Kylo Ren to convince him to return to his family.

FAMILY LIFE

After the Battle of Endor, Han and Leia marry and have a son named Ben. Feeling restless, Han spends much time away from home, starting a shipping business and racing ships. They send Ben away to train with Luke to become a Jedi. When Ben turns to the dark side and renames himself Kylo Ren, Han and Leia have difficulty coping and separate. Han returns to smuggling with Chewbacca, but having lost the *Falcon,* ends up piloting the *Eravana*—a bulk freighter. In the Western Reaches, they are reunited with their old ship and plunged back into galactic events. When Han helps destroy Starkiller Base, he confronts Kylo Ren. Han reaches out to his son, asking him to come home, but his son kills him.

timeline

THE EMPIRE ERA

Joining up
Fleeing his homeworld of Corellia, Han joins the Imperial Navy as a cadet where he is given the family name, Solo.

Smuggler's luck
Solo wins the *Millennium Falcon* from Lando Calrissian in a game of sabacc on Numidian Prime.

Debt to Jabba
Han dumps the illicit cargo he is carrying for Jabba the Hutt before the *Millennium Falcon* is boarded by Imperials.

▲ Meeting at Mos Eisley Cantina
Han meets Luke Skywalker and Obi-Wan Kenobi on Tatooine, an encounter that changes his life forever.

Medal of honor
After rescuing Princess Leia and aiding in the Battle of Yavin, Solo is awarded a medal by the Rebel Alliance.

Incident on Ord Mantell
Han encounters a bounty hunter, which reminds him that his troubles with Jabba are far from over.

▲ Battle of Hoth
Now a captain in the Rebel Alliance, Han rescues Luke Skywalker and helps Leia and the droids escape from the Empire.

▲ Incident on Cloud City
Captured by Darth Vader, Han is frozen in carbonite and turned over to Doba Fett.

Jabba's debt collected
The Hutt finally has his prize. Han hangs in Jabba's palace until sentenced to death by way of the Sarlacc.

▲ Battle of Endor
As General Solo, Han successfully leads the Endor mission to destroy the second Death Star's shield generator.

THE NEW REPUBLIC ERA

Happily married
Han Solo and Leia Organa are married in a quiet ceremony on Endor.

New father
Leia gives birth to their son Ben Solo, about a year after the Battle of Endor.

Smuggling again
Han Solo and Leia separate after Ben joins Snoke and the First Order. Han returns to his scoundrel past.

Final act
Han Solo sacrifices everything for his family, and dies on Starkiller Base at the hands of his own son.

QI'RA

APPEARANCES S, FoD **SPECIES** Human **HOMEWORLD** Corellia
AFFILIATION White Worms, Crimson Dawn

Like many wayward children on Corellia, Qi'ra falls in with the White Worms gang. She and Han are sent by Lady Proxima to manipulate an auction between the White Worms, Kaldana Syndicate, and Droid Gotra. Though Qi'ra is promoted to Head Girl by Proxima as a result, she and Han (who have fallen in love) decide to escape.

Later, Han steals a small sample of valuable coaxium and tries to run away with Qi'ra. They are chased to Coronet Spaceport by Proxima's lieutenant Moloch. Though Han makes it through security, Qi'ra is captured. Proxima sells Qi'ra to slave dealer Sarkin Enneb, and he in turn sells her to the crime syndicate Crimson Dawn. Impressed by her tenacity and resourcefulness, Dryden Vos offers her a position in Crimson Dawn—but only if she swears her life to him. She agrees and becomes his second-in-command. He then sends her on a mission to Ord Mantell, where she outsmarts the bounty hunter IG-88 and pirate Hondo Ohnaka.

Han comes back into Qi'ra's life, accompanied by Tobias Beckett and Chewbacca. She helps save their lives by formulating a heist on Kessel to steal a hoard of coaxium—all to replace what they owe an angry Dryden Vos. She accompanies the three and hires Lando Calrissian and his *Millennium Falcon* to transport them. Thanks to her planning and Teräs Käsi combat skills, the mission is a success. When they return to meet Dryden however, Beckett double-crosses them all, stealing the coaxium and leaving Han and Qi'ra to deal with Dryden. Qi'ra betrays and kills her former master. She tells Han to pursue Beckett, promising to follow. Nevertheless, she knows she cannot escape Crimson Dawn but decides that Han can be free if she remains. Thus Qi'ra contacts Dryden's master, Maul, and flies off to meet him, leaving Han behind.

Keeping up appearances
Her time with Crimson Dawn has made Qi'ra adept at hiding her true intentions. She easily fools the Pyke Syndicate.

Unexpected reunion
Han is shocked to find Qi'ra working with Dryden Vos, assuming she would still be stuck on Corellia. She is equally shocked to learn he has joined Beckett's gang.

LADY PROXIMA

APPEARANCES S **SPECIES** Grindalid
HOMEWORLD Corellia **AFFILIATION** White Worms

The head of the White Worms is Lady Proxima, a larva-like matriarch who lives in a cistern at the center of their den. Her criminal gang controls the black market in Coronet City, taking in humanoid children known as "Scrumrats" who work as slaves. Proxima takes in young Han and Qi'ra, but when Han fails at his assignment and keeps his stolen coaxium for himself, Proxima is determined to teach him a painful lesson. Han escapes with Qi'ra by breaking the glass above Proxima's "throne room," thus exposing her to the light and burning her photosensitive skin. Still scarred and bearing a grudge, Proxima continues to run her gang in the New Republic era.

MOLOCH

APPEARANCES S **SPECIES** Grindalid
HOMEWORLD Corellia **AFFILIATION** White Worms

Lady Proxima's lieutenant in the White Worms is the unsympathetic Moloch. Though he looks like a humanoid inside his protective face-plates and robes, he is in fact a worm-like Grindalid just like Lady Proxima herself, and he "walks" on a segmented tail. Moloch captures Han and Qi'ra after Han goes rogue on an assignment, taking them to Lady Proxima for punishment. When they escape, Moloch loads Rebolt, Syke, and their Corellian hounds into his A-A4B truckspeeder and pursues them to the Coronet Spaceport. Though Han escapes, Moloch's men manage to grab Qi'ra.

CORELLIAN HOUND

APPEARANCES S **HOMEWORLD** Corellia
AVERAGE SIZE 0.7 m (2 ft 4 in) high
HABITAT Adapted to many environments

Fast on their feet and with an excellent sense of smell, Corellian hounds are used by gangs as guards, attack-dogs, and trackers. There are many breeds. Sibians are white with a bone-like ridge along the crest from head to shoulders. The hounds are prone to fighting, and their bites are so savage that they often lose teeth, which they continuously regrow. The White Worms gang uses them to hunt down Han and Qi'ra when they flee to Coronet Spaceport. The dogs are thrown off the trail by strong scents of seafood in the fish market.

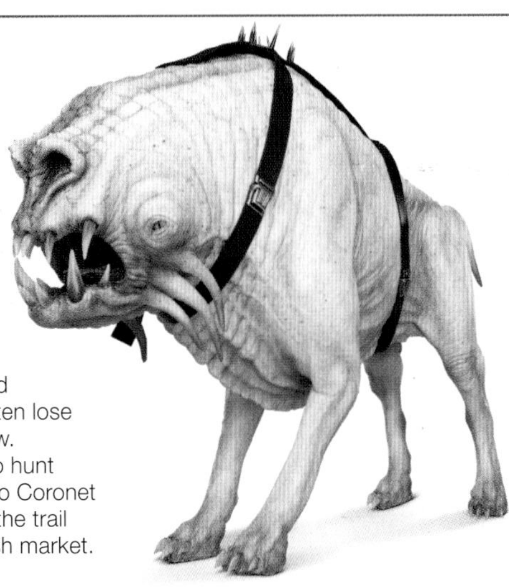

REBOLT

APPEARANCES S
SPECIES Human
HOMEWORLD Corellia
AFFILIATION White Worms

Rebolt is a member of the White Worms gang, working under Moloch. He is an experienced Corellian hound handler but deals roughly with his animals. He joins Moloch and Syke aboard their A-A4B truckspeeder to pursue Qi'ra and Han through Coronet City.

SYKE

APPEARANCES S
SPECIES Human
HOMEWORLD Corellia
AFFILIATION White Worms

Syke is the competitive colleague of Rebolt. He takes a gentler approach with their Corellian hounds, though he has a spiteful streak when it comes to Rebolt. The two White Worms gang members unleash their hounds on Qi'ra and Han at Moloch's command.

BANSEE

APPEARANCES S
SPECIES Human
HOMEWORLD Corellia
AFFILIATION White Worms

The Scrumrats are orphans and runaways that Lady Proxima's White Worms gang takes in off the street of Corellia. Bansee is their best ratcatcher, attaining the rank of Third Girl. She is ambitious and aspires to climb higher in the gang, perhaps by becoming one of Moloch's thugs.

PATROL TROOPER

APPEARANCES S **SPECIES** Human
HOMEWORLD Various **AFFILIATION** Empire

On worlds with large urban environments—particularly those with strategic importance for the government, military, and major corporations—the Empire takes control of local transit security and law enforcement. Imperial patrol troopers are the urban counterparts to the Imperial Army's biker scouts. On Corellia, patrol troopers ride Aratech C-PH patrol speeder bikes as they monitor activity in Coronet's shipyards and spaceport. A patrol trooper chases Han and Qi'ra when the two flee from Moloch, but the pursuit doesn't last long before the patrol trooper crashes.

FALTHINA SHAREST

APPEARANCES S **SPECIES** Human
HOMEWORLD Corellia
AFFILIATION Empire

Lead Transport Security Officer Falthina Sharest is a member of Corellia's emigration office, working at Coronet Spaceport. The corrupt officer agrees to a trade, allowing Han and Qi'ra to exit in exchange for their coaxium, but betrays Qi'ra when the White Worms grab her.

TOBIAS BECKETT

APPEARANCES S **SPECIES** Human **HOMEWORLD** Glee Anselm **AFFILIATION** Crimson Dawn, Beckett's crew

Tobias Beckett gains notoriety as the man responsible for Aurra Sing's death. He also runs heists for Crimson Dawn with his gang, which includes his girlfriend Val and pilot Rio Durant. He has his team run an unsuccessful scam on Honvun IV stealing identichips, only to lose them to Enfys Nest. Such failed schemes lead the crew into financial trouble. Having accrued a significant debt to Crimson Dawn's Dryden Vos, Beckett and his gang pose as mudtroopers on Mimban and steal an AT-hauler to use it in a heist on Vandor. In the process, Beckett meets Han Solo and Chewbacca and adds them to his crew. On Vandor, Beckett and the team steal priceless coaxium from the Imperial conveyex, but Enfys Nest's Cloud-Riders arrive and foil the operation. Val and Rio are both killed.

Beckett agrees to steal a coaxium hoard from Kessel for Dryden, to replace the load they previously lost. Their heist is successful, but Beckett double-crosses his own team on Savareen, taking the coaxium for himself. Han Solo pursues Beckett and kills him.

Straight shooter
Amid the chaos of the battlefield on Mimban, Beckett, in disguise as an Imperial officer, demonstrates his incredible skills as a gunslinger.

VAL

APPEARANCES S **SPECIES** Human
HOMEWORLD Unknown
AFFILIATION Beckett's crew

Val's father was a musician and named her after an instrument called the valachord. She and Tobias Beckett—her partner in crime and romance—have a running joke that he will one day learn to play one. They do jobs for Dryden Vos, which brings them into conflict with Enfys Nest. After Nest deprives them of their haul of identichips, Val and Beckett pose as mudtroopers on Mimban and steal a ship to use in a conveyex heist on Vandor. During their Vandor mission Val is caught by deadly Viper droids. Rather than risk her team getting caught too, she blows up the conveyex bridge, sacrificing herself.

RIO DURANT

APPEARANCES S **SPECIES** Ardennian
HOMEWORLD Ardennia **AFFILIATION** Freedom's Sons, Beckett's crew

Amiable Rio Durant is a four-armed pilot who originally works for Freedom's Sons, an army employed by the Galactic Republic during the Clone Wars. After the formation of the Empire, he turns to crime. Rio tries unsuccessfully to steal the speeder bike of Tobias Beckett and Val, and is offered a place in their crew instead. After meeting Han Solo on Mimban, Rio convinces Beckett to take Solo and Chewbacca on as new crew members. Rio flies the crew's ship during their heist on Vandor, but the craft is boarded by Cloud-Riders. Rio is mortally wounded in a blaster fight.

MUDTROOPER

APPEARANCES S **SPECIES** Human
HOMEWORLD Various **AFFILIATION** Empire

Mudtroopers are members of the Imperial Army appointed to swampy, war-torn worlds. The assignment is not a glamorous one. Mudtroopers such as Han Solo are often given the duty as punishment for poor service and insubordination. Some are local forces who fought for the Republic during the Clone Wars, now fighting side-by-side with stormtroopers. On Mimban the Empire battles Mimbanese guerillas in an effort to secure the planet. Tobias Beckett's gang takes advantage of the chaos—posing as mudtroopers, they steal an Imperial AT-hauler.

RANGE TROOPER

APPEARANCES S **SPECIES** Human
HOMEWORLD Various **AFFILIATION** Empire

Range troopers are among the Empire's toughest soldiers, assigned to rugged, cold-weather frontier worlds. On Vandor, they are ordered to guard the Empire's 20-T railcrawler conveyex transport in its delivery of refined coaxium. High speeds on ever-changing tracks winding through mountains and tunnels—all in rough weather—make it difficult to monitor conditions outside the train. Range troopers must personally investigate, clinging to the train surface with their magnetomic gription boots. Confronted by Tobias Beckett and his gang, their efforts prove futile.

ENFYS NEST

APPEARANCES S **SPECIES** Human **HOMEWORLD** Unknown **AFFILIATION** Cloud-Riders

Sixteen-year-old Enfys Nest is descended from a long line of freedom fighters. Her homeworld is devastated by the Five Crime Syndicates; chief among them Crimson Dawn. She inherits her role as leader of the Cloud-Riders (a pirate swoop-bike gang) and her elaborate armored costume from her mother, upon the latter's death.

After the Cloud-Riders' raid on Gargon, the Empire begins to piece together information that Enfys Nest is amassing resources to fund a rebel uprising. Meanwhile, Enfys makes herself a thorn in the side of Tobias Beckett, tricking his gang into stealing a load of identichips. Enfys shows up again to steal coaxium from Beckett during his heist on Vandor, only to lose the haul in an accident. Enfys further tracks Beckett, Han Solo, Qi'ra, and Chewbacca to Savareen. There she reveals her identity and her purpose—to fight Crimson Dawn's brutality. She convinces them to help her. After a fight with Dryden Vos and killing the traitorous Beckett, Han Solo turns over the priceless coaxium to Enfys. She in turn delivers the coaxium to Saw Gerrera, who uses it to fund his rebel Partisans.

Foe turned friend
Confronted by Enfys Nest and her Cloud-Riders on Savareen, Han realizes that instead of ruthless criminals, they are actually noble freedom fighters.

On the edge
Dryden is highly volatile and unpredictable. He is a ruthless killer who hides his true nature behind a mask of calm gentility.

DRYDEN VOS

APPEARANCES S **SPECIES** Near-human **HOMEWORLD** Unknown **AFFILIATION** Crimson Dawn

Dryden Vos acts as the public leader of Crimson Dawn, allowing his employer, Maul, to remain anonymous. Dryden has a temperament that flashes instantly from calm to bloodthirsty. The only warnings are the striations on his face, which burn crimson red with elevated blood pressure and adrenaline. The underworld kingpin appreciates a lavish lifestyle, traveling in his yacht, *First Light*, with an entourage of security enforcers, ship's crew, and menial servants.

When Tobias Beckett fails to deliver the coaxium he owes, Dryden is determined to kill him. Fortunately for Beckett, his crew-member, Han Solo, is a quick thinker and they come up with a plan to acquire replacement coaxium from Kessel. Dryden assigns his trusted lieutenant Qi'ra to accompany them.

Later, Han Solo, Chewbacca, and Qi'ra return, but are unaware that Beckett has secretly warned Dryden that they plan to double-cross him. Beckett arrives soon after, but departs with the coaxium (and Chewbacca, held at blasterpoint), leaving Solo, Qi'ra, and Dryden to fight it out. Qi'ra betrays Dryden however, killing him and taking over his criminal operation.

WEAZEL

APPEARANCES I, S **SPECIES** Human **HOMEWORLD** Tatooine **AFFILIATION** Hutt cartel, Cloud-Riders

Weazel works as an agent for the Hutts on Tatooine, and is in the crowd when Anakin Skywalker famously wins the Boonta Eve Classic podrace. Seeing the ills caused by the crime syndicates (and now the Empire), Weazel renounces his old life and joins the Cloud-Riders. He is Enfys Nest's second-in-command and best spy.

MARGO

APPEARANCES S **SPECIES** Imroosian **HOMEWORLD** Imroosia **AFFILIATION** Crimson Dawn

The concierge aboard Dryden Vos' *First Light* is an Imroosian female named Margo. She sees to all his guests' needs and greets Beckett, Han Solo, and Chewbacca when they first arrive together. Her chalk-like skin is heat resistant, an advantage on her hot, volcanic homeworld (a place she is in no hurry to return to).

TAYSHIN AND MODA MAXA

APPEARANCES S **SPECIES** Human **HOMEWORLD** Eshan **AFFILIATION** Cloud-Riders

The Maxa sisters learn how to survive in harsh conditions when the Droid Gotra incites a gang war on their homeworld. Both later join the Cloud-Riders. Tayshin, the elder of the two, is a skilled martial artist, while Moda is a talented pilot.

LULEO PRIMOC

APPEARANCES S **SPECIES** Gallusian **HOMEWORLD** Unknown **AFFILIATION** None

A singing superstar before the Clone Wars, with hits such as "Your Love is Gravy" and "Carve Your Name in My Heart," Luleo Primoc now sings with Aurodia Ventafoli, suspended in a repulsorlift flask filled with formaldehyde. He was once a holovid star, seated atop a humanoid exo-suit.

AEMON GREMM

APPEARANCES S **SPECIES** Hylobon **HOMEWORLD** Unknown **AFFILIATION** Crimson Dawn

Aemon Gremm is Dryden Vos' chief bodyguard and captain of his security team. He and his fellow Hylobons are fiercely loyal to Vos and highly aggressive toward anyone they perceive as a threat to his operations. Gremm takes all the credit for his team's work though, which is a source of friction.

AURODIA VENTAFOLI

APPEARANCES S **SPECIES** Human **HOMEWORLD** Unknown **AFFILIATION** None

The best-selling recording artist Aurodia Ventafoli is in high demand. Dryden Vos hires her as his singer-in-residence on the *First Light* for a time, with the help of a huge retainer fee. The "Chanteuse of the Stars" duets (aided by a multi-vocoder) with the diminutive singer, Luleo Primoc.

ASTRID FENRIS

APPEARANCES S **SPECIES** Human **HOMEWORLD** Yir Tangee **AFFILIATION** Smuggler

One of the many shady smugglers that hang out at the notorious Fort Ypso Lodge, Astrid Fenris is an amoral con artist from Yir Tangee. She runs a profitable scam selling Vandor ice labeled as valuable R'alla mineral water.

THERM SCISSORPUNCH

APPEARANCES S **SPECIES** Nephran **HOMEWORLD** Nepotis **AFFILIATION** Independent entrepreneur

Therm is a regular at the Lodge in Fort Ypso. As he loses money gambling with Lando Calrissian his blood boils, and thoughts of snapping the smooth-talker's neck cross his mind, but his hard exoskeleton helps him hide any emotion.

L3-37

APPEARANCES S **MANUFACTURER** Various (self-upgraded)
TYPE Custom pilot droid **AFFILIATION** Lando Calrissian

The *Millennium Falcon* owes much of its legendary performance to L3-37. L3 begins life as an astromech, later upgrading her own body with components from protocol droids and other unusual sources. Her brain has likewise evolved, with coding from espionage and protocol droids overlaid upon her original astromech architecture. There is no other droid quite like L3. She is uniquely self-aware and passionate about droid rights, leading to constant confrontations with "organics." L3's owner/partner Lando Calrissian is willing to overlook her eccentricities due to her exceptional co-piloting skills. In truth, the two develop an unusually close master-droid bond. After starting a droid revolution on Kessel, L3 is damaged beyond repair in the resulting chaos. Her brain is uploaded into the computer of the *Millennium Falcon*, thus becoming a permanent part of the ship. She performs the calculations that allow Han Solo and the crew to make the Kessel Run in less than 12 parsecs, and execute other amazing feats in their future adventures.

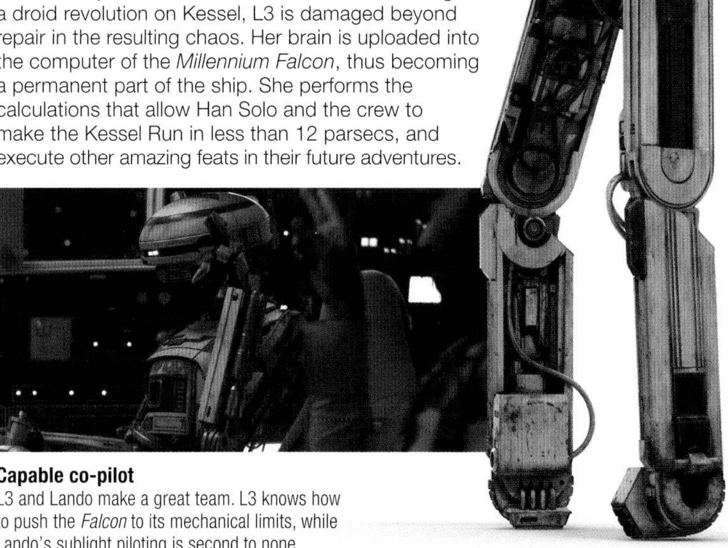

Capable co-pilot
L3 and Lando make a great team. L3 knows how to push the *Falcon* to its mechanical limits, while Lando's sublight piloting is second to none.

WG-22

APPEARANCES S
MANUFACTURER Veril Line Systems **TYPE** Modified EG-series power droid **AFFILIATION** Fort Ypso Lodge

Ralakili runs a violent droid-fighting pit at the Fort Ypso Lodge. He's been spiteful toward droids ever since the Clone Wars. The modified Gonk droid WG-22 can power his mechanical weaponry with his own internal power generator.

FD3-MN

APPEARANCES S
MANUFACTURER Unknown
TYPE Unknown
AFFILIATION Fort Ypso Lodge

Droids are modified with crude weapons and thrown into the fighting pit without consent. Most are disoriented and don't want to be there, but FD3-MN realizes that she actually quite likes it. Unfortunately gladiator droids don't tend to last long.

SIX EYES

APPEARANCES S **SPECIES** Azumel
HOMEWORLD Unknown **AFFILIATION** None

Argus "Six Eyes" Panox is an Azumel gambler and occasional customer at the Lodge at Fort Ypso. His eye stalks move independently, gaining him a reputation for looking at other sabacc players' cards. His five-chambered stomach requires him to eat frequently.

DAVA CASSAMAM

APPEARANCES S **SPECIES** Elnacon
HOMEWORLD Nacon **AFFILIATION** None

A sabacc-playing regular at the Lodge, Dava Cassamam is an ammonia-breathing Elnacon who wears a transparisteel dome and breathing apparatus when she is away from home. She is easygoing, and relaxed by Lando Calrissian, a smooth talker who effortlessly relieves her of her currency during their games.

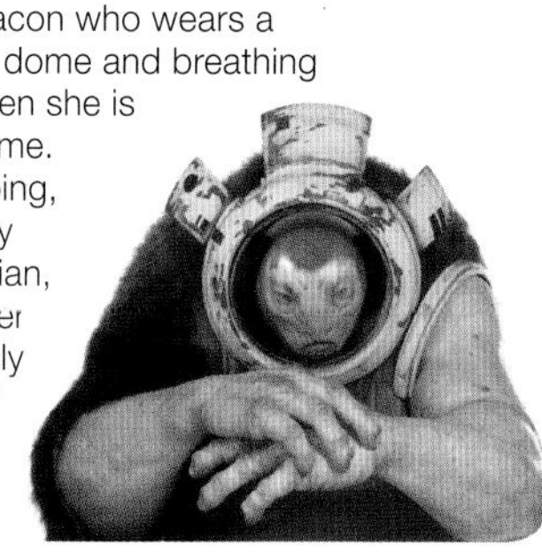

QUAY TOLSITE

APPEARANCES S
SPECIES Pyke
HOMEWORLD Kessel
AFFILIATION Pyke Syndicate

The director of operations at the Kessel Mines is Quay Tolsite. He is the local representative for the Pyke Syndicate, which leases the mines from King Yaruba of Kessel. The selfish Pyke is unconcerned with the well-being of his laborers, as long as they are capable of satisfying production targets. Tolsite enjoys his authority and privilege, embezzling money and spice from business transactions, but he pays a price. The mine environment is caustic and hard on Pyke physiology, so he and the other Pykes wear protective suits.

DD-BD

APPEARANCES S **MANUFACTURER** Unknown
TYPE Adminmech **AFFILIATION** Pyke Syndicate

The adminmech DD-BD is an enthusiastic droid who works on a Morseerian pirate ship until the vessel is impounded by the Empire. He is then sold to the Pyke Syndicate and sent to Kessel. There, L3-37 liberates him from his restraining bolt and gives him ideas about starting a revolution.

SENNA

APPEARANCES S
SPECIES Gigoran
HOMEWORLD Gigor

Senna is one of a number of Gigorans who are rounded up on his homeworld by Zygerrian slavers, sanctioned by the Empire. He committed no crimes, but members of his species are desired as slave laborers on Kessel due to their strength. The poisonous conditions in the mine have stained his formerly white fur.

SAGWA

APPEARANCES S
SPECIES Wookiee
HOMEWORLD Kashyyyk

The gallant Wookiee Sagwa protects his people from Imperial soldiers in the tree city of Rwookrrorro on Kashyyyk. He is imprisoned by the Empire and sent to the mines of Kessel. During an uprising he aids Chewbacca and Han Solo.

TAK

APPEARANCES S
SPECIES Human
HOMEWORLD Coruscant

Tak is a con artist who robs the elderly on Coruscant. He is arrested when he tries to fleece the Princess of Kessel and is sent to work in the mines on her world. When L3-37 encourages a droid riot, Tak escapes in the chaos.

SUMMA-VERMINOTH

APPEARANCES S **RANGE** Si'Klaata Cluster and Akkadese Maelstrom
AVERAGE SIZE 7400 m (24278 ft 3 in) long

Shrouded in the gas clouds surrounding Kessel are enormous creatures of legend—the summa-verminoths—that can potentially live for a thousand years. With trailing tentacles and mantles full of eyes, they snatch wayward ships foolish enough to stray from the Kessel Run. When the crew of the *Millennium Falcon* take a shortcut through the Akkedese Maelstrom they are nearly swallowed by one of these mythic monsters. They distract it by ejecting the ship's escape pod and then lure it to its doom in the gravity well known as the Maw.

"Smuggler? Such a small word. I'm more of a... galactic entrepreneur." LANDO CALRISSIAN

LANDO CALRISSIAN

Beginning as a hustler, ending as a galactic hero, Lando Calrissian comes out on top, thanks to a winning smile, charm, and a little flattery.

APPEARANCES S, Reb, V, VI, IX **SPECIES** Human **HOMEWORLD** Unknown **AFFILIATION** Rebel Alliance

SPORTSMAN AND SMUGGLER

Lando Calrissian prides himself on being an exceptional "sportsman" and looking good doing it. He is a charismatic swindler and gambler who owns the heavily modified freighter, the *Millennium Falcon*. His ship reflects Lando's own impeccable style and preference for the finer things in life. But expensive tastes come at a price and Lando often turns to gambling or illegal commissions to pay off his debts. He is joined on these jobs by his loyal, but loudly opinionated, droid co-pilot L3-37. Lando is an expert and confident sabacc player, thanks largely to the hidden card he often has up his sleeve. However, Lando's luck runs out when he takes part in a smuggling run to Kessel that brings Han Solo and Chewbacca onto the *Falcon* for the first time. By the end of the heist, his immaculate ship is almost unrecognizable, L3-37 is destroyed, and Lando abandons Solo and returns to his old ways. At another sabacc game, this time on Numidian Prime, Solo swindles the master and wins the *Falcon* from Lando.

Bitter defeat
The game of Sabacc where he loses the *Falcon* to Han haunts Lando for years.

False front
Lando welcomes his friend Han Solo with a jovial facade to hide the Empire's presence on Cloud City.

BARON ADMINISTRATOR OF CLOUD CITY

Lando's fortune changes when he wagers big and wins control of Cloud City, in the atmosphere above the planet Bespin. His life takes a dramatic turn toward more reputable pursuits as he becomes Baron Administrator of the gas mining and luxury destination. His situation sours, however, when the Empire arrives and he is forced to turn his friend Han and his companions over to Darth Vader in exchange for the city's freedom. He watches as Solo is frozen in carbonite, but when it appears that Vader intends to dishonor their deal, Lando implements a city-wide evacuation with the aid of Lobot, helping his friends escape. Nonetheless, the frozen Han is taken by the bounty hunter Boba Fett and delivered to Jabba the Hutt.

A CHARMING CON MAN

Having lost the *Falcon*, Lando embarks on a variety of business ventures across the galaxy. On Lothal, he buys land from local kingpin Cikatro Vizago to set up an illegal mining operation. Later, after winning the astromech Chopper from Zeb Orrelios, he bargains with the crew of the *Ghost* to help him con the slaver Azmorigan out of a puffer pig (Lando insists the pig is necessary for his latest convoluted scheme). He also helps the crew make illegal starship transponders to aid their escape from an Imperial blockade—this time in exchange for three military-grade shield generators. Not all of Lando's schemes work out for the best. On the Imperial colony world Castell, Lando and his loyal friend Lobot take a heist job from the nefarious Papa Toren to pay off a debt. The so-called easy job turns out to be perilous when they discover the space yacht they are robbing is owned by Emperor Palpatine and is full of Sith artifacts.

Business concluded
Having recovered her astromech, Hera Syndulla lets Lando know that she is less than impressed with his methods.

IN JABBA'S EMPLOYMENT

Lando helps orchestrate an elaborate mission to rescue Han, who is frozen in carbonite and hanging from a palace wall, from the Hutt gangster on Tatooine. Gaining employment as a skiff guard in Jabba's palace thanks to an underworld contact, Lando waits for Chewbacca and Leia Organa (disguised as the bounty hunter Boushh) to arrive on the desert world. However, the plan falls apart when Leia is discovered freeing Han from the carbonite, and she and Han are taken prisoner. Luke Skywalker arrives and attempts to persuade Jabba to release Han and Leia, but is captured, too, forcing the friends to resort to their last contingency plan. When Jabba takes Han, Luke, and Chewbacca out to the Dunes Sea to feed them to the Sarlacc, Lando is aboard one of Jabba's skiffs to help them escape. At the last moment, he and Han, Luke, and Chewbacca fight off Jabba's henchmen, while Leia Organa kills the Hutt. Afterward they all depart Tatooine.

Skiff guard
Lando disguises himself as just another vibro-wielding thug in Jabba's service. His ruse brings him fearfully close to the jaws of a Sarlacc.

In the war room
Lando and his friends listen intently to the mission briefing aboard *Home One.*

GENERAL CALRISSIAN

Wanted by both the Empire and the Hutt crime family, Lando decides to wholeheartedly commit to the Rebellion. Now a general, he attends the rebel briefing on *Home One*, the Mon Calamari flagship, where Mon Mothma, Admiral Ackbar, and General Crix Madine detail plans to sabotage the shield generator on the Forest Moon of Endor, destroy the second Death Star, and kill the Emperor. Lando and his co-pilot, Nien Nunb, fly the *Falcon* inside the Death Star, where they detonate the battle station's core, destroying it. After this decisive victory, the Empire falls into chaos, and the war finally ends in triumph a year later at the Battle of Jakku.

Living by his wits
Lando's smooth-talking and magnetic personality are infamous, and his charms have stolen more than just hearts. He is particularly adept at talking his way out of difficult or dangerous situations.

timeline

THE EMPIRE ERA

Locked up
During a mission smuggling weapons to Petrusian freedom fighters on Kullgroon, the *Millennium Falcon* is impounded by the Empire and taken to a holding yard on Vandor.

Lucky hand
Lando meets Han Solo on Vandor and beats him at sabacc using a hidden card up his sleeve.

▲Kessel
Lando accepts a job to smuggle a crew to Kessel. The errand costs Lando his co-pilot and ultimately, his ship.

Arrival on Lothal
Lando Calrissian lands on Lothal, where he acquires a plot of land from Cikatro Vizago, which he plans to mine.

Winning hand
Lando meets Garazeb Orrelios, who loses the droid Chopper to him in a game of sabacc at Old Jho's Pit Stop.

Mining days
After using the crew of the *Ghost* to help him acquire precious cargo from Azmorigan, Lando tries his hand at mining.

▲Cloud City
Lando turns to more respectable endeavors and becomes the Baron Administrator of Cloud City, a wealthy mining facility and luxury destination.

▲Betrayal of Han Solo
When Darth Vader arrives on Cloud City, Lando is forced to make a deal to hand over his friend to the Empire.

Rescuing Han Solo
Lando helps his new friends rescue Han Solo from the gangster Jabba the Hutt on Tatooine.

Battle of Tanaab
Lando defeats a pirate fleet at Tanaab. His "little maneuver" makes a big impression on rebel leadership.

Death Star assault
Flying his old ship, Lando leads the mission to destroy the second Death Star during the Battle of Endor.

THE NEW REPUBLIC ERA

Naboo
Lando commands the Alliance fleet against the Empire at Naboo, saving the planet from widespread destruction during Operation: Cinder.

Sinister plot
Lando and Han stop Fyzen Gor's plan to infect every droid in the galaxy with a virus that turns droids against their masters.

Desperate call
Decades after the fall of the Empire, Lando's solitary lifestyle is interrupted when he once more finds himself called upon to help save the galaxy.

"Stop whining. We're here to protect you." LOTHAL STORMTROOPER

STORMTROOPERS

Stormtroopers have replaced the clone armies of the Republic as expendable foot soldiers of the Empire. Their endless numbers serve across the galaxy, enforcing the Emperor's will.

APPEARANCES S, Reb, RO, IV, V, VI, FoD **SPECIES** Human **HOMEWORLD** Various **AFFILIATION** Empire

RECRUITMENT AND TRAINING

Though not necessarily the army's deadliest weapons, beneath their white armor, stormtroopers are loyal Imperial citizens. Most are naturally born men and women, who volunteer (or are conscripted) and rigorously train in Imperial academies. After the rise of the Empire, clone soldiers are gradually phased out due to their accelerated aging process. Most clones retire, but a few remain as advisers and trainers. Clone soldiers, though genetic copies, vary in personality and are surprisingly individualistic. Naturally born soldiers, in contrast, are trained and conditioned to forsake both individualism and empathy. In many ways, stormtroopers function like human droids.

Recruitment poster
This common propaganda poster on Lothal, used to recruit stormtroopers, reads "Galactic Empire: Help end the rebellion—Enlist today!" *(right)*. A garrison of stormtroopers attacks the rebel forces *(below)*.

Behind the mask
Stormtroopers appear anonymous in their armor. This leads to an overall lack of accountability and also creates occasional opportunities for spies to impersonate soldiers.

Search for the droids
Obi-Wan Kenobi uses his Jedi powers of persuasion to get past a stormtrooper roadblock in Mos Eisley.

Officious gatekeeper
A stormtrooper officer manages the cell block where Princess Leia is held on the first Death Star.

MAINTAINING SECURITY AND ORDER

Stormtroopers are stationed on strategic worlds throughout the galaxy. On planets like Lothal, Tatooine, and Coruscant, they serve a variety of functions, including guarding mining operations, factories, and commercial interests important to the Empire. They also maintain societal order and monitor politically sensitive areas—stamping out all signs of rebellion. Their power, built on fear within local populations, creates an atmosphere of abuse and corruption. Some use their positions for personal gain, taking advantage of the helpless citizens in their charge. Others, whether due to blind obedience or brainwashing, carry out atrocities in the name of Emperor Palpatine.

Overwhelming numbers
An Imperial walker and stormtroopers surround Han and Chewbacca during the Battle of Endor.

ON THE BATTLEFIELD

Stormtroopers are the backbone of the Imperial Army, waging war on rebel insurrection. In battle, stormtroopers are equipped with BlasTech E-11 blasters and DLT-19 heavy blaster rifles, a thermal detonator, grappling hook, comlink, and surplus ammunition. Stormtroopers are dreaded by civilian populations—not only for their brutality but also their fanaticism to press on regardless of cost. They are trained to disregard fallen comrades in battle and to engage the enemy no matter the odds. When the Republic transitions into the Empire, stormtroopers are summoned to bring the remaining Separatist worlds into line. Later skirmishes are mostly small in size—the results of isolated rebel cells, indigenous politics, Jedi sightings, piracy, and other underworld activity—until the dawn of the Rebel Alliance. As the Galactic Civil War expands, so does the involvement of stormtroopers in warfare, culminating in the Empire's defeat at the Battle of Endor.

DIVERSITY OF STORMTROOPERS

Stormtroopers include human men and women, but very rarely, if ever, nonhuman individuals. Outside of combat and security details, stormtrooper officers wear distinctive black caps, boots, and dress tunics. Their code cylinders, rank plaques, officers' disks, and uniform style conform to the Imperial Navy's standards. Officers in field units wear orange, black, and white pauldrons to indicate rank (unfortunately for stormtroopers, this boldly visible formality puts them at risk and many lose their lives to snipers). There are specialized units of stormtroopers, such as snowtroopers, shoretroopers, scout troopers, sandtroopers, and death troopers—each employs unique armor to support its niche combat roles. Army pilots may also be promoted from within their ranks.

TIE FIGHTER PILOTS

APPEARANCES S, Reb, RO, IV, V, VI **SPECIES** Human
HOMEWORLD Various **AFFILIATION** Empire

The Empire's black-suited pilots fly the full range of TIEs, including fighters, bombers, interceptors, and less common models. Only a small minority of cadets in the Academy's pilot-training program actually graduate with commissions. They comprise an elite class within the Imperial Navy and have a notorious superiority complex. Nonetheless, they make great sacrifices. TIE fighter pilots are trained to complete their missions at all costs, disregarding their own survival.

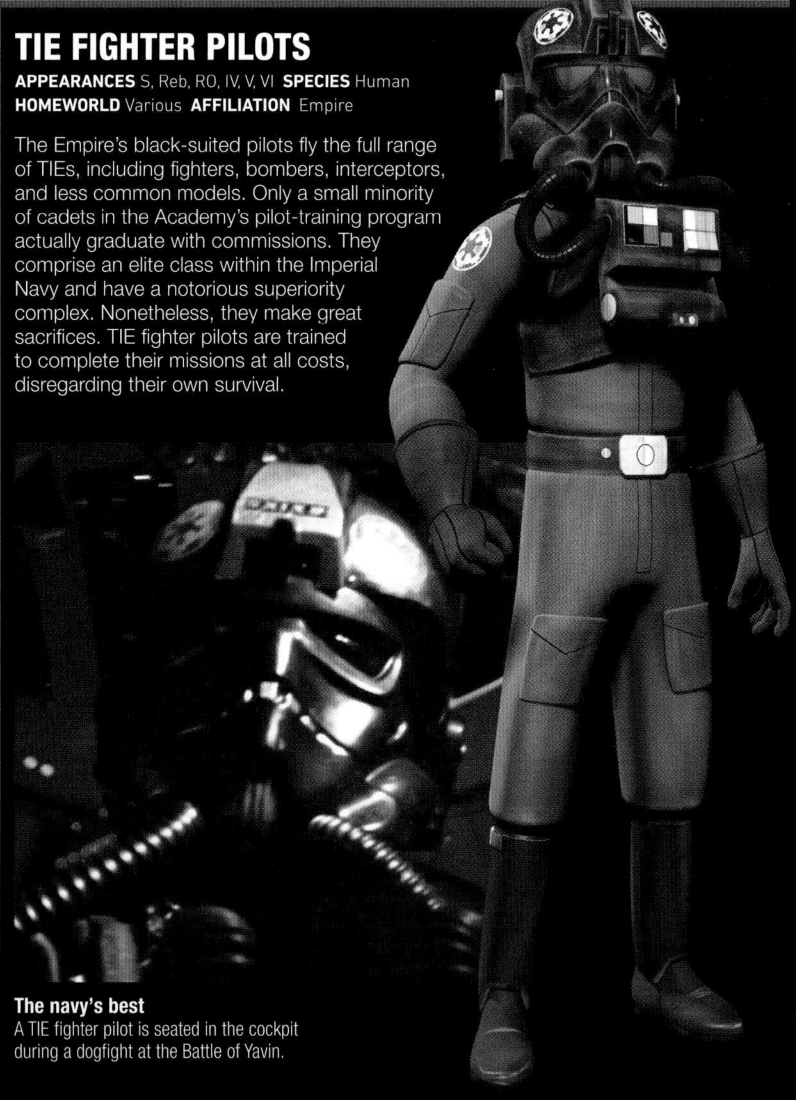
The navy's best
A TIE fighter pilot is seated in the cockpit during a dogfight at the Battle of Yavin.

Jaig eyes
Kanan begins to wear a mask after he is blinded by Maul on Atollon. It is decorated with Jaig eyes, which also adorn Captain Rex's clone trooper helmet.

KANAN JARRUS

APPEARANCES Reb **SPECIES** Human
HOMEWORLD Coruscant **AFFILIATION** Jedi, Rebel Alliance

Caleb Dume (alias Kanan Jarrus) is raised on Coruscant and becomes Depa Billaba's Jedi Padawan. While at the Jedi Temple, he also receives lessons from various Jedi, including Obi-Wan Kenobi and Yoda. He accompanies his master on many missions during the Clone Wars, including to Kardoa and Mygeeto. Kanan is but a teenager when Chancellor Palpatine issues Order 66, branding the Jedi traitors and ordering them to be assassinated. On Kaller, Billaba sacrifices her own life to get Caleb to safety, when her clone officer, Commander Grey, turns on the duo. Caleb goes into hiding and assumes a new name, Kanan Jarrus. To avoid detection by the Empire, he abandons his Jedi teachings and learns how to survive from scoundrel Janus Kasmir.

Eventually Kanan settles on the planet Gorse, where he lives in a modest room at the Asteroid Belt, a cantina owned by Okadiah Garson. Kanan works for a company called Moonglow Polychemical, which mines volatile thorilide in the crystal interior of Cynda, the moon above Gorse. Kanan leads a day-to-day existence until two people change the status quo: Count Denetrius Vidian and Hera Syndulla. The amoral Count is sent by the Emperor to improve thorilide production, and does so with catastrophic consequences. Renegade Twi'lek Hera, on the other hand, is intent on combating the Empire's atrocities.

Kanan is attracted to Hera, who sparks a gradual change in him, steering Kanan back toward the values of his Jedi past. After thwarting Vidian's dark plans, he joins her on the *Ghost*. Their new rebel crew grows with the addition of Sabine Wren and Garazeb Orrelios. The team gravitates to the Outer Rim world of Lothal, where the Empire is pillaging local mineral resources to build new military machines.

During a mission, Kanan encounters Ezra Bridger, a Force-sensitive orphan living on the streets of Capital City. Sensing Ezra's potential, Kanan invites him to join them. Kanan is reluctant to become Ezra's master, having never completed his own training to become a full Jedi Knight. Nevertheless, Kanan teaches Ezra the ways of the Force through a series of lessons during their many missions against the Empire.

One such lesson takes the duo to Lothal's Jedi temple. While meditating there, Kanan sees a vision of a Jedi Temple guard, who tells him that Ezra Bridger will fall to the dark side. Kanan's instinct is to do all he can to save Ezra from this fate; however, he eventually realizes that he cannot protect Ezra from all things. In that moment, Kanan fully embraces his new role of mentor and finally becomes a full Jedi Knight.

Constantly hunted by Vader's Inquisitors, Kanan and Ezra travel to Malachor in search of a way to defeat them. Instead, they find Maul, who attempts to make Ezra his apprentice. Maul strikes Kanan with his lightsaber, permanently blinding the Jedi. Although Kanan loses his vision, this incident only strengthens his bond with the Force. The Force-sensitive being known as the Bendu later teaches Kanan how to "see" through the Force.

As the *Ghost* crew continue to strike against the Empire and join the newly formed Rebel Alliance, Ezra's homeworld of Lothal increasingly falls under the Empire's iron grip. The crew attempt to break the Empire's hold, but Kanan's partner, Hera, is captured during their attack. She is then tortured at the Imperial Armory Complex by Governor Pryce. A rescue attempt frees Hera, but costs Kanan his life. In a final act of heroism, Kanan uses the Force to shield his comrades from a wall of flames that destroys the Imperial complex.

Jedi missions
After many duels, Kanan finally defeats the Grand Inquisitor aboard the *Sovereign (right)*. During a Force vision, Kanan is knighted by an entity appearing to be a Jedi Temple guard *(below)*. In his final moments, Kanan sees his family one last time *(bottom)*.

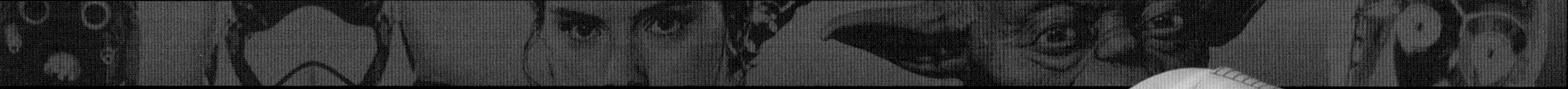

HERA SYNDULLA

APPEARANCES Reb, FoD **SPECIES** Twi'lek
HOMEWORLD Ryloth **AFFILIATION** Rebel Alliance

Hera Syndulla is a scion of an influential family on Ryloth. She saw her planet ravaged by violent conflict during the Clone Wars, only to see the clone troopers who once helped Ryloth's freedom fighters turn and enslave them for the Empire. Her own world is oppressed by the Empire and riddled with corruption at the highest levels. Inspired by her revolutionary father, Cham Syndulla, Hera leaves her world behind on a quest to find other like-minded individuals and build a movement to oppose the Empire.

On a scouting mission to Gorse, Hera meets a gunslinging Jedi-in-hiding named Kanan Jarrus. When Kanan plays a key role in thwarting a plot devised by Imperial Count Vidian, Hera realizes his potential as a partner and invites him to join her aboard her ship, the *Ghost*. Over several adventures, Hera adds other members to her rebel crew, including Imperial ex-cadet and weapons expert Sabine Wren, a Lasat survivor named Zeb Orrelios, and an orphaned Force-sensitive named Ezra Bridger. Together with Hera's astromech droid, Chopper, the team forms a surrogate family. Hera is the nurturing mentor and leader of the group, encouraging the others to do their best. She also functions as the team's ace pilot and getaway driver in their struggles against the Empire.

Hera conducts many of the team's missions in cooperation with a mysterious contact called Fulcrum. As their mission objectives become increasingly ambitious, the crew of the *Ghost* becomes increasingly curious about Fulcrum's identity. Sabine in particular questions Hera's cooperation with Fulcrum, but when the two are shipwrecked on an asteroid with deadly fyrnocks, they reach a new understanding of mutual trust and reliance.

After a series of missions on Lothal, Hera and her crew join another group of rebels, known as Phoenix Squadron. Eventually, Hera rises to the rank of Phoenix leader, taking part in a variety of missions, including the Blockade of Ibaar and Battle of Garel. On a mission in the Ryloth system, Hera is reunited with her father when her group captures an Imperial fighter carrier. The carrier becomes the new flagship for the squadron's A-wing fighters.

Natural flyer
Hera is one of the best star pilots in the galaxy. She can fly a range of freighters and starfighters and easily pilots Quarrie's Blade Wing prototype.

Hera's piloting skill and diplomacy serve the Rebellion well during a mission to Shantipole to acquire a prototype starfighter known as the Blade Wing. This powerful ship is designed by a Mon Calamari engineer by the name of Quarrie, who gives Hera the privilege of conducting the ship's first flight test. The starfighter proves capable of taking out an Imperial cruiser by itself and breaking blockades. It thus becomes the prototype for all future B-wing development.

The crew of the *Ghost* takes an important mission to escort Senator Mon Mothma to a budding rebel fleet above Dantooine. From the *Ghost*'s cockpit, Mothma announces the formation of the Alliance to Restore the Republic to the galaxy, giving Hera a front row seat to one of the most important moments in the Galactic Civil War.

Hera continues to serve the Rebel Alliance, even after suffering the loss of her Jedi partner Kanan, and gives birth to their son, named Jacen Syndulla, who already shows piloting aptitude at a young age. Chopper also remains by her side as she takes part in some of the most important battles against the Empire. After her promotion to general, she pilots the *Ghost* at the Battle of Scarif, the Rebellion's first major victory against the Empire. Following the Battle of Yavin, Hera is given command of a Mon Calamari star cruiser, which she names *Geist*, and escapes the Imperial assault on the Mako-Ta Space Docks. Hera also serves at Echo Base on Hoth and later fights at the Alliance's major victory at Endor.

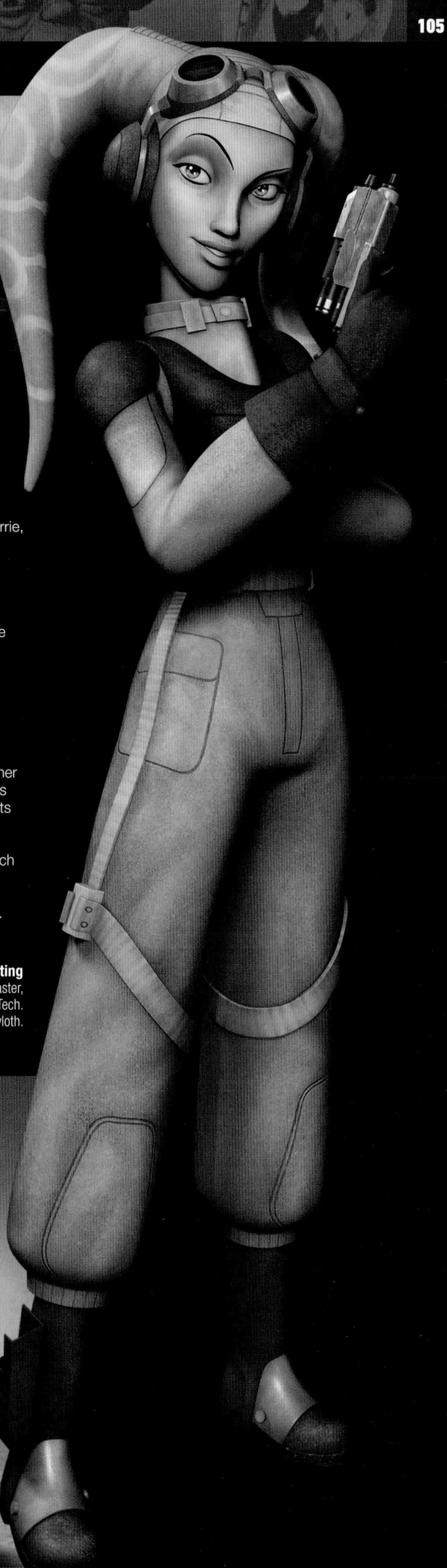

Freedom fighting
Hera carries a Blurrg-1120 holdout blaster, manufactured by Eirriss Ryloth Defense Tech. It is named for a local creature on Ryloth.

Special relationship
There is a special bond between Kanan and Hera that becomes more important to them as their fight against the Empire escalates.

Facing Thrawn
Hera's first encounter with Grand Admiral Thrawn is in her family home on Ryloth, which has been occupied by the Empire *(above top)*. She blows up the building as she escapes. During the Siege of Atollon, Hera takes command of Phoenix Squadron, following Jun Sato's sacrifice. She works with fellow rebel leader Jan Dodonna to plan an escape from Thrawn's blockade surrounding the planet *(above)*.

Versatile droid
Chopper's mechanical arms not only allow him to manipulate the ship's controls but also to engage TIE fighters.

CHOPPER (C1-10P)

APPEARANCES Reb, RO, FoD **MANUFACTURER** Industrial Automaton **TYPE** Astromech droid
AFFILIATION Rebel Alliance

Chopper (C1-10P) is owned by Hera Syndulla and is an integral member of her rebel cell, despite his cantankerous, self-centered, and eccentric nature. Chopper is largely made of replacement parts. On the outside, his leg struts are mismatched and his paint is worn. His internal circuitry is a bit of a mess as well. Yet Hera refuses to part with him because of his resourcefulness as the *Ghost*'s chief mechanic, and perhaps because of her own sentimentality.

Chopper is always ready for challenges. Like every astromech, he has an extendable arm to interface with computers, manipulate doors, and fly ships. Like other C1 models, Chopper also has three robotic arms to manage objects like handles, buttons, and even blasters. Unlike later models, he has a retractable wheel instead of a third leg, and he can activate a booster rocket from the same socket.

During the Clone Wars, the astromech serves as a navigator droid for the Republic Navy until his Y-wing is shot down on Ryloth. Chopper is destined for the scrap heap, but Hera recovers the droid and spares him this fate. Not surprisingly, Chopper develops a lifelong distaste for flying in Y-wings.

While he may at times be difficult, Chopper is dedicated to the rebel cause and has proven himself on missions. He often aids the crew of the *Ghost* as a lookout, and for such a diminutive droid he is unusually brave, facing stormtroopers in battle.

Since droids are regularly overlooked by organic beings, Chopper carries out many missions disguised as an Imperial droid. This disguise allows him to sneak into the Imperial Academy on Lothal, an Imperial communications ship, an Imperial Interdictor cruiser, and even Grand Admiral Thrawn's field headquarters on Ryloth.

The entire Phoenix fleet has reason to be grateful to him when it is saved by his resourcefulness. The rebels are seeking a new hidden base, desperate to find a place where the Empire won't find them. Little do they know they are heading straight into a trap. Just in time, Chopper befriends an Imperial protocol droid named AP-5 and removes his restraining bolt. Thankful for Chopper's friendship, AP-5 reveals the plot to him and offers the rebels an alternative option on the remote planet Atollon. They name their new home Chopper Base in honor of the droid's heroism.

Even after the rebels liberate Lothal, Chopper sticks by Hera's side while she serves with the Alliance. Operating from the Great Temple on Yavin 4, he joins her on the *Ghost* at the Battle of Scarif. Chopper remains the constant companion of Hera and her son Jacen long after the Empire is defeated. Being around Hera and Kanan's child even brings out the old astromech's playful side.

New friends
Chopper meets a fellow Republic veteran, named AP-5, during a rebel mission and persuades him to join the cause. They have a fraught and argumentative friendship.

Imperial paint job
Thanks to Sabine's painting skills, Chopper can quickly be disguised as an Imperial droid.

Hacked droid
Unfortunately, Chopper's identity as a rebel infiltrator is discovered by an Imperial communications officer aboard an IGV-55 surveillance vessel. Chopper is hacked during a mission to Killun Station and forced to turn against his friends. Luckily, Hera manages to regain control of her droid and destroys the hacker's ship.

ZEB (GARAZEB ORRELIOS)

APPEARANCES Reb **SPECIES** Lasat
HOMEWORLD Lasan **AFFILIATION** Rebel Alliance

Garazeb "Zeb" Orrelios is a vital member of the rebel crew aboard the *Ghost*. Despite his large size and brutish appearance, Zeb is thoughtful and sensitive, particularly to the plight of the weak and helpless. Nonetheless, Zeb gruffly speaks his mind, often not as tactfully as he should. The Lasat's tendency to act before he thinks leads Zeb and the crew into a lot of Imperial entanglements; fighting with stormtroopers becomes one of his favorite pastimes. His impulsiveness also contributes to a sporadic gambling problem, which at one point leaves Zeb in debt to Lando Calrissian and results in the rest of the crew having to help him sort things out.

Zeb's Lasat anatomy gives him distinct physical advantages over humans. His digitigrade legs allow him to generally jump farther, run faster, and move more quietly than his human friends. His heavy build makes him stronger, and his large finger pads aid in climbing. In addition, his sizable eyes and ears give him superior senses.

Zeb has a tragic past. While a captain of the Lasat High Honor Guard, Zeb's homeworld is razed by the Empire, which murders nearly all of its citizens. When Zeb encounters Alexsandr Kallus and discovers that the Imperial Security Bureau (ISB) agent actually participated in this atrocity, the two become bitter enemies and have several violent clashes.

Zeb's own tragedy makes him sympathetic to the suffering of others. Even in a desperate situation, he refuses to use the Empire's own brutal weapons against it, having witnessed the effects of its horrific T-7 disruptors firsthand on Lasan. Nonetheless, Zeb never runs from a fight.

On a mission to gain valuable intelligence on decommissioned Republic bases, Zeb and the Spectres travel to Seelos to meet with clone Captain Rex and his compatriots. The clones agree to help the rebels on one condition: The crew must help them on a joopa big-game hunt. Little does Zeb know that this involves using him as live bait, as joopas have a particular taste for Lasats. Fortunately, the gamble pays off when Captain Rex joins their crew.

During a later mission, Zeb is shocked to meet two fellow refugees from his homeworld. The survivors speak of an ancient Lasat legend of a mythical planet named Lira San. They believe that, with Zeb's help, they can reach Lira San and begin their lives anew. Zeb's bo-rifle points the way, far beyond the Outer Rim, as the planet lies behind an imploded star cluster, a hazardous maze that cannot be traversed by normal navicomputers. While other ships would be destroyed in such a maelstrom, the *Ghost* is protected by an energy field emanating from Zeb's staff. They emerge on the other side of the cluster to find Lira San, the original Lasat homeworld, inhabited by other Lasat. The journey tests Zeb's spiritual beliefs and shows him that he is not the last of his people after all.

Eventually, Zeb finds peace even with his sworn enemy Kallus. After they both crash on the moon of Bahryn, Zeb comes face to face with the ISB agent. To survive the moon's icy conditions, the two have to work together and, in due course, become friends. Their friendship means so much to Kallus that he later joins the Rebellion.

Zeb continues to serve in the Rebel Alliance throughout the Galactic Civil War, becoming closer to Kallus. After the war ends, Zeb takes Kallus to Lira San to meet his people, helping Kallus come to terms with his former role in devastating Lasan and its inhabitants.

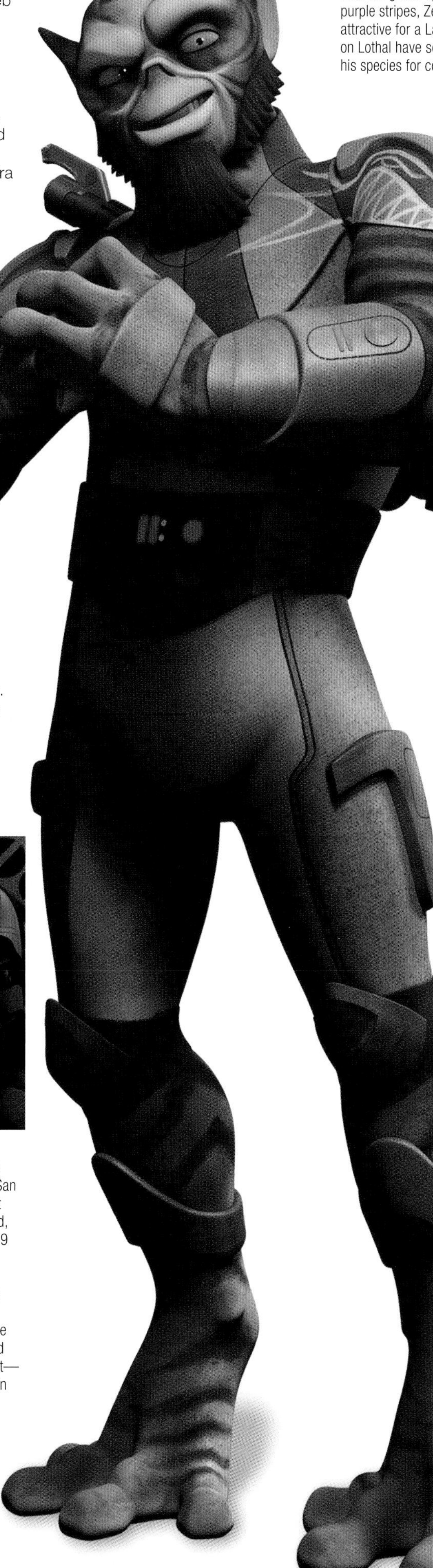

Handsome brute
With his green eyes and prominent purple stripes, Zeb is considered attractive for a Lasat, but few on Lothal have seen others of his species for comparison.

Rebel warrior
Zeb uses his bo-rifle to pilot the *Ghost* to Lira San *(above left)*. While most of his allies are offworld, Zeb must stop an E-XD9 infiltrator droid from revealing the location of Chopper Base to the Empire *(above)*. During the campaign to liberate Lothal, Zeb faces Grand Admiral Thrawn's agent—a lethal Noghiri assassin named Rukh *(left)*.

Artistic visionary
Sabine has a flair for art and adorns her armor, weapons, and most of the *Ghost* with paint.

SABINE WREN

APPEARANCES Reb, FoD **SPECIES** Human
HOMEWORLD Mandalore
AFFILIATION Rebel Alliance

Sabine Wren is the resident weapons specialist and artist aboard the *Ghost*. She is feisty, clever, and highly independent. Her courage and confidence are key traits of her Mandalorian heritage, though her concern for the plight of the downtrodden across the galaxy arises from her own personal journey.

Sabine excels during her training as a cadet at the Imperial Academy on Mandalore. She builds state-of-the-art weapons for the Empire; however she abandons her life on Mandalore when she discovers that one of the weapons she is developing is specifically designed to be used against her own people. When she speaks out against the Empire, Sabine is cast out by her family, and turns to a life of bounty hunting, partnering with her friend Ketsu Onyo.

After Onyo abandons her, Sabine becomes a rebel and in time joins the *Ghost* crew. Sabine's relationships aboard the *Ghost* are important to her, and she relies heavily on her friends, despite her strong-willed and self-sufficient nature. They have replaced the family that she lost on Mandalore. She looks up to Hera and Kanan as mentors and considers Zeb an older brother. She gets along with Chopper well enough, and she attributes Ezra's awkward teenage mannerisms to attraction. Her bad experiences while at the Imperial Academy mean that Sabine doesn't like being kept in the dark about things. However, a shared experience on a monster-filled asteroid helps her to put more faith in Hera's leadership.

As the battle against the Empire drags on, Sabine learns that she cannot escape her past. Ezra's encounters with Maul lead Sabine to find the Darksaber, an ancient Mandalorian weapon that Maul stole from her people during the Clone Wars.

Trials on Atollon
Thanks to Kanan's training, Sabine develops her own fighting style with the Darksaber on Atollon.

She trains with Kanan Jarrus to become an adept lightsaber wielder and decides to use the Darksaber to rally her people.

Sabine's return to her family on Mandalore is a cold one. Mandalore remains loyal to the Empire and Sabine's defection from the Academy is a serious embarrassment to her mother, Ursa, the leader of Clan Wren. Sabine defeats Imperial Viceroy Gar Saxon in combat, a symbolic victory against the Empire's puppet ruler that returns her family to a place of respect among the other clans. She declines to become Mandalore's new leader, but stays on her homeworld for a time to help fight in a civil war against Saxon's brother and the remaining Imperial troops.

Sabine's Mandalorian forces prove vital during the Battle of Atollon. Their arrival to combat the Imperial fleet allows the surviving rebels there to flee the planet. Sabine also displays great leadership qualities by uniting Clan Wren with Clan Kryze—led by Bo-Katan Kryze. Sabine turns the Empire's Arc Pulse Generator (a weapon she designed years before) against Imperial troops, ensuring their victory over Clan Saxon and ending the civil war on Mandalore. Sabine gives Bo-Katan the Darksaber, installing her as leader of the Mandalorian clans.

With her family ties reestablished, Sabine returns to her adoptive family to help fight the Empire across the galaxy. She helps Ezra liberate Lothal from the Empire, but when Ezra calls upon a pod of purrgil to destroy the Imperial fleet, he disappears afterward with the creatures. To honor her missing friend, Sabine remains on Lothal, living in Ezra's old home to keep an eye on the planet and protect it. After the Galactic Civil War, Ahsoka Tano and Sabine set off to find Ezra.

Old friend
Sabine meets her old friend Ketsu Onyo during a mission to rescue a rebel courier. Onyo is a bounty hunter trying to capture the courier, but Sabine persuades Onyo to abandon the bounty and help her instead.

EZRA BRIDGER

APPEARANCES Reb, FoD **SPECIES** Human
HOMEWORLD Lothal **AFFILIATION** Rebel Alliance

Ezra's parents, Mira and Ephraim Bridger, disappear when he is 7 years old, taken by the Empire for sending illegal broadcasts over the HoloNet. Growing up, Ezra manages on his own, taking odd jobs for shady characters like Ferpil Wallaway or Bossk the bounty hunter and stealing to survive. He lives in an abandoned communications tower just outside of Capital City, where he keeps his Imperial helmet collection, a small speeder, and pilfered gadgets. He has little hope for the future until he encounters a group of rebels. Ezra falls in with Kanan Jarrus, Hera Syndulla, Zeb Orrelios, Sabine Wren, and their droid, Chopper, when he tries to steal the same Imperial speeder shipment they are after. Having boarded their ship, the *Ghost*, to escape pursuing TIE fighters, Ezra finds his life changed forever.

The rebels become like a family to Ezra. Kanan recognizes Ezra's abilities to sense things before they happen and perform extraordinary physical feats. When Ezra finds Kanan's lightsaber and activates his Jedi holocron with the Force, Hera encourages Kanan to take Ezra on as his Padawan. Ezra shows promise right away, but he is undisciplined and impatient, and his ability to manipulate the Force is erratic, coming in powerful bursts that concern Kanan. With Kanan's help, Ezra locates a hidden Jedi temple where Ezra confronts his fears, attachments, and his desire for revenge against those responsible for his parents' disappearance. He also finds a kyber crystal and builds his own unusual lightsaber.

Soon after, the *Ghost* crew hacks the holonet and Ezra broadcasts an inspirational message of rebellion that is spread across the sector. However, Kanan is captured in the process, so the rebels launch a desperate rescue mission to Mustafar. Thanks to the help of a rebel cell named Phoenix Squadron, they are successful and join the group afterward. The crew also meets former Jedi Ahsoka Tano, who becomes another of Ezra's mentors.

After escaping Darth Vader himself on Lothal, Ezra doesn't return to his homeworld for some time. Eventually, he travels back and meets former Governor Ryder Azadi, who tells Ezra that his parents heard his speech and launched a prison break. They helped to free other prisoners, but lost their lives. Ezra comes to accept their fate and helps secure reinforcement corvettes for Phoenix Squadron from Princess Leia Organa. On a subsequent mission to steal fuel for the *Ghost*, Ezra bonds with a pod of purrgil, whale-like beasts that travel through hyperspace.

Seeking to destroy the Sith, Ezra uses the Force to commune with Yoda, who informs him that he may find answers on Malachor. Alongside Kanan and Ahsoka, Ezra enters the Sith temple on the planet. He encounters the mysterious Maul, who attempts to claim Ezra as his young apprentice. Ezra manages to secure a Sith holocron and faces Vader once again in battle. Vader destroys Ezra's first lightsaber and Ezra only escapes thanks to Ahsoka, who remains to duel the Sith and never rejoins the rebels.

Following the mission to Malachor, Ezra builds a new, more traditional, lightsaber. He is later promoted to lieutenant commander and entrusted with leading his first mission to Reklam Station, where his team must steal Y-wings. Unfortunately, it doesn't go to plan, and Ezra's command is suspended. Soon after, Maul kidnaps Ezra's friends, demanding his help in exchange for their lives. Together, Maul and Ezra merge a Jedi and Sith holocron and discover that Obi-Wan Kenobi is alive on Tatooine. Ezra heads to the planet to warn Obi-Wan about Maul, but the Jedi Master proves more than capable of dispatching the former Sith Lord.

All of Ezra's training and experience helps him when he returns to his homeworld to free it from the Empire, alongside the rest of the *Ghost* crew. Partway through their campaign, Kanan sacrifices himself to save Hera, Ezra, and Sabine from death. While upset at his mentor's passing, Ezra has a vision of a talking Loth-Wolf named Dume, who tells Ezra that he needs to head to the former Jedi Temple to protect it. There, he enters the World between Worlds, a place in the Force where one can alter past events, and saves Ahsoka from being killed by Vader on Malachor. Together, they stop Darth Sidious from gaining control of the dimension. The Sith Lord later attempts to win Ezra over by showing him a vision of his parents. Displaying great maturity, Ezra knows he has to let go of the past and does not fall for the Sith's ruse. Ezra then confronts Grand Admiral Thrawn on the bridge of the Star Destroyer *Chimaera* and reveals his secret plan. Arriving out of hyperspace, a pod of purrgil lays waste to Thrawn's blockade. The creatures entangle the *Chimaera*, which is launched into hyperspace. Thrawn and Ezra are carried at lightspeed to an unknown destination. Ezra's sacrifice allows his ragtag group of allies to free Lothal of Imperial oppression at last.

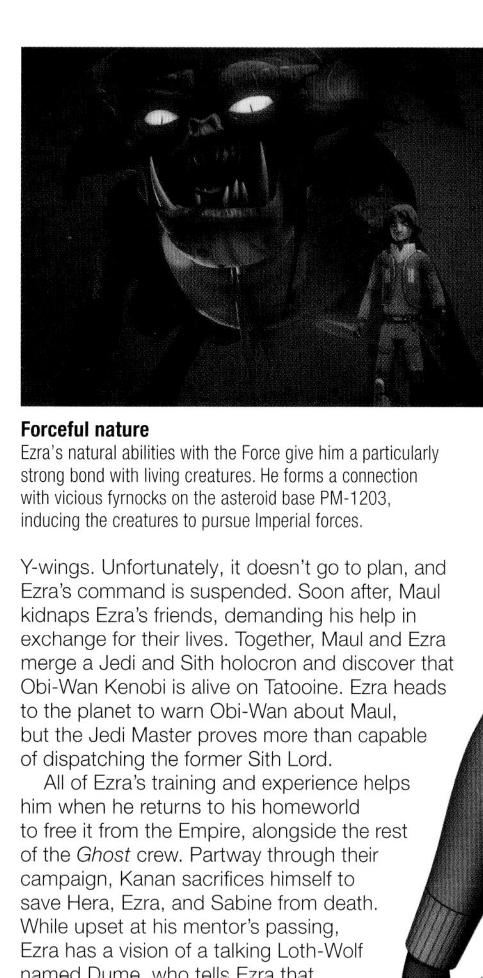

Forceful nature
Ezra's natural abilities with the Force give him a particularly strong bond with living creatures. He forms a connection with vicious fyrnocks on the asteroid base PM-1203, inducing the creatures to pursue Imperial forces.

Capable hero
During his time with the *Ghost* crew, Ezra matures into a confident and capable rebel leader, who secures a significant rebel victory against the Empire on Lothal.

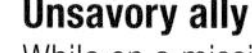

Unsavory ally
While on a mission, Ezra meets Hondo Ohnaka for the first time. The untrustworthy pirate declares Ezra the first "pirate Jedi." Hondo is fond of Ezra and joins his fight to free Lothal.

BARON VALEN RUDOR

APPEARANCES Reb **SPECIES** Human **HOMEWORLD** Corulag **AFFILIATION** Empire

Baron Valen Rudor, code name "LS-607," is a highly decorated TIE fighter pilot of Lothal's Imperial Navy. He is cocky, self-obsessed, and insufferably arrogant. Nonetheless, he has terrible luck and is increasingly bitter about it. His constant run-ins with the rebels always end badly. On his first encounter, he is shot down by the *Ghost*, and when Ezra Bridger finds his crashed TIE, Ezra steals Rudor's helmet and flight gadgets. Zeb Orrelios also separates Rudor from his ship more than once, and his chance to fly the latest TIE Advanced is sabotaged on Empire Day.

Years later, Rudor is given Old Jho's Pit Stop to run after its former owner is executed for being a rebel operative. He is suspicious of two citizens in his bar, who are actually Ezra and his fellow rebel Sabine Wren in disguise. Rudor nearly orders their arrest, but relents when Lothal resident Jai Kell gives him a sum of credits. When the Lothal rebels use an unsealed hatch in the Pit Stop to escape through the sewers, Rudor informs the investigating death trooper that he had no clue the hatch wasn't sealed.

"You'll be sorry! Or dead, you'll be dead!"

VALEN RUDOR

MYLES GRINT

APPEARANCES Reb **SPECIES** Human **HOMEWORLD** Lothal **AFFILIATION** Empire

Taskmaster Myles Grint is a man of few words who relies on his size to intimidate others on Lothal. He follows Commandant Aresko's lead and bullies both citizens and officers of lower rank. Fortunately, his incompetence contributes to the rebels' ability to operate successfully on Lothal. When Governor Tarkin arrives, he orders the Inquisitor to put a decisive end to Grint's succession of mistakes.

Unpleasant demeanor
Grint is always ready to bully lower-ranking officers and the citizens of Lothal when asked.

Bullying the locals
Grint samples a jogan fruit while he and Commandant Aresko harass a vendor in one of the capital's open markets.

CUMBERLAYNE ARESKO

APPEARANCES Reb **SPECIES** Human **HOMEWORLD** Lothal **AFFILIATION** Empire

Commandant Cumberlayne Aresko is an egotistical and unsympathetic manager of military operations on Lothal. Together with Taskmaster Grint, he oversees the local Imperial Academy and ceremonies on Empire Day. Aresko overestimates his own importance, however. He is not as clever as he imagines himself, which is a failing that contributes to his eventual downfall. He first informs Agent Kallus of the rebel activity in the capital, and when he repeatedly fails to put a stop to it, the Inquisitor hastens the end of his career.

YOGAR LYSTE

APPEARANCES Reb **SPECIES** Human **HOMEWORLD** Garel **AFFILIATION** Empire

Supply Master Yogar Lyste is an ambitious young Imperial officer posted on Lothal, charged with overseeing supplies on the planet. He also occasionally transports prisoners. His duties are continually disrupted by the rebels, which only inspires him to redouble his efforts. After the Siege of Lothal, he hosts Princess Leia Organa when she arrives on Lothal with three cruisers. Leia claims that the ships contain aid for Lothal's citizens, but Lyste is suspicious, so he orders the ships impounded. He fails to prevent the rebels stealing the vessels or to uncover Leia's duplicity. When Grand Admiral Thrawn arrives, Lyste assists him when he investigates sabotage at the Imperial Armory Complex. Later, Agent Kallus, who is secretly a rebel agent, frames Lyste as a spy to escape capture. Lyste is dragged away to an unknown fate.

IMPERIAL COMBAT DRIVER

APPEARANCES Reb **SPECIES** Human **HOMEWORLD** Various **AFFILIATION** Empire

Imperial combat pilots are well trained at the Imperial academies and envied by stormtroopers for their well-armored vehicles. These overconfident pilots are required to drive a range of vehicles, including speeders and Imperial troop transports, but there are specialized corps for some walkers and tanks. The smart drivers wear body armor to protect them from potential armed resistance.

CIKATRO VIZAGO

APPEARANCES Reb **SPECIES** Devaronian **HOMEWORLD** Devaron **AFFILIATION** Broken Horn Syndicate, Lothal rebels

Kingpin of Lothal's underworld, Cikatro Vizago is head of the Broken Horn Syndicate. Vizago deals in black market goods, particularly stolen Imperial weapons shipments. The crew of the *Ghost* often runs missions and trades with him for cash, supplies, or valuable information. When *Ghost* crewmember Kanan Jarrus is kidnapped by the Inquisitor, Vizago offers Ezra Bridger a lead in exchange for a favor at some point. Later, Vizago takes a mission from crime lord Azmorigan, but ends up being tricked by notorious pirate Hondo Ohnaka and imprisoned aboard his own ship, the *Broken Horn*. With Ezra's help, Vizago reclaims his ship and expels the intruders. Vizago later tries to smuggle the *Ghost* crew to Lothal in exchange for a number of puffer pigs. When the rebels are noticed by the Empire they manage to escape, but Vizago isn't so lucky. He is captured and forced to work on a Mining Guild ore crawler that is soon taken over by the rebels. Then, Vizago joins the rebellion and helps to liberate Lothal from the Empire.

Discreet gangster
Vizago examines a stolen shipment of E-11 blasters brought to him by Kanan Jarrus.

Smart operator
With rarely a hair out of place, Kallus takes his personal grooming very seriously.

Loyal leader in charge
Kallus orders his troops to fire on the Jedi *(left)* and contacts the Inquisitor about the Jedi *(above)*.

ALEXSANDR KALLUS

APPEARANCES Reb **SPECIES** Human
HOMEWORLD Coruscant
AFFILIATION Empire, Rebel Alliance

Agent Alexsandr Kallus is a member of the Imperial Security Bureau (ISB), a secret police organization that monitors loyalty to the Empire. He trains under Wulff Yularen, becoming his star pupil. After graduating, Kallus' first mission is to Onderon, where his troops are ambushed by a Lasat warrior. He is paralyzed in the initial foray and is forced to witness the Lasat kill his soldiers. During the sacking of Lasan, Kallus personally orders the use of the horrific T-7 ion disruptors on the Lasat, and is given a bo-rifle by a Lasat Honor Guard that he defeats. Soon after, Kallus and bounty hunter IG-88 fail to capture Han Solo for his actions on Savareen.

Kallus is sent to Lothal to investigate increasing rebel activity. He first encounters the *Ghost* and its crew when they attempt to rescue Wookiee prisoners. Kallus later runs into them again on Kessel, where he discovers Kanan Jarrus is a Jedi and Ezra Bridger is his presumed Padawan. Kallus contacts the Grand Inquisitor to aid in the hunt for the two Jedi. Kallus crosses paths with the rebels next when they attempt to sell some stolen T-7 ion disruptors to a crime lord on Lothal. Kallus infuriates the Lasat rebel Zeb Orrelios when the two cross paths. Kallus nearly beats Zeb in combat, but Ezra saves Zeb at the last possible moment, and the rebels escape.

Despite his best efforts during many encounters, Kallus is unable to destroy the rebel cell on Lothal. Kallus earns Governor Tarkin's displeasure, but is given another chance to prove himself and helps capture Kanan when the rebels broadcast a message on the HoloNet.

After the *Ghost* crew rescues Kanan and leaves Lothal, Kallus confronts them numerous times across the galaxy—including on Seelos, Ibaar, Garel, Nixus, and even in Wild Space. Each time, they continue to elude him. On his final attempt, Kallus tries to trap the rebels on an Imperial construction module orbiting Geonosis. He duels Zeb and follows him into an escape pod. They both end up crash-landing on Bahryn, a frozen moon orbiting Geonosis, and Kallus breaks his leg. They have to work together to survive the hostile environment and the ferocious bonzami inhabiting it. Kallus and Zeb end up bonding, regaling each other with stories of their past. When Zeb is picked up by the rebels, Kallus turns down an offer to join them. He eventually returns to the Empire, although he begins to doubt his affiliation.

Following Bahryn, Kallus becomes an undercover rebel spy. Using the code name "Fulcrum," he secretly supplies information to the rebels, including that there are Imperial pilots willing to defect at Skystrike Academy. When rebel Sabine Wren infiltrates the Academy and locates the would-be rebels, Kallus ensures they all escape, asking Sabine to tell Zeb that they're even now. During Grand Admiral Thrawn's investigation into sabotage on Lothal, Kanan, Ezra, and fellow rebel Chopper are undercover, trying to find out what new, top-secret weapon is being developed there. Kallus reveals to them that he is "Fulcrum."

After the investigation, Thrawn suspects there is an Imperial mole, so calls upon his old ally and Kallus' former mentor Wulff Yularen to help. Upon hearing this, the rebels try to save Kallus, but he stays to help from the inside, implicating Yogar Lyste as the rebel agent. Privately, Thrawn believes Kallus is the mole, so manipulates Kallus into sending a transmission to the rebels. Thrawn apprehends him, revealing that Kallus has accidentally provided Thrawn with the rebel base's location on Atollon. Thrawn captures Kallus and forces him to watch as he attacks the rebels orbiting the planet. When Governor Pryce orders for Kallus to be thrown out of an airlock, Kallus overpowers Pryce's guards. Kallus leaves the ship in an escape pod that is then picked up by the *Ghost* crew during their retreat.

Kallus becomes a captain in the Rebel Alliance based on Yavin 4. He also joins the *Ghost* crew to liberate Lothal from the Empire. At the end of the Galactic Civil War, Zeb takes his now close companion Kallus to Lira San, the previously lost Lasat homeworld where Zeb's people are thriving. Zeb tells the relieved Kallus that he is welcome to live among them.

Rebel at heart
Calling Kallus a traitor, Arindha Pryce orders him to be killed *(left)*. After fighting for the Alliance during the war, Zeb shows Kallus that he hadn't destroyed all of his people *(above)*.

IMPERIAL CADET

APPEARANCES Reb **SPECIES** Human
HOMEWORLD Various **AFFILIATION** Empire

When the Republic is consolidated into the Empire, clone troopers are phased out and a new military force is formed from cadets who enroll in Imperial academies. The main campus is the Royal Imperial Academy on Coruscant. Smaller worlds like Lothal may host junior academies with cadets who go on to serve in local civic roles, or like Zare Leonis, go on to senior academies to be trained as an officer. Notable Imperial academies are located on Arkanis, Corellia, Carida, and Mandalore, among other worlds.

THE GRAND INQUISITOR

APPEARANCES CW, Reb **SPECIES** Pau'an **HOMEWORLD** Utapau **AFFILIATION** Empire

Chains of Command
The Grand Inquisitor is a skilled fighter, and his standing allows him to command the other Inquisitors, stormtroopers and most Imperial officers.

Intelligent and discerning, the Pau'an that becomes the Grand Inquisitor used to be a Jedi Temple guard. While serving the Order, he detests Chief Librarian Jocasta Nu for blocking him from having full access to the Archives. During the Clone Wars, he is one of the guards that brings Jedi Barriss Offee to a military trial, where former Jedi Ahsoka Tano is accused of Offee's crime of bombing the Jedi Temple. Due to the treatment of Barriss and Ahsoka, he becomes disillusioned with the Jedi.

Following Order 66, he is recruited by Darth Sidious and becomes the Grand Inquisitor, responsible for leading the other members of the Inquisitorius. All armed with double-bladed lightsabers, the Inquisitors' initial mission is to kill surviving Jedi. The Grand Inquisitor loses a duel to Darth Vader during their first meeting, and is displeased when Sidious places the Inquisitorius in Vader's charge. On Vader's orders, the Grand Inquisitor reads the Archives to discern any possible leads on the surviving Jedi, developing an encyclopedic knowledge of his former brethren. He is interrupted on one occasion by an irate Nu who duels him because of his lack of respect for the holobooks. He gets the best of her, but is stopped by Vader from delivering the final blow. Confused and angry, the Grand Inquisitor begins fighting his master. Nu takes her chance to wipe the Archives, depriving him of further reading, and then knocks the Inquisitor out by burying him under a pile of holobooks. Vader kills her soon after.

Eventually, the Inquistorius start Project Harvestor to find Force-sensitives to train into future Inquisitors. The group also tries to convert any surviving Jedi, but kills any that refuse. One of these victims is captured Jedi Master Luminara Unduli, who is executed in the Grand Inquisitor's presence in the Spire on Stygeon Prime. He spreads rumors that she is still alive and uses her remains, which have a lingering Force presence, to lure in any surviving Jedi.

A year into the Emperor's reign, the Inquisitorius learns of another possible Jedi survivor on Raada. While the Grand Inquisitor wishes to hunt the target himself, he is required elsewhere so sends the Sixth Brother. When the Grand Inquisitor later travels to Raada, he is displeased to discover that the planet's rebellious farmers and the supposed Jedi, who is actually Ahsoka, have escaped and that the Sixth Brother is dead. The Grand Inquisitor informs Vader that there is evidence of another unknown Jedi survivor.

Years later, the Grand Inquisitor kidnaps Dhara Leonis from Lothal for Project Harvestor, torturing her in a cell on Arkanis. After Imperial Security Bureau Agent Kallus discovers the Jedi Kanan Jarrus and his presumed Padawan, Ezra Bridger, Kallus notifies the Grand Inquisitor, who sets a trap at the Spire, having ensured that Kanan and Ezra believe Unduli is held captive there. Despite having never met Kanan, the Grand Inquisitor identifies Kanan's master as Depa Billaba and the weaknesses of his fighting style. He exploits this knowledge to great effect, and Kanan and Ezra barely escape.

Soon after, the Grand Inquisitor visits the Lothal Academy to discover if two recruits are Force-sensitive. He finds out that one of them, Dev Morgan, is actually Ezra Bridger on a rebel mission. Ezra escapes alongside another potential recruit. The Grand Inquisitor also meets Zare Leonis, who is Dhara's brother and claims to be Force-sensitive. Following the Empire Day celebrations, the Grand Inquisitor tracks Kanan and Ezra to Fort Anaxes where he duels them. Ezra brushes with the dark side in order to save Kanan and evade him. Then, the Grand Inquisitor transfers Zare to the Arkanis Academy to see if he is Force-sensitive and a rebel. He begins extracting information from Zare, but he has to return to Lothal suddenly, stopping their discussion.

Later, Kanan allows himself to be captured in order to save his friends and is interrogated by the Grand Inquisitor in a failed attempt to see if the Jedi is linked to a larger rebellion. After being freed from his cell by Ezra, Kanan finally proves himself a Jedi Knight when he defeats the Grand Inquisitor, who willingly falls to his death. He warns Kanan that he has no idea what he has unleashed and that some things are more frightening than death.

The Inquisitor's trap
Kanan Jarrus and the Inquisitor duel in the crypt of Jedi Luminara Unduli at the Imperial prison on Stygeon Prime.

MAKETH TUA

APPEARANCES Reb **SPECIES** Human
HOMEWORLD Lothal **AFFILIATION** Empire

Minister Maketh Tua is a government official who often serves as a stand-in for Governor Arihnda Pryce, where she is charged with protecting the Empire's industrial interests. Tua presides over Lothal's Empire Day celebrations when Pryce is invited to Coruscant for the occasion. She introduces Sienar Fleet Systems' new advanced TIE fighter and its pilot, Baron Valen Rudor, but things go horribly wrong when the *Ghost* crew attack. After Tua and Agent Kallus fail multiple times to capture the rebels, Grand Moff Tarkin arrives on Lothal to personally put a stop to the rebellion. Tua is horrified when he orders the execution of two Imperial officers in front of her. Fearing for her life after a visit from Darth Vader, Tua tries to defect by offering the *Ghost* crew information on rebel sympathizers and the Emperor's plans for Lothal. The Empire expects her betrayal and rigs her shuttle to explode, killing Tua just as the *Ghost* crew try to extract her.

Imperial proxy
Though patriotic, Maketh Tua is nonetheless a self-absorbed and ineffectual leader.

GALL TRAYVIS

APPEARANCES Reb **SPECIES** Human
HOMEWORLD Unknown **AFFILIATION** Empire

Gall Trayvis appears to be a renegade, on-the-run senator who transmits anti-Imperial broadcasts over the HoloNet, inspiring rebels across the galaxy. At times, he encourages protest, such as boycotting Empire Day; at other times, he passes on valuable information. He informs the *Ghost* crew that Jedi Luminara Unduli is being held prisoner at the Imperial prison on Stygeon Prime. Later, he hints at a secret visit he plans to make on Lothal. During his trip, however, Trayvis reveals he is a double agent, serving the Empire, so the *Ghost* crew leave him behind. Trayvis is later interviewed on HoloNet News, stating that he is committed once more to the Empire and denouncing the Lothal rebels.

ZARE LEONIS

APPEARANCES Reb **SPECIES** Human
HOMEWORLD Uquine **AFFILIATION** *Ghost* crew

Originally from a Core World, Zare Leonis and his family settle quickly on Lothal. Zare befriends fellow grav-ball teammembers Merei Spanjaf and Beck Ollet. After Zare enters the Junior Academy for Applied Sciences, his sister Dhara, training at Lothal's Academy for Young Imperials, mysteriously disappears. Zare and Ollet later witness Imperial stormtroopers firing on non-violent protesters, which inspires Ollet to rebel against the Empire and leads to his arrest.

A year later, Zare enters the Imperial Academy, secretly hoping to discover Dhara's fate. When Ezra Bridger goes undercover at the Academy, Zare helps him steal an Imperial decoder. Determined to find his sister, Zare stays at the Academy, feigning firing at Ezra and Jai Kell when they escape. Zare is commended for trying to stop them, and receives a visit from the Grand Inquisitor himself who wants to hear about his former friends. Zare mentions his sister Dhara and pretends to be Force-sensitive. Following this meeting, Zare provides intel to Ezra's rebel group.

Soon after, the Grand Inquisitor returns and announces that Zare is being transferred to the prestigious Academy on Arkanis, where Zare believes Dhara is being held. Zare joins the exclusive Commandant's Cadets group by pretending to kill a fellow cadet, whom he actually helps escape. Zare meets Ollet, who has been brainwashed, once more and reveals that Zare is a traitor. For his final meal before his execution, Zare requests Ollet's presence and he manages to break Ollet's brainwashing. Together, they get Zare out of his cell, and Spanjaf and Ezra's rebels arrive to rescue him. Zare manages to find Dhara, and they escape the Academy, thanks to Ollet's sacrifice, with their rescuers. The siblings are transported to Garel, where they are reunited with their parents. Working alongside the Statura family and the Spanjafs, the Leonises dedicate themselves to freeing Garel from Imperial occupation.

Proud display
Zare wears a cadet uniform and helmet from the Imperial Academy. The gray and white uniforms are symbols of unity, solidarity, discipline, and prestige.

FYRNOCK

APPEARANCES Reb **HOMEWORLD** Asteroids
SIZE Variable **HABITAT** Shadows, caves

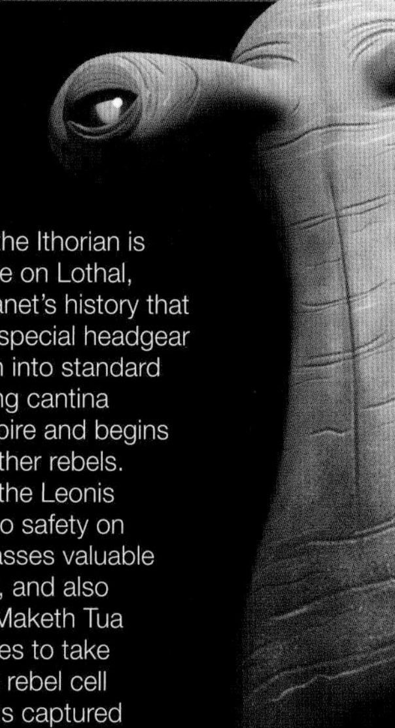

Fyrnocks are silicon-based life-forms that live on large asteroids with thin atmospheres. Afraid of the light, they dwell in shadows and hibernate for long periods until disturbed, when they spring awake and attack prey with their sharp claws and teeth. Their meals are infrequent; they feed mostly on mynocks, small space slugs, and other creatures of the asteroid belts. When Sabine Wren and Hera Syndulla are stranded on an old Republic asteroid base, they are swarmed by fyrnocks that have infested the facility. The two barely escape, but Kanan Jarrus notes the location in case the creatures could be useful later.

OLD JHO

APPEARANCES Reb
SPECIES Ithorian
HOMEWORLD Ithor
AFFILIATION Lothal rebels

Owner of Old Jho's Pit Stop, the Ithorian is one of the first settlers to arrive on Lothal, and there is little about the planet's history that he doesn't know. Jho carries special headgear that translates Ithorian speech into standard Basic. The wise and fascinating cantina owner has no love for the Empire and begins helping the *Ghost* crew and other rebels. Jho uses his freighter to ferry the Leonis family and the Spanjaf family to safety on Garel. He also occasionally passes valuable information to the *Ghost* crew, and also puts willing Imperial defector Maketh Tua in touch with them. Jho decides to take an active role in Ryder Azadi's rebel cell on Lothal. Unfortunately, Jho is captured when trying to help the group escape a raid and is executed by the Empire.

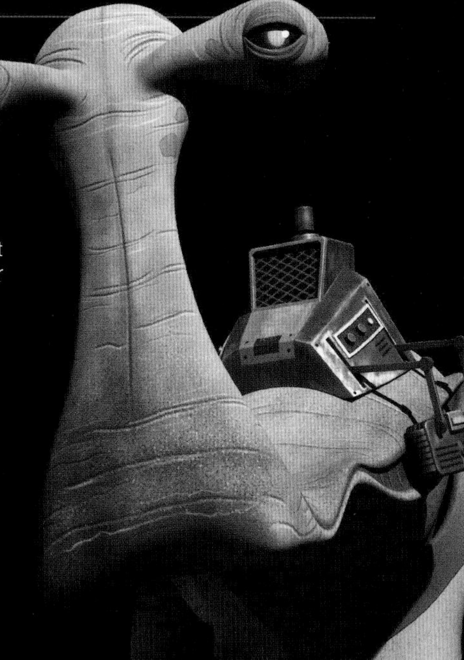

LOTH-CAT

APPEARANCES Reb **HOMEWORLD** Lothal
AVERAGE SIZE 0.94 m (3 ft 1 in) long
HABITAT Grasslands

Loth-cats are small predators that live in family groups. Their striped brown coats allow them to blend into Lothal's grassy plains where they hunt Loth-rats and other pests. It is believed that Loth-cats may be the wild ancestors of tookas, a feline species commonly found on Coruscant. Loth-cats are curious and often friendly—they've even been known to "adopt" wayward droids. Stormtroopers find them to be a nuisance, however, and sometimes use the quick-footed, temperamental cats for target practice.

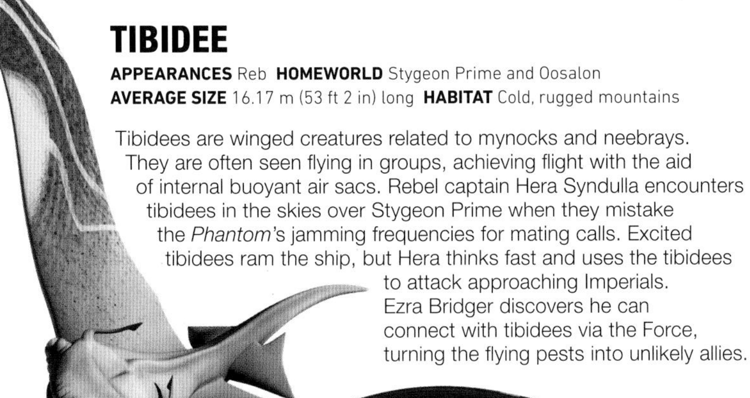

TIBIDEE

APPEARANCES Reb **HOMEWORLD** Stygeon Prime and Oosalon
AVERAGE SIZE 16.17 m (53 ft 2 in) long **HABITAT** Cold, rugged mountains

Tibidees are winged creatures related to mynocks and neebrays. They are often seen flying in groups, achieving flight with the aid of internal buoyant air sacs. Rebel captain Hera Syndulla encounters tibidees in the skies over Stygeon Prime when they mistake the *Phantom*'s jamming frequencies for mating calls. Excited tibidees ram the ship, but Hera thinks fast and uses the tibidees to attack approaching Imperials. Ezra Bridger discovers he can connect with tibidees via the Force, turning the flying pests into unlikely allies.

JAI KELL

APPEARANCES Reb **SPECIES** Human
HOMEWORLD Lothal
AFFILIATION Empire, rebels

Jai Kell is a cadet at Lothal's Academy for Young Imperials. When Ezra Bridger infiltrates the Academy pretending to be a cadet, he accidentally draws dangerous attention to Jai. The Imperial leaders suspect Jai might be Force-sensitive, so call upon the Grand Inquisitor to investigate. Ezra and fellow cadet Zare Leonis help Jai escape. At the time, Jai resents Ezra and Zare for ruining his Imperial career, but he ends up joining Lothal's rebels and helping to liberate his homeworld.

ADMIRAL KASSIUS KONSTANTINE

APPEARANCES Reb **SPECIES** Human
HOMEWORLD Coruscant **AFFILIATION** Empire

Konstantine is an arrogant admiral in the Imperial Navy, serving under ISB Agent Kallus, the Inquisitors, and Grand Admiral Thrawn at various times. He repeatedly fails to stop the rebels in the Lothal system and Iron Squadron at Mykapo. His blunders are topped by his refusal to obey Thrawn's orders at the Battle of Atollon. There, he pursues rebel Commander Sato's ship, *Phoenix Nest*, which rams the admiral's *Interdictor*-class Star Destroyer and destroys them both, bringing an end to Konstantine's military career and his life.

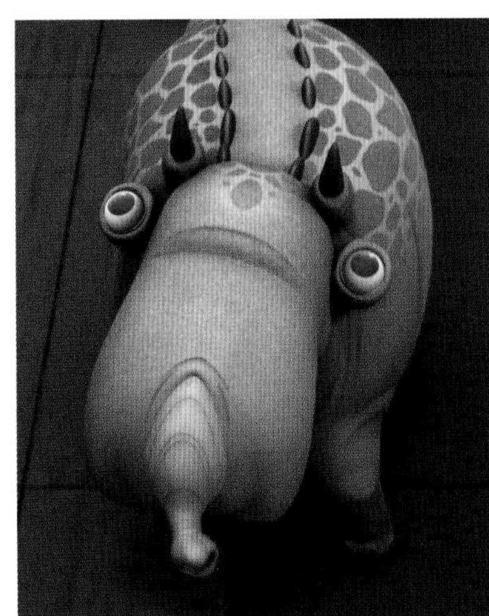

PUFFER PIG

APPEARANCES Reb
HOMEWORLD Various
AVERAGE SIZE 0.9 m (2 ft 11 in) long
HABITAT Captivity (farms and mining operations)

Puffer pigs are domesticated livestock valued by the Mining Guild for their ability to sniff out costly mineral deposits. Their bacon is also prized as food. Puffer pigs have the odd habit of inflating to many times their original size when they are startled. Lando Calrissian acquires a puffer pig from Azmorigan (to use in his new Lothal mining venture), and relies on the *Ghost* crew to smuggle it through Lothal's Imperial blockade. The crew later smuggles the pigs once more, selling them to Cikatro Vizago.

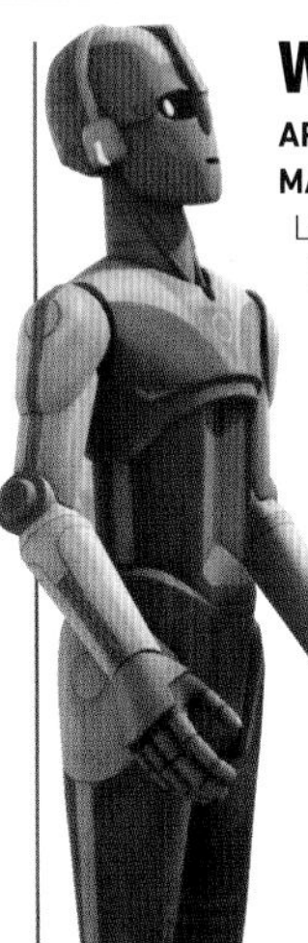

W1-LE

APPEARANCES Reb
MANUFACTURER Lothal Logistics Limited **TYPE** Modified RQ protocol droid

Lando Calrissian has owned "Willie" (W1-LE) since the Clone Wars. His memory was transferred from another droid into his current RQ protocol droid shell. Willie manages the operations at Lando's mining camp on Lothal and stands in for his boss, Lando, when he is away.

BROM TITUS

APPEARANCES Reb
SPECIES Human
AFFILIATION Empire

Brom Titus is an unlucky admiral in the Imperial Navy. He oversees an experimental gravity well test program, but his ship is destroyed by Commander Sato's rebel cell. His Reklam Station is also wrecked by Ezra Bridger, and his ship, the *Marauder*, is destroyed by rebel leader, Saw Gerrera.

AZMORIGAN

APPEARANCES Reb **SPECIES** Jablogian
HOMEWORLD Nar Shaddaa **AFFILIATION** Slaver

Lando Calrissian makes a deal with the repulsive kingpin, Azmorigan, to acquire a puffer pig in exchange for a slave. Lando manipulates rebel leader Hera Syndulla into playing along. Hera escapes, however, and leaves Azmorigan holding a serious grudge against them all. He gets a chance to settle this grudge when instead of dealing with crime lord Cikatro Vizago during a deal, he is unexpectedly confronted by *Ghost* crewmember Ezra Bridger and wanted pirate Hondo Ohnaka. Azmorigan tries to kill them, but they escape with his goods and credits. Much later, Azmorigan lets his grudges with Hondo and the *Ghost* crew slide in order to smuggle goods off a stranded Imperial cargo ship orbiting Wynkahthu.

JUN SATO

APPEARANCES Reb **SPECIES** Human
HOMEWORLD Mykapo **AFFILIATION** Rebels

Jun Sato is the leader of the Phoenix rebel cell and an ally of Bail Organa and Ahsoka Tano. Sato commands the Phoenix Squadron of A-wings from his ship, *Phoenix Home*, which is later destroyed by Darth Vader. Afterward, Sato bases his command aboard the *Liberator*, and later *Phoenix Nest*. Sato welcomes the crew of the *Ghost* into his cell, and Hera Syndulla soon leads his starfighter squadron. Sato establishes a rebel base on Atollon, but when Imperial Grand Admiral Thrawn attacks, Sato sacrifices his own life so that Ezra Bridger can escape to help.

JOOPA

APPEARANCES Reb **HOMEWORLD** Seelos **AVERAGE SIZE** 21 m (68 ft 11 in) long **HABITAT** Underground

Fearsome wormlike creatures named joopas live under the salt crusts of Seelos. They have an array of red eyes and a gaping mouth lined with mandibles. Joopas sense their prey by feeling their vibrations. The joopa thrusts its slimy tongue to the surface, wraps it around its unsuspecting prey, and yanks it underground. When Captain Rex, Wolffe, and Gregor retire to Seelos, they spend their days "slinging" (fishing) for joopas. The giant worms are a prize delicacy and the clones recruit rebel Zeb Orrelios to help, though he is nearly eaten alive.

EG-86

APPEARANCES Reb **MODEL** EG-series power droid **AFFILIATION** Rebels

Friendly and keen, EG-86 is a rebel courier droid who is transporting secret information when he arrives on Garel. Thanks to the help of the *Ghost* crew, he completes his mission and delivers the intel to R2-D2 on Havoc Outpost.

QUARRIE

APPEARANCES Reb **SPECIES** Mon Calamari **HOMEWORD** Mon Cala **AFFILIATION** Rebels

Quarrie is a Mon Calamari shipwright who resides on Shantipole where Hera Syndulla and her crew seek his help. He provides them with his Blade Wing prototype and upgrades their shuttle. Later, he helps the rebels turn his prototype into the manufacturable B-wing starfighter line.

FIFTH BROTHER

APPEARANCES Reb **SPECIES** Unknown **HOMEWORLD** Unknown **AFFILIATION** Inquisitorius

A former Jedi, the Fifth Brother joins the Emperor's organization of Inquisitors. He is tasked with hunting down surviving Jedi, serving first under the Grand Inquisitor and then Darth Vader. The arrogant, brutish Fifth Brother is given charge of Admiral Konstantine, and, along with the Seventh Sister, is ordered to capture Kanan Jarrus and Ezra Bridger and locate Ahsoka Tano. After repeated failures, the Inquisitors track them to Malachor and summon Vader. However, the Fifth Brother is bested by Maul in lightsaber combat.

SEVENTH SISTER

APPEARANCES Reb **SPECIES** Mirialan **HOMEWORLD** Mirial **AFFILIATION** Inquisitorius

A former member of the Jedi Order, the Seventh Sister joins the Inquisitors after the Empire is founded. She employs some unusual methods on her missions, including the use of ID9 seeker droids for recon and a unique Force ability that enables her to deliver painful scratches to opponents. The Seventh Sister is also under orders to locate Force-sensitive children. When the Grand Inquisitor is defeated, she hopes in vain to replace him. The Seventh Sister is ordered to pursue Kanan Jarrus, Ezra Bridger, and Ahsoka Tano. While on their trail, she is eliminated by Maul on Malachor.

KETSU ONYO

APPEARANCES Reb, FoD **SPECIES** Human **HOMEWORLD** Shukut **AFFILIATION** Black Sun, rebels

Ketsu Onyo is a former Imperial Cadet and artist on Mandalore. She and her friend, Sabine Wren, escape the academy and become bounty hunters. After a disagreement, Ketsu leaves Sabine for dead and joins the criminal organization Black Sun. The two meet again when Ketsu is contracted by Black Sun to retrieve rebel droid EG-86 on Garel. They fight at first, but after being forced to work together, part on good terms. Though Ketsu declines Sabine's initial offer to join the rebels, she later agrees to sign up. Ketsu helps her allies obtain much needed fuel, facilitating their escape from Grand Admiral Thrawn on Atollon, and later joins the team that frees Lothal.

RYDER AZADI

APPEARANCES Reb **SPECIES** Human **HOMEWORLD** Lothal **AFFILIATION** Rebels

Ryder Azadi is the Governor of Lothal until he is deposed by the machinations of Arindha Pryce. He supports the dissident broadcasts of Ephraim and Mira Bridger. They all end up imprisoned together, however when they escape, the Bridgers are killed. After seeing a Force vision of his parents, Ezra follows a mysterious white Loth-Cat to Ryder, who informs Ezra of his parents' fate. Ryder builds a small resistance movement on Lothal and aids the *Ghost* crew. Ryder and his Lothal rebels later liberate their world from Imperial control with the help of Ezra and the rest of his crew.

WHITE LOTH-CAT

APPEARANCES Reb **HOMEWORLD** Lothal **AVERAGE SIZE** 0.94 m (3 ft 1 in) **HABITAT** Grasslands

Ezra Bridger meets a mysterious white Loth-cat that acts as a guide for him and seems to have a strong connection to the Force. In their first encounter, the Loth-cat leads Ezra to the former Lothal Governor, Ryder Azadi (Ryder and the Loth-cat are friends). On their next meeting, the cat helps Ezra and Sabine Wren hide a hyperdrive from a crashed TIE/d defender elite. The Loth-cat also introduces Ezra to a white Loth-wolf, another creature with a very strong Force connection. On their third meeting, the Loth-cat helps Ezra and Zeb Orrelios relocate their hyperdrive.

FENN RAU

APPEARANCES Reb **SPECIES** Human **HOMEWORLD** Concord Dawn **AFFILIATION** Republic, Journeyman Protectors, rebels

Fenn Rau serves the Republic during the Clone Wars, helping to train clone pilots and fighting alongside them. During the Imperial era, Rau serves as leader of the Journeyman Protectors who guard the planet Concord Dawn. When the rebels seek safe passage past his planet, Rau and the Protectors attack. The skirmish ends with Rau captured. Rau discovers that Viceroy Gar Saxon has destroyed the Protectors, so he joins the rebels and helps train Sabine Wren. Later, he aids them on missions and supports Bo-Katan Kryze as leader of the Mandalorians.

CHAVA

APPEARANCES Reb **SPECIES** Lasat
HOMEWORLD Lasan **AFFILIATION** Lasats

The old shaman known as "Chava the Wise" is a refugee from the planet Lasan after it was destroyed by the Empire. She and her companion, the High Honor Guardsman Gron, are rescued by the crew of the *Ghost*. Well versed in the prophecies of her people, Chava believes fellow Lasat Zeb Orrelios is the key to finding their new homeworld. Together, they embark on a treacherous journey to Lira San, the legendary refuge of their people. Chava and Gron settle there with millions of other Lasats, later welcoming Zeb back, along with his friend, Alexsandr Kallus.

PURRGIL

APPEARANCES Reb
HOMEWORLD Deep space
AVERAGE SIZE 5.5 m (18 ft 1 in) high, 30 m (98 ft 5 in) long **HABITAT** Space (attracted to gas deposits)

Large whalelike creatures known as purrgil have long been a menace to deep-space travelers. They float into hyperspace lanes and cause collisions that tear ships apart. The rebel crew of the *Ghost* encounters a pod of these intelligent creatures flocking to a deposit of Clouzon-36 gas at a Mining Guild refinery. Purrgil breathe the gas, which they use as biofuel to travel through hyperspace. Ezra Bridger develops a strong bond with the purrgil king and his pod. Ezra later calls on the purrgil to pull Grand Admiral Thrawn and himself into the great unknown.

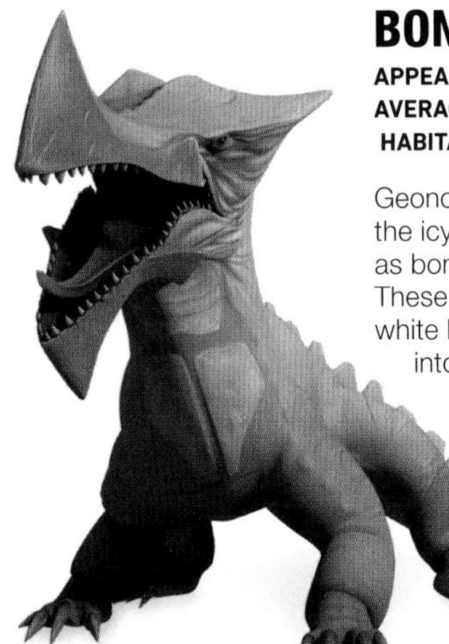

BONZAMI

APPEARANCES Reb **HOMEWORLD** Bahryn
AVERAGE SIZE 4.75 m (15 ft 7 in) high, 13 m (42 ft 8 in) long
HABITAT Subterranean ice caverns

Geonosis is orbited by 15 moons, one of which is the icy Bahryn. Large, armor-plated beasts known as bonzami live in cave systems on the moon's surface. These predators hunt both alone and in packs. Short, white hair covers their armor and allows them to blend into their icy habitat, should they encounter prey that can see in the dark. Their steady footsteps and loud screeches give warning as they approach. ISB Agent Kallus and the rebel Zeb Orrelios survive an encounter with a bonzami when they are marooned on Bahryn together.

KRYKNA

APPEARANCES Reb **HOMEWORLD** Atollon
AVERAGE SIZE 2 m (6 ft 7 in) high **HABITAT** Deserts and caves

Large, spiderlike predators called krykna wander the barren wastes of Atollon, hunting snaillike dokmas. They live in underground colonies where they store food and lay their eggs. When Commander Sato's rebel cell establishes a base on Atollon, the fierce krykna pose an immediate problem. The rebels discover that the krykna are repelled by sensor beacons, so they set up a beacon perimeter to hold the creatures at bay. Kanan Jarrus and Ezra Bridger are unable to connect with the creatures via the Force. It is only when an ancient being known as the Bendu teaches Kanan to rid himself of negative emotions that they are able to calm the krykna.

AP-5

APPEARANCES Reb **MANUFACTURER** Arakyd Industries **TYPE** RA-7 protocol droid
AFFILIATION Empire, Rebels

The protocol droid AP-5 is a military analyst for the Republic during the Clone Wars. When the Republic is transformed into the Empire, AP-5 is relegated to tracking inventory aboard Imperial Cargo Transport 241. He befriends the rebel droid Chopper when he finds him stowed away aboard the ship. AP-5 defects to join the rebels and provides them with an excellent location for their new rebel base on Atollon. AP-5 remains loyal to his new rebel friends, keeping inventory on their base before relocating with them to Yavin 4.

Face-to-face
Bendu is incredibly large, dwarfing Kanan and Ezra.

MORAI

APPEARANCES Reb **HOMEWORLD** Unknown
AVERAGE SIZE 0.2 m (7.9 in) long
HABITAT Unrestricted by habitat

A mysterious convor bird named Morai follows Ahsoka Tano across the galaxy, watching over her. The creature has a strong connection to the Force and a spiritual link to the Daughter of Mortis. Morai can be seen with depictions of the Daughter, and may be either her servant or a manifestation of the powerful Force wielder. Morai is present in the "World between Worlds" when Ezra Bridger enters via the Lothal Jedi temple, and she encourages him to save Ahsoka from certain death at the hands of Darth Vader.

BENDU

APPEARANCES Reb **SPECIES** Unknown **HOMEWORLD** Atollon **AFFILIATION** The Force

Bendu is an ancient creature with a powerful connection to the Force. He is attuned to the "middle," with neither an affinity to the light (Ashla) nor the dark (Bogan) side. Bendu is friendly to Kanan Jarrus and Ezra Bridger. He serves as a mentor to Kanan, until the Jedi oversteps his bounds and calls Bendu a coward for not intervening in the Battle of Atollon. Bendu manifests a great storm about him and unleashes his power upon Thrawn's forces and the rebels alike, demanding that they all leave his world. Thrawn commands his AT-ATs to fire at the heart of the storm, sending Bendu crashing to the ground. One with the Force, Bendu utters a prophecy of Thrawn's demise (which comes true), just before vanishing.

EIGHTH BROTHER

APPEARANCES Reb **SPECIES** Terrelian Jango Jumper **HOMEWORLD** Terrelia **AFFILIATION** Inquisitorius

The Eighth Brother is a former member of the Jedi Order who serves the Emperor as one of his Inquisitors, assigned to hunt the Jedi. Darth Vader orders the Eighth Brother to locate Maul (known as "The Shadow"). The Eighth Brother tracks Maul to the Sith temple on Malachor, where he finds more than he bargained for: Kanan Jarrus, Ezra Bridger, and Ahsoka Tano. During the resulting conflict, Kanan damages the Eighth Brother's lightsaber. The Eighth Brother leaps from the temple, using his spinning laser sword to fly, but it malfunctions and he appears to fall to his death.

IMPERIAL SUPER COMMANDOS

APPEARANCES Reb **SPECIES** Human **HOMEWORLD** Various Mandalorian worlds **AFFILIATION** Empire

Mandalorian warriors under the command of Viceroy Gar Saxon serve as Imperial Super Commandos. They wipe out the Journeyman Protectors as retribution for assisting the rebels. Saxon forces Tristan Wren, brother of Sabine, to join the commandos and prove his family's loyalty. However, Tristan eventually turns against Saxon, resulting in Saxon's death. The resulting Mandalorian civil war sees Tiber Saxon (Gar's brother) as the new leader of the commandos.

MELCH

APPEARANCES Reb **SPECIES** Ugnaught **HOMEWORLD** Bespin **AFFILIATION** Empire, Hondo Ohnaka

Melch is an Ugnaught slave, known as "Laborer 429," on the Empire's Reklam Station, before becoming an associate of Hondo Ohnaka and Azmorigan. Melch and Hondo assist the rebels, led by Hera Syndulla and Ezra Bridger, in their liberation of Lothal from the Empire.

VULT SKERRIS

APPEARANCES Reb **SPECIES** Human **HOMEWORLD** Unknown **AFFILIATION** Empire

Vult Skerris is a commander in the Imperial Navy. He serves as a flight instructor at Skystrike Academy, training cadets such as Wedge Antilles and Derek Klivian. Serving under Grand Admiral Thrawn, Skerris tests the prototype TIE/d defender elite. His ship is destroyed during a dogfight with rebel pilot Hera Syndulla over Lothal.

ARINDHA PRYCE

APPEARANCES Reb **SPECIES** Human **HOMEWORLD** Lothal **AFFILIATION** Empire

Arindha Pryce rises to a prominent position in the Galactic Empire. She starts her career managing Pryce Mining, but has to hand over her family's business to the Empire, thanks to the scheming of Lothal's Governor Ryder Azadi. Pryce accepts a role in Senator Domus Renking's office in Coruscant, but he fires her, and she goes on to join the Higher Skies Advocacy Group. Pryce schemes revenge against Azadi and Renking, while forming an alliance with Imperial Officer Thrawn. In exchange for becoming Governor of Lothal, Pryce sells her employer out to Grand Moff Tarkin and betrays her homeworld by providing critical information on it. Minister Maketh Tua often serves as Pryce's proxy, as the governor often visits Coruscant. Pryce gains notoriety by stopping the Batonn Insurgency, but her hold over Lothal is threatened by growing rebel activity. She requests the recently promoted Grand Admiral Thrawn's help combating the rebels and works alongside him on many missions. She earns his displeasure when she destroys the Lothal Fuel Depot to eliminate rebel Jedi Kanan Jarrus, because this brings Thrawn's TIE defender program to a halt. During the liberation of Lothal, Pryce remains aboard the Imperial Complex as it rises above the planet. She perishes when rebel Sabine Wren destroys the facility.

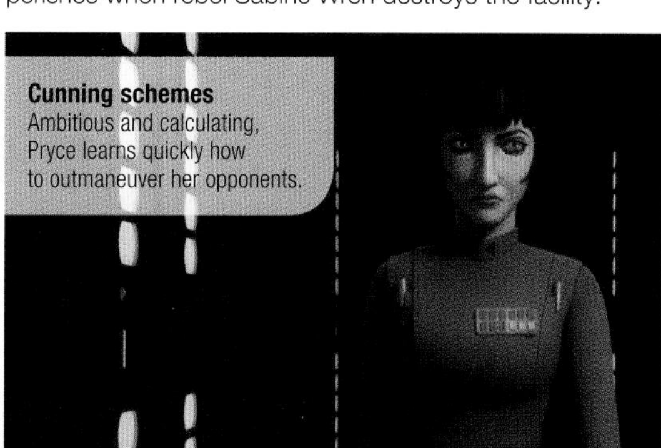

Cunning schemes
Ambitious and calculating, Pryce learns quickly how to outmaneuver her opponents.

THRAWN

APPEARANCES Reb **SPECIES** Chiss **HOMEWORLD** Csilla **AFFILIATION** Chiss Ascendancy, Empire

Mitth'raw'nuruodo, otherwise known as Thrawn, is an intelligent member of the mysterious Chiss Ascendancy, an empire that controls part of the galaxy's Unknown Regions. He is charged with exploring the galaxy's Outer Rim to figure out if the Republic would make a suitable ally for his people against a new threat. During the Clone Wars, he helps Anakin Skywalker find his missing wife Padmé Amidala on Batuu. In the process, they find a factory making experimental battle droids for the Separatists and clone trooper armor. Mysteriously, both the droids and the armor are impervious to lightsabers. From these experiences, Thrawn deduces that the Republic is not a suitable ally.

Years later, Thrawn feigns his exile from the Ascendancy in order to infiltrate the Empire to see if it may make a better ally than its predecessor. He is found by the Empire in Wild Space and taken to the Emperor, who is impressed by his knowledge of the Unknown Regions and his tactical abilities. Thrawn is sent to the Royal Imperial Academy on Coruscant and later joins the Imperial Navy. Upon defeating his nemesis, Nevil Cygni, Thrawn is made Grand Admiral, with command of the Seventh Fleet, and is tasked with eliminating rebel insurgencies. Thrawn is renowned for the insights he gains into his enemies by understanding their philosophy, art, and culture. He also starts developing the TIE defender starfighter, a superior ship that easily outmatches any rebel vessel. While the defender is being developed on Lothal, Thrawn sets out to capture the sector's local rebels, leading to the Battle of Atollon and the defeat of rebel Commander Jun Sato.

After this victory, the Emperor directs Thrawn and Darth Vader to investigate a disturbance in the Force on Batuu. There they find the warlike Grysk using Force-sensitive Chiss children as slaves. They free the children, but in the process Thrawn deduces Vader's true identity, and Vader uncovers Thrawn's first loyalty to the Chiss Ascendancy. Thrawn then turns his attention on the rebels, who launch a campaign to liberate Lothal. He is irritated when Governor Arihnda Pryce thoughtlessly orders that her troops fire upon the Capital City's fuel tanks to kill the rebel leaders. While they take out Jedi Kanan Jarrus, the act stops production on the TIE defender. Regardless, the rebels succeed in liberating Lothal, and Ezra Bridger uses a pod of purrgil to pull himself and Thrawn away into deep space.

MART MATTIN

APPEARANCES Reb **SPECIES** Human **HOMEWORLD** Mykapo **AFFILIATION** Rebels

Rebel Commander Jun Sato's nephew, Mart Mattin, is the leader of Iron Squadron, though it is comprised of only one ship: a YT-2400 light freighter, *Sato's Hammer*. Mart and his crew (Gooti Terez, Jonner Jin, and R3-A3) are an irritant to the Imperials in the Mykapo system. When his ship is damaged by Admiral Kassius Konstantine, Mart is rescued by the *Ghost* crew and joins his uncle's rebel cell. Mart plays a part in the liberation of Lothal, entrusted with a secret mission from Ezra Bridger to summon the purrgil.

JONNER JIN

APPEARANCES Reb **SPECIES** Human **HOMEWORLD** Mykapo **AFFILIATION** Iron Squadron, Rebel Alliance

Steely Jonner is a member of Mykapo's rebel Iron Squadron. When they are warned of an impending Imperial arrival, leader Mart Mattin refuses to depart, but teammates Jonner, Gooti Terez, and R3-A3 escape with the *Ghost* crew. They are reunited on Atollon however, and join the Rebel Alliance.

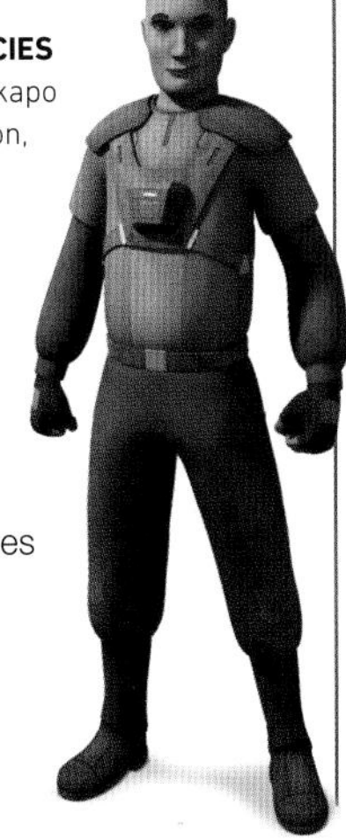

GOOTI TEREZ

APPEARANCES Reb **SPECIES** Theelin **HOMEWORLD** Mykapo **AFFILIATION** Iron Squadron, Rebel Alliance

Courageous Gooti Terez is a loyal member of the Iron Squadron cell, fighting against the Empire. Her team destroys an Imperial patrol with the help of the *Ghost* crew. Though she and her teammates evacuate onboard the *Ghost*, they must later return and rescue their leader, Mart Mattin, from the Imperials.

KLIK-KLAK

APPEARANCES Reb **SPECIES** Geonisian **HOMEWORLD** Geonosis **AFFILIATION** Hive of Karina the Great

Klik-Klak becomes one of the last remaining Geonosians after his people are exterminated by the Empire in order to keep the Death Star's construction a secret. Klik-Klak hides underground and builds a small droid army. Saw Gerrera and his Partisans arrive to investigate the Geonosian disappearance. Fearing discovery, Klik-Klak's droids wipe out all but Saw. The *Ghost* crew arrives looking for Gerrera and captures Klik-Klak. Ezra Bridger's efforts uncover evidence of the Empire's deeds on Geonosis. Out of pity they free Klik-Klak, who carries a single Geonosian egg, which later hatches a new queen.

TARRE VIZSLA

APPEARANCES Reb **SPECIES** Unknown **HOMEWORLD** Unknown **AFFILIATION** Jedi, House Vizsla, Mandalore

Before the Empire's formation, the first Mandalorian to join the Jedi Order is Tarre Vizsla. He creates the Darksaber, which House Vizsla uses to unite Mandalore under its rule.

SEEVOR

APPEARANCES Reb **SPECIES** Trandoshan **HOMEWORLD** Trandosha **AFFILIATION** Mining Guild

Seevor manages Mining Guild vehicle Crawler 413-24. This is hijacked by the *Ghost* crew and his slave laborers are freed. During a fight with Ezra Bridger, Seevor falls into a smelter and is vaporized.

URSA WREN

APPEARANCES Reb **SPECIES** Human **HOMEWORLD** Krownest **AFFILIATION** Clan Wren

Mandalorian Countess Ursa Wren is leader of Clan Wren, mother of Sabine and Tristan, and wife of Alrich. She is a former member of Death Watch and loyal to House Vizsla. When Sabine flees the Imperial Academy, it brings shame upon her family and Ursa is forced to serve Viceroy Gar Saxon and the Empire. When Ursa is reunited with Sabine, she betrays her daughter's rebel friends, offering to trade them to Saxon for Sabine's pardon. Saxon does not keep his word and Ursa shoots him to save Sabine. After this Clan Wren allies with Sabine and the rebels.

TRISTAN WREN

APPEARANCES Reb, FoD **SPECIES** Human **HOMEWORLD** Krownest **AFFILIATION** Clan Wren (formerly Imperial Super Commandos)

Tristan is the brother of Sabine Wren. When Sabine abandons her place at the Imperial Academy, Tristan is forced to join Gar Saxon's Imperial Super Commandos to prove his loyalty. Tristan is ordered to wipe out Clan Wren when his sister returns, but he sides with his family instead. During the Battle of Atollon he helps attack a Star Destroyer, allowing the Phoenix rebel cell to escape. During the Mandalorian civil war, Tristan and his mother are nearly killed by a weapon designed by Sabine. As the war expands, he and Clan Wren pledge their allegiance to Lady Bo-Katan.

ALRICH WREN

APPEARANCES Reb **SPECIES** Human **HOMEWORLD** Krownest **AFFILIATION** Clan Wren

When Aldrich marries Ursa Wren, he takes her clan name as his own. Unlike his wife and children, Alrich is an artist rather than a warrior (although his daughter Sabine inherits his creative nature). When Sabine leaves the Imperial Academy, Alrich is held on Mandalore as a veritable political prisoner. After Clan Wren sides with Sabine and the rebels against the Saxons, Alrich is transported to Sundari for execution. Sabine and her friends successfully rescue her father just in time. As the Mandalorian civil war expands, Alrich encourages his wife to refrain from attacking Tiber Saxon's Star Destroyer herself.

LOTH-WOLF

APPEARANCES Reb **HOMEWORLD** Lothal **AVERAGE SIZE** 2.6 m (8 ft 6 in) tall, 5.85 m (19 ft 2 in) long **HABITAT** Grasslands and mountains

Loth-wolves have a close relationship with the original inhabitants of Lothal. Ancient drawings in the Jedi temple and southern caves depict them together. Yet the mysterious creatures are so seldom seen during the time of the Empire that many believe them extinct. Loth-wolves have a strong connection with the Force, the energy of the planet, and the "World between Worlds." They can travel vast distances in seemingly no time. They also aid the rebels and play an indispensable role in the liberation of the planet.

WHITE LOTH-WOLF

APPEARANCES Reb **SPECIES** Loth-wolf **HOMEWORLD** Lothal **AFFILIATION** Lothal, the Loth-wolves

The White Loth-wolf is the alpha of a pack of wolves on Lothal. He is finely attuned to the will of the Force and driven to protect the planet. The Loth-wolf serves as a guide to Kanan Jarrus and Ezra Bridger. He has the ability to render people unconscious when he wishes to conceal events, but he can also communicate by speaking Basic. After the death of Kanan Jarrus, the White Loth-Wolf introduces a grieving Ezra Bridger to a large wolf named Dume—a Force manifestation of Kanan Jarrus' will after his death.

RUKH

APPEARANCES Reb **SPECIES** Noghri
HOMEWORLD Honoghr
AFFILIATION Empire (Grand Admiral Thrawn)

Grand Admiral Thrawn's most trusted bodyguard and assassin is an unrelenting, calculating Noghri named Rukh. The brute has excellent eyesight and smell, and is exceptionally strong and agile. A cloaking device allows him to hunt invisibly, too. Thrawn calls upon Rukh to hunt the rebels on Lothal. Rukh is instrumental in capturing General Hera Syndulla, but not all of his missions are successful. He is overpowered and humiliated by Sabine Wren and Garazeb Orrelios (Zeb), but they naively release him. During the liberation of Lothal, he is electrocuted while fighting with Zeb inside the Imperial Complex.

VERIS HYDAN

APPEARANCES Reb **SPECIES** Human
HOMEWORLD Ossus **AFFILIATION** Empire

Minister Veris Hydan is an exalted advisor to Emperor Palpatine. Though not a Force-wielder himself, he is a skilled archaeologist and scholar of ancient Sith and Jedi lore. Hydan is assigned to excavate the Lothal Jedi temple and find an entrance to the mysterious "World between Worlds." Though Ezra Bridger escapes into the Force realm, Hydan captures Sabine Wren and forces her to decipher the temple's Mortis mural. Sabine escapes though, and when the portal is closed again, Hydan is lost in a chasm that swallows up the temple.

JACEN SYNDULLA

APPEARANCES Reb
SPECIES Human-Twi'lek hybrid
HOMEWORLD Lothal
AFFILIATION Rebel Alliance

Jacen Syndulla is the son of Twi'lek Rebel General Hera Syndulla and the late Jedi Knight Kanan Jarrus. He is also the grandson of Twi'lek freedom fighter Cham Syndulla from Ryloth. He inherits his unique green hair and green ear-tips from his mother. Jacen grows up during the Galactic Civil War, never having met his father, but surrounded by love from the people (and droid Chopper) he calls his family. He is a member of the *Ghost*'s crew from an early age, known by the call sign "Spectre 7."

LYRA ERSO

APPEARANCES RO **SPECIES** Human
HOMEWORLD Aria Prime
AFFILIATION Erso family

After graduating from the University of Rudrig, Lyra works as a guide for Galen Erso's scientific team on an expedition on Espinar. She and Galen are married on Coruscant and their daughter Jyn is born on Vallt during the Clone Wars. The family is taken prisoner during the conflict, but rescued by Orson Krennic. Both Lyra and Galen are offered jobs by Krennic, at which point Lyra begins to suspect the Empire of great evil. The family escapes to Lah'mu, hiding there for four years. When Krennic finds them, Lyra bravely draws a blaster but is shot by a death trooper.

ORSON CALLAN KRENNIC

APPEARANCES RO **SPECIES** Human **HOMEWORLD** Lexrul **AFFILIATION** Republic, Empire

Orson Krennic is born in Sativran City on Lexrul during the Galactic Republic era. He is placed in the Future Program on Brentaal where he befriends fellow student, Galen Erso. Krennic joins the Republic Corps of Engineers and helps Galen to get hired at the Institute of Applied Sciences. Krennic progresses into the top-secret Republic Special Weapons Group and begins to research development of the Death Star, using plans captured from Geonosis. Krennic immediately realizes the project needs the talents of his friend Galen. Krennic pressures Galen to research kyber crystals for the Death Star's superlaser. With progressive successes, the ambitious Krennic is promoted to Director of the Advanced Weapons Research Division of the Imperial Security Bureau. Grand Moff Tarkin orders a test fire of the Death Star on the Holy City of Jedha. When rebels steal the Death Star plans from Scarif, Tarkin obliterates the entire facility, including Krennic and all present—both Rebel Alliance and Imperials.

Lofty ambitions
Proud Krennic longs for recognition and an audience with the Emperor. He resents Tarkin's interference. When Krennic has the chance to meet Lord Vader, however, his low position in the hierarchy is made clear.

GALEN WALTON ERSO

APPEARANCES RO **SPECIES** Human
HOMEWORLD Grange **AFFILIATION** Erso family, Empire (against his will)

As a child prodigy, Galen Erso excels at his early studies—especially math and science. While enrolled at the Republic Futures Program, he befriends architecture student Orson Krennic. The two work on Coruscant and Galen becomes renowned as a crystallographer, receiving numerous scientific awards. He and his wife, Lyra, have a daughter, Jyn. Krennic manipulates Galen into researching kyber crystals for his Death Star weapons program. Growing wary of the Empire, Galen and his family flee to Lah'mu, but Krennic tracks them there and forces Galen to return to his work on the Death Star—alone. Lyra is killed and Jyn safely hidden, to be raised by their friend Saw Gerrera. Knowing he can't escape Imperial service, Galen builds a fatal flaw into the Death Star that he hopes will be exploited by the rebels. Galen is reunited with his daughter one last time at the Imperial facility on Eadu, as he lies dying in her arms, wounded by a rebel bombing raid.

Family in exile
Jyn's health and happiness are more important to Galen than anything else. His research has often taken him away from her, so on Lah'mu, while hiding out from the Empire, he tries to make up for lost time.

"This is our chance to make a real difference."

JYN ERSO

JYN ERSO

A rebel, vagrant, criminal, and hero, Jyn Erso is torn from her family as a child and raised by a revolutionary. She runs away only to be pulled back into a fight for the galaxy, after which she becomes a legend.

APPEARANCES RO, FoD **SPECIES** Human **HOMEWORLD** None **AFFILIATION** Partisans, Rebel Alliance

WAYWARD EARLY LIFE

Jyn Erso is born on Vallt, to parents Galen and Lyra Erso. She spends her early life moving around due to her father's scientific work for the Empire, living on Lokori and Coruscant. Wary of the Empire's growing power, her family flees to Lah'mu. When they are tracked down by Imperial Director Orson Krennic, Galen instructs Jyn to hide in a pre-prepared location. Lyra is killed and Galen is taken away, and assumed dead by Jyn. Jyn is rescued by family friend Saw Gerrera and grows up as a member of his rebel "Partisans" and one of his best fighters, meeting the infamous freedom fighter Enfys Nest along the way. Saw and Jyn part ways and she lives as a criminal with many aliases. Eventually arrested by the Empire, Jyn is sent to an Imperial labor camp on Wobani. There, the Rebel Alliance breaks her out and brings her to Yavin 4. Initially mistrustful of them and their cause, Jyn learns her father is alive and developing a superweapon for the Empire.

Lah'mu farewells
Lyra embraces her daughter, knowing she may never see her again, and gifts her a kyber crystal necklace to remind her of the power of the Force.

LOOKING FOR SAW

The rebels need Jyn to find her old mentor Saw and acquire a message sent to him by Galen Erso. Jyn flies with Captain Cassian Andor and his droid companion K-2SO to Jedha to search for Saw. They enter the Holy City and meet Chirrut Îmwe and Baze Malbus, who save them from stormtroopers. A skirmish erupts with Saw's Partisans, and the group is captured by Saw's troops. Jyn is taken to Saw for a reunion and persuades him to play her father's message. Galen reveals that he has built a fatal flaw into the Empire's new planet-killer, known as the Death Star. When the Death Star fires upon and destroys the Holy City, Saw instructs Jyn to leave him behind. Jyn and her new friends (including Bodhi Rook, former Imperial pilot and friend of Galen) escape in Cassian's U-wing.

Surrogate father
Jyn looked to Saw as her replacement father, but felt betrayed by him when he abandoned her, not knowing it was for her own safety.

Preceding reputation
Although Mon Mothma agrees with Jyn, she cannot act without her allies' support, the majority of which are unwilling to trust the word of a known criminal.

CHASING A FAMILY LEGACY

After crash-landing on Eadu, where they hope to find Jyn's father, Jyn learns that Cassian intends to assassinate him. She rushes to find Galen, climbing up to the secret Imperial research facility. Before she can reach him, Galen is fatally wounded by a sudden rebel bombing raid. Father and daughter are reunited for just a moment, before he dies in her arms. Cassian pulls her away and the team escapes, flying on to the rebel headquarters on Yavin 4. There, Jyn makes an impassioned plea to the Rebel Alliance leaders, begging them to sanction an infiltratation of the Imperial data vault on Scarif to steal the Death Star plans now—before it is too late. The rebel council isn't convinced though. They vote against Jyn's proposal, leaving her further disillusioned.

THE FATAL BATTLE OF SCARIF

To Jyn's surprise, Cassian assembles a squadron of volunteer soldiers for the mission and they depart for Scarif—against orders. Now working as a unit whose members trust one another, they slip through the planet's shield gate and arrive at the landing pad. Jyn, Cassian, and K-2SO then sneak inside the Citadel Tower. Once inside the data vault, Jyn and Cassian search through the file names for the Death Star plans, stopping at "Stardust," Galen's nickname for Jyn. They retrieve the data tape and climb the tower to the transmitter. Despite facing a last-minute attempt to stop them by Imperial Director Krennic, Jyn and Cassian successfully transmit the plans to the rebel fleet. As they descend the tower, the Death Star fires on Scarif, sending a shockwave that obliterates everything.

Undercover
Cassian and Jyn assume Imperial disguises—Jyn as a technician—and work together with K-2SO to gain access to the Scarif vault.

From child soldier to rebel

Under Saw's tutelage, Jyn quickly learns how to fight. She excels at hand-to-hand combat skills, such as with her trusty truncheons, among other survival skills. Saw prizes Jyn as his greatest warrior.

timeline

▲ Life on Coruscant
Jyn spends her early childhood on Coruscant, while her father works on the Empire's top-secret project "Celestial Power."

Parents taken from Jyn
Jyn hides in a secret hatch located in a cave on Lah'mu, where Saw Gerrera finds her.

Alone again
Saw Gerrera abandons Jyn on Tamsye Prime, leaving her bitter and distrustful of others.

Facing troopers on Garel
Compassionate Jyn helps a girl being bullied by stormtroopers, and returns her pet Tooka.

Run-in with Sabine
Jyn finds a holomap on Garel belonging to rebel Sabine Wren, which leads stormtroopers to chase her.

Adventures on Ord Mantell
A Fandral child steals Jyn's kyber-crystal necklace, but when Jyn realizes he is just hungry, she takes pity on him.

▲ Recruited by rebels
Jyn is abducted by the Rebel Alliance and briefed at their Yavin 4 headquarters by Cassian Andor, Mon Mothma, and General Draven.

Last meeting with Saw
Jyn meets Saw again in the Catacombs of Cadera on Jedha just before the Holy City is destroyed. He worries she has come to kill him.

▲ Finding Galen Erso
Jyn is reunited with her father, Galen, at the Imperial facility on Eadu just before his death. This loss lights a new fire inside her.

▲ "Rogue One" is born
Cassian Andor assembles a team of volunteers to steal the Death Star plans, because "Rebellions are built on hope."

Scarif undercover
After Bodhi Rook distracts the Imperial gaze from them, Jyn dons a ground technician uniform to sneak inside the Scarif facility.

▲ Death of a hero
Jyn and Cassian await the Death Star's shockwave after sending the Death Star plans to Admiral Raddus' ship, the *Profundity*.

CASSIAN JERON ANDOR

APPEARANCES RO **SPECIES** Human **HOMEWORLD** Fest **AFFILIATION** Rebel Alliance

As a child during the Clone Wars, Cassian Andor fights against the Galactic Republic's military expansion. These experiences, combined with personal losses, mean he quickly grows up battle-hardened. After the formation of the Empire, Cassian is recruited by General Draven to become an agent for the Rebel Alliance. On a mission to Wecacoe, Cassian captures the Imperial security droid K-2SO and reprograms him. The two are henceforth constant companions and go on many missions together. In his role as Intelligence officer Cassian has used many aliases.

During one mission, on a trip to the Ring of Kafrene, Cassian learns from an informant, Tivik, that Imperial scientist Galen Erso sent his old friend (and ostracized rebel) Saw Gerrera information about the Empire's new planet-killing superweapon. Cassian, along with K-2SO, is assigned to accompany Galen's daughter, Jyn, to Jedha to find Saw. During a skirmish in the Holy City they meet natives Baze Malbus and Chirrut Îmwe, before they are all captured by Saw's troops. Cassian encounters Imperial defector Bodhi Rook in Saw's jail while Saw gives Jyn her father's message, which reveals a ruinous flaw in the Death Star. Realizing word of the Death Star has leaked, the Imperials use the superweapon to destroy the Holy City. Cassian, Jyn, and their new friends flee just in time.

They all travel to Eadu, where Cassian has been given a secret directive to assassinate Galen Erso. His conscience prevents him from following through, though Galen is soon killed in a bombing raid.

Cassian and his team return to Yavin 4 and, against orders, assemble a squad to steal the Death Star plans on Scarif. Once they arrive, Cassian, Jyn, and K-2SO pose as Imperials to reach the data vault. There they acquire the plans but must transmit them to the rebel fleet from atop the communications tower. As they climb, Cassian is wounded. Jyn continues alone, but upon reaching the top is trapped by Director Orson Krennic. Cassian, not willing to give up at this vital moment, shoots him, allowing Jyn to successfully send the plans to the rebels. As they do, the Death Star fires on Scarif. Cassian and Jyn die heroes in each other's arms.

"Rebellions are built on hope."

CASSIAN ANDOR

Undercover issues
Cassian and Jyn must overcome their mutual trust issues to work well together. The atmosphere between them when they arrive on Jedha is decidedly frosty.

DEATH TROOPERS

APPEARANCES Reb, RO **SPECIES** Human (modified) **HOMEWORLD** Various **AFFILIATION** Empire

Death troopers are elite soldiers altered in a top-secret program to boost stormtrooper performance beyond normal human limitations. Emperor Palpatine chooses their name to capitalize on rumors of Imperial experiments leading to the reanimation of necrotic tissue. Death trooper squads act as bodyguards and enforcers for high-ranking Imperial officers such as Governor Wilhuff Tarkin, Grand Admiral Thrawn, Darth Vader, and Director Krennic. They are also assigned to guard classified shipments of kyber crystals. Death troopers participate in warfare on Atollon, Eadu, and Scarif.

BENTHIC TWO TUBES

APPEARANCES S, RO **SPECIES** Tognath **HOMEWORLD** Yar Togna **AFFILIATION** Cloud-Riders, Partisans

Benthic "Two Tubes" flees his planet with his eggmate, Edrio, when it is overrun by the Empire. Benthic then joins Enfys Nest's Cloud-Riders to fight the Crimson Dawn crime syndicate. He takes part in their raid on Vandor, attempting to steal a coaxium shipment, and then a skirmish on Savareen to recover another supply. Thereafter Benthic joins Saw Gerrera's Partisans on Jedha. He interrogates Bodhi Rook and delivers him to Saw, but must evacuate when the Holy City is destroyed. During the Galactic Civil War, he meets Princess Leia Organa and forms a new partnership between the Partisans and Rebel Alliance.

OOLIN MUSTERS

APPEARANCES RO **SPECIES** Blutopian **AFFILIATION** Rebel Alliance

Also known as "Nail" and "Kennel," Oolin Musters is a member of the Rebel Alliance. She is captured by the Empire and imprisoned on Wobani, finding herself cellmates with Jyn Erso. She threatens to kill Jyn. When Jyn is rescued, Musters escapes and makes her way to Jedha.

RUESCOTT MELSHI

APPEARANCES RO **SPECIES** Human **AFFILIATION** Rebel Alliance

Sergeant Ruescott Melshi is a friend of Cassian Andor and member of the Rebel Alliance. He leads an extraction team to rescue Jyne Erso from a labor camp on Wobani. Later, he helps assemble a team of rebel volunteers for Jyn and Cassian, and is killed in the Battle of Scarif.

EDRIO TWO TUBES

APPEARANCES Reb, RO **SPECIES** Tognath **HOMEWORLD** Yar Togna **AFFILIATION** Partisans, Cavern Angels

Edrio "Two Tubes" and his eggmate, or brother, Benthic, get their nicknames from the pair of breathing tubes they wear. They flee their homeworld after the Empire takes control. Edrio joins Saw Gerrera's Partisans and bombs the Empire's Jalindi relay. In the process he destroys the light cruiser *Marauder* and rescues rebels Ezra Bridger and Sabine Wren. Edrio and Saw then destroy a large kyber crystal in the Tonnis sector, and with it two Imperial ships. Edrio is killed when the Death Star test-fires on the Holy City of Jedha.

BODHI ROOK

APPEARANCES RO **SPECIES** Human **HOMEWORLD** Jedha **AFFILIATION** Empire, Rebel Alliance

Bodhi Rook is a gentle soul who was raised on Jedha. Bodhi enrolls in the Terrabe Sector Service Academy, hoping to become an Imperial starfighter pilot, yet is unable to continue that course due to poor test scores. Instead, Bodhi is assigned to fly Imperial cargo shuttles.

In time, Bodhi begins to have misgivings about his service to the Empire. He befriends rogue Imperial scientist Galen Erso, who encourages Bodhi to defect and deliver a secret message intended for his daughter Jyn Erso to rebel extremist Saw Gerrera on Jedha. Bodhi approaches Saw's Partisans but is taken prisoner. They take him to their headquarters in the Catacombs of Cadera, where Bodhi finally meets Saw. Paranoid Saw does not believe Bodhi's tale and uses a terrifying Mairan named Bor Gullet to frighten and interrogate Bodhi, profoundly impacting Bodhi's mental state.

When motley rebel crew Cassian Andor, Jyn Erso, Baze Malbus, and Chirrut Îmwe are also captured by Saw's forces, Jyn is given her father's message detailing a fatal flaw in the Death Star. At that same moment the superweapon fires on Jedha's Holy City. Bodhi escapes with his fellow prisoners and helps them fly to Eadu to meet Galen. From there they fly to Yavin 4, where Cassian assembles a team—including Bodhi—to infiltrate the Imperial facility on Scarif and steal the Death Star plans. As they leave Yavin 4, Bodhi applies a call sign to the team: "Rogue One."

Bodhi uses his Imperial insight to get the team through Imperial security and the shield gate above Scarif. He stays with their ship while Cassian, Jyn, and K-2SO go to steal the plans. As the battle begins, Bodhi feeds the Imperials misleading reports and alerts the Rebel Alliance fleet that they must destroy Scarif's shield gate so they can receive Jyn's transmission of the Death Star plans. After successfully making contact, Bodhi is killed in an explosion.

Facing foes
During the Battle of Scarif, Bodhi must hook his stolen shuttle up to the Imperial communications network. This brings him into direct conflict with the Imperial forces he used to work with.

BOR GULLET

APPEARANCES RO **SPECIES** Mairan **HOMEWORLD** Maires **AFFILIATION** Partisans

Bor Gullet is a member of a bulbous, tentacled Mairan species. Mairans can read minds and sense intentions by wrapping their tentacles around the cranium of an individual, so are used by some groups to interrogate prisoners. The process is extremely unpleasant and sometimes used as a form of torture. Prolonged exposure can cause memory loss and even insanity. The effects of short-term exposure are reversible. Saw Gerrera keeps Bor Gullet in a den at his headquarters on Jedha, using the creature to interrogate pilot Bodhi Rook.

Pessimistic pilot
K-2SO and Cassian are approved for solo or tandem U-wing flights. At the start of their missions K-2SO likes to calculate the low odds of their success.

K-2SO

APPEARANCES RO **MANUFACTURER** Arakyd Industries **TYPE** KX-series security droid **AFFILIATION** Empire, Rebel Alliance

Rebel agent Cassian Andor acquires security droid K-2SO from an Imperial stormtrooper detachment on Wecacoe. Cassian manages to wipe his memory and reprogram K-2SO to serve the rebels, albeit with some quirks—K-2SO is unfailingly blunt and has a propensity to violence. The two work closely together on subsequent missions, including spending time with Wookiees.

K-2SO accompanies a rebel extraction team to free Jyn Erso from the prison labor camp on Wobani. Back on Yavin 4, K-2SO expresses displeasure namely because Jyn, a captured criminal, is allowed to keep a weapon but Cassian doesn't trust him with one. The trio travels to Jedha to look for Saw Gerrera, who holds vital intel. K-2SO is left behind to guard their ship, but disapproves of this instruction and disobeys Cassian, following them and preventing them from almost being arrested by Imperials. Cassian orders him to return to their U-wing, which means K-2SO is able to rescue them when the Death Star destroys the Holy City. K-2SO then helps them fly to Eadu, where a storm leads them to crash. While Cassian leaves to find Jyn's father, scientist Galen Erso, K-2SO observes that Cassian's blaster was in the sniper configuration, revealing Cassian's secret intention to kill Galen. While Jyn runs off, K-2SO helps steal an Imperial cargo shuttle for the team's escape.

After forming a volunteer team to invade Imperial base Scarif—home of the valuable Death Star plans—K-2SO, Cassian, and Jyn pose as Imperials to sneak inside the Imperial security complex, where K-2SO disables a fellow KX-series droid and acquires a map of the complex from its memory banks. They proceed to the data vault. K-2SO is able to take over the control computer while Jyn and Cassian search for the Death Star plans. Jyn provides K-2SO with a blaster, which greatly pleases him. As she and Cassian continue on to the tower so they can transmit the Death Star plans to the rebels, stormtroopers infiltrate the vault. K-2SO seals the doors and fights off the stormtroopers as long as he can in order to buy Jyn and Cassian time, but he is eventually destroyed.

ANTOC MERRICK

APPEARANCES RO **SPECIES** Human
HOMEWORLD Virujansi
AFFILIATION Rarified Air Cavalry, Rebel Alliance

Antoc Merrick is the lead pilot of the Virujansi planetary defense force. When the new Imperial-appointed governor replaces the ruling council, Merrick retires and instead joins the Rebel Alliance, earning the rank of general with oversight over all Starfighter Command. Merrick flies a T-65B X-wing as Blue Leader at the Battle of Scarif. He and his Blue Squadron penetrate the shield gate and fight along the surface of Scarif. He destroys several Imperial AT-ACTs, but his X-wing is shot down by TIE strikers and he is killed.

DAVITS DRAVEN

APPEARANCES RO **SPECIES** Human
HOMEWORLD Pendarr III
AFFILIATION Rebel Alliance

During the Clone Wars, Davits Draven is a member of the Galactic Republic's military intelligence. His colleagues become Imperial officers, but Draven joins the Rebel Alliance and is trained as a field operative. Draven makes difficult decisions as a spy and top intelligence officer. He unravels Galen Erso's connection to the Death Star as part of Operate Fracture, ordering the rescue of Jyn Erso and assassination of Galen. After the Battle of Yavin he takes charge of the interrogation of Grakkus the Hutt. On a later mission, Draven is killed by Darth Vader.

IMPERIAL WEAPONS TECHNICIAN

APPEARANCES Reb, RO, IV, VI **SPECIES** Human
HOMEWORLD Various **AFFILIATION** Empire

Imperial weapons technicians, also known as gunners, are usually cadets taken from the Imperial Navy's pilot training programs who either have not graduated to full pilot status or are past their prime and have not risen in rank sufficiently to receive a command. They operate weaponry such as turbolasers, ion cannons, and the Death Star's superlaser and experimental technology like the gravity wells on the Imperial Interdictor. Black uniforms are common, but technicians in experimental programs may wear other colors.

WEETEEF

APPEARANCES RO **SPECIES** Talpini
HOMEWORLD Tal Pi **AFFILIATION** Partisans

Talpini Weeteef Cyu-Bee is a member of Saw Gerrera's Partisans on Jedha. He is an explosives expert, using his sticky bombs to take down Imperial vehicles, and is an excellent marksman too. Jyn Erso and Cassian Andor get caught in a skirmish where Weeteef targets an Imperial patrol and does much damage.

BEEZER FORTUNA

APPEARANCES RO **SPECIES** Twi'lek
HOMEWORLD Ryloth **AFFILIATION** Partisans

Beezer is a cousin of Bib Fortuna, the majordomo of Jabba the Hutt. He is inspired by fellow Twi'lek freedom fighter Cham Syndulla to fight his planet's oppressors. Beezer is imprisoned by the Empire in the Ryloth city of Lessu but freed by Saw Gerrera's Partisans. He becomes Saw's strategist on Jedha.

CHIRRUT ÎMWE

APPEARANCES RO **SPECIES** Human **HOMEWORLD** Jeda
AFFILIATION Guardians of the Whills, Partisans, Rebel Alliance

Chirrut Îmwe and his friend Baze Malbus are members of the near-extinct Guardians of the Whills, and sworn to protect the Temple of the Whills in Jedha's Holy City. Chirrut believes strongly in the Force. He has great respect for the old Jedi Order and seems to have an innate Force connection, allowing him to sense things before they happen—a sort of vision without eyesight (he is blind). After the Empire comes to Jedha, Chirrut and Baze join Saw Gerrera's Partisans on one condition—that the group provides supplies for their orphanage. The Partisan's violent methods only create more orphans, however. Chirrut and Baze then look to transport the orphans offworld. They steal an Imperial shuttle for their plan, but when the Partisans want it for an attack, Chirrut and Baze leave the group.

When the Rebel Alliance sends Jyn Erso, Cassian Andor, and K-2SO to Jedha, Chirrut encounters Jyn in the market by sensing her kyber-crystal necklace. He and Baze save the rebels from stormtroopers, only to be kidnapped by Gerrera's militia. When the Death Star destroys the Holy City, Chirrut and Baze escape aboard Cassian's ship. They fly to Eadu to find Jyn's father, where Chirrut warns Jyn that the Force suggests Cassian is about to kill someone (likely her father). A skirmish between the rebels and Empire follows, in which Chirrut's Force connection helps him to shoot down a TIE fighter.

Back on Yavin 4, Chirrut and Baze volunteer for Jyn's mission to steal the Death Star plans on Scarif. They lead a team setting explosives to lure stormtroopers away from the data vault. Chirrut sets out alone in the midst of the battle to flip the landing zone's master switch, necessary for the rebels to transmit the Death Star plans to their fleet. Chirrut is successful, but hit by an explosion. He dies in Baze's arms.

Weapons master
Zamo-shiwo martial artist Chirrut is able to take down many stormtroopers on Jedha with his staff. On other ocassions he is a deadly aim with his lightbow *(left)*.

One with the Force
Chirrut's calm belief in the Force is sometimes a source of mockery for his pragmatic, battle-hardened friend Baze. But it brings him courage and strength even in the face of certain defeat during the Battle of Scarif.

BAZE MALBUS

APPEARANCES RO **SPECIES** Human **HOMEWORLD** Jeda **AFFILIATION** Guardians of the Whills, Partisans, Rebel Alliance

Gruff Baze Malbus serves the Guardians of the Whills in Jedha's Holy City, alongside his close friend Chirrut Îmwe. When the Empire arrives, its forces seal the temple and disband the Guardians, an act that causes Baze to become disillusioned with his faith and past calling. Baze and Chirrut join Saw Gerrera's Partisans and insist the Partisans help them care for the city's orphans. The duo steals an Imperial Sentinel and plan to transport the orphans off Jedha and away from the fighting, but this causes friction among the Partisans and they depart the group on bad terms. Baze becomes a freelance assassin, but remains close to Chirrut.

When Cassian Andor, Jyn Erso, and K-2SO arrive on Jedha, Chirrut tries to save them from stormtroopers and Baze steps in to help, though all of them are then captured by the Partisans. When the Death Star fires on Jedha, Baze and Chirrut escape aboard Cassian's ship with their new friends. They fly to Eadu to find Jyn's father, Galen, and then on to Yavin 4 to discuss Galen's revelations about the Empire's Death Star.

Though Rebel Alliance High Command refuses to sanction a mission to Imperial base Scarif to steal the Death Star plans, Baze and Chirrut are inspired by Jyn's call to action and volunteer for her forbidden venture. On Scarif, the two lead a team to lure soldiers away from the data vault while Cassian, Jyn, and K-2SO sneak inside. Chirrut walks out amidst the ensuing battle and is hit by an explosion. Chirrut assures Baze that if he looks to the Force, he will always find Chirrut there. He then dies in Baze's arms. Knowing he cannot survive the battle, Baze clings to the Force and his friend's words and boldly charges the Imperial soldiers to face his own death.

Battle ready
Baze has traded the monklike clothes of the Guardians of the Whills for battle armor. He is never without his customized repeating blaster, which he unleashes on advancing Imperials on Scarif *(left)*.

IMPERIAL TANK PILOT

APPEARANCES RO **SPECIES** Human **HOMEWORLD** Various **AFFILIATION** Empire

Imperial tank pilots are a specialized corps of drivers that operate TX-225 combat assault tanks. On Jedha, these tanks carry kyber crystals in orange transport containers. The tanks require a minimum crew of three: the driver, gunner, and commander (identified by gray shoulder markings). There are many iterations of their armor incorporating design improvements and customized to match the requirements of each vehicle. Most are light and flexible to allow pilots to squeeze into cramped driving compartments.

TAM POSLA

APPEARANCES S, RO **SPECIES** Human (cyborg) **HOMEWORLD** Milvayne **AFFILIATION** Milvayne Authority, bounty hunter

Tam Posla is a galactic law enforcement officer who goes beyond the call of duty and becomes a bounty hunter. He comes to Jedha to investigate reports of kidnapping, humanoid trafficking, and horrific surgical experiments committed by "Roofoo" (Dr. Evazan) and "Sawkee" (Ponda Baba). He later joins Doctor Chelli Aphra's team of mercenaries, which raids the laboratory of deceased Techno Union leader Wat Tambor and kidnaps Rebel Alliance General Hera Syndulla to gain access to the Tarkin Initiative's Hivebase-1. In a later misadventure he tries to arrest Aphra, but is killed by the droid Triple Zero (0-0-0). Polsa's body is later reanimated by a Force-sensitive space fungus.

WOAN BARSO

APPEARANCES RO **SPECIES** Human **HOMEWORLD** Unknown **AFFILIATION** Refugee Relief Movement

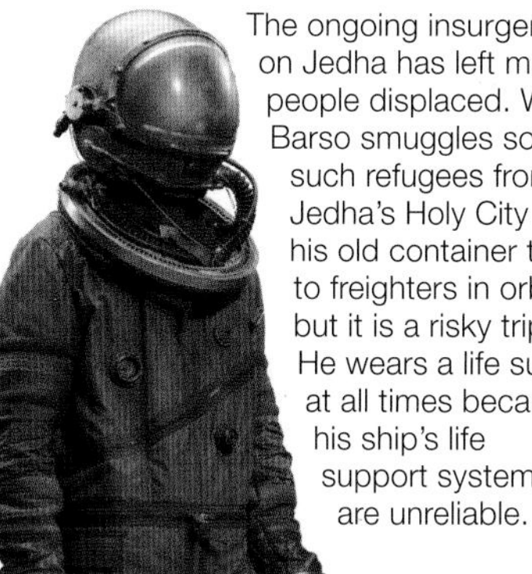

The ongoing insurgency on Jedha has left many people displaced. Woan Barso smuggles some such refugees from Jedha's Holy City in his old container tug, to freighters in orbit, but it is a risky trip. He wears a life suit at all times because his ship's life support systems are unreliable.

CAYSIN BOG

APPEARANCES RO **SPECIES** High-gravity humanoid **HOMEWORLD** Teres Lutha Minor **AFFILIATION** Mercenary

Caysin Bog is blown apart in a Partisan strike on Jedha and then reassembled by Dr. Cornelius Evazon (going by the name "Roofoo"). He escapes the desolation of Jedha and works with his partner Tam Posla and Doctor Chelli Aphra on a contract to loot the laboratory of deceased Techno Union leader Wat Tambor on Skako Minor. From there the team kidnaps Rebel Alliance General Hera Syndulla to use in a trade and gain access to the Empire's Hivebase-1. Once inside, Aphra causes Bog's death to gain a personal advantage, which enrages Tam Posla.

FEYN VANN

APPEARANCES RO **SPECIES** Human **HOMEWORLD** Tri-Barr Station **AFFILIATION** Nordoxicon Unlimited, Empire

Feyn Vann is a renowned engineer from Nordoxicon recruited to develop a series of deflector arrays that channel hypermatter streams from the Death Star's main reactor to the crystalline firing array. He is killed alongside his peers by death troopers on Eadu at the command of Imperial Director Orson Krennic.

ADMIRAL RADDUS

APPEARANCES RO **SPECIES** Mon Calamari
HOMEWORLD Mon Cala **AFFILIATION** Nystullum city government, Royal Court of King Lee-Char, Mon Cala Mercantile Fleet, Rebel Alliance

As mayor of Nystullum on Mon Cala, Raddus advises King Lee-Char and defends Mon Cala from Governor Tarkin's Imperial invasion. When the Empire takes control of the planet, Raddus takes part in the Mon Calamari exodus, commanding the Nystullum government city-ship, the *Profundity*. Raddus joins the Rebel Alliance and commands their navy as Admiral. He also serves on the Alliance High Council, though rarely meets with the committee in person on Yavin 4, appearing remotely as a hologram instead. Raddus is a pragmatist, and frustrated by some of the Alliance's dallying. As a person of action, he rushes to support Jyn Erso and Rogue One at the Battle of Scarif—and his ship receives her transmission of the Death Star plans. The *Profundity* is boarded by Darth Vader and Raddus is believed killed. Princess Leia's ship, *Tantive IV*, escapes with the plans on board. The Resistance flagship is later named in Raddus' honor.

"I say we fight!"
ADMIRAL RADDUS

Act first
Raddus takes the initiative to re-route the *Profundity* and support the Rogue One team on Scarif even without authorization.

NOWER JEBEL

APPEARANCES RO **SPECIES** Human
HOMEWORLD Uyter **AFFILIATION** Imperial Senate, Rebel Alliance, New Republic

Cautious Senator Jebel serves on the Imperial Senate after the formation of the Galactic Empire, but secretly, he is acting as Minister of Finance for the Rebel Alliance. He keeps this role after the formation of the New Republic and restoration of the Senate.

VASP VASPAR

APPEARANCES RO **SPECIES** Human
HOMEWORLD Taldot Sector
AFFILIATION Imperial Senate, Rebel Alliance

Senator Vaspar secretly serves as the Minister of Industry for the Rebel Alliance Cabinet in their civil government. He is responsible for management of resources and does not believe the rebels have the capability to take on the first Death Star.

TYNNRA PAMLO

APPEARANCES RO **SPECIES** Human
HOMEWORLD Taris **AFFILIATION** Imperial Senate, Rebel Alliance

Senator Pamlo is the Rebel Alliance's Minister of Education. She works closely with Alliance Intelligence to investigate the sacking of Lasan and the desolation of Geonosis. When Jyn Erso proposes going after the Death Star, she worries her own world could be destroyed in retaliation.

ANJ ZAVOR

APPEARANCES RO, IV
SPECIES Human
HOMEWORLD Majoros
AFFILIATION Rebel Alliance

Colonel Zavor is a Rebel Alliance officer working at Fleet Command. He acts as a liaison between Admiral Raddus and Alliance headquarters during the Battle of Scarif. Zavor is present during the Battle of Yavin and the awards ceremony that follows.

GENERAL RAMDA

APPEARANCES RO **SPECIES** Human
HOMEWORLD Rine-cathe 111 **AFFILIATION** Empire

Eager to be working near the heart of Imperial action, General Sotorus Ramda oversees the military presence on Scarif. The island is considered by many to be a leisurely place for older officers to wait out retirement in paradise. General Ramda helps create this image, being a lax and somewhat incompetent bureaucrat. His younger, dissatisfied subordinates conspire to send critical reports against him to Coruscant. Ramda baulks when Director Krennic demands to see all of Galen Erso's communications, exasperated by the extent of work it would require. He perishes when the Death Star fires on Scarif.

IMPERIAL DECK TECHNICIAN

APPEARANCES S, RO **SPECIES** Human
HOMEWORLD Various **AFFILIATION** Empire

The ground crew on Imperial bases such as Scarif and Mimban are known as deck technicians. They are a specialist division of Imperial technicians, trained as mechanics to keep ships in good working order and direct ship traffic. They may also pilot various vessels when local logistics make safe take offs and landings difficult. Jyn Erso disguises herself as an Imperial deck technician in order to sneak into the Empire's Citadel and data vault, along with Cassian Andor and K-2SO during the Battle of Scarif.

ZAL DINNES

APPEARANCES RO **SPECIES** Human
HOMEWORLD Tierfon **AFFILIATION** Rebel Alliance, Tierfon Yellow Aces

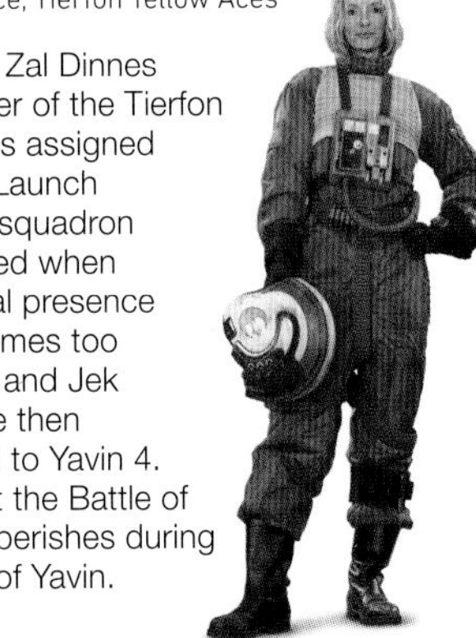

Rebel pilot Zal Dinnes is a member of the Tierfon Yellow Aces assigned to Tierfon Launch Base. Her squadron is disbanded when the Imperial presence there becomes too great. She and Jek Porkins are then transferred to Yavin 4. She flies at the Battle of Scarif but perishes during the Battle of Yavin.

LIEUTENANT ADEMA

APPEARANCES RO
SPECIES Human
HOMEWORLD Toria-vic Nebula, Planetoid A.17
AFFILIATION Empire

Zealous Lieutenant Mytus Adema is stationed in the Citadel command center on Scarif when Rogue One infiltrates their facility and steals the Death Star plans. He is fooled by misleading reports of rebel activities during the affair, but correctly notes Jyn Erso and Cassian Andor accessing the data vault.

SHORETROOPER

APPEARANCES RO **SPECIES** Human
HOMEWORLD Various **AFFILIATION** Empire

Coastal defender stormtroopers, otherwise known as shoretroopers, are a relatively uncommon class of Imperial trooper. They are stationed to patrol the edge of oceanic environments on tropical worlds such as Scarif. Their armor is designed to withstand corrosive aquatic environments, reduce sun glare, and repel excess moisture. Most shoretroopers are sergeants and able to command squadrons of standard stormtroopers. Higher ranks are distinguished by colored stripes on their chest and shoulders. Squad leaders wear a kama around their waist and sport a blue strip on their chest and shoulders. Captains have a mostly blue chest plate.

DOCTOR CHELLI APHRA

APPEARANCES Other **SPECIES** Human **HOMEWORLD** Unknown
AFFILIATION University of Bar'leth, Archaeological Association, Darth Vader, Triple-Zero and Beetee-One, Black Krrsantan

Amoral, ambitious Chelli Lona Aphra is an innovative archaeologist working for her own gains across the galaxy. Her father is a scholar obsessed with an ancient and forgotten Force-sensitive order called the Ordu Aspectu, and for a long period of time is estranged from his wife Lona and his daughter as he prioritizes his research. Left feeling abandoned, Chelli grows up mostly alone with her mother, until Lona is tragically killed by raiders. Having earned her doctorate in archaeology from the University of Bar'leth—not by legitimate research, but by outsmarting her Sava (professor)—Chelli, now Doctor Aphra, meets Sana Starros and the two become constant companions.

After graduation, Aphra is hired by the Droid Gotra to recover the Beetee-One assassin droid "blastomech" prototype (BT-1), the Triple-Zero matrix (0-0-0), and a forgotten "portable battle droid factory" on Geonosis. This work leads to her being recruited by none other than Darth Vader, much to Aphra's surprise, to help him build his own private army. She installs the Triple-Zero matrix into a protocol droid and he in turn helps her awaken the sleeping Beetee-One. Aphra turns the droids over to Vader and then helps him acquire the droid factory. When Aphra is no longer needed, Vader plans to kill her. Aphra tries to outsmart the Sith Lord by telling the Emperor of their partnership first, but Vader pushes her out of an airlock and subsequently believes her dead. However, Aphra has arranged for the Wookiee bounty hunter Black Krrsantan, Beetee-One, and Triple-Zero to pick her up in a ship.

Aphra continues her archaeological adventures with a variety of associates. When her father reappears in her life she works with him to investigate the Ordu Aspectu and recover the ancient consciousness of a Force-wielding being named Rur. She also has a turbulent relationship with Imperial Captain Magna Tolvan, who she double-crosses on more than one occasion, finally leaving Magna with her memories of their affair wiped to ensure their mutual survival.

Her engineering handiwork turns against her when she is forced to work for Triple-Zero. She assembles a crew of mercenaries, under the droid's orders, and kidnaps rebel General Hera Syndulla, using her to infiltrate the Empire's Hivebase-1 and recover Triple-Zero's memories. Aphra is captured, imprisoned and escapes, only to find herself and Triple-Zero caught in a twisted game controlled by Doctor Cornelius Evazan.

Unlikely allies
Aphra openly admires Lord Vader who, on first meeting, she finds even more interesting than she had hoped.

Rebel run-in
When Aphra secures the trust of Luke Skywalker, his rebel friends remain suspicious of her. When she must eventually betray and abandon Luke, the event causes her guilt.

COMMANDER IDEN VERSIO

APPEARANCES *Star Wars*: Battlefront II
SPECIES Human **HOMEWORLD** Vardos
AFFILIATION Empire, Black Squadron, Inferno Squad, Rebel Alliance, Danger Squadron, New Republic, Resistance

Iden Versio is a top-class graduate from the Imperial Academy on Coruscant. She becomes a TIE fighter pilot for the Empire during the early days of the Galactic Civil War and fights in the Battle of Yavin. Her father, Admiral Garrick Versio, forms a Special Forces commando unit called Inferno Squad following the destruction of the Death Star and installs her as its commander. She and her teammates (including Gideon Hask, Seyn Marana, and Del Meeko) infiltrate the Dreamers (the remnants of Saw Gerrera's Partisans) and eliminate them. Inferno Squad fights at the Battle of Endor, observing the destruction of the second Death Star from the moon's surface.

Following the death of the Emperor, "Operation: Cinder" is activated and Iden's homeworld of Vardos is one of many targeted by the Empire's climate disruption arrays. Unable to comply with the Empire any longer, she rebels against her father's command. She and teammate Del Meeko defy orders, taking their ship, *Corvus*, and surrender to the Rebel Alliance. They fight for the rebels in the remaining battles of the Civil War, alongside the leader of Danger Squadron, Shiv Suurgav. At the Battle of Jakku, Iden manages to shoot down Hask and finds her father aboard the *Eviscerator*. Though he insists on going down with his ship, Iden and her father reconcile before they are finally parted.

In the years following the Battle of Jakku, Iden and Del marry and have a daughter named Zay. When Del goes missing, Iden, Shiv, and Zay search for him. They wind up back on Vardos, where Iden encounters Hask, now a First Order officer. Iden and Zay follow Hask aboard his Star Destroyer, *Retribution*, and steal schematics for the powerful First Order Dreadnought. Hask reveals that he murdered Del. The two fight and Iden kills Hask, though she is mortally wounded in the process. Iden Versio dies in her daughter Zay's arms. Shiv and Zay then escape to D'Qar, delivering the Dreadnought schematics to Resistance pilot Poe Dameron.

Today the Rebellion dies
Prior to the Battle of Endor, Commander Iden Versio infiltrates a rebel ship, the *Invincible Faith*. She destroys an intercepted Imperial tranmission that is being decoded on the vessel and which would have revealed the Empire's trap above Endor.

Top-secret orders
Following the surprising Imperial defeat over Endor, Iden Versio is given new orders by her father that are critical to the success of "Operation: Cinder."

IMPERIAL FLEET TROOPERS

APPEARANCES RO, IV, VI
SPECIES Human **HOMEWORLD** Various
AFFILIATION Empire

Imperial fleet troopers are members of a special branch of the Empire's Navy created by Grand Moff Tarkin. They form the backbone of security aboard multiple vessels, and are trained extensively in combat. Many also receive training in operations support to increase their utility to their captains. The troopers are easily recognized by their distinctive helmets and are utilized on the Death Star and Death Star II, with some being responsible for piloting and firing the battle stations as ordered.

R5-D4

APPEARANCES II, IV
TYPE Astromech droid
MANUFACTURER Industrial Automaton **AFFILIATION** None

R5-D4, also known as "Red," is a white, red, and blue droid scavenged by Jawas and carried aboard their sandcrawler on Tatooine. They sell R5-D4 to Owen Lars, but his motivator immediately malfunctions. This gives C-3PO the opportunity to recommend R2-D2 to Lars and Luke Skywalker instead.

SANDTROOPER

APPEARANCES IV, RO **SPECIES** Human
HOMEWORLD Various **AFFILIATION** Empire

Sandtroopers are specialized Imperial stormtroopers, trained and equipped to serve in arid environments such as Tatooine. Their armor is equipped with cooling units, long-range comlinks, anti-glare lenses, extra rations, and a water supply. All sandtroopers wear colored pauldrons to indicate their rank—black indicates enlisted troopers, white is for sergeants, and orange is for unit leaders.

"These aren't the droids we're looking for."

SANDTROOPER

WUHER

APPEARANCES IV **SPECIES** Human
HOMEWORLD Tatooine **AFFILIATION** None

Wuher is a bartender at the Mos Eisley Cantina. As an orphan, he works his way off the streets by studying the biochemistries of various species and mixing them the most desirable drinks. He has a strong dislike of droids and installs a droid detector to keep them out.

GENERAL TAGGE

APPEARANCES IV **SPECIES** Human
HOMEWORLD Tepasi **AFFILIATION** Empire

Born into nobility and privilege, General Tagge is chief of military operations aboard the first Death Star. Unlike some of his colleagues, he has wary respect for the Rebel Alliance. Prior to the Battle of Yavin, Tagge departs the Death Star to look into Princess Leia's mention of a rebel base on Dantooine. Following the Death Star's destruction, Tagge is promoted to the Grand General of the Imperial army with authority over Darth Vader himself. Tagge becomes responsible for Imperial expansion into the Outer Rim, so tasks Vader with eliminating any criminal cartels that haven't allied with the Empire. Tagge begins using Doctor Cylo's powerful cyborg operatives on missions, but they betray him, taking control of a Super Star Destroyer. After Vader wipes out the threat, Tagge is demoted by the Emperor and placed under Vader's command. The Sith Lord promptly kills him.

ADMIRAL MOTTI

APPEARANCES IV **SPECIES** Human
HOMEWORLD Seswenna
AFFILIATION Empire

Admiral Conan Antonio Motti hails from a wealthy and powerful family in the Outer Rim. He commands the Star Destroyer *Steel Talon*, and is also the head of naval operations aboard the Death Star, under Grand Moff Tarkin. He foolhardily challenges Darth Vader on his failure to discover the secret Rebel Alliance base, which earns him a Sith Force choke. His arrogant overconfidence in believing the battle station to be invincible results in his death.

PONDA BABA

APPEARANCES RO, IV **SPECIES** Aqualish
HOMEWORLD Ando **AFFILIATION** Smuggler

Ponda Baba is the pirating partner of Doctor Evazan. He rescues Evazan from a bounty hunter and the two begin smuggling spice for Jabba the Hutt. Together, they travel to Milvayne, going on a crime spree there, and to Jedha, where Baba takes a dislike to Jyn Erso and Cassian Andor. A drunken thug, Baba picks a fight with Luke Skywalker in the Mos Eisley Cantina, and loses his arm when Obi-Wan Kenobi intervenes. Evazan tries, and fails, to reattach his arm, which eventually ends up in the hands of Milvaynian bounty hunter Tam Polsa. Baba and Evazan go their separate ways for a time, until they meet once more when Evazan, who has retrieved Baba's arm, contacts him. Together, they watch rogue archaeologist Doctor Aphra and evil protocol droid Triple-Zero's exploits on Milvayne and hire mediocre hunters Winloss and Nokk to kill Aphra.

"Whoever heard of a bander who didn't gamble?"

FIGRIN D'AN

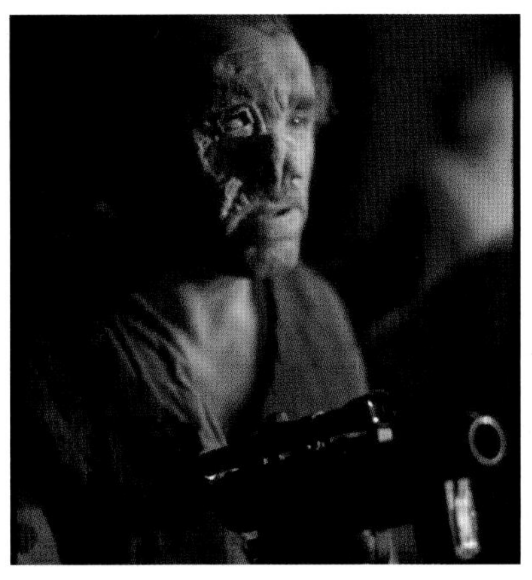

DOCTOR EVAZAN

APPEARANCES RO, IV **SPECIES** Human
HOMEWORLD Alsakan **AFFILIATION** Smuggler

Once a promising surgeon, Doctor Evazan is now notorious for conducting cruel medical experiments. Evazan is nearly killed and horrifically scarred by a bounty hunter, until Ponda Baba saves him. Working for Crimson Dawn leader Dryden Vos, Evazan begins making the Decraniated—cyborg humanoid servants completely purged of their identities. Soon after, Baba and Evazan move to Jedha where they continue to create Decraniated from survivors of the Partisans attacks. They leave the city prior to its destruction. Obi-Wan Kenobi and Luke Skywalker encounter the troublemaker in the cantina on Tatooine and he unsuccessfully tries to reattach Baba's severed arm after Obi-Wan cuts it off. Wanting to escape his multiple death sentences, Evazan forms a new identity as a shape-shifter named Lopset Yas, but he is imprisoned by the Empire alongside morally gray archaeologist Doctor Aphra. He only reveals his true identity when he has escaped and captured Aphra and Aphra's nemesis, murder droid Triple-Zero. For fun, he puts bombs in Aphra and Triple-Zero that are set to explode if they get too far apart, and settles down to watch the ensuing antics from afar through Triple-Zero's eyes.

MOMAW NADON

APPEARANCES IV **SPECIES** Ithorian
HOMEWORLD Ithor **AFFILIATION** Rebel Alliance

Momaw Nadon is a male Ithorian ("Hammerhead") and rebel sympathizer exiled on Tatooine. His presence there is punishment for revealing the secrets of Ithorian agricultural technology to the Empire, even though his doing so saved his homeworld from destruction. On Tatooine, he cultivates a hidden garden in the mountains south of Mos Eisley, where he conceals rebel operatives. He is present at the Mos Eisley Cantina on the fateful day Luke Skywalker and Obi-Wan Kenobi first meet Han Solo and Chewbacca.

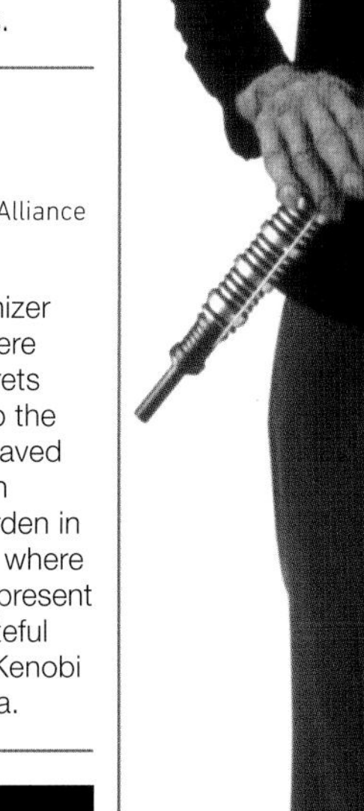

THE MODAL NODES

APPEARANCES IV **SPECIES** Bith
HOMEWORLD Bith **AFFILIATION** None

The Modal Nodes is a popular band that brings in the crowds at the Mos Eisley Cantina. Regular band members include Figrin D'an (on Kloo horn), Nalan Cheel (on Bandfill), Doikk Na'ts (on Fizzz, aka Dorenian Beshniquel), Tedn Dahai (on Fanfar), Tech M'or (on the Ommni box), Ickabel G'ont (on the Double Jocimer), and Sun'il Ei'de (on drums). The wholly instrumental band specializes in jazzy musical forms. The Nodes arrives on Tatooine to play for Jabba the Hutt in his palace as recompense for D'an's debts to the crime lord. When Jabba frees the band, its members stay on Tatooine to earn some money. The Nodes is performing at the cantina when Luke Skywalker and Obi-Wan Kenobi enter the establishment looking for a pilot to take them to the Alderaan system.

FIGRIN D'AN

APPEARANCES IV **SPECIES** Bith
HOMEWORLD Bith **AFFILIATION** None

"Fiery" Figrin D'an is the overbearing band leader of the Modal Nodes. As a Bith, his brain has a fine aptitude for music and his high manual dexterity is well suited to playing a range of instruments. Though he favors the Kloo horn, D'an also plays a mean Gasan string drum. D'an is a keen gambler, and his debts are the reason the band has to play for Jabba on Tatooine.

GARINDAN

APPEARANCES IV **SPECIES** Kubaz
HOMEWORLD Kubindi **AFFILIATION** Various

Garindan is taken from Kubindi by the Empire and forced to become a spy. He eventually escapes, but can't return home and is forced to work as an informant in Mos Eisley for the highest bidder. Imperial authorities hire Garindan to locate R2-D2 and C-3PO. He quickly picks up their trail and uses a comlink to alert the Empire that Luke Skywalker, Obi-Wan Kenobi, and the droids plan to meet Han Solo in docking bay 94.

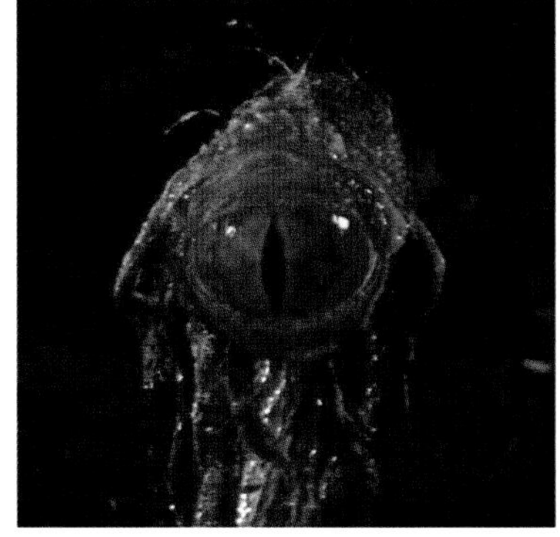

DIANOGA

APPEARANCES IV **HOMEWORLD** Vodran
AVERAGE SIZE 7 m (23 ft) long
HABITAT Sewers, swamps

Dianogas spread themselves across the galaxy by climbing aboard starship bilges and stowing away in their garbage tanks. They can now be found in sewers in many spaceports. Luke encounters a dianoga in the trash compactor on the Death Star and is nearly drowned and eaten by the beast.

JAN DODONNA

APPEARANCES Reb, RO, IV **SPECIES** Human
HOMEWORLD Commenor
AFFILIATION Republic, Rebel Alliance

General Jan Dodonna serves in the Republic Navy aboard a *Venator*-class Star Destroyer during the Clone Wars. Soon after the Empire's formation, Dodonna defects from the Imperial Navy to join the rebels. He leads the Massassi Group, a rebel team based on Yavin 4 that joins the Rebel Alliance. Dodonna and a portion of his forces join Phoenix Squadron at its base on Atollon. The two groups are about to launch a joint assault on Lothal but are interrupted by a surprise Imperial attack on the planet. Many rebels are killed, and only a few ships escape to regroup on Yavin 4.

Dodonna is on Yavin 4 during the Battle of Scarif. Following the victory, Dodonna identifies the Death Star's single flaw and commands the assault on the battle station from Yavin's command center. After the Death Star's destruction, Dodonna orders the evacuation of the base.

A year later, Dodonna is present at the Mako-Ta Space Docks when the fleet of Mon Cala cruisers arrives to be retrofitted into Alliance warships. He is given command of a ship named *Republic*. Unfortunately, the rebels are betrayed by the Shu-Torun, who sabotage the ships, rendering them inoperative. Soon after, the Empire arrives to obliterate the rebels. Thanks to a mission led by Davits Draven and Princess Leia Organa, Dodonna is given the access codes to regain control of the *Republic* and promptly orders that his vessel jumps to hyperspace. He returns and saves many of his allies, but the *Republic* is destroyed, and Dodonna goes down with his ship.

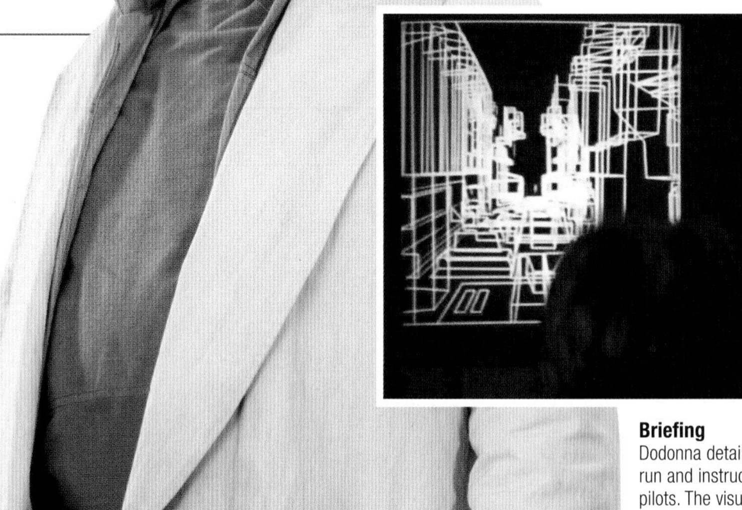

Briefing
Dodonna details the Death Star's trench run and instructs the rebel starfighter pilots. The visuals come directly from the plans R2-D2 carried.

JON VANDER

APPEARANCES Reb, RO, IV **SPECIES** Human **HOMEWORLD** Onderon
AFFILIATION Rebel Alliance

Jon "Dutch" Vander is a former Imperial pilot who defects to the rebels when he is ordered to bomb rebel-friendly areas of his home planet. Vander becomes the leader of Gold Squadron, a rebel unit of Y-wings, and helps transport rebel leader Mon Mothma to Dantooine where she officially forms the Rebel Alliance. Vander and his squadron fight during the Battle of Scarif, helping to destroy the planet's shield gate. Prior to the Battle of Yavin, Vander questions General Dodonna during their briefing, but leads his squadron in the assault on the Death Star. He is shot down and killed by Darth Vader during the mission.

GARVEN DREIS

APPEARANCES RO, IV **SPECIES** Human **HOMEWORLD** Virujansi
AFFILIATION Rebel Alliance

A former member of the Rarified Air Cavalry on Virujansi, Garven "Dave" Dreis leads the X-wing Red Squadron during the Battle of Scarif and the Battle of Yavin. When Gold Squadron fail in its trench run on the Death Star, Dreis misses hitting the battle station's exhaust port, and his X-wing is destroyed by Darth Vader.

BIGGS DARKLIGHTER

APPEARANCES IV **SPECIES** Human **HOMEWORLD** Tatooine
AFFILIATION Rebel Alliance

Biggs Darklighter is a childhood friend of Luke Skywalker. They often fly T-16 skyhoppers in Beggar's Canyon together. Biggs leaves Tatooine to attend an Imperial Academy and become a TIE pilot. After graduation he abandons his commission and joins the Rebel Alliance. He returns to Tosche Station on Tatooine to tell Luke of his plans, before traveling to Yavin 4. There he meets Luke again, and the two fly as part of X-wing Red Squadron in the mission to destroy the Death Star. Biggs is one of the last pilots killed in the battle, his ship destroyed by Darth Vader.

JEK PORKINS

APPEARANCES IV **SPECIES** Human
HOMEWORLD Bestine IV
AFFILIATION Rebel Alliance

Jek Porkins is a pilot and trader who abandons his homeworld when the Empire moves in and develops a new military base there. He flies as Red Six during the Battle of Scarif and the Battle of Yavin. During the assault on the Death Star, his X-wing is struck by debris, causing malfunctions that leave his ship slow and unresponsive. His X-wing then explodes when it is hit by TIE fighter fire.

WEDGE ANTILLES

APPEARANCES Reb, IV, V, VI **SPECIES** Human **HOMEWORLD** Corellia **AFFILIATION** Empire, Rebel Alliance, New Republic

"Copy, Gold Leader. I'm already on my way out."

WEDGE ANTILLES

Wedge Antilles grows up on Corellia, where he works as a pilot and mechanic. He joins the Empire and receives training at the prestigious Skystrike Academy to train to become an elite TIE fighter pilot. After witnessing Imperial atrocities, Wedge and his friend Derek "Hobbie" Klivian wish to defect to the rebellion and are recruited into Phoenix Squadron by Sabine Wren. Wedge goes on an undercover mission to gain clearance codes from an Imperial base on Killun 71. He flies during the Battle of Atollon in an A-wing and is one of the few survivors from Phoenix Squadron, going on to join the Massassi Group on Yavin 4.

After joining Red Squadron, Wedge becomes fast friends with fellow pilots Jek Porkins and Biggs Darklighter. While he doesn't participate in the Battle of Scarif, Wedge relays the order to the other pilots to redeploy to the planet. Days later, Wedge flies as Red Two when his squadron meets the approaching Death Star. Wedge is one of the three pilots who participate in the final trench run, but his X-wing is damaged, forcing him to retreat. He and Luke are the only two survivors of Red Squadron. They both continue to serve under the new Red Leader Arhul Nara and come to trust each other completely. Wedge goes on to participate in the successful missions to Giju, Tureen VII, and Mon Cala.

During the Imperial attack on the rebel forces at Mako-Ta Space Docks, Wedge joins Luke's newly formed Rogue Squadron, disobeying General Dodonna's orders and helping to ensure many rebels survive. Following the mercy mission to Oulanne, Wedge successfully recruits ex-imperial pilot Thane Kyrell to the Rebellion. At the Battle of Hoth, Wedge flies a T-47 airspeeder. He and his gunner, Wes Janson, successfully bring down the first AT-AT by tripping the walker with a tow cable. Wedge and Janson board X-wings and escort the final rebel ship to safety.

Wedge is later promoted to Commander and becomes Red Leader. He attends the Rebel Alliance briefing at *Home One* and is charged with leading Red Squadron during the Battle of Endor. He is one of several X-wing pilots to fly into the second Death Star, accompanying the *Millennium Falcon*. They narrowly escape after destroying the battle station's main reactor. Afterward, Wedge joins the celebration on Endor at the Ewoks' Bright Tree Village.

Following the festivities, Wedge becomes a captain in the New Republic military and goes on a reconnaissance mission to discover Imperial supply lines. Wedge and his ship are captured above Akiva by Imperial Admiral Rae Sloane, and Wedge is tortured while in captivity. Thanks to rebel pilot Norra Wexley and her allies, Wedge is rescued and reunites with the Republic on Chandrila. While recovering from his ordeal, Wedge becomes close to Norra and trains her son, Temmin Wexley, to be a X-wing pilot. He also forms Phantom Squadron and leads his pilots during the Liberation of Kashyyyk and the Battle of Jakku. After the war's conclusion, Wedge becomes the lead instructor of a flight academy on Hosnian Prime.

Skilled survivor
Wedge is the only pilot to fly in and survive all of the Rebellion's major battles since the Battle of Yavin, including the Battle of Hoth *(right)* and the Battle of Endor *(above)*.

DAVISH "POPS" KRAIL

APPEARANCES IV **SPECIES** Human
HOMEWORLD Dantooine
AFFILIATION Rebel Alliance

Davish Krail is a veteran Y-wing pilot who flies as Gold Five under Jon Vander in Gold Squadron during the Battle of Yavin. He accompanies Tiree and Vander in the first trench run to the Death Star's exhaust port. He aborts the unsuccessful attempt after his friends are killed, but his ship is blown up by Darth Vader, though after he manages to alert Red Squadron.

DEX TIREE

APPEARANCES IV **SPECIES** Human
HOMEWORLD Onderon
AFFILIATION Rebel Alliance

Dex Tiree flies as Gold Two and is Dutch Vander's wingman in the Y-wing Gold Squadron during the Battle of Yavin. While beginning the trench run in an effort to blow up the first Death Star, his ship is the first to be hit by Darth Vader's TIE Advanced x1, and he is electrocuted by a power surge just before his Y-wing explodes.

TAUNTAUN

APPEARANCES V, VI
HOMEWORLD Hoth
AVERAGE SIZE 2 m (9 ft) tall
HABITAT Snow plains

Rebel soldiers discover tauntauns living in ice caves while building Echo Base. Tauntauns are easily domesticated and used as pack animals. Well adapted for cold, they have thick scales and fur, and can slow their metabolism to survive Hoth's freezing nights. Han Solo keeps an injured Luke Skywalker alive by placing him inside a dead tauntaun.

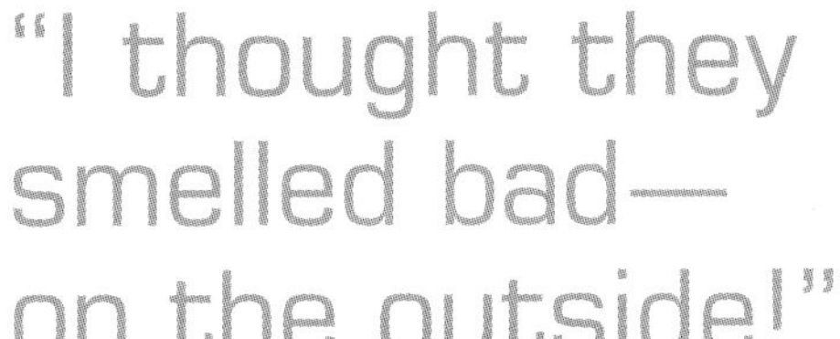

"I thought they smelled bad— on the outside!"

HAN SOLO

WAMPA

APPEARANCES CW, V, FoD **HOMEWORLD** Hoth
AVERAGE SIZE 3 m (10 ft) tall
HABITAT Snow plains

As the top predators on Hoth, wampas generally prey upon tauntauns, but do not hesitate to attack humans or their settlements. Their thick white fur protects them from the intense cold and allows them to sneak up on prey undetected. Wampas drag victims back to ice caves where they are later torn apart at leisure.

ADMIRAL OZZEL

APPEARANCES V **SPECIES** Human
HOMEWORLD Carida **AFFILIATION** Empire

A veteran of the Clone Wars, Kendal Ozzel is a Rear Admiral in the Imperial Navy. He is promoted to Admiral following the Battle of Yavin and commands Darth Vader's flagship, the *Executor*. Ozzel displays poor judgment and frequently irritates Vader. Ozzel is present for the assault on the Mako-Ta Space Docks. When an Imperial probe droid finds evidence of life on Hoth, Ozzel doubts the proof at first, then fails in a bid to surprise the rebels there. Vader accuses him of being "as clumsy as he is stupid," before executing him.

TRIPLE-ZERO

APPEARANCES Other **MANUFACTURER** Custom
TYPE Protocol droid **AFFILIATION** Darth Vader, Doctor Aphra, Beetee-One

Rogue archaeologist Doctor Aphra breaks into Wat Tambor's quarantine vault to steal a dangerously brilliant personality matrix known as 0-0-0. She installs the matrix in the protocol droid chassis. After he is activated, the murder-loving droid assists Aphra in awakening the "blastomech" Beetee-One. Triple-Zero, as the droid calls himself, serves as an aid to Aphra and her new master, Darth Vader, for a time. Later, he runs his own crime syndicate on Son-Tuul and blackmails Aphra into working for him. Thanks to Doctor Evazan, Triple-Zero is forced to work with Aphra once more on Milvayne.

GENERAL RIEEKAN

APPEARANCES V **SPECIES** Human
HOMEWORLD Alderaan
AFFILIATION Rebel Alliance, New Republic

A fighter for the Republic during the Clone Wars, General Carlist Rieekan becomes a founding member of the Rebel Alliance. Offworld when Alderaan is destroyed, he assumes command at Echo Base on Hoth. When Vader's forces strike, he delays them long enough for rebel transports to evade capture, and then escapes himself. During the Battle of Jakku, he launches a plan to try to persuade some Imperial ships to defect and join the New Republic cause.

ZEV SENESCA

APPEARANCES V **SPECIES** Human
HOMEWORLD Kestic Station
AFFILIATION Rebel Alliance

Zev Senesca locates Luke Skywalker and Han Solo when they become lost overnight on Hoth's ice fields. Zev flies as Rogue Two during the Battle of Hoth, but he and his gunner are both killed during the conflict when their snowspeeder is blasted by several Imperial walkers.

BEETEE-ONE

APPEARANCES Other **MANUFACTURER** Tarkin Initiative **TYPE** Blastomech **AFFILIATION** Darth Vader, Doctor Aphra, Triple-Zero

BT-1 (Beetee-One) is fitted with numerous high-power weapons not normally found in similar-looking astromechs. After BT-1 is assembled by the Tarkin Initiative, he kills everyone at the Imperial base and causes it to self-destruct. Doctor Aphra finds him in space and fits him with behavioral inhibitors, but is unable to wake him. She uses Triple-Zero to re-activate him and the droids serve Aphra and Darth Vader. When Triple-Zero goes rogue, BT-1 continues to act as a sidekick of sorts. He is destroyed by Darth Vader aboard the Accresker Jail, but is rebuilt by a Force-sensitive and sentient fungus possessing Tam Polsa.

ADMIRAL PIETT

APPEARANCES V, VI **SPECIES** Human
HOMEWORLD Axxila **AFFILIATION** Empire

Firmus Piett hails from the Outer Rim Territories. He rises through Imperial ranks thanks to his quick thinking and ability to shift blame for his own mistakes. He serves as a junior captain under Grand Moff Tarkin and eventually becomes a captain aboard Darth Vader's flagship, the *Executor*, until his commanding officer, Ozzel, is executed for incompetence. Promoted to the rank of Admiral by Vader himself, Piett pursues the *Millennium Falcon* through an asteroid field following the Battle of Hoth. Soon after, Piett orders Imperial officer Ciena Ree to lead a TIE fighter patrol of the Hudalla system to investigate rebel activity. Piett's distinguished career ends abruptly when an A-wing crashes into the *Executor*'s bridge during the Battle of Endor.

GENERAL VEERS

APPEARANCES V **SPECIES** Human
HOMEWORLD Denon **AFFILIATION** Empire

General Maximilian Veers is the mastermind behind the Imperial assault on Echo Base during the Battle of Hoth. From the cockpit of his AT-AT, *Blizzard One*, he leads the attack that destroys the rebel shield generator, before infiltrating their base with his snowtroopers.

DEREK "HOBBIE" KLIVIAN

APPEARANCES Reb, V **SPECIES** Human
HOMEWORLD Ralltiir
AFFILIATION Empire, Rebel Alliance

Derek "Hobbie" Klivian is a distinguished rebel pilot who began his career as an Imperial cadet at Skystrike Academy with Wedge Antilles. Both Wedge and Hobbie wish to defect to the rebellion, and they are extracted by an undercover rebel named Sabine Wren. Alongside Wedge, Hobbie joins Phoenix Squadron and survives the Battle of Atollon. Much like the way, Sabine assisted him, Klivian goes undercover on the *Rand Ecliptic* and helps Imperial pilot Biggs Darklighter defect. He is stationed on Yavin as standby pilot for Red Squadron and goes on to join Luke Skywalker's Rogue Squadron. He flies alongside Luke as his wingman in the Battle of Hoth but dies when his ship is shot down and crashes into *Blizzard One*—the lead Imperial walker.

SPACE SLUG

APPEARANCES V
HOMEWORLD Unknown
AVERAGE SIZE 900 m (2,952 ft) long
HABITAT Asteroids

Space slugs are solitary, silica-based lifeforms that dwell in asteroid caves, living on the mineral-rich deposits found in their habitats. Largely dormant, these gargantuan slugs are also known to prey on passing ships. On one such occasion, Han Solo pilots the *Millennium Falcon* into an asteroid field in a desperate attempt to elude his Imperial pursuers, only to be nearly swallowed by one of these opportunistic feeders.

Belly of the beast
A space slug uses all its energy to lunge at a passing ship.

MAJOR DERLIN

APPEARANCES V, VI **SPECIES** Human
HOMEWORLD Tiisheraan **AFFILIATION** Rebel Alliance

Major Bren Derlin leads the Alliance's mission to Omereth to extract slicer Drusil Bephorin's family, which is only successful thanks to Luke Skywalker's assistance. Derlin then works as a security chief and a member of Alliance Intelligence at Echo Base on Hoth. He gives the order to close the base door when Han Solo and Luke Skywalker become lost outside, to avoid putting the whole base at risk. He later serves as the unit leader in the Battle of Endor.

WES JANSON

APPEARANCES V **SPECIES** Human **HOMEWORLD** Taanab
AFFILIATION Rebel Alliance

Lieutenant Wes Janson flies as rear gunner for fellow pilot Wedge Antilles during the Battle of Hoth. They use their speeder's harpoon and tow cable to bring down the first AT-AT in the attack on Echo Base.

DAK RALTER

APPEARANCES V **SPECIES** Human
HOMEWORLD Kalist VI
AFFILIATION Rebel Alliance

A rebel pilot in Rogue Squadron, Dak Ralter serves as Luke Skywalker's gunner during the Battle of Hoth. Born into a family of political prisoners in an Imperial penal colony, Ralter escapes, harboring bright ambitions that he will never realize—he is killed when his snowspeeder is destroyed by an AT-AT.

SNOWTROOPER

APPEARANCES V **SPECIES** Human
HOMEWORLD Various
AFFILIATION Empire

Snowtroopers are elite stormtrooper regiments equipped for combat and survival in the extreme cold. Modeled after the Republic's former clone cold assault troops, which served in frigid environments like Orto Plutonia, Rhen Var, and Toola during the Clone Wars, their insulated suits and heated breather masks are powered by battery packs that last up to two standard weeks. Deployed in General Veers' attack on Echo Base in the Battle of Hoth, and brandishing E-11 blaster rifles and E-web heavy repeating blaster cannons, snowtroopers are a formidable match for rebel soldiers. Their equipment includes ice boots, an insulated belt cape, polarized snow goggles, grappling hooks, ion flares, and a homing beacon.

MYNOCK

APPEARANCES V **HOMEWORLD** Unknown
AVERAGE SIZE 2 m (7 ft) long
HABITAT Various

Mynocks are space parasites that survive on a ship's power cables and energy conductors. If they are not cleared quickly, they can fully drain a craft's power. When mynocks are ingested by a giant space slug, they can live inside their host's gut, sharing its meals.

4-LOM

APPEARANCES V **MANUFACTURER** Industrial Automaton **TYPE** LOM-series protocol droid **AFFILIATION** Bounty hunter

4-LOM is a protocol droid who serves aboard a luxury ship until his programming is overwritten and he turns to a life of crime and bounty hunting. 4-LOM soon partners with bounty hunter Zuckuss, tracking down bounties in their ship, the *Mist Hunter*. On Valtos, they try to catch Han Solo, but Han and Chewbacca trick them to rescue one of their captives and escape in the *Millennium Falcon*. In the *Mist Hunter*, Zuckuss and 4-LOM give chase, but both ships crash onto a dangerous planet. While the smugglers try to help them, Zuckuss and 4-LOM double-cross them, so are left behind. Years later, Darth Vader hires a team of bounty hunters, including 4-LOM, to locate the *Falcon*.

ZUCKUSS

APPEARANCES V **SPECIES** Gand **HOMEWORLD** Gand **AFFILIATION** Bounty hunter

Zuckuss, a bounty hunter who often works together with 4-LOM, is Force-sensitive and one of the first traditional findsman tracking experts to leave his planet. Along with 4-LOM, Zuckuss tries, and fails, to capture Han Solo and Chewbacca for Rekias Nodo. Years later, Zuckuss is hired on more than one occasion by Darth Vader: firstly to retrieve Doctor Aphra from the Rebel Alliance and secondly to join the hunt for the *Millennium Falcon* after the Battle of Hoth.

IG-88

APPEARANCES V, FoD **MANUFACTURER** Holowan Laboratories **TYPE** Assassin droid **AFFILIATION** Bounty hunter

Obsessed with hunting and killing, IG-88 is a rogue assassin droid and a chief rival of Boba Fett. During the Imperial era, IG-88 and pirate Hondo Ohnaka work together to try to collect the bounty on Crimson Dawn lieutenant Qi'ra, but Qi'ra captures them instead. After escaping, IG-88 is soon hired by Imperial Agent Kallus to hunt down Han Solo, nearly catching him. On a mission to Garel, IG-88 ends up being shot at by stormtroopers, even though he is working for the Empire. Years later, IG-88 hunts the *Millennium Falcon* and Han Solo once more for Darth Vader, and he ends up being defeated by Boba Fett. Decades later, IG-88 meets mercenary Bazine Netal who wants information on the *Falcon* since she is now hunting the ship.

CAPTAIN NEEDA

APPEARANCES V **SPECIES** Human **HOMEWORLD** Coruscant **AFFILIATION** Empire

Lorth Needa is a ruthless officer who serves the Republic in the Clone Wars when Chancellor Palpatine is kidnapped by General Grievous during the Battle of Coruscant. As commanding officer of the Imperial Star Destroyer *Avenger*, he takes part in the search for the rebels' secret base. After losing the *Millennium Falcon* while pursuing it through an asteroid field, Darth Vader Force-chokes him to death.

LOBOT

APPEARANCES V **SPECIES** Human cyborg **HOMEWORLD** Bespin **AFFILIATION** Rebel Alliance

While working for the Empire, Lobot has an AJ^6 construct installed into his head that helps him complete calculations quicker but comes at the cost of losing some of his personality. He later stops working for the Empire and befriends the smuggler Lando Calrissian. Lando and Lobot lead a small crew to steal the *Imperialis*, which they later discover belongs to the Emperor. When Lobot opens a locked room in the ship, he is gravely wounded by two Royal Guards. Lando places him in a bacta tank to heal, while their colleagues dispatch the guards. To escape the ship, Lobot lets the AJ^6 construct take full control, sacrificing what remains of his personality. Later, Lando becomes the Baron of Cloud City on Bespin and Lobot becomes his chief administrative aide and helps free Leia, Chewbacca, and C-3PO from Imperial custody. Lando leaves with the rebels and Lobot remains behind, fighting the Empire. Lobot and Lando are reunited following the Battle of Endor, when Lando returns to liberate Cloud City. While removing some Imperials from the Bolo Tanga room, Lobot helps Lando decide upon a present to give the heavily pregnant Leia.

MOFF JERJERROD

APPEARANCES VI **SPECIES** Human **HOMEWORLD** Tinnel IV **AFFILIATION** Empire

Tiaan Jerjerrod supervises construction of the second Death Star. When the project falls behind schedule, the Emperor sends Darth Vader to put additional pressure on the Moff. Jerjerrod commands the battle station's superlaser during the Battle of Endor. He perishes when the rebels detonate the Death Star's reactor core.

OOLA

APPEARANCES VI **SPECIES** Twi'lek **HOMEWORLD** Ryloth **AFFILIATION** None

Bib Fortuna kidnaps Oola and has her trained in exotic dancing. She becomes so enthralled with his stories of the grandeur of Jabba's palace that she turns down opportunities to escape. When Fortuna presents her to Jabba as his personal dancer, the Hutt lavishes unwanted attention upon her and keeps her chained to his throne. When she refuses his advances, he furiously drops her into his pet rancor's pit, where she meets a horrible end.

Trained dancer
Oola is a trained Ryloth dancer who is forced to entertain Jabba and his entourage.

BOUSHH

APPEARANCES FoD **SPECIES** Ubese **HOMEWORLD** Uba IV **AFFILIATION** Bounty hunter

A well-known bounty hunter from Uba IV, Boushh encounters wanted rebels Princess Leia and Chewbacca on Ord Mantel. A fight breaks out between the rebels and Boushh, who wants to collect a bounty on them. After defeating Boushh with Maz Kanata's help, Leia steals his armor to use as a disguise to infiltrate Jabba's Palace.

SALACIOUS B. CRUMB

APPEARANCES VI **SPECIES** Kowakian monkey-lizard **HOMEWORLD** Kowak **AFFILIATION** Jabba's palace

Salacious Crumb is the jester of Jabba's court. He begins his time with Jabba as a stowaway thief aboard the Hutt's ship, but Bib Fortuna manages to capture him. Henceforth Crumb sits beside Jabba and mercilessly teases captives. His shrill, irritating laughter amuses Jabba immensely.

8D8

APPEARANCES VI **MANUFACTURER** Verpine Roche Hive **TYPE** Smelter droid **AFFILIATION** Jabba's palace

8D8 is a cruel industrial droid owned by Jabba the Hutt. He tortures other droids to ensure that they know their place in the palace, sometimes tormenting just for fun. The 8D-series droids resent the more sophisticated protocol and astromech droids and tend to be bullies.

EV-9D9

APPEARANCES VI **MANUFACTURER** MerenData **TYPE** Supervisor droid **AFFILIATION** Jabba's palace

EV-9D9 is Jabba's sadistic droid overseer. Her programming is corrupted, but she manages to avoid the manufacturer's recall and continues working in the Hutt's murky dungeons. She assigns R2-D2 to Jabba's sail barge and C-3PO to be the new interpreter.

DROOPY McCOOL

APPEARANCES VI **SPECIES** Kitonak **HOMEWORLD** Kirdo III **AFFILIATION** None

Droopy McCool is the lead horn player in Jabba's house band. His real name is an unpronounceable series of whistles, but the band's manager, Max Rebo, gives him his stage name. Lonely, Droopy plays his chidinkalu flute and longs for the company of other Kitonaks.

RANCOR

APPEARANCES VI **HOMEWORLD** Unknown **AVERAGE SIZE** 5 m (16 ft) high **HABITAT** Grottos, plains

Jabba's rancor is a birthday gift from Bib Fortuna. The rancor lives in a chamber below Jabba's throne room and is cared for by Malakili, the resident monster handler. When angry, Jabba likes to drop victims through a trapdoor and into the rancor's den, where they are eaten whole by the beast. When Luke Skywalker finds himself in the rancor's clutches, he is able to kill the monster by dropping a secondary gate on its head. Malakili has a bond with the ferocious but semi-intelligent creature and is heartbroken when it dies.

MAX REBO

APPEARANCES VI **SPECIES** Ortolan **HOMEWORLD** Orto **AFFILIATION** None

Max Rebo is the leader of his eponymous band, famous for playing at Jabba's palace. Whenever Jabba wishes, Rebo plays his red ball jet organ, accompanied by the other musicians. His two passions are music and food, which make him easily exploitable. When he brokers a deal with Jabba to play for free meals only, he infuriates the rest of the band. While on a trip to Mos Eisley, Rebo encounters his estranged brother, Azool Phantelle, who has stolen money on Jabba's turf. They are both chased by angry citizens and stormtroopers, until Rebo throws his brother's stolen money into the street. Jabba forces Azool to be a walking drinks table to pay for his crimes.

BARADA

APPEARANCES VI **SPECIES** Klatooinian **HOMEWORLD** Klatooine **AFFILIATION** None

A slave and mechanic owned by Jabba the Hutt, Barada is responsible for all of the gangster's repulsorlift vehicles. Despite his life of enforced servitude, Barada is reasonably content with his lot until Luke knocks him into the Pit of Carkoon, where he will be digested by the Sarlacc for 1,000 years.

GAMORREAN GUARD

APPEARANCES CW, VI **SPECIES** Gamorrean **HOMEWORLD** Gamorr **AFFILIATION** Jabba's Palace

Jabba the Hutt employs a contingent of Gamorreans as his henchmen and palace guards. They are typically armed with primitive axes and vibro-lances. Gamorreans are not considered to be very bright, requiring constant management by Jabba's head of security, Ephant Mon. Outside of Jabba's circle, Gamorreans are aligned with clans which are each led by a matron and a warlord. In Gamorrean culture, females farm and hunt while brutish males wage epic wars.

SARLACC

APPEARANCES VI **HOMEWORLD** Tatooine **AVERAGE SIZE** 3 m (10 ft) wide, 100 m (328 ft) long **HABITAT** Desert

One of Jabba the Hutt's favorite pets, the mighty Sarlacc nests in the Pit of Carkoon. From above, only the Sarlacc's mouth is visible. The rest of the enormous creature, including its vast stomach, is buried deep in the sand. When Jabba's prisoners are dropped into the monster's pit, the Sarlacc's tentacles grab them and drag them into its mouth. Rows of hundreds of spear-like teeth prevent the prisoner from climbing out, and the Sarlacc swallows its prey whole. Han, Luke, and Chewbacca are taken to the pit for execution, but with help from friends, manage to escape.

A gruesome fate
Jabba's slave Kithaba is snatched by the Sarlacc.

KLAATU

APPEARANCES VI **SPECIES** Kadas'sa'Nikto
HOMEWORLD Kintan
AFFILIATION Jabba the Hutt

Klaatu is one of several Kadas'sa'Nikto who serve Jabba the Hutt, repairing the crime lord's skiffs. A gambler, Klaatu enjoys watching the executions in the rancor pit beneath Jabba's throne. During the failed executions of Han Solo and Luke Skywalker at the Great Pit of Carkoon, he watches from the top deck of Jabba's sail barge as Luke Force leaps from a skiff to the barge. The Jedi scales the side to confront Klaatu, slicing his weapon in half and forcing Klaatu to flee inside the vessel. Seconds later, Leia Organa fires the sail barge's cannon at the deck before escaping the barge with Luke. Klaatu is killed in the ensuing explosion.

Endor patrol
The environment on the forest moon of Endor suits the biker scouts' specialized light armor and swift, agile 74-Z speeder bikes.

SCOUT TROOPER

APPEARANCES Reb, VI **SPECIES** Human
HOMEWORLD Various **AFFILIATION** Empire

Scout troopers are highly trained soldiers of the Empire, specializing in reconnaissance and sniping. The Imperial scout troopers were preceded by the clone scout troopers of the Galactic Republic. The scouts provide excellent long-range fire for their stormtrooper counterparts. Darth Vader's personal Death Squadron includes a complement of scout troopers, whose priority is to aid the Sith Lord in squashing the Rebel Alliance along with its sympathizers and secret allies. Scout troopers are stationed on Endor, where the second Death Star is under construction.

On the forest moon, scout troopers on patrol are taken by surprise and defeated by a small team of rebel soldiers. This same band of rebels attacks the bunker holding the shield generator that protects the Death Star in orbit. The scout troopers fight back, briefly subduing the rebels, before a tribe of Ewoks comes to the latter's aid. The defeated scouts are taken prisoner by the rebels, who successfully destroy the generator and the second Death Star shortly thereafter.

GENERAL CRIX MADINE

APPEARANCES VI **SPECIES** Human
HOMEWORLD Corellia **AFFILIATION** Rebel Alliance, New Republic

Crix Madine begins his military career as a well-respected leader of an Imperial commando unit, but he eventually defects to the Rebel Alliance. He is made a general and is responsible for covert operations. After Bothan spies deliver intelligence on the second Death Star being constructed over the Endor moon, Madine plans the assault against the Empire's latest battle station. He enlists recently freed Han Solo to lead an elite unit of highly trained commandos that will be inserted onto the forest moon in a stolen Imperial shuttle to destroy the shield generator protecting the second Death Star. Following the success of Solo's mission and the Rebel Alliance's resounding victory against the Empire, Madine is placed in charge of the newly formed New Republic Special Forces. He orders a small unit to investigate the Imperial presence on the planet Akiva. A year after the Battle of Endor, Madine attends the Liberation Day festivities on Chandrila and is believed killed during the surprise Imperial attack.

TEEBO

APPEARANCES VI **SPECIES** Ewok
HOMEWORLD Forest moon of Endor
AFFILIATION Bright Tree Village

After his scouting party captures the rebel strike team in a net trap, Teebo pokes Han with his spear to ensure compliance. In return, Teebo gets zapped twice by R2-D2 when he releases the droid from its bonds. During the Battle of Endor, Teebo sounds the Sacred Horn of the Soul Trees, giving the signal for the Ewoks to attack. In the celebration following the destruction of the second Death Star, Teebo plays percussion on stormtrooper helmets and bonds with R2-D2.

WICKET W. WARRICK

APPEARANCES VI, FoD **SPECIES** Ewok
HOMEWORLD Forest moon of Endor
AFFILIATION Bright Tree Village

When Wicket discovers a human woman unconscious in the woods, he remains wary until she offers him part of a ration bar to eat. Hearing the approach of Imperial scout troopers, he grabs his spear, ready for combat. When the troopers fire at them, Wicket and the woman—Leia—hide behind a log. Wicket rolls out of sight as one of the scout troopers threatens Leia with his blaster. He attacks the trooper's legs, giving Leia a chance to knock out her assailant, grab her blaster, and shoot the other Imperial trooper before he can escape.

Wicket decides to bring his new friend Leia to the Ewok village. En route, they save two of Wicket's fellow villagers from stormtroopers. When they arrive at Bright Tree Village, Leia is treated as an honored guest. Wicket and Paploo accompany Leia and the rebel commando squad to a ridge overlooking the Imperial landing platform and reveal a "secret" entrance to the shield generator bunker on the other side of the ridge. The rebels mount a sneak attack on the bunker, but are outnumbered by the Imperial soldiers waiting for them. When the rebels are led back out of the bunker at gunpoint, Wicket returns with an army of Ewoks to free them.

After the Battle of Endor, Wicket attends the festivities to celebrate the victory. The day after, Wicket joins Han Solo's strike team to destroy an Imperial base on the far side of the moon. Wicket also works with fellow Ewok Princess Kneesaa, Leia, and Luke Skywalker to defeat a gigantic Gorax. Wicket gives Leia a gift of a serpent-puzzle-plant acorn before she leaves his home.

CHIEF CHIRPA

APPEARANCES VI, FoD **SPECIES** Ewok
HOMEWORLD Forest moon of Endor
AFFILIATION Bright Tree Village

Son of Chief Buzza, Chirpa is a hunter for the Bright Tree Village tribe. When Buzza informs Chirpa that baby Ewoks (named woklings) have been stolen from the village, Chirpa works with Logray and Ra-Lee to rescue them. Chirpa eventually takes over as Chief of the Council of Elders and marries Ra-Lee. They have a daughter named Kneesaa together.

At the time of the Battle of Endor, scouts from the village capture key members of the rebel strike team sent to the forest moon, including C-3PO. Like the other Ewoks, Chirpa believes the shiny metallic droid is a prophesied golden god and initially agrees with the shaman Logray that several of the captives should be cooked alive in a sacrificial ceremony. Luke Skywalker tells C-3PO to order the Ewoks to release them, and when they refuse, Luke covertly uses the Force to levitate the droid into the air. Awed by this fearsome display of divine power, Chirpa orders the rebels freed immediately. C-3PO then tells the tribe the story of the rebels' struggles against the evil Empire, prompting Chirpa to declare the rebels honorary members of the tribe. Together, the Ewoks and rebels defeat the Imperial forces guarding the shield generator. Kneesaa goes on to succeed him as Chief.

Bold leader
At first skeptical of the rebel intruders on the forest moon, Chief Chirpa allies with them to defeat the Imperial soldiers.

LOGRAY

APPEARANCES VI **SPECIES** Ewok
HOMEWORLD Forest moon of Endor
AFFILIATION Bright Tree Village

Logray is shaman Makrit's apprentice for the Bright Tree Village tribe of Ewoks. Along with Chirpa and Ra-Lee, he discovers that Makrit plans to sacrifice the three of them and some kidnapped baby ewoks to a Gorax named the Great Devourer. Thanks to Ra-Lee's ingenuity, they escape and Makrit is devoured instead. Then, Logray takes over as the shaman for the tribe. When the captured members of the rebel strike team are brought to the village, Logray orders that Han, Luke, Chewbacca, and R2-D2 be cooked alive as a ritual sacrifice to "the Golden One," the shining protocol droid C-3PO, whom the Ewoks revere as a legendary deity.

PAPLOO

APPEARANCES VI **SPECIES** Ewok
HOMEWORLD Forest moon of Endor
AFFILIATION Bright Tree Village

Like his friends Teebo and Wicket, Paploo is a skilled Ewok scout. The trio leads the rebel strike team to the location of the bunker containing the planetary shield generator for the second Death Star orbiting the forest moon. While others debate the best plan for seizing the bunker from the Imperial soldiers, Paploo sneaks forward and steals an Imperial scout trooper's speeder bike. His diversion provides the strike team with the element of surprise as they launch their attack.

NIEN NUNB

APPEARANCES VI, VII, VIII **SPECIES** Sullustan **HOMEWORLD** Sullust **AFFILIATION** Rebel Alliance, Resistance

Sullustan smuggler Nien Nunb is a decorated and long-serving member of the Rebel Alliance. Days after the Battle of Yavin, Nien uses his ship the *Mellcrawler* to help his friend Evaan Verlaine and Princess Leia Organa smuggle persecuted Alderaanians off of his homeworld to safety. Years later, Nien helps the insurrection on Sullust against the Empire that liberates the planet.

During Operation: Yellow Moon, Nien and Leia work with three other rebels (Kidi Aleri, Lokmarcha, and Antrot), using the *Mellcrawler* for transport. Their mission is to deflect the Empire's attention away from the massing Alliance fleet above Nien's homeworld—Sullust. When the team is captured and held aboard the Star Destroyer *Shieldmaiden*, Leia, Nien, and Kidi escape on an Imperial shuttle the *Tydirium*, but Lokmarcha and Antrot sacrifice themselves, and the *Mellcrawler* is destroyed. After the operation, Nien gets a new ship named the *Mellcrawler II*. With his frequent co-pilot and fellow rebel Shriv Suurgav, Nien crash-lands the *Mellcrawler II* on a living island that tries to eat them and their ship. They escape being devoured, but the Imperials who also crash aren't so lucky.

Prior to the Battle of Endor, the Rebel Alliance fleet masses at the planet Sullust before launching into hyperspace to reach the site of the assault on the second Death Star. Nien's longtime friend Lando Calrissian plans to fly the *Millennium Falcon* inside the second Death Star to make a direct attack on the vulnerable power core within the unfinished structure, and asks Nien to be his co-pilot for the crucial mission. Nien lives up to Lando's trust in him, displaying great skill at flying the highly customized freighter. Days after the victory over Endor, Nien and Lando travel to Naboo in the *Mellcrawler II* along with a small rebel fleet to help Leia stop the planet's destruction by the Empire.

Decades later, Nien sends his friend Leia a message of support when New Republic Senator Casterfo reveals to the galaxy that Leia's biological father is Darth Vader. Soon after, Nien is present when Leia announces the formation of the Resistance to protect the galaxy, becoming one of its original members. Taking the rank of Lieutenant Commander, Nien primarily flies starfighters and participates in the assault on the First Order's Starkiller Base. Afterward, he attends Han Solo's funeral on D'Qar prior to the Resistance's evacuation of their base. Following the lethal First Order assault on the Resistance forces on Crait, Nien is one of a handful of survivors to escape aboard the *Falcon*. As he did three decades before, Nien takes his place in the cockpit as co-pilot once more, this time sitting alongside Chewbacca.

Flying buddies
With Nunb and Lando at the helm, the *Millennium Falcon* stages a direct assault on the Death Star's power core.

Suspicious colleague
Tam Ryvora is very suspicious of Kaz since he seemingly lacks any knowledge of starfighter mechanics.

"Get ready to be impressed."

KAZUDA XIONO

Ulterior motives
Kaz befriends fellow aspiring ace Jace Rucklin on the *Colossus.* Little does he realize that Jace actually wants to use Kaz, hoping to steal some of Yeager's hyperfuel for an upcoming race.

KAZUDA XIONO

APPEARANCES Res **SPECIES** Human **HOMEWORLD** Hosnian Prime
AFFILIATION New Republic, Resistance, Team *Fireball*

Kazuda "Kaz" Xiono is the young and excitable son of New Republic senator Hamoto Xiono. Kaz's father uses his influence to get his son enrolled in the New Republic Military Academy and then commissioned as a starfighter pilot. When the New Republic uncovers information about the First Order's interest in the planet Castilon, Kaz and two other pilots are sent to rendezvous with Poe Dameron of the Resistance and pass on this intelligence. However, they are intercepted by Major Elrik Vonreg flying a red TIE interceptor. Kaz orders his wingmates to retreat, intending to take on the First Order pilot himself. Fortunately for Kaz, Poe Dameron arrives and helps Kaz force Vonreg to flee back to the First Order.

Poe Dameron offers Kaz a place in the Resistance as a spy, stationing him on Castilon's *Colossus* refueling platform to uncover the First Order's interest in the station. Poe introduces Kaz to Jarek Yeager, an old friend and the owner of a starship repair shop. Yeager grudgingly hires Kaz as a mechanic, despite his lack of skills, to provide cover for Kaz's mission. Kaz works with mechanics Neeku Vozo and Tam Ryvora. Neeku takes Kaz's dreams of becoming the best pilot in the galaxy literally, gossiping with the platform residents and getting Kaz enrolled in a race. Kaz reluctantly accepts the challenge, but, flying Yeager's *Fireball*, crashes at the end of the race.

Owing to this incident, and the fact that Kaz is little help around the garage, Tam is frustrated at first with Kaz. However, in time, they become friends. He proves his worth when a customer arrives at the garage and starts acting suspiciously—Kaz discovers that the customer is spying for Kragan Gorr's pirate gang, which has repeatedly raided the station.

Kaz finally gets a lead on the First Order when Hype Fazon invites him and Tam to Doza Tower. Kaz spies on a meeting between Vonreg and the station administrator, Imanuel Doza, and learns that the First Order is offering to protect the station and provide fuel in exchange for use of the platform. Kaz then helps two children from Tehar, who are hiding on the *Colossus*, to escape the First Order.

Later, Poe and Kaz rescue Synara San, the survivor of a freighter overrun with Kowakian primates, and bring her back to the platform. San is secretly a pirate spy who facilitates further raids on the station. Meanwhile, Kaz makes friends with the captain's daughter, Torra Doza, who unwittingly helps Kaz spy on her father.

On their next mission, Kaz, Poe, BB-8, and CB-23 investigate a mysterious set of coordinates and discover an abandoned First Order base, Station Theta Black. Just before the station is destroyed by the First Order, Kaz and the others discover it was mined for dedlanite to make blasters. General Organa and Kaz agree that although this intel will do little to persuade the New Republic Senate of the First Order's threat, the information is still useful for their cause.

The pirate attacks on *Colossus* increase, so Captain Doza is forced to come to an arrangement with the First Order to protect the platform, but the group's presence quickly turns into a hostile occupation led by Commander Pyre. Kaz comes to realize that Synara is a pirate spy, but still helps her flee.

After Kaz and Poe return from a mission to the Dassal system, Poe leaves the *Colossus* with BB-8, and CB-23 remains with Kaz. As the First Order locks down the platform, Kaz and Yeager barely escape capture, and in the process alienate Tam—whom they have excluded from their Resistance activities. Kaz, Yeager, and Neeku launch a plan to submerge the *Colossus* so they can swim up to the First Order's communication jammer on Doza Tower and disable it in order to contact the Resistance. Even though Yeager is captured, they are successful and Kaz contacts Leia, who informs him that she cannot send help.

Kaz then decides to form his own resistance cell on the platform. The group realizes that the station is actually a ship with a Class 2 hyperdrive. While sneaking inside Doza Tower to free Yeager, Kaz and Torra witness a transmission of the destruction of Hosnian Prime by Starkiller Base. Kaz is horrified by the realization that he has lost his home and his parents, and becomes even more determined to fight back. Pyre realizes that he is losing control, so he evacuates the station with his ground troops and Tam just as the *Colossus* rises out of the water.

The Ace Squadron, Yeager, and Kaz rush to their ships and battle the First Order starfighters. Synara also arrives with the pirates to aid the *Colossus*. When a First Order Star Destroyer arrives and begins bombarding the *Colossus*, Kaz orders everyone to return to the station. With Vonreg on Yeager's tail, Kaz saves his mentor by blowing up his nemesis. Kaz and Yeager return to the platform, which jumps into hyperspace. They believe they are on their way to meet the Resistance on D'Qar—but Neeku informs him their destination is uncertain.

JAREK YEAGER

APPEARANCES Res **SPECIES** Human
HOMEWORLD Unknown
AFFILIATION Rebel Alliance, New Republic, Team *Fireball*

Gifted pilot Jarek Yeager flies for the Rebel Alliance and later the New Republic. After the Galactic Civil War, he competes in starfighter races alongside his brother, Marcus Speedstar. The two have a friendly, if reckless, racing rivalry—until tragedy strikes. Jarek's wife and child are killed when Marcus' ship spins out of control during a race after he modifies his speeder to get an edge. Jarek holds his brother responsible for the deaths and immediately ends their relationship.

Jarek retires to the *Colossus* supertanker with his droid, R1-J5, and opens a garage. Although Jarek himself gives up racing, his team of mechanics—Neeku Vozo and Tam Ryvora—work on an old ship, the *Fireball*, hoping to compete in races at the station. When his old friend Poe Dameron asks him to provide cover for a Resistance spy, Kazuda Xiono, Jarek reluctantly hires Kaz as part of his team. Kaz knows nothing about being a mechanic, which causes Jarek more than a few headaches! Yeager allows Kaz to fly the *Fireball* in a race, making Tam unhappy because Yeager had promised the ship to her. In other respects, Yeager holds Kaz at a distance, telling him that he has no interest in Kaz's mission: spying on the First Order.

Yeager's brother Marcus, now a famous racer, arrives at the station to compete in the Platform Classic. To generate more hype and money from the race, Captain Doza, the station's administrator, pressures Jarek to face off against Marcus. After some persuasion, Jarek accepts and flies against him. During the race, Marcus apologizes once again. Jarek lets Marcus win so his brother can use the prize money to rescue his teammate, Oplock, from the Guavian Death Gang. Although Jarek is not ready to forgive his brother entirely, at least the two of them part on better terms.

Always remembers
Yeager keeps a holopicture of himself with his deceased wife and daughter in his garage. The holopicture was taken of the three of them at Black Spire Outpost on Batuu.

Back in the saddle
Even though Yeager hasn't raced publicly in years, he gets back in his craft to fly against his brother. When the *Colossus* is being attacked by the First Order, he boards his ship once more to defend his home.

Against the First Order
Beyond providing a cover for Kaz, Yeager doesn't want any involvement with the Resistance. However, when the First Order tries to arrest Team *Fireball*, Yeager stands against the First Order.

NEEKU VOZO

APPEARANCES Res **SPECIES** Nikto **HOMEWORLD** Kintan
AFFILIATION Team *Fireball*

Cheery and optimistic, Neeku Vozo is one of Jarek Yeager's *Fireball* mechanics and is always willing to see the best in others. Neeku is a unusual fellow, since he doesn't understand analogies or figures of speech. He takes everything he hears literally, leading to frequent misunderstandings, hilarious situations, and wild misadventures. Neeku is also incredibly logical and smart, and these traits make him a skilled mechanic.

Neeku soon becomes acquainted with Resistance spy Kazuda Xiono when he arrives at the *Colossus*. At first, Neeku unintentionally makes things difficult for Kaz by telling everyone Kaz is the greatest pilot in the galaxy. He also gets Kaz entered into the station's next starfighter race. Kaz is not thrilled about competing in this dangerous event, but he finishes—more or less.

Neeku has a knack for making peculiar friends. When Kaz is searching for Kel and Eila, two fugitive children from Tehar, Neeku introduces Kaz to his friends, the Chelidae, engineers on the *Colossus* whom he believes can help. Neeku helps Kaz communicate with them, and they then assist with finding the children. When Neeku and Kaz discover the children are hiding from the First Order, Neeku coordinates a plan with the Chelidae to fake Kel and Eila's deaths to keep them safe.

When Marcus Speedstar arrives at the station to race in the Platform Classic, he brings his friend, a Mountain Nikto named Oplock. Neeku and Oplock hit it off right away, even though Kaz and Tam find Oplock's way of communicating a bit off-putting. Later, Neeku adopts a strange sea creature from the oceans of Castilon that he names Bibo. After its gigantic mother starts attacking the *Colossus*, Neeku returns Bibo to her.

Joining the Resistance
When the First Order takes over the *Colossus* station, Commander Pyre attempts to arrest Team *Fireball*, who must go into hiding *(left)*. After the group realizes that no help will come, Neeku joins Kaz's local resistance cell *(above)* and helps to activate the station's hyperdrive so they can escape the First Order.

Consoling a friend
Tam offers Neeku consolation when he has to return his new pet, Bibo, to its mother—a gigantic rokkna that is threatening the station.

R2-C4

APPEARANCES Res **MANUFACTURER** Industrial Automaton **TYPE** Astromech
AFFILIATION New Republic, Resistance

R2-C4 flies with Kazuda Xiono in his T-85 X-wing when Kaz faces off against the First Order's Major Elrik Vonreg. R2-C4 is left with the Resistance when Kaz is recruited as a spy on the *Colossus*.

Joining the First Order
While her colleagues escape the First Order, Tam is captured. She is interrogated by Agent Tierney of the First Order Security Bureau, and is upset to learn of Kaz's secret affiliation to the Resistance. Before the First Order is forced to evacuate *Colossus*, Tierney offers Tam a place with the First Order—and Tam reluctantly accepts.

TAMARA "TAM" RYVORA

APPEARANCES Res **SPECIES** Human **HOMEWORLD** Kuat
AFFILIATION Team *Fireball*

Tamara "Tam" Ryvora is the daughter of a famous racer on Kuat. She leaves her homeworld to become a racer herself. Tam arrives at *Colossus* station, where she becomes friends with Hype Fazon; however, the two grow apart when Hype earns a place in Ace Squadron.

Tam loses her own ship in a race after borrowing against the craft's full value in order to make vital repairs. To make a living, she then becomes a member of Jarek Yeager's mechanics team. Tam sees repairing the team's *Fireball* ship and making it fit to race again as a second chance at realizing her own dreams.

When Kazuda Xiono arrives and Yeager makes him part of the team, Tam is irritated by his obvious lack of mechanical skills and poor attitude to hard work. She takes his criticism of the *Fireball* personally, and is further annoyed when he flies the ship in a race and crashes it, so that it needs further repair work. Nonetheless, she and Kaz slowly become friends as they continue to work together.

Tam meets Hype Fazon once again when he invites her and Kaz up to Doza Tower, where he now lives. Kaz, working secretly as a Resistance spy, is only too eager to accept the invitation, hoping to gather useful intelligence. While in Aces lounge, Tam and Hype get into a bitter argument when he pours scorn on the *Fireball*. Infuriated, Tam storms off—it seems that their friendship will not easily be rekindled.

Tam soon befriends Synara San, completely unaware that this newcomer to the station is a pirate spy working for Kragan Gorr. When Gorr's gang attacks *Colossus* once again—this time with the aid of Synara's transmissions—Tam risks her own life rushing to help Synara amid the chaos. Although Tam's concern is actually misplaced, this generosity of spirit makes a strong impression on Synara.

R1-J5

APPEARANCES Res **MANUFACTURER** Industrial Automaton **TYPE** Astromech
AFFILIATION Team *Fireball*

R1-J5 is Jarek Yeager's antique astromech. Long ago, his outer shell rusted away, leaving a skeletal frame that exposes all of his essential components.

R1-J5 is an obsolete model, and his programming has acquired a few glitches over the decades. The droid once served as Yeager's racing co-pilot (evidenced by the pilot's helmet slung over his head). R1-J5 is also loyal to Yeager's *Fireball* team of racers and mechanics; however he doesn't immediately take a liking to newcomer Kazuda Xiono—though he softens in time. Most of R1-J5's duties consist of retrieving tools, conveying messages, and running errands. R1-J5 also keeps an eye on all of Yeager's belongings, leading to the discovery that Jace Rucklin has stolen Yeager's hyperfuel. When Yeager races his brother in the Platform Classic, R1-J5 serves as Yeager's co-pilot. R1-J5 later joins the fight against the First Order, both in and out of Yeager's starfighter.

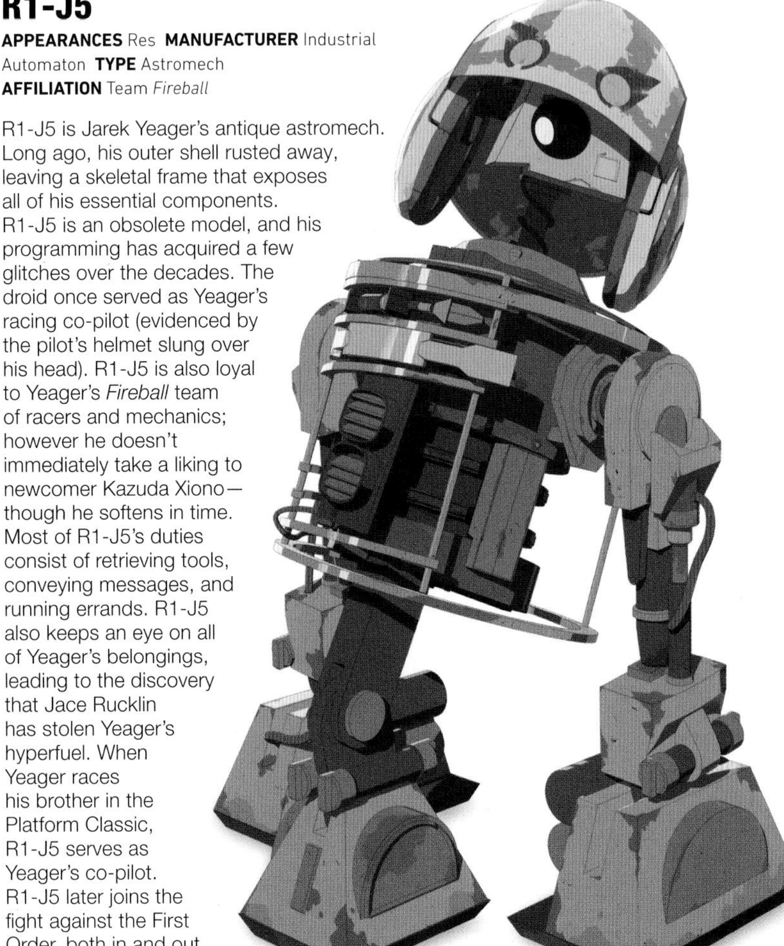

MAJOR VONREG

APPEARANCES Res **SPECIES** Human **HOMEWORLD** Unknown
AFFILIATION First Order

Major Elrik Vonreg is distinguished by his red TIE fighter pilot armor and matching red First Order TIE interceptor. Vonreg is a renowned fighter pilot, not afraid to take on an entire squadron of New Republic X-wings. When he encounters the likes of Poe Dameron and Kazuda Xiono, however, he is forced to retreat, allowing the Resistance to learn of the First Order's interest in Castilon. Meanwhile, Vonreg and Commander Pyre persuade Captain Phasma to use the pirate Kragan Gorr and his gang to harass the *Colossus* station. Vonreg later visits the supertanker, accompanying a shipment of fuel. He meets with Captain Doza, and tries to convince the station administrator that the *Colossus* needs the First Order to protect it. As their meeting concludes, Vonreg discovers that they are being spied upon by Kaz. Responding to a First Order probe droid's call for reinforcements in the Dassal system, Vonreg faces Poe and Kaz from his ship once more, but flees when they destroy his escorts. When the *Colossus*' pilots fight back against the First Order's occupation, Vonreg joins the air battle. He nearly annihilates Jarek Yeager, but Kaz shoots him down before he can land the final shot.

Vonreg to the rescue
When the First Order pays the Warbirds to kidnap Torra Doza, Major Vonreg travels to their ship. Vonreg then turns on them, "rescuing" Torra in order to return her to her father, Imanuel, and win his favor.

TORRA DOZA

APPEARANCES Res **SPECIES** Human
HOMEWORLD Unknown
AFFILIATION Ace Squadron

Torra Doza is the daughter of the *Colossus* station's administrator, Captain Imanuel Doza. They live in the Doza Tower together with the droid R23-X9 and Torra's pet, Buggles. Torra is a member of Ace Squadron and pilots the *Blue Ace* starfighter, which she also uses in local races. She befriends Kazuda Xiono, and even goes so far as to help him sneak around the Tower despite suspecting he is a spy. After her suspicions are proven correct, she helps Kaz in his fight against the First Order.

R23-X9

APPEARANCES Res
MANUFACTURER Industrial Automaton (customized) **TYPE** Astromech
AFFILIATION Torra Doza, Ace Squadron

While R23-X9 may look similar to an R-series astromech, it is actually a rarer model, built especially for Torra at great cost. It serves as her co-pilot and is painted blue to match her uniform and ship.

4D-M1N

APPEARANCES Res **MANUFACTURER** Unknown
TYPE Protocol droid **AFFILIATION** Torra Doza

4D-M1N serves as a nanny droid for Torra Doza, keeping an eye on her for her father, Imanuel. 4D-M1N switches to sentry mode if an intruder is detected. When the First Order threatens Imanuel, she falls in battle trying to defend him.

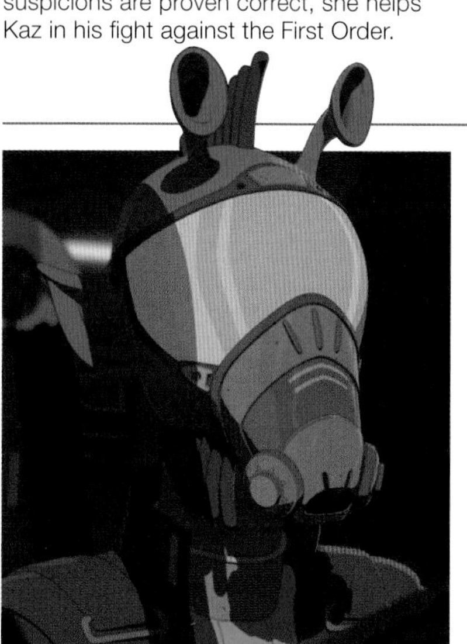

HYPE FAZON

APPEARANCES Res **SPECIES** Rodian
HOMEWORLD Rodia **AFFILIATION** Ace Squadron

Hype Fazon flies the *Green Ace*, with the call sign "Ace One," and is the top racer in Ace Squadron—with a big ego to match. Hype has numerous sponsors, evidenced by their logos all over his ship. Despite his boastfulness, Hype has a strong moral core—for example, he refuses to take part in duties that aid the First Order. Hype used to be close friends with Tam Ryvora, but the two have grown apart. When he hears her negative opinion of him, he tries to mend their friendship but fails. He does not take well to the First Order's occupation, being temporarily captured, and joins the fight against the group.

BO KEEVIL

APPEARANCES Res **SPECIES** Kel Dor
HOMEWORLD Dorin **AFFILIATION** Ace Squadron

Bo Keevil is a member of the *Colossus* station's Ace Squadron who chooses his words carefully. Keevil is a confident aviator who flies a difficult craft to handle—the *Yellow Ace*. He is also a show-off with a mysterious past. His life-support mask is of a kind typically worn by his Dorin species when they travel offworld, since oxygen is toxic to them and their ocular membranes dry out quickly. Their thick, leathery skin allows them to survive the vacuum of space—which is a handy adaptation for a pilot like Keevil.

FREYA FENRIS

APPEARANCES Res **SPECIES** Human
HOMEWORLD Yir Tangee
AFFILIATION Ace Squadron

Freya Fenris is a serious and skilled pilot based on Castilon's *Colossus* station. Flying *Red Ace* with Ace Squadron, she defends the platform against pirate raids by Kragan Gorr's gang alongside fellow aces Bo Keevil, Hype Fazon, Griff Halloran, and Torra Doza. Although the odds are against them, they fend off swarms of pirates, with secret help from Resistance spy Kazuda Xiono, who jams the pirates' radio signals. Like the other Aces, Freya competes in local races to pass the time—and in hopes of winning some extra credits.

R4-G77

APPEARANCES Res **MANUFACTURER** Unknown
TYPE Astromech **AFFILIATION** Ace Squadron

Ace Squadron pilot Hype Fazon loves his droid, R4-G77. The astromech is part of a new line that uses repulsorlift technology to move around. Hype's "baby" R4 has several mechanical arms, including a grasping claw and electro-shock prod. He also has an attitude—when Flix and Orka try to fix his bad motivator, R4 doesn't react well!

SC-X2

APPEARANCES Res **MANUFACTURER** Unknown
TYPE Unknown **AFFILIATION** Ace Squadron

Bo Keevil's astromech is an unusual ball droid model that rolls on a track for better traction and direction control. Keevil's droid stays steadfastly by his side at all times. It carries a supply of emergency parts for Keevil's life-support mask inside its body, among other handy gadgets.

R5-G9

APPEARANCES Res **MANUFACTURER** Industrial Automaton **TYPE** Customized astromech
AFFILIATION Ace Squadron

Much like his flashy customized ship, Halloran's droid is a customized Imperial astromech. While it has an astromech's body and navigational skills, it combines the precision of an FX-series medical droid with the observational skills (and range of nasty tricks) of a probe droid.

T3-K10

APPEARANCES Res **MANUFACTURER** Duwani Mechanical Products **TYPE** Astromech
AFFILIATION Ace Squadron

Freya Fenris' astromech droid is a modern twist on an ancient but efficient droid line that is back in style. This droid makes quick navigational calculations with little fuss. T3-K10 is a capable engineer and is suited to co-piloting larger starships, too.

GRIFF HALLORAN

APPEARANCES Res **SPECIES** Human **HOMEWORLD** Unkown
AFFILIATION Ace Squadron

Griff Halloran flies *Black Ace*, a racing ship derived from an old Imperial TIE fighter, and his uniform bears some resemblance to that of an Imperial TIE fighter pilot's. Griff also sports Imperial crest tattoos on both his arms. His appearance naturally leads the residents of the *Colossus* to conclude that he could well be a former Imperial pilot. He grimly cultivates this impression—enjoying the intimidating effect he has on others—by neither confirming nor denying questions about his possible Imperial past. Nonetheless, he is a dependable defender of the *Colossus* and a formidable racer.

FIRST ORDER STORMTROOPER

APPEARANCES Res, VII, VIII **SPECIES** Human
HOMEWORLD Various **AFFILIATION** First Order

Unlike the Galactic Republic, which utilized a clone army, and the Imperial Army, which was largely composed of a volunteer force instructed in academies, the First Order trains its stormtroopers from birth, with a strict education and training regimen that amounts to brainwashing. First Order stormtroopers are given serial numbers rather than names—and any glimmer of individuality is quickly crushed.

As Palpatine's evil Empire collapses, Counselor Gallius Rax selects two dozen orphans from Jakku, his homeworld, to be trained as soldiers. Following Rax's death in the Battle of Jakku, a small Imperial remnant flees to the Unknown Regions. A young Armitage Hux is put in charge of the child soldiers, whom he trains to become the First Order's initial squad of stormtroopers.

However, the real mastermind behind the First Order's future stormtrooper armies proves to be Armitage's father, Brendol Hux. Impressed by the training, devotion, and effectiveness of the Galactic Republic's clone army, but dissatisfied with the Imperial stormtroopers' clumsiness and unreliability, Brendol devises a program to indoctrinate children from birth. He thus creates an even more effective force than the previous Imperial Army or the Grand Army of the Republic.

While on Parnassos, Brendol Hux encounters Phasma, who claims to be her planet's greatest warrior. She volunteers to join the First Order and become a stormtrooper. In due course, Phasma and Armitage conspire to murder Brendol. With Brendol dead, they take control of Project Resurrection, the stormtrooper program, and employ Jinata Security to kidnap infants to become the next generation of troopers.

Performing a much more important role than her title of "Captain" would suggest, Phasma trains the First Order's stormtroopers to be ruthless killing machines, blindly following orders no matter how morally suspect. She teaches her charges to have no sympathy for others—including each other. Stormtroopers who fail in their duty deserve the most severe punishments, even death. Those who challenge her authority in any way are branded traitors and soon face the laser axes of stormtrooper executioners.

The defection of FN-2187 (Finn) is of great concern to Phasma and Hux, raising serious questions about loyalty within the stormtrooper ranks. It also causes First Order leader Kylo Ren to propose that a new clone army might serve the First Order better than Phasma's stormtroopers. Phasma desperately seeks to apprehend and execute FN-2187, but her defeat at his hands aboard the *Supremacy* emphasizes the threat that he poses to the corps' morale.

Every stormtrooper is issued an F-11D blaster rifle and an SE-44C blaster pistol. There is a wide variety of specialist divisions, tailored to different modes of warfare and fighting environments, including flametroopers, snowtroopers, heavy stormtroopers, and scubatroopers. There are probably specialist forces—which the Resistance has yet to encounter—for other environments.

Target apprehended
First Order stormtroopers completely despise all Resistance agents.

Passionate masses
Legions of First Order stormtroopers celebrate Armitage Hux's historic speech prior to the firing of Starkiller Base's superweapon.

AUNT Z

APPEARANCES Res **SPECIES** Gilliand
HOMEWORLD Crul
AFFILIATION Aunt Z's Tavern

Z'Vk'Thkrkza, known as Aunt Z to the patrons of her tavern on the *Colossus*, is a purveyor of great food, drinks, advice, and information. She also takes bets on the local races. Aunt Z is fun and friendly, but she can also be rather direct, and she knows how to cut through the "bantha poodoo"! Aunt Z is tough, too, breaking up bar fights and squelching robberies. Comfort food remains key to her business, evidenced by the waffle tattoo on her upper left arm, crossed by a knife and spatula. She has to temporarily flee the station when she is wanted by the First Order, but returns to save her home.

BOLZA GROOL

APPEARANCES Res **SPECIES** Klatoonian
HOMEWORLD Klatooine
AFFILIATION Independent

Bolza Grool is a gorgmonger (a seller of tasty gorg amphibians) with a market stall on the *Colossus*. Bolza and Kaz Xiono start out on the wrong foot, but later Bolza sponsors him in races.

GLITCH

APPEARANCES Res **MODEL** Hospitality droid
MANUFACTURER Unknown
AFFILIATION Aunt Z's Tavern

G1-7CH, otherwise known as "Glitch," is a service droid that works at Aunt Z's Tavern on the *Colossus* station. He serves drinks in the bar and helps Aunt Z determine the odds of races for her betting service.

ORKA

APPEARANCES Res **SPECIES** Chadra-Fan
HOMEWORLD Chad **AFFILIATION** The *Colossus* Office of Acquisitions

Orka and his partner, Flix, run the Office of Acquisitions on the *Colossus* station with the help of their trusty pit-droid, GL-N. He is also a knowledgeable repairer of astromech droids. Kaz Xiono barters with them—mostly with the business-savvy, but kind, Orka—when he needs speeder parts. Their first deal sends Kaz on a hunt for tasty gorgs. Orka and Flix go on to develop a good relationship with Kaz and he even minds their shop (in exchange for parts) while they are away.

FLIX

APPEARANCES Res **SPECIES** Gozzo
HOMEWORLD Drahgor III **AFFILIATION** The *Colossus* Office of Acquisitions

Flix works with his partner Orka in the *Colossus* station's dungeon-like Office of Acquisitions. They buy most of their parts from scavengers who recover them from the bottom of Castilon's sea. Quieter than Orka, Flix handles the administrative aspects. He's a stickler for numbers and for keeping the office organized—the opposite of Orka. He and Orka are both used to dealing with rough characters on the station, but they try to flee when the First Order occupies the platform. Kaz tries to get their help to free the *Colossus*, but they wish him luck and hide instead.

CAPTAIN DOZA

APPEARANCES Res **SPECIES** Human
HOMEWORLD Unknown **AFFILIATION** Empire, the *Colossus*

Captain Imanuel Doza is a former captain in the Galactic Empire and the administrator of the *Colossus* station on Castilon during the time of the New Republic. Imanuel's wife was a pilot for the Rebel Alliance during the Galactic Civil War. His daughter, Torra Doza, is a pilot racer in Ace Squadron at the station. The First Order pressures Doza to place *Colossus* station under its protection and control. He gives in when the pirate attacks on the platform increase, but later realizes this was a mistake and joins the fight against the First Order forces on the station.

HALLION NARK

APPEARANCES Res **SPECIES** Neimoidian
HOMEWORLD Cato Neimoidia
AFFILIATION Kragan Gorr's pirate gang

Hallion Nark comes to *Colossus* platform needing ship repairs at Yeager's garage. He is actually a spy for Kragan Gorr's pirate gang. Nark escapes the station just before a "triple dark" outage.

JACE RUCKLIN

APPEARANCES Res **SPECIES** Human
HOMEWORLD Unknown
AFFILIATION Rucklin's team

Jace Rucklin and his team (Lin Gaava and Gorrak Wiles) are racers at the *Colossus* station on Castilon. Rucklin befriends Kaz Xiono to trick him into stealing Jarek Yeager's hyperfuel. The fuel causes his speeder to explode, forcing Rucklin to work in Doza Tower to recoup the costs.

KRAGAN GORR

APPEARANCES Res **SPECIES** Quarren
HOMEWORLD Mon Cala **AFFILIATION** Warbirds

Tough and ruthless, Kragan Gorr leads the pirate gang named the Warbirds. His group is hired by the First Order to harass the *Colossus* station on Castilon in order to pressure its captain, Imanuel Doza, to submit to the First Order's protection. Gorr uses Hallion Nark to infiltrate the station so that his gang can attack. After Hallion is exposed, another Warbird, Synara San, is welcomed into the station crew. Kragan's gang attacks the *Colossus* again, but is run off when Kaz Xiono and Jarek Yeager get the station's turbolaser targeting computer working. When Kaz pleads for help against the First Order, Kragan and the Warbirds answer the call and board the *Colossus* before it jumps to hyperspace.

KEL AND EILA

APPEARANCES Res **SPECIES** Human
HOMEWORLD Tehar **AFFILIATION** Independent

Kel and his younger sister Eila flee from their planet when the First Order, led by Kylo Ren, kills their people, including their parents. The children stow away aboard a ship and end up at the *Colossus* station on Castilon. When the First Order discovers there are Teharan survivors, it offers a bounty for Kel and Eila, claiming the children are runaways from an important First Order family. Kaz Xiono and the *Colossus'* Chelidae engineers help the children fake their own deaths. The children escape the First Order's clutches and live in hiding in engineering section with the Chelidae.

KOWAKIAN APE

APPEARANCES Res **HOMEWORLD** Kowak
AVERAGE SIZE 2.4 m (8 ft) high
HABITAT Highland jungles

Kowakian apes are brutish genetic cousins of monkey-lizards. These dangerous creatures have a sour disposition and a mighty roar. Kragan Gorr's pirate gang is surprised by a cargo hold full of Kowakian primates when they try to loot a Darius G-class freighter near the planet Castilon. What they expect to be priceless cargo turns out to be a menagerie of Kowakian monkey-lizards and one very angry Kowakian ape. The ape eats most of the pirates; only Synara San manages to survive.

MARCUS SPEEDSTAR

APPEARANCES Res **SPECIES** Human
HOMEWORLD Unknown **AFFILIATION** Marcus Speedstar's racing team

Marcus is the estranged brother of Jarek Yeager, and is responsible for the accidental deaths of Jarek's family. Marcus comes to the *Colossus* to see Jarek and race in the Platform Classic. He uses the prize money to pay off a debt with the Guavian Death Gang.

R4-D12

APPEARANCES Res **MANUFACTURER** Industrial Automaton **TYPE** Astromech **AFFILIATION** Marcus Speedstar's racing team

R4-D12 is a cone-headed astromech droid belonging to racer Marcus Speedstar. The R-series droid provides navigational assistance during races, anticipating potential obstacles and forecasting multiple alternate outcomes.

SYNARA SAN

APPEARANCES Res **SPECIES** Mirialan
HOMEWORLD Mirial **AFFILIATION** Warbirds

Synara San is a member of Kragan Gorr's pirate gang and is his co-pilot during an early raid on Castilon's *Colossus* station. When she and her crewmates try to loot a freighter, they find it overrun with Kowakian monkey-lizards and a giant ape. She hides in a cargo crate, but her fellow pirates are devoured. Synara is discovered unconscious by Kaz Xiono and Poe Dameron, who mistake her for one of the ship's original crew. They take her back to the *Colossus*, where she recovers and works as a salvager—and as a spy for Gorr. She unexpectedly becomes friends with mechanic Tam Ryvora, who rushes to aid Synara when Kragan Gorr attacks the station again. Synara has to knock out one of the pirates to maintain her cover.

With the First Order suspecting that there is a pirate spy on the *Colossus*, Kaz learns that Synara is the spy and fears that she will be exposed. Thanks to Kaz and Neeku's help, Synara leaves the station aboard an escape pod and reunites with the Warbirds. Kaz later pleads for help against the First Order, and Synara convinces the Warbirds to help the *Colossus*. Aboard the pirate's flagship, the *Galleon*, Synara leads the Warbirds against the First Order. When a First Order Star Destroyer enters orbit and attacks the station, the *Galleon* lands in one of the *Colossus*' hangar bays. Synara and the Warbirds flee with the platform's residents to an unknown destination.

BUGGLES

APPEARANCES Res **HOMEWORLD** Naboo
SIZE 70 cm (2 ft) high

Buggles is a six-legged voorpak pet belonging to Torra Doza. Buggles lives with Torra in Doza Tower on Castilon's *Colossus* station. The voorpak isn't entirely housebroken and occasionally runs loose around the station. Voorpaks are popular with the aristocracy of Naboo. Their soft fur, light weight, pleasant odor, and generally friendly disposition make them ideal pets. Wild voorpaks live in rocky outcrops on hillsides, where they raise litters of up to five pups. Despite their cute appearance, voorpaks are carnivores, catching prey with their sharp teeth.

BIBO

APPEARANCES Res **HOMEWORLD** Castilon
SIZE 30 cm (1 ft) long **HABITAT** Open seas

When Synara San salvages a Clone Wars-era Z-96 shipwreck and brings it back to the *Colossus*, Neeku finds a small creature inside. Though Synara, Tam, and Kaz find the gelatinous, tentacled creature rather ugly and smelly, Neeku immediately falls in love, naming it Bibo. Neeku's new, chaotic pet tries to eat everything in Yeager's garage, including tools, ship parts, fuel, and even the astromech named Bucket. When Bibo wanders off, Neeku and Tam find him in the arms of Eila in engineering. She has had visions that Bibo will bring calamity to the station.

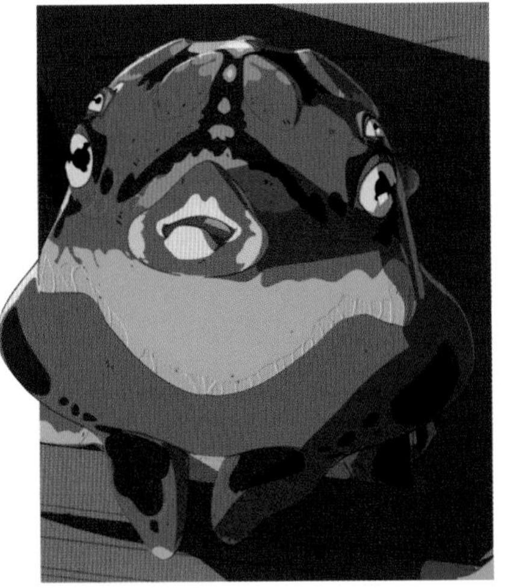

BITEY

APPEARANCES Res **HOMEWORLD** Castilon
SIZE 20 cm (8 in) long

Resistance spy Kazuda Xiono bargains with Flix and Orka at the *Colossus* Department of Acquisitions, agreeing to provide them with food in exchange for some ship parts. Kaz heads to the market, where he acquires a live gorg for their lunch. By the time Kaz returns, Flix and Orka have already eaten, but they still honor the deal, and decide to keep the gorg as a pet instead of eating him later. He earns the name Bitey due to his habit of biting fingers and electrical wiring with his jagged teeth. This behavior proves useful to Kaz when he uses Bitey to foil the thieving Teroj Kee.

ROKKNA

APPEARANCES Res **HOMEWORLD** Castilon
AVERAGE SIZE 220 m (722 ft) long
HABITAT Open seas

Rokknas are large sea creatures that lurk deep in the seas of Castilon. These terrifying leviathans have four eyes, six tentacles, and a gaping beak. Thankfully, they are not normally violent, but will attack if provoked, especially if their young are taken. Rokknas are seldom seen emerging from the depths, until a baby rokkna is accidentally taken as a pet by Neeku Vozo on the *Colossus*. Its mother is distressed by her baby's disappearance, and uses her sense of smell to track it to the station. The mother then begins attacking the *Colossus*, so Neeku hands over the baby to save the station.

SPEAGULL

APPEARANCES Res **HOMEWORLD** Castilon
AVERAGE SIZE 66 cm (2 ft) long **HABITAT** Water

Speagulls are water birds native to Castilon that are often seen flying or perching on ships, such as the *Galleon*, and platforms—including the *Colossus* station. They are skilled swimmers, and their natural diet consists of fish, crustaceans, and other aquatic creatures. However, they are known to beg, or even steal, scraps from the residents of the *Colossus*. Like most animals on Castilon, the birds have four eyes, which allows them to hunt for food and keep watch for predators at the same time. Their blue-and-white plumage keeps them camouflaged, whether they are seen from above or below, flying or swimming underwater.

CHELIDAE

APPEARANCES Res **HOMEWORLD** Castilon
AFFILIATION *Colossus* station

Slow-moving and peaceful, the Chelidae are a mysterious group of beings who work behind the scenes as engineers and caretakers aboard the *Colossus* station. They are a friendly bunch, but do take a long time to communicate or do anything in general. Neeku Vozo is good friends with the Chelidae and introduces them to Kazuda Xiono when he needs help hiding Kel and Eila—two children from Tehar who are running from the First Order. The Chelidae offer the two kids shelter and go on to help Neeku and Kaz free the station from First Order occupation.

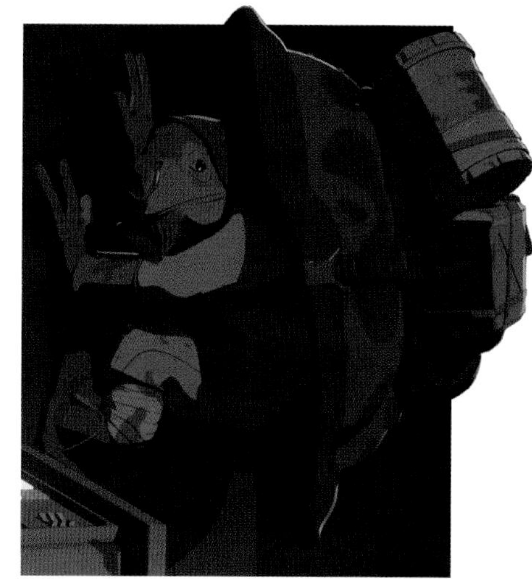

COMMANDER PYRE

APPEARANCES Res **SPECIES** Human **HOMEWORLD** Unknown
AFFILIATION First Order

Ruthless and efficient, Commander Pyre is a distinguished First Order leader who wears distinctive golden stormtrooper armor and a black pauldron on his right shoulder. He takes part in the negotiations between Captain Imanuel Doza of the *Colossus* station and the First Order, along with Major Erik Vonreg and Captain Phasma. He and Vonreg persuade Phasma to use Kragan Gorr's pirate gang to harass the *Colossus* and pressure Captain Doza into seeking protection from the First Order. These efforts fail at first, and Pyre has to explain why to Phasma, diminishing her confidence in their plan. Later, Pyre leads the search for the Teharan children, Kel and Ella, who are hiding on the station. He fails to apprehend them, tricked by Kaz Xiono and others into thinking that they have drowned. Then, the First Order pay the pirates to kidnap Imanuel's daughter Torra, but betray them and rescue her instead.

After the First Order returns Torra to the *Colossus*, Imanuel allows Pyre to lead a garrison of his troops on the station. Pyre quickly occupies the station, arresting citizens that get in their way and trying to apprehend the Resistance agents.

Following the near complete submergence of the *Colossus* beneath Castilon's oceans, Pyre personally leads a trooper contingent to investigate why the First Order's communication jammer has stopped working. He engages the culprits, Kaz and Yeager, in a firefight and captures Yeager. Pyre eventually realizes that he has lost control of the station, so orders his garrison to evacuate. He also calls upon First Order reinforcements, including a Star Destroyer, to aggressively take over the station, but the *Colossus* escapes to hyperspace.

AGENT TIERNY

APPEARANCES Res **SPECIES** Human
HOMEWORLD Unknown
AFFILIATION First Order

Agent Tierny is a member of the secretive First Order Security Bureau who is sent to the occupied *Colossus* station and charged with rooting out any Resistance spies. Rather than employing aggressive interrogation tactics, Tierny uses her well-honed guile on Team *Fireball* member Tam Ryvora. She exposes the fact that Tam's friends have been lying to her and then manipulates her into joining the First Order. With the Resistance regaining control of the *Colossus*, Tierny resorts to her pair of RK-3 blasters as she flees the platform with Tam.

CB-23

APPEARANCES Res **MANUFACTURER** Industrial Automaton **TYPE** BB-series Astromech droid
AFFILIATION Resistance, Team *Fireball*

CB-23 is a ball droid astromech assigned to Resistance Captain Poe Dameron while his own droid, BB-8, is helping Kaz Xiono on the *Colossus* station. CB-23 is loyal and resourceful, and though she chafes at BB-8 initially, the two droids become fast friends. She accompanies Poe, along with Kaz and BB-8, to investigate a Darius G-class freighter overrun with Kowakian monkey-lizards—and a monstrous Kowakian ape. While trying to escape these creatures, CB-23 discovers a survivor, Synara San. CB-23 again accompanies Poe and Kaz to investigate Station Theta Black. While the other three explore the station, CB-23 flies their X-wings into the surrounding asteroid field to hide them. She later returns to retrieve them after the First Order arrives, and they fly back to base. After accompanying Poe, Kaz, and BB-8 to the Dassal system, CB-23 replaces BB-8 on the *Colossus*, and she assists Kaz in defeating the First Order occupation.

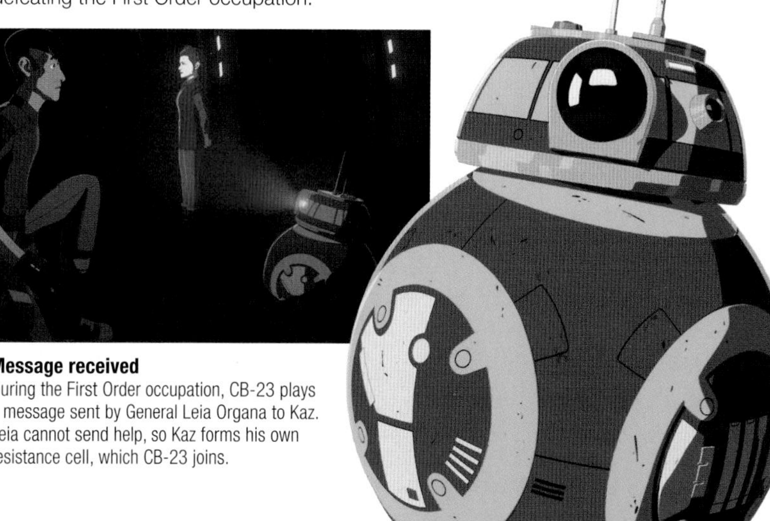

Message received
During the First Order occupation, CB-23 plays a message sent by General Leia Organa to Kaz. Leia cannot send help, so Kaz forms his own resistance cell, which CB-23 joins.

FIRST ORDER SCUBA TROOPER

APPEARANCES Res **SPECIES** Human **HOMEWORLD** Various **AFFILIATION** First Order

On aquatic worlds the First Order employs specialist SCUBA troopers to patrol military installations and occupied areas. These fighters are equipped with underwater blasters, flippers, breathing apparatus, air-tight armor, and lights to help with visibility underwater. When the *Colossus* station is submerged on Castilon, SCUBA troopers deploy to search for Resistance activity, and encounter Kazuda Xiono and CB-23, who only escape thanks to Neeku Vozo's inervention.

"We've pulled crazier stunts than this."

POE DAMERON

POE DAMERON

He thinks of himself as the best pilot in the galaxy, and he might be right. General Leia Organa sees even more than that, though—a future leader of the Resistance—if he can get his head out of his cockpit.

APPEARANCES Res, VII, VIII, IX **SPECIES** Human **HOMEWORLD** Yavin 4 **AFFILIATION** New Republic, Rapier Squadron, Resistance, Black Squadron

BLACK SQUADRON

Poe Dameron is the son of Sergeant Kes Dameron and Lieutenant Shara Bay. He is raised on Yavin 4, listening to stories of Rebel Alliance heroes Luke Skywalker, Princess Leia, and Han Solo. Like his mother, Poe becomes a pilot. He flies as commander of the New Republic's Rapier Squadron. But Poe grows frustrated with the New Republic's inaction against the growing threat of the First Order, so he joins General Leia Organa's Resistance. Flying now as Black Leader, Poe is tasked with locating Lor San Tekka and finding the map to Luke Skywalker. Poe also meets an eager pilot named Kazuda Xiono (Kaz) and recruits him to uncover the First Order's activities at *Colossus* station on the planet Castilon. Poe introduces Kaz to his friend, Jarek Yeager, and leaves his droid, BB-8, to help him. Later, Poe retrieves BB-8 and goes on to meet Lor San Tekka.

Black Leader
Poe leads the small Black Squadron on many missions, including to Kaddak, Spalex, and Cato Neimoidia.

JAKKU TO STARKILLER

On Jakku, Lor San Tekka gives Poe part of a map that leads to Luke Skywalker's whereabouts. As they speak, the First Order arrives. Knowing his capture is imminent, Poe gives the map to BB-8 and tells him to flee. Poe is imprisoned on Kylo Ren's *Resurgent*-class Star Destroyer, the *Finalizer*. Luckily, a stormtrooper named FN-2187 (Finn) wants to desert the First Order and needs a pilot. Together, they steal a Special Forces TIE figher and crash-land on Jakku. Poe wakes up alone and makes his way back to D'Qar. Later, he is reunited with BB-8 and Finn. Poe leads a squadron of Resistance X-wings in a strike against the First Order's Starkiller Base. He targets the facility's thermal oscillator, causing a chain reaction that destroys the entire planet.

Black One
Poe's unique T-70 X-wing starfighter, *Black One*, has black and orange markings.

RECKLESS FLYBOY

After the battle, the First Order arrives above D'Qar to retaliate. Poe comes up with a plan to distract them so the Resistance can evacuate. He destroys all the surface weapons on the First Order's dreadnought, *Fulminatrix*, hoping to provide an opportunity for Cobalt Squadron to bomb it. Though successful, all Resistance bombers are destroyed in the process. General Organa demotes Poe for disobeying her orders to fall back and for causing heavy and needless losses. When the Resistance discover that the First Order is tracking them through hyperspace, Poe, Finn, and companion Rose Tico hatch a plan to sneak aboard the First Order flagship and disable the tracker. As part of this, Poe sends Finn, Rose, and BB-8 to Canto Bight. Meanwhile, Leia is injured in a bombing orchestrated by Kylo Ren, and Vice Admiral Holdo takes command. Holdo refuses to tell Poe her plans and Poe suspects she is not working in their best interests. He leads a mutiny against her, and is surprised when Leia wakes from a coma and stuns him with a blaster for insubordination.

Mutual distrust
Poe and Vice Admiral Holdo don't see eye-to-eye. Holdo thinks Poe is too impulsive, while Poe doesn't completely trust the temporary Resistance leader.

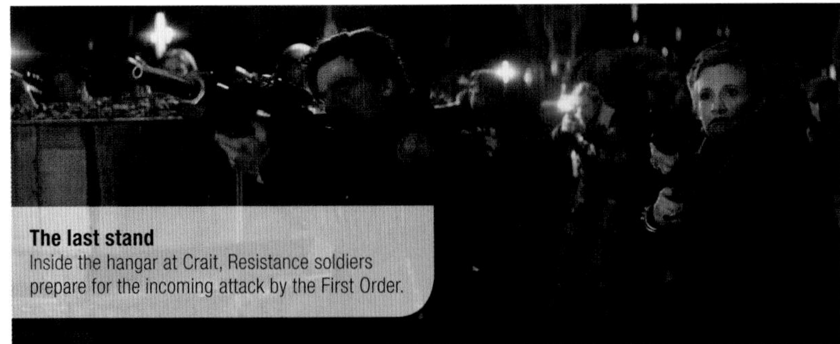

The last stand
Inside the hangar at Crait, Resistance soldiers prepare for the incoming attack by the First Order.

SENSIBLE LEADER

Poe wakes up in an escape shuttle with Leia and learns that Holdo had constructed a plan with Leia's blessing. They are now on their way to an abandoned rebel base on Crait. There, Poe is reunited with BB-8, Finn, and Rose. When the First Order arrives, Poe leads the charge from his V-4X-D ski speeder against their superlaser siege cannon. Having learned his lesson over D'Qar however, Poe realizes they cannot win, and orders the Resistance pilots to turn back rather than risk sacrificing everyone again. When the Resistance appears trapped and all seems lost, Poe follows some native vulptex creatures and leads the Resistance survivors out of the cave through a hidden tunnel where they meet Rey and the *Millennium Falcon*, escaping the First Order.

Cockpit hero
Poe aggravates his superiors with his arrogant attitude and reckless battle tactics. However, his willingness to take risks and try out new ideas is what makes him one of the top Resistance pilots. By practicing a little restraint, Poe may reveal his leadership potential.

timeline

▼ Birth of Black Squadron
Poe Dameron recruits Temmin Wexley, Jessika Pava, Kun, L'ampar, and Oddy Muava to form Black Squadron and search for Lor San Tekka.

Suralinda's secret plan
Poe goes to Pheryon to meet his reporter friend Suralinda Javos, who surprises him by asking to join the Resistance.

Meeting Kaz
After a skirmish with First Order Major Elrik Vonreg, Poe recruits New Republic pilot Kazuda Xiono to the Resistance.

Station Theta Black
Poe introduces Kaz to General Organa, who orders them to investigate the First Order's activities at an abandoned mining facility.

Map to Skywalker
Poe meets Lor San Tekka on Jakku, looking for "a chance." San Tekka believes the map "will begin to make things right."

▲ Kylo interrogates Poe
Kylo Ren learns BB-8 has the map, after performing a painful mental Force probe on Poe.

Poe meets Finn
Finn breaks Poe out of captivity and they steal a Special Forces TIE fighter to escape.

▲ Friends reunited
Believing each other dead, Poe and Finn have a surprise reunion on the D'Qar landing pad.

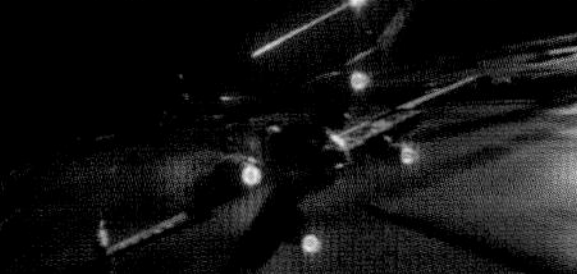

▲ Poe's folly
While the Resistance escapes D'Qar, Poe risks everything to destroy a First Order dreadnought—a tragic choice that changes him for the better.

Poe's demotion
Poe earns General Organa's ire after the Resistance bombers are destroyed. Vice Admiral Holdo lacks confidence in him as a result.

▲ Mutiny on the *Raddus*
Poe leads a mutiny against Vice Admiral Holdo. He is joined by fellow pilot C'ai Threnalli and Lieutenant Kaydel Ko Connix.

Battle of Crait
Using outdated ski speeders, Poe leads the charge against the First Order's superlaser siege cannon. He quickly comes to his senses and retreats before suffering massive casualties.

"The droid... stole a freighter?"

KYLO REN TO LIEUTENANT MITAKA

BB-8

Loyal, brave, and persistent, BB-8 is a selfless and dependable droid who always aims to please. He is loyal to his master, and to whomever his master lends him.

APPEARANCES Res, VII, VIII, IX, FoD **MANUFACTURER** Industrial Automaton **TYPE** BB-series astromech droid **AFFILIATION** New Republic, Rapier Squadron, Resistance, Black Squadron, Team Fireball

EARLY SERVICE

Belonging to ace pilot Poe Dameron, BB-8 is an astromech droid specializing in navigation, ship repairs, and systems support for starfighter pilots. Both serve in the New Republic's Rapier Squadron, until they are recruited to the Resistance by its leader—General Leia Organa. Poe, with BB-8 beside him, founds Black Squadron, and Leia charges the team with locating explorer Lor San Tekka. Once they find him and ask for his assistance in their search for Luke Skywalker, Poe lends BB-8 to his new spy recruit, Kazuda Xiono (Kaz). Dameron tasks the pair with investigating First Order activity on the *Colossus* refueling station on the planet Castilon. When San Tekka informs the Resistance that he has the map, Poe retrieves BB-8 from Kaz to recover the intel on Jakku.

Colossus cover
Kaz and BB-8 join Poe's friend Jarek Yeager's maintenance crew—Team Fireball.

Lone scavenger
Rey lives on her own on Jakku. It is with reluctance that she allows BB-8 to stay.

LOST ON JAKKU

In Jakku's Tuanul village, BB-8 and Poe meet Lor San Tekka and acquire the map. When the First Order arrives, BB-8 and Poe try to escape in Poe's X-wing but to no avail. Poe gives BB-8 the map and tells him to flee, promising to find him later, before Poe is captured by Kylo Ren. Left to fend for himself, BB-8 wanders through the desert, where he is snared by the scavenger Teedo. BB-8 is rescued by a kinder scavenger, Rey, who begrudgingly allows him to stay with her. At Niima Outpost, some thugs try to steal BB-8, but Rey fights them off. After the melee, BB-8 spots Finn wearing Poe's jacket, and after a brief tussle, all three find themselves being chased by stormtroopers and TIE fighters. They make a daring escape aboard an abandoned *Millennium Falcon*.

DELIVERING THE MAP

Out in space, the *Falcon* is intercepted by Han Solo. After a scuffle with rathtars and criminal gangs, BB-8 shows Han the map to Luke Skywalker. Han refuses to travel to his estranged wife Leia, but takes BB-8, Rey, and Finn to Maz Kanata on Takodana. However, chaos erupts when the First Order arrives. Fortunately, the Resistance turns up and fights the First Order, but Kylo Ren kidnaps Rey. After the battle ends, BB-8 travels to D'Qar with the others and is finally reunited with Poe. While the Resistance realizes that BB-8's map is incomplete, the group has to focus on the First Order—who is preparing to use Starkiller Base to destroy D'Qar. In *Black One*, BB-8 and Poe join the assault on the superweapon. Thanks to the ground team, they can deliver the critical shot that destroys the base. Afterward, they return to D'Qar, R2-D2 powers up just in time to help BB-8 piece together the map to Luke.

Two droids are better than one
R2-D2 has been storing a piece of the map for years. When he powers up, he is able to complete BB-8's map.

Canto Bight
BB-8 is not used to the strange luxuries and creatures of the Canto Casino.

FLIGHT OF THE RESISTANCE

When the First Order attacks the D'Qar base, the Resistance is forced to evacuate. BB-8 goes to extraordinary lengths to keep Poe's ship functioning during the battle. They rejoin the Resistance aboard the *Raddus*, but it is attacked by Kylo Ren, and BB-8 is nearly blown apart. It comes to light that the First Order is tracking the Resistance through hyperspace, so BB-8, Finn, and Rose Tico head to Canto Bight in search of the "Master Codebreaker" to help disable the First Order's tracking system. Unfortunately, Finn and Rose are arrested at the casino; instead of rescuing them, BB-8 finds himself with criminal slicer DJ. They steal a ship and rescue Finn and Rose. All four sneak aboard the First Order's flagship *Supremacy*, but DJ betrays them and they are captured. BB-8 saves Finn and Rose by hijacking an AT-ST. They escape to Crait, where BB-8 is reunited again with Poe.

Resourceful droid
BB-8 is an innovative and intelligent droid who does his utmost to help his allies complete their missions. He has six tool-bay disks that can easily be swapped out for others carrying different tools.

timeline

Mission to Megalox Beta
When Poe travels to Megalox Prison to question Grakkus the Hutt, BB-8 and his droid friends cause havoc.

Mission to Kaddak
BB-8 and Poe are joined by C-3PO to retrieve a droid spy, but First Order Agent Terex intervenes and BB-8 must swing into action.

Signal from Sector Six
Poe Dameron, Kaz Xiono, BB-8, and CB-23 investigate a distress signal and must contend with a ship overrun by Kowakian monkey-lizards.

▲ First Order arrives
BB-8 spots the First Order troop transports coming toward Tuanul, where they wipe out the village.

BB-8 meets Rey
Outside Rey's home, Teedo loads BB-8 onto his luggabeast, but Rey takes pity and intervenes.

Finn gets the thumbs up
Finn reveals he's lying about being a part of the Resistance, but the former stormtrooper convinces BB-8 to tell Rey the Resistance is on D'Qar.

▲ Meeting Han Solo
Aboard the *Millennium Falcon*, BB-8 shows Han Solo a partial holomap leading to Luke Skywalker.

▲ Reunited with Poe
BB-8 is reunited with Poe Dameron on D'Qar following the Battle of Takodana.

Completing the map
R2-D2 finally awakens and reveals he has the rest of the map leading to Luke's location.

▲ Standoff over D'Qar
BB-8 works his magic in Poe's X-wing as they take out the surface weapons on the First Order's dreadnought, the *Fulminatrix*.

Misadventure in Canto Casino
On Canto Bight, Dobbu Scay mistakes BB-8 for a gambling machine and drops coins into his slots.

◀ Aboard the *Supremacy*
BB-8 rolls clumsily in a makeshift "disguise" aboard the First Order's flagship, the *Supremacy*. However, First Order droid BB-9E isn't fooled.

Unexpected foe
Captain Phasma and Finn, formerly stormtrooper FN-2187 *(below)*, have developed a hostile relationship because of Finn's insubordination.

Fearsome reputation
Phasma is known for being merciless. She is one of the commanders of the First Order forces *(above)* and is not used to being disobeyed.

CAPTAIN PHASMA

APPEARANCES Res, VII, VIII **SPECIES** Human **HOMEWORLD** Parnassos **AFFILIATION** First Order

Captain Phasma is a ruthless warrior. She cares only about her own advancement and survival having not the slightest regard for others—even if they are on the same side as her. Phasma grows up on Parnassos, a primitive, desolate world where her clan must fight to protect its territory. Phasma single-handedly engineers the death of her entire clan, including her parents, so that she and her brother Keldo may survive and join the stronger Scyre clan. When First Order officer Brendol Hux crash-lands on her world, Phasma sees another opportunity and volunteers—as the planet's greatest warrior—to join the First Order.

Although she prefers the title "Captain," Phasma's functional rank is much higher, with her leading beside General Armitage Hux and Kylo Ren from Starkiller Base. Phasma coordinates high-profile spies and field agents, including the self-serving Terex. When he proves unwieldy, she has Terex subdued with cybernetic implants. Phasma also oversees First Order interests at the *Colossus* fueling station on Castilon. Her primary role, however, is as the leader of the First Order's stormtroopers. As such, she manages the training of FN-2187 (Finn), whom she finds highly capable yet frustratingly uncooperative. She repeatedly orders him not to assist weaker team members, and he fails to follow orders to fire upon civilian targets.

Together with Kylo Ren, Phasma leads the attack at Tuanul on Jakku, where she orders her stormtroopers to eliminate the remaining villagers. When FN-2187 fails to comply, and goes so far as to remove his helmet without permission, she orders him to submit to an evaluation. Nonetheless, Phasma is surprised when he deserts the First Order and escapes to Jakku with Resistance captive Poe Dameron. Phasma meets Finn again on Starkiller Base, where he and Han Solo capture her. Although she puts up a superficial fight, Phasma readily submits and drops the shields on Starkiller Base—thus dooming the First Order—hoping to save herself. But she is dropped in a trash compactor after serving her purpose.

Phasma escapes the trash compactor and Starkiller Base before the planet explodes. However, she discovers that Lieutenant Sol Rivas had accessed the same computer terminal she'd used to lower the shields. In an effort to cover her tracks, she blames her deeds on him and takes a TIE pilot (TN-3465) with her to assassinate him. Afterward, she ruthlessly kills her loyal pilot as well.

Phasma encounters Finn again when he and his accomplice, Rose Tico, sneak aboard the First Order flagship *Supremacy*. She takes perverse pleasure in overseeing their execution, telling the executioners to "make this hurt." When Resistance leader Vice Admiral Holdo rams the *Supremacy* in the *Raddus*, the execution ceremony is thrown into disarray. Phasma and Finn are thrown into combat, and though she appears to be the superior fighter, Finn manages to send her falling into the fiery depths of the ship.

Tough training
Captain Phasma personally oversees the training of the stormtroopers. She is an unforgiving captain.

LOR SAN TEKKA

APPEARANCES VII **SPECIES** Human **HOMEWORLD** Unknown
AFFILIATION Church of the Force, New Republic, Resistance

Explorer Lor San Tekka is not a Jedi, but he believes in their ideals as a member of the Church of the Force. He explores many remote worlds and ancient and contemporary places of religious significance, including the Crèche on Ovanis. After the Battle of Endor, Lor San Tekka assists Luke Skywalker in the search for long-forgotten Jedi knowledge. He is imprisoned on Cato Neimoidia after breaking into the Neimoidians' vaults and examining a relic of significance to Force-wielders. He is put on trial and due to be executed, but General Organa and Poe Dameron rescue him. However, San Tekka is kidnapped by First Order Agent Terex, who ejects him into space. Lor San Tekka is rescued by Black Squadron and brought to D'Qar, where he disappoints Leia, confessing that he does not know the whereabouts of Luke Skywalker, although given time he may discover it. Soon after, he notifies Leia that he has a map fragment that may point to the lost Jedi's location. Poe Dameron meets him in Tuanul Village on Jakku. There, San Tekka turns over the map to Poe before the First Order arrives and Kylo Ren murders him.

Brutal punishment
Kylo Ren demands the map from Lor San Tekka, but the old man merely expresses his disappointment in what Kylo Ren has become.

FN-2003

APPEARANCES VII **SPECIES** Human
HOMEWORLD Unknown
AFFILIATION First Order

FN-2003, also known as Slip, is a friend of FN-2187 (Finn) and the weakest member of their team. Slip is killed on Jakku. Before his death, he wipes a bloody handprint on Finn's helmet.

FN-2199

APPEARANCES VII **SPECIES** Human
HOMEWORLD Unknown **AFFILIATION** First Order

FN-2199 (Nines) is a former comrade and friend of Finn. At the Battle of Takodana, Nines spots Finn, who has deserted the First Order, and yells "Traitor!" Then he brandishes a Z6 riot control baton and fights Finn, who is wielding a lightsaber. Nines is shot and killed by Han Solo.

FIRST ORDER FLAMETROOPER

APPEARANCES VII, VIII **SPECIES** Human
HOMEWORLD Various **AFFILIATION** First Order

Slow-moving First Order flametroopers work in tandem with standard stormtroopers. They are equipped with D39-incinerators, which incorporate a double-barreled D-93w flame projector gun connected by hoses to a set of fuel tanks carried on a backpack. Flametroopers are used regularly by the First Order. Agent Terex deploys them against an egg worshipped by the Crèche, inadvertently hatching it. Kylo Ren and Captain Phasma utilize them to burn down Tuanul Village on Jakku.

FIRST ORDER HEAVY TROOPER

APPEARANCES VII, VIII **SPECIES** Human
HOMEWORLD Various **AFFILIATION** First Order

First Order heavy troopers require substantial strength to carry their hefty FWMB-10 repeating blasters (otherwise known as megablasters), and wear web gear fitted with additional ammunition. Manufactured by the Sonn-Blas Corporation, their blaster cannons feature barrel-cooling shrouds and integrated fold-out stands. The blasters are also mounted on infantry vehicles as their primary weapons. While their rate of fire is slower than standard stormtrooper blasters, FWMB-10s pack a big punch, and are capable of neutralizing Resistance vehicles with a single, well-placed shot. Heavy troopers are commonplace on Starkiller Base and the *Supremacy*.

FIRST ORDER SPECIAL FORCES TIE FIGHTER PILOT

APPEARANCES Res, VII, VIII **SPECIES** Human
HOMEWORLD Various **AFFILIATION** First Order

The First Order's Special Forces include elite TIE fighter pilots who answer directly to upper command levels. They are assigned special TIE/sf fighters with room for two pilots. Their helmets are distinguished by red markings. Internally, the helmets also have advanced targeting systems. A typically aggressive Special Forces pilot pursues Rey and Finn as they pilot the *Millennium Falcon* over Jakku, racing through the wreckage of the Super Star Destroyer *Ravager*. Notable Special Forces TIE pilots include Major Elrik Vonreg, who dresses in all-red armor.

FIRST ORDER TIE FIGHTER PILOT

APPEARANCES Res, VII, VIII **SPECIES** Human
HOMEWORLD Various **AFFILIATION** First Order

The First Order values its pilots much more than the Empire ever did. TIE fighter pilots are given more extensive training and much improved craft to fly in the era of the First Order. They undergo strict training from childhood, much like stormtroopers. Many pilots grow up on Star Destroyers and space stations, never setting foot on a planetary surface until adulthood, if ever. Cadets who fail to pass strict requirements for vision, reflexes, and other fundamental flight skills may graduate to become shuttle pilots, gunners, or technicians instead.

FIRST ORDER SNOWTROOPER

APPEARANCES VII, VIII **SPECIES** Human
HOMEWORLD Various **AFFILIATION** First Order

First Order snowtrooper gear is designed for cold-weather warfare, with waterproof insulated body gloves, armor, and helmets. These troopers wear fewer armor plates (made of betaplast) than regular stormtroopers, to allow increased movement in difficult snowy conditions. Additional features include a heavy kama wrapped around their waist and a pack that holds survival gear and supplies battery power. Snowtroopers fight at the battles of Starkiller Base and Crait. Their polarized visor and suit temperature regulators are an advantage in the hot, glaring sun of Crait's salt flats.

"FN-2187!...That's the only name they ever gave me!" FINN TO POE

FINN

Finn's life as a stormtrooper teaches him to obey orders and put the First Order above all else. However, an awakening on Jakku presents him with an opportunity to choose a new path as a hero.

APPEARANCES VII, VIII, IX, FoD **SPECIES** Human **HOMEWORLD** Unknown **AFFILIATION** First Order, Resistance

FN-2187

Like all First Order stormtroopers, Finn is taken from his family at a very young age. He never sees them again, and is raised instead with other stormtrooper cadets. He is not afforded any sort of individual personal identity or even a name—instead he is simply designated "FN-2187." While in training, Finn is considered a model stormtrooper and even commended by Captain Phasma. However, she orders Finn to stop helping his best friend FN-2003, who is weak and jeopardizes Finn's entire team. In this respect, Finn's concern for others leads to his own existential crisis later when he is ordered by Phasma to fire upon innocent civilians.

Standard armor
FN-2187 wears the typical uniform of a First Order stormtrooper.

ESCAPE FROM THE FIRST ORDER

In his first battle, Finn can't bring himself to terminate the Tuanul villagers on Jakku and realizes he must leave the First Order. Aboard the *Finalizer*, Finn frees a captive Resistance pilot, Poe Dameron, so that Poe can fly them to safety in a stolen TIE fighter. After crashing on Jakku (and being parted from Poe), Finn meets Rey and BB-8. Together they leave the planet aboard the *Millennium Falcon*. Ashamed of his past as a stormtrooper, Finn pretends to be a member of the Resistance in order to gain Rey's trust. Confiding his true identity to BB-8, Finn persuades the droid to disclose the location of the Resistance base. Shortly afterward, their ship is boarded by Han Solo and Chewbacca, and Finn is almost eaten when Han's cargo of monsters escapes.

Escaping Jakku
After their intended escape vessel is destroyed by TIE fighters, Rey, Finn, and BB-8 dash toward their second choice—the *Millennium Falcon*.

Traitor
Finn defends himself from FN-2199's vicious attack.

MEETING ON TAKODANA

Han Solo takes Finn, Rey, and BB-8 to Takodana to meet wise tavern owner Maz Kanata. She urges them to stand up to the First Order and fight. Having seen the power of the enemy firsthand, a scared Finn admits his ruse and abandons his friends. He attempts to leave the planet with the pirate Sidon Ithano, but the First Order arrives and attacks Maz's castle. This time Finn has no choice but to fight, with a lightsaber given to him by Maz. Stormtrooper FN-2199—Finn's former comrade and squad mate—confronts Finn and declares him a traitor. Finn is knocked down, but saved by Han Solo.

Making an entrance
Chewbacca keeps a look-out as Finn and Han assess how they can sneak into Starkiller Base.

STARKILLER MISSION

Finn panics when he sees Kylo Ren leave Takodana with a captured Rey aboard his shuttle. Whether Finn actually believes in the Resistance cause, or is motivated solely to rescue Rey, he becomes a member when he agrees to help the Resistance infiltrate Starkiller Base. After reuniting with Rey there, Finn proves his mettle when he is confronted by Kylo. Prepared to make the ultimate sacrifice to save his friend, Finn draws Luke Skywalker's old lightsaber and engages the dark side warrior in combat. Finn is severely injured during the fight, and is taken to the Resistance base for treatment. Rey leaves Finn there, believing they will see each other again.

JOURNEY TO CANTO BIGHT

The Resistance fleet is being chased by the First Order, which uses hyperspace tracking technology to follow their every move. Running out of time and fuel, Finn, Rose Tico, and BB-8 journey to the city of Canto Bight in search of a master codebreaker who can help them disable the tracker. There they meet a slicer named DJ who claims he can break into any system. Finn uses his knowledge of the First Order's flagship, the *Supremacy*, to sneak the team on board, but their mission falls apart when they are spotted and captured.

Unexpected allies
Though their first meeting is strained, Rose and Finn are brought closer together on their mission to Canto Bight.

FIGHTING THE FIRST ORDER

Finn's capture aboard the *Supremacy* brings him face to face with his former commander, Captain Phasma. Calling on his training as a stormtrooper cadet, Finn faces Phasma in melee combat, ultimately defeating his opponent. Finally realizing that his loyalty lies with his Resistance friends, Finn rejoins them to make a final stand on Crait. There, he pilots a ski speeder in an effort to delay the advancing ground forces. A last-minute maneuver by Rose saves him in the heat of battle, allowing them to escape aboard the *Millennium Falcon* to fight another day.

Final reckoning
Captain Phasma has always taken Finn's defection as a personal insult, and wants revenge after he humiliated her on Starkiller Base. The final duel between the two is viciously personal.

Borrowed jacket
Poe's jacket is the only trace Finn can find of his new friend in the ruins of the TIE fighter crash on Jakku. He uses the jacket to shield his head from the hot sun and later wears it. At their eventual joyful reunion, Poe tells Finn to keep it.

timeline

First encounter
FN-2187 (Finn) is sent by Captain Phasma to put down a protest in a mining colony at Pressy's Tumble.

▲ Slip's death
After witnessing his friend FN-2003 ("Slip") fall in battle, FN-2187 fails to follow Phasma's orders on Jakku.

▲ First meeting
Needing a pilot to help him flee the Star Destroyer *Finalizer*, FN-2187 helps Resistance leader Poe Dameron escape.

Finn is born
Finn (FN-2187) receives his new name from Poe Dameron as they speed toward Jakku aboard a stolen TIE fighter.

Chance encounter
After Finn crashes in the Goazon Badlands, BB-8 encounters him in Niima Outpost and recognizes the jacket he is wearing as Poe's.

Escape from the *Eravana*
The *Millennium Falcon* is intercepted by Han Solo and Chewbacca. Finn and Rey get caught in the middle of a fight between underworld gangs and ravenous rathtars.

Pirate's life
Maz Kanata unnerves Finn when she stares into his eyes. Finn invites Rey to run away with him, but she keeps her promise to help BB-8.

Battle with the First Order
Finn wields a lightsaber in battle for the first time, but finds that a former squad mate is his equal in close combat.

▲ Resistance member
Finn is reunited with Poe Dameron on D'Qar. He helps the Resistance leaders plan their attack on Starkiller Base.

◀ Recovery
After his duel with Kylo Ren, Finn is left in a coma. Rey leaves him in the care of Resistance doctors.

Uncertain loyalty
Finn considers leaving the Resistance in order to save Rey, but Rose convinces him to stay and help.

Casino night
Finn and Rose cause significant damage to the city of Canto Bight by releasing a herd of fathiers from their holding pens. They ride one of the creatures to safety.

◀ Infiltration
Finn uses his knowledge of the *Supremacy* to sneak aboard, in an attempt to deactivate the First Order's hyperspace tracker.

"Let the past die. Kill it if you have to."

KYLO REN TO REY

KYLO REN

Though his lineage includes the brightest heroes as well as the darkest villain of recent history, Force-wielding Kylo Ren chooses to terrorize the galaxy as the evil servant of Supreme Leader Snoke.

APPEARANCES VII, VIII, IX **SPECIES** Human **HOMEWORLD** Chandrila **AFFILIATION** First Order, Knights of Ren

EARLY LIFE

One year after the Battle of Endor, Ben Solo is born to Princess Leia Organa and General Han Solo in Hanna City, Chandrila. His parents' busy professional lives (coupled with their decision to send him away to be trained by his uncle, Luke Skywalker) leave Ben feeling abandoned. Leia does not tell him that his grandfather, Anakin Skywalker, became Darth Vader. She intends to address the painful truth when Ben is much older. Regrettably, Ben learns the truth, and is confronted with the reality that his whole family has deceived him about their lineage and connection to the dark side of the Force.

End of the Empire
After the destruction of the second Death Star, Leia and Han pursue a romantic relationship.

TURN TO DARKNESS

Trained by Luke as part of a new generation of Jedi, Ben studies the light side of the Force. However, Ben later turns against his master and destroys Luke's other students. Now known as Kylo Ren, he learns about the dark side of the Force from the First Order's mysterious Supreme Leader, Snoke. Snoke's teaching blends traditions of both the dark and the light sides—a tension that causes dangerous instability within Kylo. He becomes a promising pupil to Snoke and the master of the Knights of Ren. Kylo also looks to the past for inspiration. His crossguard lightsaber is modeled after an ancient lightsaber blade from the time of the Scourge of Malachor. He even communes with the charred relic of Vader's mask, seeking visions of the power of the dark side.

Gaining information
Kylo Ren manages to probe Rey's mind and discovers she has seen the map that shows Luke's location.

THE SEARCH FOR SKYWALKER

Tasked by Snoke to hunt down the missing Luke Skywalker, Kylo follows Resistance pilot Poe Dameron to Jakku for his meeting with Lor San Tekka. Kylo fails to secure Tekka's map pinpointing Luke's location, but captures Poe to question him. Kylo learns that the map is stored within a BB-series droid, who is accompanied by Rey. After tracking the droid to Takodana, Kylo succeeds in capturing Rey, but during her interrogation she resists him. Through this encounter Kylo learns that Rey's strong Force abilities rival his own.

TRIAL AND FAILURE

Snoke is concerned Kylo will waver when he has an inevitable confrontation with his father. However, Kylo resolves to prove himself to Snoke and become immune to the light side. When Kylo finally meets Han on Starkiller Base, he strikes his father down. Kylo is wounded by Chewbacca, but chases after Rey and Finn in order to retrieve his grandfather's lightsaber from Finn. After he brutally wounds Finn in a duel, Kylo is stunned to watch Rey retrieve Anakin's lightsaber with the Force, and then best him in combat. Rey scars Kylo's face, but their duel is cut short as the planet's surface begins to disintegrate following the Resistance's attack. Snoke orders General Hux to retrieve the defeated Kylo, so that he may receive his final training from Snoke personally.

SUPREME LEADER

After their humiliating defeat at Starkiller Base, Supreme Leader Snoke is displeased with Kylo for being bested in combat by Rey and failing to find Luke Skywalker. Viciously taunting him, Snoke brands Kylo a failure—a serious error in judgment that leads to his apprentice killing him and declaring himself the new Supreme Leader. When his attempt to recruit Rey to his cause fails, Kylo turns his attention to annihilating the Resistance. Just when he has them cornered on Crait, he falls for Luke Skywalker's misdirection, realizing too late that he is fighting nothing more than a Force projection of his old master. Kylo's miscalculation allows the Resistance to escape yet again.

Blinded by anger
Enraged by the apparent return of his hated former master, Kylo throws all caution aside and tries to kill Luke. He does not realize that Luke is simply trying to distract him.

Jedi Killer
Much like his grandfather and uncle before him, Kylo possesses formidable lightsaber skills. He puts his talent in combat to use by annihilating Luke's Jedi students.

timeline

A new era
Ben Solo is born in the spotlight to an important family of leaders in the Rebellion and the New Republic.

Extended family
Despite flashes of unpredictability, young Ben shows great affection for his family including his "uncle" Lando Calrissian.

Jedi training
Leia sends her son Ben away to be trained by his uncle, Luke Skywalker.

Traitor
Ben turns against Luke and joins Snoke. He takes the name Kylo Ren and a new identity as a leader in the First Order.

Assault on Jakku
Kylo arrives on Jakku and captures Lor San Tekka, but a brief interrogation of the old man leaves him frustrated.

▲ Forceful interrogation
Kylo interrogates Poe Dameron using the Force and learns that a BB unit is carrying the map to Skywalker.

Kidnap on Takodana
Kylo Ren leads the attack on Takodana and captures Rey. He believes finding BB-8 is no longer necessary.

Rey resists Kylo
During Rey's interrogation, she turns the tables and reveals Kylo's fear—that he will never be as powerful as Darth Vader.

▲ Snoke's demand
When Snoke learns of Rey's abilities in the Force, he orders Kylo to bring her to him.

Family reunion
Han Solo pleads with his son to come home, believing that Ben is struggling against the darkness and can be saved.

Humiliating defeat
Caught off guard once again by Rey's capabilities, Kylo is left shamed and wounded in the snow on Starkiller Base.

Unmasked
After a scolding from Supreme Leader Snoke, Kylo lashes out in anger and destroys his own helmet. Kylo's face is marked with a long scar, evidence of his failed encounter with Rey on Starkiller Base.

Starfighter strike
Kylo Ren leads a fighter attack on the Resistance flagship, *Raddus*, nearly killing his mother during the raid.

Apprentice no more
Snoke connects Kylo and Rey's minds in an attempt to locate Luke Skywalker's hiding place, but Kylo cuts him down before he can act on the information.

Deceptive duel
Pursuing the remnants of the Resistance, Kylo Ren attempts to strike down his former master, Luke Skywalker, only to discover that he has been fighting a Force projection.

"Today is the end of the Republic."
GENERAL HUX

Never enough
Hux is one of the First Order's highest ranking officers, but he would do anything to outrank Kylo Ren.

ARMITAGE HUX

APPEARANCES Res, VII, VIII, IX **SPECIES** Human
HOMEWORLD Arkanis **AFFILIATION** First Order

Armitage Hux is the illegitimate son of Commandant Brendol Hux, an Imperial officer. Brendol is an Imperial Academy instructor who devises a new program to conscript and train stormtroopers from birth. He is an uncaring father who shows no kindness to his son. When their homeworld is overtaken by the Rebel Alliance, Brendol takes his young son, Armitage, to Jakku. Following the Battle of Jakku, the Huxes escape to the Unknown Regions of the galaxy with Admiral Rae Sloane to build a new Empire.

Armitage is given charge of the young stormtroopers, and commands them with brutality, demanding absolute loyalty and obedience. His malicious tendencies and delusions of grandeur grow as he matures and rises through the ranks of the First Order. Later, he and Captain Phasma conspire together and assassinate his father, Brendol.

General Armitage Hux has a fierce rivalry with Supreme Leader Snoke's apprentice, Kylo Ren. Hux values the military might of the First Order rather than Kylo's devotion to the mystical Force. Hux seeks to prove himself and win favor with Snoke in order to diminish Kylo's standing. To this end, he pursues the droid BB-8 and the map to Luke Skywalker. As the commander of Starkiller Base, he pleads with Snoke to let him destroy the Hosnian system—the seat of government for the Galactic Republic. When Snoke agrees, Hux delivers a passionate speech to his forces before firing the superweapon and obliterating Hosnian Prime. His next target is the Resistance base on D'Qar. However, when Starkiller is attacked by the Resistance and about to be destroyed, Snoke orders Hux to bring Kylo Ren and come to him.

Following the destruction of Starkiller Base, Hux oversees the retaliatory attack on D'Qar. Though the assault decimates the base, the Resistance escapes and Poe Dameron destroys the First Order's prized dreadnought destroyer. Snoke is displeased with Hux at first, but when Hux explains his overarching plan, Snoke is most pleased. Hux has devised a novel way to track the Resistance through hyperspace, preventing his enemies from escaping.

Resistance spies Rose Tico and Finn are captured when they infiltrate Snoke's flagship, the *Supremacy*, and attempt to deactivate Hux's hyperspace tracker. Hux orders their execution and then leaves to fire upon the Resistance's escaping craft, thanks to information obtained by the double-crossing slicer, DJ. Hux is caught by surprise though, when Resistance flagship *Raddus*, piloted by Vice Admiral Holdo, collides with the *Supremacy*, breaking it apart. In the chaos, Hux runs to Snoke's throne room only to find the Supreme Leader dead and Kylo Ren unconscious. Hux tries to take advantage of the opportunity to kill Kylo, but his rival awakes and chokes him into submission. To ensure his own survival, Hux becomes Kylo's lackey, and operates as his second-in-command at the Battle of Crait.

Rivalry's end
Kylo Ren's Force powers prove more than a match for Hux, who must submit to a new master.

UNKAR PLUTT

APPEARANCES VII, FoD **SPECIES** Crolute
HOMEWORLD Crul **AFFILIATION** Independent entrepreneur

The cantankerous, selfish Unkar Plutt leaves his watery homeworld after a shady business deal falls apart. The "Blobfish," as he comes to be known, settles on Jakku and starts a business buying scraps from the local scavengers. In the course of business, a young girl named Rey is left with him. She begins working directly for him at first, becoming his top scavenger. Later, Unkar steals the *Millennium Falcon* from the criminals known as the Irving Boys, and makes a few modifications as it sits under a tarp by his Concession Stand. Unkar eventually becomes the top junk dealer at Niima Outpost, driving out all his competitors and controlling all commerce there. When Rey discovers the droid BB-8, Unkar offers to buy him, but Rey declines. In response, Unkar sends his thugs to steal the droid—but Rey fights them off. After Rey steals the *Millennium Falcon*, Unkar tracks her to Takodana and confronts her at Maz's Castle. Chewbacca comes to her aid, however, and rips off one of Unkar's arms.

Good for business
Rey is Unkar's top scavenger, so he orders his thugs to make sure others don't interfere with her.

UNKAR'S THUGS

APPEARANCES VII, FoD **SPECIES** Various humanoids **HOMEWORLD** Jakku
AFFILIATION Unkar Plutt

Unkar Plutt employs a small group of thugs, armed with vibro-shivs and blasters, who work for him around Niima Outpost on Jakku. He uses them to do his dirty work, such as breaking up unauthorized commerce, stealing from uncooperative scavengers, and sabotaging any aspiring competitors. The amoral ruffians hide under hoods, wraps, and goggles, but everyone around the Outpost knows who they really are. Unkar's thugs cause occasional trouble for Rey, especially when they try to take BB-8 from her by force in the market.

BOBBAJO

APPEARANCES VII **SPECIES** Nu-Cosian
HOMEWORLD Jakku
AFFILIATION Critters of all kinds

The kindly old Bobbajo carries a menagerie of pets on his back, including a worrt named J'Rrosch, several gwerps and pishnes, a lonlan, and two zhhee. He travels from village to village on Jakku telling fantastical stories about his adventures with his creatures. In one story he takes responsibility for the destruction of the Death Star, though only children take him seriously. Bobbajo occasionally has dealings with Unkar Plutt and has run into Rey at the Concession Stand in Niima Outpost.

SARCO PLANK

APPEARANCES VII **SPECIES** Melitto
HOMEWORLD Li-Toran **AFFILIATION** Various

The self-serving Sarco Plank is a scavenger who guides Luke Skywalker to the Temple of Eedit on Devaron. He intends to use Luke to open the temple and then take the treasures inside for himself. Once Luke serves his purpose, Sarco Plank attacks him—but to no avail. Sarco ends up trapped inside the temple. After freeing himself, he relocates to Jakku and works as an arms dealer and bounty hunter. His bad luck continues there. Sarco competes with Rey to claim salvage rights on the wreck of the Star Destroyer *Spectral*, but ultimately fails.

NIGHTWATCHER WORM

APPEARANCES VII, FoD **HOMEWORLD** Jakku
AVERAGE SIZE 20 m (66 ft 7 in) **HABITAT** Sand dunes

Also known as sandborers and Arcona night terrors, Jakku's nightwatcher worms are nocturnal creatures that live under the sand. Sensing vibrations, they poke an eyestalk with glowing red eyes above the surface to investigate. Their small eyes are deceptive: they give no indication of the large creature with a gaping mouth below. Nightwatcher worms prefer to eat ship parts and wayward droids, but they also eat living prey. A nightwatcher worm takes an interest in BB-8, forcing Rey to outsmart it. The worm becomes an unintended ally when it eats the pesky Teedo's speeder.

STEELPECKER

APPEARANCES VII **HOMEWORLD** Jakku
HABITAT Sand dunes and rock outcrops near wreckage

Amid the ship debris scattered in the dunes on Jakku, scavenger birds called steelpeckers flutter about looking for metal objects to consume. Their talons and beaks are coated in iron, allowing them to break off bitesize chunks of metal to swallow. A steelpecker gizzard typically contains vanadium, corundum, and osmiridium to aid in digestion. Steelpecker guano is a prized commodity for Jakku's settlers. It is exported and used in the production of starship hulls.

HAPPABORE

APPEARANCES VII, FoD **HOMEWORLD** Various (domesticated)
AVERAGE SIZE 5.9 m (19 ft 2 in) long **HABITAT** Various (adaptable)

Happabores are large, docile, piglike creatures, often raised as livestock on Devaron and Jakku. They can store large quantities of water in their bloodstreams, which allows them to drink only infrequently. Happabore hides are tough and well-armored on their dorsal side for protection from the sun and predators. On Jakku, Finn drinks from a happabore trough in Niima Outpost and Rey is forced to deal with them when she scavenges in the dunes. On Devaron, happabores also serve as a means of transportation for residents like Sarco Plank.

"I didn't know there was this much green in the whole galaxy." REY TO HAN

REY

Alone on a desert world, Rey believes she is nothing more than a lowly scavenger, forever waiting for a family that never comes. When she discovers a hidden power within her, she must harness this power to help her newfound friends—and the galaxy.

APPEARANCES VII, VIII, IX, FoD **SPECIES** Human **HOMEWORLD** Jakku **AFFILIATION** Resistance

MYSTERIOUS EARLY LIFE

At an early age, Rey is abandoned on Jakku and left in the charge of Unkar Plutt. She works for the junk boss by scavenging for parts and supplies from Jakku's Starship Graveyard from the Galactic Civil War. Rey lives by herself in Hellhound 2, a wrecked Imperial AT-AT that she renovates in the Goazon Badlands, and survives by trading her finds for food and water rations. Unusually for residents of Jakku, Rey is not looking to work her way off the backwater planet, as she believes that one day her family will return for her. While waiting indefinitely for them to come back, Rey practices flying a few ships, including a Ghtroc 690 light freighter. Rey is planning to sell it to Unkar—until it is stolen.

Home sweet home
The Hellhound 2's intact heat shielding protects Rey from the harsh conditions of a Jakku day.

A FATEFUL ENCOUNTER

One evening, after finishing her dinner of polystarch and veg-meat, Rey hears a commotion in the dunes. She rushes to find the droid BB-8 in distress, and rescues him from a greedy Teedo. Taking pity on the wayward droid, Rey shelters the astromech before taking him to Niima Outpost. BB-8 recognizes the jacket of his former master, now worn by Finn. Rey confronts Finn, believing him a thief, but he claims he is part of the Resistance. When First Order stormtroopers arrive, hunting for BB-8, the trio relies on Rey's piloting skills to escape Jakku aboard Unkar's *Millennium Falcon*.

Teedo
Atop a cybernetic luggabeast, Teedo captures BB-8 in a net near the Kelvin Ravine. Rey rescues the droid from the brutish scavenger.

TAKODANA AND THE FORCE

The *Millennium Falcon* is intercepted by Han Solo and Chewbacca, who take Rey and Finn to Maz Kanata's castle on Takodana. They hope that pirate Maz can get BB-8, who carries a map to Luke Skywalker's location, delivered to the Resistance. In Maz's castle, a lightsaber that once belonged to Luke and Anakin Skywalker calls to Rey through the Force. When Rey touches it, she sees a Force vision and hears voices from beyond the grave. Fleeing in fear, Rey is captured when the First Order arrives on Takodana.

Elder advice
Maz tries to console a frightened Rey, explaining that her visions are a result of her connection to the Force.

STARKILLER BASE AND DESTINY

On Starkiller Base, Kylo Ren probes Rey's mind with the Force. He senses her affinity for Han Solo and her fantasies about a mysterious island, but she is strong in the Force and fights him, preventing Kylo from retrieving the map to Skywalker in her memory. Now embracing her Force abilities, Rey uses a mind trick on her stormtrooper guard, who sets her free. After Rey rejoins her friends and witnesses Han Solo's death, Rey and Finn are confronted by Kylo Ren. Finn is gravely wounded by Kylo, but Rey claims Skywalker's blade as her own. She confounds Kylo with her fighting skill, and defeats him. After the destruction of Starkiller Base, Rey seeks out Skywalker, hopeful that he will train her as a Jedi.

Duel on Starkiller Base
Rey stands victorious above the wounded Kylo Ren.

SURPRISE ON AHCH-TO

Rey's arrival on Ahch-To does not go as expected. Rather than meeting a great hero of the Rebellion, she finds an ill-tempered old man, content to live out his final days in solitude without connection to the Force. Skywalker refuses to train her, instead agreeing to give her just three lessons to show her the folly of the Jedi. Rey believes that if she cannot convince Skywalker to aid the Resistance, then turning Kylo to the light side is their only hope. She departs to meet Ren, secretly taking ancient Jedi texts with her to preserve the history of the Jedi.

Unexpected answers
A gloomy sea cave on Ahch-To tempts Rey with revelations about her past. But what it shows her leaves Rey even more confused.

Awakened hero
Talented Rey possesses an unusually strong connection to the Force. Much like the legendary Anakin Skywalker, she is also an expert mechanic and pilot.

FACING SNOKE

Kylo Ren takes Rey straight to Supreme Leader Snoke, who encourages Kylo to strike her down as the final test in his training. Instead, Ren turns on his own master, killing him with Skywalker's lightsaber. Snoke's Praetorian Guard rush to avenge him, but Rey and Kylo work in unison against the elite warriors. With Snoke and his guard defeated, Rey asks Kylo to help her save the Resistance, but he refuses to be redeemed. She escapes to rejoin the Resistance on Crait, arriving just in time to clear their retreat and ferry the survivors away aboard the *Millennium Falcon*.

False dawn
Kylo turning on Snoke seems to confirm Rey's dearest hope—that Kylo can be redeemed. Though the pair fight Snoke's guards together, it is soon revealed that Kylo is only motivated by his own ruthless ambition.

timeline

Abandoned
A tiny Rey watches helplessly as a starship pulls away, marooning her on the unfamiliar world of Jakku.

Starship study
Rey learns to pilot starships using a scavenged computer and flight simulator program found among the wrecks of the Starship Graveyard.

A new path
Rey rescues BB-8 from Teedo and gets herself mixed up in a struggle between the First Order and the Resistance.

Change of plans
Intending to steal a quadjumper, Rey changes her plans when it explodes and she, Finn, and BB-8 must flee Jakku in the *Millennium Falcon.*

▲ Meeting a legend
Rey meets Han Solo and Chewbacca, and learns that the stories about Luke Skywalker and the Jedi are actually true.

Awakening
Rey discovers Luke Skywalker's lightsaber in an old chest. The awakening she receives is a truth she does not wish to face.

Capture by Kylo
Using the dark side of the Force, Kylo Ren immobilizes Rey and kidnaps her from the forests of Takodana.

▲ Force interrogation
Rey fights Kylo as he probes her mind, learning as much about him as he does about her.

Growing powers
Rey successfully attempts a Jedi mind trick, manipulating a stormtrooper into removing her restraints and leaving her his blaster.

Loss of Han Solo
Rey is devastated to witness the death of Han Solo at the hands of Kylo Ren inside Starkiller Base.

Duel in the snow
Rey bewilders Kylo by ignoring his offer to teach her. Instead she trusts in the Force and humiliates him in lightsaber combat.

Arrival at Ahch-To
Rey travels to the watery world of Ahch-To and meets Luke Skywalker on the cliffs of a rugged island.

Master no more
Rey is surprised to discover that Luke has shut himself off from the Force and is unwilling to train her. Skywalker senses in Rey a raw power that he has not felt since training Ben Solo.

Force connection
Rey develops a mysterious connection with Kylo Ren through the Force, allowing them to communicate from across the galaxy.

Searching for truth
Entering a mysterious cavern on Ahch-To, Rey believes she can finally learn who her parents are, but finds only an illusion of the Force.

Abandoning Ahch-To
Upon learning how Skywalker failed his apprentice years before, Rey leaves Ahch-To in hopes that she can still turn Kylo towards the light. She meets him on Supreme Leader Snoke's flagship.

Lightsaber lost
After their duel against Snoke's guards, Rey and Kylo grapple for control of Luke Skywalker's lightsaber, breaking it in two. Rey carries the pieces with her to Crait.

TEEDO

APPEARANCES VII, FoD **SPECIES** Teedo **HOMEWORLD** Jakku **AFFILIATION** None

Teedos are small, reptilian beings that subsist as scavengers in Jakku's dunes. Though selfish in their dealings with other species, they do not maintain individual identities. They are all named Teedo and share a telepathic link and a collective experience. Rey is forced to deal with unpleasant Teedos often. She rescues BB-8 from an especially irritating Teedo riding a luggabeast near her home. A short while later, the Teedo again tries to steal BB-8 from Rey. She lures him to a wrecked Star Destroyer where she knows a nightwatcher worm lurks—and the Teedo is nearly eaten.

LUGGABEAST

APPEARANCES VII, FoD **HOMEWORLD** Various **AVERAGE SIZE** 2.31 m (7 ft 7 in) high **HABITAT** Adaptable (domesticated)

Luggabeasts are cybernetically enhanced beasts of burden. Salvaged machine parts and chemical injections are used to augment the strength and stamina of the animals. They are given food and water through tubes and have no need to drink or eat otherwise. On Jakku, luggabeasts are used by Teedos and settlers to travel between outposts and scavenge the starship graveyard. Teedos specialize in breeding and adapting the creatures on Jakku, but similar cyborg beasts of burden produced from other species are used throughout the galaxy.

RATHTAR

APPEARANCES VII **HOMEWORLD** Twon Ketee **AVERAGE SIZE** 6.09 m (20 ft) long (including tentacles) **HABITAT** Swamps

Among the most feared predators in the galaxy, rathtars are large, tentacled creatures with a voracious appetite. Their gaping mouths are lined with teeth that are continually replaced. Though rathtars have small brains, they are social animals and hunt effectively in packs. A rathtar's deadly reputation makes it a prized catch for smugglers and big game hunters. Maul observes poachers being eaten by a pack before killing several rathtars himself. Han Solo and Chewbacca smuggle several rathtars, but they get loose and cause havoc.

TASU LEECH

APPEARANCES VII **SPECIES** Human **HOMEWORLD** Nar Kanji **AFFILIATION** Kanjiklub

Tasu Leech is the leader of the criminal Kanjiklub gang. In cooperation with the rival Guavian Death Gang, he locates Han Solo's ship, the *Eravana*, and boards it with his men. Han Solo borrowed 50,000 credits from Kanjiklub and has not paid his debt—for the second time. Tasu Leech intends to take BB-8 and anything else of value, splitting the profit with the Guavians. When Rey releases Han's cargo of rathtars, it causes violent chaos on the ship, allowing Han, Chewbacca, Rey, Finn, and BB-8 to escape.

BALA-TIK

APPEARANCES VII **SPECIES** Human **HOMEWORLD** Unknown **AFFILIATION** Guavian Death Gang

On the planet Kaddak, in a city known as the Sliver, Kanjiklub's Tasu Leech overhears C-3PO say that Han Solo owes the Guavian Death Gang money. Tasu then confers with Bala-Tik, the frontman for the Guavians. The two rival gangs agree to work together and collect the money Han Solo owes them. After tracking Han Solo to Nantoon, Bala-Tik and his enforcers board Han's ship, the *Eravana*. There, an angry Bala-Tik demands the credits Han Solo owes them, but he is unprepared to face the rathtars set loose on the ship.

GUAVIAN DEATH GANG ENFORCER

APPEARANCES Res, VII **SPECIES** Human (augmented) **HOMEWORLD** Various **AFFILIATION** Guavian Death Gang

The Guavian Death Gang's enforcers are humans who swear allegiance to the organization and in return receive cyborg augmentations and chemical injections to boost their effectiveness as killers. Enforcers communicate with each other via high-frequency data bursts transmitted by the disk in the center of their "face." Bala-Tik always travels with a contingent of enforcers, including on his visits to Kaddak and in his confrontation with Han Solo. Guavians have also been observed on *Colossus* station on Castilon.

COLONEL DATOO

APPEARANCES VII **SPECIES** Human **HOMEWORLD** Unknown **AFFILIATION** First Order

Colonel Erich S. Datoo is in command of the primary fire control room on Starkiller Base. He is responsible for discharging the energy burst that destroys the Hosnian system. He next aims the weapon at the planet D'Qar, home to the Resistance headquarters, but Starkiller Base is destroyed before he can hit his target.

CHIEF PETTY OFFICER UNAMO

APPEARANCES VII **SPECIES** Human **HOMEWORLD** Unknown **AFFILIATION** First Order

Chief Petty Officer Nastia Unamo serves on the bridge of the *Resurgent*-class Star Destroyer *Finalizer*, under the command of Kylo Ren and General Hux. She supervises the bridge crew and tracks the stolen TIE fighter flown by Poe Dameron and FN-2187 to their crash site on Jakku.

KORR SELLA

APPEARANCES VII **SPECIES** Human **HOMEWORLD** Hosnian Prime **AFFILIATION** Resistance

Korr Sella is an intern for New Republic Senator Leia Organa, and later joins the Resistance as a commander. Sella acts as General Leia Organa's envoy to the New Republic Senate. She attempts to warn them of the growing threat from the First Order, but she is too late. Sella is killed when Starkiller Base destroys Hosnian Prime.

GA-97

APPEARANCES VII **MANUFACTURER** Reiffworks Droid Restoration **TYPE** GA servant droid **AFFILIATION** Resistance

GA-97 is an operative working for C-3PO, stationed in Maz Kanata's castle on Takodana. When BB-8 shows up with Han Solo, Chewbacca, Rey, and Finn, GA-97 notifies C-3PO. The message results in Poe Dameron and his X-wing squadron arriving on Takodana to battle the First Order.

SNOKE

APPEARANCES VII, VIII **SPECIES** Unknown
HOMEWORLD Unknown **AFFILIATION** First Order

Supreme Leader Snoke is a practitioner of the dark side of the Force. Though he is not a Sith, he has studied their teachings and other ancient lore of Force-users. He is arrogant and overconfident, like Emperor Palpatine before him, and these weaknesses likewise prove his undoing. From the shadows, Snoke watches the rise and fall of the Empire and the legendary saga of Darth Vader and Luke Skywalker. When the Empire falls, its remnants seek refuge in the Unknown Regions of the galaxy. There, they find their way using the accumulated knowledge of Grand Admiral Thrawn and the aid of a mysterious, purple-robed race known only as the "navigators." Concealed in the Unknown Regions, the Imperial survivors prepare for a future war and become known as the First Order. Snoke's power grows and his rise to prominence in the organization takes the surviving Imperial leadership by surprise.

Snoke begins to train apprentices to serve him. The most promising is Luke Skywalker's nephew and Jedi acolyte, Ben Solo. Snoke turns him to the dark side and Ben becomes Kylo Ren, master of the Knights of Ren. Wishing to eliminate his greatest threat, Snoke commands Kylo Ren to locate and destroy Luke Skywalker. Snoke also senses an awakening in the Force, but is unsure of the source.

Snoke warns Kylo that the droid carrying the map they seek to Luke Skywalker is aboard the *Millennium Falcon* with Kylo's father, Han Solo. While Snoke has encouraged Kylo to face Solo, Snoke warns him that he has never faced such a difficult test.

On Snoke's orders, the First Order uses its Starkiller superweapon to destroy the New Republic's capital in the Hosnian system and prepares to wipe out the Resistance on D'Qar. Meanwhile, Rey's identity is discovered, and Snoke orders Kylo to bring her to him. However, after Kylo murders Han Solo, Kylo is defeated by Rey and Starkiller Base is destroyed.

Snoke becomes dissatisfied with Kylo Ren after his defeat at the hands of Rey. He ridicules Kylo as "a boy in a mask," which fills his young apprentice with rage. Snoke is pleased when Kylo finally brings Rey before him on his flagship *Supremacy*, which restores some of Snoke's confidence in his student. Snoke notes that Rey has risen from the light side of the Force to match Kylo, though he had always assumed Kylo's equal would be Luke Skywalker.

Nonetheless, Snoke underestimates Rey's ability and overestimates Kylo's loyalty. When he orders Kylo to eliminate Rey in his presence, Snoke is unable to sense Kylo's intent to ally with the girl, against him. Kylo uses the Force to turn Rey's lightsaber (resting beside Snoke's throne) toward his master and cuts him in half. Snoke's Praetorian Guards attempt to avenge their fallen master, but are defeated by Kylo and Rey. To Rey's horror, Kylo then seizes control of the First Order, becoming its new Supreme Leader.

Distant figure
Though he wields immense power, Snoke prefers not to place himself in harm's way. He commands from the shadows, communicating with his subordinates via holograms, often projected at a vast size to further reinforce his might.

"There has been an awakening. Have you felt it?"

SNOKE TO KYLO REN

Death of a tyrant
In his dealings with Kylo and Rey, Snoke forgoes his usual caution—a decision that costs him dearly. He is so confident in the strength of his Force abilities that he views neither of them as a real threat, only realizing his folly when it is far too late.

MAZ KANATA

APPEARANCES VII, VIII, IX, Fod **SPECIES** Unknown
HOMEWORLD Takodana **AFFILIATION** Independent entrepreneur

Maz Kanata was born over a thousand years before the war between the First Order and the Resistance. Though not a Jedi herself, she does have a strong but subtle connection to the Force. Maz is a former pirate, master storyteller, and the proprietor of a castle tavern on the shores of Nymeve Lake on Takodana.

Maz is a longtime friend of Han Solo and Leia Organa. Notably, she helps Leia rescue Han from Jabba the Hutt by suggesting Leia use the outfit of the bounty hunger Boushh as a disguise to infiltrate Jabba's palace.

Around 30 years later, Han arrives at Maz's castle with Rey, Finn, and BB-8. He asks Maz to deliver them to Leia, but Maz refuses, believing it's time for Han to join the fight himself. Meanwhile, Rey wanders into the dungeons and discovers Luke Skywalker's lightsaber packed away in a chest. Maz appears after Rey has a Force vision. She urges Rey to take the lightsaber and to seek Luke Skywalker, but Rey refuses and runs away. Shortly afterward, the First Order attacks Maz's castle, and in the ensuing battle Maz gives the lightsaber to Finn, urging him to use it. Although her castle is destroyed, after the battle she tells her new friends not to lose hope, and remains on Takodana to clean up.

Maz very quickly returns to her old life of action and adventure, getting caught up in a blaster fight she refers to as a "union dispute." In the midst of this, Finn, Rose Tico, and Poe Dameron contact her for advice about finding someone who can break them into Snoke's flagship, and she directs them toward Canto Bight.

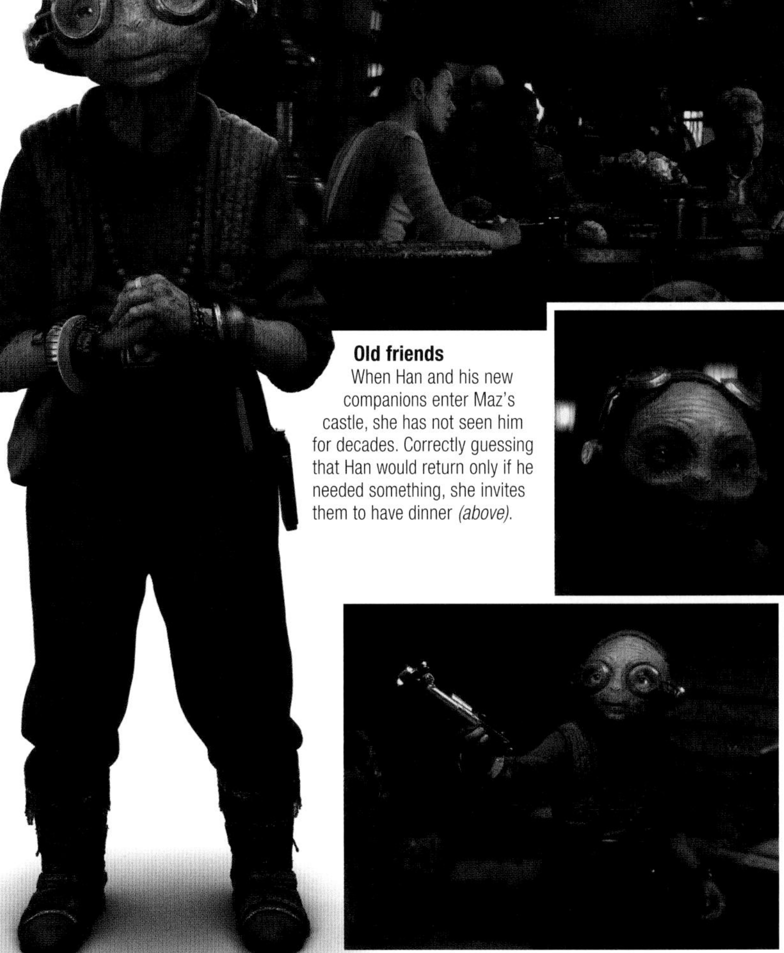

Old friends
When Han and his new companions enter Maz's castle, she has not seen him for decades. Correctly guessing that Han would return only if he needed something, she invites them to have dinner *(above)*.

Battle joined
Maz tells Han, Finn, and Rey that there is only one fight—the fight against darkness, which has taken many different forms over the years *(above)*. Rey, after exposure to Luke Skywalker's lightsaber, flees the castle, but Maz gives the lightsaber to Finn, hoping to rekindle the heroism that she senses in his heart *(left)*.

BAZINE NETAL

APPEARANCES VII **SPECIES** Human **HOMEWORLD** Chaaktil **AFFILIATION** Independent bounty hunter

"Bazine Netal" (her name is an alias) spends her early childhood in an orphanage in Chaako City on Chaaktil. She is adopted by the pirate Delphi Kloda, who raises her at his combat school and teaches her martial arts. Badly burned in her first mission, she now wears a cowl to cover her scars. Working as a bounty hunter and First Order spy, Netal becomes an associate of Grummgar. While the two are lounging at Maz's castle, she watches BB-8 and Rey arrive with Han Solo, and notifies the First Order. She is later hired to hunt down the *Millennium Falcon*, so travels the galaxy to learn more about the ship.

SIDON ITHANO

APPEARANCES VII **SPECIES** Delphidian
HOMEWORLD Delphidian Cluster
AFFILIATION Sidon Ithano's crew

Captain Sidon Ithano, also known as "the Blood Buccaneer," "the Crimson Corsair," and "the Red Raider," is one of the best pirates in the Outer Rim. His nicknames are derived from his red Kaleesh helmet. He locates the abandoned Separatist ship *Obrexta III*, hoping to find a lost horde of Count Dooku's kyber crystals. Instead, he finds a frozen clone trooper and data pinpointing many forgotten Separatist bases. While visiting Maz Kanata's castle, Finn tries to negotiate passage offworld with Sidon and his first mate, Quiggold, just before the First Order attacks.

ME-8D9

APPEARANCES VII **MANUFACTURER** Unknown
TYPE Protocol droid **AFFILIATION** Maz's castle

ME-8D9, or "Emmie," is an ancient droid believed to have once belonged to the Jedi Order during the Old Republic era, thousands of years ago. If so, she may be one of the castle's original inhabitants. She later became an assassin, but has softened in her old age and now serves as a translator and security officer in Maz's castle. She even breaks up a fight between a First Order pilot and Resistance pilot prior to the war between the two enemies. ME-8D9 is present when the First Order destroys the castle, bringing her millennia there to a sad end.

TRINTO DUABA

APPEARANCES IV, VII
SPECIES Stennes Shifter
HOMEWORLD Stennaros
AFFILIATION Independent

Trinto Duaba is a vagrant traveler about whom little is known. His species has an innate ability to use the Force to pass invisibly through crowds. He is present at Chalmun's Cantina in Mos Eisley when Obi Wan and Luke Skywalker meet Han Solo. He is also present decades later when Han Solo brings Finn, Rey, and BB-8 to meet Maz Kanata on Takodana. When Maz's castle is destroyed by the First Order, Trinto manages to slip through the chaos unharmed and seek refuge.

QUIGGOLD

APPEARANCES VII **SPECIES** Gabdorin
HOMEWORLD Gabdor
AFFILIATION Sidon Ithano's crew

Quiggold is the first mate of Captain Sidon Ithano's pirate crew. When searching for a lost shipment of kyber crystals, they find a clone trooper named Kix, frozen in stasis. While at Maz's castle, Finn tries to negotiate transportation with Quiggold and Sidon Ithano to get offworld.

GRUMMGAR

APPEARANCES VII **SPECIES** Dowutin
HOMEWORLD Dowut **AFFILIATION** Free agent

Grummgar is a mercenary and big game hunter known for his poaching escapades on the planet Ithor. His specialty is hunting multi-legged, venomous predators called Molsume. He frequently relaxes at Maz Kanata's castle and is a known associate of Bazine Netal.

GWELLIS BAGNORO

APPEARANCES VII **SPECIES** Onodone
HOMEWORLD Unknown **AFFILIATION** Independent entrepreneur

Gwellis Bagnoro is a secretive customer often seen at Maz Kanata's castle with his pet barghest, Izby. He is an expert forger, specializing in transit documents. His species is mysterious—perhaps originating in the Unknown Regions.

WOLLIVAN

APPEARANCES VII **SPECIES** Blarina
HOMEWORLD Rina Major **AFFILIATION** Independent entrepreneur

Wollivan is a galactic explorer who sells his knowledge of hyperspace navigation, unexplored worlds, and scavenged treasures to make a living. He has something of a gambling problem, though, and for that reason he likes to hang out at Maz Kanata's castle more than is sensible.

PRASTER OMMLEN

APPEARANCES VII **SPECIES** Ottegan
HOMEWORLD Ottega
AFFILIATION Sacred Order of Ramulus

Praster Ommlen is a former weapons smuggler who gives up his life of crime to become a monk in an Ithorian religion (Ithorians, or "Hammerheads," are related to Ottegans). He offers spiritual advice to customers at Maz's Castle and observes the destruction of Hosnian Prime from just outside.

STRONO TUGGS

APPEARANCES VII **SPECIES** Artiodac
HOMEWORLD Takodana
AFFILIATION Maz's castle

Strono "Cookie" Tuggs has served as the cook in Maz's castle for hundreds of years. When his sous chef Robbs Ely is murdered and his recipe book stolen, Cookie sets up a cooking contest among his other chefs to see if one uses Ely's recipes—which would identify him as the killer.

TEMMIN WEXLEY

APPEARANCES VII, IX **SPECIES** Human
HOMEWORLD Akiva **AFFILIATION** Rebel Alliance, New Republic Defense Fleet, Resistance, Black Squadron, Blue Squadron

Temmin "Snap" Wexley's father, Brentin, is arrested by the Empire when Temmin is still young. His mother, Norra, joins the Rebel Alliance, leaving him alone. Temmin spends his childhood as a junk dealer and reconstructs a battle droid named Mister Bones to be his companion. In the aftermath of the Battle of Endor, while still a teenager, Temmin joins the Rebel Alliance and hunts Imperial fugitives with his mother. He fights at the climactic Battle of Jakku and becomes a starfighter pilot for the New Republic. He later joins the Resistance and assists Poe Dameron in the search for Lor San Tekka and the Battle of Starkiller Base. Before the Resistance evacuation of D'Qar, General Organa orders Wexley to leave and search the galaxy for any surviving New Republic military commanders.

Recon chief
Snap is one of the most skilled reconnaissance pilots in the Resistance. Knowing this, Leia sends him to gather as much information as possible about Starkiller Base.

JESSIKA PAVA

APPEARANCES VII **SPECIES** Human **HOMEWORLD** Dandoran
AFFILIATION Resistance, Black Squadron, Blue Squadron

Jessika Pava is known as "the Great Destroyer" by Resistance droids due to her unfortunate habit of losing astromechs to enemy fire during X-wing dogfights. As a child on Danderon, her family was captured by pirates and sold into slavery. Jessika idolized Luke Skywalker as a child and follows in his footsteps, joining the Resistance and flying an X-wing. As a pilot she flies under the command of Poe Dameron in both Black and Blue Squadrons. She helps her commander search for Lor San Tekka, who is believed to know how to find Luke, and goes on to fly her X-wing as Blue Three at the Battles of Takodana and Starkiller Base. After the destruction of Starkiller Base, General Organa sends Jessika with Temmin Wexley to search for any remaining Resistance operatives and New Republic military commanders in the Outer Rim.

Blue Three
Above Starkiller Base, Jess provides Poe with vital cover as he makes his final attack run on the thermal oscillator. Many of her squadron mates are shot down.

ELLO ASTY

APPEARANCES Res, VII **SPECIES** Abednedo
HOMEWORLD Abednedo **AFFILIATION** New Republic Defense Fleet, Resistance, Cobalt Squadron, Red Squadron

Ello Asty originally flies patrols and performs in air shows as a member of the New Republic Defense Fleet on Hosnian Prime. He joins Leia Organa's Resistance, also based on Hosnian Prime, before they relocate to D'Qar. There, Ello communicates with Poe Dameron's spies, including Kazuda Xiono, when Poe is unavailable. He also pilots his T-70 X-wing starfighter in the Resistance's Red Squadron, flying as Red Six. Ello takes part in the Battle of Starkiller Base, but is killed during the attack on the base's thermal oscillator.

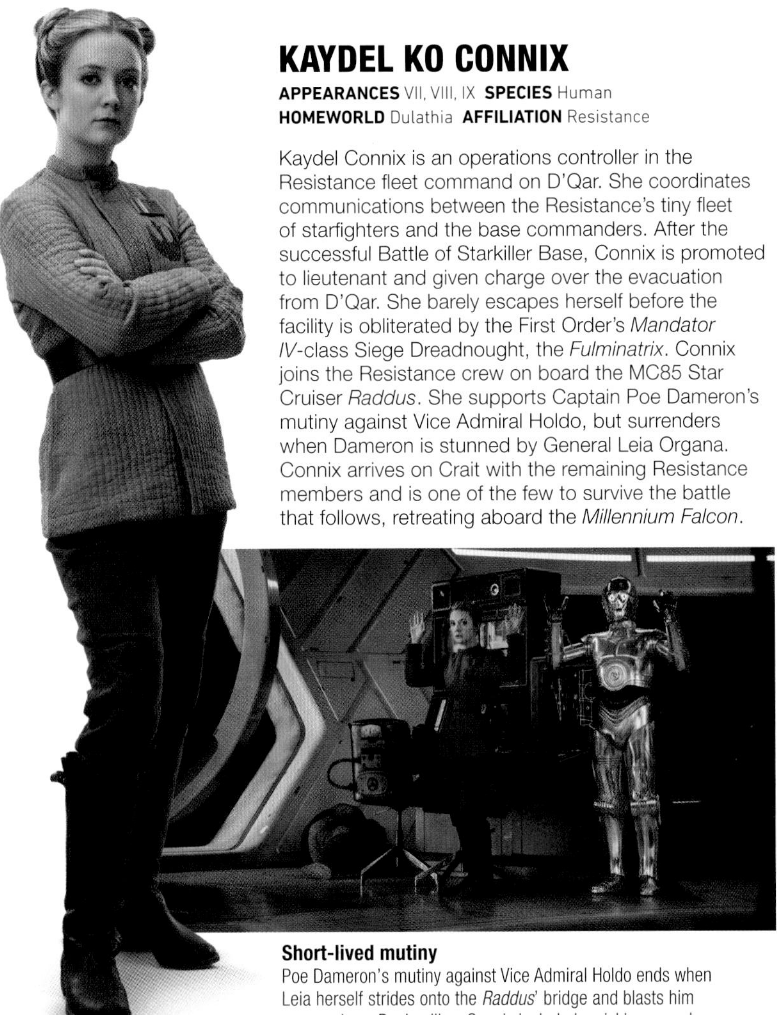

KAYDEL KO CONNIX

APPEARANCES VII, VIII, IX **SPECIES** Human **HOMEWORLD** Dulathia **AFFILIATION** Resistance

Kaydel Connix is an operations controller in the Resistance fleet command on D'Qar. She coordinates communications between the Resistance's tiny fleet of starfighters and the base commanders. After the successful Battle of Starkiller Base, Connix is promoted to lieutenant and given charge over the evacuation from D'Qar. She barely escapes herself before the facility is obliterated by the First Order's *Mandator IV*-class Siege Dreadnought, the *Fulminatrix*. Connix joins the Resistance crew on board the MC85 Star Cruiser *Raddus*. She supports Captain Poe Dameron's mutiny against Vice Admiral Holdo, but surrenders when Dameron is stunned by General Leia Organa. Connix arrives on Crait with the remaining Resistance members and is one of the few to survive the battle that follows, retreating aboard the *Millennium Falcon*.

Short-lived mutiny
Poe Dameron's mutiny against Vice Admiral Holdo ends when Leia herself strides onto the *Raddus*' bridge and blasts him unconscious. Poe's allies, Connix included, quickly surrender.

U.O. STATURA

APPEARANCES VII **SPECIES** Human **HOMEWORLD** Garel **AFFILIATION** Rebels, Resistance

U.O. Statura first takes up arms as a teenager, battling the Empire on Garel. Decades later he serves as an admiral in the Resistance, based at their headquarters on D'Qar. After a career in scientific research, he is well suited to planning the Battle of Starkiller Base, and correctly identifies the base's weakness: its thermal oscillator.

HARTER KALONIA

APPEARANCES VII **SPECIES** Human **HOMEWORLD** Unknown **AFFILIATION** Resistance

Dr. Harter Kalonia treats Leia Organa during her pregnancy. Later, as a major in the Resistance, she is stationed in the Resistance Command Center on D'Qar. Here she serves as Leia Organa's personal assistant and chief medical officer, and she tends the combat injuries sustained by Chewbacca and Finn.

CALUAN EMATT

APPEARANCES VII, VIII **SPECIES** Human **HOMEWORLD** Unknown **AFFILIATION** Rebel Alliance, Resistance

Caluan Ematt is a friend of Princess Leia Organa and lieutenant in the Rebel Alliance during the Galactic Civil War. He leads an elite recon unit called the Shrikes that locates potential new bases for the rebels. Ematt is also a member of Han Solo's strike team during the Battle of Endor. Later, he becomes a founding member of the Resistance, though he remains a double agent in the New Republic military, recruiting for the Resistance. After the Battle of Starkiller Base he is promoted from Major to General. Ematt goes on to fight at the Battle of Crait.

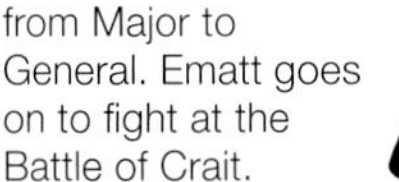

VOBER DAND

APPEARANCES VII, VIII **SPECIES** Tarsunt **HOMEWORLD** Suntilla **AFFILIATION** Resistance

Vober Dand serves as a controller in the Resistance Ground Logistics Division. He is highly organized and rigid about sticking to protocol—leading to arguments with fellow staff and commanders alike. He is stationed at the Resistance Command Center on D'Qar during the Battle of Starkiller Base and participates in the evacuation that follows. He survives the devastating attack on the Resistance flagship, the *Raddus*, and witnesses Vice Admiral Holdo take command.

PZ-4CO

APPEARANCES VII, VIII **MANUFACTURER** Serv-O-Droid, Inc. **TYPE** Protocol droid **AFFILIATION** Resistance

"Peazy" is a blue protocol droid designed to resemble the long-necked humanoid Tofallid species. She stores immense tactical data in her memory banks and works as a communications specialist in the Resistance headquarters on D'Qar. She convinces General Organa (after weeks of pestering) to begin recording her memoirs, beginning with Operation: Yellow Moon, which took place just before the Battle of Endor.

B-U4D

APPEARANCES VII, VIII **MANUFACTURER** Unknown **TYPE** Loading droid **AFFILIATION** Resistance

"Buford" (B-U4D) is a starfighter maintenance droid working for the Resistance on D'Qar. He is a tireless member of the ground crew, and assists in the base's evacuation.

TALLISSAN LINTRA

APPEARANCES VIII **SPECIES** Human **HOMEWORLD** Pippip 3 **AFFILIATION** Resistance, Blue Squadron

Lieutenant Tallissan "Tallie" Lintra is one of the best pilots in the Resistance, and flies an RZ-2 A-wing as Blue Leader. She survives the evacuation of D'Qar, but not Kylo Ren's attack on the fleet.

PAIGE TICO

APPEARANCES VIII **SPECIES** Human **HOMEWORLD** Hays Minor **AFFILIATION** Resistance, Cobalt Squadron

Paige Tico is the older sister of Rose Tico. The two grow up in the Otomok system where they witness the brutality of the First Order and escape to join the Resistance. Paige serves as a gunner aboard the bomber Cobalt *Hammer*, taking part in missions against pirates in the Cassandra Sector and a relief operation in Atterra. During the evacuation from D'Qar, Paige's bomber attacks the First Order Dreadnought *Fulminatrix*. With her crew incapacitated, Paige singlehandedly drops the bomber's payload and destroys the enemy vessel. Though the explosion also takes Paige's life, her sacrifice allows the Resistance to escape.

C'AI THRENALLI

APPEARANCES VII, VIII **SPECIES** Abednedo
HOMEWORLD Abednedo
AFFILIATION Resistance

C'ai Threnalli is a male Abednedo Resistance pilot stationed on D'Qar. After waving Rey off on her mission to find Luke Skywalker, he assists with the evacuation and continues to fly as Poe Dameron's wingman—he also supports Poe's mutiny against Vice Admiral Holdo. Threnalli survives the Battle of Crait and escapes aboard the *Millennium Falcon*.

LARMA D'ACY

APPEARANCES VIII **SPECIES** Human
HOMEWORLD Warlentta
AFFILIATION Resistance

Hailing from Warlentta, Larma D'Acy is a Resistance commander who is recruited to the cause by General Organa herself. One of the few officers to survive Kylo Ren's attack on the *Raddus*, she supports Vice Admiral Holdo when she takes command of the Resistance fleet. D'Acy survives to escape from Crait with the remaining Resistance members.

EDRISON PEAVEY

APPEARANCES VIII **SPECIES** Human
HOMEWORLD Unknown
AFFILIATION Empire, First Order

Edrison Peavey serves in the Imperial Navy during the Emperor's reign. He later commands the First Order Star Destroyer *Finalizer*, reporting to General Armitage Hux (whom he secretly views with contempt). He is present during the attack on D'Qar, and forms part of Kylo Ren's entourage on his command shuttle at the Battle of Crait.

MODEN CANADY

APPEARANCES VIII **SPECIES** Human
HOMEWORLD Unknown
AFFILIATION Empire, First Order

Moden Canady begins his military career in the Imperial Navy as commander of the Imperial Star Destroyer *Solicitude*. After the Galactic Civil War he joins the First Order and becomes captain of the Siege Dreadnought *Fulminatrix*, serving with Edrison Peavey under General Armitage Hux. He is resentful of his young and incompetent First Order crew, who lack the training and experience of his former Imperial shipmates. He and all aboard the *Fulminatrix* perish in a Resistance bomber attack ordered by Poe Dameron.

ALCIDA-AUKA

APPEARANCES VIII **SPECIES** Lanai
HOMEWORLD Ahch-To **AFFILIATION** None

Alcida-Auka is the matron of the Lanai Caretakers of Ahch-To's temple island. Her people are matriarchal, passing down their titles and roles from mother to daughter. The females care for the Jedi temple ruins while the males fish out at sea, returning home for periodic festivals.

FIRST ORDER FLEET GUNNER

APPEARANCES VIII **SPECIES** Human
HOMEWORLD Various **AFFILIATION** First Order

Pilots, engineers, and gunners all start at the First Order's academies with the same basic training regimen and are assigned specializations according to their demonstrated aptitude. Fleet gunners like Brun Obatsun wear black uniforms similar to Fleet Engineers, and are stationed in weapons control centers across the *Supremacy*'s exterior. Targeting data is projected directly onto their visors. Other visual information is cut out to reduce distraction. The gunners fire a constant barrage of plasma bursts as the Resistance fleet flees D'Qar.

PORG

APPEARANCES VIII **HOMEWORLD** Ahch-To
AVERAGE HEIGHT 18 cm (10 in)
HABITAT Islands and open seas

Sea birds are the dominant life-form on Ahch-To. Porgs are birdlike creatures that dwell in the rocky cliffs of the planet's islands and coastal zones. They dive into the sea and use their large, telescopic eyes to help them catch small fish, which they feed to their young (known as porglets). Porg offspring are often hatched as pairs, in nests tended by their mother and father. Porgs are considered quite tasty by some species, and are sometimes hunted by the resident Lanai and visitors to the islands.

FIRST ORDER SHUTTLE PILOT

APPEARANCES VIII **SPECIES** Human
HOMEWORLD Various **AFFILIATION** First Order

First Order shuttle pilots form an elite unit tasked with transporting high-ranking officers, dignitaries, and wealthy First Order families with considerable influence. Such assignments are coveted by older First Order pilots who are less concerned with forging careers in battle than providing for their families through high-paid but mundane flight schedules. The exception are pilots serving military officials such as Kylo Ren in his *Upsilon*-class command shuttle. These pilots face battle situations on a regular basis.

THALA-SIREN

APPEARANCES VIII **HOMEWORLD** Ahch-To
AVERAGE HEIGHT 5.4 m (18 ft)
HABITAT Coastal areas

Thala-sirens are sea mammals with four flippers used for swimming. They are generally docile and come ashore to rest and bask in the sun. Mothers, also known as sea sows, nurse their young on the rocky shores of Ahch-To's islands. With no predators on land, the sows allow Luke Skywalker to approach and milk them. Their mammary glands produce green milk, which is salty and has a hint of the large kelp they feed upon. Large Thala-bulls are a worry to the unwatchful. They use their large tusks to lunge at intruders to their territory.

SNOKE'S NAVIGATORS

APPEARANCES VIII **SPECIES** Unknown
HOMEWORLD Unknown Regions
AFFILIATION First Order

Snoke's otherworldly "navigators" are ancient alien beings from the Unknown Regions. They are first discovered by the remnants of the Empire that flee into the Unknown Regions, and are soon hired as guides. The tall, seemingly mute beings serve Snoke in his throne room aboard the *Supremacy*, where they build his oculus viewing scope and advise him on hyperspace routes and the curiosities of space. They communicate using inaudible pulses of energy in wavelengths unperceivable to humans, but visible to navigator eyes.

ROSE TICO

APPEARANCES VIII, IX, FoD **SPECIES** Human **HOMEWORLD** Hays Minor **AFFILIATION** Resistance, Cobalt Squadron

Rose and Paige Tico grew up in the Otomok system on Hays Minor. Their people were enslaved by the First Order and forced to mine their own planet before it was bombed by the First Order to test its weapons. The two sisters are very close, wearing matching pendants. The medallions are made of valuable Haysian smelt, and represent their homeworld, but to Rose and Paige, they are symbols of their love for each other and good luck charms. The sisters escape, joining the Resistance together. They are assigned to Cobalt Squadron, with Rose as a mechanic and Paige as a gunner.

Paige is killed during the attack on D'Qar, but Rose is left no time to mourn. While guarding the escape pods aboard the *Raddus*, she encounters Finn, who is trying to escape so that he can find Rey. She stuns him, but when he can speak again, their discussion turns to the Resistance fleet's pursuit by the First Order—and how they might escape the predicament. They meet with Poe Dameron and discuss a plan to sneak aboard the First Order flagship *Supremacy* and disable its tracker. They call Maz Kanata, who tells them to find someone known as the "Master Codebreaker" in Canto Bight.

Rose, Finn, and Poe's droid, BB-8, arrive and search the Canto Casino for the Codebreaker, but are soon arrested. Rose and Finn are imprisoned and BB-8 is thrown out. In their jail cell they meet a slicer (hacker) named DJ, who offers to fill the role of the Codebreaker. They decline, and DJ opens the cell to let them all out, parting ways. Rose and Finn head to the racetrack stables where they steal a fathier, riding amidst a stampede through the old city. Once outside town, they are trapped on a cliff. Luckily, BB-8 and DJ arrive on a stolen ship and rescue them. Unable to find the Master Codebreaker, they agree to hire DJ instead. Successfully boarding the *Supremacy*, the three don First Order officer uniforms to sneak through the ship. They reach the tracker but are apprehended. Sentenced to death, Rose and Finn discover at their execution that they were betrayed by DJ. Fortunately, their punishment is interrupted when Resistance Vice Admiral Holdo rams the ship at lightspeed, and then BB-8 seizes control of an AT-ST and rescues them. The three escape and rejoin the Resistance remnant on Crait. The First Order soon arrives and besieges the base where they are sheltering, so Rose and Finn join Poe's wing of ski speeders to face the First Order. As they head toward the First Order's superlaser siege cannon, Poe realizes their attack is futile and calls it off. However, Finn keeps going. Rose suddenly charges his ship to stop him, declaring, before passing out, that they'll win the war by saving the ones they love. The Resistance retreats and escapes aboard the *Millennium Falcon*, where Finn tends to the unconscious Rose.

Inauspicious meeting
When Rose first meets Finn, she has already heard tales of his heroism. On learning he plans to desert, however, her excitement turns into righteous fury.

In disguise
Despite her deep hatred for the regime that enslaved her homeworld, Rose is forced to wear the uniform of a First Order major to infiltrate Snoke's flagship.

Old wounds
As their mission progresses, Rose and Finn find they have much more in common than they first imagined.

"We are the spark that will light the fire that will restore the Republic."

VICE ADMIRAL HOLDO

VICE ADMIRAL HOLDO

APPEARANCES VIII **SPECIES** Human **HOMEWORLD** Gatalenta **AFFILIATION** Apprentice Legislature, Rebel Alliance, Resistance

Like all Gatalentans, Amilyn Holdo is free spirited and highly intellectual. As a young woman, she serves as a member of the Imperial Senate's Apprentice Legislature on Coruscant. There she meets Princess Leia Organa and they become good friends. While on Pamarth, Leia confides to Holdo that she is part of the rebellion against the Empire. Shortly afterward, Holdo helps Leia find safe passage to the Paucris system, allowing her to warn the rebel fleet of an impending Imperial attack.

Decades later, as the threat of the First Order looms, Holdo joins the Resistance as a Vice Admiral and is given command of the *Free Virgillia*-class Bunkerbuster *Ninka*. Prior to the evacuation of D'Qar, she briefs the Cobalt and Crimson bomber squadrons on the destruction of Hosnian Prime and Starkiller Base. She equips both squadrons for battle and then assists in the evacuation of the Resistance base.

When General Organa is incapacitated and most of the Resistance leadership killed, Vice Admiral Holdo transfers to the Resistance flagship, the *Raddus*, and takes command of the surviving Resistance forces. From the start, there is friction between her and Poe Dameron, who has recently been demoted for his rash decisions that caused tremendous losses for the Resistance. Holdo declines to inform Poe of her plan to reach Crait and evacuate the Resistance to the planet below. Poe grows ever more suspicious of her intentions and launches a mutiny, taking Holdo into custody. When Leia awakens, she grabs her blaster and stuns Poe, putting an end to the mutiny.

Holdo wishes Leia and the Resistance goodbye, and remains on the *Raddus* to buy them time. When the First Order fires upon the helpless Resistance transports, Holdo makes a valiant choice. She sacrifices herself by ramming the *Supremacy* at lightspeed, cutting it in half and allowing her friends to escape to Crait.

Final sacrifice
Holdo pilots her ship toward the *Supremacy*, grimly determined to destroy it and save her friends.

Desperate times
When Holdo takes command of the Resistance, the situation could hardly be worse. The First Order is relentlessly pursuing them, and total annihilation seems inevitable.

PRAETORIAN GUARD

APPEARANCES VIII **SPECIES** Human
HOMEWORLD Various
AFFILIATION Supreme Leader Snoke

Supreme Leader Snoke's elite Praetorian Guards are his personal security soldiers. They accompany him everywhere, guarding his throne room and residence. Their red plastoid armor and luxurious red robes are a deliberate nod to Emperor Palpatine's Royal Guards, mimicking the splendor and Imperial power that they once symbolized—the title "Praetorian Guard" itself dates back to the 14th Emperor of Kitel Phard. The Praetorians' identities are kept hidden so that they cannot be bribed or blackmailed to betray their sacred duty. Their personal histories have even been wiped from the First Order's records. The guards are trained in a variety of martial arts, including Teräs Käsi, Echani, Bakuuni Hand, and Nar Kanji techniques, so they can face physical threats of all kinds.

The mag-coils in the Praetorians' heavy armor plating generates a magnetic field that deflects blaster fire and even causes glancing lightsaber blows to bounce away (although a direct lightsaber thrust will still penetrate). The armor is uncomfortable at best, and the energy from the mag-coils causes lingering pain in the wearer. Praetorian weapons include Bilari electro-chain whips (which form pikes when at rest), twin joining vibro-arbir blades, vibro-voulges, and electro-bisentos. Their blades are energized to counter lightsabers in duels, and their edges vibrate at a high frequency to increase their cutting performance.

Praetorians are trained to consider everyone a possible threat, including Snoke's advisors and his own apprentices. Hidden behind their opaque visors, they keep a watchful eye on all who approach the Supreme Leader. The Praetorians stand at attention in Snoke's throne room on his flagship *Supremacy* when Kylo Ren brings Rey before him. Snoke's overconfidence leads him to keep the guards at bay. When their master is suddenly slain by Kylo Ren, they rush to avenge him. Fighting in four pairs, their strength and skill rivals that of both Rey and Kylo, but all are cut down in an epic battle.

DJ

APPEARANCES VIII **SPECIES** Human
HOMEWORLD Unknown **AFFILIATION** Himself

DJ's alias stands for "Don't Join." He believes there are no good or bad sides—the First Order and Resistance are two sides of the same coin. He is a criminal slicer (hacker) who uses his skills to steal money from the wealthy on Canto Bight. He creates a false persona named Denel Strench to take the blame for his crimes. DJ is arrested after cheating at Eclipse casino games and getting into a vehicular accident in front of police. At the time of his arrest, a gambling droid uncovers DJ's alter ego, exposing his charade. While in jail, DJ meets Resistance members Rose Tico and Finn. They all escape and go their separate ways, but DJ and BB-8 team up and end up rescuing the other two. In need of a slicer, Rose and Finn hire DJ to help them sneak aboard the First Order flagship *Supremacy* using his stolen yacht *Libertine*. Once aboard, the three are captured and it's revealed he sold them out in exchange for his own freedom and a substantial payment.

"Live free, don't join." DJ

LEXO SOOGER

APPEARANCES Other
SPECIES Dor Namethian
HOMEWORLD Askkto-Fen IV
AFFILIATION None

A former assassin, Lexo Sooger is now the celebrity masseur at Zord's Spa and Bathhouse. When Sooger finds a human left on his doorstep, he takes her in and names her Lula. One of his treatments is disrupted by a stampede of fathiers, thanks to Finn and Rose Tico.

COUNTESS ALISSYNDREX

APPEARANCES VIII
SPECIES Unknown
HOMEWORLD Cantonica
AFFILIATION Canto Casino

The Contessa (Countess) Alissyndrex delga Cantonica Provincion is a keen fan of the fathier races on Canto Bight. She and her husband, who is rarely seen, are the figureheads of the city. Her gorgeously engorged shoulders hold the priceless Onyx Bands of Cato Neimoidia.

DOBBU SCAY

APPEARANCES VIII **SPECIES** Unknown
HOMEWORLD Unknown **AFFILIATION** None

Alcoholic offworlder Dobbu Scay spends much of his gambling time inebriated. Unable to maintain any self-control in the face of the vast array of distractions at Canto Bight's casino, Dobbu has already lost most of his spending money when he meets BB-8. Mistaking the astromech for a slot machine, he empties his coins into BB-8's diagnostic slot before the droid rolls away. Fortunately for Dobbu, he is able to recoup his losses later when panicked patrons drop their winnings during the fathier stampede.

SLOWEN LO

APPEARANCES VIII
SPECIES Abednedo
HOMEWORLD Cantonica
AFFILIATION None

Beach-dwelling Canto Bight citizen Slowen Lo makes vast sums of money selling high-quality driftwood art. He is irritated when Finn and Rose Tico illegally land their ship on the beach at Canto Bight and so informs the police, getting them thrown in jail.

YASTO ATTSMUN

APPEARANCES VII **SPECIES** Unknown
HOMEWORLD Listehol **AFFILIATION** None

Tyrranical Baron Yasto Attsmun is a wealthy aristocrat who hosts frequent Canto Bight parties with infamous guests aboard his yacht, *Undisputed Victor*. One such party ends with the murder of an arms dealer. The Baron has aspirations of a relationship with club owner Ubialla Gheal.

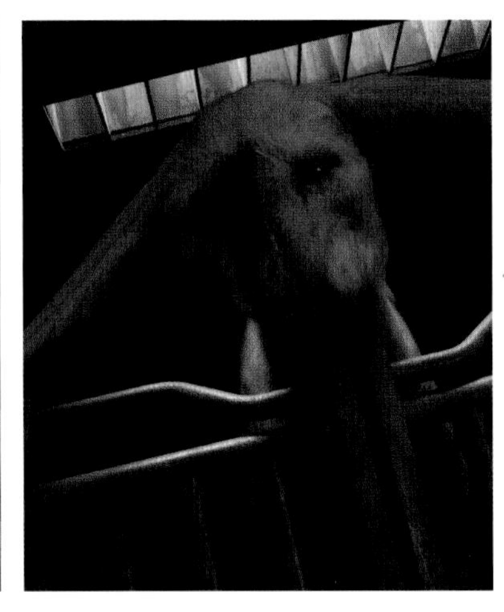

FATHIER

APPEARANCES VIII **HOMEWORLD** Various worlds (domesticated) **AVERAGE SIZE** 3 m (9 ft 10 in) high at shoulder **HABITAT** Grasslands

Fathiers are bred (and abused) on planets such as Cantonica for races, where large sums of money are wagered. The rides are fast (speeds of 75 kilometers per hour and higher are the norm) and dangerous. Falls can kill a jockey, and stumbles can maim a fathier, rendering it useless to the owners. The animals are intelligent and naturally gentle, preferring to live in herds. Rose Tico and Finn steal a fathier to escape the police during their mission to Canto Bight, causing a stampede through the city.

THAMM

APPEARANCES VIII **SPECIES** Troglof
HOMEWORLD Troglofa **AFFILIATION** Canto Casino and Racetrack

The most popular croupier at the Canto Casino is named Thamm. He has a reassuring demeanor that makes casino patrons feel comfortable, as if he is a close friend. Thamm is a member of a rare species with tentacle-like arms and is small enough to stand directly on the tables. He can move his eye stalks independently to keep an eye on players and make sure nobody is breaking the rules. He is also notable for his unusual, but pleasant, natural odor.

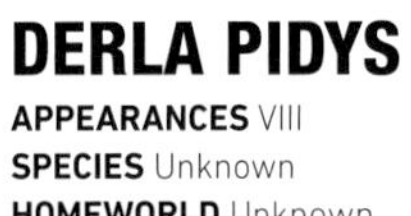

DERLA PIDYS

APPEARANCES VIII
SPECIES Unknown
HOMEWORLD Unknown
AFFILIATION None

A legendary sommelier, Derla Pidys is a frequent visitor to Canto Bight and the best at her trade in the sector. From Naboo to Orto Plutonia, she picks up her wares, selling them, often with an embellished origin, to enraptured clients. On one visit, she aims to acquire an unusual, rare vintage known as the "Wine of Dreams" from the equally odd Grammus sisters.

KEDPIN SHOKLOP

APPEARANCES Other **SPECIES** Wermal
HOMEWORLD Werma Lesser
AFFILIATION VaporTech

After spending 102 years as a vaporator salesman, polite Kedpin Shoklop wins a trip to Canto Bight as his reward for being named Salesbeing of the Year. His first vacation in a century doesn't go so well though. He gets caught up with a criminal and ends up in jail.

THODIBIN, DODIBIN, AND WODIBIN

APPEARANCES VIII **SPECIES** Suerton **HOMEWORLD** Chanceuxi
AFFILIATION Themselves

The "Winning Three"—Thodibin, Dodibin, and Wodibin—have a reputation around the Canto Bight casino for their unusually long lucky streaks. It is believed that the trio can somehow affect probability in their favor. The casino security keeps a close watch but has never observed any criminal activity. The Suerton is a reptilian species well known across the galaxy for being inexplicably fortunate in all things.

GRAMMUS SISTERS

APPEARANCES VIII **SPECIES** Unknown
HOMEWORLD Uknown **AFFILIATION** None

Twins Rhomby and Parallela Grammus have an undeniably strong bond and are performance artists frequently seen in the Canto Bight casino. They appear to enjoy attracting lots of attention with their unusual attire, claims that they are from another dimension, and the unknown language that they use between themselves. When a clerk at their current hotel fails to tell them apart, they are despondent and demand that the manager gives them the clerk as a souvenir. The sisters use their new souvenir as a servant to relay their complicated requests.

TEMIRI BLAGG

APPEARANCES VIII **SPECIES** Human
HOMEWORLD Cantonica **AFFILIATION** None

Temiri Blagg is one of many street children left on Cantonica by wayward guardians who come for the gambling and other fleeting pleasures. He is placed under the charge of Bargwill Tomder to work in Canto Bight's stables. The Force-adept boy encounters Rose Tico and Finn as they flee from police custody. He and his friends, Oniho Zaya and Arashell Sar, decide to help them, releasing the entire herd of fathiers to cause confusion as Finn and Rose flee on one of the animals. Later, the children learn of the Battle of Crait, and long for such adventures themselves.

BARGWILL TOMDER

APPEARANCES VIII **SPECIES** Cloddogran
HOMEWORLD Galagolos V **AFFILIATION** Canto Casino and Racetrack

Cantankerous Cloddogran Bargwill Tomder is altogether unlovable. Festering, smelly, and plague-ridden, Tomder has no concern for his personal health or hygiene. He has charge of the Canto Bight stables at the city's large, money-spinning racetrack, where he oversees stalls of valuable fathiers and a motley crew of urchins, all of whom he exploits to his own advantage. Determined to prove his management skills to his employers, Tomder uses his four arms to crack his whip and inspire both animals and slave children to get back to work.

VULPTEX

APPEARANCES VIII **HOMEWORLD** Crait
AVERAGE SIZE 51 cm (20 in) tall
HABITAT Salt flats, rock outcrops, and caves

Hot and arid, the salt flats of Crait are nonetheless home to many creatures, including small predators called vulptices. Their crystalline fur, an adaptation to the mineral-rich environment, is a defense mechanism against larger predators. This covering acts as armor and produces a jingling sound to warn other vulptices about danger. Most active at dusk and dawn, vulptices congregate in cave dens at night. The friendly creatures lead the Resistance to an alternate cave exit during the Battle of Crait, thus enabling them to escape the First Order.

STORMTROOPER EXECUTIONER

APPEARANCES VIII
SPECIES Human **HOMEWORLD** Various
AFFILIATION First Order

As part of their regular duties, stormtroopers are commanded to act as anonymous executioners. Their armor carries no individual rank or identifying insignia other than the black carbon finish on their shoulders and helmet that designates their role. Executioners carry a laser ax with eight collapsible claws, forming two sets of monomolecular energy ribbons. Public executions of the disloyal are held regularly, as an example to anyone who may be wavering in their support for the First Order.

BB-9E

APPEARANCES VIII **MANUFACTURER** Industrial Automaton **TYPE** BB-series Astromech droid
AFFILIATION First Order

First Order droids are treated like gadgets and service machines rather than friends and companions, as in the Resistance. A cold and methodical droid with a mean streak, BB-9E spots BB-8, Finn, and Rose aboard the *Supremacy* and immediately reports their suspicious activity.

ZORII BLISS

APPEARANCES IX
SPECIES Human
HOMEWORLD Kijimi
AFFILIATION Spice Runners of Kijimi

As Han Solo once proved, even the scoundrels of the galaxy can take sides when it seems all hope is lost. Zorii Bliss, the tough, no-nonsense leader of the Spice Runners of Kijimi, may find that staying neutral in the war between First Order and Resistance comes with too high a price.

D-O

APPEARANCES IX
MANUFACTURER Babu Frik
TYPE Custom droid
AFFILIATION Resistance

This small, rolling droid has been cobbled together from the spare parts in a droidsmith's workshop. Skittish and impressionable, D-O quickly becomes fixated on BB-8, following his new friend around and trying to copy him.

JANNAH

APPEARANCES IX
SPECIES Human
HOMEWORLD Kef Bir
AFFILIATION Resistance-allied

Jannah is a fierce and principled freedom fighter. She leads a tribe of brave and noble warriors on an ocean moon. Her skills with an energy bow are second to none, and her bravery and athleticism in battle are legendary.

SITH TROOPER

APPEARANCES IX
SPECIES Human
HOMEWORLD Various
AFFILIATION First Order

The First Order's Sith troopers are an elite army created with a single purpose—to complete the conquest of the galaxy. They are inspired by and draw their power from a dark and ancient legacy. Sith troopers are fanatically loyal, are highly trained in all forms of combat, and carry a devastating arsenal of heavy weapons.

THE KNIGHTS OF REN

APPEARANCES VII, IX **SPECIES** Unknown
HOMEWORLD Unknown
AFFILIATION Loyal to Kylo Ren

The Knights of Ren are Kylo Ren's most deadly and mysterious servants. With their bodies encased in rusty, battered armor and their faces permanently concealed beneath ominous masks—echoing that of the new Supreme Leader himself—even their species remains a mystery. What is obvious to anyone who witnesses them in action is that their fighting skills and martial prowess are without equal. Each Knight is armed with a lethally effective and unique weapon, suited to either long range or close-quarter combat.

BEHIND THE SCENES

"[*Star Wars*] is finally about people and not finally about science… I think that's what makes it so accessible." Harrison Ford, 1977

It may be set in a galaxy far, far away, but it is the characters that have made *Star Wars* compelling for generations of fans. These people have fantastical origins, but they struggle with issues familiar to everyone: greed versus honor, duty versus desire, good versus evil. When combined with amazing practical makeup and groundbreaking visual effects, *Star Wars* has made space fantasy characters seem believable and relatable like never before.

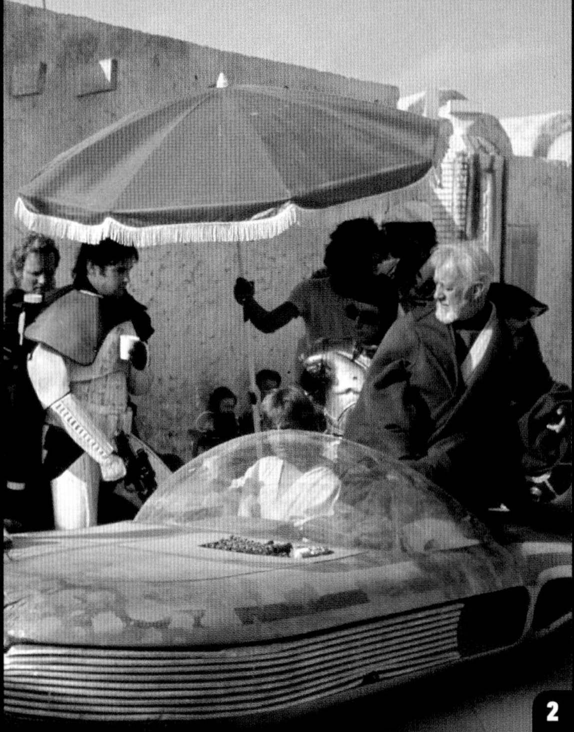

Concept illustrator Ralph McQuarrie's first concept illustration for Deak Starkiller and Darth Vader's lightsaber duel on a rebel ship was created in consultation with George Lucas and helped hone the look of the characters **(1)**. Mark Hamill (Luke Skywalker) and Alec Guinness (Ben Kenobi) are shielded from the searing Tunisian sun while they take a welcome break from filming in March 1976 **(2)**. In *A New Hope*, the bantha was played by a trained elephant named Mardji in an elaborate costume **(3)**.

Makeup artist and creature designer Stuart Freeborn puts the finishing touches on a sculpture of Yoda, whose face was based on his own and that of Albert Einstein, as well as conceptual art by McQuarrie and Joe Johnston. Freeborn helped create several notable aliens for *Star Wars*, including some of the cantina aliens (many of whom were created by Rick Baker), Chewbacca, and Jabba the Hutt **(4)**.

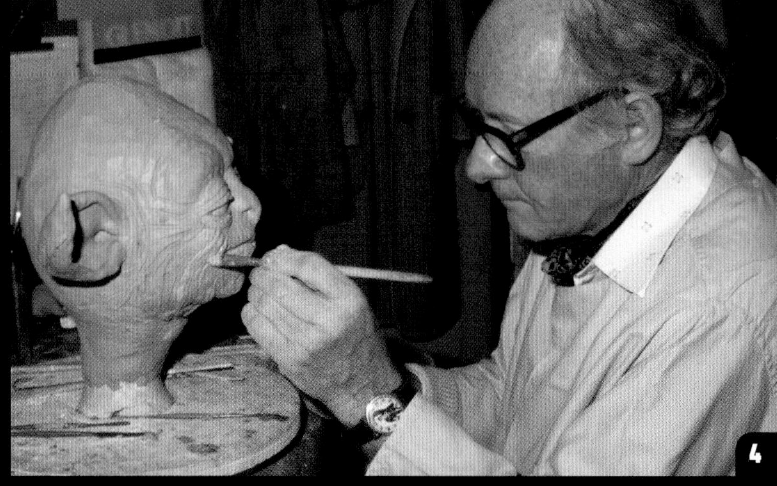

Harrison Ford and Peter Mayhew, in his Chewbacca costume, on the set of *Star Wars:* Episode V *The Empire Strikes Back* **(5)**. Mark Hamill rehearses the Cloud City fight scene with Darth Vader swordmaster Bob Anderson, who played Darth Vader in the dueling scenes. **(6)**. Mask of the Mon Calamari leader, Admiral Ackbar, a part-puppet, part-mask creation for *Return of the Jedi,* developed by the ILM Monster Shop. The mask was controlled and performed by puppeteer Tim Rose, on loan from the Jim Henson Company **(7)**.

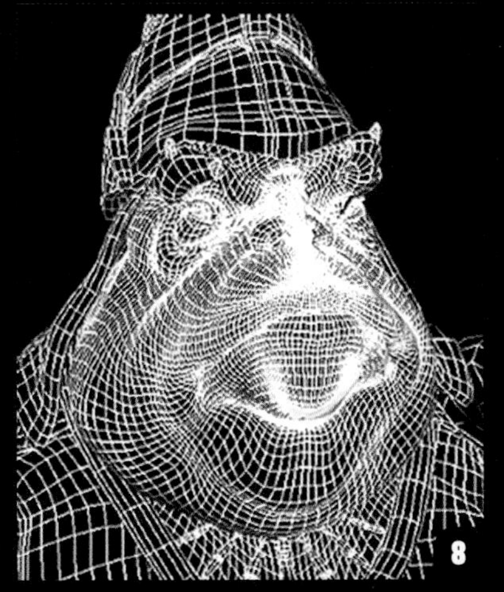
8

9

A wire frame rendering of Boss Nass, one of ILM's most challenging computer-generated creations **(8)**. George Lucas directs Silas Carson as Nute Gunray for the Naboo Palace scenes in Italy **(9)**. Ian McDiarmid and Natalie Portman film against a bluescreen for a Naboo scene in *The Phantom Menace* **(10)**. Early costume concept art by Dermot Power for Anakin Skywalker for *Star Wars:* Episode II *Attack of the Clones* **(11)**.

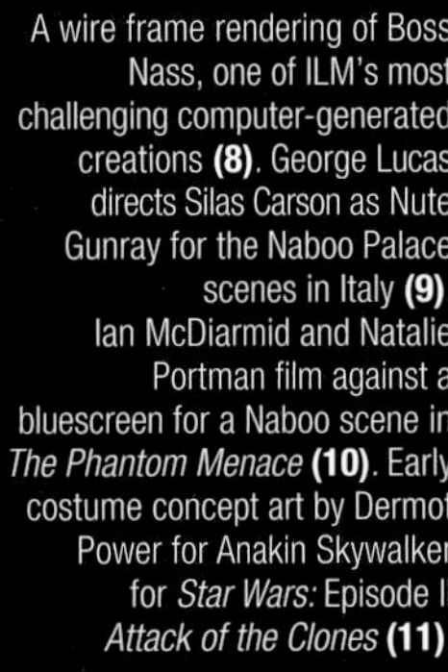

10

11

12

13

Dermot Power's concept art for *Attack of the Clones* depicts a female Sith warrior, a character who finally appears as the fierce assassin Asajj Ventress in the animated TV series *Star Wars: The Clone Wars* **(12)**. Hayden Christensen in a pick-up shot from the final day of shooting *Revenge of the Sith* at Elstree Studios **(13)**. J.J. Abrams (top center) oversees the cast read-through of *Star Wars: The Force Awakens* at Pinewood Studios with (clockwise from right) Harrison Ford, Daisy Ridley, Carrie Fisher, Peter Mayhew, Producer Bryan Burk, Lucasfilm president and producer Kathleen Kennedy, Domhnall Gleeson, Anthony Daniels, Mark Hamill, Andy Serkis, Oscar Issac, John Boyega, Adam Driver, and writer Lawrence Kasdan **(14)**.

14

Puppeteers operate mechanized porgs on location on Skellig Michael, Ireland during filming of *Star Wars:* Episode VIII *The Last Jedi* **(15)**. Director Rian Johnson (far right) poses for a photo on the *Millennium Falcon* set at Pinewood Studios with (left to right) John Boyega, producer Ram Bergman, Carrie Fisher, Oscar Isaac, Daisy Ridley, Lucasfilm President Kathleen Kennedy, Billie Lourd, Anthony Daniels, Joonas Suotamo, Jimmy Vee, and Paul Kasey **(16)**.

15

16

LOCATIONS

Countless habitable worlds are scattered throughout the farthest reaches of the galaxy. Each one has its own geography, flora and fauna, secrets, and surprises.

Long ago, hyperspace explorers established coordinates and trade routes for thousands of star systems, many of which have at least one habitable planet or moon. Since then, many new systems have been charted. Some of these far-flung worlds feature architectural wonders and are home to intelligent indigenous civilizations, while others are undeveloped and populated almost entirely by wild creatures. Some worlds feature diverse terrain, while others are so dominated by a single geographical feature that they are described as sand, ice, jungle, or water planets.

More than a trillion citizens reside on the planet Coruscant, which is considered the heart of the Core Worlds, the galactic hub of culture, education, fine arts, technology, and finance. But because of economic or legal restrictions, or political oppression imposed by the prevailing government, many choose to live in the Outer Rim, beyond the influence of the Republic, the Empire, or the New Republic.

"The pride I feel for this planet cannot be put into words." SUPREME CHANCELLOR PALPATINE

NABOO

A small and geologically unique world, Naboo's surface consists of swampy lakes, rolling plains, and green hills. The river cities are resplendent with classical architecture and greenery, while the underwater Gungan settlements are exotic examples of hydrostatic bubble technology.

APPEARANCES I, II, CW, III, VI, FoD **REGION** Mid Rim **SECTOR** Chommell **SYSTEM** Naboo **PRIMARY TERRAIN** Plains, swamps, forests

ARCADIAN DESTINATION

Boasting some of the most idyllic meadows and scenic waterfalls on Naboo, the Lake Country is one of the planet's most remote inhabited regions, with a sparse population made up mostly of farmers, shaak herders, and glass craftworkers. Sealed off from Naboo's underground waterways and caverns, the lakes here are safe from large aquatic monsters. In springtime, the Festival of Glad Arrival transforms the meadows into a setting for colorful pageants and musical performances. Although the fertile land is regularly flooded by its rivers, the area is pleasantly dry in summer. Padmé Amidala's family maintains a retreat on the island of Varykino in the Lake Country.

Trade routes
For generations, Gungans have used bongo submarines to explore and navigate the network of underwater tunnels that snake through the planet Naboo.

THE CORE

Lacking a molten core, the small, ancient planet of Naboo is a conglomerate of large, rocky bodies permeated by caves and tunnel networks. These largely water-filled networks create numerous swampy lakes on the planet's surface, which lead deeper into its structure. The native Gungans have developed submersible transports to traverse the caves and tunnels, but most hesitate to venture deep into the planetary core, which is infested with enormous, ravenous sea beasts. However, hardy Gungan navigators regard certain networks through the core as time-honored trade routes and the most expedient avenues from one area of Naboo to another.

Peaceful planet
Although Naboo's sparse human population embraces peace and tranquillity, they and the indigenous Gungans navigate an uneasy relationship for hundreds of years until they ally to defend their verdant world.

BATTLE OF NABOO

Following a blockade by the Trade Federation, Queen Amidala returns to Naboo hoping to save her people. She leads the resistance with the help of Jedi Qui-Gon Jinn and Obi-Wan Kenobi, Anakin Skywalker, and the indigenous Gungans. While the Gungan military lures the droid army away from the capital, Amidala and the Jedi head to infiltrate Theed Palace, where Trade Federation leader Nute Gunray is stationed. However, Darth Maul appears and engages the two Jedi, leading them into the city's power generator for an epic duel that ends in Qui-Gon's death and Maul's apparent demise. Meanwhile, young Anakin finds his way to the Droid Control Ship, destroying it from the inside and deactivating the droid armies. At the same time, in the Theed Palace throne room, Amidala arrests Gunray and forces him to sign a new treaty.

Dangerous decoy
The Gungan army bravely engages with the enormous droid army on the Great Grass Plains, just south of Theed.

THE GUNGAN SACRED PLACE

Built by the Elders, the Gungan Sacred Place is an ancient monument north of the Lianorm Swamp. For generations, Gungans have gathered in this area during times of discord or when the leaders anticipate great danger. The monument is accessed by a hidden entrance, which leads to a path that emerges in a clearing beneath a dense forest canopy. The remains of gigantic statues and monolithic heads, some displaced by the roots of primeval trees, appear to alternately rise from and rest upon the hallowed grounds, from which outsiders are normally forbidden.

Urgent union
During the Trade Federation invasion of Naboo, Jar Jar Binks brings Queen Amidala to meet Boss Nass at the Gungan Sacred Place *(top)*. There, the Gungans and the Naboo agree to an alliance against their enemies. Little is known about the reptilian humanoids called the Elders *(above)*, who waged war with ancient Gungans and left numerous monuments on Naboo.

Symbolic spectacle
The Festival of Light's fireworks are artfully controlled bursts that represent significant historic moments in Naboo's association with the Republic.

FESTIVAL OF LIGHT

An annual event, the Festival of Light celebrates the anniversary of when Naboo joined the Galactic Republic. In the city of Theed, the celebration is traditionally observed with a public ceremony that includes an elaborate laser light show and fireworks display. During the Clone Wars, Supreme Chancellor Palpatine returns to his homeworld to attend the festival in its 847th year, even though he is aware he may be targeted for assassination. Knowing that to shrink from such duty would be to admit fear of the enemy, Palpatine trusts the Jedi to protect him during the festival.

OPERATION CINDER

Weeks after the Battle of Endor, the Emperor's contingency plans, including Operation Cinder, are activated. Following the Emperor's posthumous orders, Naboo is one of many planets marked for destruction. The Empire targets Naboo with climate disruption arrays that will render the planet uninhabitable. Led by Princess Leia, a small force of N-1 starfighters attacks the arrays, and, with the help of Rebel Alliance reinforcements, destroys them. The Empire then launches a ground assault on Theed that is repelled by the Alliance forces.

Climate control
A disruption to the temperate climate of Naboo would be catastrophic.

Cultured capital
Theed's universities cultivate artists, educators, and politicians who are dedicated to public service—with one notable exception.

THEED

APPEARANCES I, II, CW, III, VI, FoD
LOCATION Naboo

Originally a farming village nestled along the banks of the Solleu River, Naboo's capital city, Theed, is built at the edge of a great plateau where the Solleu runs toward a spectacular waterfall. Fed by underground tributaries that flow from the planet's core, the river travels through and around Theed so that nearly every vantage point in the city has water views. For generations, Naboo traders have used the waterways to occasionally meet with Gungans. Many of the city's buildings have columned facades and domed roofs. Theed's harmonious architectural style reflects the peaceful culture and ways of the city's founders and citizens.

During the blockade of Naboo, this peace is disrupted as the city is occupied by the Trade Federation. The people of Naboo suffer in detention camps under the Federation, until they are freed by the combined Gungan and Naboo forces after the Battle of Naboo. At the end of the Clone Wars, the city holds the funeral for the beloved former queen and senator, Padmé Amidala.

After the Battle of Endor, an Imperial faction launches an attack on Naboo, landing forces in Theed. This ground assault is repelled by Princess Leia and members of the Rebel Alliance.

THEED ROYAL PALACE

APPEARANCES I, II, CW, III, VI **LOCATION** Theed, Naboo

Resting serenely atop a plunging cliff face lined with waterfalls is the immense Theed Royal Palace, Naboo's seat of power. The city of Theed radiates from the palace, and it is often the terminus of grand parades. The ancient and majestic building serves as the residence of Naboo's elected sovereign, as well as the meeting place of Naboo's Royal Advisory Council. The palace is a mighty structure, with strong lines and an imposing presence, but it is also decorated with delicate, ornate finishes that are a testament to Naboo's sensitivity to art and culture. The palace is protected by the Naboo Palace Guard, although given Naboo's pacifist nature, the trained troops rarely need to mobilize. During the blockade of Naboo, Viceroy Nute Gunray of the Trade Federation occupies the palace. He is captured during the Battle of Naboo by Queen Amidala. Years later, Count Dooku infiltrates the palace to try to capture the Supreme Chancellor during the 847th Festival of Light ceremony. Following the Battle of Naboo, an ion pulse cannon is installed to protect Theed. It is activated when the Empire attacks the city during Operation Cinder.

Palatial sanctuary
Theed Royal Palace enjoys commanding views from its cliff-face sanctuary *(left)*. The city's main thoroughfare, the Palace Plaza, is a wide, pedestrian-only avenue that stretches from the Royal Palace to the palace courtyard *(above)*.

ROYAL PALACE THRONE ROOM

APPEARANCES I, II
LOCATION Theed Palace, Theed, Naboo

The Royal Palace's original designers and contemporary curators eschew any display of bulky, inelegant machinery, but the building has many subtly blended technological features. The throne room is protected by ornate blast doors, an interplanetary communications system, and hidden compartments for weapons in case of an emergency. A composite holoprojector is built into the throne room's floor, along with a large viewscreen on the wall, which allows Queen Amidala and her Advisory Council to converse with dignitaries from other worlds.

Captured throne
During their occupation of Naboo, Neimoidians confer with Darth Sidious' hologram in the throne room.

OTOH GUNGA

APPEARANCES I, CW
LOCATION Lake Paonga, Naboo

Deep below the surface of Lake Paonga is the largest Gungan city on Naboo, Otoh Gunga. The city resembles a glittering cluster of jewel-like bubbles and is the crowning achievement of unique Gungan technology. The Gungans grow the building material for their cities, and the elegant structures contained within the bubbles consist of curving forms that appear alive. The bubbles are hydrostatic force fields that contain breathable atmospheres for the city's inhabitants. Though the bubbles are rigid enough to keep the water out, they can be safely passed through by Gungans swimming to and from the city at special portal zones.

During the Trade Federation's occupation of Naboo, the Gungan leader Boss Nass ignores the battle droid threat, believing Otoh Gunga is safe. But when the battle droids encroach on Gungan territory and invade Otoh Gunga, they force the Gungans to abandon their underwater city. The Gungans hide in the nearby forests where the Gungan Sacred Place is located, and eventually ally with Queen Amidala and the Naboo people.

Following the defeat of the Trade Federation, overcrowding becomes a prime concern for Boss Nass and the Gungan Rep Council. The increased Gungan tolerance of visiting offworlders results in Otoh Gunga becoming a tourist attraction and, surprisingly, a favored destination for honeymooning vacationers. After Padmé steps down as queen, one of her former handmaidens, Eirtaé, travels to Otoh Gunga to learn about Gungan technology.

Gungan engineering
Gungans combine bubble wort catalyst and stabilized plasma in electrostatic field generators to create the permeable hydrostatic bubbles needed to keep their city dry *(above)*. Otoh Gunga's amphibious inhabitants use specially designed portal zones to enter and exit the submerged city *(right)*.

THEED HANGAR

APPEARANCES I, CW
LOCATION Theed, Naboo

Attached to one side of Naboo's Theed Palace, a spacious hangar serves as the headquarters of the Royal Naboo Security Forces and Starfighter Corps, and houses the sleek yellow Naboo N-1 starfighters as well as the queen's gleaming Royal Starship. Separated from the hangar by a heavy blast-proof door, the neighboring power generator supplies the hangar's spacecraft with plasma energy through underground conduits. The hangar is equipped with air traffic control, tactical computer stations, and a secret subterranean tunnel link to the palace. During the Battle of Naboo, Queen Amidala and her allies use the tunnels to infiltrate Theed, allowing them to reach the hangar and liberate the air traffic controllers and pilots from their droid captors. The pilots scramble to their N-1 starfighters and swiftly leave the hangar to join the fight. Eventually, the hangar is closed as fighter operations are moved out of the palace and later the Empire demilitarizes Naboo. During Operation Cinder, Princess Leia, Queen Soruna, and rebel pilot Shara Bey enter the hangar, finding old N-1 starfighters that they board to protect Naboo from destruction by the Empire.

"Well, if there's a bright center to the universe, you're on the planet that it's farthest from."

LUKE SKYWALKER

TATOOINE

Far from the Core Worlds, the inhospitable desert planet Tatooine is of little interest to either the Old Republic or the subsequent Empire. Ironically, this dusty world is home to two generations of Skywalkers, who are instrumental in bringing down both galactic governments.

APPEARANCES I, II, CW, III, Reb, IV, VI **REGION** Outer Rim Territories **SECTOR** Arkanis **SYSTEM** Tatoo **PRIMARY TERRAIN** Desert, mesas, buttes, canyons

Negotiations
Although Jedi have little reason to visit Tatooine, Obi-Wan Kenobi meets with Jabba the Hutt during the Clone Wars to discuss a delicate situation involving Jabba's abducted son, Rotta.

Sand planet
Isolated and almost entirely devoid of water, Tatooine is a world of dry air and parched soil. The planet's silicate surface reflects the light of its suns so intensely that legends tell of its original explorers first mistaking the planet for a third, smaller sun. Indigenous sentient life includes the scavenging Jawas and the fearsome Tusken Raiders. Creatures found roaming the desert include banthas, rontos, dewbacks, scurriers, womp rats, krayt dragons, and eopies.

LAWLESS WORLD

Beyond the interests of the Republic or Imperial laws, Tatooine is largely controlled by the Hutts, whose shady operations bring many spacers, bounty hunters, and thieves to the planet's few port cities. Despite the planet's criminal activity and hardworking settlers' attempts to extract a living from the unforgiving environment, sporadic colonization efforts have resulted in only scattered communities, separated by vast gulfs of wilderness.

Infinite wastes
Tatooine's surface is a seemingly endless desert environment cooked by the intense energy of twin yellow suns. Only the sporadic rocky mesas, canyons, and arroyos break up the monotony of seemingly endless shifting dunes.

DESERT SCAVENGERS

Long before the Hutts took control of Tatooine, mining colonies searched the sand planet for precious minerals and ores. When Tatooine metal proved to have unwanted metallurgic properties, the mines were shut down and the miners abandoned most of their equipment, including mobile transports used for hauling and refining ore. Much to the remaining colonists' surprise, the native Jawas quickly claimed and salvaged these "sandcrawlers," making them an important part of their culture. Jawas use the large, treaded vehicles not only as an armored defense against the elements and Tusken Raiders, but for transporting trade goods, including refurbished droids made from scavenged parts, to remote outposts. The sandcrawlers' smelting reactors, originally designed to melt processed ore, have been modified to produce salable ingots. Although Tusken Raiders have no interest in computer technology, they also scavenge—and more often steal—metal they can shape into weapons and masks.

Nomadic traders
Scurrying outside their sandcrawler, Jawas present various droids for sale to moisture farmer Owen Lars.

KRAYT DRAGONS

According to Jawa folklore, the great Tatooine desert known as the Dune Sea was once a true ocean. Ancient fossil-bearing rock and eroded canyons seem to confirm the Jawas' stories, but most of Tatooine's inhabitants still find it hard to believe water ever flowed on the planet's arid, sand-covered surface. Despite the scarcity of water, Tatooine boasts many indigenous creatures, the largest of which are krayt dragons, represented by two species: the relatively common canyon krayt, which dwells in rock caves and canyons, and the much larger greater krayt, which submerges itself in the shifting sands and uses its powerful limbs to swim through the dunes.

Skeletal remains
Shortly after arriving on Tatooine, the droid C-3PO shuffles past the sand-scoured skeleton of a greater krayt dragon that rests in the Jundland Wastes.

MOISTURE FARMS

Water vaporators are not only the most energy-efficient devices used to gather water on Tatooine, they are the most crucial piece of equipment for colonists' survival. Although a single vaporator may cost up to 500 credits, some colonists invest in multiple units to establish their own moisture farms. Independent farmers often use surplus water for their small hydroponic gardens, but few gardens yield enough to make substantial profits. Vaporators require frequent maintenance as well as security systems to deter Tusken Raiders.

Vaporator fields
Luke surveys his uncle's farm and vaporators *(right)*, which are strategically spaced to collect moisture *(above)*.

Crowded hovels
Abandoned by the mining companies that first colonized Tatooine, the cheap hovels in Mos Espa's slave quarter provide only the most basic shelter for downtrodden slaves.

Tearful farewell
On the street outside their home, Anakin Skywalker says goodbye to his mother, Shmi.

MOS ESPA

APPEARANCES I, II
LOCATION Tatooine

On the lip of the Dune Sea, down a canyon called the Xelric Draw, the city of Mos Espa is a serpentine sprawl of low-level buildings with thick walls and domed roofs to defend against the scorching heat of the planet's twin suns. One of the few port cities on Tatooine, Mos Espa is larger than Mos Eisley spaceport and is known for its wide streets, bordered by many shops and stalls. Among the dwellings, workspaces, and commercial operations, the city also boasts many entertainment areas, including the famed Mos Espa Grand Arena, which can almost hold the city's entire population. Although wealthy Hutts, including Jabba, keep residences in Mos Espa, most of the inhabitants are settlers and subsistence earners who eke out meager livings as best they can.

Because neither the Galactic Republic nor the Trade Federation has any jurisdiction over Tatooine, and because Tatooine has few valuable natural resources, the only real wealth in Mos Espa is tied up in gambling and offworld trade, especially in the lucrative black market. The influx of commercial ventures fuels Mos Espa's growth, quickly transforming it into the largest city on Tatooine and the desert planet's de facto capital. Many outlanders believe they may avoid paying high tariffs by doing business in Mos Espa, but because Tatooine is controlled by the devious Hutts, few travelers save money at the spaceport. The inexpensive hotels and cantinas exist primarily to lure traders, spacers, and unwitting tourists into the Hutts' casinos and gambling dens, where they can easily lose their earnings and even life savings within hours. Few losers complain because they know the Hutt-owned establishments are staffed by security personnel who don't take kindly to troublemakers. However, the rise of the Empire prompts the Hutts to revise their business schemes, and Jabba shifts his interests to Mos Eisley, causing Mos Espa to decline.

Although slavery is outlawed in Republic space, it persists on worlds outside the Republic's authority. An entire section of Mos Espa's outskirts has been transformed into a slave quarter. Slaves function more as prestige possessions than cheap laborers, and owners part with them only reluctantly. Slaves are sometimes used as capital in business transactions. Nearly all slavery operations in Mos Espa are controlled by Hutt gangsters, who, as with all their illegal ventures, regard slavery as a useful institution.

Return to Mos Espa
Padmé Amidala's yacht delivers Anakin to a Mos Espa docking bay *(right)*, and the two take a droid rickshaw to Watto's shop *(above)*.

WATTO'S SHOP

APPEARANCES I, II
LOCATION Mos Espa, Tatooine

Although Watto promotes his establishment as a parts dealership, everyone in Mos Espa calls it a junk shop. The property is ideally situated near the spaceport's busiest docking bays and service hangars, and it is well known to many podracers. Originally, the shop's main building was an unremarkable squat dome, but Watto has added a distinctive bell-shaped top, which provides additional living and working space and attracts customers because of its unusual appearance and greater height than neighboring buildings. The dome's apex forms a comfortable perch for Watto and is similar to the muck nests of his home planet. The shop is one of the most successful of its kind in Mos Espa. Watto attributes his success to four things: inflated prices, stolen stock, slaves, and no questions asked. Like most Mos Espa merchants, Watto accepts only local currency.

Inside Watto's shop, merchandise ranges from desirable rare parts to fully operational droids. His selection of droids and droid parts includes GNK power droids, DUM-series pit droids, astromechs, and shell plating for Cybot Galactica protocol droids. An R1-type shopkeeping drone handles most of the routine business operations, while Watto's slave, Anakin, repairs and cleans machinery, allowing Watto to dedicate more time to his gambling interests.

Watto has also amassed a collection of podrace memorabilia, including many rare trophies. Outside the shop, an arched portal serves as the entrance to the scrapyard, where Watto stores the bulk of his merchandise, including larger items like podracer engines, landspeeder turbines, and empty cargo containers. Near the scrapyard's entrance, Watto maintains a constantly shifting pile of largely useless scrap, which he leaves outside for Jawa scavengers. Although Watto prefers paying customers, he has a certain respect for Jawas, as they have taught him much about salvaging ruined vessels and protecting technology from heat and sand.

Slave labor
Holding machinery for repairing and cleaning mechanical apparatus and technology, the curved tables inside Watto's shop double as display shelves for various parts for sale *(above)*. Anakin's natural talent for repairing machinery makes him one of Watto's most prized possessions *(left)*.

Tour of the scrapyard
Hoping to obtain an unusual hyperdrive component, the Jedi Qui-Gon Jinn follows Watto into the scrapyard behind Watto's shop.

"Start your engines!" BEED

MOS ESPA GRAND ARENA

Financed by the Hutts, the Mos Espa Grand Arena is home to the Boonta Eve Classic, the largest annual podrace held on Tatooine. The arena's podracing track is one of the most famous in the Outer Rim Territories and attracts competitors and spectators from all over the galaxy.

APPEARANCES | **LOCATION** Outskirts of Mos Espa, Tatooine

Podrace fans

Over 100,000 beings fill the Mos Espa Grand Arena to capacity for the Boonta Eve Classic. They file into the grandstand seats, crowd into broad viewing platforms, or cluster into the upper tiers to witness the high-speed spectacle. Many hope to win big after hitting the betting windows and playing the odds.

Sand rock construction
Straddling the junction of the Xelric Draw and the Northern Dune Sea, the arena's amphitheater is built into the natural curve of a steep-walled canyon.

PODRACER HANGARS

Originally constructed as a series of enclosed bays, each of which serviced a single podracer, the arena's hangars have been expanded as the sport has grown in popularity. The dividers between the bays have been removed to accommodate additional podracers and to keep up with the number of entrants. While the hangars are used for vehicle maintenance and last-minute tune-ups before a race, they also provide a place for podracer pilots, their wealthy fans, and their sponsors to place unregulated, high-stakes bets with one another.

Bustling pit droids
Inside a hangar, teams of pit droids are constantly on the move, assisting podracer mechanics in preparation for the Boonta Eve Classic.

WATTO'S BOX

Mos Espa's wealthier residents and guests can afford private viewing boxes separated from the rest of the rabble. Toydarian junk merchant Watto hosts viewing parties for his friends and gambling partners in his own private box. Because only a small fraction of the racetrack passes the arena, Watto's box is equipped with viewscreens that broadcast transmissions from aerial cam droids, enabling Watto and his cronies to monitor each podracer's progress. The most opulent viewing box is reserved for the ruling Hutts, particularly Jabba, grandmaster host of the Boonta Eve Classic.

Heavy losses
Watto places huge bets on podracing champion Sebulba to win the Boonta Eve Classic. He is confident at first, but ends up a big loser when his own slave, Anakin Skywalker, wins the race.

No turning back
As the podracer pilots move into position on the arena's starting grid, none dwell on the fact that the Boonta Eve Classic has the highest mortality rate of all podrace competitions in the galaxy.

STARTING GRID

The formal race ceremony begins with a parade of flag-bearers, each carrying a podracer's distinctive emblem as they line up before the starting grid. The system for determining the starting lineup at the Boonta Eve Classic is the subject of much speculation and argument among podracing aficionados. Allegedly developed by expert race officials, the system actually involves a baffling mix of performance statistics, outright bribery, and random chance. After the flag-bearers clear the grid, the podracers' massive engines roar to life, seemingly hungry for the chance to charge along at speeds exceeding 700 kilometers (435 miles) per hour. Eighteen podracers enter the fateful competition that results in a major upset for Sebulba the Dug and a great victory for Anakin, who wins not only the event but also his freedom. A mere seven pilots manage to cross the finish line.

BEN KENOBI'S HOME

APPEARANCES IV **LOCATION** Jundland Wastes, Tatooine

Obi-Wan "Ben" Kenobi lives in an abandoned moisture prospector's hut on a bluff surrounded by the Western Dune Sea. The house has one main room above ground and is built on top of a sheltered cave, which Obi-Wan uses as a little workshop and cellar to store food. Here, Obi-Wan reveals to Luke Skywalker that his father was a Jedi. After they leave Tatooine and Obi-Wan dies on the Death Star, Luke returns to the hut, but he is attacked by bounty hunter Boba Fett. Luke defeats Boba and leaves with Obi-Wan's journal. Darth Vader and Doctor Aphra later arrive to inspect the hut, with Vader sensing Luke's strength with the Force. Aphra sets off a molecular bomb to remove any trace of their visit. Years later, Luke returns once more to find components for his second lightsaber.

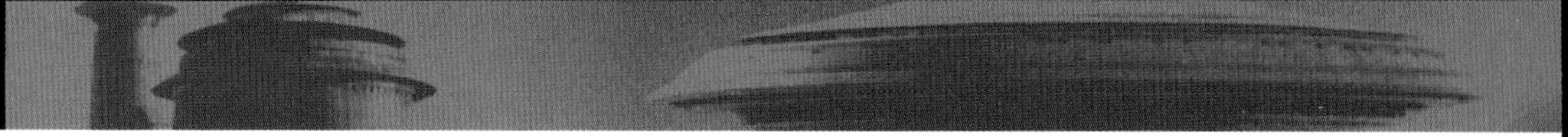

"The entire planet is one big city." RIC OLIÉ

CORUSCANT

Situated in the heart of the galaxy, Coruscant is the seat of government for the Galactic Republic and the subsequent Empire. Completely covered by skyscrapers, the planet has a population of over one trillion, including many powerful and influential politicians and industrialists.

APPEARANCES I, II, CW, III, VI, FoD **REGION** Core Worlds **SECTOR** Coruscant subsector, Corusca sector **SYSTEM** Coruscant **PRIMARY TERRAIN** Urban cityscape

Shimmering "surface"
Viewed from orbit, Coruscant resembles a great, glittering sphere and appears to promise prosperity for all. Sunlight dances across the gleaming skyscrapers' uppermost levels, which are home to the wealthiest citizens. But beneath this veneer, the city-world descends thousands of levels to impoverished, dangerous areas untouched by the sun for millennia.

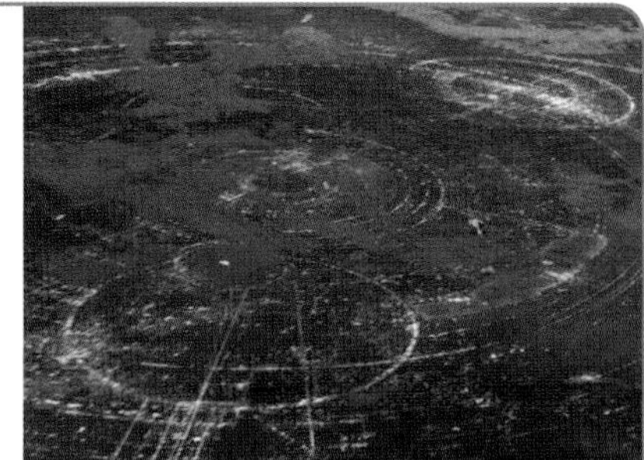

Urban growth
The crisis on Naboo and the Clone Wars dramatically impact Coruscant's Senate District, as the call to bolster the Galactic Republic's stability results in new buildings to house thousands of pro-Republic and war-effort departments.

SKYSCRAPER SPRAWLS

Over many thousands of years, Coruscant's surface has become completely buried under the foundations of immense, densely clustered skyscrapers. The enormous structures reach so high into the atmosphere that tenants require piped-in purified gasses for breathing in upper-level complexes, a luxury only the affluent can afford. Several kilometers down, the lower levels are a worldwide maze of treacherous alleys where the most impoverished dwell. Citizens from above and below intermingle in myriad nightclubs, gaming houses, bars, and entertainment establishments that cater to alien species.

Global megalopolis
Exhausted of all natural resources, Coruscant is entirely dependent on outside support to survive.

AIR TRAFFIC

Coruscant's skies are filled with unending repulsorlift traffic. Most skylanes are autonavigated, with vehicles traveling on preprogrammed routes to minimize risk of collisions. Large passenger ships join the fastest traffic in the highest skylanes, while smaller air taxis crisscross these routes to take high-paying riders directly to their destinations. Tour operator pilots demand high fees for taking wide-eyed offworlders on breathtaking cruises over the planet. Even in the depths of night, Coruscant is alive with glittering lights and rivers of traffic, a bustling megalopolis that refuses to sleep.

Freighter lanes
Unending streams of freighters deliver food and other necessities.

THE WORKS

A large sector and industrial area in Galactic City, the Works is a once-great manufacturing district, recognized as a major source of production for spacecraft parts, construction droids, and building materials. But centuries ago, increasingly high costs on Coruscant prompted most manufacturers to shift their operations to offplanet facilities. Now, the Works largely consists of long-abandoned buildings and empty warehouses, many appropriated by criminals. A derelict hangar in the Works is an ideal site for clandestine meetings between Darth Sidious and Darth Tyranus.

Abandoned towers
Toxic waste leaves large areas of the Works entirely uninhabitable.

Jubilant celebrations
Fireworks light up Coruscant's sky after Palpatine's death.

CIVIL WAR

Following Emperor Palpatine's death there are celebrations across much of Coruscant. Soon after, a civil war breaks out between the Imperial forces and the citizens loyal to them and the rebellious citizens, supported by New Republic troops. Grand Vizier Mas Amedda, the nominal successor to the Emperor, is imprisoned in the Imperial Palace by forces loyal to the Emperor's protégé, Gallius Rax. Following the Battle of Jakku, Amedda represents the Empire and signs the Galactic Concordance, a peace treaty ending the Galactic Civil War. Coruscant then joins the New Republic with Amedda installed as a puppet leader of its provisional government.

PALPATINE'S APARTMENT

APPEARANCES | **LOCATION** 500 Republica, Galactic City, Coruscant

Within the upper levels of the most prestigious and exclusive residential tower in the Senate District on Coruscant, Senator Palpatine keeps an apartment that offers majestic views, yet is modest in comparison with the residences of other sectorial representatives. The apartment consists of an expansive suite of rooms, most of which are decorated in hues of scarlet, Palpatine's preferred color, and with unusual art objects that reflect his worldly point of view. To ensure the complete safety of his guests, Palpatine outfits each room with discreet surveillance and security systems, which enable him to know immediately whether his guests have any special requirements or require assistance.

Calming influence
Devoid of vibrant colors or ostentatious decorations, Palpatine's apartment is designed to pacify argumentative visitors and make every guest feel assured of their host's diplomatic authority.

"I'm on my way to the Jedi Temple to start my training, I hope." ANAKIN SKYWALKER

JEDI TEMPLE

Since being reclaimed from the Sith 1,000 years ago, the Jedi Temple has been the home of the Jedi Order on Coruscant. Part school and part monastery, the Temple houses facilities for training and meditation, dormitories, medical centers, and archives that contain extensive data from across the galaxy.

APPEARANCES I, II, CW, III, VI, FoD **LOCATION** Galactic City, Coruscant

Jedi dispatch Standing in the center of the High Council chamber, Obi-Wan Kenobi and Anakin Skywalker receive orders from the Council.

HIGH COUNCIL CHAMBER

The Jedi High Council, the governing body of the Jedi Order, convenes within one of the Jedi Temple's outer spires. The circular High Council chamber holds a ring of 12 seats, one for each of the Jedi Masters who serve as Council members. Monitoring galactic events and contemplating the nature of the Force, the Council has final authority on Jedi missions on behalf of the Republic and also determines whether prospective Jedi candidates are worthy of training. While advanced communications networks keep the Council apprised of galactic events, its members also rely on the Force to sense disturbances and anticipate situations that may require their help. During the Clone Wars, the Council uses the High Council chamber to consider battle strategies and coordinate troops.

The Temple A massive ziggurat rising from one of the highest levels on Coruscant, the Jedi Temple is instantly recognizable by its distinctive crown of five spires. The Jedi Order also maintains chapter houses and other temples throughout the galaxy.

Giving instruction
While teaching Jedi younglings from the Bear Clan, Yoda confers with Obi-Wan.

TRAINING YOUNG JEDI

Prior to a Padawan's pairing with a Jedi Master, young Jedi—also known as Jedi younglings—are taught in a communal group called a clan. At any given time inside the Jedi Temple, 10 different clans undergo instruction in the ways of the Jedi under the tutelage of Jedi Master Yoda. Each clan consists of up to 20 younglings, ranging in age from 4 to 8 and comprising a number of different species. Anakin is a rare example of a Padawan student who skips the clan stage of training by joining the Jedi Order as an older child.

JEDI ARCHIVES

Inside the Jedi Temple, incredible amounts of data are stored electronically and holographically in the Jedi Archives, possibly the single largest source of information in the galaxy. Jedi scholars and investigators use the carefully organized data in their studies or their missions. Besides standard data tapes and holobooks, the Archives contain holocrons, which are polyhedral-shaped devices that store phenomenal amounts of data. These are housed in a vault prohibited to non-Jedi.

Guardians of knowledge
Jocasta Nu, the chief librarian of the Jedi Archives, assists Obi-Wan *(above left)*, who searches the Archives for information about the mysterious Kamino system *(above)*.

TEMPLE UNDER SIEGE

To help Palpatine conquer his enemies, his new apprentice, Darth Vader, storms the Jedi Temple with his elite clone trooper special forces in tow. They cut down the Jedi ranks within the Temple, not sparing the younglings who cower in the empty Jedi Council chamber. Palpatine also broadcasts a false emergency transmission across space, notifying distant Jedi that the war is over and instructing them to return to the Temple. Seeing through this trap, Jedi Masters Obi-Wan and Yoda infiltrate the Temple and modify the transmission, warning the remaining Jedi to stay away.

Stalking Jedi
At Supreme Chancellor Palpatine's command, the newly appointed Sith Lord Darth Vader leads Anakin's former battalion, the 501st Legion, on a killing mission inside the Jedi Temple.

IMPERIAL PALACE

After the Jedi Purge, Palpatine orders the Jedi Temple to be repaired and redecorated. He renames his enemy's former stronghold the Imperial Palace and rules his Empire from within it. As a public ruler, he holds many lavish balls at the Palace and meets with individuals he finds interesting. In secret, Palpatine moves many of his Sith artifacts to the Palace and orders the excavation of an old Sith shrine where he plans to discover the dark side's final secrets, together with Darth Vader. Following Palpatine's death, his loyal follower and potential successor, Grand Vizier Mas Amedda, is imprisoned in the Palace by Imperial forces loyal to Counselor Gallius Rax. Amedda is eventually liberated by a group of young rebels, who ensure he reaches the New Republic.

After the fall
Following Palpatine's death, celebrations erupt across the planet. The Palace, however, remains a stronghold of the Imperial forces stationed on Coruscant.

Galactic representatives
Each box in the Galactic Senate Chamber contains a delegation from an important world or sector in the Republic. The democratic ideals of the Senate are put to the test every time the legislative process degenerates into arguing and pointless bureaucracy.

GALACTIC SENATE CHAMBER

APPEARANCES I, II, CW, III
LOCATION Senate District, Coruscant

The Galactic Senate Chamber is the nerve center of political activity on Coruscant. The huge open area is lined with 1,024 pods arrayed in concentric circles, each pod housing a delegation from an important planet, sector, or political body. The pods are outfitted with anti-gravity repulsorlifts, so that when a politician wishes to address the assembled Senate, his or her pod detaches from the wall and floats into the open air in the middle of the chamber. The entire structure is fitted with voice-amplifying microphones and automatic translators, and hovercams constantly flit about to record the proceedings for the official record. At the centermost point of the Galactic Senate Chamber is the podium of the Supreme Chancellor. This is where the elected leader of the Republic sits to hear arguments from every representative, usually joined in the podium by the vice chancellor and a senior administrative aide. The podium retracts into the floor when not in use, giving the chancellor access to a suite of rooms where business can be conducted between Senate sessions.

The Galactic Senate Chamber is the site of many of the most crucial events in the latter years of the Republic. It is where Queen Padmé Amidala of Naboo, upset over the lack of political help in ending the Trade Federation's blockade of her homeworld, calls for a Vote of No Confidence in the leadership of Supreme Chancellor Valorum. After the Battle of Naboo, Padmé joins the Senate as the representative from Naboo, playing a role in the debate over whether the Republic should adopt the Military Creation Act in response to the growing threat of Count Dooku's Separatist movement. At the end of the Clone Wars, Palpatine gives a speech in the Galactic Senate Chamber in which he declares himself Emperor. Jedi Master Yoda confronts Palpatine, and the two have a stunning clash of Force powers inside the chamber that results in Yoda fleeing the fight. Once the chamber is repaired, the newly formed Imperial Senate holds meetings here, but they have little to no influence over the Emperor's plans.

Power play

Senator Palpatine slyly manipulates Queen Amidala into pushing for Chancellor Valorum's removal from office. Amidala introduces the Vote of No Confidence in Valorum's leadership, leading to Palpatine's election as the new Supreme Chancellor. The queen believes this will be a good move for Naboo, since Palpatine is a native of her homeworld, but it has dire consequences for the galaxy as Supreme Chancellor Palpatine slowly brings the Senate under his control and ensures that he is given stronger executive powers.

"Order! We shall have order!" **MAS AMEDDA**

Fight to the death
After the defeat of his Master, Qui-Gon *(right)*, Obi-Wan Kenobi struggles to pull himself out of the reactor shaft while Maul attacks *(above)*.

THEED POWER GENERATOR

APPEARANCES I **LOCATION** Theed, Naboo

Located within the capital city of Theed on Naboo, the power generator is where the planet's natural plasma reserves are refined and used as a source of efficient energy. The building also houses hangar facilities for the starfighters of the Royal Naboo Security Forces. The power generator is a clean, brightly illuminated location of towering columns and dangerous drops. During the Battle of Naboo, Obi-Wan Kenobi and Qui-Gon Jinn chase Darth Maul into the power generator and engage in a fierce lightsaber duel. A series of laser gates separates the Jedi, allowing Maul to get the upper hand and kill Qui-Gon. Obi-Wan defeats Maul and casts his body into a reactor shaft.

SENATE OFFICE BUILDING

APPEARANCES II, CW, III
LOCATION Senate District, Coruscant

The Senate Office Building houses administrative facilities used by legislators on Coruscant, including the offices of the Supreme Chancellor. Landing facilities constructed directly into the side of the building allow senators and guests to come and go freely. Senate Guards provide protection while senators such as Bail Organa, Padmé Amidala, and Onaconda Farr hold discussions with their allies and opponents concerning upcoming pieces of legislation. During the Separatist Crisis and the Clone Wars, many important meetings are held in the Senate Office Building, including debates on the wisdom of the Military Creation Act.

Legislative District
The Senate Office Building is close to the Galactic Senate Chamber for the convenience of its representatives.

Always busy
Starships and airspeeders are constantly arriving and departing, taking senators to important meetings.

CHANCELLOR PALPATINE'S OFFICE

APPEARANCES II, CW, III **LOCATION** Senate District, Coruscant

The office of the Supreme Chancellor of the Republic is located in one of the highest levels of Coruscant within the well-guarded Senate Office Building. It consists of several rooms, featuring red-paneled walls and decorated with bronze statues, bas-relief murals, and other rare and exotic artworks. One piece of sculpture on Palpatine's desk secretly contains his red-bladed lightsaber. During the Clone Wars, Mace Windu and three other Jedi Masters arrive in Palpatine's office to place the chancellor under arrest. He defends himself using his dark side powers. Palpatine's office is also where Anakin's conversion from Jedi to Sith takes place.

PADMÉ'S CORUSCANT APARTMENT

APPEARANCES II, CW, III, FoD
LOCATION Senate District, Coruscant

Padmé Amidala uses this apartment after she becomes Naboo's representative to the Galactic Senate. Spacious and luxurious, it is located in the upper levels of the Coruscant cityscape. Just prior to the Clone Wars, assassin Zam Wesell tries to kill Padmé by placing two venomous kouhuns in her apartment.

CORUSCANT UNDERWORLD

APPEARANCES II, CW
LOCATION Lower Levels, Coruscant

The Coruscant underworld is a term used to describe the lower levels of the city, where sunlight seldom reaches and crime is a constant danger. Nightclubs, taverns, and casinos are common in the better-trafficked areas of the underworld. Brightly colored signs offer illumination regardless of the time of day, while thugs and pickpockets lurk in dark corners preying on pedestrians. Senators and Jedi Knights rarely travel into the underworld unless they have good reason.

After dark
The Coruscant underworld is a dangerous place to travel for those who are alone or unarmed.

Mind trick
In the club, Obi-Wan is confronted by a patron offering him death sticks. With the Force, he convinces the dealer to go home and rethink his life.

OUTLANDER GAMBLING CLUB

APPEARANCES II **LOCATION** Entertainment District, Coruscant

One of the most popular gambling establishments in Coruscant's lower-level Entertainment District, the Outlander Club is a busy place where patrons can place wagers on games of chance and the outcomes of sporting events across the galaxy. With so many people circulating in and out of the club's doors, it is a perfect spot for fugitives to escape unwanted attention or for criminals to sell illegal goods. Just prior to the Clone Wars, Obi-Wan and Anakin pursue assassin Zam Wesell into the Outlander Club. Wesell tries to blend in, but Obi-Wan finds her and cuts off her arm.

DEX'S DINER

APPEARANCES II **LOCATION** CoCo Town, Coruscant

The restaurant operated by Dexter Jettster is a stopover for residents of the CoCo Town neighborhood of Coruscant. The diner is small but usually jam-packed, and offers a variety of filling, unhealthy foods and endless cups of Jawa juice. The droid WA-7 and the human Hermione Bagwa work in the diner as waitresses, and Dex himself often fills the role of chef. Just prior to the Clone Wars, Obi-Wan visits Dex's Diner to ask its proprietor about a dart used to silence bounty hunter Wesell. Dexter, who worked at a mining operation on Subterrel before opening his restaurant, identifies the weapon as a rare Kamino saberdart. This clue leads Obi-Wan to Kamino, where he discovers a secret clone army.

Foot traffic
Dex's Diner occupies a bustling location where customers can drop in at any time, day or night.

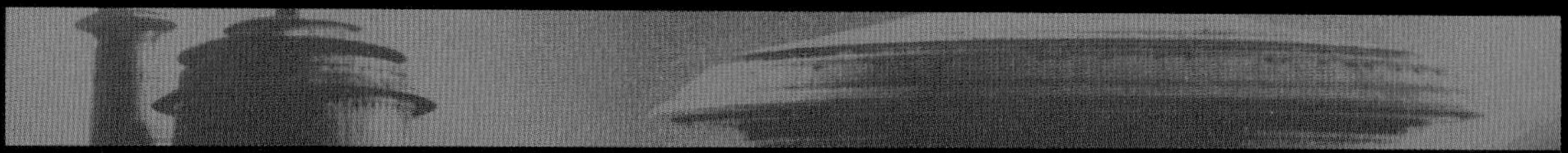

KAMINO

APPEARANCES II, CW **REGION** Outer Rim
SECTOR Unknown **SYSTEM** Kamino
PRIMARY TERRAIN Oceans

Kamino is a watery world located far beyond the Outer Rim, just south of the Rishi Maze. It is the home of the Kaminoans, tall, pale-skinned beings with large eyes who have a talent for genetic manipulation. Over the years, the Kaminoans developed cloning laboratories on their homeworld and their clone creations began appearing on outlying worlds such as the mining planet of Subterrel. The weather patterns of Kamino are frequently rocked by storms and lightning blasts, but the stilt cities of the Kaminoans are built to withstand high winds and pounding waves. The capital of Kamino is Tipoca City, which also houses the most advanced cloning laboratories anywhere on the planet. Kamino is home to a wide variety of aquatic life, including aiwhas, flying cetaceans ridden by the Kaminoans as mounts.

Shortly after the Battle of Naboo, Darth Sidious sets in motion his plan to take control of the galaxy by setting off a false war. Jedi Master Sifo-Dyas places an order with the Kaminoans for a massive clone army. Darth Sidious uses this to his advantage, getting Count Dooku to order Sifo-Dyas' assassination and then assume the Jedi's identity. Dooku then recruits bounty hunter Jango Fett as the genetic template for the army's creation. Fett agrees to live on Kamino for the next decade to provide samples and help train the newly grown soldiers. The deletion of Kamino's coordinates from the Jedi Archives ensures no one will interfere with the project until it is nearly complete.

Eventually Obi-Wan Kenobi tracks down Kamino's location and meets with Kaminoan Prime Minister Lama Su, who assumes he has come to take delivery of the clone army. Obi-Wan also encounters Jango Fett and his cloned son Boba Fett, who flee the planet so as not to attract Jedi attention. Obi-Wan's pursuit of them leads to the Battle of Geonosis that marks the start of the Clone Wars. The Republic happily accepts the clone soldiers grown on Kamino, and these troopers become the backbone of the newly formed Grand Army of the Republic. The Separatists quickly move to cut the clone army off at its source; General Grievous and Asajj Ventress lead a full-scale attack on Kamino, using *Trident*-class drill assault craft to damage the defenses of Tipoca City and aqua droids to execute an underwater assault. The mission ends in failure for the Separatists, but the Order 66 programming contained in the clone troopers soon leads to the downfall of the Jedi. Following the Empire's formation, the cloning factories are shut down and the clone troopers are slowly phased out of the Imperial Army.

Isolated
Kamino's distant location keeps it safe until the Separatists target it during the Clone Wars.

"Kamino? It's not a system I'm familiar with." **JOCASTA NU**

Weather-proofed
The buildings on Kamino have sloping roofs to deflect wind, rain, and ocean spray. The stilts that support the structures are strong, leaving little risk of damage to the Kaminoans or their delicate experiments *(right)*. A Kaminoan on an aiwha mount approaches the elevated expanse of Tipoca City *(above right)*.

TIPOCA CITY

APPEARANCES II, CW **LOCATION** Kamino

Tipoca City is the capital city of Kamino and the site of its most important cloning facility. As Kamino's governmental center, Tipoca City contains offices used by Prime Minister Lama Su and other high-ranking administrators, but many of its buildings are occupied by Kaminoan geneticists and filled with the advanced equipment needed to grow and train clones. The buildings of Tipoca City are constructed on stilts in the vast expanse of the Kaminoan oceans, made from reinforced materials with a streamlined architectural style designed to diffuse the impact of waves and the planet's storms. Landing platforms are usually exposed to the elements, but the doors leading to the city's interior are always watertight. The city's sloped roofs are topped with communications antennas and lightning rods.

The Kaminoans begin work on the Republic's clone army approximately 10 years before the Battle of Geonosis, and they alter each clone's genetic structure so that they age at twice the standard rate. With new batches of clones being produced every year, Tipoca City is soon filled with clones ranging from infancy to adulthood. Each age group requires a different set of instructional programs and training gear. The younger clones receive flash learning in the subjects of military strategy and galactic history, while older clones are permitted to suit up in armor and participate in simulated firefights. These advanced training theaters are part of the Tipoca City Military Complex, which also houses the Central Armory, where thermal detonators, DC-15 blaster rifles, and other weapons are stored. War games held in the Military Complex can involve low-risk, holographic opponents or are set to live-fire settings in which severe injury is a real risk. Elsewhere in the Military Complex are testing facilities for heavy equipment, including six-legged AT-TEs, two-legged AT-RTs, AV-7 anti-vehicle cannons, and low-flying LAAT/i gunships.

Bounty hunter Jango Fett lives in Tipoca City for nearly a decade following his selection as the genetic donor for the Republic's clone trooper army. He abandons his apartment after Obi-Wan tracks him to Kamino.

Following the Battle of Geonosis, Tipoca City's cloning laboratories become one of the Republic's most vital assets. Turbolaser emplacements are used to successfully defend Tipoca City during the Clone Wars, though the city does suffer structural damage from the drills of the Separatist attack craft.

Surprise inspection
Taun We and Prime Minister Lama Su take Obi-Wan on a tour of the city's cloning facilities *(above)*. Aging clone "99," a trooper who grew too rapidly, handles general maintenance duties *(left)*.

Attack on Kamino
Separatist Trident ships land near Tipoca City and unleash their droid passengers *(far left)*, while clone troopers scramble to intercept the threat and defend their birthworld from the Separatists *(left)*.

LAKE COUNTRY

APPEARANCES II **LOCATION** Naboo

The Lake Country is a very beautiful and extremely isolated area on Naboo. Surrounded by mountains, the locale is situated in a valley dotted with numerous picturesque lakes. Vacationers, including Queen Padmé Amidala and her handmaidens, often visit the Lake Country to view its waterfalls and open grasslands filled with wildflowers. Herds of harmless shaaks graze openly in the bucolic meadows. Just prior to the Clone Wars, Padmé chooses the Lake Country as a safe hiding spot for herself and Anakin Skywalker following an attempt on her life.

NABOO LAKE RETREAT

APPEARANCES II
LOCATION Lake Country, Naboo

Located in the Lake Country area of Naboo, the lake retreat called Varykino has a long history of use by the Naberrie family. Before she became known as Queen Amidala, the young Padmé Naberrie spent her summers there. The villa occupies a small island in the center of a lake, reachable by gondola speeders, and an old man named Paddy Accu serves as its caretaker. Padmé and Anakin grow close while spending time at the retreat and later return to be married in secret.

Bad feeling
Jango Fett isn't happy about Obi-Wan's intrusion into his apartment and the way the Jedi questions him.

JANGO'S APARTMENT

APPEARANCES II
LOCATION Tipoca City, Kamino

Jango Fett's home for 10 years, this small apartment in Tipoca City on Kamino is given to the bounty hunter by the Kaminoans for his participation in the cloning project. Jango keeps his accommodation simple, hiding his armor out of sight and displaying no trophies from his hunts. A large window on one wall offers a spectacular view of the churning ocean that stretches out to the horizon. Boba Fett also lives in the apartment with his father, until Obi-Wan's investigation causes the pair to flee Kamino.

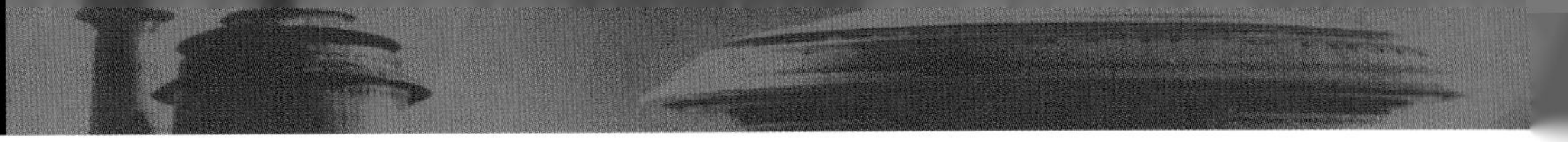

"The droid foundry seems to be working at full capacity. I am going to go down and investigate." **OBI-WAN KENOBI**

GEONOSIS

An arid world of red skies and forbidding mountains, Geonosis is the Outer Rim home of an insectoid species known throughout the galaxy for its skill at manufacturing deadly battle droids.

APPEARANCES II, CW, Reb **REGION** Outer Rim **SECTOR** Arkanis **SYSTEM** Geonosis
PRIMARY TERRAIN Rocky wastes, deserts

SEPARATIST STRONGHOLD

The Geonosians arm the Trade Federation before the Battle of Naboo, manufacturing the battle droids that fight the Gungans. When Count Dooku orchestrates the rise of the Separatist movement, he enlists Geonosian leader Poggle the Lesser to help produce an automated army to make war with the Republic. In secret, the Geonosians help develop the plans for a planet-shattering battle station. Geonosis becomes one of the most valuable planets in Dooku's Confederacy and plays host to a meeting of top Separatist leaders before Obi-Wan discovers the scope of the threat and warns the Jedi Council.

Ultimate weapon
The Geonosians begin work on a battle station that can destroy planets, later called the Death Star.

Tricky flying
The rocky rings surrounding Geonosis are a navi hazard, but can be used as obstacle courses by who wish to shake off their pursuers.

ALL-OUT WAR

The Republic responds to Obi-Wan's summons with an attack force of Jedi and clone troopers. The Battle of Geonosis is the first conflict of the Clone Wars and sees the use of heavy artillery and other advanced war machines on both sides. After a fierce fight, the Republic emerges victorious, but many Separatist forces evacuate to fight another day. Dooku abandons Geonosis following a lightsaber duel with Master Yoda, then travels to Coruscant to report to Chancellor Palpatine (Darth Sidious) that the war has begun as planned.

Heavy equipment
Republic AT-TEs and clone troopers rout the Separatist defenders in the first Battle of Geonosis *(above)*, assisted by gunships that are picking up troopers and Jedi commanders on the battlefield *(left)*.

RETAKING THE PLANET

The triumphant Republic occupies Geonosis, but clone troopers are soon needed elsewhere. As soon as the Republic relaxes its grip, the Separatists sweep in and seize the planet. Republic war leaders have no choice but to attack the planet to prevent the Separatists from bringing the factories back up to full capacity. By the time the Republic armada is ready, Poggle the Lesser has completed a new, advanced droid factory that becomes the primary target for the Republic invasion. Jedi warriors destroy the factory and force Poggle to take shelter in the Geonosian cave network of Karina the Great. The Republic captures Poggle, who agrees to order the Geonosians to build their original battle station design for them. The construction continues when the Republic transitions into the Empire, and some builders attempt sabotage. Eventually, the Empire moves their battle station from Geonosis' orbit.

GENOCIDE OF THE GEONOSIANS

Wanting to keep the Death Star a secret, Grand Moff Tarkin orders Geonosis to be sterilized with poison, killing 100 billion beings. A single drone survivor, named Klik-Klak, safeguards the last known queen egg deep underground. Two years before the Battle of Yavin, the *Ghost* crew and rebel Saw Gerrera discover Klik-Klak and the egg, and proof of the genocide. While Klik-Klak remains on the planet, the rebels escape an Imperial patrol but lose the proof they need to convince the galaxy. After the Battle of Yavin, Darth Vader returns to Geonosis to discover the hatched queen. Unfortunately, she is infertile so she cannot bring her species back. Instead, she produces mechanical children from a droid factory "womb" with which she augments herself. Vader steals her factory but leaves the queen alive.

Return to Geonosis
When Poggle the Lesser and his Geonosians take back their homeworld, the Republic must fight a second time.

Lone survivor
Desperate to ensure the survival of his species, Klik-Klak is initially wary of the rebel visitors and sends battle droids to attack them.

"It just isn't fair. I'm never gonna get out of here!" LUKE SKYWALKER

LARS MOISTURE FARM

A humble homestead in a desolate corner of Tatooine, the Lars moisture farm becomes a home for Shmi Skywalker and her grandson, Luke, before being destroyed by the Empire.

APPEARANCES II, III, Reb, IV **LOCATION** Near Jundland Wastes, Tatooine

Conference
Cliegg Lars informs Anakin Skywalker that his mother is a captive of the Tusken Raiders *(right)*. Later Anakin bids farewell to his slain mother at her graveside *(below)*.

Secret message

After his uncle purchases the droids R2-D2 and C-3PO from Jawas, Luke brings the pair to the garage, or tech dome, attached to the moisture farm. Here, he cleans the droids with equipment kept in his workshop, removing carbon scoring from R2's chassis and treating C-3PO to an oil bath. During his examination of R2-D2, Luke discovers a mysterious recording. The astromech droid claims the holographic vision of Princess Leia Organa is a private message for Obi-Wan Kenobi, and after Luke removes his restraining bolt, the little droid runs away in the dead of night. Luke and C-3PO follow him, hoping to recover the fugitive before Luke's uncle realizes what has happened. They thus avoid the stormtrooper attack that destroys the homestead.

CLIEGG AND SHMI

Located near the Jundland Wastes, the Lars moisture farm belongs to Cliegg Lars in the years before the Clone Wars. With his son, Owen, Cliegg uses the vaporators installed on the property to draw water from the atmosphere and grow small food crops. Cliegg soon buys the slave Shmi Skywalker from Watto and marries her. Just prior to the Battle of Geonosis, Tusken Raiders kidnap Shmi while she is out gathering mushrooms at the homestead's perimeter. A search party finds no trace of her, and Cliegg loses his leg to a Tusken trap. Anakin finally locates his mother, but not in time to save her life.

Dreaming of something more
Luke Skywalker becomes a talented bush pilot in his T-16 skyhopper, fueling his hopes that his uncle will let him leave the moisture farm behind and begin a new life away from Tatooine as an Academy cadet.

CHANGE OF HANDS

After a funeral is held for Shmi, Anakin leaves Tatooine behind. Cliegg mourns the loss of his wife and soon follows her into death. This leaves the Lars moisture farm the property of Owen Lars, who maintains the estate with the help of his wife, Beru. The couple gets a surprise when Anakin's former Jedi Master, Obi-Wan Kenobi, visits them, carrying Anakin's infant son, Luke. Owen doesn't want to get mixed up in any further complications involving the Jedi, but he and Beru reluctantly agree to take Luke in and become his guardians, acting as his aunt and uncle as he grows into adulthood. Obi-Wan remains on Tatooine to watch over the boy, despite Owen's disapproval.

Looking to the future
Beru and Owen agree to raise Luke.

Providing sustenance
Beru Lars prepares a meal in the homestead's kitchen.

RAISING LUKE

Luke becomes a great pilot, racing his T-16 skyhopper through Beggar's Canyon and dreaming of joining the Academy. Owen tries to protect Luke by keeping him on the moisture farm year after year. Owen's purchase of the droids C-3PO and R2-D2 from Jawas leads Imperial stormtroopers to the homestead in search of the plans hidden in R2-D2's memory banks. A stormtrooper squad executes Owen and Beru. Weeks later, Darth Vader and Doctor Aphra inspect the farm, searching for a trace of Vader's son, Luke Skywalker.

No place for visitors
The droid factory is a hazardous environment of extreme temperatures, corrosive chemicals, and industrial equipment.

GEONOSIS DROID FACTORY

APPEARANCES II **LOCATION** Geonosis

The planet Geonosis is of great value to the Separatists, primarily for the massive factories built into its crust that produce seemingly endless ranks of military-grade battle droids. The largest droid factory is capable of churning out B1 battle droids and their bulkier cousins, B2 super battle droids, all with minimal supervision by organic operators. The factory is almost entirely automated and rarely shuts down for any reason. This reduces the factory's safety margin to almost nothing and allows the Geonosians to make as many droids as possible. It also makes the environment a death trap for any unlucky beings who wander into its machinery. The factory is a whirl of activity and a clamor of noise at all hours, with assembly lines snaking from level to level and the constant motion of machinery stamping rigid patterns into metal sheets. Waste materials are continuously fed into the factory and melted down, only to be poured into new molds so the process can start again. Large cargo droids, propelled by anti-gravity repulsorlifts, ferry supplies from one assembly station to the next. The factory is located underground and is detectable at the surface only by telltale plumes of smoke wafting out of vents.

When Obi-Wan Kenobi arrives on Geonosis to investigate Separatist activity, the sight of the droid factory confirms his suspicions that Count Dooku is arming for war against the Republic. He informs the Jedi Council of his findings but is captured by Dooku's Geonosian allies. Anakin Skywalker and Padmé Amidala follow Obi-Wan to Geonosis and endure a terrifying trip through the factory. Anakin's lightsaber is destroyed by one of the stamping machines, while C-3PO suffers the indignity of having his head removed and placed on a battle droid frame.

"Machines building machines! How perverse!"

C-3PO

Automated assembly line
The factory largely runs itself and requires little supervision from the Geonosians.

"Let the executions begin!"

POGGLE THE LESSER

GEONOSIS EXECUTION ARENA

Also known as the Petranaki arena, this place is a source of entertainment for Poggle the Lesser and his Geonosians, who cheer as helpless victims are devoured by monsters such as the acklay, nexu, and reek.

APPEARANCES II **LOCATION** Desert plains near droid foundry, Geonosis

Awaiting the end
Chained to tall, massive columns, Padmé, Anakin, and Obi-Wan look like easy prey for the execution monsters.

Arena beasts
Anakin uses the Force to tame a reek, which carries him on its back. He is pursued by Geonosian guards riding thick-skinned orrays.

CRUEL SPECTACLE

An open-air amphitheater close to Poggle the Lesser's seat of power, the execution arena is the site of the scheduled execution of Obi-Wan, Anakin, and Padmé following their capture by Geonosian forces. While Count Dooku watches in satisfaction, the three captives are chained to posts and left to the mercies of a clawed acklay, a horned reek, and a sharp-toothed nexu. Though they manage to free themselves, it seems only a matter of time before they perish.

JEDI RESCUE

Alarmed by the captives' plight and the news of a massive Separatist buildup, the Jedi launch a two-pronged rescue mission. First, Mace Windu gathers a squad of 200 Jedi to fly to Geonosis and slip into the execution arena. At Mace's signal, the Jedi ignite their lightsabers while Mace faces off against Count Dooku inside Poggle the Lesser's viewing platform. Any hope that the standoff might end without bloodshed vanishes when bounty hunter Jango Fett springs into action to defend Dooku. Geonosian warriors follow Fett's lead, and soon the stands erupt in chaos as the Jedi defend against their insectoid attackers. Anakin, Obi-Wan, and Padmé join the struggle as the battle spills onto the arena floor, where Mace beheads Jango Fett with his lightsaber.

Stopping the action
The sudden arrival of the Jedi brings a halt to the gruesome festivities.

REINFORCEMENTS ARRIVE

Just when the tide begins to turn against the Jedi, the second stage of their mission begins. Master Yoda, newly arrived from Kamino, leads an army of clone troopers into the arena aboard a fleet of LAAT/i gunships. The Separatists respond with more battle droids, and soon the violence cannot be contained within the confines of the arena—the desert plains become the next battlefield as the Battle of Geonosis kicks into high gear.

Air attack and ground assault
A Republic gunship takes aim at Separatist cannons *(far left)*. After gaining a new body in the droid factory, C-3PO marches into the execution arena as part of a legion of battle droids *(left)*.

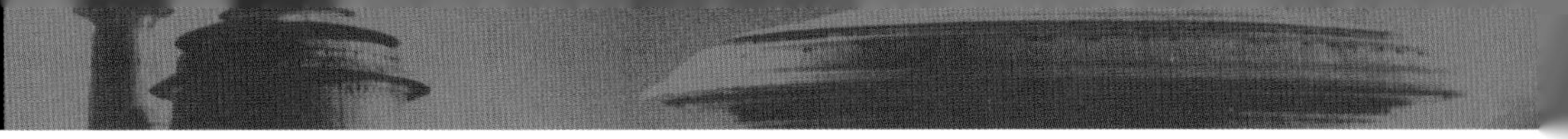

"Lando Calrissian and poor Chewbacca never returned from this awful place." C-3PO

JABBA'S PALACE

This iron-walled fortress beyond Tatooine's Dune Sea is home to one of the galaxy's vilest gangsters. But the palace isn't enough to protect Jabba the Hutt from Luke Skywalker.

APPEARANCES CW, VI **LOCATION** Northern Dune Sea, Tatooine

Built to last
The elevated position of Jabba's palace offers long-distance views of any approaching threats. In the shadow of the palace, a hungry worrt scans for passing prey animals.

Nosy guardian
C-3PO is startled by the surveillance droid built into the palace's gate.

IMPENETRABLE FORTRESS

Jabba the Hutt has attracted many enemies. His palace, designed to keep out unwanted visitors, is located in a remote part of Tatooine and protected by a huge gate guarded by a TT-8L/Y7 gatekeeper droid. These precautions don't keep out Maul and Savage Opress, who invade the palace during the Clone Wars and force Jabba to join their Shadow Collective.

Walking into danger
C-3PO is right to be afraid of what awaits them in Jabba's palace. R2-D2 is as confident as ever, reassuring his friend that they have nothing to worry about.

A LIFE OF DECADENCE

Most of the time, Jabba carefully controls who has access to the interior of his palace. His majordomo, Bib Fortuna, screens anyone who gets past the gate. Most of the welcomed guests are bounty hunters, criminal associates, or entertainers. In his throne room, Jabba sits on a dais to watch his dancers move to the sounds of the Max Rebo Band. If anyone displeases him, Jabba hits a button that triggers a trap door, sending the victim tumbling into the rancor pit below, to be devoured by the beast.

Palace entertainment
The dancers and musicians of Jabba's court do not stop performing *(below)*, even when one of them is fed to Jabba's pet rancor. While his aide Bib Fortuna offers whispered advice, Jabba gleefully accepts C-3PO as his new interpreter droid and dresses Leia in the garb of a palace slave *(right)*.

Deep freeze
Disguised as the bounty hunter Boushh, Leia is determined to rescue Han from his carbonite prison.

RESCUE MISSION

Angry with Han Solo for dumping a valuable cargo of spice, Jabba the Hutt puts a price on the smuggler's head. When Boba Fett delivers a slab of carbonite containing Han Solo in hibernation, Jabba puts the trophy on display. Princess Leia and Luke Skywalker arrive at the palace to rescue their friend, but Jabba, one step ahead of them, captures the princess and drops Luke into his rancor pit. Luke manages to kill the beast, so Jabba decrees his prisoners will instead be executed at the Great Pit of Carkoon. Jabba and his entourage leave the palace in the luxury sail barge *Khetanna*, but Jabba meets a fatal end.

TETH

APPEARANCES CW **REGION** Outer Rim **SECTOR** Baxel **SYSTEM** Teth **PRIMARY TERRAIN** Cliffs, jungles

Teth is controlled by the Hutts. Prior to the Naboo blockade, Jedi Qui-Gon Jinn and Obi-Wan Kenobi travel to Teth to stop the Hutts, who are stealing Republic agricultural shipments. During the Clone Wars, Separatist agents kidnap Jabba the Hutt's son, Rotta, and retreat to a cliff-top fortress on Teth. Republic forces find them, triggering the Battle of Teth and securing Rotta's rescue. Later, Ziro the Hutt escapes from captivity on Nal Hutta and visits his father's grave on Teth to retrieve a secret holojournal. Ziro is betrayed by his companion, Sy Snootles, who shoots him and takes the journal.

RYLOTH

APPEARANCES CW, Reb **REGION** Outer Rim **SECTOR** Gaulus **SYSTEM** Ryloth **PRIMARY TERRAIN** Deserts, plains, mountains

Ryloth is inhabited by the Twi'leks. During the Clone Wars, Orn Free Taa represents the planet in the Galactic Senate. When the Separatists invade, Mace Windu leads the effort to liberate Ryloth from Techno Union foreman Wat Tambor. Mace brokers an alliance between Orn Free Taa and his rival, insurgent Cham Syndulla, and ultimately wins a Republic victory. After the Empire comes to power, Cham forms the Free Ryloth Movement to attempt to liberate his homeworld from its tyranny. On one occasion, he fails to kill the visiting Emperor and his apprentice, Darth Vader. Years later, Cham helps his daughter, Hera, to steal an Imperial carrier orbiting Ryloth. Hera later blows up her old family home in order to escape the Empire with her father and her allies. When the Empire is defeated, Ryloth does not join the New Republic and becomes independent.

Listening post
Rishi Station is filled with communications equipment designed to detect secure military transmissions.

RISHI STATION

APPEARANCES CW **LOCATION** Outer Rim **SECTOR** Abrion
SYSTEM Rishi **PRIMARY TERRAIN** Rocks, craters

This barren moon in the Rishi system is the site of a Republic outpost during the Clone Wars. It is staffed by a small team of clone troopers who monitor transmissions to determine whether the Separatists plan to attack Kamino. When Separatist commando droids take control of Rishi Station, a squad of clones led by Captain Rex and Commander Cody recaptures the base after suffering many losses.

Idyllic world
Maridun is a peaceful planet untouched by war, until the arrival of Separatist general Lok Durd.

MARIDUN

APPEARANCES CW **REGION** Outer Rim **SECTOR** Rolion
SYSTEM Maridun **PRIMARY TERRAIN** Grasslands, forests

The grassy world of Maridun is home to the peaceful settlement of Lurmen as well as dangerous animals like mastiff phalones. During the Clone Wars, Anakin is among the Jedi and clone troopers who crash-land on the planet. The Jedi agree to help the Lurmen tribe defend itself against the forces of Separatist general Lok Durd. Their coordinated effort destroys Durd's life-exterminating defoliator weapon.

"I am sending you to the Mustafar system in the Outer Rim. You will be safe there." **GENERAL GRIEVOUS**

MUSTAFAR

A place of ashen skies and glowing lava, Mustafar is one of the harshest environments in the galaxy and the site of Darth Vader's fateful duel with Obi-Wan Kenobi.

APPEARANCES CW, III, Reb, RO **REGION** Outer Rim **SECTOR** Atravis **SYSTEM** Mustafar **PRIMARY TERRAIN** Volcanoes, lava flows

WORLD OF FIRE

Wishing to harvest rare minerals from the molten lava on Mustafar, the Techno Union builds mining facilities that incorporate energy shields to protect the machinery from the intense heat. During the Clone Wars, Darth Sidious orders bounty hunter Cad Bane to kidnap Force-sensitive children and take them to Mustafar, but Anakin and Ahsoka Tano foil his plans. Late in the war, General Grievous sends the members of the Separatist Council to Mustafar to stay hidden from the Republic.

Surrounded by fire
The administrative buildings on Mustafar offer spectacular views of erupting lava geysers. Mustafar's molten rock contains rare and valuable minerals, making mining in such a harsh environment worth the risks.

DUEL OF BROTHERS

With the Separatist Council now an easy target, Darth Sidious sends his new apprentice, Darth Vader, to Mustafar to execute its members. After completing the evil deed, Vader remains on the planet, where his wife Padmé Amidala finds him. Vader accuses her of conspiring with Obi-Wan Kenobi to work against him, and when Obi-Wan emerges from Padmé's ship, Vader believes his suspicions have been confirmed. Vader and Obi-Wan engage in an epic duel of Force powers and lightsaber swordplay that spills from the control rooms out onto the precarious catwalks spanning the lava river. With its energy shields damaged, most of the mining facility is consumed by volcanic eruptions. Obi-Wan eventually reaches the safety of a rocky shore and warns Vader not to attack him while he holds the high ground.

Separatist Council
The leaders of the Separatists believe they will be safe on Mustafar, never suspecting they have been led into a trap.

VADER'S FATE

The former apprentice doesn't listen and leaps at Obi-Wan to kill him. Obi-Wan strikes, removing Vader's legs and arm and leaving him defeated at the edge of a lava lake. The heat causes Vader's clothing and skin to catch fire, and a heartbroken Obi-Wan departs the planet, believing Vader has died. Darth Sidious arrives soon after, retrieving his critically injured apprentice and taking him to a medical facility on Coruscant. There, Vader receives treatments that not only save his life but transform him into a terrifying cyborg.

Barely alive
Emperor Palpatine arrives on Mustafar in time to save Darth Vader from death and transport him to Coruscant where he rebuilds him as an armored cyborg.

SITH RETREAT

During the Imperial era, Darth Vader erects a foreboding castle on Mustafar above an ancient Sith shrine on the planet, killing countless Mustafarians who attempt to stop him. Vader's castle becomes the final destination for many Jedi survivors of Order 66. When Jedi and rebel Kanan Jarrus is captured on Lothal, he is taken aboard Grand Moff Tarkin's Star Destroyer, *Sovereign*, to Mustafar. While in orbit over the planet, the crew of the *Ghost* rescues him. Former Jedi Ahsoka Tano and a small rebel fleet arrive in time to cover Kanan and his friends as they make the jump to hyperspace.

TIE fighter flight
In two stolen TIE fighters, most of the *Ghost* crew flees the Imperial Star Destroyers, hoping allies will return to save them.

MALASTARE

APPEARANCES CW **REGION** Mid Rim
SECTOR Dustig **SYSTEM** Malastare
PRIMARY TERRAIN Forests

Malastare is the homeworld of the Dug species, though humans and Grans have migrated there. The planet is known for its history of vicious wars, dangerous podracing, and vital fuel reserves. Ainlee Teem, a Gran from Malastare, is nominated in the election for Supreme Chancellor after the invasion of Naboo. During the Clone Wars, Malastare's fuel deposits are fought over by the Republic and Separatists. During a massive ground battle, the Republic deploys an electro-proton bomb that immobilizes Separatist droids. The bomb awakens the last Zillo Beast, which goes on a rampage. Fearing an apocalypse, the Dugs insist the Republic exterminate the monster. The Republic has other plans, capturing the virtually invulnerable creature for study on Coruscant.

Fuel wars
Across Malastare, vast fuel reserves flow into depots through an extensive network of pipelines *(left)*. When the Separatists and the Republic are drawn into fierce conflict over the fuel, the Republic detonates an electro-proton bomb to disable the Separatist droids *(below)*, but the blast also unleashes the Zillo Beast, long believed to be extinct.

CATO NEIMOIDIA

APPEARANCES CW, III **REGION** Colonies **SECTOR** Quellor **SYSTEM** Cato Neimoidia **PRIMARY TERRAIN** Canyons

Famed for its bridge cities, Cato Neimoidia is the headquarters of the notorious Trade Federation. Several Jedi visit the planet briefly, including Anakin Skywalker, Obi-Wan Kenobi, Ahsoka Tano, and Plo Koon, who is shot down by one of his own clone pilots over the planet when Order 66 is executed. Following the Clone Wars, much of the planet's wealth is lost during the Trade Federation's collapse, so the planet's Neimoidians adapt and offer their empty, and incredibly secure, vaults for hire. Galactic adventurer Lor San Tekka is imprisoned here when he tries to break into one of the vaults, but he is eventually rescued by Resistance leader General Leia Organa and her forces.

SALEUCAMI

APPEARANCES CW, III **REGION** Outer Rim **SECTOR** Suolriep
SYSTEM Saleucami **PRIMARY TERRAIN** Desert, swamps

A world of mixed terrain, from dank swamps to arid deserts, Saleucami hosts settlers wishing to avoid the Clone Wars. Clone deserter Cut Lawquane makes the planet his home, taking up farming with his adopted family. Saleucami is also the location of Stass Allie's final mission, when troops blast her speeder bike after Order 66 is given, killing the Jedi Master.

SCIPIO

APPEARANCES CW **REGION** Core Worlds **SECTOR** Albarrio
SYSTEM Albarrio **PRIMARY TERRAIN** Mountains

Enveloped in ice and snow, the planet Scipio's hardened mountain fortresses shield massive vaults, which secure the InterGalactic Banking Clan's wealth against all manner of threats. The clan is controlled by the Muuns, who constitute the managing Council of Five. In the Galactic Senate, the Banking Clan's interests are represented by Senator Rush Clovis from Scipio, who proposes a senatorial auditing team to investigate the suffering on Bromlarch. Years later, he leaves the Senate after his plot with the Trade Federation's Lott Dod to construct battle droid factories for the Separatist Droid Army is revealed. Clovis returns to power by exposing corruption and fraud in the Council of Five, compelling the Muuns to name him the new head of the Banking Clan conglomerate. Both the Galactic Republic and the Separatists send ambassadors to Scipio to ensure their respective agendas are safeguarded from further corruption. Clovis' appointment ends quickly, however; he is killed during a Separatist attack on the planet.

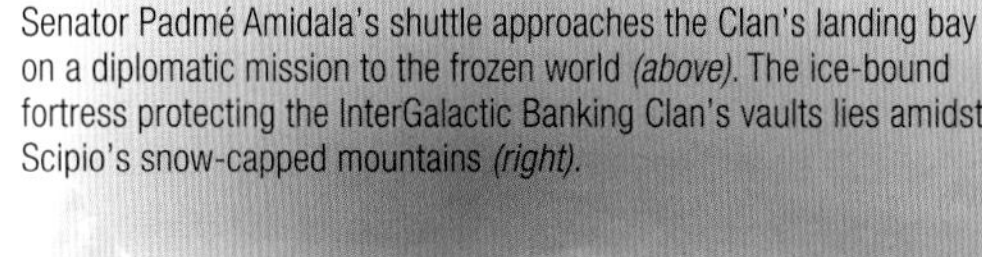

Frozen assets
Senator Padmé Amidala's shuttle approaches the Clan's landing bay on a diplomatic mission to the frozen world *(above)*. The ice-bound fortress protecting the InterGalactic Banking Clan's vaults lies amidst Scipio's snow-capped mountains *(right)*.

MANDALORE

APPEARANCES CW, Reb, FoD **REGION** Outer Rim
SECTOR Mandalore **SYSTEM** Mandalore
PRIMARY TERRAIN Deserts, urban

Centuries of war have made Mandalore a wasteland. Under the leadership of Duchess Satine Kryze, the New Mandalorians faction tries to leave behind the planet's violent past. Terrorist groups like Death Watch, however, demand that Mandalore return to its warrior roots. When the Duchess declares Mandalore's neutral position in the Clone Wars between the Galactic Republic and the Separatists, Death Watch, now aligned with Maul and his Shadow Collective, stage a coup and seize control of Mandalore. After the Republic liberates the planet from Maul, Satine's sister, Bo-Katan, is declared the planet's ruler. She is soon betrayed by Clan Saxon, whose member Gar Saxon takes over the planet and pledges his allegiance to the Empire. Years later, Clan Wren, and later Bo-Katan, lead a rebellion against Clan Saxon.

SUNDARI, MANDALORE

APPEARANCES CW, Reb **LOCATION** Mandalore

Sundari is the domed capital city of the planet Mandalore during the reign of Duchess Satine Kryze's New Mandalorian government. Situated in the desert, the bio-dome protects the city from the harsh environment that resulted from the Mandalorian wars. Death Watch attacks the city during the terrorists' bid to regain control of Mandalore. Years later, rebel Sabine Wren leads an assault on a Star Destroyer stationed at the city to destroy an old prototype weapon of hers that is capable of vaporizing Mandalorian armor and the warriors wearing it.

ALDERAAN

APPEARANCES CW, III, IV **REGION** Core Worlds
SECTOR Alderaan **SYSTEM** Alderaan
PRIMARY TERRAIN Mountains

One of the most picturesque planets of the Core Worlds, Alderaan is home to wildflower-speckled grasslands that sweep upward into ancient mountain ranges capped with snow. Its cities, designed to enhance and preserve the planet's natural beauty, have become epicenters for culture and education, both highly valued by Alderaanians.

In the days of the Galactic Republic, Alderaan is a prominent planet in galactic affairs. When the invasion of Naboo ends the tenure of Chancellor Valorum with a Vote of No Confidence in the Galactic Senate, one of the nominees to succeed him is Senator Bail Antilles of Alderaan.

At some point prior to the Clone Wars, Queen Breha Organa is coronated and marries Alderaan's new Senator, Bail Organa. Breha and Bail befriend both Senator Mon Mothma of Chandrila and Senator Padmé Amidala during this time. During the Separatist crisis, Bail is a leading member of Chancellor Palpatine's Loyalist Committee, which strives to maintain the integrity of the Republic. When the Jedi and the Senate learn that an army of clones has secretly been created for the Republic, Bail speaks out against a rush to war. Unfortunately, the Senate votes emergency powers to Supreme Chancellor Palpatine and the Grand Army of the Republic invades Geonosis, beginning the Clone Wars.

During the war, Alderaan hosts a conference dedicated to the plight of the conflict's refugees. Senator Amidala is the keynote speaker. Jedi Padawan Ahsoka Tano has a vision of Padmé's murder and joins her on Alderaan, where she successfully prevents an assassination attempt by bounty hunter Aurra Sing.

Near the end of the Clone Wars, Bail joins Padmé and Mon as vocal senators opposed to the chancellor's continually expanding powers. After Palpatine declares himself Galactic Emperor, Bail aids the fleeing Jedi and, with Breha, adopts Padmé's newborn daughter Leia to raise her as their child.

Bail and Breha publicly hold true to the Alderaan's pacifist nature, but realize that armed conflict is the only way to stop the Empire. They play a large role in forming the Rebel Alliance, hosting rebel sympathizers at banquets, uniting many rebel cells, and even secretly funding the cause. All the while, they strive to maintain plausible deniability of their membership to the outlawed organization.

Prior to the Battle of Scarif, Bail returns to Alderaan to prepare his people for armed conflict. But Grand Moff Tarkin, who has always suspected their true affiliation, needs to make a dramatic political statement with the Death Star. For that reason, and inspired by the presence of Princess Leia Organa as a prisoner aboard the space station, he selects Alderaan as the first target. The Death Star's massive laser annihilates the planet, killing Breha, Bail, and billions of other Alderaanians.

Now only an asteroid field, known as the Alderaanian Graveyard, remains of the once-proud world. The Empire blockades the graveyard until their defeat at the Battle of Endor. Soon after, the Alderaan Flotilla, a small fleet of Alderaanians who were offworld when the Death Star fired, travels to the graveyard. They search for any remnants of their homeworld amongst the asteroids. Thanks to Leia, the survivors are given scrap from the Death Star that they can use to build a space station as a new home in the asteroid field.

> "Alderaan is peaceful.... You can't possibly—"
>
> **LEIA ORGANA TO GRAND MOFF TARKIN**

Mountain palace
Skilled architects blend the cityscape design into the beautiful, sweeping backdrop of the local snow-capped mountains.

"You will never find a more wretched hive of scum and villainy." **OBI-WAN KENOBI**

MOS EISLEY SPACEPORT

On the remote desert world of Tatooine, far from the bright center of the galaxy, the dingy city of Mos Eisley serves as the planet's principal spaceport.

APPEARANCES CW, IV, VI **LOCATION** Great Mesra Plateau, north of Anchorhead, Tatooine

City of hangars
With no main landing facility, arrivals must berth in one of the 362 hangars around the spaceport *(above)*. Between flights, travelers head for a local cantina *(right)*.

DESERT OASIS

Southeast of the barren Jundland Wastes and not far from the palace of the ruthless crime lord Jabba the Hutt, Mos Eisley's wind-worn appearance belies its true nature as a thriving spaceport. Countless varieties of starships travel in and out of the city daily, bringing with them pilots, passengers, and cargo, both lawful and highly illegal. Goods traders and parts dealers share the dusty streets with dewbacks and wanted fugitives. Precious amid the desert, water is what binds Mos Eisley together. The main distribution plant sits in the heart of the city. From there, a patchwork of duracrete and plastoid buildings spreads outward, born of the lack of central planning in a spaceport that grew haphazardly and that does not even have a main landing facility.

Quiet streets
The usually bustling streets become nearly deserted once Imperial stormtroopers take up posts around the city. No one wants to be scrutinized too closely by the Empire.

Evading capture
Obi-Wan's Jedi mind trick helps Luke and the droids evade a checkpoint *(above)*. Hunting for the stolen Death Star plans, Imperial stormtroopers patrol the streets *(right)*.

IMPERIAL OCCUPATION

Ordinarily such a pit of crime would attract little attention from the forces of the Galactic Empire, but all that changes when two droids carrying crucial stolen Imperial intelligence—the plans to the Death Star battle station—vanish in the nearby desert. A detachment of Imperial stormtroopers arrives to lock down the city. Obi-Wan Kenobi brings Luke Skywalker, C-3PO, and R2-D2 to the spaceport to seek passage to Alderaan. The Jedi Master's quick-thinking use of the Force allows them to slip past stormtroopers who are patrolling the streets. Then it is a matter of finding a pilot willing to risk Imperial entanglement.

Hunk of junk
At Docking Bay 94, Luke is not impressed with the *Millennium Falcon*.

SMUGGLER'S PARADISE

Amid the hustle and bustle of the spaceport, smuggling activities carry on with nary a second glance. Trafficking in spice and illegal weapons brings great rewards to those willing to take the risks involved, though corrupt customs officials are generally willing to overlook such transgressions for a fee. After a haul, Han Solo and Chewbacca secure the *Millennium Falcon* in Docking Bay 94 at the spaceport, little suspecting that their departure will be far more eventful—a narrow escape from the blaster fire of Imperial stormtroopers pursuing the freighter's passengers.

Den of iniquity
Cantina clientele hustle up their next paying job *(above)* or relax along the bar for a drink and some downtime *(left)*.

MOS EISLEY CANTINA

APPEARANCES CW, IV **LOCATION** Mos Eisley, Tatooine

The Mos Eisley Cantina is favored by star pilots laying over on Tatooine before their next journey into space. On any given day, aliens of numerous species relax within its dimly illuminated confines, whispering secrets over strong drinks. Patrons range from legitimate cargo haulers to all manner of criminals, gangsters, and bounty hunters, and among such a throng, sudden outbursts of violence are no surprise. During the Clone Wars, a vicious blaster fight breaks out when Chairman Papanoida, leader of the Pantorans, arrives to liberate his kidnapped daughter Chi Eekway, who has been taken by the bounty hunter Greedo on behalf of the Separatists. All of her captors die in the rescue, except for Greedo, who manages to escape. Later in the war, Sith-acolyte-turned-bounty-hunter Asajj Ventress is biding her time over a drink in the cantina when she notices a tremendous bounty posted for the fearsome brothers Savage Opress and Maul. She locates their ship, inadvertently aiding the rescue and escape of Jedi Knight Obi-Wan Kenobi. Two decades pass before desert hermit Obi-Wan needs swift passage to Alderaan to bring Luke and the stolen Death Star plans to the Rebel Alliance. In the cantina, he discovers an old friend of Master Yoda, the Wookiee Chewbacca, now first mate on the *Millennium Falcon*. In a grimy booth, captain Han Solo agrees to transport the passengers for a sizable fee. Moments later, Greedo accosts Han at gunpoint and Han shoots him dead under the table.

Hot spot
The Mos Eisley Cantina is the gathering place for patrons from all walks of life *(left)*, entertaining them with the rollicking tunes of the Modal Nodes *(below)*.

RAXUS

APPEARANCES CW **REGION** Outer Rim **SECTOR** Tion Hegemony **SYSTEM** Raxus **PRIMARY TERRAIN** Plains, hills, ocean

Raxus hosts the Separatist Parliament during the Clone Wars. Hoping for a peaceful resolution of the grievances stated by the Confederacy of Independent Systems, Padmé Amidala secretly travels to Raxus to meet with her longtime friend, former Republic senator Mina Bonteri. Padmé's bodyguard Ahsoka Tano is initially skeptical but soon recognizes the integrity of Mina and her son, Lux. Padmé and Bonteri strike an accord, but Count Dooku sabotages their pact. Later in the war, Dooku's former apprentice, Asajj Ventress, and Jedi Master Quinlan Vos attempt to assassinate Dooku at an award ceremony in his honor on Raxus. They are unsuccessful, however, and Dooku captures Vos. Raxus suffers under the Emperor's galactic reign, perhaps in part due to its previous Separatist affiliation. Eventually, the planet's rulers have to fully surrender their autonomy to the Empire.

MORTIS

APPEARANCES CW **REGION** Wild space **SECTOR** Unknown **SYSTEM** Chrelythiumn **PRIMARY TERRAIN** Caverns, forests, mountains

An ancient monolith of unknown origin, from the outside Mortis appears to be a black octahedron with red lines etched upon its surface. Once inside, visitors discover a seemingly terrestrial realm, ranging from verdant forests and stone fortresses to deep caverns and floating mountains. Disconcertingly, the terrain sometimes mutates as travelers cross it. On Mortis, the flow of the Force is especially strong; some believe Mortis may be the very origin of the Force itself.

Foreboding landscape
Dathomir's central star casts an eerie red glow across its fog-shrouded terrain covered in twisted vegetation.

DATHOMIR

APPEARANCES CW, Reb **REGION** Outer Rim **SECTOR** Quelii **SYSTEM** Dathomir **PRIMARY TERRAIN** Forests, swamps

Dathomir is a planet that few people visit willingly. Illuminated by the eerie scarlet light of its red sun, its continents are thick with swamps and forests. Hundreds of years before the Clone Wars, the Fromprath species lived on Dathomir until the Nightsisters, a group of witches, forced them offworld and took over the planet. From a massive stone fortress, the Nightsisters wield ancient magic fueled by the planet's power, and they are capable of supernatural feats rivaling the Force talents of the Jedi and Sith. Also dwelling on Dathomir, separate from the all-female witch clan, are Zabrak males known as Nightbrothers. When necessary, Nightsisters venture to the Nightbrother village to select the most suitable mates from among them.

Years prior to the blockade of Naboo, Darth Sidious visits Dathomir and meets the Nightsister known as Talzin. He offers to take her on as his apprentice, but the Sith Lord betrays her and kidnaps her son Maul instead. The pirate Hal'Sted later arrives on Dathomir, and Talzin has to give him the young Asajj Ventress to save the clan.

By the time of the Clone Wars, Mother Talzin is the spiritual leader of the Nightsisters. Sidious views Talzin as a growing threat to his plans for galactic domination, but she is not the only Nightsister who troubles the Sith Lord: Ventress is now Count Dooku's apprentice, and Sidious demands her death when her dark-side abilities grow dangerously powerful. After Dooku attempts to murder Ventress, she returns to Dathomir and enlists the aid of the clan to seek revenge upon the Sith. Mother Talzin uses her magic to turn Ventress' selected apprentice, Savage Opress, into a vicious, Force-powered warrior. Ventress and Opress are unable to defeat Dooku, who sends General Grievous and his droid army to annihilate the Nightsister clan. Despite their best efforts, including awakening an undead horde of Nightsister zombies to fight the battle droids, all of the Nightsisters but Talzin and Ventress are massacred. Talzin and Sidious then wage a proxy war via Opress and Maul, whose mental and physical prowess has been restored by Talzin's magic at great cost to herself.

While on a mission to assassinate Dooku, Ventress and Jedi Master Quinlan Vos travel to Dathomir. Here, Ventress trains Vos in the dark side, forcing him to kill the Sleeper, an ancient and powerful creature that resides deep beneath the water in the Nightsisters' fortress. After Ventress falls saving Vos' life, Vos and Jedi Obi-Wan Kenobi return her body to Dathomir, laying it in the water which turns green as it sinks into it.

At some point after, Maul and Talzin attempt to sacrifice Dooku on the planet so Talzin can regain her power, but Grievous and Sidious intervene. In the end, Talzin sacrifices herself so her son can escape.

During the Imperial era, Maul forms a new criminal organization called Crimson Dawn, running the operation from Dathomir. He orders one of his lieutenants, Qi'Ra, to report to him there. Years later, after leaving the planet, Maul returns to Dathomir with Jedi Ezra Bridger. They perform some Nightsister magick inside the fortress and receive more clarity on a Force vision they both shared. The ritual awakens two Nightsister ghosts who possess Ezra's allies Sabine Wren and Kanan Jarrus. Ezra frees them by destroying the Nightsisters' altar.

LOLA SAYU

APPEARANCES CW **REGION** Outer Rim **SECTOR** Belderone **SYSTEM** Lola Sayu **PRIMARY TERRAIN** Volcanic

The purple hue of Lola Sayu might be considered beautiful, were it not for the fact that much of the planet's southern hemisphere consists of nothing more than a gaping hole where the sphere is shattered. Much of the planet's remaining crust is crisscrossed with countless cracks, like a broken eggshell. This inhospitable world, controlled by the Separatists during the Clone Wars, hosts the Citadel, an impenetrable prison.

THE CITADEL

APPEARANCES CW **LOCATION** Lola Sayu

Built centuries before the Clone Wars by the Galactic Republic, the Citadel prison is designed to hold the most difficult-to-restrain inmates—even rogue Jedi Knights. In Separatist hands, under the command of sadistic warden Osi Sobeck, it houses the Confederacy's highest-value detainees, including Captain Tarkin and Jedi Master Even Piell. In addition to the prison's imposing sheer walls and labyrinthine design, the Citadel is guarded by commando droids, electro-mines, and vicious anoobas.

WASSKAH

APPEARANCES CW **REGION** Mid Rim **SECTOR** Mytaranor **SYSTEM** Kashyyyk **PRIMARY TERRAIN** Forests

This verdant moon is controlled by a gang of Trandoshan hunters who kidnap individuals and release them into the dense foliage of the forests, after which hunting parties track and slay the desperate captives as trophies. Ahsoka Tano is briefly trapped on Wasskah, where she teams up with several kidnapped Jedi younglings, the mighty Chewbacca, and his Wookiee allies, to defeat the Trandoshans.

ONDERON

APPEARANCES CW **REGION** Inner Rim **SECTOR** Japrael **SYSTEM** Japrael **PRIMARY TERRAIN** Jungles

To guard against the creatures that fill Onderon's jungles, the planet's primitive human inhabitants build fortified settlements that eventually expand into enormous walled cities like the capital, Iziz. At the start of the Clone Wars, King Ramsis Dendup is deposed by Sanjay Rash, who allies with Count Dooku. A citizen rebellion led by siblings Steela and Saw Gerrera against Rash's rule receives covert aid from the Jedi and succeeds in overthrowing him. Insurgent leader Lux Bonteri goes on to represent Onderon in the Senate. When the Republic transforms into the Empire, Saw renames his rebel group the Partisans and begins viciously attacking the occupying forces. In one such attack, Imperial Agent Kallus watches powerless as his squad of stormtroopers is cut down in front of him. Saw eventually leaves his homeworld, declaring it lost.

THE BOX

APPEARANCES CW **LOCATION** Serenno

Criminal mastermind Moralo Eval designs the Box as the ultimate, deadly test of intelligence and skill. Housed at Count Dooku's palace on the planet Serenno, the gigantic cubical structure contains a constantly shifting series of obstacle courses and traps spanning five levels. Dooku invites 12 of the galaxy's finest bounty hunters to be tested, five of whom move on to undertake a mission to kidnap Supreme Chancellor Palpatine on Naboo.

ILUM

APPEARANCES CW **REGION** Unknown Regions **SECTOR** 7G **SYSTEM** Ilum **PRIMARY TERRAIN** Arctic

Entirely frozen over, the inhospitable world of Ilum is the principal source of kyber crystals, found in many lightsabers. An ancient Jedi temple marks the exit from the dim caverns where the crystals are located, and it's here that Jedi younglings are brought for a ritual to find a crystal individually suited to them. When the Empire takes over, they destroy the temple so they can easily access the crystals for their own destructive use and begin strip-mining the planet.

ABAFAR

APPEARANCES CW **REGION** Outer Rim **SECTOR** Sprizen **SYSTEM** Unknown **PRIMARY TERRAIN** Desert

Abafar's most memorable feature is the seemingly endless wasteland known as the Void. Uncannily flat and barren, its unnaturally uniform orange hue, due to particulates in the atmosphere, can drive even the most strong-willed individuals mad. The Galactic Republic's database file on Abafar notes large indentations crisscrossing the planet's surface. Settlements such as Pons Ora have grown up around mining operations that extract rhydonium, a rare, volatile fuel.

UMBARA

APPEARANCES CW **REGION** Expansion Region **SECTOR** Ghost Nebula **SYSTEM** Umbara **PRIMARY TERRAIN** Hills

The dangerous planet Umbara earns the moniker "the Shadow World" because so little sunlight reaches its surface. The near-human species that inhabit the planet are known for their advanced technology. During the Clone Wars, Umbara secedes from the Republic after the assassination of its senator, Mee Deechi, resulting in an invasion by the Grand Army to retake the planet. During the Imperial era, the rebel leader known as Nightswan incites a rebellion on the planet, and an Imperial fleet is sent to quell it. The Umbarans surrender fully and their planet falls under direct Imperial rule.

MON CALA

APPEARANCES CW **REGION** Outer Rim **SECTOR** Calamari **SYSTEM** Calamari **PRIMARY TERRAIN** Oceans

The oceanic world of Mon Cala is home to two sentient aquatic species: the Mon Calamari and the Quarren. Although the two share a long history of differences, mutual respect keeps their planet united under the reign of a single king and a single representative in the Galactic Senate. In the Clone Wars, Senator Tikkes, a Quarren, defects to the Separatists and is replaced by Tundra Dowmeia, a loyalist Quarren, and later Meena Tills, a Mon Calamari. During Prince Lee-Char's accession to the throne, civil war breaks out, but the young leader is able to heal the schism. A year into the Emperor's rule, Lee-Char, under the influence of a morally questionable Jedi Purge survivor, leads a rebellion against the Empire. This is swiftly quashed by Grand Moff Tarkin and Darth Vader. Lee-Char is imprisoned on Strokill Prime, so Regent Urtya takes over as leader. Years later, Urtya meets members of the Rebel Alliance who attempt to persuade him to give the Mon Cala Mercantile Fleet to their cause. When he declines, they try to save Lee-Char, but the former king dies. They record Lee-Char's dying words and pass them to Urtya, who broadcasts them across the oceans. The Empire kills him for his rebellion, but the fleet joins the Alliance.

BARDOTTA

APPEARANCES CW **REGION** Unknown **SECTOR** Unknown **SYSTEM** Unknown **PRIMARY TERRAIN** Mountains

Bardotta is home to a spiritual order of peaceful mystics called Dagoyan Masters. Due to previous bad experiences with Jedi seeking to take younglings for training on Coruscant, the Bardottans distrust the Jedi Order. When Dagoyan Masters begin disappearing, Queen Julia fears an ancient prophecy is being fulfilled and seeks help from her friend Jar Jar Binks. He arrives with Mace Windu, to vouch for the Jedi Master's honor, just before Julia vanishes. Jar Jar and Windu rescue Queen Julia and thwart the Frangawl cult's grim plan to drain the Force essence from the Dagoyan Masters.

"Mudhole?! Slimy?! My home this is!" YODA

DAGOBAH

Covered in swamps and dense jungles, Dagobah teems with life and the Force. Here, Luke Skywalker is trained in the ways of the Jedi by Master Yoda.

APPEARANCES CW, V, VI, FoD **REGION** Outer Rim **SECTOR** Sluis **SYSTEM** Dagobah
PRIMARY TERRAIN Swamps

Dangerous passage
Dagobah is unassuming from space, but the trip down to the planet's surface is treacherous, as vehicles must negotiate violent lightning storms and poor visibility.

Murky exile
Luke crashes his X-wing in a swamp during his dangerous descent to the planet's surface.

LIVING FORCE

Late in the Clone Wars, while meditating, Yoda hears the voice of the dead Jedi Master Qui-Gon Jinn, who claims he is part of the living Force. The other Jedi worry about Yoda's mental state, but Qui-Gon implores Yoda to travel to Dagobah alone. With the help of Anakin Skywalker, Yoda escapes the Jedi Temple in his Jedi starfighter. Upon reaching Dagobah, Yoda meditates and again hears Qui-Gon, who explains that Dagobah is one of the purest places in the galaxy with strong manifestations of the living Force. Led by a cloud of fireflies to a dark cave, Yoda has a vision of Jedi being struck down by a shrouded Sith Lord. Yoda collapses in despair outside the cave. Qui-Gon consoles him with words of hope and offers to guide Yoda to an understanding of how the Jedi will ultimately prevail.

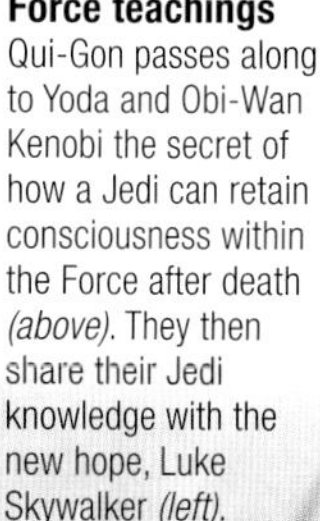

Force teachings
Qui-Gon passes along to Yoda and Obi-Wan Kenobi the secret of how a Jedi can retain consciousness within the Force after death *(above)*. They then share their Jedi knowledge with the new hope, Luke Skywalker *(left)*.

Awaiting his student
After the Clone Wars, Yoda returns to Dagobah to live in a small hut in the swamp while he waits to train Luke.

EXILE PLANET

After his trials by the mysterious Force Priestesses, Yoda understands that a victory over the Sith will not come during the Clone Wars. When Supreme Chancellor Palpatine is revealed as a Sith Lord, Yoda fights but does not defeat him. Yoda retreats with Bail Organa to Polis Massa, where they rendezvous with Obi-Wan and Padmé Amidala. Padmé gives birth to twins—the children of former Jedi Anakin Skywalker, now Sith apprentice Darth Vader—and then dies. Yoda and Obi-Wan decide to separate the children, keeping them hidden from the Sith until the time is right to reveal them. Before he departs for his exile on Dagobah, Yoda introduces Obi-Wan to the teachings of Qui-Gon. Yoda continues to study the Force while the children grow into adulthood.

TRAINING GROUNDS

Dagobah itself proves to be part of Luke's Jedi trials. Storms and dense fog create rough landing conditions, and his X-wing crashes into a swamp. A seemingly primitive life-form tests his patience at camp, but Luke is eager to meet Yoda, so he tolerates the interloper. Upon arriving at the creature's hut, Luke's irritation is unmistakable. The creature voices his concerns about training Luke to Obi-Wan's ghostly voice, thereby revealing that he is in fact the Jedi Master. Yoda reluctantly agrees to train Luke in the ways of the Force, despite sensing in him traits similar to his father. The swamps serve as the training grounds for Yoda's new apprentice. Deep in the jungle, Yoda tests Luke's readiness by sending him into the Cave of Evil that he had entered years before during the Clone Wars. As Luke's powers grow, he has a vision of his friends in danger. He resolves to leave Dagobah without completing his training, but promises to return.

Balance in the Force
To help Luke to further his Force abilities, Master Yoda guides him on stamina and balance.

CAVE OF EVIL, DAGOBAH

APPEARANCES CW, V **LOCATION** Dagobah

Infused with dark side Force energy, the Cave of Evil on Dagobah manifests visions of possible dark futures. Guided by the disembodied voice of the deceased Qui-Gon Jinn, Yoda enters the cave near the end of the Clone Wars and has a vision of the destruction of the Jedi Order that overwhelms him. Years later, Yoda tests Luke Skywalker by taking him to the cave. Luke has a vision in which he faces Darth Vader and strikes him down. The Sith Lord's helmeted head hits the floor, and the damaged face shield reveals Luke behind the mask.

Man in the mask
Luke sees his own face in the damaged helmet of Darth Vader, after confronting the Sith Lord's apparition in the cave.

STYGEON PRIME

APPEARANCES Other, Reb **REGION** Outer Rim **SECTOR** Nuiri **SYSTEM** Stygeon **PRIMARY TERRAIN** Mountains

Stygeon Prime is an inhospitable world with towering snow-capped mountain peaks. This fearsome terrain makes the planet the perfect location for a maximum-security facility to house the most dangerous, high-value prisoners. During his years as both Supreme Chancellor and Emperor, Darth Sidious exerts dominion over Stygeon Prime's prison, the Spire. After Maul returns from exile during the Clone Wars to lead his criminal organization, the Shadow Collective, Sidious confronts his former apprentice on Mandalore and defeats him in single combat. Maul is then incarcerated at the Spire.

THE SPIRE

APPEARANCES Other, Reb **LOCATION** Stygeon Prime

The Spire is one of the galaxy's most imposing prisons. During the Clone Wars, Mandalorian commandos are able to break Maul out of his confinement there, but only because Darth Sidious permits the escape in order to set a trap for Maul's patron, Mother Talzin. Years later, the Spire is under Imperial control when former Jedi apprentice Kanan Jarrus is lured there with the promise of rescuing Jedi Master Luminara Unduli from captivity. The Inquisitor is waiting for him, however, and they fight a vicious duel.

Planned escape route

Prison break
Kanan leads his team of Zeb, Sabine, and Ezra *(left)* in a mission to infiltrate the Spire *(above)*.

ORD MANTELL

APPEARANCES FoD **REGION** Mid Rim **SECTOR** Bright Jewel **SYSTEM** Bright Jewel **PRIMARY TERRAIN** Mountain chains

Ord Mantell orbits the blue star Bright Jewel and houses a base of operations for the Black Sun crime syndicate. Prior to the Separatist crisis, Jango and Boba Fett are hired to capture a woman who has run away to try and join the Black Sun on Ord Mantell. During the Clone Wars, the Separatists attack the planet as part of Darth Sidious' plot to drive a wedge between Maul and his Black Sun allies. During the Imperial era, Qi'ra captures Hondo Ohnaka and IG-88 on Ord Mantell when they try to apprehend her. Years later, Princess Leia, Chewbacca, and R2-D2 meet Maz Kanata on the planet and knock out bounty hunter Boushh. They steal his outfit so Leia can impersonate Boushh to rescue Han Solo.

Many moons
One sun and nine moons give Utapau a distinctive skyline *(below)*. Tidal effects on the planet's subterranean oceans vary wildly, depending on the positions of the moons in relation to one another *(right)*.

UTAPAU

APPEARANCES CW, III **REGION** Outer Rim
SECTOR Tarabba **SYSTEM** Utapau
PRIMARY TERRAIN Sinkholes

Located in the remote Tarabba sector of the Outer Rim, the arid, windswept planet Utapau is pitted with enormous sinkholes and surrounded by numerous moons. Its surface is mainly desert terrain, but the bottoms of the sinkholes contain pools of water that support life on the planet. Utapau is home to the Pau'an and the Utai, collectively referred to as Utapauns, and also a more primitive life-form, the Amani. Utapauns dwell in cities that line some of the sinkholes, while the Amani are often found in villages out on the plains. The cities, which expand into the caves and crevasses beneath the planet's surface, are supported by mining operations that excavate valuable minerals.

Although the planet tries to remain neutral during the Clone Wars, the death of a Jedi in Pau City brings Obi-Wan Kenobi and Anakin Skywalker to Utapau. They uncover a Separatist plot to purchase a rare enormous kyber crystal from Sugi arms dealers. Crystals of this size were believed to be the stuff of legend, but Obi-Wan and Anakin witness its incredible power firsthand. Before General Grievous can take the crystal from the Utapau system, Obi-Wan and Anakin destroy it rather than let it fall into Separatist hands.

In the final days of the Clone Wars, Darth Sidious orders key Separatist leaders to gather on Utapau. When Obi-Wan returns to Utapau in search of Grievous, Tion Medon, the port administrator of Pau City, tips the Jedi off to the Separatists' presence. Obi-Wan sends his astromech droid R4-G9 back to the Republic fleet in his starfighter. With the help of the varactyl Boga, Obi-Wan tracks down Grievous and challenges him to a duel. During their battle, Republic forces arrive and battle the droid army. Obi-Wan defeats Grievous, only to be attacked by the clones in his command when Order 66 is issued.

During the Imperial era in a cave on the planet, crazed Pau'an surgeon Fyzen Gor augments a medical droid with organic parts from his dead best friend. He continues experimenting on the droid until it has the devastating capability to turn all the droids in the galaxy against their organic masters. Over the next two decades, smugglers Han Solo and Lando Calrissian have separate run-ins with the unusual pair, but Lando kills them both two years after the Battle of Jakku, eliminating the dangerous threat.

"Chancellor Palpatine thinks Grievous is on Utapau."
KI-ADI-MUNDI

Sinkhole city
Obi-Wan's Jedi starfighter descends into the sinkhole of Pau City when he is searching for General Grievous, who is rumored to be on the planet.

GALAXIES OPERA HOUSE

APPEARANCES III **LOCATION** Coruscant

The Galaxies Opera House is located in the upper levels of the Uscru District on Coruscant. The venue is favored by Supreme Chancellor Palpatine, who has a private box in a premier viewing location in the main theater. During a performance of the acrobatic opera *Squid Lake* by a Mon Calamari troupe, a pivotal meeting between Anakin and the chancellor takes place. Palpatine tells Anakin the Sith legend of Darth Plagueis the Wise, who sought to control death.

"Good relations with the Wookiees, I have." YODA

KASHYYYK

The Wookiees of Kashyyyk are fierce warriors loyal to the Republic and the Jedi. Their determination and courage has made their homeworld a battleground for galactic domination.

APPEARANCES III **REGION** Mid Rim **SECTOR** Mytaranor **SYSTEM** Kashyyyk **PRIMARY TERRAIN** Forests

REPUBLIC LOYALISTS

For many years, Kashyyyk has been a prominent world represented by respected members of the Galactic Senate. Renowned for their strength and ferocity in battle, Wookiees do not hesitate to fight when the need arises. However, they are also firm believers in peace and justice. Their arboreal homeworld of Kashyyyk reveals the Wookiees' technical prowess and artistic vision. Wookiee cities are built upon the planet's mighty trees, their architecture interwoven with the beauty of the canopy. Wookiee aircraft, such as an ornithopter resembling a fearsome insect, also reflect the planet's hues, as do their weaponry and battle armor. Anyone who believes a Wookiee is merely a primitive beast will soon discover their mistake.

Battle ready
Captain Merumeru and his Wookiee warriors prepare to defend Kashyyyk.

Where forest meets sea
The Wookiees come down from their tree cities to defend key locations at sea level.

Under attack
As Republic forces arrive to assist the Wookiees *(left)*, fierce warriors rally to defend their homeland from the droid army *(below)*.

BATTLE OF KASHYYYK

Its location on key hyperspace lanes makes Kashyyyk a strategic objective in any galactic conflict. Late in the Clone Wars, the Separatists launch a massive invasion of the planet with battle droids and heavy artillery. The Jedi Council know that an immediate defensive response by the Grand Army of the Republic is required, and Yoda volunteers to lead the counteroffensive, based on his strong relationships with Wookiee leaders. The clone troopers and war droids engage in a vicious battle on the beaches outside the vital city of Kachirho.

RISE OF THE EMPIRE

When Darth Sidious gives the command to execute Order 66, Kashyyyk is one of many worlds where the Republic's clone troopers turn against the Jedi. Yoda senses the nearly simultaneous deaths of hundreds of Jedi across the galaxy. When Commander Gree approaches, the Jedi Master senses the danger and cuts him down in self-defense. With clones still swarming the planet, Tarfful and Chewbacca escort Yoda to an escape pod. As a result of the Wookiees' long-standing loyalty to the Republic and the Jedi Order, the new Galactic Empire visits great brutality upon Kashyyyk, conquering the planet. Many Wookiees are enslaved, and the Empire implants them all with inhibitor chips to hurt them if they disobey. Some Wookiees are taken offworld to construct the Death Stars or to the spice mines of Kessel, where the harsh working conditions dramatically shorten the Wookiees' life spans.

Order 66
Yoda defends himself when the clones turn against the Jedi on Darth Sidious' command.

Devastated planet
At least half of Kashyyyk's forests are ruined by the Imperial occupation and the subsequent bombardment. Thankfully, after the liberation, nature begins to reassert itself.

THE LIBERATION OF KASHYYYK

After the Battle of Endor, Kashyyyk remains in the tight control of an Imperial faction led by Grand Moff Tolruck. When Chewbacca and Han Solo learn of an opportunity to free the planet, they try to act upon it, but it is an Imperial trap. While Han escapes, Chewbacca is captured and held in Ashmead's Lock prison on Kashyyyk. Han leads a team to infiltrate Ashmead's Lock and free Chewbacca and the other prisoners. Chewbacca, Han, and a portion of the team stay on Kashyyyk and manage to access Tolruck's base. Here, they hack the control module for the inhibitor chips, freeing all the Wookiees. Many Wookiees rise up against their captors, so the orbiting Star Destroyers decide to bombard the planet. Upon hearing of the attack, the New Republic launch a fleet to help defeat the Imperial faction and finally free Kashyyyk.

KACHIRHO

APPEARANCES III **LOCATION** Kashyyyk

Kachirho is a coastal city on Kashyyyk that spirals around the trunk of an enormous wroshyr tree near the Wawaatt Archipelago. Two piers and docks extend out from the city into the freshwater lagoon. The center of Wookiee hyperspace mapping, Kachirho is led at the time of the Clone Wars by the chieftain Tarfful. Most other cities on the planet are protected by dense foliage, but the wide-open area around Kachirho makes it an optimal landing site when the Separatists attack Kashyyyk late in the Clone Wars. Kachirho's neighbors come by the thousands from land and sea to defend the city from the droid invasion.

POLIS MASSA

APPEARANCES III **REGION** Outer Rim **SECTOR** Subterrel **SYSTEM** Polis Massa **PRIMARY TERRAIN** Asteroid

Polis Massa is the field of asteroids that remains following the destruction of a planet of the same name. The Archaeological Research Council of Kallidah settles Polis Massa Base and begins an archaeological mining project to uncover the mysteries of the cataclysm. The Kallidahin eventually become known as Polis Massans.

Far from important hyperspace lanes, Polis Massa Base serves as an emergency sanctuary for the Jedi after Order 66. There, Padmé Amidala gives birth to the twins Luke and Leia and then dies. Along with Senator Bail Organa, Yoda and Obi-Wan Kenobi determine their plans for the future of the Jedi Order. The Polis Massans continue to support rebels against the Empire, with their site acting as a secret rebel base.

Remote hideaway
The asteroid field proves an ideal location for the Jedi to regroup after Order 66.

CORELLIA

APPEARANCES S **REGION** Core Worlds **SECTOR** Corellian Sector **SYSTEM** Corellia **PRIMARY TERRAIN** Oceans, forests, and sprawling urban centers

The people of Corellia are legendary explorers. In the early histories of their world, adventurers set out across the seas to discover new continents or catch epic hauls of fish to sell in the harbor markets of Coronet City—as they still do today. Their shipyards build renowned starfighters, capital battleships, and commercial freighters prized throughout the galaxy. With these ships the Corellians journey across the galaxy and colonize countless other worlds. When the Empire takes over Corellia, it converts Sienar Fleet Systems factories into manufacturers of Imperial TIE fighters, Star Destroyers, and other weapons of galactic war.

Corellia's coastal cities are managed with efficiency. Ports, industry, commerce, and residential centers are located on platforms called "pills" connected by bridges. All military, commercial, and personal travel is directed through Coronet Spaceport. There, the local security agency manages emigration in coordination with the Imperial Security Bureau. Emigration officers sit in well-protected booths, carefully scrutinizing passengers to make sure they have Imperial-approved papers. Those without influential Imperial ties or connections to one of the powerful families in the manufacturing industry all spend their lives dreaming of leaving Corellia for a better life. An Imperial recruitment center is situated in the space port to remind potential emigrants that there are always opportunities to see the galaxy as a member of the Imperial military.

Putrid sewer
Corellia does not have a glamorous reputation. Scrumrat Han spends his childhood dreaming of escaping its corrupt and dirty urban center, Coronet, only to realize he must return to rescue his friend Qi'ra.

"This guy is nuts. No one goes back to Corellia."
RIO DURANT, ABOUT HAN SOLO

DEN OF THE WHITE WORMS

APPEARANCES S **LOCATION** Coronet City, Corellia

Not far from Coronet Spaceport, Lady Proxima's White Worm gang makes its den in an abandoned industrial site amidst one of the poorest areas of the city. Cobbling together old housing modules, access pipes, and factory scrap, the labyrinth of passages leads to a central, shadowy sinkhole where Proxima and her offspring soak in a cistern of churning water. The hideout houses all of Proxima's thugs and the scrumrat street children she takes in to carry out her black-market business ventures.

MIMBAN

APPEARANCES S **REGION** Expansion Region **SECTOR** Circarpous **SYSTEM** Circarpous **PRIMARY TERRAIN** Mud fields, rainforests, and swamps

During the Clone Wars, the Separatist army takes an interest in Mimban's bountiful mineral resources. A squad of clone troopers train the Mimbanese to fight, promising later freedom. When the Republic becomes the Empire, the planet is stripped of its lush jungles and mined for dolovite and hyperbaride. As a result, the atmosphere is polluted and the landscape razed to mud. The Mimbanese rise up from their subterranean dwellings and make war on the Empire in an effort to free their devastated world.

VANDOR

APPEARANCES S **REGION** Mid Rim **SECTOR** Sloo **SYSTEM** Unknown **PRIMARY TERRAIN** Snowy mountain ranges and frozen seas

Vandor is a pristine frontier world renowned for its fresh air and untapped resources. A small population of settlers and prospectors live in wooden shanties and lodges along the snowy mountain slopes surrounding Fort Ypso. Explorers and adventurers come to start a new life or escape troubles. However, the Empire takes an interest in an old Banking Clan vault, and begins to establish a small presence. Tobias Beckett's gang robs the Imperial 20-T Railcrawler conveyex transport there for its valuable coaxium cargo.

FORT YPSO

APPEARANCES S **LOCATION** Vandor

Established by the Ypsobay Trading Company (before the organization collapsed due to financial problems), Fort Ypso is a frontier outpost in the alpine wilds of Vandor. Fur traders, Iridium mining prospectors, smugglers, and homesteaders come to the rustic wooden Lodge owned by Tibbs Ospe for meals, drinks, and to assemble teams for their next adventures into the wilderness. There is entertainment, too—the sabacc table is popular (Lando Calrissian is a regular), as are the droid gladiator matches run by Ralakili. A resident Nithorn singer adds to the atmosphere.

KESSEL

APPEARANCES S, Reb **REGION** Outer Rim Territories **SECTOR** Kessel **SYSTEM** Kessel **PRIMARY TERRAIN** Primeval forests, rocks, mines

One half of the former paradise world of Kessel is dominated by spice mines. The opposite hemisphere, marked by lush forests and the palatial estates of King Yaruba and the royal family, is kept clearly separate from the infamous mines, which are sustained by slave labor. The spice is a valuable commodity traded by the galactic underworld, and one such dealership group, the Pyke Syndicate, controls the mines during the early years of the Empire. They turn the medicinal mineral known as Kessel spice into a powerful narcotic, consumed on their own world of Oba Diah and sold throughout the galaxy. The Empire keeps an eye on operations, taking a more direct involvement in mining affairs after the theft of coaxium by Tobias Beckett's crew on behalf of Crimson Dawn. During the Empire's later administration, rebel Hera Syndulla and the crew of the *Ghost* rescue Wookiee prisoners sent to labor in the mines.

Toxic atmosphere
Spice-mining releases dangerous toxins into the environment. Byproduct kessoline poisons the water supplies and its use as a fossil fuel produces noxious gas.

Falcon flight
It is from Kessel, having stolen coaxium and needing to leave in a hurry, that Han Solo completes his legendary Kessel Run. He and his companions liberate some coaxium but also draw attention by freeing slave miners and droids at the same time.

KESSEL SPICE MINES

APPEARANCES S, Reb **LOCATION** Kessel

The Pyke Syndicate's Kessel spice mines are overseen by Quay Tolsite, who maintains hired thugs to mind prisoners and watch for smugglers trying to steal spice and other valuable minerals. The Mining Guild also has agents at the mines, working in cooperation with the Pyke operation. All wear heavy protective gear to shield them from the corrosive environment and radiation. While Quay Tolsite manages the business end, he uses a large droid crew to keep the mines running efficiently, day and night. The hard labor is carried out by slaves provided by the Empire in exchange for mineral resources. Many of the slaves, such as the Wookiees, are rebel troublemakers. Others are convicted criminals.

KESSEL RUN

APPEARANCES S **LOCATION** Kessel

The Kessel Run is a trade route passing through the Akkadese Maelstrom and the Si'Klaata Cluster, terminating at the planet Kessel. The way is marked by beacons, mapping out the most stable path through the treacherous swirling debris. Straying from this proven course means almost certain obliteration, whether by impact with asteroids, being sucked into gravity wells (the worst of which is the "Maw"), or being devoured by summa-verminoth. Han Solo manages to fly the *Millennium Falcon* through a shortcut, completing the Kessel Run in a record 12 parsecs (if rounding the number down).

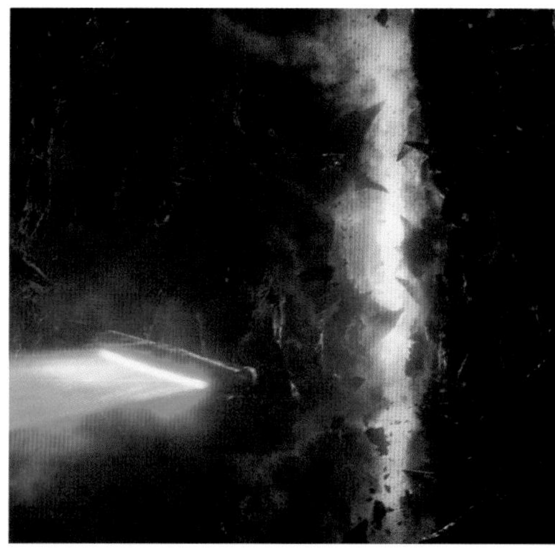

SAVAREEN

APPEARANCES S **REGION** Outer Rim Territories **SECTOR** Savareen **SYSTEM** Savareen **PRIMARY TERRAIN** Deserts and oceans

Savareen is a sparsely populated, arid world of sweeping sand dunes and rocky peaks. The inhabitants have a small depot by the sea, unknown to the Empire, where they refine coaxium and sell a popular local brandy. When the village rises up against Crimson Dawn, the syndicate removes their tongues as punishment. Later Tobias Beckett, Han Solo, Chewbacca, Qi'ra, and Lando Calrissian arrive after stealing coaxium from Kessel for Crimson Dawn. They are met by Enfys Nest and the Cloud-Riders, who convince Han, Chewbacca, and Qi'ra to side with them rather than the crime syndicate.

NUMIDIAN PRIME

APPEARANCES S **REGION** Mid Rim **SECTOR** Bright Jewel **SYSTEM** Numidian **PRIMARY TERRAIN** Jungles, rivers, and seas

Numidian Prime is a tropical world with beautiful rainforest vistas and a warm, comfortable environment for human habitation. It is both an exotic resort destination for those who look to relax in rustic, natural settings, and a hideout for smugglers and the disreputable. Lando Calrissian retreats here after his Kessel Run deal with Han Solo and Qi'ra falls apart. Solo follows him there and beats Calrissian in a hand of sabacc, thus winning the *Millennium Falcon* from him.

"Lothal is just as important to our Empire as any world in the galaxy."

MAKETH TUA

LOTHAL

Lothal would seem to be just another insignificant, sparsely populated backwater in the Outer Rim. However, the Imperial Star Destroyer in orbit, as well as the Sienar Fleet Systems factories and a stormtrooper garrison in the capital, all suggest otherwise.

APPEARANCES Reb **REGION** Outer Rim Territories
SECTOR Lothal **SYSTEM** Lothal
PRIMARY TERRAIN Prairies, mountains, seas

QUIET LIFE ON THE OUTER RIM

Before the arrival of the Empire, Lothal is an agricultural society. Farmers cultivate rolling prairies and moisture vaporators draw water to grow jogan, melons, gourds, grains, and other crops. Towns like Kothal, Jalath, and Tangletown are small and the citizens diverse, including humans, Feeorins, Bardottans, Xexto, Balosars, Anx, Ruurians, and Ithorians. While gangsters, bounty hunters, and slavers are a problem, and gladiator matches are frowned upon in Lothal culture, most early settlers are more concerned with Loth-wolves and sabercats. There is a small Jedi presence, their temple hidden among ancient catacombs in the mountains. Lothal is peaceful and quiet, of little concern to major powers in the galaxy.

Tarkintown

Impoverished refugees find shelter in run-down Tarkintown, named after Grand Moff Tarkin, the Governor of the Outer Rim Territories. Tarkin evicts farmers from their homes when he appropriates their land for new industries to benefit the Empire. The shantytown is a haven for smugglers and criminals as well, many of whom take advantage of the desperate locals. The *Ghost* crew like to donate supplies—stolen from the Empire—to the needy townspeople. During the Siege of Lothal, Darth Vader orders Agent Kallus to imprison its inhabitants and destroy the town as its people had accepted the *Ghost* crew's aid.

Home on the range
Prairie grass dances in Lothal's afternoon winds, hiding Loth-cats hunting Loth-rats below ancient rock formations *(below)*. Near the remote settlement of Jhothal, smoke rises from a Lothal homestead's chimney under a double moonrise *(right)*.

THE EMPIRE ARRIVES

Everything changes when the Empire, pushing farther into the Outer Rim, arrives on Lothal, which lies on its new trade route. It establishes a port and base on Lothal, but also comes to exploit the planet's mineral wealth. The citizens—those in smaller towns and the farmers in the countryside—receive no benefit from the Empire's presence, especially when the Empire starts appropriating land and evicting settlers to build mines and factories. Those who speak out are imprisoned, and some are never seen again. Mines strip the land bare, leaving gaping holes in the landscape. Meanwhile, the Imperial Governor Arihnda Pryce manages everything from the shadows.

Serve and protect whom?
Stormtroopers are concentrated in Capital City, where they guard the Empire's headquarters, government buildings, the Imperial Academy, and Sienar Fleet Systems factories. Meanwhile, average citizens struggle to maintain their own safety and security, having to deal with corrupt stormtroopers and Imperial officials.

Policing the city
Stormtroopers chase rebels after they steal speeder bikes and an important weapons shipment.

A SPARK OF REBELLION

The Empire is quick to move on any sign of dissent from the locals. Merchants who resist are immediately arrested. Mira and Ephraim Bridger, who run dissident broadcasts on the HoloNet, are among the many citizens taken away by authorities. At the Imperial Academy, students who stand out with unusual abilities—believed to be Force-sensitives—mysteriously disappear. Despite the risks, some citizens do their part to resist, and a small rebel cell begins to stand out. Led by Hera Syndulla and Kanan Jarrus, the *Ghost* crew fight against the Imperial machine managed by Minister Maketh Tua and military officers Grint and Aresko. Its activities draw the attention of the ISB's Agent Kallus, the Grand Inquisitor, and Governor Tarkin.

In the spotlight
Concerned about this world, which is vital to his plans, the Emperor sends more of his forces to Lothal.

SIEGE OF LOTHAL

After the rebels obliterate an Imperial Star Destroyer orbiting Mustafar, Darth Vader himself comes to Lothal to quash the rebels. The planet is placed under a blockade and no ships are allowed to leave without Imperial sanction, and its citizens are also subject to strict curfew. Eventually the *Ghost* crew manage to escape the planet, but cannot rescue Tua, who attempts to defect. Afterward, former Governor Ryder Azadi forms a new rebel cell, sabotaging many vehicles being produced in the Armory Complex.

Standing up
Alongside the Rebel Alliance troops, Lothal's citizens stand up against the Empire.

LIBERATION

After years of Imperial occupation and the stripping of its raw materials, Lothal's environment is on the brink of collapse. With the help of pilots from the Rebel Alliance, the *Ghost* crew lead a final assault to free Lothal, annihilating the Imperial Planetary Occupation Facility and Governor Pryce along with it. Thanks to the help of a pod of purrgils, they destroy Thrawn's blockading fleet and Imperial rule on Lothal comes to an end. After the Galactic Civil War, the planet's environment is restored and its people return to a life of relative peace.

CAPITAL CITY

APPEARANCES Reb **LOCATION** Lothal

Some of Lothal's citizens are thrilled when the Empire first arrives. Land barons, government officials, the wealthy elite, and those with military ties all benefit handsomely. Trade is tightly regulated, which creates many new opportunities for smugglers, organized crime, and corruption within the local government.

The economy of Capital City booms as mining operations bring back valuable minerals, metals, and crystals to refineries in the city. Processed materials in turn supply the factories building TIE fighters, Imperial troop transports, and AT-DPs. The factories in and out of the city, however, spew toxic gasses and slowly poison the rivers and seas.

The Imperial Armory Complex at the center of the city works in secret to develop the TIE/d defender starfighter. This special weapons program is of considerable interest to Grand Admiral Thrawn, who values the defender's survivability in combat with Rebel Alliance fighters- a result of its superior armament and deflector shield.

Those who live in the capital—humans, Rodian, Aqualish, Gotals, Ugnaughts, Ithorians, Chagrians, Houks, and others—face constant surveillance, excessive taxation, and harassment. Propaganda campaigns dominate the media to control public opinion, while citizens are forced to attend mandatory displays of Imperial patriotism and participate in rigged local elections. Travel and communications are monitored, and patrols of stormtroopers, AT-DPs, and ITTs ensure everything stays in order within Capital City.

Apart from risky pursuits like bounty hunting or podracing, a young person's best hope is getting accepted by Lothal's Academy for Young Imperials and graduating as an officer. Some, however, turn to illegal activities, such as smuggling, piracy, or joining a rebel cell. Others get along as best they can, buying and selling in open markets, working in the Empire's factories, and trying not to be noticed.

Nonetheless, leisure pursuits continue in the shadow of the city's Imperial Command Center. The shopping district offers art from Naboo, Alderaan, and Bith and the latest fashions imported from Coruscant, as well as restaurants with chefs from all over the galaxy. For the wealthy, luxury housing is available in skyscrapers above the shops. Nearby stadiums are popular for fans of grav-ball, too.

Aesthetic influence
Citizens walk among the curved towers and stadiums of Lothal *(above)*. Lothal's Capital City *(below)* has a lot of architectural similarities to other mining economies, like those found on Bespin and Garel.

EZRA'S ROOST

APPEARANCES Reb **LOCATION** Lothal

Ezra Bridger lives in an abandoned communications tower outside Lothal's Capital City. The tower is accessed through a room at the base, where Ezra stores his speeder. An elevator shaft leads to the top, exiting onto a circular balcony where Ezra can see all the way to the city and the sea beyond. The balcony encircles several empty rooms, one of which holds the bunk where Ezra sleeps and stores his helmet collection and various pilfered gadgets. When Lothal becomes too dangerous for Ezra, he leaves his home and joins the *Ghost* crew. ISB Agent Kallus, now secretly working for the Rebel Alliance, uses the tower to send intelligence to the rebels. Later Ezra and the rebels return to free Lothal, using the tower as a reconnaissance point to plan their assault on the Imperial Armory Complex.

Vantage point
Ezra has a great view from his tower, but it is so isolated that he would be trapped if the Empire ever discovered him there.

ANAXES

APPEARANCES CW, Reb **REGION** Core Worlds
SECTOR Azure **SYSTEM** Azure
PRIMARY TERRAIN Forests and rocky canyons

Anaxes hosts an important Republic shipyard that is attacked by Separatist Admiral Trench during the Clone Wars. This military stronghold later serves as a base of operations for the "Bad Batch" when they investigate the Separatists' use of Captain Rex's battle strategy algorithm. Later in the war, the planet is obliterated, but a portion of the Republic's fort survives on planetoid PM-1203. Fulcrum (Ahsoka Tano) and Hera Syndulla use it as a supply exchange point, but, by that time, the base is overrun by fyrnocks. Ezra Bridger turns this to his advantage in a confrontation with the Grand Inquisitor.

OLD JHO'S PIT STOP

APPEARANCES Reb **LOCATION** Jhothal, Lothal

Old Jho's Pit Stop, and the outpost where it is located, far from Lothal's capital, is named for its Ithorian owner. The tavern serves food and drinks, several of which are favorites of Kanan Jarrus. One of the bar's notable features is its Clone Wars-era memorabilia, including the nose of the LAAT/i *Crumb Bomber*. The *Ghost* crew uses the Pit Stop as a safe harbor to repair their ship. When the Empire cracks down on Lothal's rebel activity, the cantina has to serve Imperial patrons and broadcast Imperial propaganda.

LOTHAL JEDI TEMPLE

APPEARANCES Reb **LOCATION** Lothal

Lothal's Jedi temple is an ancient religious site hidden in the far north. The location is powerful in the Force and a source for kyber crystals. Jedi Master Yoda makes contact with Ezra Bridger, Kanan Jarrus, and Ahsoka Tano over successive visits there. In addition, Kanan accepts the mantle of Jedi Knight here during a vision. The temple requires a master and apprentice to work together to open it. Most of the multi-level building, which predates contemporary teachings of the Jedi, sits underground. At its deepest levels are paintings of Loth-wolves and the mysterious ancient inhabitants of Lothal—and a mystical gateway to the World between Worlds.

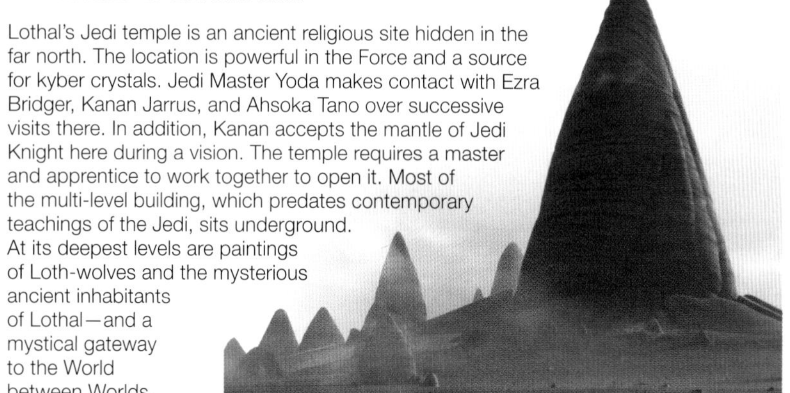

GAREL

APPEARANCES Reb, FoD
REGION Outer Rim Territories
SECTOR Lothal **SYSTEM** Garel
PRIMARY TERRAIN Mountains, deserts

Garel is a rocky world dominated by large spiral cities built amid mesas and desert plains. Situated directly on the Empire's newly established trade route through the Outer Rim, Garel is a primary exchange point for weapons shipments. The droids R2-D2 and C-3PO become entangled with the *Ghost* crew when they intercept one such Imperial shipment there. The rebel cell Phoenix Squadron temporarily hides on Garel, until the Empire attacks them, and they are forced to flee. Years later, Garel is liberated by local rebels.

CONCORD DAWN

APPEARANCES Reb **REGION** Outer Rim Territories **SECTOR** Mandalore **SYSTEM** Concord Dawn **PRIMARY TERRAIN** Rocky

After enduring centuries of war, Concord Dawn suffered a devastating blast that destroyed much of its southern hemisphere. The remaining planetoid is the birthplace of notable scoundrels such as Rako Hardeen. Fenn Rau and his Journeyman Protectors control Concord Dawn under the authority of the Empire. However, when Fenn Rau aligns with the rebels, Viceroy Gar Saxon and the Imperial Super Commandos wipe out the Protectors and take their place as the dominant military force in the system. Viceroy Saxon maintains a secret base on the third moon of Concord Dawn.

ATOLLON

APPEARANCES Reb **REGION** Outer Rim Territories **SECTOR** Lothal **SYSTEM** Atollon
PRIMARY TERRAIN Deserts and coral forests

Atollon is a world once covered by ancient seas that have long since evaporated, leaving vast deserts and coral forests. The most impressive corals to survive are the gargantuan plated coral trees. Some animal life, such as krykna spiders and little dokma, have adapted to survive in the hot sun without benefit of standing water. The planet is also home to the Force-wielding Bendu, a being who prefers to be left in peace. Deep underground lie vast aquifers supporting subterranean life and mysteries yet to be discovered. The Phoenix rebel cell establishes a base on Atollon, after it is driven from Garel by the Empire. The planet is known to inhabitants of the sector in legends and ancient artwork, but hidden in an unexplored portion of the Lothal sector and obscured in the Empire's databases.

New home
Phoenix Squadron member Dicer sets up a sensor on the North Face near Chopper Base (*right*). The plated coral trees dominate the Atollon landscape (*below*).

LIRA SAN

APPEARANCES Reb **REGION** Wild Space
SECTOR Unknown **SYSTEM** Lira San

Lira San is the ancestral homeland of the Lasat people. It is hidden behind an imploding star cluster and absent from astronomical charts. A portion of the population left millennia ago, resettling on Lasan. They lost all memory of Lira San other than a mysterious prophecy about one day returning to a promised homeworld. The Empire scorched the surface of Lasan, and few Lasats escaped. The Lasat Garazeb "Zeb" Orrelios and the *Ghost* crew help surviving refugees Chava and Gron locate Lira San by working through the prophecy. There, they are reunited with their people.

CHOPPER BASE

APPEARANCES Reb **LOCATION** Atollon

Chopper Base is a rebel operations center named for Hera Syndulla's droid, C1-10P (Chopper). He befriends an Imperial protocol droid named AP-5, who defects and helps the rebels find a safe location to hide from the Empire. Commander Sato's Phoenix rebel cell establishes its base in the tallest plated coral tree in the middle of a vast desert. Establishing the base is challenging: the rebels contend with carnivorous krykna spiders who gobble up some of the first scouts to arrive, and later face an Imperial EX-D infiltrator droid sent to expose them. Ultimately, Grand Admiral Thrawn discovers the base's location and launches a devastating attack. Commander Sato sacrifices himself and the Phoenix flagship so the survivors can retreat to Yavin 4.

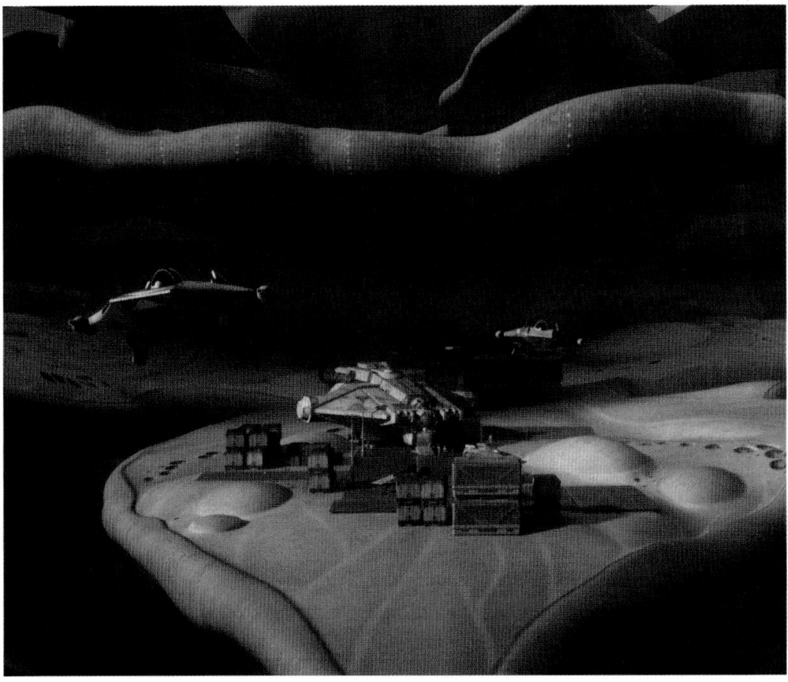

DANTOOINE

APPEARANCES Reb **REGION** Outer Rim Territories **SECTOR** Raioballo **SYSTEM** Dantooine **PRIMARY TERRAIN** Forests, grassy plains, and great lakes

During the Clone Wars, Jedi Master Mace Windu leads the Republic against the Separatist droid army on Dantooine. In the Imperial era, Senator Mon Mothma arranges for rebel representatives to meet in orbit of Dantooine, leading to the formation of the Rebel Alliance. Dantooine is briefly a Rebel Alliance base; it is abandoned for Yavin 4. When Imperial Governor Tarkin demands Princess Leia reveal the location of the Rebel Alliance base, she names Dantooine. General Tagge investigates and learns she is lying. Infuriated, Tarkin orders her execution.

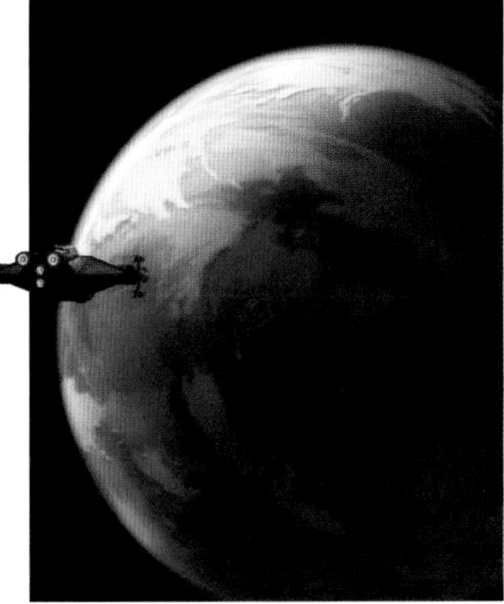

MALACHOR

APPEARANCES Reb **REGION** Outer Rim Territories **SECTOR** Chorlian **SYSTEM** Malachor **PRIMARY TERRAIN** Barren, rocky wastes

Malachor is a desolate world controlled by the Sith of antiquity. An ancient battle between the Sith and the Jedi results in a legendary cataclysm referred to as the "Scourge of Malachor." Afterward, Jedi are forbidden to travel there, and Malachor data is removed from the Jedi Archives. Darth Sidious takes his apprentice, Darth Maul, to Malachor to investigate a Sith temple. They inhale the ash of dead Force-users to conjure visions. Years later, Yoda beckons Ezra Bridger to go there, where he meets Maul.

MALACHOR SITH TEMPLE

APPEARANCES Reb **LOCATION** Malachor

Beneath the surface of Malachor is a Sith temple where a battle between Sith and Jedi raged thousands of years ago. During the struggle, the temple's internal superweapon misfired and obliterated both forces, leaving their charred remains as a memorial, forever locked in stone. Lightsabers and armor lay strewn about. The temple can only be entered by a master and apprentice working in cooperation. Ezra Bridger and Maul work together to reach the center and retrieve a Sith holocron. Ezra then places the holocron in a chamber at the temple pinnacle, where an ancient female Sith presence informs him of the temple's destructive purpose. Ezra and his master, Kanan Jarrus, escape (as does Maul), but Ahsoka Tano stays to fight Darth Vader. The temple explodes, but both survive. Ahsoka then embarks on a spiritual journey beneath the temple that changes the course of her life.

Knowledge is power
At the top of the Sith temple *(below)*, Ezra places the holocron in a pyramid that activates the superweapon *(right)*.

SYNDULLA RESIDENCE

APPEARANCES Reb **LOCATION** Ryloth

The home of the Syndulla clan is located in Ryloth's Tann Province. During the Clone Wars, a Republic Y-wing crashes in the front yard. Hera Syndulla pulls the droid Chopper out of the wreckage and repairs him. Later, her father, Cham Syndulla, is forced to abandon their home during a war with the Empire. Imperial Grand Admiral Thrawn directs Captain Slavin to convert the residence into the local Imperial headquarters. Hera later attempts to retrieve her family's Kalikori totem, but Admiral Thrawn seizes it. After being captured, Hera has to blow up her former home, so she can escape the Empire.

KROWNEST

APPEARANCES Reb **REGION** Outer Rim Territories **SECTOR** Mandalore **SYSTEM** New Kleyman **PRIMARY TERRAIN** Rugged mountains and alpine forests

Krownest is a chilly but habitable world under the administration of Mandalore. Winters last for much of the year, but fortunately local plants are mostly evergreen and produce a natural antifreeze that allows them to grow, even under snow. The wildlife has naturally adapted to the cold, thanks to thick, furry coats and large reserves of fat. Clan Wren makes its ancestral home on Krownest, in idyllic, isolated family estates.

WREN STRONGHOLD

APPEARANCES Reb **LOCATION** Krownest

Clan Wren's seat of authority is an estate on Krownest, carefully guarded by clan members. The minimalist mansion of steel and glass overlooks snow-covered mountains and a frozen lake. The great hall has a large banquet table situated below the throne for the clan leader. In the tradition of ancient Mandalorian culture, the manor includes rooms for sparring and physical training. Sabine Wren grows up here before leaving for the Imperial Academy. Her mother Ursa Wren is the ruling matriarch.

LOTHAL RESISTANCE CAMP

APPEARANCES Reb **LOCATION** Lothal

The Spectres' rebel camp is hidden in the mountains of Lothal's northern hemisphere. When it is discovered by the Imperials, they bomb the area and the rebels must seek the aid of the Loth-wolves to flee. The wolves take them through subterranean passages to an ancient habitation in the southern hemisphere, hidden on a canyon cliff. The walls there are decorated with hieroglyphics similar to those found within the lower levels of Lothal's Jedi temple. Their new camp serves the rebels in the last days before they drive the Empire from Lothal.

THE WORLD BETWEEN WORLDS

APPEARANCES Reb **LOCATION** Unknown

The World between Worlds is a mysterious spiritual realm flowing from the Force and located outside the bounds of time and space. The Lothal Jedi temple, itself older than modern Jedi traditions, is one gateway to it. Emperor Palpatine, aware of the realm, sends Minister Veris Hydan to excavate the temple and look for its gateway. He uncovers a mural of the legendary Force-wielders of Mortis, but cannot decipher it. Sabine Wren and Ezra Bridger are successful however, and Ezra enters a gateway encircled by Loth-wolves. Inside, Ezra finds a plane with portals to significant Force events. Finding Ahsoka Tano confronted by Vader through one such portal, Ezra pulls her into the World between Worlds and saves her life. They are interrupted by Palpatine, who attempts to penetrate the boundaries of the realm. Ahsoka and Ezra escape, after which the temple disappears. Later, Palpatine reconstructs a piece of the temple, trying to trick Ezra into opening the gateway for him, but Ezra declines and destroys it.

Doorway from death
Ezra saves Ahsoka's life by reaching through a portal and pulling her from Malachor into the World between Worlds.

LOTH-WOLF DEN

APPEARANCES Reb **LOCATION** Lothal

Kanan Jarrus, Ezra Bridger, and the crew of the *Ghost* become acquainted with a small pack of legendary Loth-wolves. Their austere den is located in the mountainous wilds of Lothal, beneath a large rock spire. It is deep enough to be impervious to Imperial bombing runs from above. The walls of this cave den are decorated with paintings of the ancient indigenous peoples coexisting with the wolves. The den is interconnected with cave passages leading to many strange places on Lothal—and perhaps beyond, via the World between Worlds.

ERSO HOMESTEAD

APPEARANCES RO **LOCATION** Lah'mu

When Galen Erso and his family flee from Director Krennic and the Empire, their friend Saw Gerrera helps them create a new life on Lah'mu. The Erso family home sits on 65 hectares of farmland. Most of the structure is buried underground and constructed by Galen and Lyra Erso themselves. Power and heating to the home is directed from geothermal vents. The local water supply is too high in minerals to be potable, so drinking water is drawn from moisture vaporators. Lah'mu's fertile soil is quite suitable for the family's large gardens however, tended with the assistance of an SE-2 worker droid. Galen, Lyra, and their daughter, Jyn, lead a happy life there for four years. Jyn experiences a pleasant, albeit lonely, childhood on Lah'mu, until Krennic and his death troopers arrive.

Making a home
Jyn's sleeping bunk *(above)* and the main living area *(below)* are functional, with minimal personal items.

LAH'MU

APPEARANCES RO **REGION** Outer Rim Territories **SECTOR** Railballo
SYSTEM Lah'mu **PRIMARY TERRAIN** Mountains and forested lowlands

Lah'mu is an unspoilt world rich in minerals and rainfall, making it an ideal environment for agriculture. Much of this is due to heavy volcanic and geothermal activity, especially in the Eastern hemisphere. Too far for most from hyperspace routes, it is occupied by only a few hundred homesteaders. The Republic encourages human settlers who are trying to escape the violence of the Clone Wars to resettle here, but they are soon forgotten. This sense of neglect makes it an ideal hiding place for the Erso family.

RING OF KAFRENE

APPEARANCES RO **REGION** Expansion Region **SECTOR** Thand **SYSTEM** Kafrene **PRIMARY TERRAIN** Space station amidst rocks and ice

Former mining colony the Ring of Kafrene is a trading post at the junction of the Rimma Trade Route and the Biox Detour. It was established by wealthy investors who failed to realize that the asteroid had few ore deposits of value, and their venture went bankrupt. The "Ring" connects two planetoids and has a diverse community of merchants, though many of the residents dwell in squalor. Cassian Andor is sent on a mission here to investigate Imperial kyber crystal shipments, and meets informant Tivik in backstreets patrolled by stormtroopers.

JEDHA

APPEARANCES RO **REGION** Mid Rim **SECTOR** Terrabe **SYSTEM** Jedha **PRIMARY TERRAIN** Deserts, mesas, and mountains

Jedha is the desolate moon of the planet NaJedha, its landscape dotted with sandstone mesas. Locked in a continuous winter, the climate is chilly, but not uncomfortable. Most of the year the sandy valleys and lowlands are barren, with only occasional rain torrents. The planet is rich in kyber crystals, and, partly for that reason, it has been home to many religions, including in recent millennia the Jedi and Church of the Force, who congregate at the Holy City and the Temple of the Kyber. In fact, the kyber resources are the main reason why the Empire seized control of Jedha in the first place. After the Battle of Yavin, the Rebel Alliance comes to the shattered moon to try to re-forge old alliances, while the remaining Partisans try to save what remains.

Natural stone
Jedha's sandstone is a source of once great but now dilapidated statues of Jedi, the Whills, and other ancient practitioners of the Force.

WOBANI

APPEARANCES RO **REGION** Mid Rim **SECTOR** Bryx **SYSTEM** Wobani **PRIMARY TERRAIN** Barren hills and processing plants

Wobani is the site of an Imperial labor camp where prisoners harvest and process underground reservoirs of tibanna and other valuable gasses. When Princess Leia is 16 years old, she visits Wobani on a humanitarian mission. She is dismayed by the treatment of the indigenous people by the Empire, and brings 100 refugees to Alderaan. Later, as an Imperial prisoner, Jyn Erso is sentenced to hard labor on Wobani in camp LEG-817, but she is rescued from a prisoner transport turbo tank by the Rebel Alliance and taken to Yavin 4.

JEDHA CITY

APPEARANCES RO **LOCATION** Jedha

Jedha City, also known as the Holy City or NiJedha, sits atop a mesa overlooking a desolate valley. Stormtroopers perch on the backs of long-legged creatures, called spamel, scrutinizing pilgrims who come to visit the temples and religious sites. To enter the city, guests must make an exhausting climb to gates near the top of the city's sandstone walls. Once inside, they find the citadel is divided into the Old City and the New City, which is still some 5,000 years old. At the front of the Old City sits the Temple of the Kyber. The streets are always crowded with pilgrims, priests, monks, tourists, sellers of trinkets, and street-food vendors. Stormtroopers and tanks patrol the streets, searching for Partisan rebels and anyone attempting to smuggle kyber crystals offworld. Jedha City was destroyed by the Empire during the test-firing of its superweapon, the Death Star, which it passed off as a mining accident.

Marketplace melting pot
Despite heavy Imperial occupation, everyday life continues on Jedha. Merchants sell sanctioned and blackmarket goods in the markets and pilgrims *(right)* seek spiritual answers.

CATACOMBS OF CADERA

APPEARANCES RO **LOCATION** Jedha

The Catacombs of Cadera are ancient tombs carved from a rock formation about a day's walk from Jedha's Holy City. They and the surrounding ruins were formed by a long-forgotten civilization. In more recent centuries the Catacombs were occupied by a monastery of the Church of the Contained Crescent, but they too vacated the site before it became occupied once again; this time by Saw Gerrera and his militant Partisans. The Catacombs are finally destroyed when the Death Star fires upon the Holy City.

TEMPLE OF THE KYBER

APPEARANCES RO **LOCATION** Holy City of Jedha

Known as the Temple of the Kyber, the Temple of the Whills, or simply the Kyber Temple, Jedha's most holy site was sacred to the ancient Jedi and those who follow their teachings concerning the Force. The triangular temple tower rises high above the city. Vader's Castle on Mustafar is designed using similar principles. When the Empire takes control of Jedha, it shuts the temple and turns out its guardian monks. A bountiful source of kyber crystals, the temple's vast underground stores are looted by the Empire to power the Death Star's superweapon. The temple is destroyed when the Death Star obliterates the Holy City.

"The moon with the rebel base will be in range in 30 minutes."

DEATH STAR INTERCOM

YAVIN 4

Yavin 4 is the fourth moon of an uninhabitable red gas giant. No native sentient life inhabits the moon, and with no known mineral resources of significance, Yavin 4 has avoided the attention of the Empire.

APPEARANCES Reb, RO, IV **REGION** Outer Rim Territories **SECTOR** Gordian Reach **SYSTEM** Yavin **PRIMARY TERRAIN** Jungles

Canopy cover
A rebel soldier stationed above the forest canopy scans for incoming ships. Allies are signaled for landing instructions inside the base of the temple ruins.

PRISTINE ENVIRONMENT

Yavin 4 is covered by an impenetrable rainforest of purple-barked Massassi trees, climbing ferns, grenade fungi, and bioluminescent orchids. Woolamanders cradle their young in the canopy above, and their mating calls echo through the forest late at night. Stintaril rodents hunt in packs through the trees, overwhelming the roosting golden whisper birds. Runyip forage on the floor below, harassed by ravenous piranha beetles. Below ground, leviathan grubs feed on Massassi roots for 300 years before emerging as one of the largest carnivores in the forest. In the swamps, armored eels prey on brightly colored lizard crabs, which are caught and absorbed by bulbous anglers perched on buttress tree roots above the muck. Unspoiled by industry, pollution, or colonies of settlers, Yavin 4 retains one of the galaxy's richest and most diverse ecosystems.

SECRET REBEL BASE

During the Emperor's reign, military leader Jan Dodonna sets up a rebel cell on Yavin 4, which becomes one of the biggest within the wider network of rebel groups. Dodonna and his team find ancient towering ruins left by the Massassi, an extinct slave race once ruled by the Sith. Dodonna decides to honor the Massassi by naming his rebel cell after them. Rebel engineers convert one of the largest structures into a base of operations. Inside are living quarters, meeting and services rooms, and landing bays for the fleet. A hidden power station 2 kilometers (1¼ miles) away supplies the base and provides shields and ion cannons sufficient to hold off an attack from most battleships.

Hidden signs
The Massassi group is unaware of the Great Temple and the surrounding structures' link to the Ordu Aspectu, an ancient splinter group of the Jedi Order.

Haunted temple For a time, the *Ghost* and its crew are based at the Great Temple.

Crucial message Private Tenzigo Weems races toward Mon Mothma to inform her that rebels are on Scarif.

ORGANIZING A REBELLION

After rebel leader Mon Mothma formally announces the Rebel Alliance, a portion of the Massassi group and Phoenix Squadron are defeated on Atollon by the Empire. Phoenix Squadron is practically wiped out by the attack, so the remnants merge with the Massassi group. Seeking to avoid detection by the Empire, Rebel Alliance High Command abandons its former base on Dantooine and moves to the Great Temple. From here, the Alliance leadership organizes non-combat missions including supply runs, reconnaissance missions, and disrupting an Imperial relay station on Jalindi. New recruits steadily join the Alliance as its leaders acquire the military machinery necessary to fight back. The Alliance avoids open warfare with the Empire, unwilling to risk the lives of civilians and rebels alike.

ATTACK ON SCARIF

Rebel intelligence stationed at Yavin 4 learns that the Empire is building a superweapon with the power to destroy entire planets. News of the Death Star's existence sparks a fierce debate among the Alliance Council, but its only hope is to recover the battle station's blueprints archived at the Imperial Security Complex on Scarif in order to discover its weakness. As Rogue One acquires the plans on the ground, the rebel fleet deploys from Yavin 4 to provide cover. The fleet take heavy losses, but win their first major victory against the Empire as Princess Leia escapes with the plans.

Protecting the Alliance At the Battle of Yavin, pilots of new X-wings fly as Red Squadron while pilots of the older Y-wings fly as Gold Squadron. Thirty rebel pilots fly past the red gas giant, but only three return.

THE BATTLE OF YAVIN

When the *Millennium Falcon* delivers Princess Leia to Yavin 4, the rebels discover her freedom comes at a high price. A tracking device has been attached to the ship and the approaching Death Star has forced their hand. The rebel fleet must launch an attack on the Imperial battle station before their base and Yavin 4 are destroyed. With R2-D2 aboard, Luke Skywalker joins the X-wing flight team in an attempt to detonate the Death Star's reactor core via an unprotected shaft. If this mission fails, the Empire will destroy Yavin 4 with its superlaser and utterly destroy the Rebel Alliance. Following their victory over the first Death Star, General Dodanna calls for the full evacuation of the base. Knowing that an Imperial counter attack is imminent, the Alliance begins scouting for a new outpost.

Monitoring the battle From their strategy center, Commander Bob Hudsol, General Jan Dodonna, Princess Leia Organa, and C-3PO monitor the assault on the Death Star.

Hail the heroes Instrumental in the success of the rebellion, the Heroes of Yavin attend the Royal Award Ceremony.

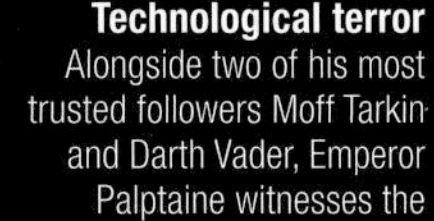

Technological terror
Alongside two of his most trusted followers Moff Tarkin and Darth Vader, Emperor Palpatine witnesses the construction of the Death Star.

BIRTH OF A SUPERWEAPON

Even before the birth of the Empire, preparations for its ultimate weapon were underway. On Geonosis, engineers working at the behest of the Sith Lord Darth Sidious created the first designs for the Death Star. When Jedi Knights and clone troopers attacked the planet, beginning the Clone Wars, Count Dooku retrieved the designs for safekeeping in the hands of the Sith. By the time the war ends and Sidious has declared himself Emperor of the galaxy, the battle station's construction began in secret above Geonosis under Director Orson Krennic and Admiral Tarkin's supervision.

That's no moon
Hyperdrive systems propel the moon-sized Death Star's lightspeed jumps to cross the galaxy.

Planet buster
The superlaser's blast is powerful enough to shatter a planet into chunks of rock.

UNDER CONSTRUCTION

While construction continued over Geonosis, work soon began on the weapon itself. Krennic coerces his friend, scientist Galen Erso, to weaponize kyber crystals for the Death Star's superweapon. While Galen feigns loyalty to the project, he secretly plans a devastating fault in a thermal exhaust port that could be used to destroy the entire station. Galen creates a holorecording explaining his actions, urging the Rebel Alliance to steal the Death Star plans from the Citadel on Scarif. Erso then persuades Imperial pilot Bodhi Rook to pass the holorecording to his old friend Saw Gerrera.

Desperate message
Deep in the Catacombs of Cadera, Galen's daughter watches her father's message; it's the first time Jyn has seen him in years.

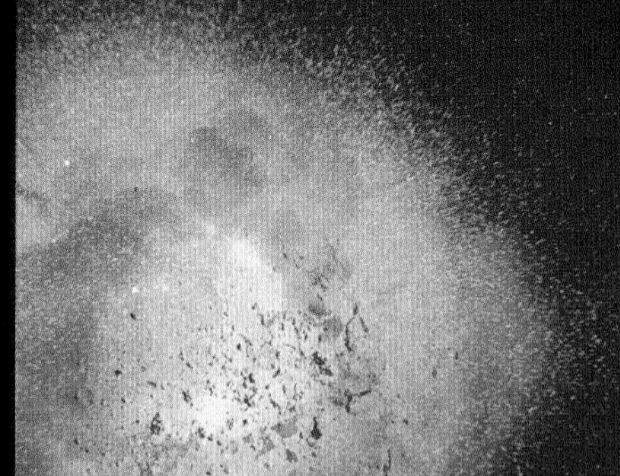

Striking fear
After Alderaan is destroyed by the Death Star, Darth Vader collects a rock from the debris. He gives it to Queen Trios of the Shu-Torun as a reminder of what the Empire does to those who resist.

TESTING THE WEAPON

The Empire learns that Bodhi has defected and traveled to Jedha City, so Tarkin orders a partial test of the Death Star's weapon on the location. The city is completely destroyed. When the Rebel Alliance attacks Scarif, Tarkin orders the Death Star to fire upon the Imperial facility containing the Death Star plans—but the destruction fails to stop the Alliance. Rebel Princess Leia is captured and brought to the Death Star, where Tarkin forces her to witness the destruction of her homeworld Alderaan, killing billions.

"This station is now the ultimate power in the universe." ADMIRAL MOTTI

THE DEATH STAR

With the embers of rebellion simmering in the Empire, Grand Moff Tarkin believes fear will keep its many planets in line. Who would dare stand against the Death Star with its power to destroy entire worlds?

APPEARANCES II, III, RO, IV **AFFILIATION** Empire

Princess rescued
Leia Organa is liberated from her cell by Han and Luke, and together they escape—into a trash compactor *(right)*. Darth Vader and his former Jedi Master, Obi-Wan Kenobi, duel one final time *(above)*.

ESCAPING THE DEATH STAR

The *Millennium Falcon*'s crew—Han Solo and Chewbacca—are hired to bring Obi-Wan Kenobi, Luke Skywalker, R2-D2, and C-3PO to Alderaan. However, they are shocked to discover that Alderaan has been blasted to rubble. Soon after, they are caught in a tractor beam and pulled into a docking bay aboard the Death Star. Amazingly, they avoid capture. After Obi-Wan parts company with the others to shut down the tractor beam, R2-D2 learns that Princess Leia is imprisoned on the Death Star, and scheduled for execution. Luke, Chewbacca, and Han hastily launch a rescue mission. They manage to free Leia, but the arrival of stormtroopers forces them all to dive into a chute that empties into a trash compactor. Fortunately, R2-D2 and C-3PO shut down the compactor before it crushes their human compatriots. Luke and Han rush Leia back to the *Falcon*, while Obi-Wan disables the tractor beam. However, when the former Jedi attempts to rejoin his allies back at the *Falcon*, he encounters Darth Vader, who engages his former master in a duel. To ensure that Luke, Leia, and the others escape, Obi-Wan allows Vader to strike him down, becoming one with the Force.

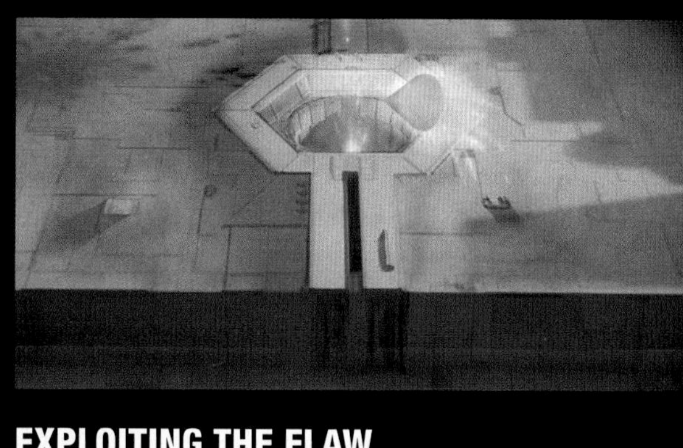

Vulnerable
The Death Star's primary weapon combines multiple laser beams *(far left)* to form a single massive blast. But two small proton torpedoes fired down a thermal exhaust port merely 2 meters (6 ft 6 in) wide *(left)* prove catastrophic for the battle station.

EXPLOITING THE FLAW

The *Falcon* and its crew travel to the Rebel Alliance base on Yavin 4, where the Alliance analyzes the Death Star plans and discovers Galen Erso's fatal flaw. When the battle station enters the planet's orbit, the rebels launch a desperate attack on the Death Star. A small number of starfighters make a bombing run at a seemingly inconsequential exhaust port in the Death Star's meridian trench. Used to hitting womp rats on Tatooine with the pneumatic cannons on his T-16 skyhopper, Luke Skywalker fires the fatal shot with the added guidance of the Force. The proton torpedoes explode when they reach the main reactor and the resulting chain reaction blows the Death Star apart.

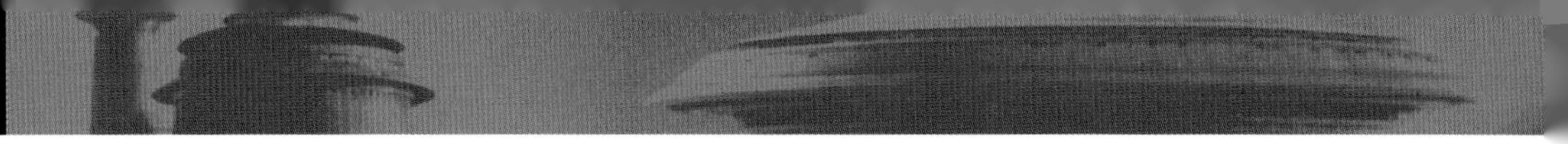

DARTH VADER'S CASTLE

APPEARANCES RO **LOCATION** Mustafar

Pleased with his apprentice's recent performance, Emperor Palpatine offers Darth Vader his own fortress in the design and location of his choosing. Vader selects Mustafar because he associates it with his connection to the dark side and his transformation from Anakin to Darth Vader. Palpatine also gifts Vader a mask containing the consciousness of an ancient Sith Lord and sculptor known as Momin, and sends his chief architect, Colonel Alva Brenne, and her aide, Lieutenant Roggo, along with Vader. During their work, the mask possesses Roggo, and under its influence, he kills Brenne. Momin projects an image of the perfect fortress and helps Vader design it, but not without trying to double-cross him. Vader is displeased at this and kills Momin's newly inhabited body, after which Momin unsuccessfully tries to possess Vader. Momin settles for a Mustafarian body to inhabit instead.

At Vader's insistence, Momin begins to design the Dark Lord's castle to channel the dark side of the Force from a locus below the sanctum, harnessing the energy to open a gateway into the Force itself. There, Vader hopes to contact his dead wife, Padmé. It takes Momin eight attempts at construction before Vader can open the gateway to the dark side as desired. At each unsuccessful attempt, Vader is frustrated and kills Momin's current body, causing him to transfer from a Mustafarian to a stormtrooper, then an Imperial officer, then a Mustafarian lava flea, and finally an Imperial construction worker before Momin completes the final design.

The fortress is built above a cave on the site of a former Sith temple in the Gahenn Plains. The cave houses the locus of the dark side of the Force. Vader's red lightsaber was forged in this cave, and later, the First Order's Supreme Leader Snoke wears a ring with obsidian carved from this same cave. Like the ancient Temple of the Kyber on Jedha, Vader's castle has twin tuning towers, both made of black obsidian. The towers channel the Force and enhance Vader's connection to it. Inside the castle is a waiting room, absent of chairs, with a view of Mustafar's treacherous volcanic landscape. The room is meant to intimidate Vader's "guests." Vader meets with important emissaries in this room, including Imperial Director Orson Krennic. At the heart of the temple is a meditation chamber guarded by the Emperor's Royal Guards, where Vader communes with the Force from inside a bacta tank, free from the confines of his terrifying black armor.

Vader's first attempts to open the gateway to the dark side cause catastrophic environmental effects around Mustafar, and Vader becomes preoccupied with the resulting Mustafarian uprising. The Mustafarians wipe out the local Imperial garrison, but Vader manages to channel the Force through his castle vortex and destroy the rioters. During this time, Momin uses the functional portal to resurrect his own original body. Momin then attacks Vader and badly injures him, but Vader crushes Momin to death with a stone slab. Alone now, Vader is able to finally enter the dark side gateway and search for his wife, but dark visions cloud his attempts. In frustration he retreats and destroys the portal. Only the cave beneath remains.

Intimidating meeting place
Vader banks on the stark architecture and inhospitable environment of his fortress to intimidate Imperial staff, such as Director Orson Krennic, and remind them of their place.

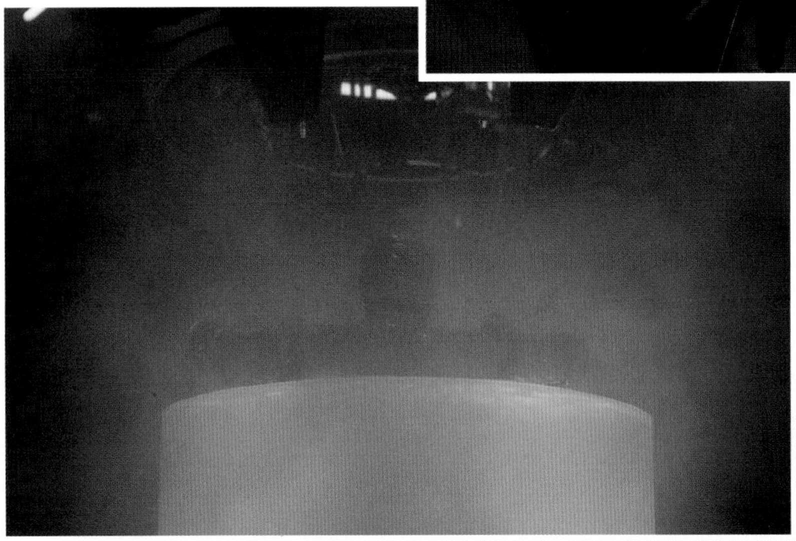

Castle keeper
Vader is attended by Vaneé *(above)*, who protects the inner sanctums of his master's fortress, such as his meditation chamber and restorative bacta tank *(left)* from prying guests' eyes.

"Mustafar is where Jedi go to die."
HERA SYNDULLA

Dangerous defenses
Architect Colonel Brenn thought the lava fields would make a stunning vista. Vader knows they provide invaluable protection.

SCARIF

APPEARANCES RO **REGION** Outer Rim Territories **SECTOR** Abrion **SYSTEM** Scarif **PRIMARY TERRAIN** Tropical coastal zones, shallow seas with coral reefs

Scarif is a tropical world far from other habitable planets. Its isolation coupled with the minerals and ore deposits in its mantle make it an ideal secret Imperial shipyard and weapons foundry. After the Death Star is moved from Geonosis, it is brought to Scarif to complete its construction under the oversight of Director Orson Krennic. Scientist Galen Erso has the immense data file containing the Death Star plans—including its fatal flaw—stored at the data vault deep in the Citadel complex, where Krennic mistakenly thinks it is safe. Many Imperials share this attitude toward the planet's impregnability.

The entire planet is secured by a deflector shield, with an access point to Scarif's surface available through a single shield gate. The gate is guarded by turbolasers, bays of TIE fighters, and multiple orbiting Star Destroyers. This high level of security is intended to prevent anyone but authorized Imperials from reaching (or departing from) the surface of the planet.

Scarif itself is peppered with volcanic island chains, atolls, coral reefs, and ever-shifting sand bars. Aquatic life is abundant. In the lagoons and reefs just around the Imperial Security Complex are more than 1,500 known species of fish. The most fearsome sea creature there is the tentacled Blixus, known to drag unmindful stormtroopers into the lagoons and eat them. Further out to sea are great fish and sea beasts capable of swallowing entire starships.

The Imperial Security Complex straddles islands connected by sandy tombolos and transit tubes. The islands are home to many birds, reptiles, and insects. Some of them are hunted, cooked, and served at the local stormtrooper mess hall.

Older officers stationed on Scarif treat their posting like an early, unsanctioned retirement. Their lackadaisical approach to their duties contributes to the Empire's loss at the Battle of Scarif, resulting in the destruction of the entire Imperial complex and loss of all personnel stationed there, initiated by the order of Grand Moff Tarkin.

Tropical battleground
The jungles of Scarif become the perfect terrain for the camouflaged rebels to hide in and confuse the Empire from.

Hive of activity
The Imperial security complex on Scarif spans a number of islands. Cargo shuttles are in constant employment to and from the many landing bases.

"Send word to the Alliance… they have to go to Scarif and get the plans."

GALEN ERSO, VIA JYN ERSO

EADU

APPEARANCES RO **REGION** Outer Rim Territories **SECTOR** Bheriz **SYSTEM** Eadu **PRIMARY TERRAIN** Rocky mountains, grasses, and scrub brush

Eadu is a harsh world with severe storms of lightning, gale-force winds, and torrential rains. The northern hemisphere is marked by tall rock spires and a near endless night due to the unpleasant weather. Ravines collect runoff and give off a stench of decay. The Imperial Kyber Refinery is hidden in this lifeless north. Fortunately the southern hemisphere, with its fertile soil, is not as inhospitable. There, about 2,500,000 Eaduans live in small villages where they raise nerf herds.

IMPERIAL KYBER REFINERY

APPEARANCES RO **LOCATION** Eadu

The secret Imperial Kyber Refinery, also known as the Eadu Energy Conversion Laboratory, is hidden among a treacherous zone of rock pinnacles shrouded in dark clouds. Rogue Imperial Galen Erso manages the facility with a team of scientists, in a program that fuses kyber crystal shards into larger matrixes and conducts research into controlled chain reactions. The project falls under the Tarkin Initiative, overseen by Director Orson Krennic. Security for the facility is overseen by Captain Magna Tolvan and it is guarded by stormtroopers from the 975th garrison.

CITADEL TOWER

APPEARANCES RO **LOCATION** Scarif

The Citadel is the focal point of the Imperial Security Complex on Scarif. It is an immense tower housing a heavily guarded cold-storage data vault, central communications dish, landing pads for high-ranking officials, and a complex control room where General Sotorus Ramda overseas daily operations. The vault contains data on countless top-secret programs, including the plans to the Death Star. It is guarded by a battalion of stormtroopers and shoretroopers, a surplus of Imperial security droids, and occasionally a contingent of death troopers accompanying visiting VIPs. Rebels Jyn Erso, Cassian Andor, and his droid, K-2SO, infiltrate the tower, steal the Death Star plans, and transmit them to the Rebel Alliance from the top of the tower via the communications dish. The tower, along with the rest of the facility, is destroyed by a single shot from the Death Star.

Secure satellite
Offworld communication from Scarif happens via the satellite dish at the very top of the Citadel Tower. The planetary shield gate prevents unauthorized transmissions, however.

"Set your course for the Hoth system. General Veers, prepare your men." DARTH VADER

HOTH

Once the Empire becomes aware of the rebels' base of operations on Yavin 4, the freedom fighters must relocate to a new secret hideaway. In their search for unlikely homes, they settle upon the cold, barren world of Hoth.

APPEARANCES V, FoD **REGION** Outer Rim Territories **SECTOR** Anoat **SYSTEM** Hoth **PRIMARY TERRAIN** Plains, mountains

A FROZEN WORLD

Hoth is a frozen, inhospitable world. Rocky mountains give birth to winding glaciers, spilling into vast fields of snow and icy tundra. Surrounded by a precarious asteroid belt, the planet is barraged by meteors. Still, life exists on the planet. Several species of tauntaun feed on lichens in glacier caves and grottos formed by the planet's heated core. Wampas hunt tauntauns and drag them back to their caves to feed their young. At night, the wind howls haunting melodies through winding burrows of sapphire ice worms.

Probe droids
The Empire disperses spies across the galaxy, looking for the rebels' secret base. Eventually a droid discovers curious signs of life on Hoth.

PERILS AT THE DOORSTEP

Hoth is fraught with dangers. While on patrol, Han Solo and Chewbacca discover one of the Empire's Viper probe droids. It self-destructs when struck by blaster-fire, but only after alerting the Imperials. Meanwhile, Luke Skywalker is attacked by a ferocious wampa and pulled back to its den. The beasts are a frequent problem for the rebels, and several remain captive at Echo Base. Though Luke escapes, he nearly freezes to death in a blizzard afterward. Yet the rebels' worst struggles are faced once the Imperial military arrives.

Ice monsters
Wampas are a hazard of being stationed on this frozen world. They have even been known to attack Echo Base in small groups.

Frozen wastes
From space, Hoth appears bleak and barren. There are no signs of civilization or significant life, making it an ideal hiding place.

Inevitable defeat
Imperial walkers descend upon the rebel forces *(top)*. At best, the rebels know they can only slow down the Empire's assault. Their real goal is to give the evacuation effort more time *(above)*.

Race to the *Falcon*
Chewbacca, Han, Leia, and C-3PO narrowly escape Echo Base.

THE BATTLE OF HOTH

General Veers is tasked with destroying the shield power generator at Echo Base. Forced to steer clear of the shield perimeter, Imperial dropships set down on the precarious Moorsh Moraine, well north of the heavily fortified rebel base. Having surrendered all element of surprise, but augmented with legions of snowtroopers, the Empire's AT-ATs, AT-STs, and speeders begin their march toward the rebel stronghold. As they move south to the foot of the Clabburn Range, they are met by the rebels' Rogue Squadron of modified T-47 airspeeders.

EVACUATION

Once Veers destroys the shield power generator, the rebels must evacuate. As their ion cannon disables the Star Destroyers above, transport ships launch the evacuation. Virtually unarmed, the rebel transports rely on starfighter escorts led by Wedge Antilles and Wes Janson. The *Millennium Falcon* takes off with the last transport, *Bright Hope*. Luke and the remaining survivors scramble to take off in their X-wings, leaving Darth Vader and his snowtroopers to scrounge through the wreckage for clues to the fleet's destination. Scavengers later arrive on Hoth to loot the wreckage from the battle.

Tired troops
Rebel soldiers wait for the oncoming battle.

"That's it. The rebels are there."

DARTH VADER

Danger comes to Echo Base
The rebel fleet prepares for battle in the hangar bay *(above)*. R2-D2 wanders the corridors of Echo Base *(right)*.

ECHO BASE

APPEARANCES V, FoD **LOCATION** Hoth

Following the Battle of Yavin, the Rebel Alliance begins searching for a new location to base its secret operations. The rebels settle on the icy planet Hoth, which is so remote that it is absent from most maps. Rebel engineers carve the command center from the ice and clear out several natural caverns (some of which contain dangerous wampas). They excavate vast bays to hold the rebel fleet of starfighters and a contingent of GR-75 medium transports, in addition to quarters for more troops and other personnel. Establishing a military installation buried in snow and ice proves challenging: frequently melting ice, shrinkage, and cave-ins mean the base needs constant maintenance. The rebels are resolute, however, and name their new home Echo Base after its remarkable acoustics.

The Alliance must not only deal with harsh environmental conditions and the eventual ground war with the Empire, but also wampa attacks, itchy tauntaun lice, and even meteor showers. To keep personnel healthy, Echo Base has a well-equipped infirmary with physicians and medical droids.

Though vital for defense, the shield generators, visible from a great distance due to their large size, guarantee eventual detection by the Empire. General Rieekan orders extra defenses to be constructed, including heavy blast doors, infantry trenches surrounding the base, and anti-personnel batteries in key locations. The base's chief defense is a sizable Kuat Drive Yards v-150 ion cannon, which fires gigantic charged-plasma bursts powerful enough to penetrate the shields of an Imperial Star Destroyer and disable its shields, weapons, and engines.

All these precautions prove necessary when an Imperial probe droid discovers the rebel presence on Hoth and the Empire launches an AT-AT assault. This eventually dooms Echo Base, putting the rebels on the run once again. Instrumental in the evacuation, the base's ion cannon disables the Imperial fleet above while the GR-75 transports ferry rebel personnel away from Hoth to temporary safety.

Mounting tension
Leia Organa monitors progress from the Echo Base control room, expressing concern about the impending battle.

HOTH ASTEROID BELT

APPEARANCES V **REGION** Outer Rim Territories **SECTOR** Anoat **SYSTEM** Hoth **PRIMARY TERRAIN** Rocks, gas pockets

The planet Hoth suffers constant meteor bombardment from the surrounding asteroid belt. The chaotic region is a favorite hiding place for pirates and smugglers, as well as a legitimate source of metal ore and minerals.

Following the battle of Hoth, the *Millennium Falcon* hides inside the belt, where the crew finds that the asteroids harbor life. Giant space slugs have formed a colony, with some specimens large enough to swallow entire starships. Mynocks infest the rocky caverns, feeding on passing starships and the wreckage of vessels that don't survive.

Cozy in the swamp
R2-D2 waits outside Yoda's home, which is too small and cluttered for him to move easily about inside *(above)*. After Luke mentions his desire to find Yoda on Dagobah, Obi-Wan Kenobi's voice speaks to Yoda and Luke inside the hut *(above left)*.

YODA'S HUT

APPEARANCES V, VI **LOCATION** Dagobah

When Yoda returns to the planet Dagobah after the ascension of Emperor Palpatine, he initially makes a camp in the E3-standard starship lifeboat that brings him there. Though the craft is small, it affords reasonable living space for a being of Yoda's diminutive size, providing shelter from the constant threat of Dagobah's unrelenting rains and persistent pests and predators. Within a year, however, the craft begins to degrade as it is slowly consumed by the swamp.

Yoda sets about building a new home made of mud, wattle, and stones. He constructs his house at the base of a great gnarltree on a knoll beside a murky lagoon. The humble dwelling includes a sitting room, kitchen area, and sleeping loft, with several windows and two circular entries. The interior is surfaced in smooth, white clay adobe, providing a clean, attractive, and dry shelter.

Yoda cooks at a small stove in the middle of his home, behind which is a storage area with windowsills covered in drying seeds, berries, and herbs. In the back of the shelter is a sink with running water, a few clay bowls and pots, and Yoda's spice collection. A loft hangs above, with sleeping mats and blankets, though Yoda sleeps on the ground level during his final years. Tools and keepsakes are stored in a nook. The rest consists of a sitting area with a wooden stump for a table.

Being so close to the lagoon, with open doors and windows, means Yoda's home is visited by many creatures. Yoda frequently finds snakes, lizards, butcherbugs, and spiny bograts scampering across the floor. He doesn't mind the company and only sweeps the venomous ones back out the door.

Yoda lives in his home for more than 20 years before Luke visits him there, twice. On his first visit, Yoda agrees to train Luke as a Jedi, and during the second, Yoda tells Luke that he must confront his father, Darth Vader. Advanced in years, Yoda then passes away in the comfort of his bed. Yoda's vacant hut is reclaimed by the swamp and the many creatures he has befriended over the years.

Not-so-safe haven
Bespin is the nearest safe haven from Hoth that Han is able to locate while fleeing from the Empire *(above)*. On the approach to Cloud City, the *Millennium Falcon* is met and escorted by a pair of cloud cars *(left)*.

BESPIN

APPEARANCES V, VI **REGION** Outer Rim Territories **SECTOR** Anoat **SYSTEM** Bespin **PRIMARY TERRAIN** Gas giant

The planet Bespin is a gas giant isolated from two sister worlds by an asteroid belt known as Velser's Ring. Bespin has no landmasses, but its upper, habitable atmosphere has a layer of breathable air, and this zone hosts a number of orbital cities, gas-mining facilities, and unique life-forms. Bespin has an unusual abundance of life for a gas planet, and the night skies are lit with bioluminescent organisms that look like twinkling stars.

In the lower atmosphere, giant beldons float in large herds. They range in size from 0.8 to 10 kilometers (½ to 6¼ miles) wide, filled with numerous orange gas bladders and propelled by fleshy fins. Long tendrils fall from their bodies, gathering atmospheric plankton and chemicals, which they metabolize into tibanna gas, a valuable commodity and the foundation of Bespin's floating cities' economies.

Algal "trees" form floating mats with stalks that descend to the lower atmosphere to gather nutrients. These algal forests produce most of the oxygen in the planet's life zone. They also provide a habitat and food source for an untold number of creatures.

Large thrantas, transplanted from Alderaan, dive majestically through the clouds, ridden by only the bravest thrill-seekers. Blue-and-red-tipped rawwks flit among the algal trees, chasing schools of air shrimp that shimmer in rainbow colors to warn others of a predator. Flocks of velkers attack beldons and feast on their buoyant flesh, attracting carrion-eating crab gliders, until the corpse slowly drifts toward the toxic planet core.

"We're a small outpost here and not very self-sufficient."

LANDO CALRISSIAN

CLOUD CITY

Floating 59,000 kilometers (37,000 miles) above Bespin's gaseous core, Cloud City is both a gas-mining facility and a luxury destination. Founded by Lord Ecclessis Figg of Corellia, it is presently overseen by Baron Administrator Lando Calrissian.

APPEARANCES V, VI **LOCATION** Bespin

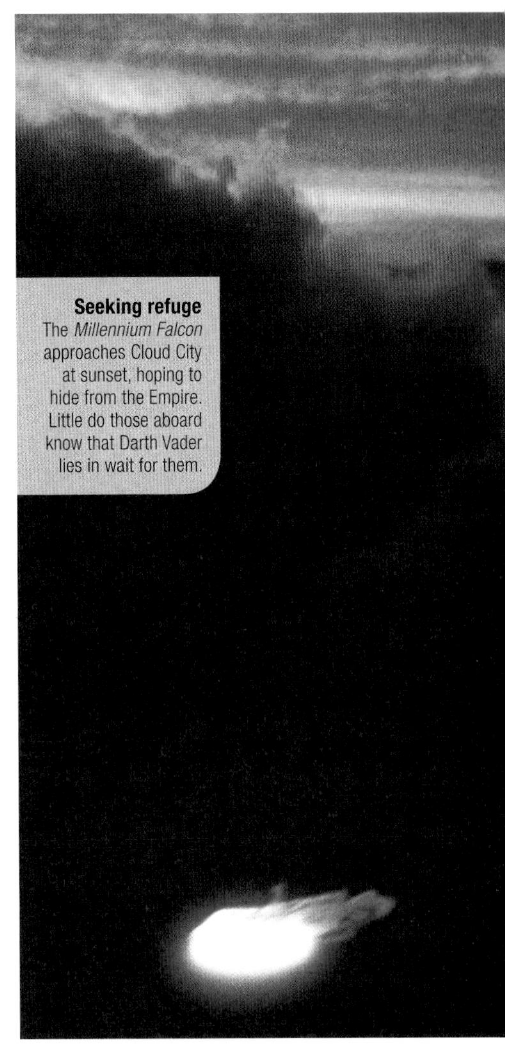

Seeking refuge
The *Millennium Falcon* approaches Cloud City at sunset, hoping to hide from the Empire. Little do those aboard know that Darth Vader lies in wait for them.

Refining in the clouds
An automated tibanna gas refinery hovers outside Cloud City.

MINING THE SKIES

Cloud City is built around a central column that rises from a gas-processing reactor at its base. The city's otherwise hollow core contains giant directional vanes that control the facility's ever-floating location. Plants around the city's outer ring process Bespin's tibanna gas for export. Cloud City employs countless freelance gas prospectors to navigate Bespin's breathable upper atmosphere. They are hired to pinpoint pockets of tibanna using their flying craft before larger contractors can locate gas eruptions. Rare and valuable tibanna gas has a variety of uses. Its anti-gravitational properties are utilized across the galaxy for numerous types of airborne craft. It is also a key component in some blasters as a conducting agent and power-output amplifier. On some worlds, the gas is even employed as a heating fuel, while non-spin-sealed tibanna is used as hyperdrive coolant.

A city for fun
The promenade of Cloud City is lined with designer shops full of imported goods, fine restaurants, bars and cafes, cinemas, and gaming rooms.

A LUXURY DESTINATION

Cloud City is an exclusive resort, attracting elite clientele and wealthy tourists who stay in stylish casino hotels and enjoy Bespin's legendary two-hour sunsets. Visitors include well-to-do politicians, celebrities, industry tycoons, gangsters, and the occasional high-ranking Imperial officer. Fortunes are made and lost in this city renowned for its nightlife, scandals, and excess. Cloud City's five million residents and visitors dwell atop its 16-kilometer-(10-mile-) wide mining facility levels. The city floats in the planet's breathable upper atmosphere, known as the "Life Zone," which is shielded and infused by a layer of airborne algae and other photosynthetic organisms.

Unsettling beauty
Princess Leia discusses her anxiety about their situation with Han Solo. Her suite is typical of the luxury resorts on Cloud City. It is coincidentally designed in white synthstone, after the architecture of her homeworld, Alderaan, and crafted in honor of Lord Figg's Alderaanian wife.

Ugnaughts: Little workers

Ugnaughts are a small species of humanoids with tusks and upturned noses. Lord Ecclesis Figg builds Cloud City with the aid of three Ugnaught tribes. When the city is complete, Figg allows the Ugnaughts to remain in residence and maintain the city for a share in its mining profits.

Sith subterfuge Darth Vader discusses arrangements regarding the capture of Han with Boba Fett and Lando.

THE IMPERIAL OCCUPATION

Anticipating the arrival of Han Solo, Boba Fett infiltrates Cloud City and alerts Darth Vader. Vader, in turn, quietly arrives with a contingent of stormtroopers and forces Lando to cooperate. Lando agrees to turn Han over to Vader in exchange for a guarantee that the Empire will not interfere with Cloud City in the future. Leia Organa notices something is amiss when her droid, C-3PO, goes missing. Chewbacca discovers the droid has been dismantled and set to be destroyed by Ugnaughts (in fact, he has been shot and memory-scanned by stormtroopers) and rescues him. Lando then leads his friends to Vader under the ruse that they are going to dinner. Upon capture, Han is thrown into a prison cell with Leia before being taken to a carbon-freezing chamber. Darth Vader then uses the rebels to lure Luke into a confrontation, where he reveals that he is Luke's father in a failed attempt to persuade him to join the dark side. While the rebels and Lando escape the city, the inhabitants suffer a continued Imperial presence. Following the Battle of Endor, the local Imperial Governor Adelhard blockades the entire sector. Thanks to Lando, Lobot, and a local resistance, Cloud City is freed.

Chamber of horrors As Han is led to the carbon-freezing chamber, Lando has second thoughts about his deal with Darth Vader to ensure the safety of his Cloud City.

CARBON-FREEZING CHAMBER

APPEARANCES V **LOCATION** Cloud City, Bespin

Carbonite storage repulsor sleds are designed for use with the carbon-freezing chamber on Cloud City to safely store and transport high-pressure gasses like tibanna. The gas is stored within a super-strong block of frozen carbonite inside the sled. Darth Vader hopes to immobilize his son, Luke, in carbonite and transport him to the Emperor. To determine whether Luke will be able to survive this carbon-freezing process, Vader decides to use Han as a test subject. After he freezes Han, Vader hands him over to bounty hunter Boba Fett, who in turn delivers him to Jabba the Hutt for a substantial reward. Although a success, the process causes chronic hibernation sickness, which afflicts Han with temporary blindness and severe disorientation when he is eventually freed. Ultimately, however, Vader fails to trap Luke.

"A small rebel force has penetrated the shield and landed on Endor." DARTH VADER

ENDOR

The fate of the galaxy is determined on a peaceful forest moon, where the Rebel Alliance obtains the aid of the most unlikely allies to defeat the Empire.

APPEARANCES VI, FoD **REGION** Outer Rim Territories **SECTOR** Moddell **PRIMARY TERRAIN** Forests, savannahs, mountains

Captured by Ewoks
The Ewok Wicket senses a scout trooper approaching *(left)*. A group of Ewoks comes to investigate the rebels caught in their net *(above)*.

HOMEWORLD OF THE EWOKS

The Moon of Endor is a sanctuary of pristine temperate forests and primitive societies that thrive there. The primeval landscape remains relatively undisturbed until the arrival of the Empire. Ewoks dwell in family huts connected by terraces, ladders, and suspension bridges. Villages are overseen by wise chiefs and tribal elders. In warm summer months, Ewoks may stay in fishing villages or hunting and farming lodges on the forest floor. Well versed in forest survival, they travel long distances on shaggy, spotted ponies and use friendly bordoks to haul loads of supplies. Ewoks soar through valleys on gliders with leather wings, but must be careful to avoid vicious blue-and-gold condor dragons.

SECRET IMPERIAL BASE

Bothan spies steal information about the second Death Star and deliver it to the rebel leadership. Not only do they discover the existence of a new Death Star, but also that it is protected by a shield generator located on Endor. Believing they can strike before the new battle station is fully operational, a team of rebel commandos led by General Han Solo sneaks past the Imperial blockade in the stolen shuttle *Tydirium*. Their mission is to destroy the Empire's facility on the moon's surface. The Imperial command bunker is located below a relay dish and guarded by Imperial walkers and a garrison of stormtroopers, scout troopers, and other officers under the command of Colonel Dyer, Commander Igar, and Major Hewex.

Imperial landing zone
Lambda-class shuttles *(left)* fly to a landing platform with turbolifts running up the legs of the installation *(below)*. AT-ATs are loaded at gates below.

RESIDENTS AND EXPATRIATES

Endor is rich with life, and Ewoks are not the only creatures of significance. Yuzzums are Endor's dreamy wanderers. Two of them catch a ride on visiting ships, making their way to Jabba's palace on Tatooine. One works there as a singer and the other as an exterminator. Aggressive Duloks dwell in the swamps, emerging to hunt Ewoks and lantern birds. The songs of munyips and ruggers can be heard as they climb through Ewok villages. Giant gorax occasionally descend from the mountains and terrorize Ewok tribes.

Yuzzums
The rifle-carrying Endor native Wam Lufba tends to the pests—some quite menacing—in Jabba's palace on Tatooine.

Bait
C-3PO and R2-D2 lure a group of troopers into an ambush, where Ewoks pummel them with stones during the Battle of Endor.

CLIMACTIC BATTLE

Though the rebels are taken prisoner by the Ewoks at their first encounter, C-3PO eventually persuades the Ewoks to join the rebel cause, to save not only their own homes and families, but the rest of the galaxy as well. The Alliance's success at the Battle of Endor, which decisively ends the rule of the Emperor, can largely be attributed to the bravery and ingenuity of the Ewoks. Their primitive culture is able to overthrow the technologically advanced Imperial army with spears and arrows, rock-throwing catapults, wooden battering rams, and rolling logs.

Change in the primeval forest
The evergreen forest of Endor is peaceful until the Empire arrives. Songs of churi and lantern birds are replaced by speeder bike engines and the clanking of AT-STs.

DEATH STAR II

APPEARANCES VI
REGION Outer Rim Territories
SECTOR Moddell **SYSTEM** Endor
PRIMARY TERRAIN Space battle station

Emperor Palpatine constructs the second Death Star, in part as an elaborate ruse. He hopes to destroy the Rebel Alliance by feigning a critical vulnerability in the Death Star, thus luring the rebels into a conflict they cannot win.

The Emperor devises a plan to let the rebels' Bothan spies obtain false information about the progress and status of the Death Star's construction. The rebels presume the battle station's superlaser will not be in operation at this stage, while in fact, the superlaser, powered by massive green kyber crystals (the same crystals which, in smaller form, are utilized in Jedi lightsabers), is fully functional. During the Battle of Endor, Palpatine surprises the rebels by ordering the Death Star to fire on one of the large Mon Calamari cruisers.

However, once the rebel strike team manages to destroy the shield generator on Endor that protects the Death Star, a small flight team, led by General Lando Calrissian on the *Millennium Falcon*, is able to enter the Death Star and destroy the battle station's main reactor core. Meanwhile, Luke Skywalker barely escapes after his father, Darth Vader, sacrifices himself to destroy the Emperor and save his son.

The second Death Star is significantly larger than the first. Its diameter is more than 200 kilometers (124 miles), compared to the original battle station's 160 kilometers (99 miles). In fact, the Death Star is nearly 3 percent the size of the moon of Endor itself. Since the Death Star is stationary and not in a synchronous orbit, it requires tremendous force to counter Endor's gravity. It utilizes a repulsorlift field created by the shield generator on Endor to maintain its position. The force generated by the Death Star creates earthquakes, tidal imbalances, and other geological disturbances on the surface below.

The Death Star has considerable defenses. Batteries include a complement of 15,000 heavy turbolasers, 15,000 standard turbolasers, 7,500 laser cannons, and 5,000 ion cannons, all of which are installed on the station's outer surface. Thousands of TIE fighters of various models are ready to deploy at all times, in addition to shuttles and ground assault vehicles such as AT-ATs and AT-STs.

Chain reaction
The Death Star's reactor core is its one vulnerability. When the rebel ships fly through the battle station's coolant shafts and detonate the core, a massive chain reaction occurs that destroys the Death Star.

EMPEROR'S THRONE ROOM

APPEARANCES VI **LOCATION** Death Star II

Emperor Palpatine's throne room is his command center and ceremonial seat of power aboard the second Death Star. Its gleaming industrial design, devoid of decorations and symbols of lavish comfort (unlike his personal offices and chambers, both here and on Coruscant), are meant to intimidate the dignitaries, subjects, and prisoners brought before him. His throne is a simple, contoured swiveling chair set in front of a viewport with enhanced magnification scanners. The dais before him is flanked by viewscreens linked to the station's computers and communications systems.

EWOK VILLAGE

APPEARANCES VI, FoD **LOCATION** Endor

Bright Tree Village perches 15 meters (50 feet) above the forest floor, where nest-like bunches of thatched huts housing nearly 200 Ewoks cling to the trunks of evergreen trees. At the village center are communal meeting areas, as well as homes for tribal elders and Chief Chirpa's family. Large huts for extended families huddle along the outer edges of the village. All are tied together by rope bridges, ladders, and platforms. In the canopy above, watchers look out for marauding gorax and condor dragons. Ewoks also launch gliders from the canopy to patrol the forests and valleys beyond. Bachelors maintain small huts below the village proper, where they keep watch for even greater dangers below.

Ewok huts are cozy inside. A cooking fire is located at the center, where meat is roasted on a spit and soups boiled in clay pots. Storerooms of food and kindling lie under the floor and woven sleeping mats and furs are stacked in lofts above. Wooden stools and baskets sit on the floor, while Ewok hoods, capes, and tools hang on the walls. Fires and torches light the village at night. The bark of the conifer trees where the Ewoks live not only provides a good insect repellent but is also highly fire resistant. The boughs also make excellent spears, bows, slingshots, glider frames, and catapult arms.

Ewoks spend much of their time in the trees, but descend to the forest floor to forage for berries, gather herbs, and hunt. A few Ewoks, such as the Warrick family, even maintain huts and lodges on the ground.

When the Rebel Alliance arrives on Endor, it is Leia Organa who first befriends the Ewok Wicket and walks with him back to Bright Tree Village. There she is welcomed with Ewok hospitality, fed, and clothed. Her rebel friends are then captured and brought to the village to be the main course in a banquet in C-3PO's honor—the Ewoks believe that the timid protocol droid is a god. Luke cleverly uses the Force to play on their superstitions and win the rebels' freedom. That night, C-3PO explains their plight to the Ewoks and persuades them to join the fight. After the battle is won, the Ewoks and the rebels return to the village to celebrate.

Village morning
The sun rises above Bright Tree Village on Endor as the Ewoks prepare for the day.

Village evening
Bonfires burn at night in the Ewok village, where the inhabitants are safe and secure from the dangers of battle elsewhere in the forest *(left)*. Meanwhile, Han and Leia share a private moment *(below)*.

Dinner party
The Ewoks carry the rebels back to their village, all of them bound except C-3PO, who receives royal treatment *(above)*. Later, the Ewoks prepare Han, Luke, and Chewbacca for a feast in C-3PO's honor *(left)*.

"Wonderful. We are now a part of the tribe." **C-3PO**

ENDOR BUNKER SECRET ENTRANCE

APPEARANCES VI **LOCATION** Endor

When Han Solo and the rebel forces debate how to infiltrate the secret entrance to the Empire's shield generator bunker, an Ewok named Paploo takes it upon himself to steal an Imperial speeder bike and create a diversion. The rebels then attempt to take the bunker and a back-and-forth ensues in which the Ewoks once again prove their worth. They are instrumental in winning the ground battle that rages outside the bunker entrance. The rebels are eventually able to trick the officers inside the bunker into opening the blast doors. Once inside, they place charges and destroy the entire complex.

Entering the bunker
Biker scouts stand guard outside the bunker entrance *(left)*. Han, Leia, and the rebel strike team invade the bunker *(above)*.

BATUU

APPEARANCES Res **REGION** Outer Rim Territories **SECTOR** Trilon **SYSTEM** Batuu
PRIMARY TERRAIN Mountains, forests, rivers, and seas

The backwater world known as Batuu is a rustic garden planet, recognized as a last stop before the mysteries and dangers of Wild Space. Batuu is a place where explorers, bounty hunters, smugglers, and trailblazers stock up on supplies before their trek, or return and tell outrageous tales of adventure. Here, heroes and scoundrels forge their origins and, if they don't make it back from their escapades, their sagas are retold as legends in the cantinas and market squares.

The countryside of Batuu is unspoiled and wild. Surabat River Valley winds though a treacherous canyon of rock spires, rapids, and hairpin turns. Though largely undeveloped, Batuu is the site of an ancient trading post called Black Spire Outpost, which has served traders even before the dawn of hyperspace travel.

Black Spire Outpost is bustling with commerce. Droid repairs are available at Mubo's Droid Depot. Merchant Row and the Market have shops bursting with local wares and galactic oddities. Docking Bay 7 receives regular freighters full of tasty delights and fascinating cargo—but beware of Docking Bay 9, which is occupied by unfriendly forces!

During the Clone Wars, Anakin Skywalker comes to Batuu to search for his missing wife, Padmé Amidala. Here, he meets Commander Mitth'raw'nuruodo (Thrawn), who agrees to help Anakin find her. In the process, they learn that Padmé has discovered a Separatist base on Mokivj. Years later, Emperor Palpatine sends Anakin, now Darth Vader, and Grand Admiral Thrawn back to Batuu to investigate a disturbance in the Force. There, they find that the Grysk, an enemy of Thrawn's own Chiss people and a potential threat to the Empire, has been kidnapping Force-adept children and holding them there for use as slaves.

During the rise of the First Order, Batuu does not escape the group's grasp. Desperate to track down the Resistance following their escape from Crait, the First Order stations a Star Destroyer in orbit above the planet. A smaller ground force patrols Black Spire Outpost, keeping an eye out for any Resistance spies. Ancient ruins sit at the edge of the trading post, providing a rendezvous point for the Resistance as they prepare to launch an attack. Despite the First Order's presence and the threat of imminent conflict, there are friends and allies to be found. Hondo Ohnaka, the infamous pirate with a big heart and an odd sense of humor, has made a deal with the mighty Chewbacca to run a transportation company from one of the outpost's docking bays, using the *Millennium Falcon*.

CASTILON

APPEARANCES Res **REGION** Outer Rim Territories **SECTOR** Unknown
SYSTEM Castilon **PRIMARY TERRAIN** Open seas and isolated islands.

Castilon is located on the border of the Outer Rim Territories and Wild Space. The most notable destination on Castilon is the *Colossus*, a refueling station and trading outpost. Smaller inhabited platforms and floating vessels are scattered around the globe.

A number of battles have been fought above Castilon over successive millennia, resulting in many shipwrecks left on the sea floor. Deep in the planet's underwater Karavian Trench live gargantuan, tentacled beasts called rokkna, with four eyes and a notable smell. One such beast terrorizes *Colossus* station when her young is accidentally taken along with a salvaged underwater wreck and then adopted as a pet by mechanic Neeku Vozo. Smaller seafood commonly caught by fishermen include sharvo fish. Native speagulls are a constant companion to fishermen, hoping for a handout or to steal a fish from their nets.

The most intelligent beings to rise from the depths on Castilon are the native Chelidae. These amphibians carry large shells on their backs and are capable of clinging to walls. Their movements are slow, as is their manner of speech. They are friendly, despite the many offworlders who have come to exploit their homeworld, and act as engineers, maintaining Castilon's *Colossus* station.

When the New Republic discovers that the First Order has taken an interest in Castilon, its leaders send pilot Kazuda Xiono to deliver the information to the Resistance captain, Poe Dameron. Though they are intercepted by the First Order's Major Elrik Vonreg, Kaz and Poe work together to fend him off. Poe then recruits Kaz to the Resistance and places him on Castilon as a spy.

"Castilon? We're on the edge of nowhere."

KAZUDA XIONO

The fast lane
Colossus is described by Resistance spy Kaz as a hangout for star pilots. During the station's Platform Classic race, pilots fly through a course of sky rings *(below right)*.

COLOSSUS PLATFORM

APPEARANCES Res **LOCATION** Castilon

The *Colossus* is a supertanker fuel depot built by the Empire and is one of the few such platforms remaining during the New Republic era. For over twenty years, the *Colossus* has been partially submerged on the ocean planet Castilon. The station's administrator is Captain Imanuel Doza, a former Imperial officer. He and his daughter, Torra Doza, reside in the elite Doza Tower.

The station is defended by Ace Squadron, a starfighter pilot team whose members spend their ample free time engaging in races such as the famous Platform Classic. Captain Doza is keen to promote the events because the spectators bring much-needed business to the station. The members of Ace Squadron (Hype Fazon, Freya Fenris, Torra Doza, Griff Halloran, and Bo Keevil) all reside in luxurious suites in Doza Tower, which has an exclusive communal lounge. *Colossus* provides more than just starship fuel. It has a large resident community with merchants selling goods in an open market. The market provides for all of the residents' and visitors' basic needs, with vendors of food, clothing, trinkets, and wares from offworld. There are dining establishments and taverns such as Aunt Z's. Lodging is also available. Resident scavengers scour the seabed for old shipwrecks and process them at the station's loading docks. They sell their finds to the Office of Acquisitions, run by Flix and Orka. Their salvages provide a source of commerce on the station—parts for racers and the station itself—and they also supply local garages like the one owned by Jarek Yeager. Resistance spy Zak Xiono works for Yeager along with co-workers Neeku Vozo and Tam Ryvora.

The engineers of *Colossus* are a group of native Chelidae. They keep the station running and prove helpful allies for Kaz Ziono, in part because they move unseen in the depths of the station and know much of what goes on in every corner.

The First Order takes a keen interest in *Colossus*, desiring to use the platform as a staging ground for their growing military in preparation for an assault on the New Republic and the Resistance. Under the oversight of Captain Phasma, Major Elrik Vonreg and Commander Pyre hire Kragan Gorr and his pirate gang to harass *Colossus*. They pressure Captain Doza into contracting with the First Order to provide protection, in exchange for use of the platform. Realizing his own Ace Squadron is insufficient to handle the recurring pirate threat, Doza reluctantly agrees. The First Order soon takes over operations and all security on the platform, confining residents and arresting troublemakers. Kaz Xiono leads his friends at the station against the First Order occupiers. They sink the station, leaving only Doza Tower above water, but this fails to dissuade the First Order. When Kaz discovers that the station is actually a ship with a capable hyperdrive, he and Neeku activate the engines while Ace Squadron fights off the First Order's TIE fighters. Synara San leads Kragan's pirates and joins the *Colossus* residents in fighting off the First Order. They all then escape aboard the *Colossus* into hyperspace—though their final destination is unknown to all.

Commercial Castilon
Colorful awnings running along the side of the *Colossus* cover the bustling marketplace *(bottom left)*, which acts as a meeting place for locals such as dock worker Orthog and friendly Arcona Garma *(left)*.

AUNT Z'S TAVERN

APPEARANCES Res
LOCATION *Colossus* station

The eponymous Aunt Z's Tavern (owned by the Gilliand Z'Vk'Thkrkza) is the most popular cantina on the *Colossus*. Aunt Z is assisted by her service droid Glitch. The tavern has seating at the bar, in alcoves around the room, and on a balcony facing Doza Tower. Entertainment includes watching local races (and betting on them), two arcade areas, a holodart system, and a jukebox. The venue is decorated with flags emblazoned with racer emblems, old battle helmets, and a reproduction of art from the nose of the *Crumb Bomber*, a Republic ship that once adorned Old Jho's Pit Stop on Lothal.

"We're not sure how to describe a weapon of this scale." TEMMIN "SNAP" WEXLEY

STARKILLLER BASE

In the shadowy far reaches of the galaxy, the First Order builds a technological terror within a planet. Starkiller Base is a new generation of superweapon that vastly exceeds the Death Star in destructive power—and threatens to end both the Resistance and the New Republic.

APPEARANCES Res, VII, FoD **REGION** Unknown Regions **SECTOR** Mobile **SYSTEM** Mobile **PRIMARY TERRAIN** Snowy mountains, forests, ice fields

STAR POWER

Once the Starkiller weapon is fully charged, it projects a beam of energy from its firing shaft through hyperspace at speeds faster than light. The blinding red beam is capable of destroying entire star systems on the other side of the galaxy. General Hux inaugurates Starkiller Base by using it to annihilate the Hosnian system, including the New Republic's capital on Hosnian Prime. Unlike the Empire's Death Star, Starkiller Base does not need to travel to the vicinity of the intended target to fire upon it with precision. This gives the First Order an unparalleled tactical advantage.

A MYSTERIOUS WORLD

Starkiller Base is the central symbol of mighty military power in Supreme Leader Snoke's expanding forces—yet it has humble origins. The planet lies hidden away in the Unknown Regions of the galaxy, visited by few explorers until its discovery by the Empire. It is a fertile world of dense forests and vibrant ecosystems, rich in natural resources, including a bountiful supply of kyber crystals that the Empire mines to fuel the Death Star's superlaser. Later, the world is discovered by the First Order, who harvests the remaining crystals and repurposes the planet as a mobile weapon of unimaginable power.

Draining a sun

The Starkiller superweapon, based on top-secret Imperial research, rapidly drains and pulls a host star's energy into its core using a collector on the surface. There, the energy is held in a containment field where it is stabilized and regulated by a thermal oscillator, before being unleashed on the intended target or targets.

Engineering masterpiece
An icy, eerie globe constructed to be a devastating weapon, Starkiller Base is a menacing benchmark of the First Order's advanced technological achievements.

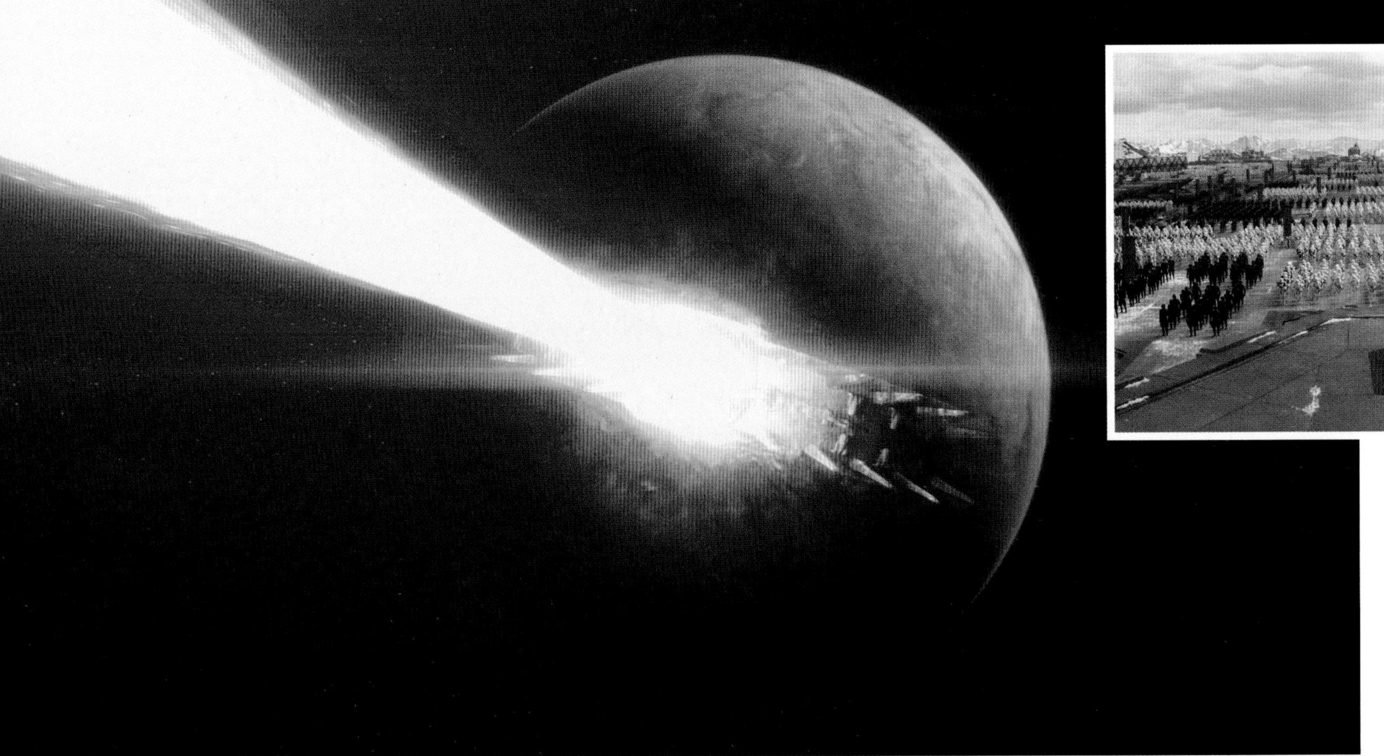

Calculating General
General Hux makes a speech to troops assembled in the parade ground before the weapon is fired. However, the destruction of Hosnian Prime is no mere display of First Order power. Hux calculates that the unexpected atrocity will force the Resistance to respond, and thus reveal the location of their secret base—and the First Order's next target.

LIFE ON THE BATTLE STATION

Starkiller Base is well guarded. Assault walkers, TIE fighters, and snowtroopers aboard speeders regularly patrol the planet's surface. Inside the base, First Order officers command impressive barracks of stormtroopers. They are supported by sentry and patrol droids, which sweep corridors, storage bays, and landing platforms. However, danger is still ever-present on the base: despite decades of research and cutting-edge technology, a planet is not an ideal vessel to hold the power of a sun. Tremendous storms and tectonic disturbances are a constant problem. Charging the weapon subjects one half of the planet's surface to dangerous radiation, while firing the weapon sends a shockwave that obliterates vast expanses of forest on the other half.

STARKILLER'S DEMISE

Threatened with the impending destruction of the Resistance base on D'Qar, Han Solo and his friends race to Starkiller Base aboard the *Millennium Falcon*. Once inside, Han, Finn, and Chewbacca capture Captain Phasma and force her to drop the Starkiller's shields. After locating Rey, who had been taken prisoner but escaped, the team detonates explosives, creating a hole in the armored housing of Starkiller's thermal oscillator. Meanwhile, pilot Poe Dameron leads a team of Resistance starfighters in an aerial assault on the base. Poe destroys the thermal oscillator, which destabilizes the containment field and causes an energy breach—demolishing the entire planet.

Angry prisoner After switching off the shields, the captive Captain Phasma warns Han and Finn that their plan will be hard to pull off, and that her troops will storm the block and kill them.

Fiery inferno A ferocious blaze rips through space as Starkiller Base explodes in a riot of color and light.

"Why does everyone wanna go back to Jakku?" FINN TO REY

JAKKU

Jakku may be a desolate junkyard planet, but this barren world plays a pivotal role in ending the Empire. Decades later, the First Order arrives in search of Luke Skywalker—and inadvertently awakens the destiny of a young scavenger named Rey.

APPEARANCES VII, FoD **REGION** Inner Rim **SECTOR** Western Reaches
SYSTEM Jakku **PRIMARY TERRAIN** Desert wastelands, sand dunes, rocky outcrops

Extreme environment

Jakku is a planet of sizzling temperatures and scorched wastes, but despite these harsh conditions, life persists. Native sentient species include the Teedo and Uthuthma, and non-sentient species include the nightwatcher worm, which tunnels through sand and attacks its prey from below, and iron-beaked carrion birds called steelpeckers. Notable immigrant settlements, apart from Niima Outpost, include Cratertown, Blowback Town, and Reestkii.

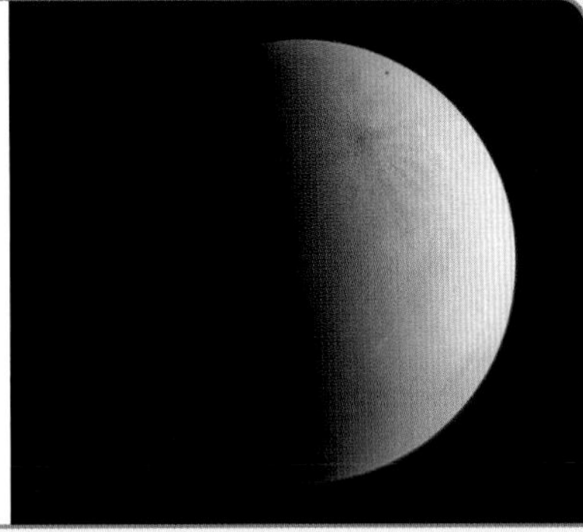

TUANUL VILLAGE

Religious hermits have a long historical presence on Jakku. Tuanul Village is a commune of followers of the Force in the remote Kelvin Ravine. Noted explorer and traveler Lor San Tekka settles in Tuanul, but a fateful meeting with Resistance pilot Poe Dameron concerning the whereabouts of Luke Skywalker also leads the First Order there. Blasters fire and dwellings burn as stormtroopers attack the village. Kylo Ren interrogates Lor San Tekka and captures Poe, before the stormtroopers are ordered to round up the villagers and kill them. Amid the resulting massacre, Poe's droid, BB-8, manages to escape with Lor San Tekka's map of Skywalker's location.

EARLY JAKKU

Once a forested world with seas full of varied life, Jakku has been rendered a barren globe by cataclysmic events. Emperor Palpatine believes ancient relics on the planet might hold a mysterious significance, so he orders an archaeological expedition. This site becomes an Imperial Observatory, housing a weapons facility, research base, and maps of secret navigational routes through the Unknown Regions. At the end of the Galactic Civil War, the New Republic discovers Imperial forces defending Jakku and the Observatory. Both sides take part in a major battle in space and on the planet itself. A portion of the Empire's forces escapes to the Unknown Regions, but, by the battle's end, the Empire has suffered a resounding defeat.

NIIMA OUTPOST

After the Battle of Jakku, profit-seeking Niima the Hutt founds an outpost to salvage hardware and supplies from the many shipwrecks, becoming one of Jakku's largest settlements. When Niima is assassinated, entrepreneur Unkar Plutt fills the void left in the local scrap trade. From his concession stand, Unkar barters food rations and water in return for Imperial and New Republic ship parts, computer systems, and supplies salvaged by scavengers of many species, including Dybrinthe, Abednedo, and humans. Lonely scavenger Rey is one such local, who searches old Star Destroyers for scrap parts, cleans them up, and trades them with greedy Unkar to earn a meager supply of food rations.

Marooned walker
An old wreck of an Imperial AT-AT walker, lying on its side in the sand, serves as Rey's home. Sitting in the shade of one of its enormous feet, Rey surveys the desert in her territory.

Starship Graveyard
Numerous ships belonging to both the New Republic and the Empire lay scattered and half-submerged in a graveyard of windswept sand dunes. The starships are a treasure trove of scrap for eager scavengers.

DANGEROUS WORLD

Jakku's deserts and settlements present all sorts of dangers. After Rey rescues BB-8 from a scrap-dealer, it's clear that the little droid would rather stick with her than take the risk of drowning in the Sinking Fields' sands or getting lost in Kelvin Ridge. The next day at Niima Outpost, Unkar's thugs attack Rey and try to steal BB-8, but Rey is more than a match for them. However, danger soon rears its ugly head again: just after Rey and BB-8 meet Finn, the First Order appears in search of the Resistance astromech. The newly formed team must dash through stalls and duck under tents to dodge TIE fighter fire before commandeering the *Millennium Falcon*. The Starship Graveyard becomes a perilous obstacle course as Rey pilots the *Falcon* through it, trying to escape the pursuing TIEs.

D'QAR

APPEARANCES VII, VIII **REGION** Outer Rim
SECTOR Sanbra **SYSTEM** Ileenium
PRIMARY TERRAIN Jungles, mountains, and plains

D'Qar is located on the edge of the Mid Rim and Outer Rim Territories, and is relatively close to both Naboo and Crait. Though there isn't any indigenous intelligent life there now, D'Qar once supported an ancient civilization, which is now extinct and whose once-great cities have long since been consumed by the jungles. D'Qar serves as a small rebel outpost during the Galactic Civil War, and then serves as the Resistance headquarters until the Battle of Starkiller Base.

TAKODANA

APPEARANCES VII **REGION** Western Reaches and Mid Rim
SECTOR Tashtor **SYSTEM** Takodana
PRIMARY TERRAIN Temperate forests and seas

Takodana is a peaceful garden world, relatively isolated between the Inner Rim and Outer Rim. It sits on a hyperspace route between Noe'ha'on and Chalcedon, and is connected to the Ring of Kafrene via the Biox Detour. Takodana is a haven for spacers and the disreputable on their way in and out of the galactic frontier. Takodana has a sparse native population of less than one million. The largest city—still relatively small—is Andui. The planet has remained neutral in major conflicts and has not seen war for centuries—until the arrival of the Empire at the end of the Galactic Civil War.

Let me do the talking
Han Solo, Rey, Finn, and BB-8 head toward Maz's castle. Han warns them not to stare "at any of it."

MAZ KANATA'S CASTLE

APPEARANCES VII **LOCATION** Takodana

Maz Kanata offers refuge from all the troubles of the galaxy. Her fortress tavern is a safe haven for the weary, the hunted, travelers, explorers, dignitaries, and galactic entrepreneurs. No fights are allowed on the premises, and any violation of Maz's cardinal rule will get guests banned or thrown into the dungeons below the castle. Maz provides food, lodging, and entertainment with live music and gambling. Her list of available services goes well beyond that however, with loans and appraisals, repairs, supplies, medical assistance, maps, and valuable information. Maz takes a percentage of all business deals made on her premises, which are collected by her droid, MD-8D9. While the first night's room and board is free, all must pay after that. The favorable conditions at the castle ensure many long-term guests, who lounge in the restaurant and bar for days on end and find it easy to forge new contacts in the cordial environment.

The castle may be relatively peaceful under Maz's ownership, but it is still a hotbed of underworld activity. Maz herself has a legendary career in piracy, despite being equally renowned for her hospitality.

She hosts high-stakes gambling, while bounty hunters, dealers in illicit merchandise, and pirates conduct unseemly deals at her tables and in private meeting rooms in the towers.

Maz's basement is full of ancient relics—cultural artifacts and historical pieces, including items associated with the Jedi and other Force-wielders—with which she feels a connection. The castle itself sits on an ancient battleground of the Jedi and Sith, and its lower levels date from the Jedi occupation of Takodana.

Maz is particularly fond of smugglers Han Solo and Chewbacca, who are frequent visitors to her castle. While listless and hungover, Han meets fellow smuggler Sana Starros just outside the castle. After dispatching some Hassk mercenaries, Sana offers him a smuggling job before leaving. When she later returns to the castle with contraband in tow and bounty hunters hot on her tail, Sana, Han, and Chewbacca have to quickly flee aboard the *Millennium Falcon*.

Following the Battle of Endor, Han returns to the castle to meet an Imperial turncoat, who will be able to help him free Kashyyyk. When the Empire arrives, Han works with Inferno Squad to stop them.

Decades later, Han brings Rey and Finn to meet his old friend Maz at her lakeside castle in hopes that she can help him transfer the droid BB-8 to Leia Organa (without actually dealing with Leia himself). The resident droid, GA-97, alerts the Resistance of BB-8's arrival at the castle, while bounty hunter Bazine Netal notifies the First Order. This castle intrigue kicks off a race between the two forces to recover the droid first. Meanwhile, Rey hears voices coming from the basement, where she finds Luke Skywalker's first lightsaber and receives a vision of her past and future. In the aftermath of the battle between the First Order and the Resistance, the castle lies in ruins.

Life in the castle
Strono "Cookie" Tuggs steps away from the kitchen to receive praise for this evening's dinner from Professor Allium and friends (*above*). Maz is reunited with her old friend Han Solo *(above left)*.

HOSNIAN PRIME

APPEARANCES Res, VII **REGION** Core Worlds **SECTOR** Unknown **SYSTEM** Hosnian **PRIMARY TERRAIN** Cities

Hosnian Prime is an urban world dominated by beautiful cities of towering architecture. It is a hub not only of government, but also commerce and education, with sprawling shopping complexes, museums, and universities.

The planet serves as a temporary capital of the New Republic. Unlike the Empire and the Old Republic before it, the New Republic is not based on Coruscant. The New Republic's temporary capital is chosen by democratic election in an effort to make member worlds feel more included. It is from Hosnian Prime that Leia Organa's parentage is leaked during her campaign for First Senator, ending her political career and leading to her focusing on the formation of the Resistance. Unimaginable tragedy strikes when the First Order destroys the entire Hosnian system using its superweapon known as Starkiller Base.

Liberty dies
General Organa's emissary, Korr Sella, watches in horror as the energy beam from Starkiller Base penetrates the atmosphere and obliterates the planet (*left*). Hosnian Prime has many large cities that are visible from space (*above*).

Resistance victory
The Resistance gathers to celebrate the destruction of Starkiller Base and welcome the strike force back.

RESISTANCE BASE

APPEARANCES VII, VIII **LOCATION** D'Qar

Following surveys of D'Qar, the Rebel Alliance builds a small outpost on the planet, but the end of the Galactic Civil War eliminates the need for a full base. When the New Republic refuses to heed Leia Organa's warnings regarding the First Order, Leia establishes the Resistance and decides to use the old Alliance base on D'Qar as its new headquarters. Leia sends engineers to expand and update the facility before moving her forces to the base. Fast-growing trees must constantly be cut back on the base to keep runways and bunker exits clear.

For years, Leia directs her small military from this base. She sends Poe Dameron and the rest of Black Squadron on a vital mission to locate Lor San Tekka, hoping that he can point them toward the secret location of her brother, Luke Skywalker.

After Hosnian Prime's destruction, the First Order target D'Qar with Starkiller Base. The Resistance moves quickly to launch an offensive against the First Order superweapon and destroy it before it can recharge. Now that the First Order is alerted to its presence on D'Qar, the Resistance know that it has no future at that location. Leia orders an immediate evacuation, but she does not leave before holding a brief funeral for her deceased husband, Han Solo. During the evacuation, which is organized by Lieutenant Kaydel Connix, the Resistance fleet waits in orbit, ready to provide safe harbor to the base personnel. Just when everything seems safe, the First Order arrive to annihilate the desperate rebels. Despite a successful escape from D'Qar, the Resistance is now pursued in space by its relentless enemy.

Lucky escape
The last U-55 loadlifter leaves the base, just as the First Order dreadnought fires upon the location.

D'Qar operations
The Resistance ground crew are hard at work repairing a power generator (*above*). C-3PO, Admiral Statura, and General Organa discuss the attack on Starkiller Base from the Resistance Command Center (*right*).

AHCH-TO

APPEARANCES VII, VIII **REGION** Unknown Regions
SECTOR Uncharted **SYSTEM** Ahch-To
PRIMARY TERRAIN Oceans and rocky islands

Mysterious Ahch-To is the home of the first Jedi temple. It has many names in ancient legends, but it is absent from nearly all star-charts—except one obtained by scholar Lor San Tekka—and thus nearly lost to legend. Luke Skywalker retreats to Ahch-To and its remote temple island, intending to live out the rest of his days in reclusive exile, until his peace is disturbed by Rey.

Ahch-To is not an easy place in which to thrive. Covered mostly by dark seas, small islands dot the surface where rough water and howling winds carve rocky ledges adorned with feeble zones of vegetation. Nonetheless, birds, fish, sea mammals, and great leviathans of the deep do flourish here. Small, flighted porgs nest in colonies along the cliffs, feeding their young with regurgitated fish and Ahch-Tonian grubs. Thala-sirens nurse their young peacefully on the rocky shores, providing a dairy source for other island residents.

Edible fish from the seas include fingerlip garpon, twinfin hyacander, and spetan channelfish. Fish are caught by the Lanais, the most intelligent species to live above the surface of the waters. They inhabit many islands and their cultures can differ significantly on each. At Luke's location—the origin point of the Jedi Order—is a settlement of Lanai matriarchs known as the Caretakers. The white-robed creatures consider it their sacred duty to maintain the ancient structures on the island and tolerate Luke's presence among them. The males, who spend most of their time out at sea, are known as Visitors. They return to the island on a monthly basis, when a festival is held with music and dancing. They share their catch with the Caretakers as well, who dry, smoke, and salt the fish in their little village.

An ancient Jedi village stands on the south side of the island, where Luke lives in a conical stone hut. After Rey arrives, she sleeps in a similar hut nearby. A landing pad is located nearby, down a long, stone stairway, where Chewbacca waits with the *Millennium Falcon*. Meanwhile, Luke's X-wing is submerged in a cove to the east.

Interrupted exile
Luke and Rey first meet in a natural amphitheater known as the Saddle on the temple island. Luke's first instinct is to drive away his Force-sensitive visitor.

Primitive existence
Luke's stone hut *(above)* in the Jedi village on the south of the temple island is built to withstand extreme weather conditions. The door is a salvaged piece of Luke's submerged X-wing.

"Do you think I came to the most unfindable place in the galaxy for no reason at all?"

LUKE SKYWALKER

FIRST JEDI TEMPLE

APPEARANCES VIII **LOCATION** Ahch-To

When Luke Skywalker's efforts to train his nephew, Ben Solo, as a Jedi end in disaster, he is distraught. He seeks out the first Jedi temple and the original Jedi teachings for answers. With much questing, he finally locates Ahch-To, an island housing the temple itself, and the tree library holding the sacred Jedi texts.

The temple sits on the highest perch at the western end of the temple island, where it has existed for untold millennia. Other temples once existed, but were destroyed by the Empire. Ahch-To's temple is a simple cave housing meditation plinths, one of which is perched just outside the west entrance, overlooking the sea. It is here that Luke eventually spends his final moments, looking out at the sunset of the planet's twin suns. In the center of the cave is a mosaic beneath a pool of water, depicting the Prime (first) Jedi at balance with the Force—in peaceful coexistence with both light and dark.

Down the temple stairs, a little to the east in a protected nook of the island, is a centuries-old uneti tree. Inside the hollowed tree is a reading chamber housing the oldest known examples of the earliest Jedi teachings. The tree is destroyed by the Force ghost of Jedi Master Yoda, but not before the books are taken by Rey.

As the birthplace of the Jedi Order, ancient Ahch-To has strange and powerful spots that are strong in the Force. In particular, Rey finds herself drawn to a natural blowhole on the eastern side of the temple island that is a dangerous source of dark side energy. There, she experiences visions of her past and future, and must face the possibilities of who she is and what she could become.

Meeting of minds
Rey has visions of Ahch-To's temple island before arriving on it. Despite having cut himself off from the Force, Luke reluctantly agrees to teach Rey the ways of the Jedi.

CANTONICA

APPEARANCES VIII, FoD **REGION** Outer Rim Territories **SECTOR** Corporate **SYSTEM** Cantonica **PRIMARY TERRAIN** Deserts

Cantonica is a desolate world, apart from the resort destination of Canto Bight, where wealthy tourists and war profiteers go to play. The landscape outside that isolated paradise is foreboding—menaced by sandstorms and scorching winds. What little vegetation exists is mainly cactus and scrub brush. Cantonica is located within the Corporate Sector—a fiefdom that allows independent systems to govern themselves. This autonomy has drawn suspicion from the Empire and the First Order but, for now, remains a safe haven for smugglers, tourists, and gamblers alike.

CANTO BIGHT

APPEARANCES VIII **LOCATION** Cantonica

Canto Bight is a playground for the wealthiest in the galaxy. The city is made up of luxury hotels, restaurants, casinos, shopping plazas, spas, racetracks, sporting events, and endless forms of decadent entertainment. Canto Bight is the planetary capital, but much of the planet is a vast wasteland with few other places of interest. The city sits on the coast of the Sea of Cantonica, boasted as the largest artificial ocean in the galaxy. After the destruction of Starkiller Base and the evacuation of the Resistance from D'Qar, rebels Finn, Rose Tico, and BB-8 come to Canto Bight to look for the Master Codebreaker. Their efforts are unsuccessful, however, and they leave the planet with the aid of an untrustworthy slicer named DJ, whom they meet in the local jail.

Maintaining an image
Beneath the beautiful, wealthy surface of Canto Bight lies a strict regime. The Canto Bight Police Department will not tolerate any infractions, corruption, or crime.

CANTO CASINO

APPEARANCES VIII
LOCATION Canto Bight, Cantonica

The Canto Casino is the crown jewel of Cantonica, lined with stained-glass windows and expensive furnishings. It includes a lavish hotel with rooms to fit every size and shape, a shopping concourse with merchandise from across the galaxy, 22 restaurants full of delights to suit every digestive sack, and, nearby, the renowned Canto Racetrack with stables for fathiers and other quick-footed beasts. The casino has private game rooms where the fortunes of entire worlds are won and lost. Guests are served exotic cocktails of all kinds by protocol waiter droids.

> "I wish I could put my fist through this whole lousy, beautiful town."
>
> **ROSE TICO**

CRAIT

APPEARANCES VIII **REGION** Outer Rim Territories **SECTOR** Unknown **SYSTEM** Crait (PZ-43 Gamma) **PRIMARY TERRAIN** Salt flats, mountains, briny seas

Crait is a remote world rich in minerals. The planet's broad flats are dusted with white salt, while just beneath the surface are reserves of blood-red rhodochrosite, ground to sand. Further below the surface, in vast caves, the same rhodochrosite elements form towering crystals.

The harsh salt flats of Crait do not promote a large diversity of life, but some species do thrive. Vulptices hunt for small animals, insects, and crystal bats that are found in rhodochrosite caves. All life is adapted to the high mineral content of the environment, and utilizes it to form exoskeletons, spines, and protective coverings. Sunken waterways channel rare rainfall to briny lakes, some connected to springs and sinkholes where fish and crustaceans breed, with large, dangerous specimens nesting deep within wells heated by hydrothermal vents.

Before the outbreak of the Galactic Civil War, Bail Organa believes the planet is an ideal place for a new rebel outpost, and authorizes the building of a small base in an abandoned mine. It isn't until a young Princess Leia investigates the Crait outpost that she discovers her parents are building a rebellion against the Empire. Not long after her visit, the site is abandoned.

During the Galactic Civil War, Leia returns with Luke Skywalker and Han Solo to look into establishing a new base, but they are attacked by the Empire's SCAR Squad. Though they fend off the Imperials, it is clear that Crait is not suitable for the Rebel Alliance. The outpost is left derelict for decades, used only by the occasional miner, working in the caves with their droids.

Leia doesn't forget about Crait, however, and keeps the small world on her radar for future use, knowing its location has fallen off many star-charts. As such, she recommends the location as a refuge for the Resistance as it attempts to escape the First Order.

Kylo Ren and his forces assault the stronghold with AT-M6 walkers, while the Resistance fights back in vain using decrepit old V-4X-D ski speeders. The confrontation culminates in a lightsaber duel between Kylo Ren and Luke Skywalker, which serves as a distraction, giving the Resistance remnant time to escape. They pass through a cave system and flee aboard the *Millennium Falcon*.

Battle-ready
As an abandoned rebel base, many fortified structures remain on Crait, including deep trenches linked to the stronghold via tunnels.

Ground disturbance
When the First Order and Resistance forces face off on Crait, the salt flats make for a dramatic battleground. The First Order's AT-M6s *(above)* and the Resistance's ski speeders *(right)* drag up the red minerals from below.

BEHIND THE SCENES

"*Star Wars* is very plot driven. Every minute and a half we're on to a new set. So you have to instantly believe in it." **Rick McCallum, producer of the Prequel Trilogy**

Space fantasy and science-fiction films may live or die based on their locations, as dubious scenery and/or obvious props can spoil the illusion. *Star Wars* has always used a combination of beautiful, real-world locations and incredible production design. From the Death Star's cavernous hangar and Tatooine's burning deserts to the snows of Hoth, the jungles of Dagobah, and the vertigo-inducing skyline of Coruscant, fans have marveled at the amazingly lifelike worlds created for the movies.

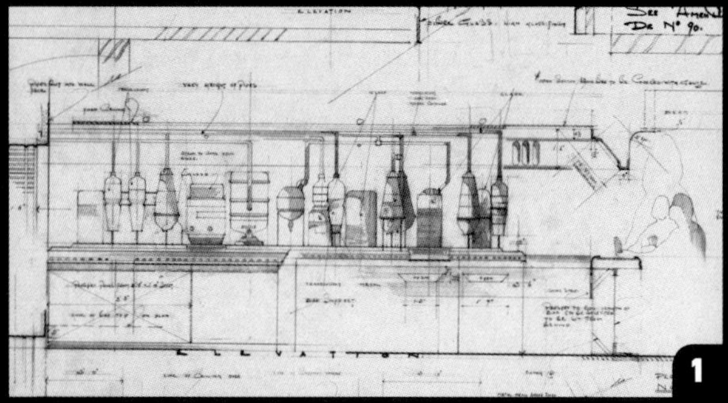

1

2

A blueprint by Alan Roderick-Jones of production designer John Barry's Mos Eisley Cantina set, showing the bar, for *Star Wars:* Episode IV *A New Hope* **(1)**. Anthony Daniels (C-3PO), Mark Hamill, Alec Guinness, and Kenny Baker (R2-D2) filming on location for Episode IV, with the Tunisian desert standing in for Tatooine **(2)**.

Shooting Han Solo's rescue of Luke Skywalker from the icy wastes of planet Hoth in Finse, Norway, for *Star Wars:* Episode V *The Empire Strikes Back*; a tauntaun puppet stands in the foreground **(3)**. At Elstree Studios, UK, the crew shoots a scene on Episode V's Dagobah jungle set, production designed by Norman Reynolds **(4)**, where Yoda trains Luke Skywalker in the ways of the Jedi.

3

5

4

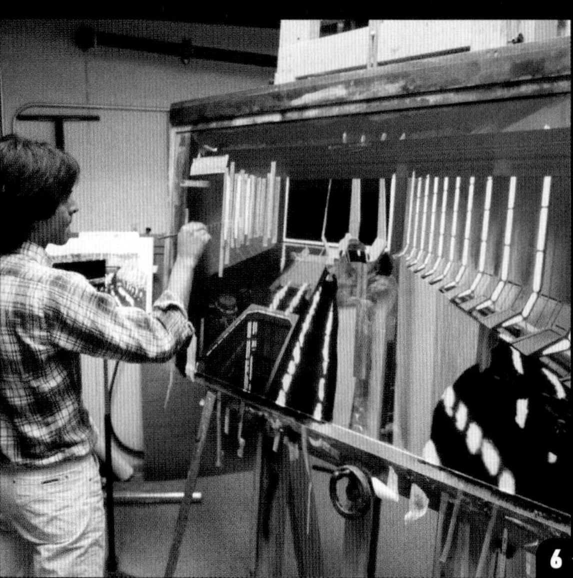

6

A detail of this production painting by Ralph McQuarrie visualizes the key elements of an entire scene: Darth Vader stands on the bridge of an Imperial Star Destroyer, a crewman, other Star Destroyers, and a distant planet lend perspective in the background **(5)**. Industrial Light & Magic matte artist Frank Ordaz works on a painting of the interior of the Death Star docking bay in *Star Wars:* Episode VI *Return of the Jedi* **(6)**.

Production designer Gavin Bocquet and director George Lucas examine a maquette model of Mos Espa on Tatooine for *Star Wars:* Episode I *The Phantom Menace* **(7)**. The spectacular Palace of Caserta in southern Italy becomes the setting for Episode I's Theed Palace on Naboo **(8)**, where several scenes were shot.

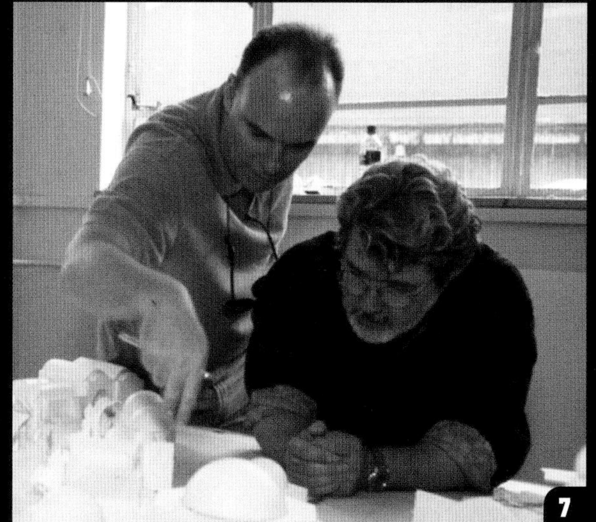

7

8

9

10

ILM model maker Grant Imahara works on the miniature set for the Coruscant street chase in *Star Wars:* Episode II *Attack of the Clones* **(9)**. ILM chief grip Tom Cloutier helps to light the Geonosis arena miniature set **(10)**.

11

Concept artist Warren Fu's pre-production painting of the Imperial rehabilitation center in *Revenge of the Sith*; Darth Sidious in the background **(11)**. Like much of the design for the animated series *Star Wars Rebels*, artist Andre Kirk's depiction of Lothal's sprawling Capital City was inspired by concept artist Ralph McQuarrie's production paintings for the original *Star Wars* trilogy **(12)**.

12

Concept artist Jon McCoy's pre-production painting of the sabacc game held at Fort Ypso lodge on Vandor during *Solo: A Star Wars Story* **(13).** A concept art painting of the *Colossus* fueling station on the planet Castilon for the animated TV series *Star Wars: Resistance* **(14)** by art director Amy Beth Christenson.

13

14

TECHNOLOGY

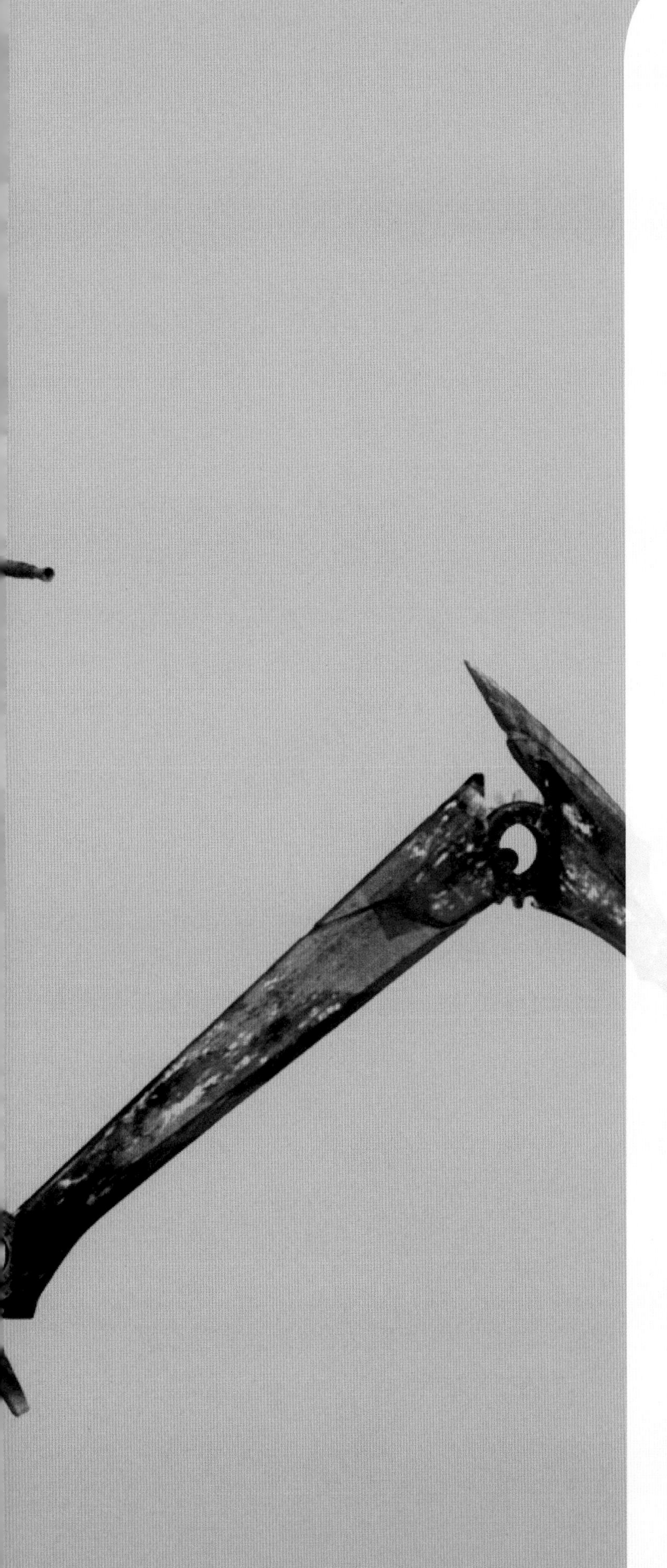

Although some cultures eschew technology, most embrace everything from basic tools and droids to sophisticated sensors and weapons systems.

Throughout the galaxy, most beings rely on various types of technology, whether advanced or primitive, to help them in their work duties as well as their everyday lives. Many utilize sensors to collect and examine data, and use energy shields and weapons for protection. They may also depend on droids for a multitude of tasks, ranging from running simple diagnostics to performing complicated medical procedures, or sending communications to flying starships.

While interplanetary trade eventually yields myriad technological developments, wars also spur innovation, as manufacturers and armorers are conscripted or compelled to develop new defensive and offensive weapons. The Jedi lightsaber is one of the most remarkable energy weapons ever made, and the system-destroying Starkiller Base is perhaps the most fearsome. However, while many technologically advanced civilizations believe that they are superior to comparatively primitive cultures, and are confident that they will easily prevail in any conflict, the Battle of Endor attests to the fact that technology alone does not guarantee victory.

"Roger, roger."

BATTLE DROID

Starship crew
General Grievous' flagship, the *Malevolence*, is crewed by 900 battle droids, who receive commands from the shipboard Central Control Computer to carry out complicated technical duties.

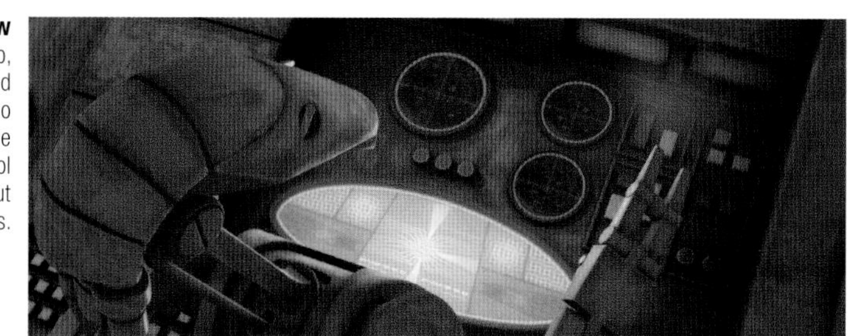

BATTLE DROID

Easily controlled, unquestioningly obedient, and inexpensive to mass-produce, battle droids are the primary troops in the Trade Federation's mechanized armies.

APPEARANCES I, II, CW, III, Reb **MANUFACTURER** Baktoid Combat Automata
MODEL B1 battle droid **TYPE** Battle droid

TECHNICAL CAPABILITY

The Trade Federation commissions battle droids with humanoid physiques for practical reasons, as this allows the droids to operate existing machinery, vehicles, and weapons originally designed for organic operators and pilots, saving the Federation unnecessary production costs or expensive retrofitting. The battle droid infantry pilots STAPs, MTTs, and AATs, as well as Trade Federation battleships and other vessels. Federation vessels that operate beyond the range of a Droid Control Ship have inboard Central Control Computers that coordinate the droid crews, enabling them to operate tactile computer consoles and communications stations.

INVASION FORCE

With their tall, gaunt, humanoid design, exposed joints, and metal finishes, battle droids bear an eerie resemblance to animated skeletons. Essentially mindless, lethal puppets, they are operated via a Central Control Computer housed in an orbital Droid Control Ship, a modified Trade Federation battleship that transmits both direct orders from the Federation's leaders and computer-automated commands. Peaceful civilizations and worlds without military defenses are easy targets for the Trade Federation. However, if a Droid Control Ship is destroyed, battle droids enter a stand-by hibernation mode that leaves them totally vulnerable.

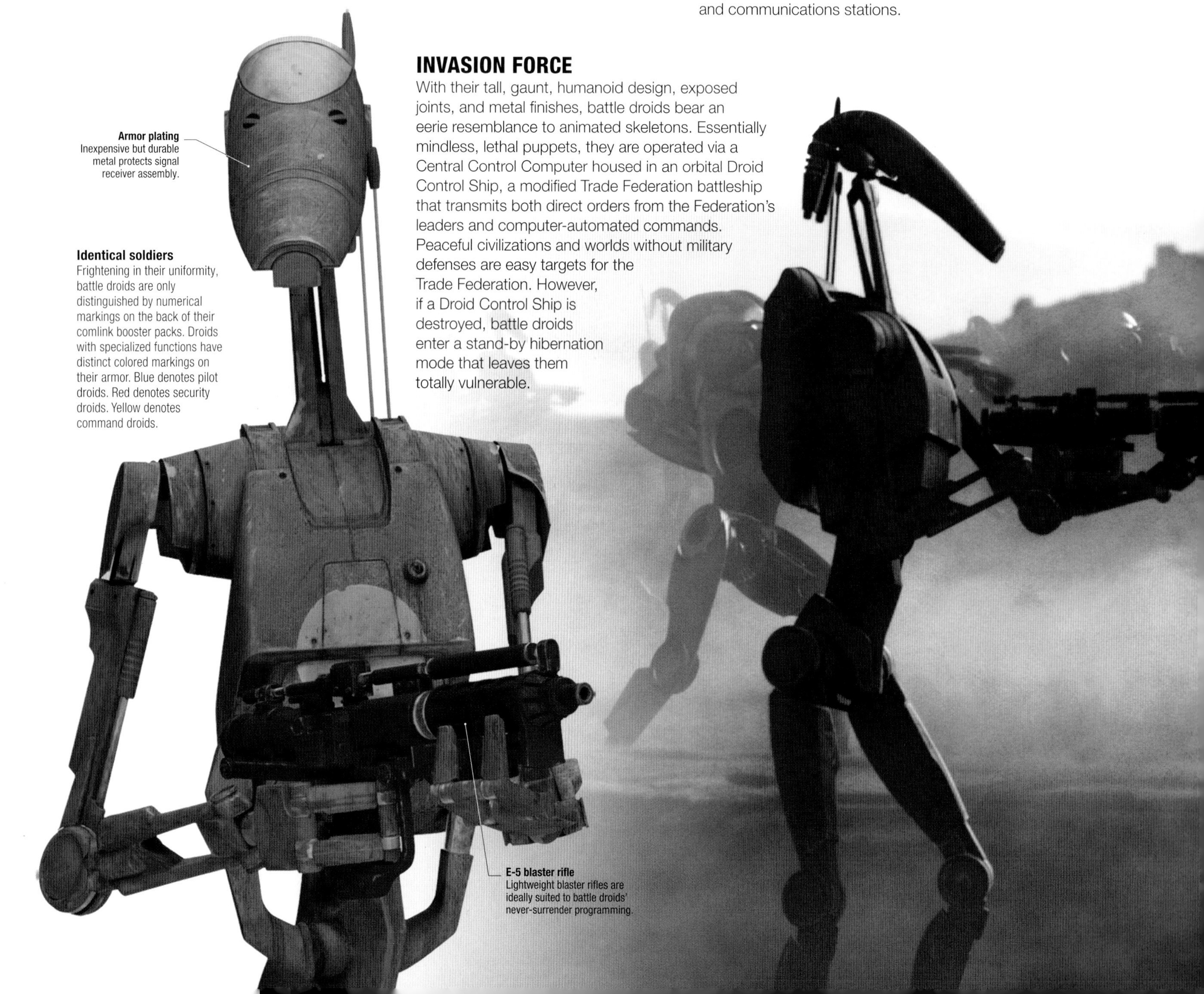

Armor plating
Inexpensive but durable metal protects signal receiver assembly.

Identical soldiers
Frightening in their uniformity, battle droids are only distinguished by numerical markings on the back of their comlink booster packs. Droids with specialized functions have distinct colored markings on their armor. Blue denotes pilot droids. Red denotes security droids. Yellow denotes command droids.

E-5 blaster rifle
Lightweight blaster rifles are ideally suited to battle droids' never-surrender programming.

Robotic army
Cheap to make, quick to assemble, battle droids roll off the production line at Baktoid Combat Automata's factories.

Covert agents
Three reprogrammed battle droids, painted blue to maintain their guise as innocuous pilots from a Separatist shuttle, follow their commander, R2-D2.

ASSEMBLY LINE

In choosing to rely on Central Control Computers to operate large armies of droids simultaneously, the budget-minded Trade Federation saves the astronomical costs that would have been required for the production of thousands of individual droid brains. The Federation contracts Baktoid Combat Automata to mass-produce B1 battle droids in the foundries-turned-factories on Geonosis.

REPROGRAMMED B1S

During the Clone Wars, Republic forces capture and disable three B1 battle droids, which are subsequently refurbished and reprogrammed to serve the Republic. After Separatists apprehend Jedi Master Even Piell and place him in a deadly prison known as the Citadel, Anakin Skywalker devises a rescue plan that involves conscripting the reprogrammed B1s to infiltrate the prison. Under the command of the astromech droid R2-D2, the B1s pilot a shuttle to deliver the other members of the rescue team to the Citadel. When a large number of enemy droids attack, the trio of B1s sacrifice themselves holding off the attack.

Calculated assault
Utilizing motion-capture data from highly trained organic soldiers, battle droids demonstrate an array of combat stances, positions, and maneuvers while fighting the newly formed Republic Army at the Battle of Geonosis.

The last battle
Much of the Agamar garrison is lost during the Imperial attack, but a small number of droids flee their holdout to face an uncertain future.

IMPERIAL ERA

After the Clone Wars end and the Separatist army is disabled, battle droids are still occasionally found throughout the galaxy, including the friendly R0-GR. Resourceful scavengers scour decommissioned Separatist factories, such as the facility on Akiva, to build droids of their own. Akivan native Temmin Wexley builds a heavily modified and lethal B1 named Mister Bones. A full garrison of battle droids remains active on Agamar after its commander, General Kalani, ignores the galaxy-wide instruction to shut down, deducing that the order is a Republic trick. Seventeen years later, the garrison is discovered by the *Ghost* crew and clone Captain Rex. Commander droid B1-268 captures the visitors, his first prisoners in two decades of service. The droids' victory is short-lived, however, as Imperial forces soon arrive, forcing the *Ghost* crew and the droids to work together to escape.

IMAGECASTER

APPEARANCES I, CW, III, FoD **MANUFACTURER** SoroSuub Corp.
MODEL SoroSuub Imagecaster **TYPE** Personal holoprojector

Commonly carried by members of the Jedi Order, the Imagecaster is a handheld, disc-shaped hologram projector, which displays three-dimensional images formed by the interference of light beams. The Imagecaster can be tuned with a comlink to carry a hologram transmission for face-to-face contact or can be used as an independent image recorder and projector. The device is sturdily constructed for field use and can hold up to 100 minutes of images. Jedi Master Qui-Gon Jinn loads his holoprojector with selected images of Queen Amidala's starship before he proceeds to the junkyard on Tatooine, where he hopes to obtain repair parts for the ship's hyperdrive.

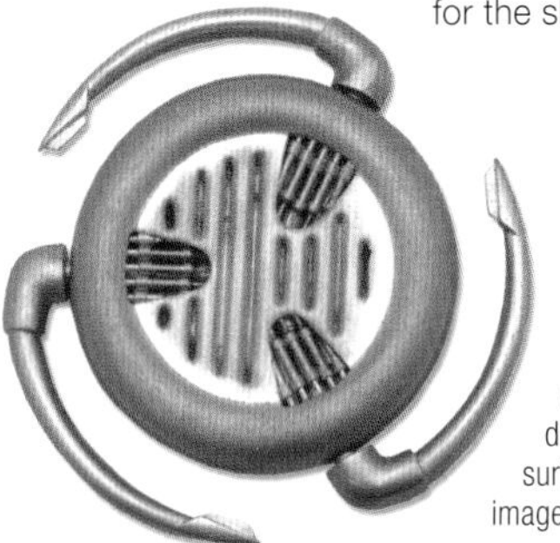

Utilitarian design
The Imagecaster's casing ring has three curved arms that rotate downward, allowing the device to stand on a level surface or link to a larger image projector.

Holographic image
Anakin Skywalker watches Qui-Gon Jinn using an Imagecaster to project a three-dimensional representation of Queen Amidala's starship.

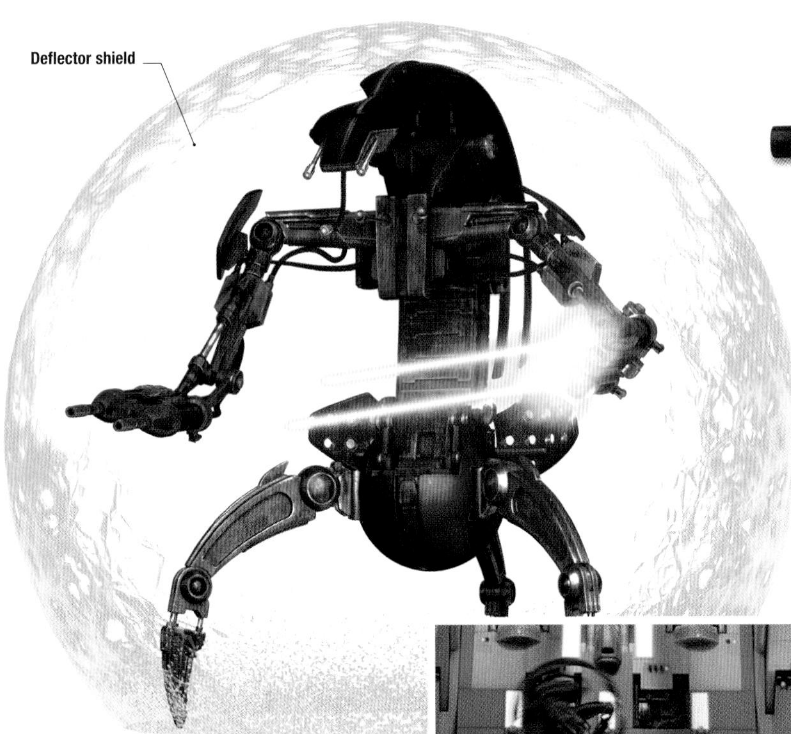

Deflector shield

Rolling mode
A droideka barrels across a starship's deck before opening fire on its target.

DROIDEKA (A.K.A. DESTROYER DROID)

APPEARANCES I, II, CW, III, Reb
MANUFACTURER Colicoids **TYPE** Battle droid

Unlike the spindly battle droid, whose humanoid frame allows a degree of versatility, the droideka is engineered with the sole function of completely annihilating its targets. Insectoid in its mix of curves and sharp angles, the droideka has heavy arms that carry immense twin blasters, which unleash destructive energy at a pounding pace. Compact deflector shield generators envelop the droid in a globe of protective energy. Although its three-legged gait is slow and awkward, the droideka can curl its body into a wheel-shaped form, which can roll on smooth surfaces at great speed. Prior to the blockade on Naboo, droidekas are used by criminal organizations, like the Xrexus Cartel, as well as large corporations, including Czerka. The Trade Federation uses droidekas aboard its starships for security and on the ground for combat operations; later they are part of the Separatist armies in the Clone Wars. During the Imperial era, droidekas continue to be used, but rarely on the same scale. On Agamar, a remnant of the Separatist droid army remains, including droidekas, who fight and then eventually ally with two Jedi and a clone.

E-5 DROID BLASTER

APPEARANCES I, II, CW, III, Reb
MANUFACTURER Baktoid Armor Workshop
MODEL E-5 **TYPE** Blaster rifle

Droid grip
The blaster is equipped with a continuous-fire trigger.

The standard-issue armament of B1 battle droids and BX-series droid commandos, the E-5 blaster rifle is a lightweight weapon with a large gas chamber that allows for powerful blasts. Based on a BlasTech design, the rifle has been reverse-engineered by Baktoid Armor for use by robotic soldiers, which will not feel the excessive heat it produces when it is repeatedly fired.

T-14 HYPERDRIVE

APPEARANCES I **MANUFACTURER** Nubian Design Collective **CLASS** 1.8
TYPE Hyperdrive

T-14 hyperdrive generators, which propel starships smoothly into hyperspace, are commonly used aboard ships produced by the Nubian Design Collective, such as the J-type 327 Nubian starship assigned to Queen Amidala of Naboo.

OBI-WAN KENOBI'S FIRST LIGHTSABER

APPEARANCES I
CREATOR Obi-Wan Kenobi
MODEL Lightsaber
TYPE Single-blade

Although visually similar to Qui-Gon's weapon, Obi-Wan's first lightsaber has a different internal mechanism. And while his kyber crystal typically emits a blue blade, it is temporarily replaced with a kohlen crystal on a mission to Pijal, causing the blade to turn orange. During a duel with Darth Maul on Naboo, Kenobi loses his lightsaber when it falls into a generator shaft.

GX-8 WATER VAPORATOR

APPEARANCES I, II, CW, III, Reb, RO, IV, VII **MANUFACTURER** Pretormin Environmental **MODEL** GX-8 water vaporator **TYPE** Moisture vaporator

Essential for survival on the desert planet Tatooine, GX-8 water vaporators coax moisture from the air by means of refrigerated condensers. Captured water accumulates on the condensers and is pumped or gravity-directed into storage cisterns. Vaporators are capable of collecting up to 1.5 liters (1½ quarts) of water per day.

PIT DROIDS

APPEARANCES I, II, CW, Reb, Res **MANUFACTURER** Serv-O-Droid, Inc. **MODEL** DUM-series pit droid **TYPE** Repair droid

Standing just over 1 meter (3 ft 3 in) tall, pit droids maintain podracer engines and cockpits, and are capable of lifting objects many times their own weight. The cheap, expendable droids run onto the racetrack to repair still-cycling superheated engines without hesitation. When not in use, they fold up into a compact stowed mode.

Tough construction
Hardened alloy casings can endure harsh Tatooine weather.

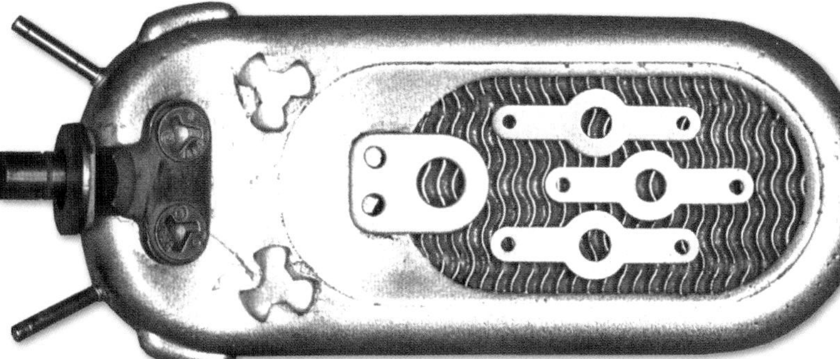

HUSH-98 COMLINK

APPEARANCES I, CW, III **MANUFACTURER** SoroSuub Corp. **MODEL** Hush-98 **TYPE** Handheld comlink

Comlinks are used for standard communication and to transmit and receive data. Many Jedi Knights are equipped with the Hush-98 comlink, which features a 100-kilometer (62-mile) range and complex security devices to prevent unauthorized interception. Built-in silence projectors allow Jedi to maintain stealth while communicating with their allies. Other components include a reception antenna, variable frequencies, encoding, and a sound-reproduction matrix. The Hush-98 is also capable of transmitting complex information such as blood sample data used to determine midi-chlorian levels.

ADVENTURER SLUGTHROWER RIFLE

APPEARANCES I, CW **MANUFACTURER** Czerka Arms **MODEL** Adventurer **TYPE** Slugthrower rifle

A projectile rifle with excellent aim over long distances, the Czerka Adventurer floods its chamber with a rich oxidizer as it detonates its shell, giving the projectile added punch and extra range. The weapon can be easily dismantled for concealed transport.

Long range
This projectile rifle can hit targets from up to 450 meters (1,476 feet).

TUSKEN RAIDER SNIPER RIFLE

APPEARANCES I, Reb, IV
MANUFACTURER Tusken Raiders
MODEL Tusken Cycler
TYPE Slugthrower

Built from stolen and scavenged parts, the Tusken Cycler is the standard projectile weapon used by Tatooine's Tusken Raiders for ranged combat. As a slugthrower-class rifle, it fires solid shots enveloped in energy instead of blaster bolts.

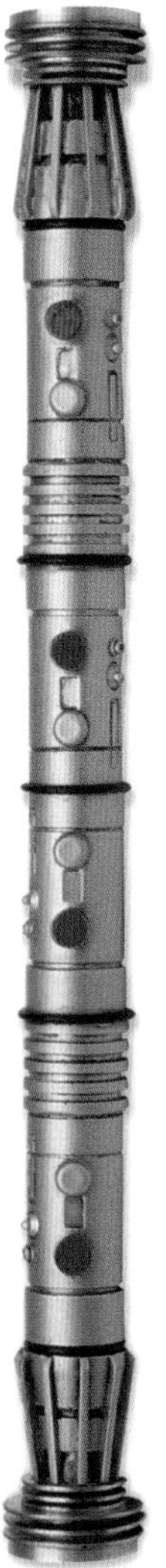

DARTH MAUL'S DOUBLE-BLADED LIGHTSABER

APPEARANCES I, CW **CREATOR** Darth Maul **MODEL** Handcrafted **TYPE** Double-bladed Sith lightsaber (two joined lightsabers)

The Sith Lord Darth Maul's primary weapon is a pair of identical red-bladed lightsabers connected at their respective pommels to form a double-bladed lightsaber. Crafted by Maul himself, the weapon contains two sets of internal components, allowing one set to act as backup for the other if necessary. Activator controls can ignite both blades simultaneously or one at a time, and each lightsaber also features blade modulation controls. The double-bladed lightsaber is traditionally used as a training device, but because it can be much more dangerous to its wielder than an enemy, most Sith have historically eschewed the weapon in favor of the single-bladed lightsaber. In Maul's expert hands, it becomes a whirling vortex of lethal energy.

It is with this blade that Maul kills his first Jedi—a Twi'lek Padawan named Eldra Kaitis. When Maul attacks the Jedi Master Qui-Gon Jinn on the planet Tatooine, Maul uses a single blade from his lightsaber during their duel but fails to strike down his opponent. Soon after, when Maul confronts Qui-Gon and his Jedi apprentice, Obi-Wan Kenobi, on Naboo, he activates both blades to fight the two Jedi at the same time. Maul slays Qui-Gon, but Obi-Wan's lightsaber cleaves through the joined pommels of Maul's weapon, leaving Maul with a single operational lightsaber. Despite Maul's deadly proficiency, Obi-Wan cuts Maul in half. Incredibly, Maul survives and manages to retain his one functional lightsaber. Years later, during the Clone Wars, Maul still possesses his weapon when he emerges from obscurity, and with it, he duels Obi-Wan and also his own former master, Darth Sidious. He loses the blade when he is defeated by Sidious.

Killing time
After years of extensive martial arts training, Maul relishes the opportunity to use his weapon against two Jedi on the planet Naboo *(left)*.

Two against one
Maul's savage prowess with two blades *(below)* is not enough to defeat Obi-Wan's single-bladed weapon.

Violent reunion
Wielding his sole remaining lightsaber, Maul resumes his duel with Obi-Wan during the Clone Wars.

ENERGY BALL (BOOMA)

APPEARANCES I, CW **MANUFACTURER** Otoh Gunga Defense League **MODEL** Gungan energy ball **TYPE** Energy weapon

Using the plasmic energy found deep in Naboo's porous crust, the Gungans have crafted a spherical grenade-type weapon they call a booma, or boomer. Made in many different sizes, these grenades are either thrown by hand, sling, or falumpaset-towed catapult. When they hit their target, their protective shells burst, releasing the plasma and a powerful electric shock.

GUNGAN PERSONAL ENERGY SHIELD

APPEARANCES I **MANUFACTURER** Otoh Gunga Defense League **MODEL** Standard issue personal energy shield
TYPE Personal energy shield

This handheld shield carried by soldiers of the Gungan Grand Army defends against light physical attacks as well as blaster fire. The ovoid-framed shield uses hydrostatic bubble technology and can deflect blaster bolts back at the shooter.

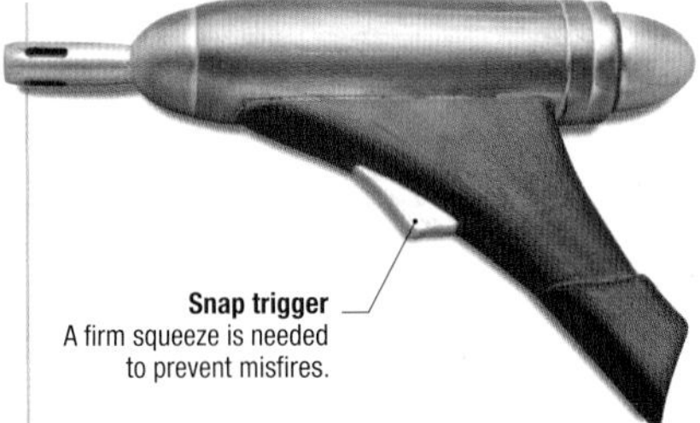

Snap trigger
A firm squeeze is needed to prevent misfires.

NABOO ROYAL PISTOL

APPEARANCES I, CW, FoD **MANUFACTURER** SoroSuub Corp. **MODEL** ELG-3A blaster pistol
TYPE Hold-out blaster

Lightweight, elegant, and functional, the SoroSuub ELG-3A is practically a standard accessory for diplomats and nobles who require a personal blaster. Padmé Amidala and her handmaidens carry the slim pistol. Most are designed for easy concealment, however there is a version with an extended barrel.

GUNGAN ATLATL

APPEARANCES I, CW **MANUFACTURER** Otoh Gunga Defense League **MODEL** Otoh Gunga standard issue atlatl
TYPE Bludgeoning/ranged weapon

Used by Gungans to launch energy balls at a greater distance than an unassisted arm can achieve, the atlatl is essentially a throwing stick that also serves as a highly effective blunt weapon. Atlatls are carved from a naturally insulating wood and can be wielded with one hand. They have a maximum range of 100 meters (328 ft) and an optimal range of 30 meters (98 ft).

KAMINOAN SABERDART

APPEARANCES II **CREATOR** Kaminoans
MODEL Handcrafted Kaminoan saberdart **TYPE** Toxic dart

Recognized by few experts outside the Outer Rim, the Kaminoan saberdart is a rare artifact. A small, fork-shaped dart with distinctive cuts on its side, it is used to deliver a deadly toxin. Although highly lethal, saberdarts may attract suspicion because they are so unique to the Kamino system.

Poison chamber
The toxins Malkite themfar and Fex-M3 can cause death in less than 10 seconds.

REMOTE

APPEARANCES II, CW, IV, Res, VII **MANUFACTURER** Industrial Automaton **MODEL** Marksman-H **TYPE** Training remote

Typically used as combat training tools, training remotes are small floating spheres equipped with relatively harmless blasters and an array of sensors. Jedi use remotes to hone their lightsaber skills, as well as their attunement to the Force. Jedi younglings usually wear vision-obscuring blast shields and use the Force to visualize a remote's location and actions, wielding lightsabers to block any incoming shots. As training sessions intensify, the remote begins to move more and more quickly and attacks with increasingly intense bursts of energy. Remotes are also extensively used by sharpshooters who want to polish their skills.

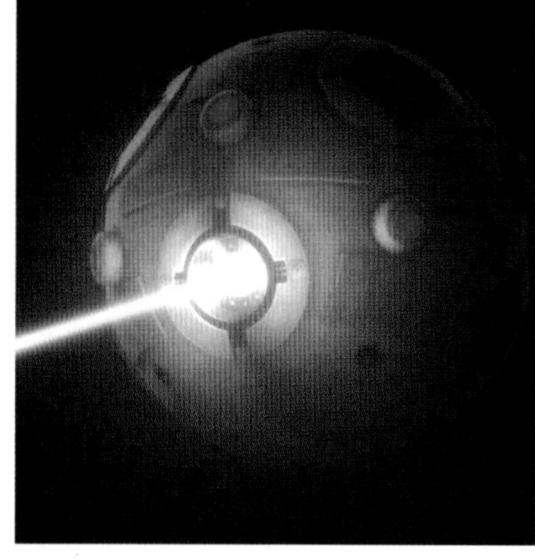

Lethal variation
Remotes can be modified to be defensive security weapons capable of firing deadly blasts of energy at intruders.

Learning tool
Ahsoka inspects Jedi initiates training with remotes aboard the *Crucible*.

Full-body protection
Armor allows clone troopers to march through deflector shield barriers and withstand hails of deadly projectiles or explosive blasts with impunity.

Design flaw
Inexperienced with human ergonomics, Kaminoans unintentionally built Phase I armor to be uncomfortable to sit in. Subsequent generations of armor correct this flaw.

PHASE I CLONE TROOPER ARMOR

APPEARANCES II, CW, III, Reb **MANUFACTURER** Kaminoan armorsmiths **MODEL** Phase I armor **TYPE** Body armor

Various types of armor have been developed for clone troopers to operate in different environments and atmospheres. The first series of clone troopers, deployed at the Battle of Geonosis, wear Phase I armor, which consists of 20 form-fitting plastoid-alloy composite plates sealed to a temperature-control body glove via magnatomic gription panels. In creating the armor, Kaminoan designers take inspiration from armor worn by the clones' genetic source, the bounty hunter Jango Fett, including his helmet with its distinctive T-shaped visor. The pressurized body glove also provides temporary protection against the vacuum of space.

DC-15 BLASTER RIFLE

APPEARANCES II, CW, III, Reb **MANUFACTURER** BlasTech Industries **MODEL** DC-15 blaster rifle **TYPE** Blaster rifle

A standard-issue weapon for clone troopers in the Grand Army of the Republic, the DC-15 blaster rifle uses a replaceable tibanna gas cartridge that yields up to 500 shots of charged plasma bolts when the weapon is set on low power. On maximum power, the DC-15 yields 300 shots and can leave a .5-meter (1½-ft) hole in any ferroconcrete wall.

Cutout handle
The hollow area in the blaster's handle minimizes weight for faster draw.

WESTAR-34 BLASTER PISTOL

APPEARANCES II, CW **MANUFACTURER** Concordian Crescent Technologies **MODEL** WESTAR-34 **TYPE** Blaster pistol

Designed for brief but intense surprise attacks at close range and custom fit for the bounty hunter Jango Fett, the WESTAR-34 blaster pistol is made of an expensive dallorian alloy that can withstand sustained-fire heating that would melt most ordinary blasters.

GEONOSIAN SONIC BLASTER

APPEARANCES II, CW, Reb **MANUFACTURER** Gordarl weaponsmiths **MODEL** Geonosian sonic blaster **TYPE** Sonic blaster

The standard sidearm of Geonosian soldiers uses oscillators to produce a powerful omnidirectional sonic blast. The weapon's energy is enveloped in a plasma-containment sphere shaped by emitter cowls that channel the sonic beam.

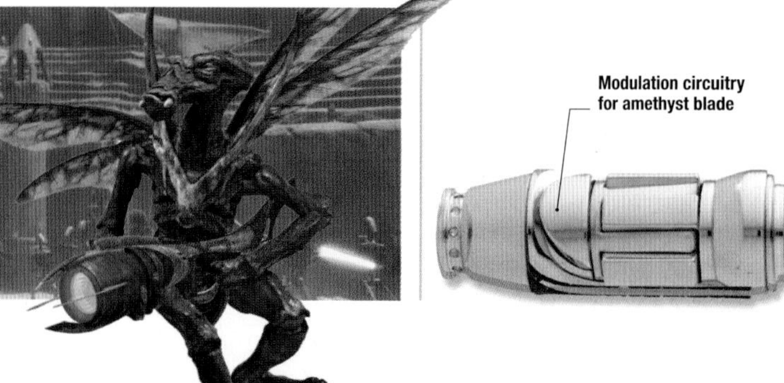

MACE WINDU'S LIGHTSABER

APPEARANCES II, CW, III **CREATOR** Mace Windu **MODEL** Handcrafted **TYPE** Jedi lightsaber

During his long career as a Jedi, Mace builds and uses at least two lightsabers, both of which produce a purple-hued blade. After many years of experience with his first lightsaber, and after being appointed a senior member of the Jedi Council, he crafts his second lightsaber using the highest standards of precision, creating a superior weapon that represents his mature abilities as a Jedi leader. Regarded as one of the best lightsaber wielders in the Jedi Order, Mace is a master of combat techniques that sometimes tread dangerously close to dark side practices.

Modulation circuitry for amethyst blade

Electrum finish denotes a senior Council member

Handgrip

"The planet is secure, sir. The population is under control."

SUPER BATTLE DROID G21

SUPER BATTLE DROID

The bulkier, stronger, and more advanced version of the standard B1 battle droid, the super battle droid is equipped with a built-in laser cannon and can operate without a command signal.

APPEARANCES II, CW, III **MANUFACTURER** Baktoid Combat Automata
MODEL B2 super battle droid **TYPE** Super battle droid

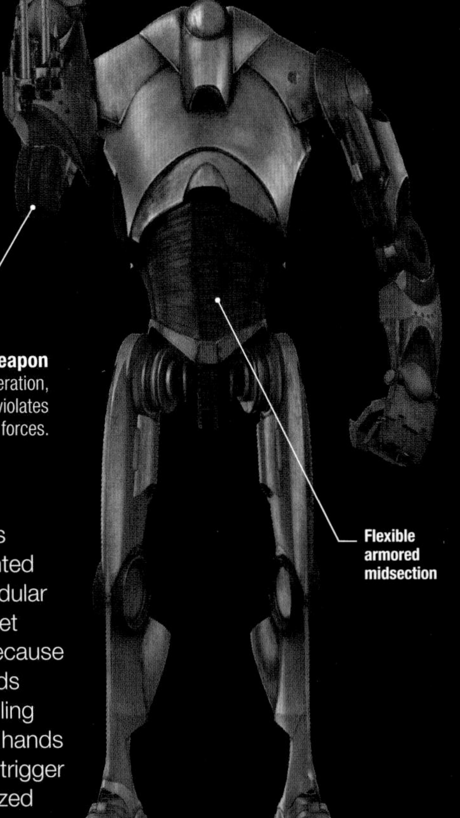

Durable
The reinforced elbow-joint bearings are hermetically sealed.

Secret weapon
Initially built in secret for the Trade Federation, the military-grade super battle droid violates Republic regulations on private security forces.

Flexible armored midsection

BUILT-IN WEAPONS

The standard B2 battle droid has built-in dual laser cannons mounted on its right forearm, which is modular and can be replaced with a rocket launcher and other weapons. Because the B2's armored monogrip hands lack fingers, it has difficulty handling standard blasters. However, the hands have built-in signal emitters that trigger the firing mechanism on specialized blaster rifles, making it easy for the droids to squeeze off shots.

IMPROVED MODEL

After the Trade Federation loses thousands of B1 battle droids at the Battle of Naboo, Federation leaders begin researching concepts for an improved battle droid. The result is the B2 battle droid, which is designed by the Techno Union. The B2 incorporates many components from the standard B1, but packages them in a much sturdier shell. The droid's delicate signal receptor—identical to B1 components—is built into its heavily armored upper chest, which also houses a basic cognitive processor. This limited intelligence enables the B2 to function semi-independently of a Droid Control Ship. However, because the B2 is not capable of complex thinking, a link with a Control Ship is required for optimum performance. Because the B2 has a high center of gravity, it utilizes programmed movement algorithms to maintain balance. The B2 also has strap-on foot tips that can be replaced with climbing claws or buoyant pods to traverse different terrains.

Jedi killers
Deployed on Geonosis to defend leaders of the Trade Federation against an invasion of Republic forces, armored B2 battle droids *(right)* deflect blaster bolts as they join B1 battle droids in an unrelenting attack on Jedi targets. But for all their ferocity, B2 battle droids can be defeated by a dauntless astromech *(below left)*.

JETPACK VARIANT

Techno Union engineers design a powerful jetpack for propelling the B2 battle droid through the air. To economize on fuel, increase range, and compensate for the B2's weight, the jetpack incorporates a compact repulsorlift. Commonly referred to as a rocket droid or jetpack droid, this variant B2 is officially designated the B2-RP (rocket pack) and is distinguished from other B2s by blue-white markings on its torso, arms, and legs. During aerial conflicts, vessels in the Confederacy of Independent Systems deploy B2-RPs, which launch themselves directly at enemy ships.

Airborne B2
A super battle droid hurtles toward its target.

Rocket trooper
A platoon of upgraded B2s *(top)* fire wrist-mounted blasters. An upgraded B2-RP *(above)* fights at the Battle of Ringo Vinda.

B2-RP UPGRADE

Introduced late in the Clone Wars, the upgraded B2-RP is dubbed the super battle droid rocket trooper, featuring a larger jetpack with two bulky thrusters that attach to the droid's shoulders and small additional thrusters secured to the ankles. The design and configuration of these thrusters give the droid greater control over its aerial maneuvers, as well as increased speed. The upgraded B2-RP also features wrist-mounted blasters on both arms.

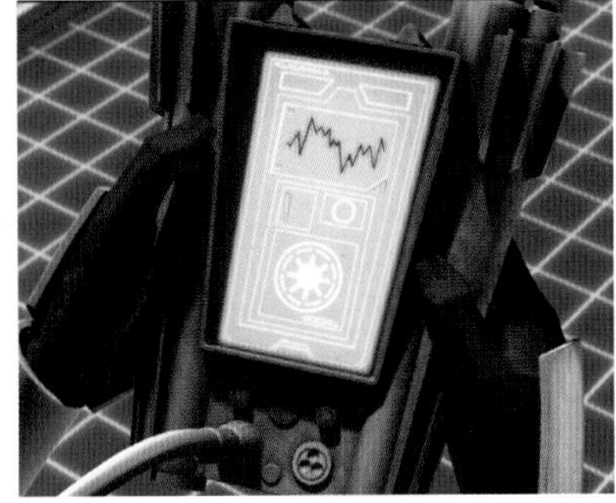

DATAPAD

APPEARANCES I, CW, III, Reb, Res, VIII **MANUFACTURER** Various **MODEL** Various **TYPE** Datapad

Datapads are common devices used for a variety of informational purposes across the galaxy. Most datapads have a display screen and an input mechanism and are capable of storing holographic data and playing it back on command.

ASAJJ VENTRESS' LIGHTSABERS

APPEARANCES CW **CREATOR** Unknown **MODEL** Handcrafted **TYPE** Sith lightsaber

Asajj Ventress wields a pair of curved-hilt lightsabers during her apprenticeship to Count Dooku, which can be combined to form a single double-bladed lightsaber. Extremely skilled with the red-bladed weapons, Ventress fights the Jedi Master Luminara Unduli during her assault on the attack cruiser *Tranquility*. Later in the Clone Wars, Ventress helps Ahsoka Tano escape from Republic authorities on Coruscant, but loses her twin lightsabers when she is ambushed by Barriss Offee. Ventress later acquires a new yellow-bladed lightsaber on the black market.

DC-17 BLASTER

APPEARANCES CW, III, Reb **MANUFACTURER** BlasTech Industries **MODEL** DC-17 hand blaster **TYPE** Blaster pistol

This heavy blaster pistol is carried by most Republic clone troopers, particularly high-ranking captains and commanders. The BlasTech DC-17 can also be outfitted with an ascension hook for scaling walls and has a built-in stun setting. The weapon is often worn in a quick-draw holster allowing for rapid response to sudden threats. Both Commander Bly and Captain Rex prefer to wield two DC-17 blaster pistols at the same time.

Firepower The standard DC-17 blaster pistol has a 50-shot capacity.

Personalized DC-17 pistols are designed to be identical and interchangeable, but commanders often customize them with unique paint jobs.

DC-15A BLASTER

APPEARANCES II, CW, III **MANUFACTURER** BlasTech Industries **MODEL** DC-15A blaster **TYPE** Blaster

One of the standard-issue weapons for clone troopers during the Clone Wars, the DC-15A is a reliable blaster rifle capable of both sustained fire and slower, long-range accuracy. The variable power output can be controlled by the clone trooper and includes a low-powered stun setting. The weapon can be mounted on a tripod. DC-15A rifles can be outfitted with sniper scopes and also work in conjunction with the holographic data readouts inside a clone trooper's helmet. During the Battle of Teth, clone troopers use ascension cables attached to their DC-15A rifles to scale high walls.

ANAKIN'S MECHNO-ARM

APPEARANCES II, CW, III, Reb, RO, IV, V, VI **MANUFACTURER** Republic **MODEL** Custom mechno-arm **TYPE** Cybernetic prosthetic

After Count Dooku cuts off Anakin's right arm on Geonosis, the Jedi Knight receives a mechanical prosthetic as a replacement. It resembles a droid arm with exposed gears and joints, and it greatly boosts Anakin's gripping strength. Electrostatic fingertips allow Anakin to retain his sense of touch.

T-SERIES TACTICAL DROID

APPEARANCES CW, Reb **MANUFACTURER** Baktoid Combat Automata **MODEL** Tactical droid **AFFILIATION** Separatists

T-series tactical droids serve an important advisory role among Separatist forces during the Clone Wars. Far smarter than most battle droids, tactical droids are designed to stay away from the frontlines and plan battle strategies from the security of a flagship or fortified headquarters. Due to tactical droids' intelligence, many commanders allow them to have full authority over Separatist military elements. This leads many T-series droids to express their superiority over all other droid models.

COUNT DOOKU'S LIGHTSABER

APPEARANCES II, CW, III **CREATOR** Count Dooku **MODEL** Handcrafted **TYPE** Sith lightsaber

Jedi Master Dooku considers himself a sophisticated duelist and builds his lightsaber with an unusual, curved hilt for greater finesse at executing precise slashes and lunges. After Dooku leaves the Jedi and joins the Sith, he replaces his lightsaber's blue kyber crystal with a red one. During a confrontation on Geonosis, Dooku easily dispatches both Anakin Skywalker and Obi-Wan Kenobi, but proves unable to gain the upper hand when facing Master Yoda. Dooku carries the lightsaber throughout the Clone Wars. He faces Anakin and Obi-Wan again while aboard the *Invisible Hand*. This time Dooku's dueling skills fail him, and he loses his head to a vengeful Anakin.

Scarlet blaze Dooku's kyber crystal produces a red blade.

Unusual shape The hilt's curved shape adds control when dueling.

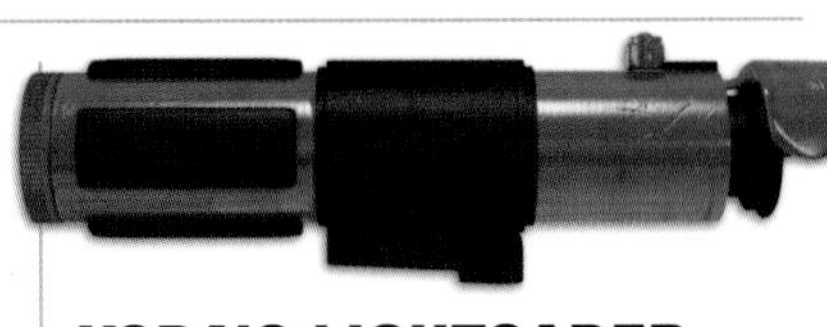

YODA'S LIGHTSABER

APPEARANCES II, CW, III **CREATOR** Yoda **MODEL** Handcrafted **TYPE** Jedi lightsaber

Yoda's lightsaber has a shorter-than-average hilt and a blade proportioned to match the Jedi Master's smaller size. Despite his age, Yoda is one of the best combatants in the Jedi Order, executing dizzying attacks from every direction. The green-bladed lightsaber serves Yoda well throughout the Clone Wars, but he loses his weapon while fighting Emperor Palpatine inside the Senate Chamber. It is publicly thrown into a furnace by Grand Vizier Mas Amedda and destroyed.

Blade stabilizing ring

REY'S LIGHTSABER

APPEARANCES CW, III, IV, V, VII, VIII, IX **CREATOR** Anakin Skywalker
MODEL Handcrafted **TYPE** Jedi lightsaber

This lightsaber, a legacy from one generation to the next, comes into existence after the Battle of Geonosis when Anakin builds a replacement for his original Jedi weapon. Anakin's second lightsaber has a blue blade and a silver hilt featuring black handgrips. He wields the weapon against the Separatists throughout the Clone Wars and uses it to defeat Count Dooku aboard the *Invisible Hand* during the Battle of Coruscant. Later, to defend Supreme Chancellor Palpatine, Anakin cuts off Mace Windu's hand. The action marks Anakin's transformation into Darth Vader, and he uses this lightsaber during the massacre at the Jedi Temple and his battle with Obi-Wan on Mustafar.

Last actions
Anakin uses his lightsaber to confront Palpatine. Very soon, he will replace this weapon with a red-bladed saber.

Duel on Starkiller Base
Rey uses her lightsaber to fight expert duelist Kylo Ren in the snow on Starkiller Base. While she has no lightsaber training, Rey holds her own and even defeats him.

Obi-Wan takes the lightsaber from his defeated opponent and keeps it for nearly two decades while he watches over Anakin's son, Luke, on Tatooine. He eventually passes the weapon on to Luke, who wields it for more than two years, fighting the Empire. On Cymoon 1, Luke faces Vader in combat for the first time. The Sith Lord briefly regains his lightsaber, recognizing it as his former weapon, but Luke manages to get the weapon back before escaping. He later learns lightsaber techniques on Hubin from Thane Markona, whose mother was a Jedi, and studies under Yoda on the planet Dagobah. When Luke faces Vader once more on Cloud City, his skills are still no match for the Sith Lord's mastery. Vader uses his lightsaber to cut off Luke's hand, sending the weapon tumbling into the depths of Cloud City.

At some point over the ensuing three decades, legendary pirate Maz Kanata gains possession of the weapon. When Rey arrives at Maz's castle on Takodana, the lightsaber calls out to Rey, who finds it in a chest in a crypt under the castle. Rey receives visions of the past through the Force, but turns down Maz's offer of the weapon as a gift. Former First Order stormtrooper Finn takes the weapon from Maz, using it to duel with his previous friend FN-2199 during the Battle of Takodana. On Starkiller Base, Finn even manages to spar with "Jedi Killer" Kylo Ren, but he is gravely wounded by Kylo. Both Rey and Kylo call upon the lightsaber, but it answers to Rey. She duels Kylo, equaling his power and striking him across the face.

Rey later travels to Ahch-To, where Luke is residing. When Rey attempts to return his lightsaber to him, Luke throws it behind him. Rey picks it up again and finally persuades Luke to train her. After honing her skills, Rey leaves Luke behind on Ahch-To and rejoins the battle against the First Order. She allows herself to be captured and is delivered to Supreme Leader Snoke aboard his flagship, the *Supremacy*. Snoke takes the lightsaber. While he orders Kylo to kill Rey, Kylo uses the Force to activate Rey's lightsaber and kill Snoke, before passing the weapon to Rey. Snoke's elite Praetorian Guards immediately attack Kylo and Rey, but the formidable duo dispatch them all. When Ren offers his hand to Rey, hoping she will join him, she rejects the advance and attempts to call the lightsaber into her grasp once more. Kylo summons it too and the lightsaber explodes between them, shattering into pieces. Rey escapes the ship with the fragments of the legendary weapon.

Like his father
Luke has never held a lightsaber before, but knows how to wield the weapon.

Stowed away
It is unknown how long Maz has kept Luke's lightsaber stored in an ancient wroshyr wood box *(below)*.

Reforged blade
Not even being torn in two could end the story of this most famous of weapons. With its fragments carefully reforged, Rey wields it against Kylo Ren once more.

Deadly battle
While aboard the *Supremacy*, Rey fights for her life alongside Kylo Ren against the deadly Praetorian Guards *(above)*.

TT-8L/Y7

APPEARANCES Reb, VI
MANUFACTURER Serv-O-Droid, Inc.
TYPE Gatekeeper droid
AFFILIATION Jabba's palace

Nicknamed "tattletales," TT-8L/Y7s are security droids installed in entryways to screen visitors and scan for weapons. Considered obnoxious and invasive, they enjoy their position of control. Jabba the Hutt has a TT-8L fitted into a hole at his front gate that questions R2-D2 and C-3PO when they first arrive.

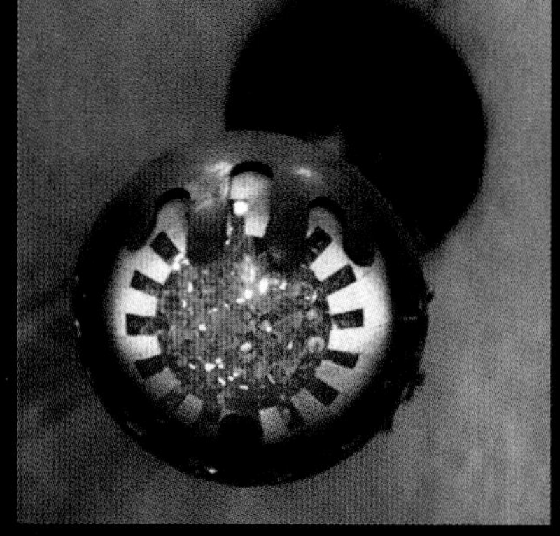

AHSOKA'S LIGHTSABERS

APPEARANCES CW, Reb **CREATOR** Ahsoka Tano
MODEL Handcrafted **TYPE** Jedi lightsaber

Ahsoka Tano's lightsabers see heavy use during the Clone Wars. The young Jedi Padawan develops a unique fighting style that incorporates a non-standard reverse grip for holding the weapon. Under Anakin Skywalker's instruction, she becomes a skilled duelist and wields her lightsaber in battles on Teth, Geonosis, and Lola Sayu, briefly losing it to a thief in the underlevels of Coruscant. Ahsoka builds a short-bladed saber to use in conjunction with her primary weapon.

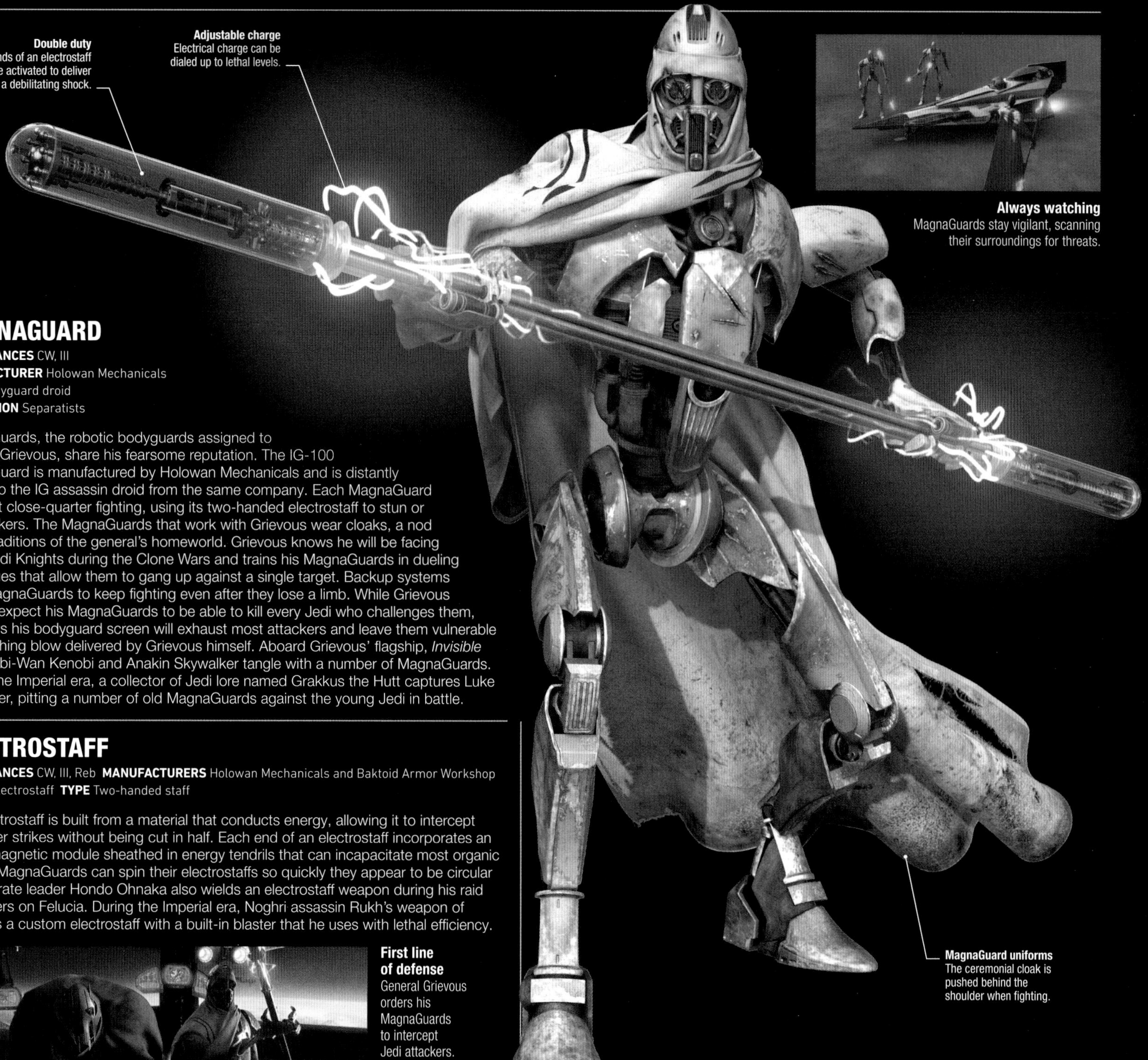

Double duty
Both ends of an electrostaff can be activated to deliver a debilitating shock.

Adjustable charge
Electrical charge can be dialed up to lethal levels.

Always watching
MagnaGuards stay vigilant, scanning their surroundings for threats.

MAGNAGUARD

APPEARANCES CW, III
MANUFACTURER Holowan Mechanicals
TYPE Bodyguard droid
AFFILIATION Separatists

MagnaGuards, the robotic bodyguards assigned to General Grievous, share his fearsome reputation. The IG-100 MagnaGuard is manufactured by Holowan Mechanicals and is distantly related to the IG assassin droid from the same company. Each MagnaGuard excels at close-quarter fighting, using its two-handed electrostaff to stun or kill attackers. The MagnaGuards that work with Grievous wear cloaks, a nod to the traditions of the general's homeworld. Grievous knows he will be facing many Jedi Knights during the Clone Wars and trains his MagnaGuards in dueling techniques that allow them to gang up against a single target. Backup systems allow MagnaGuards to keep fighting even after they lose a limb. While Grievous doesn't expect his MagnaGuards to be able to kill every Jedi who challenges them, he knows his bodyguard screen will exhaust most attackers and leave them vulnerable to a finishing blow delivered by Grievous himself. Aboard Grievous' flagship, *Invisible Hand*, Obi-Wan Kenobi and Anakin Skywalker tangle with a number of MagnaGuards. During the Imperial era, a collector of Jedi lore named Grakkus the Hutt captures Luke Skywalker, pitting a number of old MagnaGuards against the young Jedi in battle.

ELECTROSTAFF

APPEARANCES CW, III, Reb **MANUFACTURERS** Holowan Mechanicals and Baktoid Armor Workshop
MODEL Electrostaff **TYPE** Two-handed staff

The electrostaff is built from a material that conducts energy, allowing it to intercept lightsaber strikes without being cut in half. Each end of an electrostaff incorporates an electromagnetic module sheathed in energy tendrils that can incapacitate most organic beings. MagnaGuards can spin their electrostaffs so quickly they appear to be circular blurs. Pirate leader Hondo Ohnaka also wields an electrostaff weapon during his raid on farmers on Felucia. During the Imperial era, Noghri assassin Rukh's weapon of choice is a custom electrostaff with a built-in blaster that he uses with lethal efficiency.

First line of defense
General Grievous orders his MagnaGuards to intercept Jedi attackers.

MagnaGuard uniforms
The ceremonial cloak is pushed behind the shoulder when fighting.

High-ranking droid
A MagnaGuard automatically outranks any battle droid. Their presence indicates an elite Separatist commander must be close by.

Powerful pullers
Most of the equipment inside a space tug, which needs to be able to move a large ship, is devoted to keeping its tractor beam generators working.

TRACTOR BEAM

APPEARANCES CW, S, Reb, IV, V, VI, Res, VII
MANUFACTURER Various **MODEL** Tractor beam
TYPE Starship equipment

Tractor beams are a fundamental piece of technology for starships and space stations. They project a force field that can seize an object in a near-unbreakable grip and pull it into a hangar bay. Aboard warships like the Separatist heavy cruiser *Malevolence*, tractor beams are classified as offensive weapons; these beams are aimed at a fleeing craft to slow its escape or to immobilize it entirely, making it easy prey for the warship's turbolasers. Tractor beams have peaceful applications as well. Space stations use tractor beams to guide arriving vessels to safe landings, and space tugs are outfitted with powerful tractor beams for towing disabled ships.

COMMANDO DROIDS

APPEARANCES CW **MANUFACTURER** Baktoid Combat Automata
TYPE Battle droid **AFFILIATION** Separatists

Commando droids are advanced, sturdier versions of B1 battle droids, programmed with improved combat tactics and battlefield awareness and equipped with glowing white photoreceptors. Captains and other high-ranking commando droids bear white identifiers on their heads and chests. Due to a more compact head size than the B1, commando droids can fit inside clone trooper armor to execute infiltration missions. Most commando droids carry blaster rifles and stun batons, and command units wield vibroswords for one-on-one combat. After the battle of Yavin, Darth Vader and his accomplice, Doctor Aphra, steal a portable Geonosian droid factory. Vader uses it to create his own secret, private army of commando droids to battle against Doctor Cylo's cybernetic agents. Decades later, a commando droid named N1-ZX is a part of C-3PO's droid spy network, working for the Resistance until his destruction on Kaddak.

Agile adversary
A commando droid is able to move and react much faster than a standard battle droid.

Heavy armor
The droids are designed to withstand blaster fire.

Airborne
Piloting speeder bikes, commando droids blast away at their targets.

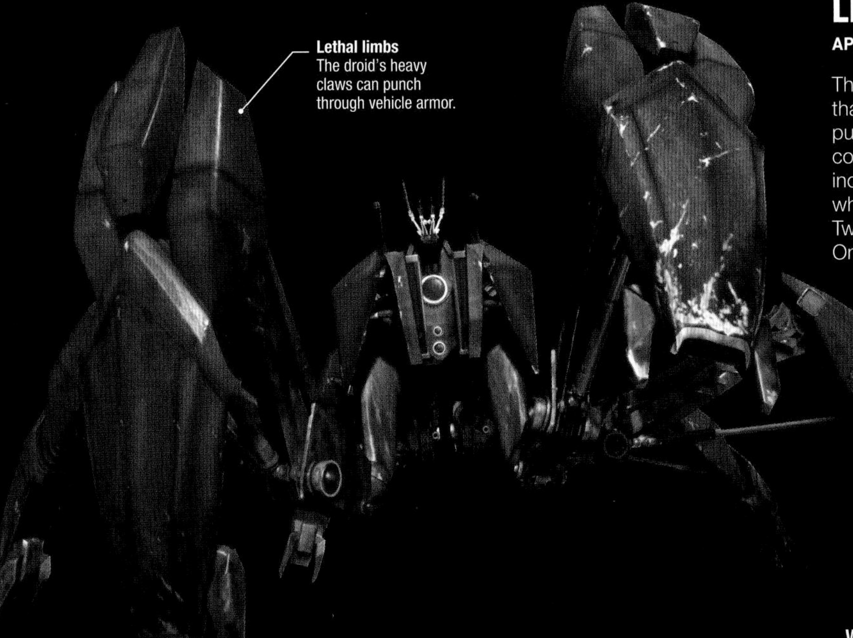

Lethal limbs
The droid's heavy claws can punch through vehicle armor.

LM-432 "MUCKRAKER" CRAB DROID

APPEARANCES CW, III **MANUFACTURER** Techno Union **TYPE** Droid tank **AFFILIATION** Separatists

The LM-432 crab droid, also known as the "muckraker," is primarily a military unit that excels at navigating swampy environments. Its six armored limbs provide secure purchase when clambering over uneven terrain, and teeth at the tips of the limbs combined with gripping prongs at the joints allow crab droids to scale steep inclines. The LM-432's face is dominated by three glowing red photoreceptors, while communications antennae keep the droid in contact with its commanders. Two blaster cannons underneath the droid's body serve as long-range threats. On Pijal, a customized crab droid is the prey during each Grand Hunt, an old tradition where the planet's future monarch proves their abilities. In the middle of Crown Princess Fanry's Grand Hunt, the prey droid viciously targets her, until she is saved by her Jedi protectors. During the Clone Wars, crab droids form part of the Separatist armies, fighting on planets across the galaxy.

Weak points
By exploiting a crab droid's blind spots, an attacker can slip past its claws and strike its vulnerable central processor.

JEDI HOLOCRON

APPEARANCES CW, Reb **CREATOR** Various
MODEL Handcrafted **TYPE** Jedi holocron

Holocrons are information-storage artifacts primarily used by the Jedi, though the Sith have their own holocron traditions. They act as repositories of vital and sensitive knowledge. Most of the data contained on a holocron is related to the nature and applications of the Force, so sharing this knowledge outside the Jedi Order is discouraged. For this reason, many holocrons are constructed with a security mechanism that permits access only to those who exhibit Force sensitivity. It is common for holocrons to resemble evenly proportioned polyhedrons, with the sides made from a crystalline material that glows when in use. A holocron's lessons are typically relayed in the form of an interactive hologram that resembles the Jedi Master who recorded the information.

Hundreds of holocrons have been created by long-vanished Jedi Masters over the centuries. The Jedi Order values these artifacts for their historical significance and their insights into teaching methods. The Order isn't willing to take chances with its holocrons and keeps them in the Jedi Archives in the Jedi Temple, with the rarest specimens locked away behind the movement-triggered lasers and heavy blast doors of the Holocron Vault. Many holocrons will not react unless paired with a specific memory crystal, and for added security, the Order does not store these items together.

During the Clone Wars, bounty hunter Cad Bane raids the Jedi Temple with the intent of penetrating the Holocron Vault. The Jedi detect his intrusion but misidentify his target, allowing Bane to slip through the temple's ventilation shafts. When the shape-shifter Cato Parasitti, Bane's compatriot, impersonates Chief Librarian Jocasta Nu, the ruse distracts the Jedi long enough for Bane to pocket the kyber holocron and exit the temple with little difficulty. After Order 66, many Jedi holocrons fall into the hands of the Sith or collectors of Jedi antiques, such as Grakkus the Hutt. Jocasta Nu survives the Purge and records a whole library of holocrons containing her extensive knowledge. She wants to rebuild the Jedi Order and dies trying to retrieve a holocron from the Jedi Temple that contains a list of known Force-sensitive children in the galaxy. Her holocron library is later found by Luke Skywalker who carries out Jocasta's last wish and establishes a new Jedi Order.

Guarded secrets
A special chamber in the Jedi Archives hosts the most valuable holocrons in the history of the Order.

"The Holocrons contain the most closely guarded secrets of the Jedi Order."

JOCASTA NU

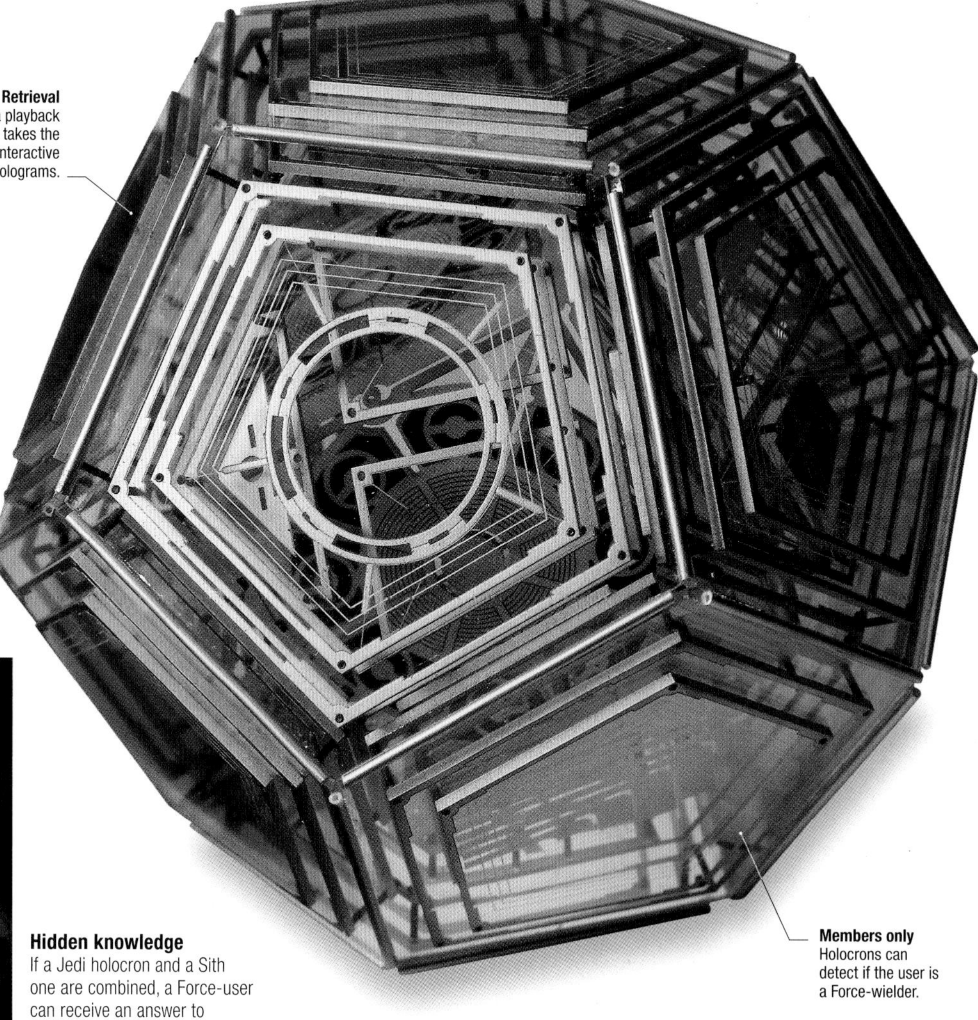

Retrieval
Data playback often takes the form of interactive holograms.

Members only
Holocrons can detect if the user is a Force-wielder.

Hidden knowledge
If a Jedi holocron and a Sith one are combined, a Force-user can receive an answer to any question they have.

KYBER CRYSTAL

APPEARANCES CW, Reb, RO, VIII, FoD
MODEL Handcrafted **TYPE** Memory crystal

Kyber crystals are rare, naturally occurring gems found on planets scattered across the galaxy. They concentrate energy in a unique manner and resonate with the Force. A kyber crystal forms the heart of a lightsaber, focusing energy into the weapon's characteristic blade. Dark side users corrupt kyber crystals, normally taken from Jedi in combat, for their lightsabers. They pour their agony into the crystals, causing them to bleed and turn red. When former Jedi Ahsoka Tano defeats the Inquisitor known only as the Sixth Brother, she takes his crystals, purifying them with the Force and turning them white. Imperial scientist Galen Erso develops a method of weaponizing massive kyber crystals, which becomes the basis of the Death Star superlaser.

GAMORREAN AX

APPEARANCES CW, VI
MANUFACTURER Various
MODEL Two-handed vibro-ax
TYPE Vibro-ax

The Gamorrean guards in Jabba the Hutt's palace carry intimidating axes as their primary weapons, a display that lets visitors know they mean business. Many of these axes contain vibration generators that improve their cutting ability, though they are just as deadly without them.

THE DARKSABER

APPEARANCES CW, Reb **CREATOR** Tarre Vizsla **MODEL** Handcrafted **TYPE** Specialty lightsaber

Hundreds of years before the Clone Wars, the first Mandalorian to enter the Jedi Order, Tarre Vizsla, creates and wields the Darksaber. It is a unique lightsaber with a sinister black blade that glows with an eerie halo. The Darksaber is later stolen from the Jedi Order by House Vizsla, who use it to unite the Mandalorians.

The artifact eventually falls into the hands of Pre Vizsla, leader of the Mandalorian Death Watch. Vizsla opposes the pacifist leader of Mandalore, Duchess Satine, and uses the Darksaber as his personal weapon. After Vizsla stages a coup to take control of Mandalore, Maul kills him and takes the weapon, ruling over Mandalore. When Darth Sidious arrives, Maul uses the Darksaber against his former master, but he is abducted by Sidious. The weapon is recovered by Maul's Mandalorian followers, who later rescue Maul and give him back the Darksaber. Maul continues to use it against the Republic when they arrive to free Mandalore from his rule. During the Imperial era, Maul stores the Darksaber in his Dathomir lair, where he and Jedi Ezra Bridger plan to use Nightsister magicks. Ezra's allies—Mandalorian Sabine Wren and Jedi Kanan Jarrus—track them there and are possessed by Nightsister spirits. Sabine wields the Darksaber against Ezra, until he is able to free her and Kanan from the Nightsisters' grip, at which point Sabine presents the Darksaber to Kanan for safekeeping. After returning to Atollon, Sabine is asked by her allies to learn how to wield the Darksaber, in hopes she will return to her family on Mandalore and unite a Mandalorian army with the Rebel Alliance. Kanan agrees to be her teacher.

Alongside Mandalorian Fenn Rau, Ezra, and Kanan, Sabine returns to her family home on Krownest with the Darksaber in hand. Once there, Imperial Viceroy Gar Saxon takes the weapon and battles Sabine, who defeats him using Ezra's lightsaber. Sabine reclaims the Darksaber to use in the ensuing Mandalorian Civil War, fighting alongside her family. She later decides the former regent of Mandalore, Bo-Katan, should use the weapon to unite Mandalore against the Empire.

Dark weapon No other lightsaber is known to have a black blade.

Deadly duels Obi-Wan battles Pre Vizsla, lightsaber against Darksaber *(above right)*. Pre Vizsla is skilled enough with the Darksaber to keep a Jedi at bay *(right)*.

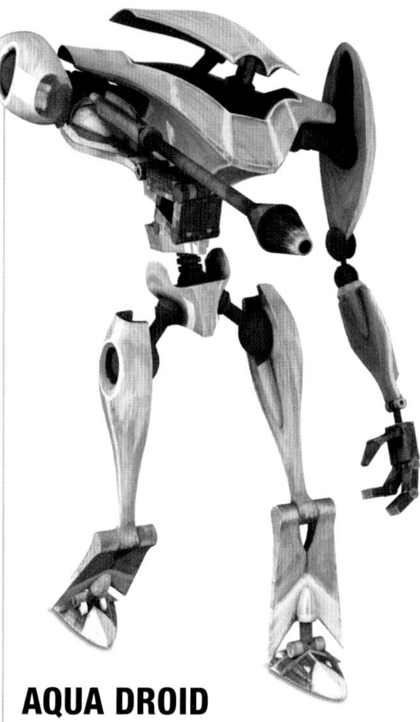

AQUA DROID

APPEARANCES CW **MANUFACTURER** Techno Union **TYPE** Droid tank **AFFILIATION** Separatists

The Separatists use aqua droids for underwater fighting on oceanic planets such as Kamino and Mon Calamari. The droids have retractable laser cannons and can move speedily while submerged, using propellers in their feet. For surprise attacks, the Separatists deploy aqua droids by hiding them in underwater starship wreckage, where they ambush their targets.

SD-K4 ASSASSIN DROID

APPEARANCES CW **MANUFACTURER** Techno Union **TYPE** Assassin droid **AFFILIATION** Separatists

SD-K4 probes are spider-like droids programmed for quiet killing. Each assassin probe moves on eight clawed legs and has multiple photoreceptors for scanning its surroundings. If cornered, it can release dozens of smaller droids through pores on its head that swarm a target and stab it with their sharp limbs. During the Clone Wars, three Separatist assassin probes attack Duchess Satine Kryze aboard the spaceliner *Coronet*, but Anakin Skywalker and Obi-Wan Kenobi successfully stop the threat.

NIGHTSISTER ENERGY BOW

APPEARANCES CW **CREATOR** Nightsisters **MODEL** Handcrafted **TYPE** Energy bow

The Nightsister energy bow has strings that are made from a plasma that emits a bright pink glow, and is designed to fire arrows made from a similar plasma material. A special group of Nightsisters, known as the Hunters, use energy bows to track down and eliminate enemies on Mother Talzin's orders. Former Sith assassin and Nightsister Asajj Ventress is given a bow when she rejoins her sisters.

ZYGERRIAN ELECTRO-WHIP

APPEARANCES CW, Reb **MANUFACTURER** Unknown **MODEL** Zygerrian electro-whip **TYPE** Shock whip

Zygerrian slavers, such as the notorious Miraj Scintel, are known throughout the galaxy for their cruelty. Their weapon of choice is the electro-whip: a metal grip with an extendable wire that glows when powered up. The whips are later used by the Galactic Empire and the Mining Guild to keep individuals they have enslaved in check.

NIGHTSISTER CRYSTAL BALL

APPEARANCES CW, Reb **CREATOR** Nightsisters **MODEL** Handcrafted **TYPE** Nightsister artifact

The Nightsisters of Dathomir have strange traditions for tapping into the Force, including the use of crystal balls to give glimpses of future events. During the Clone Wars, Nightsister shaman Mother Talzin uses a crystal ball to locate Savage Opress, and later to find his brother, Maul.

PROTOCOL DROIDS

APPEARANCES I, II, CW, III, Reb, RO, IV, V, VI, VII, VIII, IX, FoD **MANUFACTURER** Cybot Galactica **MODEL** Various **TYPE** Protocol droid

The "human-cyborg relations" protocol droids are ideal servants, able to converse in almost any language and programmed to be docile, polite, and subservient. Their translation capabilities make protocol droids invaluable in diplomacy and business negotiations, thus they are common on worlds such as Coruscant—a hub of galactic politics. Protocol droids do have a tendency to be eccentric, fussy, nervous, and fidgety. Some consider them mildly annoying—but a restraining-bolt mount and an off switch on the back of the neck are easily accessible.

While Cybot Galactica manufactures protocol droids on the factory world of Affa, the series is also available as a kit for hobbyists. Some, like Anakin Skywalker, build theirs using a motley assortment of used parts.

Protocol droids are designed to resemble humans, standing 1.67 meters (5 ft 5 in) tall and weighing 75 kg (165 lbs). They are sold in a variety of colors—including gold, red, silver, and white—and have a SynthTech AA-1 Verbo Brain, allowing them to store tremendous amounts of information in their active memory banks. TranLang III communications modules are standard features, giving them fluency in more than six million forms of communication. Upgrades to more advanced modules are also available. Cybot Galactica produces other lines of protocol droids, including the TC-series, each with their own particular abilities.

Rebel leader
The white Rebel Alliance droid K-3PO has programming upgrades to make him a battle tactics specialist. He is considered a valuable asset until he is destroyed during the Imperial assault on Hoth.

Rude droid
The silver E-3PO is fitted with a TechSpan I module that allows him to access Imperial networks. This enviable status goes to his head, however, and he is especially rude when encountering C-3PO on Cloud City.

R-SERIES ASTROMECH

APPEARANCES I, II, CW, III, S, Reb, RO, IV, V, VI, Res, VII, VIII, IX, FoD **MANUFACTURER** Industrial Automaton **MODEL** R-Series **TYPE** Astromech

Industrial Automaton's astromechs are one of the most popular lines of droids in the galaxy. They are vital to the navigation and maintenance of starships, from single-person starfighters to large vessels, and come in many shapes and sizes.

The most distinctive feature of an R-series droid is the shape of its head. The most popular R-units have dome-shaped heads, while superior versions sport transparent domes, exposing their fast-running Intellex V processors. The Empire sometimes uses R-series droids for courier duties, and tends to choose R-units with conical heads. There are budget astromechs available, which are a little taller than average, with flat-topped heads. The budget units are often riddled with defects such as bad motivators, and can be found to have difficult personalities.

Early R-series models are tall, moving slowly on a single foot. They are much less personable than later models. Later R-units are much shorter and move about on two dominant legs, with a third that can be retracted into their bodies. All R-series droids support an array of optional mechanical arms, stored away in various compartments. The R-series' range of tools depends simply on the investment of their owners. The possibilities are almost limitless, and may include grasping arms, electro-shock prods, arc-welders, and computer interface arms.

Small starfighters (especially those used by the Jedi Order, the Rebel Alliance, and Resistance) often have slots fitted for astromech co-pilots, accessible from the outside of the ship. This allows the R-series droid to monitor approaching ships or space debris while also making navigational calculations and addressing any ship damage.

Ready to serve
A number of astromechs are stationed aboard the Naboo Royal Starship in case any emergency repairs need to be carried out.

Imperial droids
The astromechs that serve the Empire are frequently memory wiped to ensure that they do not build up the personality quirks typical of some astromech lines.

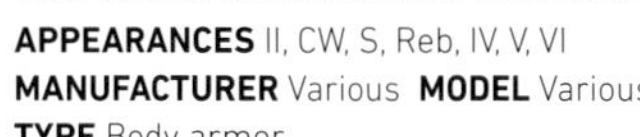

PHASE II CLONE TROOPER ARMOR

APPEARANCES CW, III, Reb **MANUFACTURER** Kaminoan Armorsmiths **MODEL** Phase II armor **TYPE** Body armor

Phase II clone armor represents the transition between Phase I clone armor, used by the Grand Army of the Republic, and stormtrooper armor, used by the Galactic Empire. The most obvious difference is the design of the helmet, which contains an advanced filtration system. The armor lacks the life-support system found in Phase I armor, requiring clone troopers to wear additional gear when venturing into areas without a breathable atmosphere. However, Phase II standard armor, with the first prototypes given to ARC troopers, is more easily customizable, and includes additional weapons, armor plating, backpacks, jetpacks, and respirators. There are also specialized variants of Phase II armor tailored to particular environments, modes of battle, and/or mission requirements. Years after Imperial troops adopt stormtrooper armor, shock troopers still continue to wear red-and-white Phase II clone armor.

MANDALORIAN ARMOR

APPEARANCES II, CW, S, Reb, IV, V, VI **MANUFACTURER** Various **MODEL** Various **TYPE** Body armor

The traditional armor of the Mandalorian people is a symbol of their culture and a special point of pride. Made of beskar, a form of iron unique to Mandalore and the moon of Concordia, it is capable of repelling Jedi lightsabers. Over the centuries the design of the armor has changed, for example, the Mandalorian crusaders used to wear helmets and robes. Mandalorian armor may also be reforged by its wearer to their exact specification and each suit is also painted to reflect its owner's affiliation. Mandalorian members of Maul's Shadow Collective wear red-and-gray armor with horns to show their allegiance to the dark side warrior. Years later, the Imperial Super Commandos wear white armor that echoes stormtrooper gear. Some suits of armor are passed down from generation to generation, much like Sabine Wren's colorful suit, which she frequently reforges and repaints to suit her tastes.

JT-12 JETPACK

APPEARANCES II, CW, Reb **MANUFACTURER** Merr-Sonn Munitions, Inc. **MODEL** JT-12 series **TYPE** Personal jetpack

The JT-12 jetpack series is a family of rocket-propelled packs that are capable of both short jumps and long-distance flight for the wearer. The average maximum jetpack speed in flight is 145 km (90.1 miles) per hour. The JT-12 jetpack series predates the Clone Wars and is used by Mandalorian factions, such as Death Watch, bounty hunters like Jango Fett, and even the Galactic Republic. The pack also features a powerful launcher that can accommodate both the MM9 and Z-6 anti-vehicle homing missile modules in its adapter slot.

IG-SERIES ASSASSIN DROID

APPEARANCES CW, V, FoD **MANUFACTURER** Holowan Laboratories **MODEL** IG-series **TYPE** Assassin droids

Produced by Holowan Laboratories, the IG-series in general is a highly aggressive range of droid models, banned by the Galactic Republic. Creating the IG-series assassin droids turns out to be a fatal mistake for the company thanks to the droids' incomplete programming. When they activate IG-88, the lethal droid turns against his creators and kills everyone in the lab. IG-88 then goes on to work as a bounty hunter, gaining notoriety throughout the galaxy comparable only to Boba Fett's.

CONTROL CHIP

APPEARANCES CW **MANUFACTURER** Kaminoans **MODEL** Custom **TYPE** Bio chip

When Jedi Master Sifo-Dyas commissions the Kaminoans to create a clone army, he also orders a bio chip to be developed and inserted into all clone embryo brains in their third stage of development. These bio-chips are originally intended to make the clones less aggressive and more compliant to orders. When Count Dooku has Sifo-Dyas killed and takes over the clone program, he orders the Kaminoans to re-engineer the bio chips to make clones comply with the Emperor's eventual Order 66 and turn against the Jedi. The Empire later uses similar chips on the Wookiees and on prisoners.

DEJARIK TABLE

APPEARANCES CW, S, Reb, RO, IV, VI, VIII **MANUFACTURER** Various **MODEL** Various **TYPE** Game

Dejarik is a table game popular throughout the galaxy, played by two combatants. Each player typically directs a selection of up to 10 holographic monsters, such as the Ghhhk, Houjix, Kintan Strider, Molator, K'lor'slug, Monnok, Scrimp, Bulbous, Ng'ok, and Mantellian Savrip, to act out battles to the death. The board is comprised of three concentric circles, with two rings segmented into 12 divisions and an inner ring acting as a single battle arena. If electronic game boards aren't available, some players use handmade monster pieces, which are almost as popular.

"I am programmed to resist intimidation."

KRAKEN

SUPER TACTICAL DROID

APPEARANCES CW, Reb **MANUFACTURER** Baktoid Combat Automata
TYPE Tactical droid **AFFILIATION** Separatists

Super tactical droids are an upgraded line based on the T-series tactical droids. They serve as generals in the Separatist Droid Army during the Clone Wars. They are not only an advancement on the previous model, but also consider themselves superior to their biological counterparts. As a result, they are both arrogant and argumentative and operate without sympathy or morality, executing ruthless strategies. Notable individuals include General Kalani, who is still active during the Imperial era; Aut-O, a Separatist fleet commander defeated by D-Squad; and Kraken, assigned to aid Admiral Trench.

BUZZ DROID

APPEARANCES CW, III **MANUFACTURER** Colicoid Creation Nest
TYPE Pistoeka sabotage droid **AFFILIATION** Separatists

Swarms of small buzz droids attack Republic ships during the Clone Wars. Vulture droid starfighters and droid tri-fighters fire jet-powered discord missiles at Republic targets, containing up to seven buzz droids, each in a shock-absorbing, spherical casing. The droids dodge their way through enemy defenses with maneuvering thrusters until they reach their targets and hatch open. Mechanical arms and cutting tools then dismantle enemy ships and droids to inflict as much damage as possible. The droids are difficult to remove from ships, and while the Republic has not developed adequate defenses against buzz droids, Jedi have found ways to work around them. During the Imperial era, some rebel forces, including the Free Ryloth Movement, deploy buzz droids in their attacks on Imperial ships. For a time, Imperial Officer Thrawn keeps a number of buzz droids to learn more about Republic-era technology.

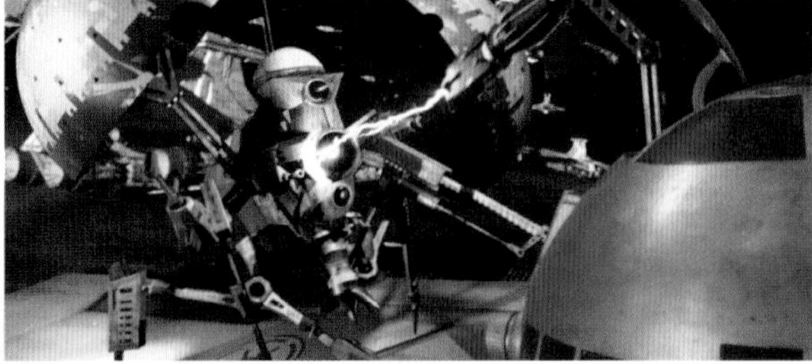

Weak spot
When a buzz droid lands on Anakin Skywalker's starfighter, R2-D2 zaps it in its most vulnerable spot: the main photoreceptor.

DARTH SIDIOUS' LIGHTSABERS

APPEARANCES CW, III
CREATOR Darth Sidious
MODEL Handcrafted
TYPE Sith lightsaber

Darth Sidious creates a pair of lightsabers during his apprenticeship under Darth Plagueis. Of discerning tastes, Sidious constructs his lightsabers using nearly indestructible phrik, a metallic compound, and an aurodium emitter, all finished with electrum. At the core of both is a corrupted kyber crystal.

He rarely uses his lightsabers—only when absolutely necessary—as it would immediately reveal his identity as a Sith. Instead Sidious prefers to exercise his powers of manipulation and use servants to carry out his dark deeds.

Secret weapon
One of Sidious' lightsabers is normally hidden inside a neuranium sculpture displayed in his office within the Senate building.

IMPERIAL TURBOLASER

APPEARANCES Reb, RO, IV, V, VI
MANUFACTURER Taim & Bak **MODEL** XX-9 heavy turbolaser **TYPE** Anti-ship emplacement weapon

The XX-9 heavy turbolaser features a rotating double-laser cannon turret mounted on a square base. The weapons are typically installed on the surface of Star Destroyers and the Death Star, where they are divided into four sections. The top level includes the turbolaser battery, while the second, lower, level houses rows of capacitor banks to store energy. The third section contains the support crew and maintenance stations, while the lowest level encloses gunnery stations and control computers.

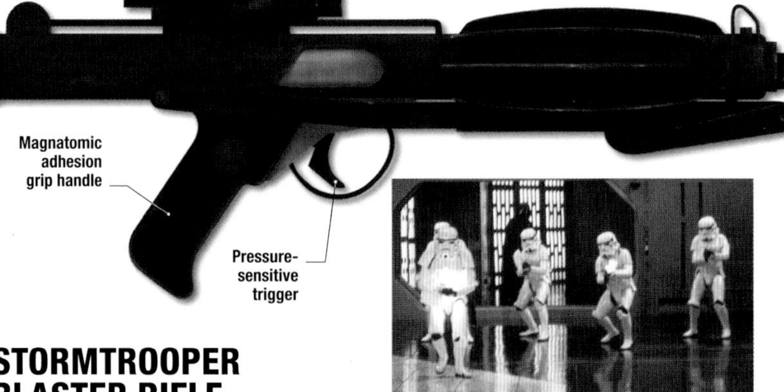

Assault weapon
Stormtroopers fire at the crew of the *Millennium Falcon* as they escape from the first Death Star.

STORMTROOPER BLASTER RIFLE

APPEARANCES S, Reb, RO, IV, V, VI, FoD
MANUFACTURER BlasTech Industries
MODEL E-11 **TYPE** Stormtrooper blaster rifle

The BlasTech E-11 is standard issue for Imperial stormtroopers. It combines lethal firepower with an impressive range in a versatile design. Most visible of the E-11's features is the telescopic range-finding sight and the folding three-position stock, which converts the pistol-sized blaster into a full-length rifle. Standard power cells carry energy for approximately 100 shots. Plasma cartridges last for more than 500 shots. Replacement power cells and gas cartridges are carried on the stormtrooper's utility belt, and the blaster also features an advanced cooling system for superior performance.

STORMTROOPER ARMOR

APPEARANCES S, Reb, RO, IV, V, VI, FoD **MANUFACTURER** Imperial Department of Military Research **MODEL** Stormtrooper armor **TYPE** Body armor

Stormtroopers are anonymously shielded in white plastoid composite armor worn over a black body glove. While most armor is fitted for humans, other forms may be manufactured to suit different body types. Armed with some of the most powerful weapons and finest armor in the Empire, stormtroopers are among the most dreaded opponents of rebel freedom fighters.

This armor protects stormtroopers from inhospitable environments, projectile weapons fire, and blaster bolts. The armor can also protect against the vacuum of space for a short period of time. Stormtrooper helmets have built-in filtration systems that extract breathable atmosphere from polluted environments. For extended operations in the vacuum of space or the filtration of potent toxins, troopers wear backpacks with extended life-support capabilities. Stormtrooper armor is generally impervious to most blast shrapnel and projectiles. It can be punctured by a powerful blaster bolt, but the armor will generally withstand glancing blasts.

Each stormtrooper is equipped with a utility belt containing a variety of equipment, including a compact toolkit, power packs, and energy rations. The belt may also contain a comlink, macro binoculars, and a grappling hook. Field troops are allowed additional ammunition and comprehensive survival equipment. Backpacks can include field communicator sets, mortar launchers, and blaster components.

Stormtroopers usually carry a thermal detonator on the back of their utility belt. Controls on the detonator are not labeled, to prevent enemy troops from activating them, but include settings for arming, blast intensity, and timing. While detonators are not normally used within ships or bases, troopers carry a full complement of such field gear to be prepared for any situation.

Sniper position knee protector plate

"I can't see a thing in this helmet!" LUKE SKYWALKER

HAN'S DICE

APPEARANCES S, IV, VIII **MANUFACTURER** Unknown **TYPE** Corellian Spike Dice

Han Solo owns a pair of dice plated in aurodium (a metal more valuable than gold) and connected by a chain. When he and Qi'ra try to escape Corellia, Han gives them to her for luck. She later gives them back during their mission to Kessel. After winning the *Millennium Falcon* from Lando Calrissian, Han hangs them in the ship's cockpit. Years later, Luke Skywalker retrieves them from the ship on Ahch-To, and then appears to give them to General Organa during the Battle of Crait. After Luke vanishes, Kylo Ren watches them likewise fade away.

RANGE TROOPER BOOTS

APPEARANCES S **MANUFACTURER** Imperial Department of Military Research **MODEL** #A7.5 Range Trooper Boots **TYPE** Magnetomic gription boots

Operating on tight schedules, range troopers accompany Imperial vehicles and convoys traveling under difficult conditions, and the shipments they protect are usually highly sensitive. On Vandor, the high-speed conveyex line must ensure timely delivery of coaxium to the Imperial vault. Range troopers have to climb outside the train to address any threats while it is in motion. Their magnetomic gription boots ensure they remain attached to the conveyex, even during sharp turns at 90 km (56 miles) per hour—and while hanging upside down.

These smart boots have sensors that monitor muscle contractions in troopers' legs to determine when to activate their magnetomic fields.

COAXIUM

APPEARANCES S, Res **MANUFACTURER** Various **TYPE** Hypermatter/Hyperfuel

Before the dawn of hyperspace travel, space mariners observe purrgil creatures breathing in Clouzon-36 gas before "jumping" away into space, moving faster than the speed of light. Upon examining dead purrgil, they find deposits of coaxium in their organs. These deposits are a metabolic product of Clouzon-36 and are what allowed the purrgil to travel through hyperspace. Coaxium is later discovered in natural deposits on worlds such as Kessel. An extremely valuable substance, coaxium is highly volatile and must be refined to render it less explosive and more stable. A tiny amount of refined coaxium is used to coat the inside of a ship's hyperdrive. When the coaxium coating is energized, it triggers a reaction that enables hyperspace travel.

BECKETT'S BLASTERS

APPEARANCES S **MANUFACTURER** BlasTech **MODELS** DG-29 and RSKF-44 **TYPE** Heavy blaster pistols

Tobias Beckett's weapons of choice are two heavy blaster pistols from BlasTech. In his dominant left hand he wields a DG-29 sideloader, which is fitted with an image-intensifying macroscope for long-distance shots. In his right hand he wields a powerful RSKF-44, an ideal firearm for short-range encounters (underworld rumors suggest this was the last thing bounty hunter Aurra Sing ever saw). Those unfortunate enough to be at the business end of either weapon will notice the barrel of each has a rainbow-ring: a clear indication of heat-exposure oxidation. Beckett gives his other weapon, another BlasTech heavy blaster pistol, the DL-44, to Han Solo.

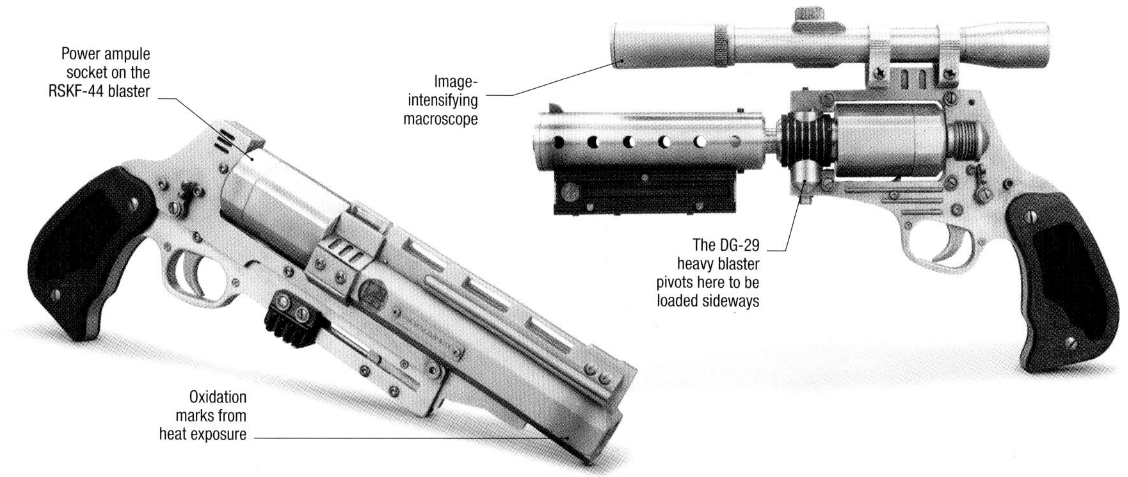

Power ampule socket on the RSKF-44 blaster

Image-intensifying macroscope

The DG-29 heavy blaster pivots here to be loaded sideways

Oxidation marks from heat exposure

ENFYS NEST'S SHIELDS

APPEARANCES S **MANUFACTURER** Unknown **MODEL** Custom **TYPE** Gauntlet shield

Enfys Nest's gauntlet shields are made of beskar (Mandalorian iron) armor plates that fan out along an articulated servo-joint. They expand with a rapid flick of her wrist and fold up in a similar manner, allowing for comfortable storage on her forearms. Beskar ore is sourced from Mandalore and its moon, Concordia. Plates of Mandalorian iron were originally developed as a protection against Jedi lightsabers. Enfys Nest is highly skilled in using her gauntlet shields to deflect blaster bolts and projectiles from hand-held weapons while sparring with her opponents.

ENFYS NEST'S HELMET

APPEARANCES S **MANUFACTURER** Unknown **MODEL** Custom **TYPE** Combat helmet

Enfys Nest wears a combat helmet traditionally passed down in her family from mother to daughter. It hides her identity (assisted by a built-in vocoder) and offers protection in battle. The helmet's horns conceal transmission antennae. The reverse eclipse emblem above the chrome visor represents a shining spotlight through eclipsing darkness. Enfys wrote a stanza of poetry above it, reading, "Until we reach the last edge, the last opening, the last star, and can go no higher."

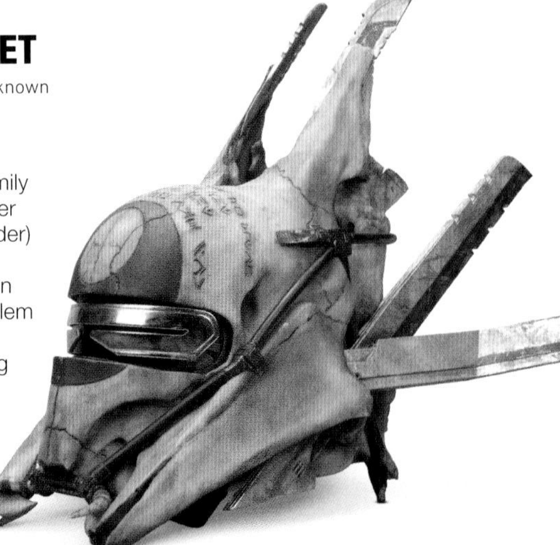

ENFYS NEST'S STAFF

APPEARANCES S **MANUFACTURER** Unknown **MODEL** Custom **TYPE** Electroripper staff

Enfys Nest prefers melee weapons to blasters. Her manifold martial arts skills stem from an upbringing that prioritizes protecting her village, family, the weak, and the defenseless against marauders and criminal gangs. Enfys' electroripper staff is a handmade weapon with a kinetite charge at the blunt end capable of producing a shock wave when slammed against a surface. The blade end is lined with a glowing energy ribbon that can incapacitate an opponent or, with a violent thrust, cut through metal.

DRYDEN VOS' KYUZO PETARS

APPEARANCES S **MANUFACTURER** Kyuzo crafters **MODEL** Custom **TYPE** Bladed weapon

Vicious crime boss Dryden Vos wields a pair of unique petars, crafted by a skilled Kyuzo blade maker to Vos' exact specifications. The double blades feature a conductive tempered carbon edge lined with a monomolecular energy cord to ensure it will slice through most targets. On the opposite side of the activator switch, bronzium knuckle guards protect Vos' clawed hands in melee combat. Rechargeable energy cells embedded in the hilt can be re-powered if placed on a recharging surface. When Vos' lieutenant, Qi'ra, betrays him, she impales Vos with one of his own petars.

DRYDEN VOS' SIGNET RING

APPEARANCES S **MANUFACTURER** Unknown **MODEL** Crimson Dawn **TYPE** Signet ring

Dryden Vos' Crimson Dawn signet ring is his most prized possession and allows him to access encrypted data networks, elite syndicate ships, and areas solely reserved for him as the public face of Crimson Dawn. Vos also uses the ring to communicate directly with the leader of Crimson Dawn, the former Sith Lord, Maul. The ring itself is made of solid bronzium, and the signet is a blood-red aurodium-cinnabar matrix. After Vos' previously trusted lieutenant, Qi'ra, kills him, she uses his signet ring to contact Maul, giving him a fake story of Vos' death.

SABACC

APPEARANCES S, Reb **TYPE** Card game

Sabacc is a card game that is popular all over the galaxy, and often accompanied by extensive betting. The goal is to win the pot of money or items of value by collecting a hand of cards with a total value of 23 or less. A sabacc deck comprises 76 cards, of which 60 cards include four suits (coins, flasks, sabers, and staves); there are 15 numbered cards per suit. The remaining 16 cards contain two sets of eight special cards with negative or null values. Lando Calrissian loses the *Millennium Falcon* to Han Solo in a variation of this game named Corellian Spike.

A pair of dice is also used when playing Corellian Spike

LANDO CALRISSIAN'S SE-14R

APPEARANCES S **MANUFACTURER** BlasTech Industries **MODEL** SE-14r **TYPE** Light repeating blaster

The SE-14r is a versatile blaster, designed to carry an optional scope, suppressor, and buttstock. It is carried by some stormtroopers, death troopers, and Imperial officers. While the SE-14r is an inexpensive blaster, famed smuggler Lando Calrissian owns a flashy model, modified to match his stylish and debonair lifestyle. It is plated in brushed chromium, an expensive material mined from one of Naboo's moons, and has a Tibrin mother-of-pearl handle. While Lando would rather avoid battles, he wields his SE-14r weapon during escapades on Kulgroon and Kessel.

E-22 RIFLE

APPEARANCES S, RO **MANUFACTURER** BlasTech Industries **MODEL** E-22 **TYPE** Blaster rifle

The double-barreled E-22 blaster rifle is commonly used by shoretroopers on Scarif and mudtroopers on Mimban. The E-22 is more powerful than the standard-issue E-11 blaster rifles carried by most stormtroopers. Its main drawback is that its recoil sleeve can become clogged, for example by Mimbanese mud.

T-21 LIGHT REPEATING BLASTER

APPEARANCES Reb, RO, IV **MANUFACTURER** BlasTech Industries **MODEL** T-21 **TYPE** Light repeating blaster rifle

The T-21 is carried by some Imperial stormtroopers. It is capable of firing powerful blasts at great distances, but it has a slow rate of fire and is difficult to aim precisely owing to its heavy recoil and lack of a targeting scope.

SABINE WREN'S ARMOR

APPEARANCES Reb, FoD **MANUFACTURER** Unknown **MODEL** Customized **TYPE** Mandalorian armor

Sabine Wren's Mandalorian armor is 500 years old. She inherits it through her clan when she comes of age, and has re-forged it at least twice. It has been worn by many legendary warriors and survived many great battles. As an artist, Sabine periodically repaints it with different designs and colors. Until the liberation of Lothal, she maintains her own signature starbird insignia on her left breastplate, though occasionally changes the colors. Her pauldrons have had a succession of different designs, but Sabine's left pauldron has always featured an animal, including, at certain points, an anooba, a fyrnock, a convor, and a purrgil.

Acquiring accessories
During Sabine's early rebel missions, she does not utilize many Mandalorian gadgets. She eventually gains a jetpack and a pair of Mandalorian vambraces.

HERA'S BLURRG-1120 BLASTER

APPEARANCES Reb, FoD **MANUFACTURER** Eirriss Ryloth Defense Tech **MODEL** Blurrg-1120 **TYPE** Holdout blaster

The Blurrg-1120, named after a creature native to Ryloth, is a versatile blaster featuring nine firing modes, including single- and double-shot. The Eirriss family, whose company manufactures the weapon, are backers of the Twi'lek freedom fighters against the Separatist occupation of Ryloth during the Clone Wars. The family continues to support Cham Syndulla and his movement to free Ryloth from Imperial oppression. Cham's daughter and rebel leader Hera Syndulla proudly wields her Blurrg-1120 blaster for years as a symbol of rebellion against the Empire.

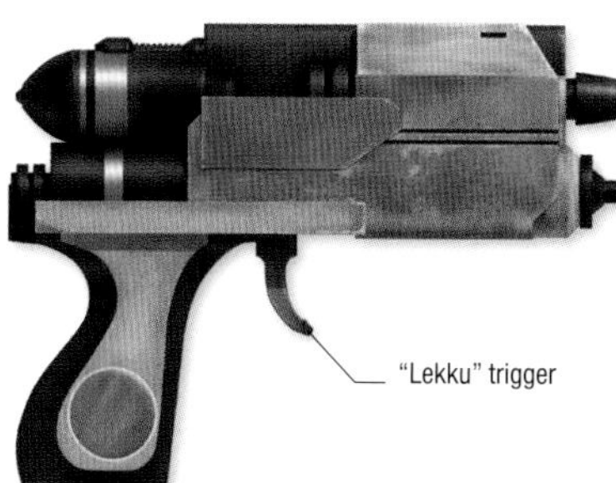

DL-18 BLASTER

APPEARANCES Reb, VI
MANUFACTURER BlasTech Industries
MODEL DL-18 **TYPE** Blaster pistol

The DL-18 is so popular among Tatooine's underworld, it is known as the "Mos Eisley special." Many of Jabba the Hutt's employees are armed with this versatile blaster pistol. The weapon is also favored by renegade Jedi Kanan Jarrus, whose pistol bears a dewback skin handle. The weapon weighs approximately 1 kilogram (2 pounds) and carries enough charge for approximately 100 shots. It has a range of accuracy up to 120 meters (394 feet).

SABINE WREN'S AIRBRUSHES

APPEARANCES Reb **MANUFACTURER** Neco Jeyrroo's Artisan Supplies **MODEL** Baobab EZ3 Airbrush **TYPE** Artist's airbrush

Artistic Sabine Wren uses a pair of airbrushes to paint and repaint her room aboard the *Ghost*, and also to leave tasteful call signs in Imperial-controlled areas. Each of Sabine's airbrushes has an adjustable nozzle to change the focus of the spray, as well as a slider below the nozzle to tweak the power and rate of spray. Five knobs on the left side of each airbrush adjust the colors. Removable cartridges of custom color sets fit into the back of them.

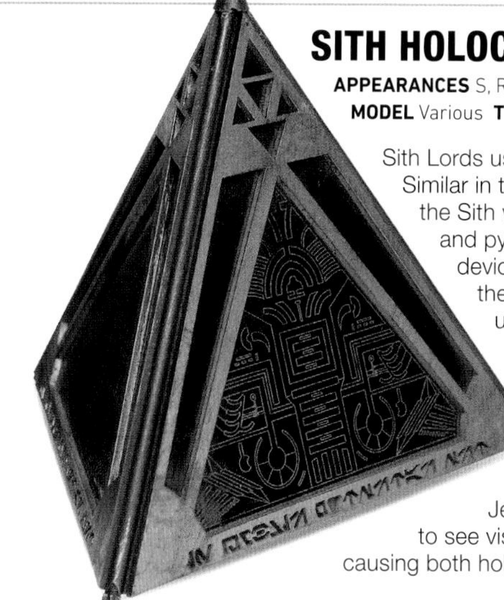

SITH HOLOCRON

APPEARANCES S, Reb **MANUFACTURER** Various Sith Lords **MODEL** Various **TYPE** Information storage device

Sith Lords use holocrons as data storage devices. Similar in their basic function to Jedi holocrons, the Sith versions are shaped like tetrahedrons and pyramids. These dangerously evil devices foster a strong connection to the Force and only someone drawing upon the dark side can open one. Ezra Bridger acquires a holocron from the Sith temple on Malachor, and as he uses it, the device begins to manipulate him. Ezra and Maul use the Sith holocron and Kanan's Jedi holocron together in an effort to see visions of what they most desire, causing both holocrons to shatter.

KANAN'S LIGHTSABER

APPEARANCES Reb **CREATOR** Kanan Jarrus **MODEL** Handcrafted **TYPE** Jedi lightsaber

Kanan originally builds his lightsaber as a Jedi Padawan. Following the enactment of Order 66, Kanan must hide his Jedi identity for 15 years, and thus keeps his lightsaber disassembled in a secret compartment until Ezra discovers it. Every time Kanan uses it, he makes himself a target for the Empire. Kanan comes to wield his saber against a range of dark side adepts, including many Inquisitors and even Darth Vader. After being blinded by Maul during a duel, Kanan uses the Force to "see," and continues to fight with his lightsaber. He loses his weapon shortly before his death, and it is recovered by Lothal's Governor, Arihnda Pryce. After her death, its whereabouts are unknown.

TIE FIGHTER PILOT HELMET

APPEARANCES S, Reb, RO, IV, V, VI, Res
MANUFACTURER Imperial Department of Military Research
MODEL TIE fighter pilot's helmet **TYPE** Pilot's helmet

TIE fighter pilots rely on their flight suits and helmets in case of hull damage to their unshielded fighters. Their reinforced black flight helmets are connected to a life-support pack hanging on their chest via a pair of gas transfer hoses. The helmet also includes ship-linked communications systems and enhanced visor displays.

WESTAR-35 TWIN BLASTERS

APPEARANCES CW, Reb, FoD **MANUFACTURER** Concordian Crescent Technologies **MODEL** WESTAR-35 **TYPE** Blaster pistols

WESTAR-35 blasters are a popular model of blaster on Mandalore that are carried by the police force as well as Death Watch during the Clone Wars. The weapons feature a high-precision barrel, rapid-fire mode, magnetic-grip handle, flash suppressor, and pressure-sensitive trigger. Sabine Wren uses a pair of custom-painted WESTAR-35 blasters throughout her time as a rebel against the Empire.

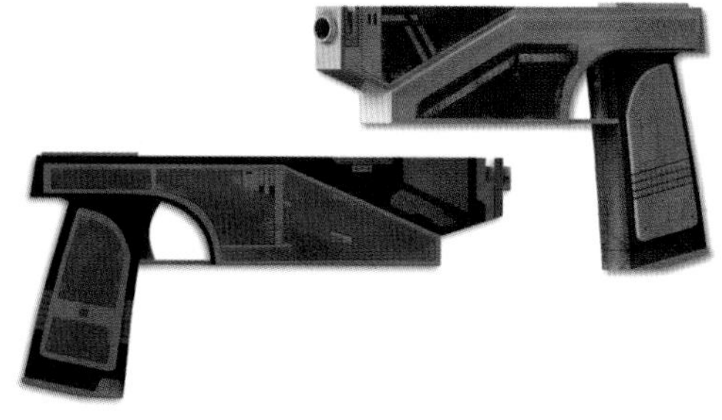

ZEB'S BO-RIFLE

APPEARANCES Reb **MANUFACTURER** Lasan-Malamut Firearms Corp. **MODEL** AB-75 **TYPE** Lasan Honor Guard bo-rifle

The Lasan bo-rifle, which is highly specialized and has a long tradition in Lasat culture, is the signature weapon of Garazeb Orrelios. Bo-rifles are used exclusively by the Lasan Honor Guard, of which Zeb is a former captain, and come in a variety of forms. Since the Empire razed Lasan, bo-rifles are rarely seen around the galaxy; much like Jedi lightsabers during the years of the Empire, bo-rifles are relics of antiquity.

Bo-rifles are nonetheless versatile weapons for violent times, and feature two modes for combat. Not only is the bo-rifle a robust and reliable ranged weapon, it can be quickly transformed into a deadly electrostaff, which is an ideal configuration for a powerful Lasan to pummel a squad of stormtroopers in close quarters.

The rifle component's power supply and discharge are similar to those of an EE-3 carbine rifle, and the tips emit electromagnetic pulses that stun opponents and neutralize ray shields. The bo-staff is activated by twisting the top handle downward, pressing both handles inward, and then activating both EMP tips. In staff mode, the weapons measure 2 meters (6½ ft) long. Zeb's firearm weighs 19 kilograms (41 lbs), requiring considerable strength to wield.

Zeb uses his weapon throughout his time as a member of the *Ghost* crew and later as part of the Rebel Alliance. When he's reunited with two surviving Lasat, Zeb helps them conduct a ritual to find the fabled Lasat homeworld, Lira San. Employing a rarely used functionality of his bo-rifle that channels the Ashla—the Lasan interpretation of the Force—Zeb is able to locate Lira San and pilot the *Ghost* through an imploded star cluster to reach the legendary planet.

"Only the Honor Guard of Lasan may carry a bo-rifle."

ZEB

EMP generator tips
The tips carry a maximum adjustable voltage of 11,000V.

Brute force
Zeb leaves a pile of stunned and pummeled stormtroopers in his wake.

His best shot
Ezra fires his energy slingshot at Agent Kallus on the planet Kessel.

EZRA'S SLINGSHOT

APPEARANCES Reb **CREATOR** Xexto tinkerer **MODEL** Handcrafted **TYPE** Wrist-mounted energy slingshot

Ezra Bridger acquired his energy slingshot from his friend Ferpil Wallaway, who owns a pawnshop on Lothal. It was constructed by another Xexto friend of Ferpil's. Slingshots of various kinds are popular on their home planet, Troiken, as the inhabitants' extra arms make them more convenient to use. Slingshots are now favored by children on Lothal as well. Pulling the virtual line back builds a low-voltage charge that can be launched accurately for long distances, and as with a Jawa ion blaster, the power is sufficient to disable droids and computer systems. Although the self-charging firing mechanism is not engineered to be lethal, it can stun a living being.

IG-RM DROID

APPEARANCES Reb **MANUFACTURER** Holowan Laboratories **MODEL** IG-RM **TYPE** Thug droid

Designed by the same corporation that created the IG-86 sentinel droids and the IG-100 MagnaGuards (the latter preferred by General Grievous), IG-RMs are the next line in aggressive security automatons. More stable than assassin droids, they require frequent instructions from their masters and are less likely to go rogue than other models. The droids are used by the Mining Guild to keep their slaves in line, and by underworld organizations. Cikatro Vizago owns quite a few IG-RMs, colorfully painted and armed with DLT-18 laser rifles. Within his Broken Horn Syndicate, the droids do much of the hard labor, fighting, and strong-arming, while Vizago manages them at a distance.

GRAND INQUISITOR'S LIGHTSABER

APPEARANCES Reb **MANUFACTURER** Unknown **MODEL** Unknown **TYPE** Double-bladed spinning lightsaber

Like his fellow—and subordinate—Inquisitors, the Grand Inquisitor uses a double-bladed red lightsaber to carry out the orders of his Sith masters. The process of construction for the Grand Inquisitor's lightsaber is unknown. It is possible that he built it himself, bleeding the kyber crystal he carried in his previous Jedi weapon, though it may have been issued to him by Darth Sidious when he persuaded the Jedi to turn to the dark side.

The lightsaber is designed pragmatically to hasten confrontation and extinguish life with absolute efficiency. In the face of the Grand Inquisitor's unorthodox technique, inexperienced Jedi become apprehensive, presenting the Grand Inquisitor with the perfect opportunity to strike.

Each Inquisitor's lightsaber functions in several modes. In crescent mode, the single-bladed lightsaber is wielded in a standard manner. In disk mode, a second blade is drawn, allowing broader fighting strokes, ideal for battling multiple combatants simultaneously. Both blades are capable of spinning around the disk by detaching from the central handle, forming an impressive wall of red lightsaber energy.

During the Grand Inquisitor's first meeting with Darth Vader, the Sith Lord breaks the Grand Inquisitor's lightsaber, but it is quickly repaired and used against Jedi Master Jocasta Nu in battle. It is unknown how many Jedi the Grand Inquisitor has extinguished in lightsaber duels over the years since Order 66. He also uses the weapon to execute non-Jedi. When the Lothal rebel cell is revealed to contain Jedi Kanan Jarrus and Ezra Bridger, the Grand Inquisitor duels the Jedi on multiple occasions. Aboard the *Sovereign*, the Grand Inquisitor is finally defeated by Kanan and his lightsaber is destroyed.

Lightsaber handle
The ribbed handle grip and lightsaber controls are set for crescent mode.

EZRA'S LIGHTSABER

APPEARANCES Reb **CREATOR** Ezra Bridger **MODEL** Handcrafted **TYPE** Jedi lightsaber-blaster hybrid

During the dark times of the Empire, many traditions of the Jedi Order are abandoned for the sake of survival. Though some wayward Jedi do make use of them, blasters have never been condoned by the Jedi Council. A Jedi would never have built a blaster into his or her own lightsaber in the past, as Ezra does. Ezra, however, is not a typical Jedi.

When he first begins his Jedi training under Kanan Jarrus, Ezra must borrow his master's lightsaber for practice. When he is ready, Ezra uses the Force to locate an ancient Jedi temple on Lothal. There, in the underground ruins, Ezra faces a series of challenges and confronts his own fears and weaknesses. When he does overcome them, a Jedi voice guides him to a blue kyber crystal—the key component required to build a lightsaber.

Ezra takes several weeks to construct his lightsaber aboard the *Ghost*, using a combination of spare lightsaber parts from Kanan, modulation circuits and an energy gate from Sabine, a donated power cell from Chopper, some extra tech Hera finds for him, and perhaps a part or two secretly acquired from Zeb's supplies. His double-bar design is unconventional for a lightsaber, but the outer bar is necessary to hold the blaster components. Having such an unusual and unproven design does pose some risk of a short-circuit at crucial moments. Since Ezra learned to build his lightsaber through trial and error, the blaster component is easily removed from the lightsaber to facilitate maintenance and repairs.

Ezra must be careful not to use his lightsaber unless there is no alternative. Doing so always draws the attention of the Empire, so having a built-in blaster function gives Ezra a safer option in violent confrontations. Ezra first uses his new lightsaber when the crew of the *Ghost* is attacked by the slaver Azmorigan on Lothal.

His master Kanan borrows the weapon to use in conjunction with his own lightsaber to defeat the Grand Inquisitor aboard the *Sovereign*. Ezra continues to wield the lightsaber, even against Darth Vader on Lothal. During the Mission to Malachor, Ezra faces Vader in battle, but the Sith Lord easily disarms him, destroying Ezra's unique weapon in the process.

Battle ready
Ezra draws his novel new lightsaber. Opponents are taken by surprise when he not only slashes and blocks, but also returns fire. When the blade is not drawn, it merely looks like a blaster, so he avoids the unwanted scrutiny of Imperials.

J-19 BO-RIFLE

APPEARANCES Reb **MANUFACTURER** Lasan-Malamut Firearms Corp.
MODEL J-19 **TYPE** Bo-rifle

Agent Alexsandr Kallus wields an unusual weapon for an Imperial officer: a Lasat J-19 bo-rifle. Kallus is presented with the weapon by one of the Lasan High Honor Guard when he defeats them in combat during the Sacking of Lasan. The bo-rifle functions equally well as a close-combat melee weapon and a long-distance blaster rifle. Its intimidating appearance makes it highly effective at scaring opponents. The J-19 is a more recent design than the bo-rifle belonging to Lasat rebel Garazeb Orrelios.

KETSU'S STAFF

APPEARANCES Reb, FoD
MANUFACTURER Ketsu Onyo
MODEL Custom **TYPE** Vibro-staff

Ketsu Onyo's vibro-staff is a deadly weapon befitting a bounty hunter. Ketsu is adept at using it as a melee weapon in close combat, but also operates it as a blaster in long-distance fights. A knuckle guard protects Ketsu's hands when sparring. The vibro-blade tip is removable and can be exchanged for blade edges, darts, laser scopes, or additional blaster modules. Ketsu created the weapon herself and frequently makes small improvements to it.

ID9 SEEKER DROID

APPEARANCES Reb **MANUFACTURER** Arakyd Industries
MODEL ID9 **TYPE** Probe droid

ID9 seekers are small probe droids designed to attach to the back of a harness, like a backpack. They may be deployed for scouting and are well suited to exploring environments inaccessible to average humanoids. These droids are adept at mimicking sounds and voice patterns. Their five articulated arms are fitted with electro-shock claws capable of stunning targets and disabling other droids. The Inquisitor known as the Seventh Sister is fond of utilizing ID9 seeker droids in her missions. Commander Iden Versio carries a similar ID10 seeker with four arms, named Dio.

AHSOKA TANO'S WHITE LIGHTSABERS

APPEARANCES Reb **MANUFACTURER** Ahsoka Tano **MODEL** Handmade
TYPE Light-side lightsabers

After Ahsoka Tano leaves the Jedi Order she fashions a new pair of lightsabers with curved hilts. Ahsoka's new lightsaber blades are now white instead of the customary blue or green. One of her lightsabers is a shoto, with a shorter blade, and used as a secondary weapon. Ahsoka tends to wield them both with a reverse grip, and uses them against the Imperial Inquisitors in multiple engagements and during her confrontation with Darth Vader on Malachor. After surviving this encounter, Ahsoka continues to carry the two lightsabers throughout the Galactic Civil War and its aftermath.

Twilight on Malachor
After years apart, Darth Vader and Ahsoka Tano are finally reunited in the Sith temple on Malachor. Ahsoka duels Vader to ensure her allies can escape.

CROSSGUARD LIGHTSABER

APPEARANCES Reb, VII, VIII
MANUFACTURER Various Force-users
MODEL Handcrafted **TYPE** Lightsaber

Crossguard lightsabers date back to an ancient cataclysmic event during the Old Republic era known as the Great Scourge of Malachor. Ezra Bridger finds an old Jedi crossguard lightsaber outside the Sith temple on Malachor, but it is too old to maintain its blade. The smuggler Sana Starros recovers a pair of crossguard lightsabers that belonged to Darth Atrius from that same era, but they are separately destroyed by Luke Skywalker and Darth Vader. Decades later, Kylo Ren constructs his own crossguard lightsaber, based on the same ancient design.

EZRA'S SECOND LIGHTSABER

APPEARANCES Reb **MANUFACTURER** Ezra Bridger **MODEL** Custom lightsaber
TYPE Jedi lightsaber

Ezra Bridger's first lightsaber is destroyed by Darth Vader at the Sith temple on Malachor. At some point Ezra builds a new lightsaber, which has a black hilt with silver highlights. Ezra is not the only one to wield his new lightsaber. On one mission Saw Gerrera briefly borrows it. Ezra eventually leaves it with teammate Sabine Wren before he and Grand Admiral Thrawn are pulled deep into space by a space-faring pod of purrgils.

DISMANTLER DROID

APPEARANCES Reb **MANUFACTURER** Industrial Automaton
MODEL DTS-series **TYPE** Demolition droid

DTS-series dismantler droids are designed to break down old ships and machinery into their basic parts, either for disposal or recycling. These droids are employed by the Empire at Reklam Station to disassemble old Republic BTL-A4 Y-wings. The droids are equipped with strong clamping claws, a razor cutter, powerful blasters, and a formidable flamethrower. Dismantler droids are programmed to attack anyone who interferes with their directives. The crew of the *Ghost* is nearly killed by a team of them while trying to steal Y-wings for the rebels.

IMPERIAL SENTRY DROID

APPEARANCES Reb **MANUFACTURER** Baktoid Combat Automata **MODEL** DT-series sentry droid **TYPE** Sentry droid

Imperial sentry droids are developed on former Baktoid Combat Automata production lines utilizing old Super Tactical Droid technology and abandoned, experimental droid schematics. Sentry droids act as automated guards aboard Imperial freighters such as the Class Four Container Transport. They operate in groups of four, with one always on patrol. Grand Admiral Thrawn uses them aboard his own ship for sparring and combat training. At times they stand guard in his personal quarters as well. Sentry droids are exceedingly strong, relentless, and have E-11 blaster rifles built into their right arms.

E-XD INFILTRATOR DROID

APPEARANCES Reb **MANUFACTURER** Imperial Department of Military Research **MODEL** E-XD **TYPE** Recon droid

The Empire's E-XD infiltrator droid is designed to resemble an RQ protocol droid while in reconnaissance mode. It appears benign as it quietly scans life-forms, vehicles, other droids, and structures—until it locates its intended target. Upon identifying its mark, the droid goes into attack mode, growing in height and drawing a variety of weapons. These droids are highly aggressive and extremely strong. If they are tampered with, an inbuilt proton warhead will explode. Rebel members Garazeb Orrelios, Chopper, and AP-5 are forced to deal with an infiltrator droid when one lands near their base on the planet Atollon.

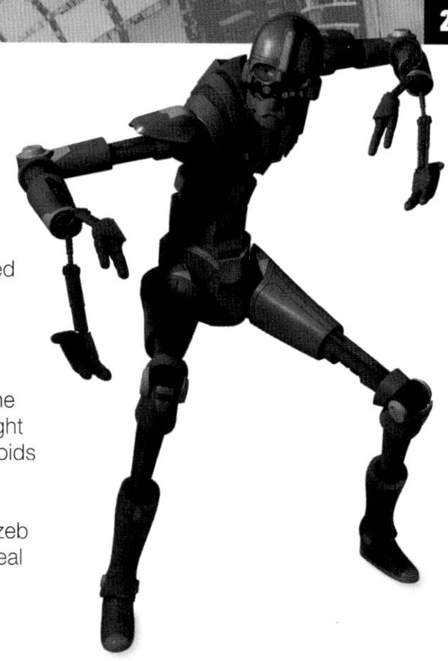

SAW GERRERA'S SUIT

APPEARANCES Reb, RO **MANUFACTURER** Unknown **MODEL** Custom **TYPE** Medical pressure suit

Saw Gerrera receives many grave injuries in his battles with the Empire. In his later years Saw's health fails to the point that he acquires a medical pressure suit to prolong his life, which includes an oxygen tank with painkillers and a respiration mask to aid his breathing as his lungs deteriorate. The suit also has atmospheric sensors to automatically adjust internal temperature, pressure, and humidity to compensate for environmental changes. As his health declines, his medical droid, G2-1B7, cares for him. The droid's programming has been modified to force it to provide Saw with medicines in dangerous quantities.

DEATH TROOPER ARMOR

APPEARANCES Reb, RO **MANUFACTURER** Imperial Advanced Weapons Research **MODEL** Death trooper armor **TYPE** Stormtrooper body armor

The precise design and specification of Imperial death trooper armor is classified. Their black armor is covered in a "reflec" polymer spray that warps electromagnetic signals and allows the troopers to pass invisibly through most sensor arrays. The helmets contain sensors and targeting systems far more advanced than those of any other troopers. These systems include image-intensifying, active-pule emitters, multi-frequency targeting, acquisition sensors, and Neuro-Saav macro-motion monitors. Implants in death troopers' body tissues provide biofeedback for the armor and likewise enable the armor to stimulate sensory organs for more intense perception of targets and their environment.

MWC-35C REPEATING CANNON

APPEARANCES RO **MANUFACTURER** Morellian Weapons Conglomerate **MODEL** MWC-35c "Staccato Lightning" repeating cannon **TYPE** Heavy repeater cannon

The MWC-35c "Staccato Lightning" repeating cannon is used by Imperial forces in crowd-control situations. Guardian of the Whills Baze Malbus steals one of these weapons to use against the Empire. The cannon employs a galven circuitry charge belt and a connected R717 refrigerant tank enabling it to fire blasts equivalent to the firepower of five laser rifles. The cannon can fire 35,000 rounds when fully charged and has two firing modes: rapid (for spraying an area) and single-burst (for delivering a more powerful, concentrated blast). This sizable weapon weighs 30 kg (66 lbs), so it requires considerable strength to operate and is difficult to aim precisely.

Rebel warrior
Baze joins the fight against the Empire on Jedha, and accompanies fellow rebel Jyn Erso to Scarif.

CHIRRUT'S STAFF

APPEARANCES RO **MANUFACTURER** Chirrut Îmwe **MODEL** Custom **TYPE** Staff

Chirrut Îmwe carries a flame-hardened walking staff made of uneti-wood. The uneti tree is sacred to the Jedi and possesses a strong inherent connection to the light side of the Force. Uneti grow at the Jedi Temple on Coruscant during the Republic era, and are said to come from seeds borne from trees at the very first Jedi temple. The end of Chirrut's staff has a metal cap with a compartment containing a tiny kyber crystal.

Surprise attack
Chirrut surprises stormtroopers by using his walking stick as an effective melee weapon.

CHIRRUT'S LIGHTBOW

APPEARANCES RO
MANUFACTURER Chirrut Îmwe
MODEL Custom lightbow **TYPE** Bowcaster

As part of his personal journey as a Guardian of the Whills, Chirrut Îmwe constructs his own lightbow. It works on the same principles as a traditional Wookiee bowcaster, and is much more powerful than a conventional heavy blaster rifle. While Chirrut may be blind, he is able to use his other senses to anticipate some events seconds before they happen—giving him a considerable advantage in combat situations.

Sure shot
Chirrut's ability to anticipate his target's next move even enables him to shoot down a TIE fighter at the secret Imperial base on Eadu.

DH-17 BLASTER PISTOL

APPEARANCES S, Reb, RO, IV, V, VI, VII, VIII, FoD **MANUFACTURER** BlasTech Industries **MODEL** DH-17 **TYPE** Medium-range blaster

Though not as versatile as Imperial military blasters, the DH-17 pistol is a well-made close-combat weapon commonly used by rebel forces for shipboard combat. Though the E-11 is favored by the Empire, sometimes their officers use the DH-17. The DH-17 is dependable on a semiautomatic setting, firing in short bursts; on automatic, the power is drained in 20 seconds.

DEFENDER SPORTING BLASTER

APPEARANCES IV, VI, VIII **MANUFACTURER** Drearian Defense Conglomerate **MODEL** Defender **TYPE** Hunting pistol

DDC's Defender sporting blasters are low-powered weapons intended for small-game hunting and self-defense. The blasters are popular with nobility and aristocrats for their lightweight design, ease of disassembly and reassembly, and their ability to be concealed. Broken down into three components, the blasters can pass through most security scans undetected. The power cell allows 100 shots per charge, though only a direct hit to a vital organ is lethal. Princess Leia Organa first learns to shoot using a Defender blaster as a teenager, displaying a rare talent for shooting. Leia uses a Defender blaster when Darth Vader boards the *Tantive IV* looking for the stolen Death Star plans. Decades later, she wields one aboard the *Raddus*, stunning a mutinous Poe Dameron.

ESCAPE POD

APPEARANCES IV **MANUFACTURER** Corellian Engineering Corp. **MODEL** Class-6 **TYPE** Six-passenger pod

CEC's Class-6 escape pods are fitted with four retro escape thrusters and six smaller maneuvering jets for fast, controlled evacuations. The emergency pods are designed to carry a maximum of six living passengers of average size. They employ a simple design with minimal equipment. The fore and aft cameras and proximity sensors aid the autopilot. They also optionally route camera feeds to the single viewport display screen. Though pods are normally off-limits to droids, during the attack on the *Tantive IV*, R2-D2 accesses an escape pod, and together he and C-3PO flee to Tatooine. They are able to escape because neither Darth Vader or his Star Destroyer sensors are able to detect that the droids are on board.

Saber fight
Darth Vader duels with his long-lost son Luke Skywalker in Cloud City.

DARTH VADER'S LIGHTSABER

APPEARANCES Reb, RO, IV, V, VI **CREATOR** Darth Vader **MODEL** Handcrafted **TYPE** Sith lightsaber

When Darth Vader first pledges loyalty to Darth Sidious, he continues to use his own Jedi lightsaber, until Obi-Wan Kenobi takes it following their duel on Mustafar. On Sidious' orders, Vader finds a surviving Jedi—Master Kirak Infil'a—whom he kills after a long battle. Vader takes the fallen Jedi's saber to Mustafar, where he pours his hate and anger into its kyber crystal, making it bleed and turning it red. Vader uses Infil'a's hilt until it is destroyed. He then fashions a new one that resembles his original Jedi hilt, but is made with a darker alloy. The lightsaber features a black-ridged handgrip, a black power cell chamber and beveled emitter shroud, a dual-phase focus crystal, a high-output diatium power cell, and the customary power and length adjustment switches.

With this new lightsaber, Vader commits many atrocities in the Emperor's name. On Malachor, Vader duels his former apprentice Ahsoka Tano, who only escapes his final strike thanks to the timely intervention of Ezra Bridger. Vader later slashes his way through rebel troops aboard the *Profundity* in an attempt to recover the stolen Death Star plans, and soon after kills his former master Obi-Wan aboard the feared battle station. The Sith Lord duels his son, Luke Skywalker, for the first time on Cymoon 1, and in a later confrontation cuts off one of Luke's hands in Cloud City. In their final confrontation, Luke momentarily succumbs to his anger and cuts off his father's hand, causing Vader's lightsaber to fall into the same energy well where Sidious eventually perishes.

Feared throughout the galaxy
Although not as limber in his new cyborg form, Darth Vader nonetheless remains the Emperor's deadliest servant.

IONIZATION BLASTER

APPEARANCES I, CW, IV, VI **MANUFACTURER** Jawas
MODEL Handcrafted **TYPE** Ion blaster pistol

Jawas construct their own ion blasters using whatever scraps they can scrounge. They begin with a stripped-down blaster power pack, and eventually add an accu-accelerator from a ship's ion drive and a droid-restraining bolt to the firing mechanism. The blasters may be fired accurately up to 12 meters (39 ft).

DLT-19 HEAVY BLASTER RIFLE

APPEARANCES S, Reb, RO, IV, V **MANUFACTURER** BlasTech Industries
MODEL DLT-19 **TYPE** Blaster rifle

DLT-19 rifles are commonly carried by Imperial stormtroopers, though bounty hunters employed as snipers also use them. As a long-range rifle, the DLT-19 is often used by sandtroopers on Tatooine and by stormtroopers aboard the Death Star. The rifle has folding sights and bipod support. It may be fired in single shots and short bursts, or be fully automatic for brief periods.

WED TREADWELL DROID

APPEARANCES II, CW, S, Reb, IV, V, VI **MANUFACTURER** Cybot Galactica
MODEL WED-15 Treadwell Droid **TYPE** Repair droid

WED Treadwells are common droids used to repair ships, machinery, and other droids. The WED's binocular visual sensors are mounted on a telescopic stalk, and multiple tool-tipped arms can be purchased separately. The droids are relatively fragile and require frequent maintenance. Jawas offer a WED-15 for sale to Owen Lars and Luke Skywalker on Tatooine.

INTERROGATOR DROID

APPEARANCES Reb, IV **MANUFACTURER** Imperial Department of Military Research
MODEL IT-O **TYPE** Interrogation droid

Illegal under the laws of the Republic, the interrogator droid is one of the technological horrors constructed in Imperial secrecy. Used by the Imperial Security Bureau without mercy, this droid meticulously exploits a prisoner's mental and physical weaknesses with its terrifying devices. It begins by injecting drugs that lessen pain tolerance and inhibit mental resistance while forcing the victim to remain conscious. Hallucinogens and truth serums ensure maximum effectiveness, and the experience is so unpleasant that most prisoners will confess on sight. Jedi Kanan Jarrus is interrogated by one IT-O aboard the *Sovereign* until the Grand Inquisitor takes over. Darth Vader subjects Princess Leia Organa to an IT-O interrogation aboard the Death Star, but she is able to resist due to her training and fortitude.

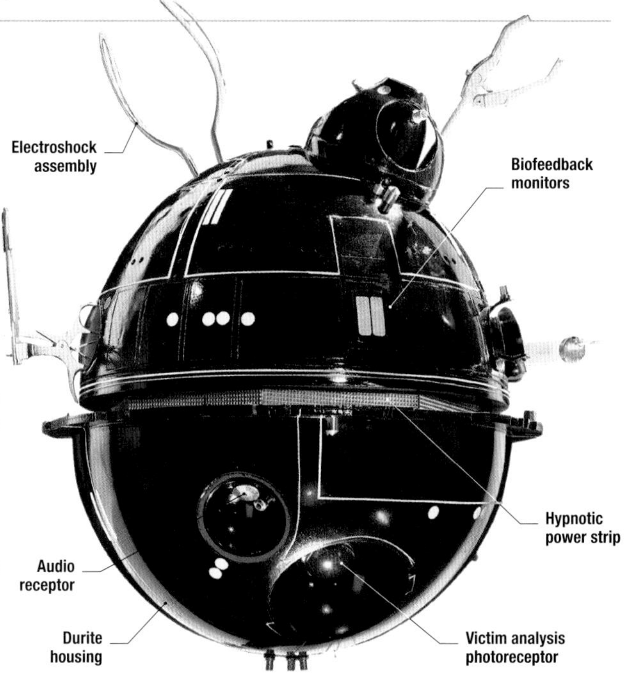

GADERFFII (GAFFI) STICK

APPEARANCES II, Reb, IV **CREATOR** Tusken Raiders
MODEL Handcrafted **TYPE** Melee weapon (staff)

Gaffi sticks are staff weapons created by Sand People using a variety of scrounged materials, though preferably durable metals. They are typically 1.3 meters (4 ft) long with a different weapon head on each end. One end is bent at a 90-degree angle, with a club head tipped by a spear point. The other end is shaped like a mace with sharpened edges. Gaffis facilitate many attack forms, from crude clubbing and stabbing to the finer staff-fighting arts.

Wookiee weapons

The Wookiee language has more than 150 words for wood—and this easily available material is used in most of their weapons, shields, and armor. Wookiees fashion a large selection of blasters that blend both traditional materials, such as wood, bone, and horn, with advanced technologies. A few popular models are even mass-produced in workshops all over Kashyyyk.

CHEWBACCA'S BOWCASTER

APPEARANCES IV, V, VI, VII, FoD **CREATOR** Chewbacca **MODEL** Handcrafted **TYPE** Wookiee bowcaster

Bowcasters are traditional weapons of Wookiees on their homeworld, Kashyyyk. They are based on ancient weapons of Wookiee culture that once employed poison darts and arrows. Bowcasters are more powerful and accurate than the average blaster, with a maximum effectiveness of up to 30 meters (98 ft). Designs vary depending on the materials used (usually wood and metal) and the crafter's artistic approach. Bowcasters fire a metal quarrel enveloped in energy, while a polarizing orb, balanced on each end of the bow, creates a magnetic field that boosts the projectile's momentum. After the cocking spring is pulled back, the trigger speeds the quarrel forward, charged with plasma energy. Chewbacca crafts several bowcasters, his most recent being an unconventional design that makes use of the frame and power pack of a stormtrooper blaster. At Han Solo's side, Chewbacca uses his weapon against a variety of foes, including Imperial stormtroopers, bounty hunters, and mynocks. Chewbacca continues to wield his bowcaster during the fight against the First Order.

Hero of Endor
Chewbacca expertly wields his Wookiee bowcaster at the Battle of Endor to fight stormtroopers, biker scouts, and Imperial officers.

VADER'S ARMOR

APPEARANCES III, Reb, RO, IV, V, VI, VII **MANUFACTURERS** Various **MODEL** Unique **TYPE** Life-support armor

After Darth Vader incurs life-threatening injuries in his duel with Obi-Wan Kenobi, he is secretly taken to the Grand Republic Medical Facility on Coruscant. While medical droids tend Vader's wounds, cyborg specialist Cylo and his team get to work, fashioning a life-support suit. Vader is fitted with armor that enables him to survive despite his badly burned body, protects him in combat, and serves to intimidate all who encounter him. The helmet provides vision-enhancement lenses, a respirator, feeding tubes, temperature regulators, and a voice projector. A chest control panel adjusts suit functions; sensor displays are visible on either side of his belt. Vader's frequent duels damage his armor, requiring him to recuperate in a bacta tank while repairs are made. Vader also likes to tweak his armor himself, displaying the engineering aptitude he has possessed since childhood.

Following Darth Vader's death aboard Death Star II, his son Luke burns his body and his armor in a funeral pyre on the forest moon of Endor. Vader's charred helmet is later taken from the pyre by an unknown individual, and decades later, his helmet comes into the ownership of his grandson, Ben Solo. Now known as Kylo Ren, dark side adept Ben talks to the relic whenever he feels tempted to rejoin the light side.

CODE CYLINDERS

APPEARANCES III, S, Reb, RO, IV, V, VI, Res, VII, VIII **MANUFACTURER** Empire and First Order **TYPE** Security device

Code cylinders are used by Imperial officers to gain access to restricted areas and high-security data networks. They record the bearer's identification, security clearance, and who has accessed what area and when. At least four categories of cylinders exist, distinguished by cap shape and color. The First Order continues to use these devices, calling them "access cylinders." General Hux's personal assassin, Captain Tritt Opan, carries a fake code cylinder full of poison for his own nefarious purposes.

A300 BLASTER RIFLE

APPEARANCES S, RO **MANUFACTURER** BlasTech Industries **MODEL** A-300 **TYPE** Blaster rifle

The A300 is one of a large line of rifles—including the A280, A280-CFE, and A310—all of which look similar. The A300 is highly customizable, with a removable shoulder stock, various sized barrel adapters, and other attachments. It is used by numerous organizations, including the Rebel Alliance and Pyke Syndicate.

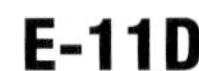

E-11D

APPEARANCES RO, Reb **MANUFACTURER** BlastTech Industries **MODEL** E-11D **TYPE** Blaster rifle

Imperial death troopers are assigned E-11D blaster rifles in addition to their SE-14R light repeating blaster pistols. This rifle features an adjustable stock and a large-bore reinforced barrel for an improved rate of fire and larger plasma blasts. However, the weapon also has a powerful recoil, making it difficult for most stormtroopers to manage.

KX-SERIES DROID

APPEARANCES RO **MANUFACTURER** Arakyd Industries **MODEL** KX-series **TYPE** Security droid

The Imperial Senate enacts a law against the building of battle droids, but Arakyd Industries, in cooperation with the Imperial military, finds a loophole by marketing the KX-series as "security droids," and omits programming to stop them harming organic beings. The KX-series is programmed to defer to military officers with the rank of lieutenant or higher, and they may act as escorts and bodyguards, as well as guards of Imperial facilities. They are capable of hard labor and translating but find these tasks tedious. Their height and strength make them intimidating to soldiers of low rank, rebel spies, and prisoners. KX-series droids are pre-programmed to operate more than 40 Imperial transport vehicles, and can quickly adapt to new ones. A data spike for accessing computer systems—and even slicing other droids—is concealed in their left fist. The New Republic has been known to reprogram KX-series droids for its own uses.

Rebel agent
K-2SO has been reprogrammed to work for the Rebel Alliance and excels at infiltrating enemy installations.

2-1B

APPEARANCES CW, III, S, Reb, RO V, VI **TYPE** Surgical droid **MANUFACTURER**: Industrial Automaton **AFFILIATION** None

Popular since the days of the Republic, Model 2-1B surgical droids are equipped with an encyclopedic memory and a great bedside manner. Their removable hands support a variety of medical devices. 2-1Bs serve both Darth Vader and Luke Skywalker during the Galactic Civil War. A unit named 2MED2 later works for the Resistance against the First Order.

FX-SERIES

APPEARANCES CW, III, V, VI **TYPE** Medical assistant droid **MANUFACTURER** Medtech Industries **AFFILIATION** None

FX-series droids provide invaluable medical assistance to 2-1B surgical droids. Designed with multiple arms, they monitor patients, perform tests, operate equipment, and recommend procedures. An FX-9 supplies Darth Vader with a blood transfusion during his reconstruction. Later, an FX-7 monitors Luke Skywalker while he receives bacta treatments.

VADER'S MEDITATION CHAMBER

APPEARANCES V **MANUFACTURER** Unknown
TYPE Life-support system

Darth Vader owns many meditation chambers across the galaxy, including one in his fortress on Mustafar and another aboard his Super Star Destroyer. Each one possesses life-support systems, enabling him to survive without wearing his helmet. Internal holoprojectors and viewscreens allow Vader to issue commands and receive communications while inside the chamber. For a time he uses a mobile chamber, which is taken by rebels when they steal Moff Tarkin's *Carrion Spike*. Vader's connection to this chamber allows him to track the ship through the Force.

AJ^6 CYBORG CONSTRUCT

APPEARANCES Reb, V
MANUFACTURER BioTech Industries
MODEL Aj^6 **TYPE** Cybernetic implant

This cyborg construct allows its wearer to access computer systems directly through a wireless link to their brain. The increased speed, broader systems access, and overall productivity boost that the implant provides has a deleterious effect on the wearer's personality, having a tendency to dominate their brain. This "lobotomy effect" has given rise to the device's other name, "Lobot-Tech headgear." Notable wearers include the Rodian Tseebo (a friend of Ezra Bridger's parents), Imperial controller LT-319, and Lobot, Lando Calrissian's friend.

BACTA TANK

APPEARANCES CW, RO, V
MANUFACTURERS Zaltin Corp., Xucphra Corp., the Vratix
TYPE Medical device

Bacta tanks are cylindrical chambers filled with bacta fluid, a gelatinous substance that encourages the rapid healing of injuries that are much too serious for the patient's body to recover from on its own. Invented by the insectoid Vratix race from the planet Thyferra, bacta is a mixture of kavam and alazhi bacteria combined with ambori fluid. Republic clones often recover from battle injuries in bacta tanks during the Clone Wars. Luke Skywalker makes a speedy recovery from a wampa attack in a bacta tank at the Rebel Alliance's Echo Base on Hoth. Darth Vader also maintains a bacta tank in his castle on Mustafar.

FORCE PIKE

APPEARANCES I, II, CW, III, Reb, RO, VI **MANUFACTURER** SoroSuub Corp.
MODEL Controller FP **TYPE** Vibro-weapon

Force pikes are a staff-type weapon with a vibroactive head capable of emitting electro-shocks that can inflict pain, stun, or even kill an opponent when used in tandem. Force pikes are famously wielded by Emperor Palpatine's Royal Guards, but are also employed by other sentries and bodyguards of high-profile persons throughout the galaxy. The Emperor's guards use them to project a force field around Force-sensitive Ezra Bridger and hold him in the air, although the young rebel is able to break free.

EG-SERIES DROID

APPEARANCES I, II, CW, S, Reb, RO, IV, V, VI, VII
MANUFACTURER Industrial Automaton
MODEL EG **TYPE** Power droids

EG-series "Gonk" droids are just one of the many varieties of power droids that serve as autonomous generators. They waddle about an area, recharging ships, machinery, and even other droids, whether they are following the command of their masters, or merely retracing a routine coded in their programming. EG droids sometimes serve as couriers and, being inconspicuous and a common sight, can easily slip in and out of hostile areas. However, their slow walking speed makes them vulnerable, especially to thieves. EG droids have been manufactured for a long time and come in many designs and colors.

MOUSE DROID

APPEARANCES CW, III, Reb, RO, IV, V, VI, VII, **MANUFACTURER** Rebaxan Columni
MODEL MSE-series **TYPE** Maintenance droid

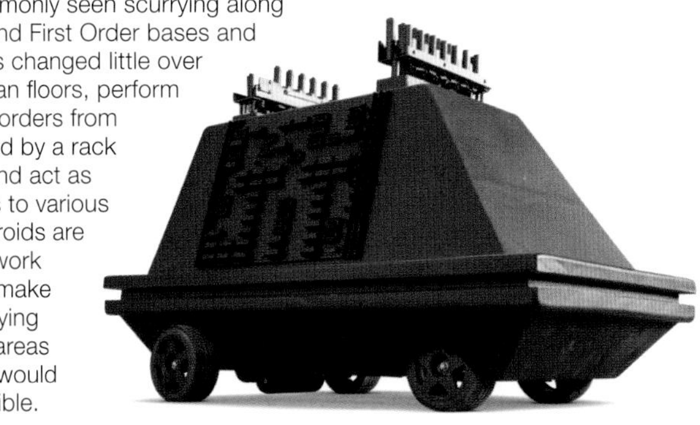

Mouse droids are commonly seen scurrying along the floors of Imperial and First Order bases and ships. Their design has changed little over the decades. They clean floors, perform as couriers, delivering orders from commanders (facilitated by a rack on their dorsal side), and act as guides, leading visitors to various destinations. Mouse droids are simple, versatile, and work quietly—qualities that make them ideal tools for spying and infiltrating secure areas or data networks that would otherwise be inaccessible.

BOBA FETT'S ARMOR

APPEARANCES IV, V, VI **MANUFACTURER** Unknown
MODEL Custom **TYPE** Mandalorian armor

Conforming to almost exact specifications of traditional Mandalorian garb, Boba Fett's armor is made of durasteel rather than the customary beskar steel, and has been heavily modified. Boba decides upon this protective gear for his bounty hunting jobs in honor of the suit worn by his bounty hunter father, Jango Fett, wearing its dents and scratches with pride. Fett's jetpack is useful for short jumps and longer flights, and is equipped with a rocket launcher that may be armed with a missile or grappling hook. His helmet is equipped with a targeting rangefinder, macrobinocular viewplate, and a motion and sound-sensor system. Fett's internal comlink allows him to summon his ship, *Slave I*, remotely and over a great distance. After the rebel insurrection aboard the *Khetanna*, some presume that Boba Fett and his armor remain within the Great Pit of Carkoon on Tatooine.

Always working
As an adult, Boba is never seen without his armor in public, even when off duty at Jabba's palace.

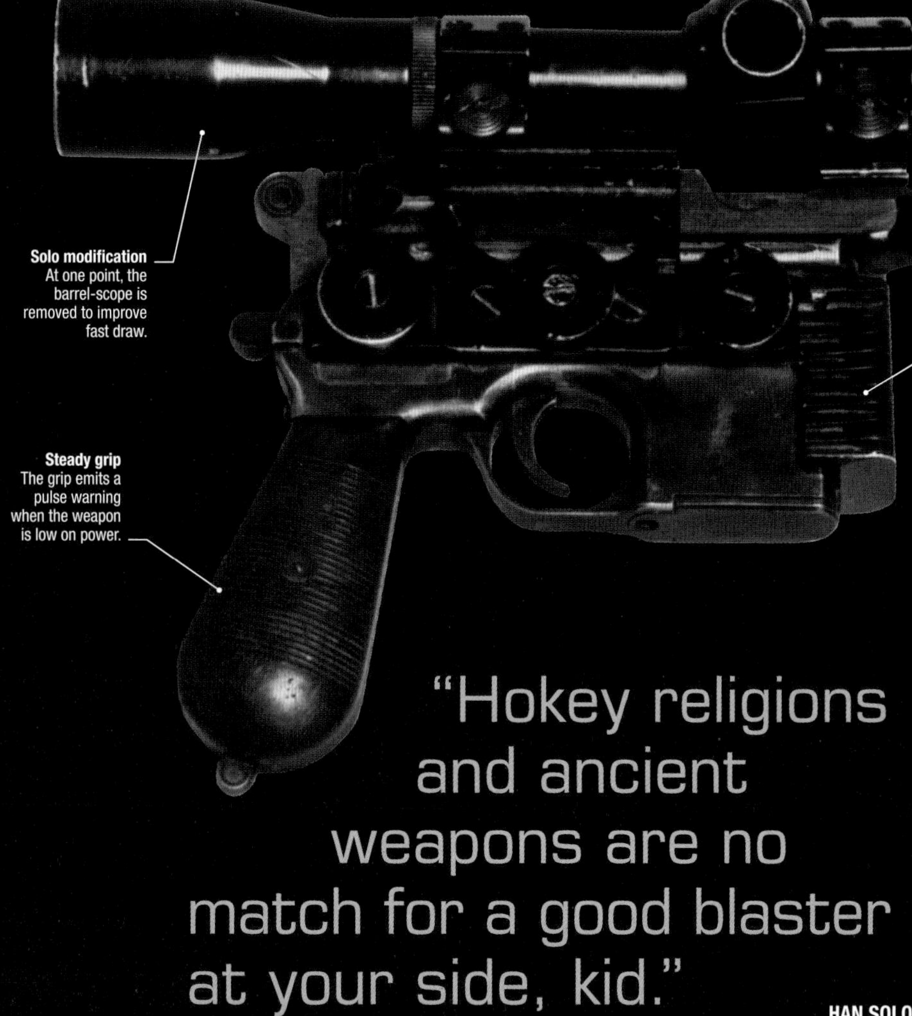

Powerful shot
The pistol fires laser bolts strong enough to pierce stormtrooper armor.

Solo modification
At one point, the barrel-scope is removed to improve fast draw.

Cooling unit

Steady grip
The grip emits a pulse warning when the weapon is low on power.

"Hokey religions and ancient weapons are no match for a good blaster at your side, kid."
HAN SOLO

HAN SOLO'S MODIFIED DL-44 HEAVY BLASTER PISTOL

APPEARANCES S, Reb, IV, V, VI, VII **MANUFACTURER** BlasTech Industries
MODEL DL-44 **TYPE** Heavy blaster pistol

A wide range of individuals make the DL-44 their blaster pistol of choice, including rebel Ezra Bridger. It offers above-average firepower for a pistol, without compromising accuracy, making it ideal for use by military forces as well as bounty hunters and smugglers. The DL-44's capacitor can charge a double-power laser bolt without overheating.

Notorious smuggler Tobias Beckett owns a DL-44 with field rifle accessories that he wields on the battlefield of Mimban. Beckett later removes the upgrades and gives the blaster to his new crewmate, Han Solo, on Vandor. After Beckett betrays Han on Savareen, Han shoots first, before Beckett can try to kill him.

Throughout his decade-spanning career, Han keeps his trusty DL-44 handy at all times, making a number of personalized modifications to his blaster pistol. Confident in his own aim, Han later removes the factory-issue motion-sensitive scope so that the pistol can be drawn faster from its holster.

During the Assault on Starkiller Base, Han Solo tries to reconnect with his wayward son Kylo Ren and persuade him to turn away from the First Order, but Kylo kills him. Han's body and his DL-44 blaster are destroyed when Starkiller Base blows up.

Bounty denied
The bounty hunter Greedo tries to abduct Han at gunpoint in the Mos Eisley Cantina on behalf of Jabba the Hutt. Instead, Han covertly draws his DL-44 beneath the table, prepared to defend himself.

Trusty blaster
Han rarely goes anywhere without his customized DL-44 blaster pistol *(center left)*, although it proves of little use against Darth Vader when the Sith Lord captures the rebels at Cloud City. Han wields it to great effect against the Imperial forces on Endor during the raid on the shield generator bunker protecting the second Death Star *(left)*.

IMPERIAL PROBE DROID

APPEARANCES S, Reb, V, VI **MANUFACTURER** Arakyd Industries
MODEL Viper probe droid **TYPE** Probe droid

Also called a probot, the Imperial probe droid is used to track down the enemies of the Empire almost anywhere in the galaxy. It can be launched from starships to travel through space in a hyperspace pod until arriving at the planet it is assigned to search. The probe droid's repulsorlift engine allows it to travel across any type of terrain, and its thrusters have silencers to prevent detection.

At 2 meters (6½ ft) in height, the probot contains numerous sensors, a holocam, six manipulator arms for taking samples, and a small mounted blaster for defense. The high-frequency HoloNet transceiver allows the probe droid to transmit information to Imperial forces even at great distances. The 11-3K is a variant on the standard probe droid that is more heavily armed, so it is often assigned to patrol duty on remote planets like Vandor.

Rebels found
Darth Vader dispatches numerous probe droids across the stars to search for the rebel base. One of the droids discovers Echo Base on Hoth and transmits visual confirmation to Vader's flagship.

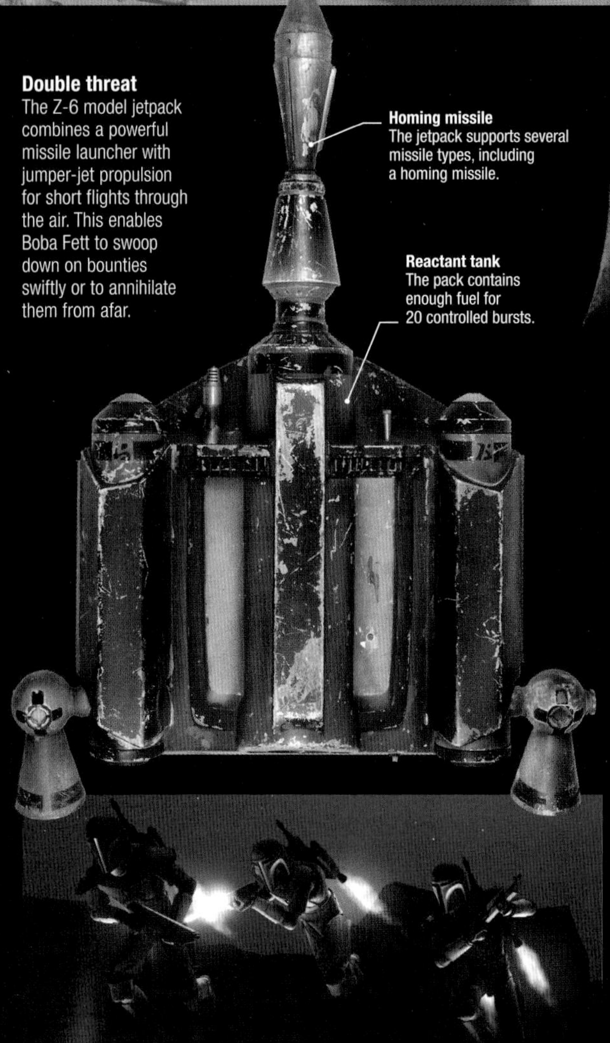

Double threat
The Z-6 model jetpack combines a powerful missile launcher with jumper-jet propulsion for short flights through the air. This enables Boba Fett to swoop down on bounties swiftly or to annihilate them from afar.

Z-6 JETPACK

APPEARANCES II, CW, Reb, IV, V, VI **MANUFACTURER** Mitrinomon Transports **MODEL** Z-6 **TYPE** Jetpack

The notorious bounty hunter Boba Fett includes the Z-6 jetpack among his usual gear. Fuel burned by the personal transportation device produces significant thrust, providing a tactical advantage during combat situations but also creating personal risk for the wearer. Gyro-stabilizers ensure that the directional thrusters provide easy maneuverability. The launcher supports two uses: as a projectile grappling hook with its cable attached to the internal winch, enabling its user to snare and haul in bounties, or as a powerful anti-vehicle homing missile. This functionality makes the Z-6 model a favorite for others, including Mandalorian commandos and Boba's father, Jango Fett.

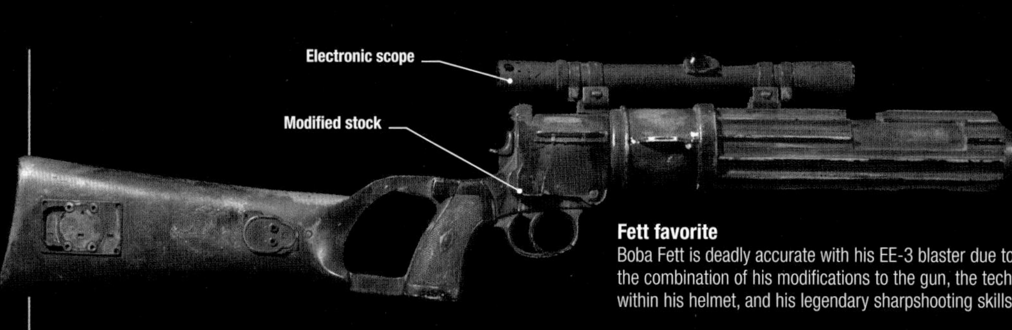

Fett favorite
Boba Fett is deadly accurate with his EE-3 blaster due to the combination of his modifications to the gun, the tech within his helmet, and his legendary sharpshooting skills.

EE-3 BLASTER RIFLE

APPEARANCES CW, IV, VI
MANUFACTURER BlasTech Industries
MODEL EE-3 **TYPE** Blaster carbine

Shorter and lighter than the E-11 blaster rifle that serves as the standard-issue weapon of Imperial stormtroopers, the EE-3 carbine rifle relies on a two-handed grip to compensate for the smaller handle attached to the barrel. The standard EE-3 has a quicker rate of fire but less accuracy and stopping power than larger rifles. Its size is its main advantage, making it a favorite of bounty hunters across the galaxy. Boba Fett carries a modified EE-3 as his preferred blaster, and the Zabrak bounty hunter Sugi wields one during the Clone Wars.

BOBA FETT'S WRIST GAUNTLETS

APPEARANCES IV, V, VI **CREATOR** Boba Fett **MODEL** Handcrafted **TYPE** Bounty hunter wrist gauntlets

Always careful to ensure he has many options at his disposal, Boba Fett wears wrist gauntlets stocked with numerous features. Their powerful weapons include the ZX miniature flamethrower from Czerka Corporation, capable of projecting a cone of fire 5 meters (16½ ft) long and 1 meter (3ft 3 in) in diameter, and the Dur-24 wrist laser from BlasTech Industries, which combines the full firepower of a standard blaster rifle with a range of up to 50 meters (164 ft). The MM9 mini concussion rocket launcher from Kelvarek Consolidated Arms fires various types of small homing missiles, such as stun rockets and anti-vehicle rockets. Fett's right gauntlet includes an extensible fibercord whip that can be fired to quickly bind up the target's limbs.

Crafty devices
Boba Fett has many tricks on his sleeves *(above left)*. At the Great Pit of Carkoon, he fires a fibercord whip from a wrist projector to ensnare Luke *(above)*.

GOLAN ARMS DF.9 ANTI-INFANTRY BATTERY

APPEARANCES V, FoD **MANUFACTURER** Golan Arms
MODEL DF.9 **TYPE** Anti-infantry battery

A fixed emplacement weapon, the DF.9's single laser cannon fires blasts capable of annihilating whole squads of approaching infantry. The cannon is effective at a distance of up to 16 kilometers (10 miles). The gunner in the 4-meter- (13-ft-) tall upper turret enjoys a full 180-degree rotation of fire. Within the durasteel armored turret, which can readily withstand blaster fire, a targeting computer technician assists with precision aim, while another ensures stable energy flow from the power generator.

LUKE SKYWALKER'S FLIGHT HELMET

APPEARANCES IV, V, VI
MANUFACTURER Koensayr
MODEL Model K-22995 helmet
TYPE Flight helmet

When Luke arrives at the secret rebel base at Yavin 4, he promptly volunteers to join the desperate attack mission against the Empire's approaching Death Star. Assigned to fly Red Five, Luke receives a standard-issue X-wing pilot's uniform for Red Squadron, including a helmet adorned with the Rebel Alliance starbird logo. The helmet has a plasteel exterior and insulated foam-lined interior. Among other features, it includes a retractable polarized visor, sensa-mic for communications, and a localized atmospheric field generator. After he destroys the Death Star, Luke continues to wear his pilot helmet on other missions in his X-wing.

A280 BLASTER RIFLE

APPEARANCES V **MANUFACTURER** BlasTech Industries **MODEL** A280 **TYPE** Blaster rifle

Considered one of the best armor-piercing blaster rifles, the A280 provides more power than other rifles at long range. During the Republic's final years, A280s are commonly used by local planetary forces, which makes them readily available on the black market. Many rebel troops wield A280s against the Empire during the Battle of Hoth. BlasTech also produces the A280C variant rifle, which is favored by Alliance commandos.

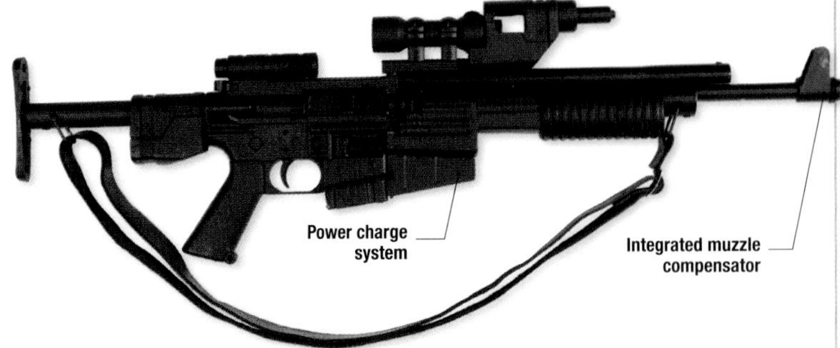

1.4 FD P-TOWER

APPEARANCES V **MANUFACTURER** Atgar SpaceDefense Corp. **MODEL** 1.4 FD **TYPE** Light anti-vehicle laser cannon

The 1.4 FD P-Tower is a fixed emplacement anti-vehicle laser cannon for use in all terrains. The single laser cannon fires from the center of the energy dish, which has 16 micropower routers spaced evenly along the edge and eight power conversion cells along the interior. The P-Tower is inexpensive, and quick and easy to produce.

Rotating base The 1.4 FD P-Tower has 360° rotation for full range of fire.

Extreme conditions The 1.4 FD P-Tower can operate in temperatures from -73°C (-100°F) to 49°C (120°F).

E-WEB REPEATING BLASTER

APPEARANCES Reb, V **MANUFACTURER** BlasTech Industries **MODEL** E-Web **TYPE** Heavy repeating blaster

The Emplacement Weapon Heavy Blaster, commonly known as an E-Web, is the most powerful repeating blaster in the Imperial arsenal. Rigid mounts counteract the kinetic energy created by the weapon's formidable firepower. Usually operated by a two-person crew, its set-up time limits its effectiveness, so some Imperial crews pre-charge the generator for faster assembly. This requires careful adjustment of the power flow to prevent an overload.

V-150 PLANET DEFENDER

APPEARANCES V, FoD **MANUFACTURER** Kuat Drive Yards **MODEL** v-150 **TYPE** Heavy ion-to-space cannon

The v-150 Planet Defender is a surface-based ion cannon designed to target starships orbiting above a planet. Often deployed in conjunction with planetary shields, it defends planets while the shields reach full power. The cannon has an optimum range of 4,000 kilometers (2,485 miles) and a maximum range of 180,000 kilometers (111,847 miles), and can disrupt Star Destroyers with a single ion bolt. However, being a stationary weapon makes the v-150 Planet Defender vulnerable to attack, and its blast shield must be retracted to utilize the cannon.

Surface-to-space firepower The v-150 Planet Defender is equipped with an independent power generator buried some 40 meters (131 feet) below the weapon placement.

LUKE SKYWALKER'S GREEN LIGHTSABER

APPEARANCES VI, VIII, FoD **CREATOR** Luke Skywalker **MODEL** Handcrafted **TYPE** Jedi lightsaber

Luke Skywalker's second lightsaber has a green blade and is the first one he built himself. After his fateful trip to Cloud City where he loses his first lightsaber, Luke constructs the saber in a cave on Tatooine, modeling it after Obi-Wan Kenobi's weapon—albeit with some simplified design elements. For the rescue of Han Solo from Jabba's Palace, the young Jedi entrusts his lightsaber to R2-D2. During their escape, the trusty astromech launches the weapon across the Great Pit of Carkoon into Luke's hand. Aboard the second Death Star, Luke uses his lightsaber in his final confrontation with Darth Vader, but refuses to succumb to the Emperor's goading to kill his father.

In the coming years, Luke continues to wield his blade as he rebuilds the Jedi Order. After sensing the dark side in his nephew, Ben Solo, Luke activates his saber above the young man while he sleeps, fully intent on killing him. Ben awakens and attacks his uncle, who immediately feels remorse. This moment leads to Ben wiping out the fledgling Jedi Order. After the Order's destruction, the whereabouts of Luke's second lightsaber are unknown.

SCOUT TROOPER BLASTER

APPEARANCES S, Reb, RO, VI **MANUFACTURER** BlasTech Industries **MODEL** EC-17 **TYPE** Hold-out blaster

A standard-issue weapon for Imperial scout troopers and patrol troopers, this compact, one-handed weapon serves as a hold-out blaster, and is optimal for short-range targets. Holstered in a scout trooper's boot or on a patrol trooper's utility belt, the pistol has a pressure-sensitive grip instead of a trigger to account for the trooper's gloves. It also has a built-in targeting scope to assist its user's aim.

Activation panel
An internal fusion reaction is activated via the control panel.

Thermite shell
Volatile baradium is contained inside a thermite casing.

CLASS-A THERMAL DETONATOR

APPEARANCES VI, Res, FoD **MANUFACTURER** Merr-Sonn Munitions, Inc. **MODEL** Class-A thermal detonator **TYPE** Thermal detonator

The Class-A thermal detonator's power and range make it illegal for use other than for authorized military purposes. The detonator has a blast radius of up to 20 meters (65 feet), though it can be tuned to limit the radius depending on the situation. Posing as the bounty hunter Boushh, Leia threatens Jabba the Hutt with disintegration when she negotiates her fee for "capturing" Chewbacca. Impressed by the bounty hunter's boldness, Jabba agrees to her terms.

SLD-26 PLANETARY SHIELD GENERATOR

APPEARANCES VI, FoD **MANUFACTURER** CoMar Combat Systems **MODEL** SLD-26 **TYPE** Deflector shield generator

The SLD-26 shield generator can protect a small moon or a large space station with a nearly impenetrable energy shield for an indefinite period of time. The Galactic Empire installs such a generator on the forest moon of Endor to protect the second Death Star during its construction phase. The Rebel Alliance sends a strike team to the moon to disable the shield generator in advance of their fleet's attack on the feared battle station. Unaware that the Emperor has set a trap for the rebels on Endor, most of the strike team, including Han Solo and Princess Leia Organa, is captured. However, with the help of the Ewoks, Chewbacca routs the troopers and frees the strike team, which destroys the shield generator, thus allowing the rebel fleet to demolish the Emperor's latest weapon.

Planetary protector
The shield generator is essential for the protection of the second Death Star, as is its destruction for the rebel victory during the Battle of Endor.

BB-SERIES DROIDS

APPEARANCES Res, VII, VIII, IX, FoD **MANUFACTURER** Industrial Automaton **MODEL** BB-series **TYPE** Astromech droid

The BB-series, used by both the Resistance and the First Order, consists of small, orb-shaped droids with heads that are magnetically attached to the upper surfaces of their bodies. The series derives this body shape from therapy droids developed during the Galactic Civil War for rebel veterans. Their outer surfaces come decorated in many colors and patterns, with a wide range of head shapes. They move by rolling their bodies and can travel at high speeds when necessary.

Like R-series and C-series astromechs, BB-series droids fit into droid slots on starfighters, aiding in navigation, weapons systems, sensor monitoring, repairs, and other ship functions. On the ground, they may also serve as guides, couriers, sentries, and spies. They speak using a variant of droidspeak, the most common astromech language, composed of beeps and other electronic sounds.

Similar to those of R-series droids, BB heads feature a single, round photoreceptor and a smaller articulated holoprojector. Fragile receiver and transmitter antennae extend from the back of the head and data ports run along the base of it. Wireless telemetry keeps the head and body of the droid in constant communication. The droids' internal gyroscopic propulsion system is self-correcting, keeping the head atop the body—most of the time. The droid bodies are sealed against contamination from outside debris. Most BB units contain six hatches with interchangeable circular tool-bay disks that support a seemingly unlimited selection of tool kits, including magnetic-tipped bolt-spinners, tow cables, torches, mechanical arms, and tools to access data terminals.

Notable BB units allied to the Resistance include Poe Dameron's loyal and ingenious BB-8 and Kaz Xiono's sassy and courageous CB-23. The sour, black-and-silver BB-9E is stationed aboard the First Order's *Supremacy*.

BB-4
The khaki-colored BB-4 is a loyal member of the Resistance and proudly wears the organization's symbol on his body.

FIRST ORDER STORMTROOPER ARMOR

APPEARANCES Res, VII, VIII, FoD **MANUFACTURER** First Order Department of Military Research **TYPE** Body armor

The First Order creates armor for its troops based on gear worn by its Imperial counterparts. Instead of plastoid composite used by their predecessors, the new regime's armor is composed of stronger, more flexible betaplast material, while the updated helmet features night-vision lenses, and targeting and communications systems. There are at least two variants of basic stormtrooper armor in use simultaneously, with differences in hue and the position of the helmet's nose plate (creating more or less black space over the mouth). It is typical for stormtroopers to wear colored pauldrons to denote rank, and some troopers, such as Captain Phasma and Commander Pyre, have armor in colors other than white. Specialist stormtroopers such as flametroopers, scuba troopers, and snowtroopers have unique armor to suit their respective battlefields.

On patrol
A squad of stormtroopers, including a flametrooper and megablaster heavy assault troopers, conduct a search on Jakku for BB-8.

In control
While Phasma is sometimes seen on the bridge of a Star Destroyer, she would much rather be in combat with her troops.

PHASMA'S ARMOR

APPEARANCES Res, VII, VIII **MANUFACTURER** Phasma **MODEL** Custom **TYPE** First Order stormtrooper armor

Captain Phasma crafts her non-standard First Order armor herself, forging it from a portion of a ship's hull that she salvages from one of Emperor Palpatine's former yachts. The armor's chromium finish gives it a silver, reflective sheen, and also protects her from heat and radiation (as it did the occupants of the old yacht). Her traditional armorweave cape also provides protection, and gives her a stylish, regal air. Phasma's gauntlets are crafted for added strength and leverage, giving her an extra-powerful punch and hand grip. Phasma believes her look is an eye-catching and intimidating symbol of old Imperial power. However, her armor fails her in battle against Finn aboard the warship *Supremacy*. Her helmet is punctured and her breastplate scorched, just before she tumbles into a fiery abyss.

PYRE'S ARMOR

APPEARANCES Res **MANUFACTURER** Unknown **MODEL** Custom **TYPE** First Order stormtrooper armor

Althletic Commander Pyre has his armor specially crafted to be more flexible. He does not wear armor around his lower torso and upper arms, exposing the black body glove he wears underneath. This provides him with increased ease of movement, but makes him more vulnerable to enemy fire. Pyre's shoes are likewise custom-designed for extra flexibility. He wears a black pauldron over his right shoulder, denoting his rank. An electrum finish gives Pyre's armor a reflective gold sheen.

PHASMA'S BLASTER RIFLE

APPEARANCES Res, VII, VIII **MANUFACTURER** Sonn-Blas Corporation **MODEL** Custom F-11D **TYPE** Blaster rifle

A year after joining the First Order, Captain Phasma orders a bespoke version of the F-11D blaster carried by all stormtroopers. Phasma's blaster features a removable buttstock, a recurved trigger guard for a double-handed grip, and larger heat dispersal vents on the barrel. The weapon also has a chromium finish to match her armor. The trigger will only fire when paired with her own gloves. The blaster is destroyed when Finn smashes it with a laser ax aboard the *Supremacy*.

Deadly shot
Phasma is very skilled not only with her F-11D blaster rifle, but all types of First Order weapons.

PYRE'S BLASTER

APPEARANCES Res **MANUFACTURER** Sonn-Blas Corporation **MODEL** Custom F-11D **TYPE** Blaster rifle

Commander Pyre uses a custom, slightly improved version of the standard F-11D that is carried by every stormtrooper in the First Order, to include an electrum finish that matches his striking gold-colored armor. The blaster also features a J20 adjustable electroscope for increased zoom and a more precise focus, as well as enlarged heat dispersal vents to prevent the gun from overheating. It is also keyed to only operate when paired with Pyre's own gloves.

The weapon's spearpoints never dull.

PHASMA'S BATON

APPEARANCES VIII **MANUFACTURER** Unknown
MODEL Custom **TYPE** Melee weapon

Captain Phasma's collection of personal weapons includes a quicksilver baton that resembles the spears used by tribes on her homeworld, Parnassos. The shaft is constructed from a collapsible micromesh matrix. When not in use, the spear retracts into a small baton with a spearhead on each end, held by a containment field. When activated, it immediately extends to full length. Phasma uses the weapon in her fateful combat with former stormtrooper Finn aboard the *Supremacy*.

FIRST ORDER TIE PILOT HELMET

APPEARANCES Res, VII, VIII **MANUFACTURER** First Order Department of Military Research
TYPE Flight helmet

Every First Order TIE fighter pilot wears a vac-seal helmet in case of a hull breach. The helmet connects, via tubing, to an air-filtration system and life-support control panel worn on the pilot's chest. Targeting sensors on either side of the helmet connect to a targeting interface projector that displays on the helmet's internal view-screen. The detachable chin unit contains a pilot comlink connected wirelessly to the ship's communication systems. Red marking on either side of the nose bridge denotes a Special Forces pilot.

KYLO REN'S HELMET

APPEARANCES VII, VIII, IX **MANUFACTURER** Unknown **MODEL** Custom **TYPE** Battle helmet

Kylo Ren's helmet is designed in the style of the Knights of Ren. It is also reminiscent of the infamous mask of his grandfather, Darth Vader, connecting Kylo to the dark side of his family heritage. The helmet conceals his former identity as Ben Solo (also obscured by the helmet's vocoder which makes his voice sound more threatening), and serves to intimidate both his enemies and his subordinates in the First Order. Beyond this and the protection it affords, the helmet has no special functions. Supreme Leader Snoke is particularly unimpressed by the helmet, calling Kylo "a boy in a mask." This infuriates Kylo, especially after his many sacrifices to please Snoke, including killing his own father. In a fit of rage, Kylo smashes the helmet in the *Supremacy*'s elevator as he descends from Snoke's throne room.

Shards of rage
Now Supreme Leader, Kylo has the fragments of his helmet reforged, perhaps trying once more to prove he is his grandfather's equal.

Helmet off
Kylo Ren ponders his helmet before he destroys it.

FIRST ORDER PROBE DROID

APPEARANCES Res **MANUFACTURER** Arakyd-Harch Technologies **MODEL** Spider probe droid
TYPE Sentry probe droid

Armed with numerous sensors, First Order probe droids watch over top-secret weapons testing grounds and other unmanned military facilities. When activated, the droids ("mothers") release smaller drones called "kids," which are equipped with blasters to dispatch detected threats. If the probe droids are destroyed or fail to eliminate the intruders, they broadcast a signal to the nearest First Order station, which scrambles a contingent of TIE fighters to their location. Poe Dameron and Kazuda Xiono encounter a probe droid while investigating a cataclysm caused by First Order activities, and barely escape.

Tuanul village
While on the hunt for the map to Luke Skywalker, Kylo Ren wields his lightsaber to strike down galactic explorer Lor San Tekka.

KYLO REN'S LIGHTSABER

APPEARANCES VII, VIII, IX **MANUFACTURER** Kylo Ren **MODEL** Custom
TYPE Crossguard lightsaber

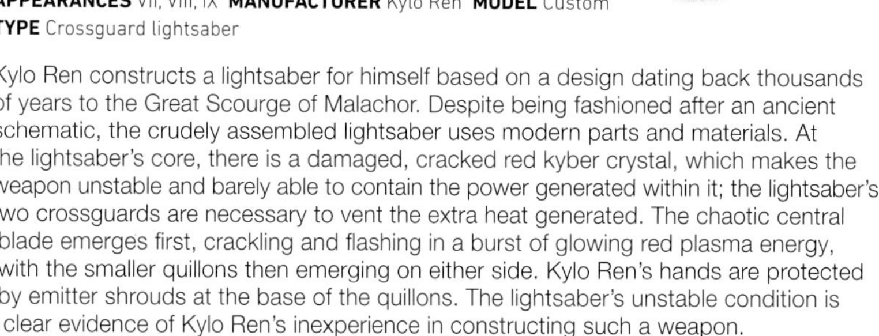

Kylo Ren constructs a lightsaber for himself based on a design dating back thousands of years to the Great Scourge of Malachor. Despite being fashioned after an ancient schematic, the crudely assembled lightsaber uses modern parts and materials. At the lightsaber's core, there is a damaged, cracked red kyber crystal, which makes the weapon unstable and barely able to contain the power generated within it; the lightsaber's two crossguards are necessary to vent the extra heat generated. The chaotic central blade emerges first, crackling and flashing in a burst of glowing red plasma energy, with the smaller quillons then emerging on either side. Kylo Ren's hands are protected by emitter shrouds at the base of the quillons. The lightsaber's unstable condition is clear evidence of Kylo Ren's inexperience in constructing such a weapon.

REY'S QUARTERSTAFF

APPEARANCES VII, VIII, FoD **MANUFACTURER** Rey
MODEL Custom **TYPE** Melee staff

Rey fashions her quarterstaff from wreckage she finds while scavenging in the dunes of Jakku. A strap allows her to sling the staff over her shoulder when she is climbing, or clip it securely to her speeder. A handhold made from scraps of an old uniform gives a secure, comfortable grip. Rey uses her quarterstaff for a variety of purposes. It serves as a trusty walking stick, ideal for testing the sands of Jakku for instability and for searching for things buried underneath. It can also be used as a weapon against bandits and thugs. The skills Rey gains with her quarterstaff also help her to wield a lightsaber; however, she is so effective with her staff that she continues to use it, even after acquiring Luke Skywalker's legendary weapon.

Giving no quarter
Rey realizes that she has to be ready at all times to defend herself at Niima Outpost on Jakku.

FIRST ORDER RIOT SHIELD

APPEARANCES VII, VIII **MANUFACTURER** Sonn-Blas Corp. **TYPE** Handheld shield

First Order riot troopers utilize lightweight composite betaplast ballistic riot shields in conjunction with Z6 riot control batons during their missions. While riot troopers are normally used to quell civil rebellions, they are also sent into battle against military targets.

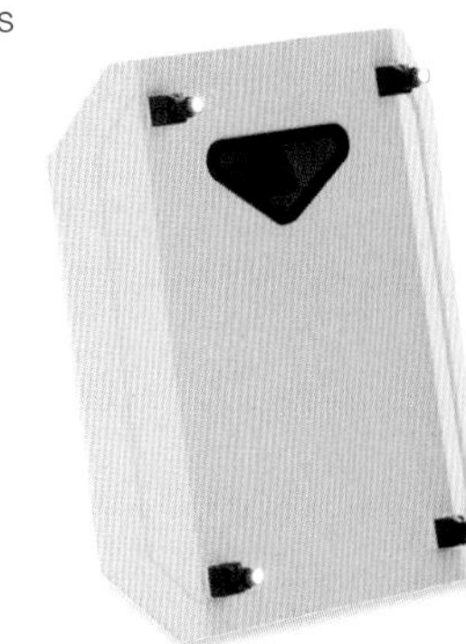

Z6 RIOT CONTROL BATON

APPEARANCES VII, VIII **MANUFACTURER** Sonn-Blas Corp.
MODEL Z6 **TYPE** Riot control baton

The Z6 Riot control baton is wielded by selected stormtroopers, usually against non-military personnel. Collapsible conductor contact veins are capable of delivering a powerful electric shock that can stun. The baton can also deflect lightsaber blades. The handle's adhesive grip pairs magnetically with a stormtrooper's gloves.

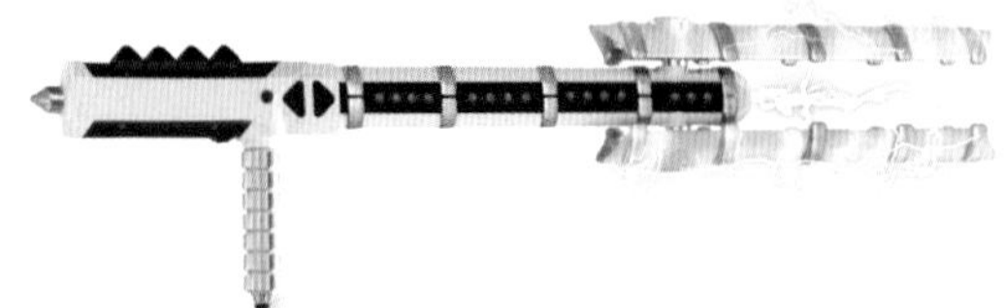

GLIE-44 BLASTER PISTOL

APPEARANCES Res, VII, VIII
MANUFACTURER Eirriss Ryloth Defense Tech **MODEL** Glie-44
TYPE Blaster pistol

The Glie-44 blaster pistol is named after Twi'lek freedom-fighter Gobi Glie. A rechargeable power cartridge slides in a front slot for convenient access. It is commonly used by Resistance members against the First Order, and is also used by civilians, police, and the military throughout the galaxy.

SE-44C BLASTER PISTOL

APPEARANCES VII, VIII **MANUFACTURER** Sonn-Blas Corp.
MODEL SE-44C **TYPE** Blaster pistol

The First Order's SE-44C is the standard-issue blaster pistol for stormtroopers. It comes with a mount for a scope and a replaceable barrel head. Some officers, such as General Hux, carry a black version made of plasteel. Captain Phasma has one finished with chromium.

REY'S NN-14 BLASTER PISTOL

APPEARANCES VII, VIII, FoD **MANUFACTURER** LPA **MODEL** NN-14 **TYPE** Blaster pistol

The NN-14's reinforced frame and large power core produce a powerful plasma bolt. Han Solo gives Rey an NN-14 blaster pistol before they enter Maz's castle on Takodana. She uses it against the First Order stormtroopers who soon invade, but Kylo Ren restrains her with the Force before she can fire at him. While their minds are linked on the planet Ahch-To, Rey fires the blaster at Kylo, but unintentionally blasts a hole in the wall of her stone hut.

D-93 FLAME-THROWER

APPEARANCES VII **MANUFACTURER** First Order Department of Military Research
MODEL D-93 **TYPE** Flame-thrower

The D-93 is used by First Order flametroopers to turn battlefields into blazing infernos, scattering the enemy, and for setting encampments alight, striking terror into their occupants. The double-barreled gun connects to a backpack containing tanks of conflagrine-14 gel, a highly volatile substance that produces a torrent of flames to a distance of up to 75 meters (246 ft). The pack contains large twin tanks of the gel, and a smaller central tank of pressurized propellant. A piezoelectrical ignition system fires the weapon.

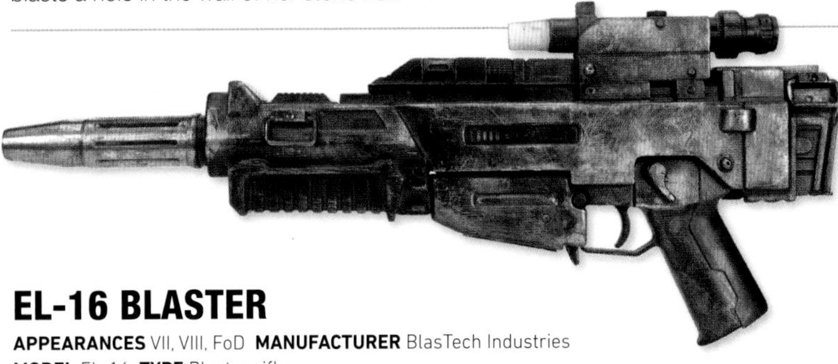

EL-16 BLASTER

APPEARANCES VII, VIII, FoD **MANUFACTURER** BlasTech Industries
MODEL EL-16 **TYPE** Blaster rifle

The EL-16 is the standard-issue blaster rifle of the Resistance. By the rise of the First Order it is an outdated weapon, but the Resistance is forced to make do with whatever meager munitions they can acquire from benefactors and secondhand weapons dealers. The EL-16HFE is a larger, heavy field version with a removable buttstock, designed for large-scale battles. Poe Dameron keeps one stowed aboard each of his X-wings. Both rifles are in use by the Resistance from its formation.

JT-000 INTERROGATOR DROID

APPEARANCES VII **MANUFACTURER** First Order Department of Military Research **MODEL** JT-000
TYPE Interrogator droid

The First Order utilizes JT-000 interrogator droids, an advanced model of torture droid based on the Empire's old IT-O units. These droids represent a violation of the New Republic's laws. The JT-000 is a perversion of advances in medical technology. It is capable of speech and able to record answers from its victims, allowing it to conduct torture-interrogation sessions without supervision. Kylo Ren keeps one on hand for when he tires of doing his dirty work himself.

FIRST ORDER SENTRY DROID

APPEARANCES Res, VII, VIII **MANUFACTURER** Rabaxan Columni **TYPE** Security droid

The First Order uses sentry droids to patrol Star Destroyers and bases, where they maintain security and watch out for spies. The droids appear small and docile as they roam about on their four rolling coasters. When they detect an intruder, however, they spring into action, dramatically increasing in height and relentlessly firing a pair of blasters. Poe Dameron, Kazudo Xiono, and BB-8 encounter these droids patrolling the First Order's secret Station Theta Black, just prior to the base's demolition.

RK-3 BLASTER

APPEARANCES Reb, Res **MANUFACTURER** Merr-Sonn Munitions, Inc. and Sonn-Blas Corp. **MODEL** RK-3 (customized) **TYPE** Blaster pistol

Major Elrik Vonreg owns a RK-3 blaster with a red finish to match his unique armor. Indicator lights at the back alert him to his weapon's power levels and the blaster bursts hit their targets with pinpoint precision. The model is also popular with Imperial officers Thrawn, Slavin, and Hask.

ACP ARRAY GUN

APPEARANCES CW, Res **MANUFACTURER** Arakyd Industries **MODEL** ACP Array Gun (customized) **TYPE** Accelerated Charged Particle Array Gun

The pirate Kragan Gorr carries a custom ACP Array Gun with a modified trigger and targeting scope. It is decorated with his gang's symbol. The weapon is more suited for close-range combat against organic opponents than droids.

FLEXPOLY BACTA SUIT

APPEARANCES VIII **MANUFACTURER** Zaltin Corp. **MODEL** Flexpoly bacta suit **TYPE** Medical device

The flexpoly bacta suit is a temporary emergency medical device that allows severely injured patients to be transported without the need of a full-sized bacta tank. The suit has sensors and tubes to autonomously circulate bacta fluid through itself and rapidly heal injuries. Finn is placed in a medically induced coma during the evacuation of the Resistance base on D'Qar. The failing, second-hand suit begins to leak its contents of life-saving bacta shortly after Finn regains consciousness. Since the Resistance is strapped for resources, it has to settle with sub-par medical equipment such as this.

SUPERLASER SIEGE CANNON

APPEARANCES VIII **MANUFACTURER** First Order Department of Military Research

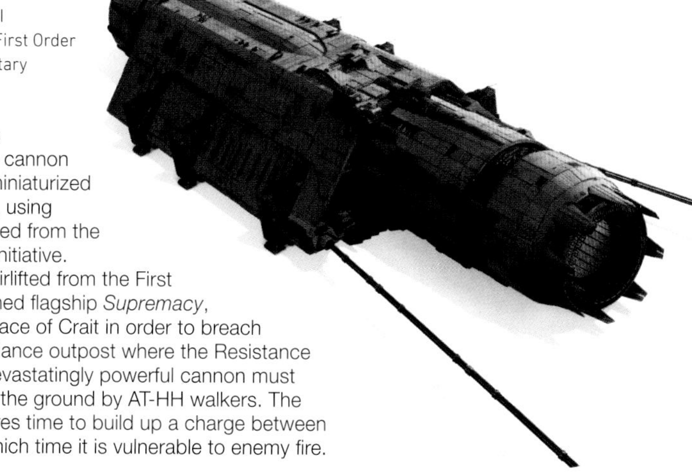

The First Order's superlaser siege cannon is essentially a miniaturized Death Star laser, using technology derived from the Empire's Tarkin Initiative. The weapon is airlifted from the First Order's demolished flagship *Supremacy*, down to the surface of Crait in order to breach the old Rebel Alliance outpost where the Resistance is hiding. This devastatingly powerful cannon must be hauled along the ground by AT-HH walkers. The superlaser requires time to build up a charge between firings, during which time it is vulnerable to enemy fire.

ELECTRO-BISENTO

APPEARANCES VIII **MANUFACTURER** Praetorian Guard **TYPE** Melee vibro-weapon

Fashioned by the Praetorian Guard, the electro-bisento is one of several weapons wielded by the Elite Praetorian Guard to defend the First Order's Supreme Leader Snoke. The tempered blade vibrates at a high frequency owing to a built-in compact ultrasonic generator. This vibro-feature makes the cutting edge even more deadly. A plasma filament also energizes the blade, allowing it to deflect lightsaber attacks. The near-indestructible phrik pole handle is likewise protected from lightsaber blows.

BILARI ELECTRO-CHAIN WHIP

APPEARANCES VIII **MANUFACTURER** Praetorian Guard **TYPE** Melee vibro-weapon

The Praetorian Guard's Bilari electro-chain whip is a solid rapier than transforms into a flexible electro-plasma chain of phrik metal. It can be used to stab, stun, flog, or restrain an opponent. The whip is designed to counter lightsabers, too, making it a formidable and versatile weapon. The Guard's gloves are insulated against the electro-pulses of the weapon. Direct contact with the skin causes burns and searing pain. Like the Guard's other weapons, the whip is proprietary and the specifications of its design are unknown even to the First Order's military engineers.

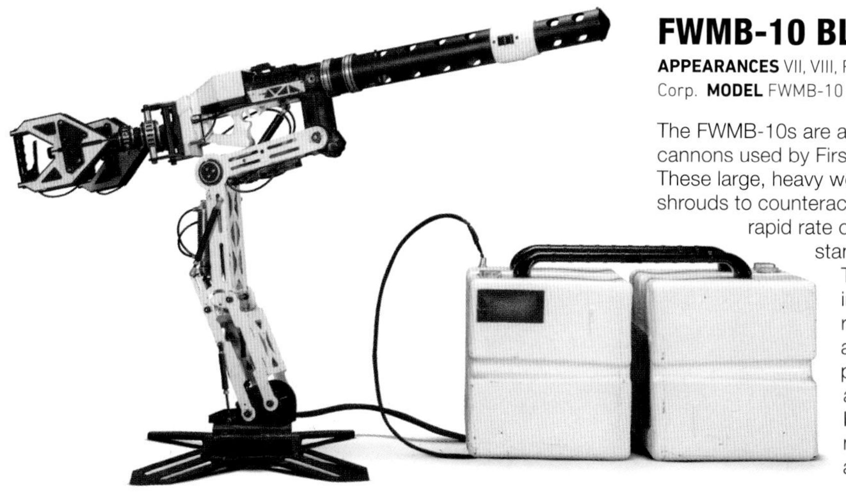

FWMB-10 BLASTER

APPEARANCES VII, VIII, FoD **MANUFACTURER** Sonn-Blas Corp. **MODEL** FWMB-10 **TYPE** Repeating blaster

The FWMB-10s are a line of repeating blaster cannons used by First Order heavy stormtroopers. These large, heavy weapons feature barrel-cooling shrouds to counteract the heat generated by their rapid rate of fire, and foldout integrated stands to support their weight. The blaster requires a high input of energy to maintain its rate of fire, so it is powered by an Ekspan Class-5B1 duplex power generator. Vehicles such as the Aratech-Loratus Light Infantry Utility Vehicle carry mounted FWMB-10 blasters as their primary weapons.

LASER AX

APPEARANCES VIII **MANUFACTURER** First Order Department of Military Research **MODEL** BL-155 Laser ax **TYPE** Executioner's ax

In the course of their executioner duties, First Order troopers swing the BL-155 Laser ax, which has four pairs of extendable claws forming four monomolecular energy ribbons. When the terrible laser ax falls, it causes its victim terrible, if mercifully brief, pain.

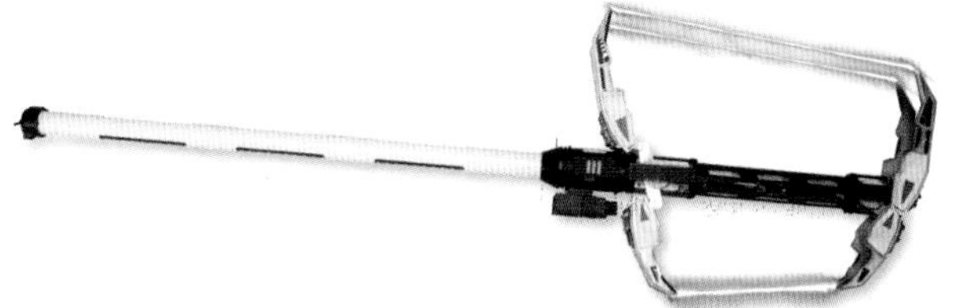

BEHIND THE SCENES

"It was crazy—spaceships, and Wookiees, and robots. It was just unlike anything that had ever been seen before." **George Lucas, creator of the *Star Wars* saga**

Technology is one of the hardest things in moviemaking to get right. Too much emphasis and it starts to overpower the characters, not enough and the film loses its otherworldly setting. Like much of the design that went into the *Star Wars* universe, the technology was created to be believable, but in ways that seem incredible. The use of robotics, cloning, and prosthetics anticipates real-world innovations, while lightsabers so pervade modern popular culture it can be strange to realize that they don't exist!

Star Wars concept illustrator Ralph McQuarrie's first production painting depicts droids R2-D2 and C-3PO on a desert planet after landing in their escape pod. At George Lucas' request, the protocol droid was redesigned to look less human and more mechanical **(1)**. Early concept costume sketches for Darth Vader by costume designer John Mollo for *Star Wars:* Episode IV *A New Hope* **(2)**.

1

2

3

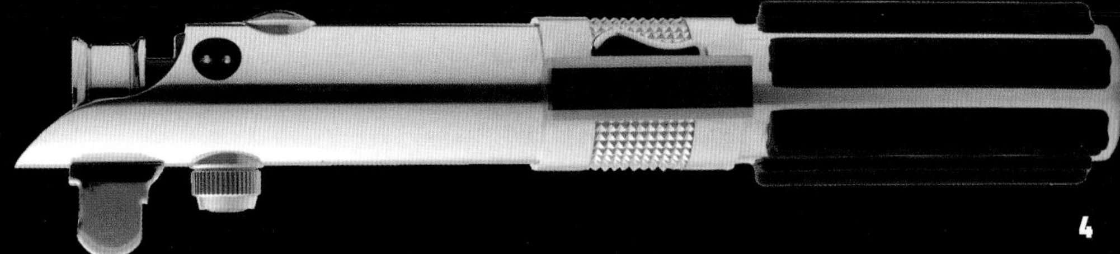
4

George Lucas shows Carrie Fisher (Princess Leia) how to hold a blaster on the Death Star set of *A New Hope* **(3)**. Inspired by the classic swashbuckling movie serials Lucas enjoyed as a boy, Luke Skywalker's lightsaber for *A New Hope* was fashioned in part from a camera flash attachment by set dresser Roger Christian **(4)**.

5

Irvin Kershner directs Dave Prowse as Darth Vader with the full-sized puppet of assassin droid IG-88 on the set of the Star Destroyer in *Star Wars:* Episode V *The Empire Strikes Back* **(5)**. Producer Howard Kazanjian with a model of an AT-ST walker, and a Boba Fett stunt double, with a miniature set on the ILM backlot for *Star Wars:* Episode VI *Return of the Jedi* **(6)**.

6

7

8

The prototype all-white super trooper armor for Boba Fett was revised in favor of a muted color scheme. Both versions of Fett's armor for *The Empire Strikes Back* were conceptually designed primarily by concept artist Joe Johnston and Ralph McQuarrie, and built by Norman Reynolds and his art department team **(7)**. A model of the second Death Star under construction, created by ILM model makers under the direction of Lucas and supervisor Lorne Peterson. The Death Star image was flipped horizontally for *Star Wars:* Episode VI *Return of the Jedi* **(8)**.

R2-D2 and an exposed C-3PO, operated by a puppeteer, take directions on a greenscreen soundstage at Leavesden Studios for *Star Wars:* Episode I *The Phantom Menace* **(9)**. ILM's animation director, Rob Coleman, studies a CG rendering of Jar Jar Binks for *The Phantom Menace* **(10)**. ILM's digital models of cyborg General Grievous and background droids in an animation or creature effects 'take,' which can be used for shape correctives or to fix interpenetrating pieces before final rendering, from *Revenge of the Sith* **(11)**.

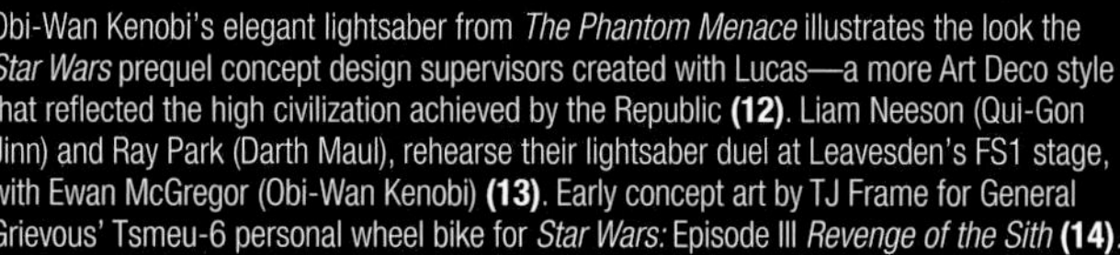

Obi-Wan Kenobi's elegant lightsaber from *The Phantom Menace* illustrates the look the *Star Wars* prequel concept design supervisors created with Lucas—a more Art Deco style that reflected the high civilization achieved by the Republic **(12)**. Liam Neeson (Qui-Gon Jinn) and Ray Park (Darth Maul), rehearse their lightsaber duel at Leavesden's FS1 stage, with Ewan McGregor (Obi-Wan Kenobi) **(13)**. Early concept art by TJ Frame for General Grievous' Tsmeu-6 personal wheel bike for *Star Wars:* Episode III *Revenge of the Sith* **(14)**.

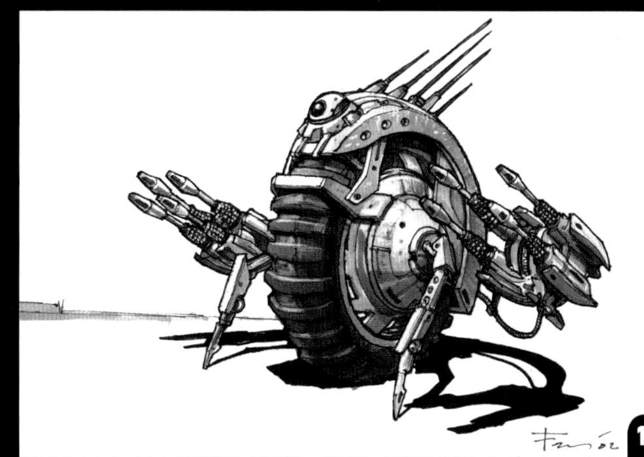

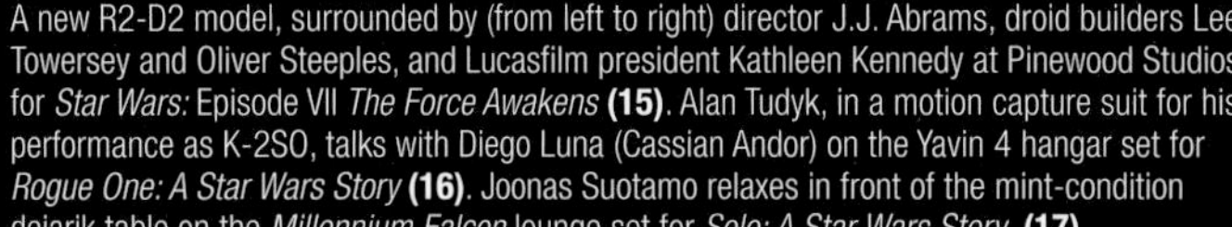

A new R2-D2 model, surrounded by (from left to right) director J.J. Abrams, droid builders Lee Towersey and Oliver Steeples, and Lucasfilm president Kathleen Kennedy at Pinewood Studios for *Star Wars:* Episode VII *The Force Awakens* **(15)**. Alan Tudyk, in a motion capture suit for his performance as K-2SO, talks with Diego Luna (Cassian Andor) on the Yavin 4 hangar set for *Rogue One: A Star Wars Story* **(16)**. Joonas Suotamo relaxes in front of the mint-condition dejarik table on the *Millennium Falcon* lounge set for *Solo: A Star Wars Story* **(17)**.

VEHICLES

Factories produce a staggering variety of vehicles for both peaceful and warlike purposes, from starships traveling at lightspeed to transporters moving with a slow, remorseless tread.

On thousands of civilized worlds, most atmospheric-propulsion vehicles utilize repulsorlift technology, which levitates vehicles and lightweight atmosphere craft via antigravitational emanations called "repulsor fields." Some repulsorlift craft are little more than engines with padded seats that travel close to the ground, while others are large luxury vessels that can skim a planet's atmospheric ceiling. For voyages between distant star systems, starships use hyperdrive technology that enables vessels to exceed lightspeed, and sublight engines for traveling at slower speeds.

During the Clone Wars, the Galactic Civil War, and the subsequent conflict between the Resistance and the First Order, many manufacturers convert transports and freighters into combat craft, and also produce entirely new vehicles that are laden with weapons. To evade the authorities that patrol the galaxy's best-known commercial routes, pirates and smugglers outfit their own vessels with powerful engines and exotic weaponry.

Deflector shield

Jedi transport
Before the dark times, red was the color of neutrality for spacecraft of the Galactic Republic.

Cockpit

Docking ring

REPUBLIC CRUISER

APPEARANCES I, CW **MANUFACTURER** Corellian Engineering Corp. **MODEL** *Consular*-class space cruiser **TYPE** Cruiser

Built in the great orbital shipyards of the Corellian Engineering Corporation, the 115-meter- (377-ft-3-in) long *Consular*-class Republic Cruiser is used by the Supreme Chancellor, members of the Galactic Senate, and the Jedi Order for diplomatic missions. The cruiser's striking scarlet color scheme declares the ship's diplomatic immunity. Typically unarmed, the cruiser features three powerful Dyne 577 radial atomizer engines, a Longe Voltrans tri-arc CD-3.2 hyperdrive, and sturdy deflector shields as protection. The bridge is located in the cruiser's forward section, just above an interchangeable diplomatic salon pod, which can eject from the cruiser in the event of emergencies.

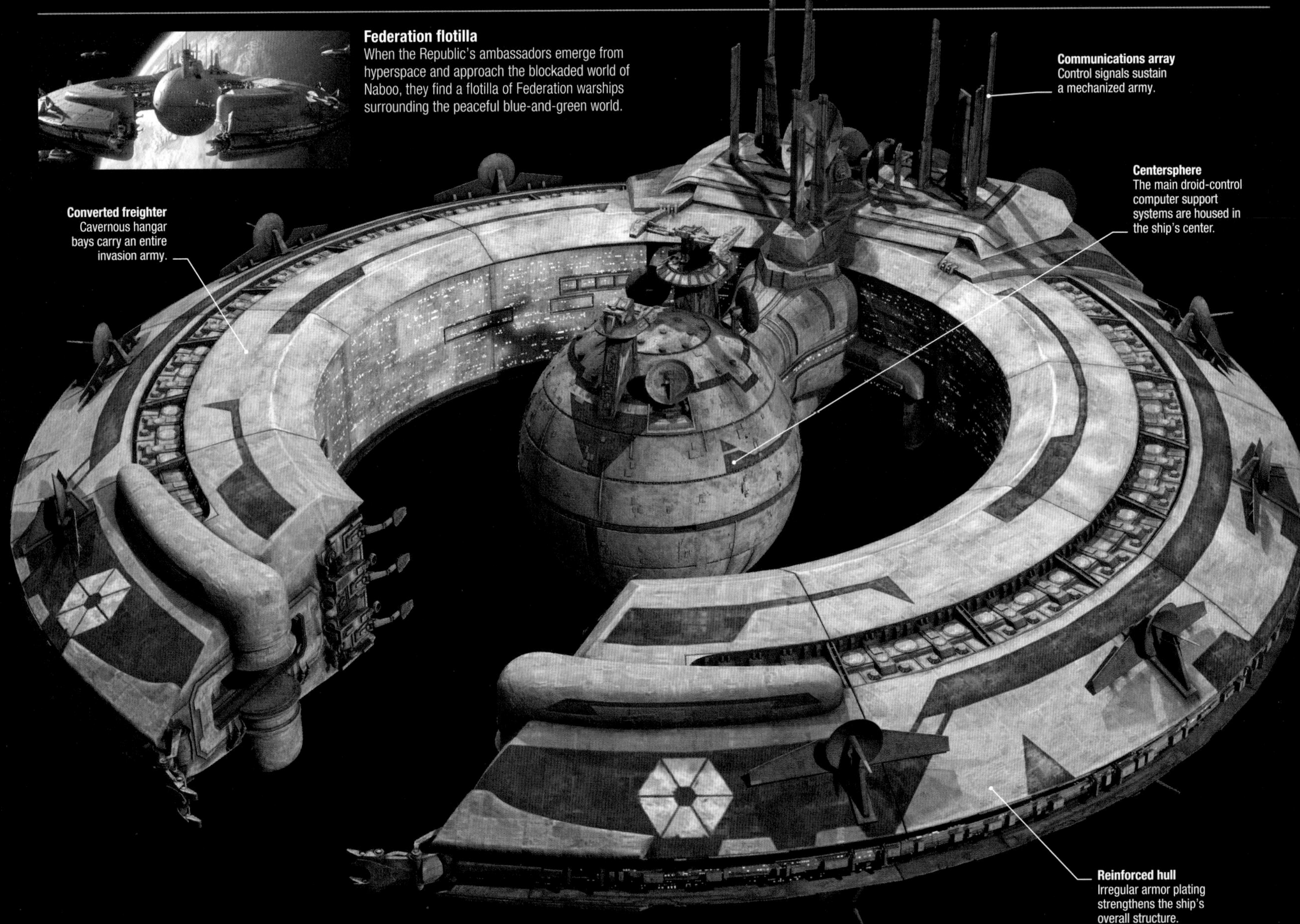

Federation flotilla
When the Republic's ambassadors emerge from hyperspace and approach the blockaded world of Naboo, they find a flotilla of Federation warships surrounding the peaceful blue-and-green world.

TRADE FEDERATION BATTLESHIP

APPEARANCES I, II, CW, III **MANUFACTURER** Hoersch-Kessel Drive Inc. **MODEL** Modified *Lucrehulk*-class LH-3210 cargo freighter **TYPE** Battleship (converted freighter)

Originally cargo freighters for the Neimoidian Trade Federation's vast commercial fleet, Trade Federation battleships are over 3 kilometers (2 miles) in diameter and hold a central sphere that contains the ship's bridge and reactor assemblies. Each battleship can carry 550 MTTs, 6,250 AATs, 1,500 troop carriers, 50 C-9979 landing craft, and 1,500 droid starfighters. Converting the freighters into warships was one of the Neimoidians' first priorities when they began secretly building their armed forces. However, the conversion has not been entirely successful, and these immense, powerful vessels have a number of weaknesses. The addition of retractable turbolasers along the equator of the ship's hull left large blind spots that small, speedy enemy vessels could exploit.

The most important vessels in the Trade Federation's fleet are the Droid Control Ships, which are used to operate the droid armies. A Control Ship is distinguished from other Federation battleships by the large communications array on its dorsal hull. Neimoidian commanders typically seal themselves in the ship's bridge while their droids handle all ship operations. Destroying a Control Ship can disable every droid in the warship's service.

Droid pilots
The effectiveness of droid starfighters has been debated in strategic circles for generations. Although droid starfighters are capable of maneuvers that would pulp even the sturdiest organic pilot, they lack the resourcefulness and cunning that living pilots bring to combat.

Wing/leg
These are locked in starfighter mode during flight.

Droid head
This contains the pilot droid's brain components.

Tapered claw
The wings extend for walker mode.

Torpedo launchers
Energy torpedoes are fired from these channels.

Separatist colors
The blue-and-white paint job is clearly visible.

Aerial combat
Droid starfighters are engineered to operate in atmospheric environments as well as outer space.

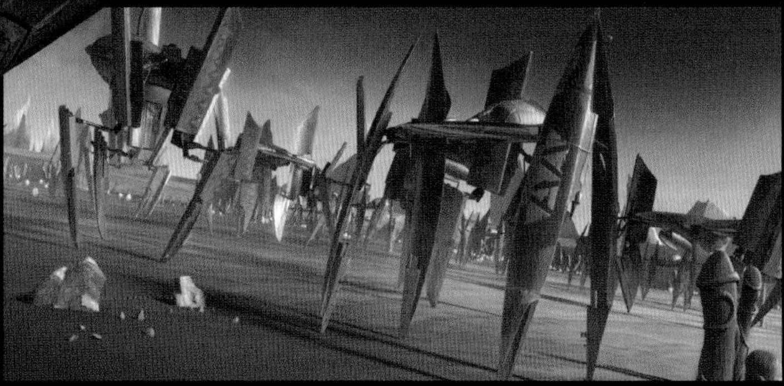

Laser armament
Each wing houses two blaster cannons.

Ambulatory starfighters
When not in flight mode, droid starfighters transform their configuration so that they can "walk" on their wings.

VULTURE DROID (DROID STARFIGHTER)

APPEARANCES I, CW, III
MANUFACTURER Xi Char Cathedral factories
MODEL Variable Geometry Self-Propelled Battle Droid, Mark I **TYPE** Droid starfighter

The Trade Federation's droid starfighters—also known as vulture droids—were designed and originally manufactured by the Xi Charrians. Like the ground-based battle droid infantry, droid starfighters are controlled by the Trade Federation's Droid Control Ship. When in starfighter mode, the droid carries four blaster cannons in its wings and two energy torpedo launchers along its forward edge, as well as buzz droid-laden discord missiles. When not in flight, the droid starfighter can transform into walking mode, allowing it to be used in surface patrols. When reconfigured for walking, the launchers are angled for anti-personnel use.

Unconventional solid fuel concentrate slugs housed in the aft fuel chamber power the droids. These slugs burn rapidly when ignited, giving the droid starfighter incredible bursts of energy but a very limited range of operation. As such, droid starfighters must operate from a nearby launch base or capital ship. When not deployed, these starfighters hang from overhead recharging racks. The Trade Federation attempts to counter any shortcomings in their automated vulture droid designs by dispatching them en masse. The Trade Federation also jealously guards its new innovations and equips the droid starfighter to protect its trade secrets. Should it lose contact with the Droid Control Ship due to a malfunction or other catastrophe, the starfighter's self-destruct mechanism is engaged, preventing it from falling into enemy hands.

TRADE FEDERATION MTT

APPEARANCES I, CW, III
MANUFACTURER Baktoid Armor Workshop
MODEL Multi-Troop Transport (MTT)
TYPE Multi-troop transport

A giant armored repulsorlift vehicle, the MTT is capable of depositing over a hundred battle droid soldiers into the thick of combat. The MTT's bulbous front end opens to reveal an articulated deployment rack, upon which rest dozens of compressed battle droids. The rack extends forward, releasing the droids into neatly organized rows. Upon activation from an orbiting Droid Control Ship, the droids unfold into their humanoid configuration. The hydraulically powered deployment rack can carry 112 battle droids in stowed configuration.

TRADE FEDERATION LANDING SHIP

APPEARANCES I, CW, III
MANUFACTURER Haor Chall Engineering
MODEL C-9979 landing craft
TYPE Landing craft

With its huge wingspan and imposing loading ramp, the Trade Federation landing ship is a daunting sight. The ship can hold heavy armor, is capable of carrying a total of 28 troop carriers, 1,114 AATs, and 11 MTTs, and requires a crew of 88 droids. The wings are removable for ease of storage and docking, and when deployed, powerful tensor field generators bind the wings to the craft and strengthen the vessel's structural integrity. Additionally, large repulsorlifts keep the ship from sagging under its own weight.

Landing-zone patrol
During the Naboo invasion, STAP-mounted battle droids survey the Great Grass Plains and transmit data to their Droid Control Ship.

SINGLE TROOPER AERIAL PLATFORM (STAP)

APPEARANCES I, CW
MANUFACTURER Baktoid Armor Workshop
MODEL Single Trooper Aerial Platform
TYPE Patrol vehicle

Deployed by the Trade Federation army's battle droids, STAPs are slim, lightweight reconnaissance and patrol vehicles armed with a pair of blaster cannons. Trade Federation engineers drew inspiration for their design from similar civilian vehicles called airhooks, which they reengineered for greater performance and reliability, and to be specifically piloted by B1 battle droids. High-voltage energy cells fuel the tiny repulsorlift craft's drive turbines, which provide the STAP with impressive speed and maneuverability.

The STAP's greatest weaknesses are its pilot's exposure to enemy fire and its fragility. Though the craft is highly agile, and transmissions from Droid Control Ships skillfully guide droid pilots, a lucky shot can quickly bring down a STAP or its pilot. As such, the vehicles are primarily relegated to patrol, "mopping up" missions, and the occasional foray into battle to harry enemy forces, while the brunt of combat is borne by heavier vehicles.

BONGO

APPEARANCES I, CW
MANUFACTURER Otoh Gunga Bongmeken Cooperative **MODEL** Tribubble bongo sub
TYPE Submarine

Organically grown through secret Gungan techniques, the bongo is a submersible vehicle used to travel the depths of Naboo's waters. Distinguished by a manta-shaped hull, the bongo's hydrostatic bubble shields keep the cockpit and cargo areas dry and filled with air. A semirigid assembly of tentacle-like fins spins to provide the bongo with thrust. In emergencies, the cockpit module can eject from the sub like an escape pod.

NEIMOIDIAN SHUTTLE

APPEARANCES I, II, CW, III, Reb, Res
MANUFACTURER Haor Chall Engineering
MODEL *Sheathipede*-class transport shuttle
TYPE Transport shuttle

The *Sheathipede*-class shuttle is typically used for short-range transit, either across a planetary surface or for ferrying passengers into orbital space where a larger ship or station awaits its arrival. The shuttle's curved insect-like landing gears lower from the ship's belly, giving the craft's legs a pincer-like appearance as it touches down. Neimoidian officials prefer models with automatic pilots because the absence of a cockpit allows for an expansive passenger cabin.

Heavy bombardment
Moving slowly along city streets, AATs prompt civilians to take refuge *(right)*. Each AAT is crewed by four battle droids: a commander, a pilot, and two gunners *(below)*.

ARMORED ASSAULT TANK (AAT)

APPEARANCES I, CW, III **MANUFACTURER** Baktoid Armor Workshop
MODEL Armored Assault Tank **TYPE** Repulsorlift battle tank

Studded with heavy artillery, the floating tanks known as AATs form the frontline of Trade Federation armored infantry divisions. The AAT's turret-mounted primary laser cannon has long-range destructive capability, and is bracketed by a pair of pylon-mounted secondary laser cannons. A pair of forward-facing short-range blaster cannons round out the AAT's energy-weapon complement. The tank also carries formidable additional weaponry: six energized projectile launchers that fire high-energy shells encased in a cocoon of plasma for incredible speed and penetrative power, specialized armor-piercing warheads, and high explosive "bunker-busting" shells.

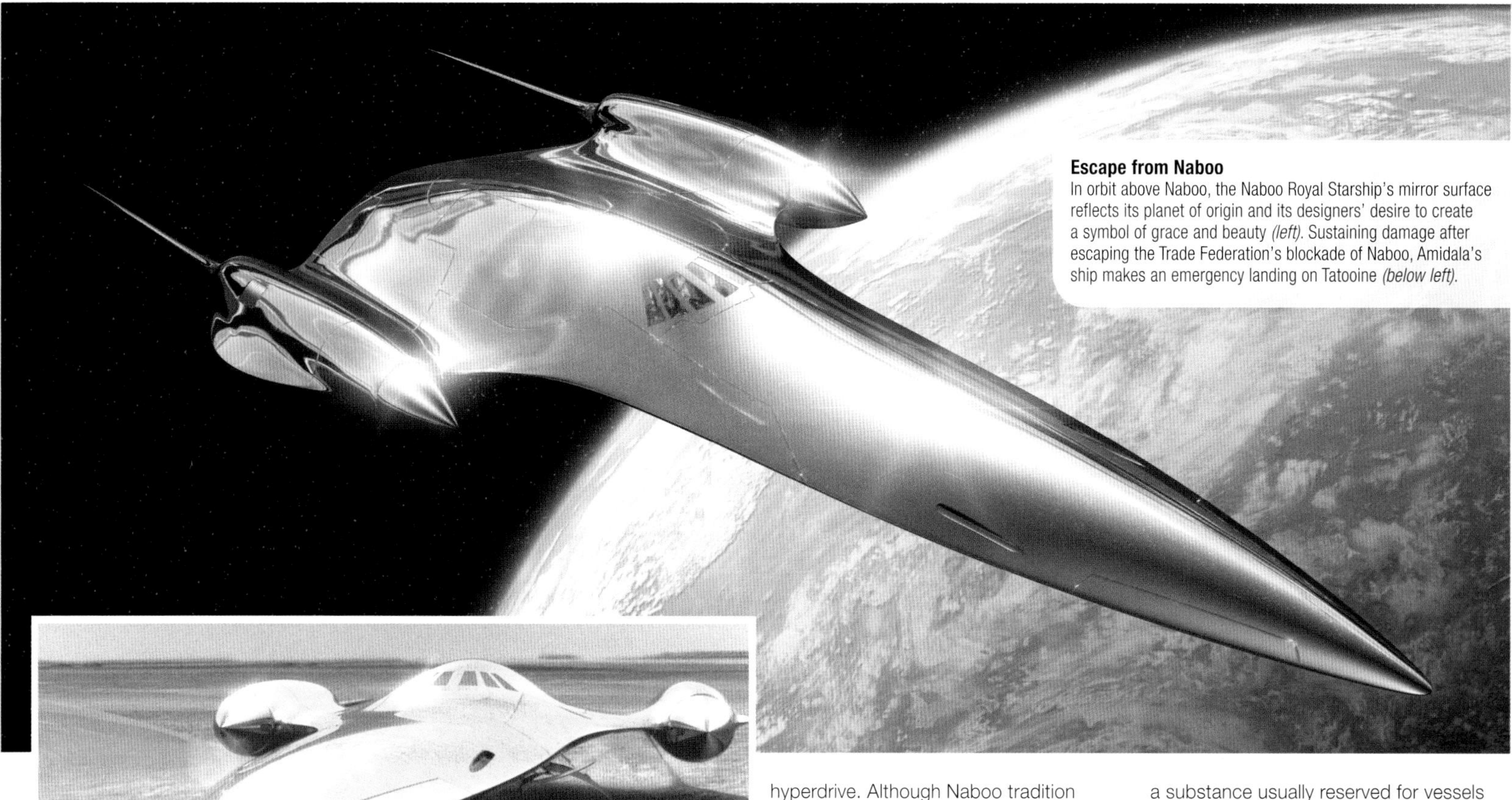

Escape from Naboo
In orbit above Naboo, the Naboo Royal Starship's mirror surface reflects its planet of origin and its designers' desire to create a symbol of grace and beauty *(left)*. Sustaining damage after escaping the Trade Federation's blockade of Naboo, Amidala's ship makes an emergency landing on Tatooine *(below left)*.

NABOO ROYAL STARSHIP

APPEARANCES I **MANUFACTURER** Theed Palace Space Vessel Engineering Corp. **MODEL** Modified J-type 327 Nubian starship **TYPE** Transport

Boasting a strikingly beautiful design that embodies the craftsmanship that prevails in the peaceful years of the Republic, the Naboo Royal Starship is at Queen Amidala's disposal for formal state visits to other planetary representatives and for royal events on Naboo. The streamlined J-type 327 Nubian vessel lacks any offensive weaponry, but does feature powerful shields and a high-performance hyperdrive. Although Naboo tradition encourages the reigning monarch to personally name the royal vessel, Amidala—by the time of the Battle of Naboo—has more important concerns than the ship's name.

The Royal Starship's unique spaceframe is handcrafted at Theed but designed around the imported Nubian sublight engine and hyperdrive propulsion system. Nubian systems are often sought by discriminating buyers and are easily acquired on most civilized worlds, but can be difficult to obtain on remote planets. The ship's gleaming finish is purely decorative and made of royal chromium, a substance usually reserved for vessels serving Naboo's monarch. The mirrored hull is hand-polished and crafted by fine artisans, not by automatons or factory equipment. The ship's interior is made with equal care and is quite spacious. From fore to aft, the vessel contains luxurious royal quarters; a forward hold; a main hold with tech station; the cockpit, which is accessible via turbolift; and the throne room, where Queen Amidala sits while in transit or to receive guests. Naboo citizens consider the entire ship a work of art. After Amidala's death, Darth Sidious gives the ship to Darth Vader, who uses it for his own purposes.

NABOO N-1 STARFIGHTER

APPEARANCES I, II, CW, III, VI, FoD **MANUFACTURER** Theed Palace Space Vessel Engineering Corp. **MODEL** Royal N-1 **TYPE** Starfighter

Starfighter hit
Although N-1 starfighters are fast and agile, they are also prone to uncontrollable spins when the engines suffer damage.

Protecting the skies and space around Naboo, the N-1 starfighter—like the Royal Naboo Starship—exemplifies the philosophy of blending art and function seen throughout Naboo technology. Its twin radial J-type engines are capped in gleaming chromium and trail long delicate finials behind the ship's single-pilot compartment. Behind the pilot, a standard astromech droid plugs into a ventrally fed socket that requires the droid to compress its legs slightly and telescopically extend its domed head through a dorsal port. The fighter features twin blaster cannons, twin fire-linked torpedo launchers, and an automatic piloting system. Senator Padmé Amidala's personal N-1 starfighter is fully plated in chromium, in acknowledgment of her former position as queen.

Ready for action
Few pilots in Naboo's Space Fighter Corps have actual combat experience, but their rigorous training prepares them for the battle against the Trade Federation.

ANAKIN'S RADON-ULZER PODRACER

APPEARANCES | **MANUFACTURER** Radon-Ulzer (engines) **MODEL** Customized repulsorlift vehicle **TYPE** Podracer

Built in secret by the young slave Anakin Skywalker, the shiny blue-and-silver podracer is smaller and leaner than all the other competing podracers in the Boonta Eve Classic. Anakin's podracer follows the same basic design found throughout the sport: a pod with a cockpit pulled by two high-powered engines. Energy binders lock the engines to each other, and durable Steelton control cables connect the engines to the pod. Seated in the cockpit, a pilot operates thruster bars that control power to the engines, and speeds can reach well over 800 kilometers (497 miles) per hour.

Because podracer pilots differ greatly in shape, size, and weight, the vehicles are heavily customized to match the requirements of the individual pilots. Pilots must have incredibly quick reflexes and very strong nerves. Anakin is the only known human to ever pilot a podracer and survive. Unlike other pilots, who invest in larger engines in the hopes of getting greater performance, Anakin salvages a pair of Radon-Ulzer 620C racing engines that his junk-dealer master, Watto, discarded, deeming them too burned out to be of any use.

Anakin develops a new fuel atomizer and distribution system that sends more fuel into the Radon-Ulzer's combustion chambers, radically increasing their thrust and his podracer's top speed to almost 950 kilometers (590 miles) per hour, which is a testament to his engineering brilliance.

Race to the finish
Anakin's Radon-Ulzer engines are capped with a trio of bright yellow air scoops that provide additional control when braking and cornering. Despite the dastardly antics of his nemesis, Sebulba, Anakin remains focused on winning the Boonta Eve Classic.

SEBULBA'S PODRACER

APPEARANCES | **MANUFACTURER** Collor Pondrat (engines) **MODEL** Customized repulsorlift vehicle **TYPE** Podracer

If reputable podracing officials were to examine Sebulba's podracer closely, they would classify it as illegal. His oversized Collor Pondrat Plug-F Mammoth Split-X engines, 7.8 meters (25 ft 7 in) in length, can achieve a top speed of 829 kilometers (515 miles) per hour. The engines are fueled by tradium power fluid pressurized with quold runium and activated with ionized injectrine. Sebulba takes pleasure in using a concealed flamethrower against competitors who dare to pass him, blasting them off course and ensuring his victory.

SITH INFILTRATOR

APPEARANCES | **MANUFACTURER** Republic Sienar Systems **MODEL** Heavily modified Star Courier **TYPE** Armed star courier

Customized in a secret laboratory, the Sith Infiltrator, dubbed the *Scimitar*, is the personal spacecraft for Darth Maul and later Darth Sidious. The craft, 26.5 meters (86 ft 11 in) in length, with folding angular wings and a rounded bridge compartment, is equipped with many weapons and instruments of evil, including six laser cannons, spying and surveillance gear, interrogator droids, and Maul's speeder bike. Powered by a curious high-temperature ion engine sublight drive system, the craft's most impressive feature is its full-effect cloaking device, which makes it invisible.

SITH SPEEDER

APPEARANCES | **MANUFACTURER** Razalon **MODEL** Modified Razalon FC-20 speeder bike **TYPE** Speeder bike

A pared-down, crescent-shaped conveyance, Darth Maul's Sith Speeder, alias the *Bloodfin*, lacks weapons or a sensor array, so all of the vehicle's energy is devoted to speed. Maul uses probe droids to find his prey, and then programs his speeder to decelerate and enter a "wait mode" should he suddenly dismount.

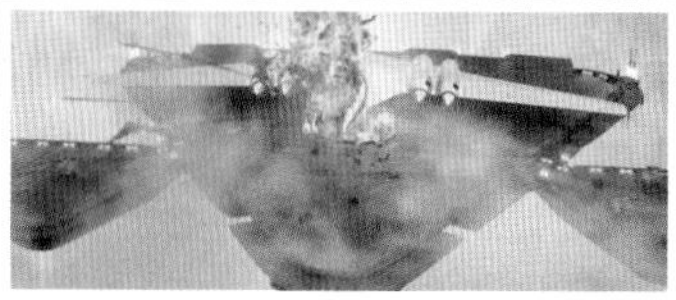

Deadly blast
The Royal Cruiser *(above)* takes a direct hit on Coruscant *(right)*.

NABOO ROYAL CRUISER

APPEARANCES II, CW **MANUFACTURER** Theed Palace Space Vessel Engineering Corp. **MODEL** Custom-built J-type diplomatic barge **TYPE** Transport (diplomatic barge)

Like the Royal Starship used by the Queen of Naboo, this chrome-hulled cruiser is a J-type vessel constructed by the Theed Palace Space Vessel Engineering Corp. The shortcomings of the previous Nubian J-type 327 are addressed with improved shield generators and paired S-6 hyperdrive generators providing adequate backup for the superluminal drive. The unarmed transport often travels under escort and can function as a fighter carrier craft, carrying up to four N-1 starfighters fitted into recharge sockets along the leading edge of its wing.

ZAM'S AIRSPEEDER

APPEARANCES II **MANUFACTURER** Desler Gizh Outworld Mobility Corp. **MODEL** Koro-2 all-environment Exodrive airspeeder **TYPE** Airspeeder

A lean getaway vessel with a pressurized cabin, Zam Wesell's airspeeder features an uncommon external electromagnetic propulsion system. The forward mandibles irradiate the air around them, inducing ionization and making it conductive. Paired electrodes electrify the airstream and magnetically propel it toward the rear of the craft, resulting in the air dragging the vessel through the skies at speeds of 800 kilometers (497 miles) per hour.

ANAKIN'S AIRSPEEDER

APPEARANCES II **MANUFACTURER** Custom special (Narglatch AirTech kit) **MODEL** XJ-6 **TYPE** Luxury airspeeder hot rod

On Coruscant, Anakin commandeers a sleek, open-cockpit airspeeder to pursue the assassin Zam Wesell. The speeder's owner, a wealthy representative of the Vorzyd sector, customized the vehicle with twin turbojet engines originally designed to function in groups of 50 aboard the gigantic bank-courier repulsor trucks of Aargau. The engines direct pressurized air through a series of thrust ducts to propel the craft.

Hyperspace booster
After the Delta-7 docks with the hyperdrive booster ring, the astromech transmits destination coordinates to the ring's navicomputer.

Enclosed cockpit
Modular options can accommodate human or alien pilots.

Bow sensors
Delta-7's bow houses scanning and communications technology.

Starfighter strikeforce
During the Clone Wars, Jedi pilots and their faithful astromechs fly Delta-7s on many missions throughout the galaxy.

JEDI STARFIGHTER

APPEARANCES II, CW, III
MANUFACTURER Kuat Systems Engineering
MODEL Delta-7 *Aethersprite*-class light interceptor **TYPE** Light interceptor starfighter

Although Jedi generally use Republic Cruisers for missions across the galaxy, some assignments call for less conspicuous transports. For this reason, and because Jedi cannot always depend on pilots to take them to their destination, all Jedi learn how to pilot starships as part of their training. Prior to the Naboo blockade, Kuat Systems Engineering unveils the Delta-7 Jedi starfighter. A wedge-shaped, single-person craft, the Delta-7 is equipped with dual laser cannons, two secondary ion cannons, and a powerful deflector shield. Despite the craft's armaments, most Jedi pilots prefer to rely on their cunning and attunement to the Force to avoid disputes and aggression, and they use weapons as a last resort.

Because the Delta-7 is too small to hold a standard navicomputer and hyperdrive, it relies on a truncated astromech droid, hardwired into the starfighter's port side, for storing navigational data, and a TransGalMeg Industries booster ring for transit through hyperspace. The astromech also provides diagnostic and repair service to the craft, as well as managing the secondary scanning and communications gear. Kuat Systems Engineering also produced the variant design of the dart-shaped starfighter: the Delta-7B *Aethersprite*-class interceptor. The Delta-7B relocated the astromech socket from the port side to just fore of the cockpit, and had a slightly enlarged hull to accommodate a full-size astromech droid. Both Anakin and Obi-Wan piloted Delta-7Bs during the Clone Wars.

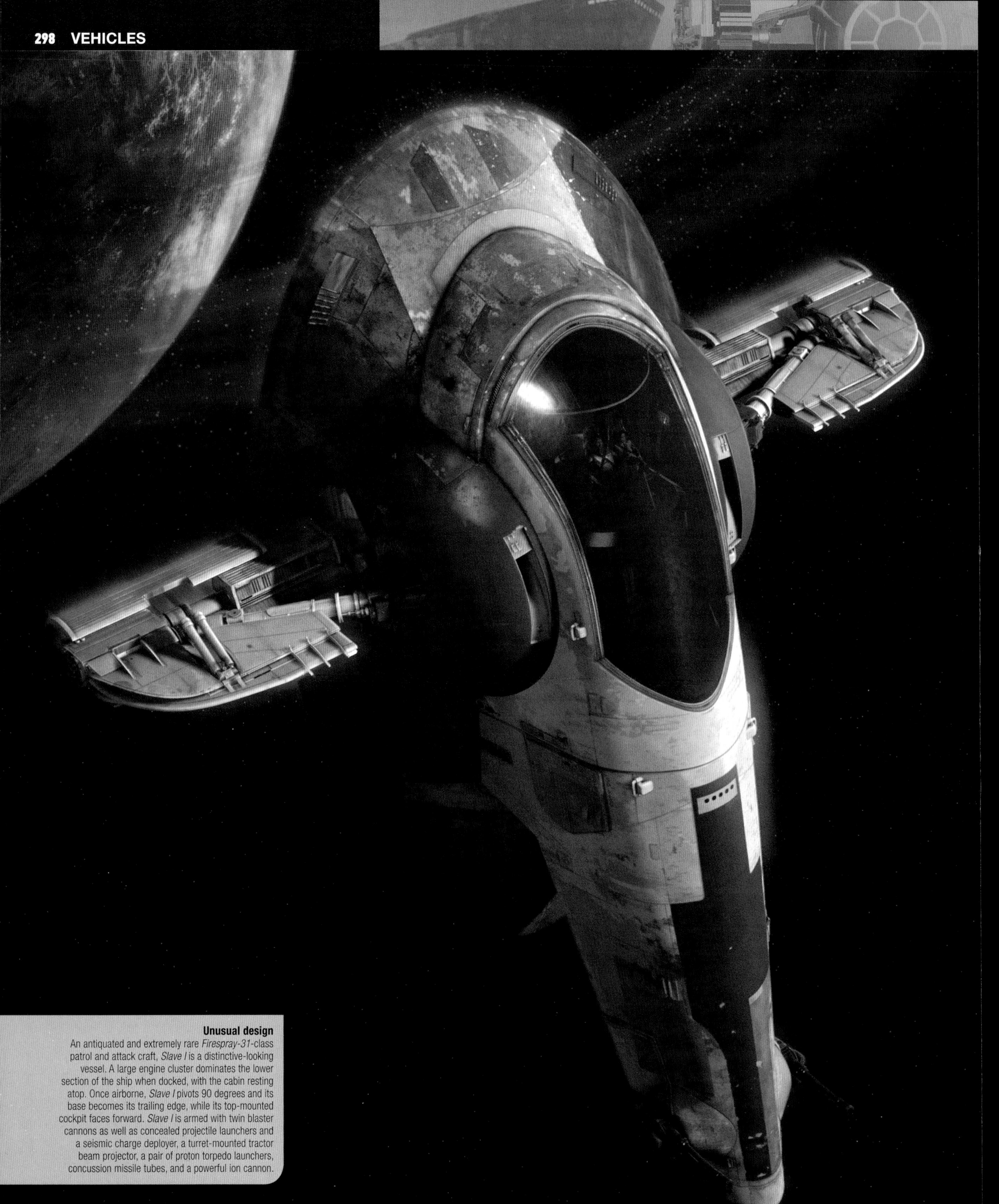

Unusual design
An antiquated and extremely rare *Firespray-31*-class patrol and attack craft, *Slave I* is a distinctive-looking vessel. A large engine cluster dominates the lower section of the ship when docked, with the cabin resting atop. Once airborne, *Slave I* pivots 90 degrees and its base becomes its trailing edge, while its top-mounted cockpit faces forward. *Slave I* is armed with twin blaster cannons as well as concealed projectile launchers and a seismic charge deployer, a turret-mounted tractor beam projector, a pair of proton torpedo launchers, concussion missile tubes, and a powerful ion cannon.

"Get him, Dad! Get him! Fire!" BOBA FETT

SLAVE I

Inherited by the bounty hunter Boba Fett from his father, Jango, the pursuit vessel *Slave I* has sophisticated anti-detection gear that ensures very few fugitives ever see their captor coming.

APPEARANCES II, CW, V **MANUFACTURER** Kuat Systems Engineering **MODEL** Modified *Firespray-31*-class patrol and attack craft **TYPE** Pursuit vessel

Training Boba Weaving through the asteroid belt surrounding Geonosis, Jango Fett fires *Slave I*'s laser cannons at Obi-Wan's Jedi starfighter *(left)*. Jango teaches his son, Boba, to pilot *Slave I (below)*.

FAMILY LEGACY

After an assassination assignment goes wrong for Jango Fett on Coruscant, the Jedi Obi-Wan Kenobi tracks Jango to Tipoca City on the water world Kamino. Jango and Boba board *Slave I* and escape to the Geonosis system, but when they realize the Jedi has pursued them, Jango launches seismic charges at Obi-Wan's starfighter. When Boba Fett eventually inherits *Slave I*, he remembers his father's deadly tactics and learns many more.

Airlock Standing in *Slave I*'s airlock, Bossk and Aurra Sing wait for Boba to exit the clone cadets' escape pod.

BOBA FETT'S CREW

After the Battle of Geonosis, Boba seeks vengeance against Mace Windu, the Jedi who struck down his father. He forms an alliance with the bounty hunters Aurra Sing and Bossk, who help him infiltrate a group of clone cadets scheduled to meet Mace on the Republic Star Destroyer *Endurance*. Boba fails to kill Mace, but critically damages the *Endurance* and winds up in an escape pod with a group of cadets. Sing and Bossk rescue Boba from the pod, and together they set another trap for Mace on the planet Vangor.

Getaway starship After rescuing young Jedi from General Grievous on Florrum, Hondo Ohnaka commandeers *Slave I* into space.

PIRATE PROPERTY

On the planet Florrum, a team of Jedi captures Boba, and Aurra Sing crashes *Slave I* while attempting to escape. The Weequay pirate Hondo Ohnaka salvages the vessel, repaints it, and adds it to his collection of starships. But after General Grievous and his droid army invade Florrum and capture Ohnaka, the Jedi Ahsoka Tano and a band of Jedi younglings rescue Ohnaka, and they escape in *Slave I*. Eventually, Boba regains ownership of *Slave I* and modifies it to transform it into the ultimate vessel for bounty hunting.

Valuable cargo Anticipating a big payout from Jabba, Boba oversees the Bespin guards who load Han onto *Slave I*.

CAPTURING HAN SOLO

On Tatooine, Boba is present when Jabba the Hutt threatens to put a bounty on the smuggler Han Solo unless he pays arrears. Shortly after the Battle of Hoth, Darth Vader also places a bounty on Han, and Boba sees an opportunity to profit twice. Piloting *Slave I*, Boba stalks Han's freighter from the Anoat system and alerts Vader that Han is heading for Cloud City. Boba and Vader arrive on Cloud City before Han and easily capture the smuggler, along with his rebel allies. After Vader freezes Han in carbonite, he allows Boba to load Han's frozen form onto *Slave I* and proceed to Tatooine, where Boba delivers Han to Jabba and collects the second bounty.

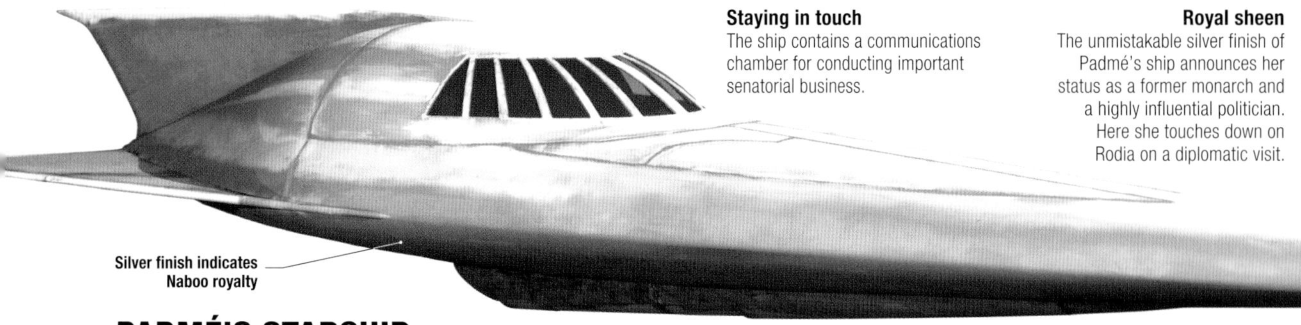

Staying in touch
The ship contains a communications chamber for conducting important senatorial business.

Royal sheen
The unmistakable silver finish of Padmé's ship announces her status as a former monarch and a highly influential politician. Here she touches down on Rodia on a diplomatic visit.

PADMÉ'S STARSHIP

APPEARANCES II, CW **MANUFACTURER** Theed Palace Space Vessel Engineering Corp. **MODEL** H-type Nubian yacht **TYPE** Luxury space yacht

The sleek yacht used by Padmé Amidala during the Clone Wars lacks weapons, but has a powerful engine bank and a strong deflector shield generator. Padmé receives the vessel after a failed assassination attempt on Coruscant destroys her royal cruiser. Senator Amidala uses her new starship to travel with Anakin Skywalker to Tatooine and Geonosis, where she witnesses the opening battle between the Republic and the Separatists. Padmé's original starship is lost when she intentionally overloads its engines to disable the Separatist cruiser *Malevolence*.

Long range
Padmé's starship is both speedy and capable of sustained travel across the galaxy, a necessity when making political visits in person.

Scrap heap
The main hold of a sandcrawler is full of half-fixed machinery and random junk.

SANDCRAWLER

APPEARANCES I, II, IV **MANUFACTURER** Various **MODEL** Sandcrawler **TYPE** Mobile desert base

Sandcrawlers are massive vehicles that crisscross the deserts of Tatooine on their wide treads. They are operated by tribes of glowing-eyed Jawas, who use the sandcrawlers as homes, workshops, and trash repositories. If a Jawa locates a droid that doesn't appear to have an owner, a scouting party will disable the roaming automaton while a magnetic tube sucks it inside the sandcrawler for storage. Jawa sandcrawlers frequently visit moisture farms, where they start impromptu auctions, though the merchandise is usually of questionable quality. Some Jawas reserve their finest goods—normally hidden away in their massive vehicles—for established customers only. The sandcrawler's thick armor is a reliable defense against sandstorms, but it can't stand up to sustained blaster fire from stormtroopers. The droids R2-D2 and C-3PO briefly spend time aboard a sandcrawler before the Jawas who seized the pair sell them to Owen Lars. When the Empire tracks the droids to that particular Jawa tribe, they reduce the sandcrawler to a smoking ruin, which is later discovered by Luke Skywalker and Obi-Wan Kenobi.

Sandcrawler on the horizon
For most Tatooine settlers, sandcrawlers are the only way they can replace their equipment. Jawas sometimes sell rare goods and will travel to even the most remote homesteads.

OG-9 HOMING SPIDER DROID

APPEARANCES II, III **MANUFACTURER** Baktoid Armor Workshop
TYPE OG-9 homing spider droid **AFFILIATION** Separatists

The OG-9 homing spider droid is a gigantic walker used by the Separatists throughout the Clone Wars. The homing spider droid moves slowly on four mechanical legs, with a powerful reactor situated in the heart of its spherical body. The top-mounted laser emplacement releases sustained-fire shots that quickly wear down a target's shields, while a bottom-mounted laser cannon keeps infantry at bay. Homing spider droids see action during the Battle of Geonosis, blasting away at Republic AT-TEs and formations of clone troopers.

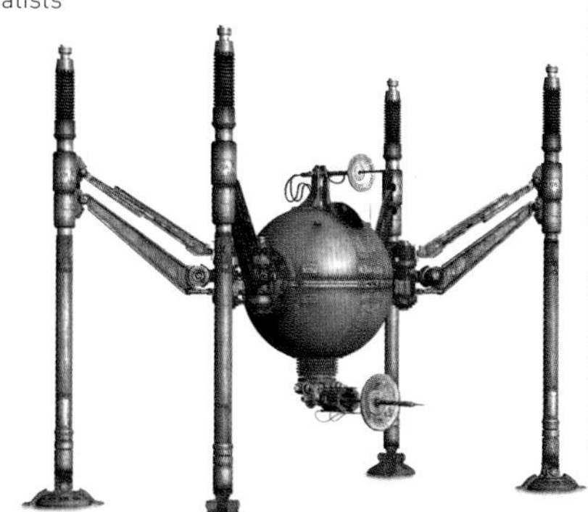

Armored hull plating

Command bridge

Warship
The Acclamator became the Republic's premier battleship at the start of the Clone Wars.

REPUBLIC ASSAULT SHIP (ACCLAMATOR-CLASS)

APPEARANCES II, CW **MANUFACTURER** Rothana Heavy Engineering **MODEL** *Acclamator*-class assault ship
TYPE Assault ship

The Republic assault ship is also known as the Acclamator. More than 700 meters (2,297 ft) long, it becomes the Republic's primary troop carrier at the start of the Clone Wars and also fills an offensive role against the Separatist navy. Each assault ship is armed with laser cannons, turbolaser turrets, concussion missiles, and heavy torpedoes, and carries ground vehicles such as AT-TE walkers. The Acclamator is capable of both ground and water landings.

Atmospheric escort
The LAAT/i gunship fills a crucial role for the Republic military, serving as both a troop carrier and an escort for ground and aerial forces. When hovering, the LAAT/i is an elevated gun platform.

Providing cover
Not only is the LAAT/i heavily armed with anti-personnel and anti-vehicle lasers, but the clone troopers who ride in it can also fire at targets using their blaster rifles.

REPUBLIC LAAT/i REPULSORLIFT GUNSHIP

APPEARANCES II, CW, III **MANUFACTURER** Rothana Heavy Engineering
MODEL Low Altitude Assault Transport/infantry **TYPE** Repulsorlift gunship

The Republic gunship is also known as the LAAT/i, for Low Altitude Assault Transport/infantry. First deployed during the Battle of Geonosis, the gunship becomes one of the most familiar Republic military vehicles during the Clone Wars. A standard gunship can carry up to 30 clone troopers and is operated by a pilot and forward gunner. Two additional clone troopers operate the bubble turrets that swing out from the troop cabin. Two more turrets are located on each wing, while three smaller laser cannons are used to scatter enemy infantry. The gunship is excellent at destroying enemy vehicles such as hailfire droids with the missiles released from the underside of each wing. A gunship can reach speeds of up to 620 kilometers (385 miles) per hour. Clone troopers grow fond of their gunships during the Clone Wars and sometimes customize them with colorful nose art.

Thrust
Twin engines can reach maximum speeds of 620 kilometers (385 miles) per hour.

"...make sure you get yourself to that landing zone in one piece."

ANAKIN SKYWALKER

Rapid deployment
The AT-TE carrier drops off its cargo and gets itself to safety as quickly as possible.

Flying solo
A single clone trooper pilots the carrier into enemy territory.

Clone Wars service
LAAT/c carriers participated in the Battle of Geonosis and returned to the planet later in the war to destroy a droid factory.

Personalized paint job
Clone troopers often decorate carriers with colorful nose artwork.

Firepower
Swiveling laser cannons are operated from the cockpit.

AT-TE CARRIER

APPEARANCES II, CW **MANUFACTURER** Rothana Heavy Engineering **MODEL** Low Altitude Assault Transport Carrier **TYPE** Repulsorlift gunship

The LAAT/c, for Low Altitude Assault Transport carrier, is a specialty variant of the LAAT gunship used to transport AT-TEs into battle. After latching onto an AT-TE with powerful magnetic clamps, the vessel's pilot ferries the heavy cargo to a designated drop zone and releases the vehicle. Two laser cannons mounted on the nose provide defense during vulnerable drop-offs.

Tanks advance
Manufactured in great numbers during the Clone Wars, AT-TEs are the backbone of Republic ground operations from the Core to the Outer Rim.

Main cannon
The AT-TE's primary weapon has its own dedicated gunner who sits above the vehicle's hull.

Command center
The command cabin houses the pilot and spotter.

Firepower
Forward guns are effective against battle droids.

All terrain
Footpads can be magnetized for scaling metal walls.

AT-TE (ALL TERRAIN TACTICAL ENFORCER)

APPEARANCES II, CW, III, Reb **MANUFACTURER** Rothana Heavy Engineering
MODEL All Terrain Tactical Enforcer **TYPE** Walker

The All Terrain Tactical Enforcer is an early example of walker technology used to great effect on the battlefield. The six-legged tanks are both assault vehicles and transports and can carry up to 20 clone troopers. Each AT-TE is operated by a crew of seven, made up of a pilot, a spotter, four gunners, and one cannon operator. The top-mounted mass-driver cannon has a slow rate of fire, but six smaller laser cannons mounted on the AT-TE's hull provide defense against enemy infantry.

Providing support
The AT-TE is excellent when used in conjunction with infantry, since it can lay down covering fire from an elevated angle.

HAILFIRE DROID

APPEARANCES II **MANUFACTURER** Haor Chall Engineering **MODEL** IG-227 *Hailfire*-class droid tank **TYPE** Tank

The IG-227 *Hailfire*-class droid tank is easily identified by its treaded, hoop-like drive wheels. The InterGalactic Banking Clan commissioned the construction of the hailfire prior to the Clone Wars, and the units saw their first combat against Republic troops during the Battle of Geonosis. A hailfire is an armored missile platform best used to destroy enemy vehicles. Each of the two launchers mounted on a hailfire can hold up to 15 guided missiles.

Rolling into battle
The hailfire is also called the wheel droid due to its maneuverable and speedy drive system *(below)*. Each missile from the droid leaves behind a trail of black exhaust that darkens the sky *(right)*.

SPHA-T

APPEARANCES II **MANUFACTURER** Rothana Heavy Engineering **MODEL** Self-Propelled Heavy Artillery Turbolaser **TYPE** Heavy artillery

The 12-legged SPHA-T is one of the biggest ground guns in the Republic's imposing arsenal. Each SPHA-T is operated by a crew of 30 clone troopers and only uses its legs when maneuvering between firing positions. When attacking an enemy target, the SPHA-T remains motionless to give the gunners added precision for aiming the extraordinarily heavy turbolaser beam.

SOLAR SAILER

APPEARANCES II, CW **MANUFACTURER** Huppla Pasa Tisc Shipwrights Collective **MODEL** *Punworcca 116*–class interstellar sloop **TYPE** Star yacht

Count Dooku's unique craft relies on a retractable sail to collect stray interstellar energies, which are directed to the ship's engines to provide a near-limitless source of fuel. The main body of the ship is a luxurious sloop with a design that closely resembles that of the Geonosian starfighter—no surprise, as Dooku had the foresight to commission the vessel from his allies on Geonosis prior to the outbreak of the Clone Wars. Dooku uses an FA-4 pilot droid to handle takeoffs and landings. Within the sailer, a secure HoloNet transceiver allows the Count to communicate with his master, Darth Sidious.

GEONOSIAN STARFIGHTER

APPEARANCES II, CW **MANUFACTURER** Huppla Pasa Tisc Shipwrights Collective **MODEL** *Nantex*-class territorial defense starfighter **TYPE** Starfighter

The needle-shaped *Nantex*-class starfighter is the primary defensive craft of the insectoid inhabitants of Geonosis. A single laser cannon is mounted between the upper and lower prongs that make up the starfighter's nose, and 100 tiny tractor beam projectors aid in precision aiming and grappling with enemy vessels at close range.

Holding the line
Republic attack cruisers, the primary defense against the Separatists, become commonly known as Jedi cruisers during the war.

REPUBLIC ATTACK CRUISER

APPEARANCES CW, III **MANUFACTURER** Kuat Drive Yards **MODEL** *Venator*-class Star Destroyer **TYPE** Star Destroyer

The Republic attack cruiser is also known as the *Venator*-class Star Destroyer and is one of the first examples of the triangular warships that would become a terrifying symbol of Imperial power. First deployed during the Clone Wars, Republic attack cruisers quickly become the most powerful capital ships in the Republic navy. Each vessel serves double duty as both a battleship and a starfighter carrier, with armaments including heavy turbolasers, laser cannons, proton torpedo launchers, and tractor beam projectors. The vessel's flight deck is built directly into the prow, providing a 0.5-kilometer- (550-yd-) long runway that allows starfighters to scramble into space the instant the bow doors are opened. An attack cruiser carries more than 420 starfighters, 40 gunships, and 24 AT-TEs, and operates with a crew of more than 7,400 personnel. Throughout the Clone Wars, Republic attack cruisers remain on the frontlines, keeping the space lanes free of Separatist interference and providing cover for landing parties of Jedi and clone troopers.

BANKING CLAN COMMUNICATIONS FRIGATE

APPEARANCES CW, III, FoD
MANUFACTURER Hoersch-Kessel Drive
MODEL *Munificent*-class star frigate **TYPE** Frigate

The InterGalactic Banking Clan operates the *Munificent*-class frigate as both a warship and a communications vessel. It is equipped for secure ship-to-ship transmissions and the jamming of enemy signals.

Hangar bays for starfighters

Elongated wings support defensive weaponry

Each frigate is operated by 200 crew but can carry up to 150,000 battle droids and often skimps on life-support systems due to the small size of its crew. Laser cannons, twin turbolasers, and ion cannons allow the frigate to put up a fight against enemy capital ships.

STEALTH SHIP

APPEARANCES CW **MANUFACTURER** Sienar Design Systems
MODEL Prototype stealth model **TYPE** Corvette

An experimental vessel developed by the Republic during the Clone Wars, the prototype stealth ship incorporates a cloaking device that renders it invisible. Additionally it is outfitted with communications antennas and gun turrets, and features an array of countermeasures to escape detection or shake missiles. During the blockade of Christophsis, the Republic deploys the stealth ship to enable a crew to reach the surface undetected and assist in Senator Bail Organa's relief mission. Anakin Skywalker decides to engage the leader of the Separatist blockade, Admiral Trench. Years later, the design of Grand Moff Tarkin's personal vessel, the *Carrion Spike*, is based on that of the stealth ship.

HYENA BOMBER

APPEARANCES CW **MANUFACTURER** Baktoid Armor Workshop **MODEL** *Hyena*-class bomber **TYPE** Bomber

Separatists use the Hyena bomber to attack warships and surface installations with high-yield explosive warheads. Hyena bombers are rarely seen during the Clone Wars, but do participate in the Battles of Christophsis and Ryloth. Like the Separatist *Vulture*-class starfighter, the Hyena bomber is controlled by a droid intelligence and is capable of splitting its wings and entering a "walking mode." The Hyena bomber carries armaments such as proton bombs, proton torpedoes, and concussion missiles, all stored in a ventral bomb bay.

Walking mode
The Hyena bomber uses its wings as limbs when taxiing from one surface location to another.

BARC SPEEDER

APPEARANCES CW, III **MANUFACTURER** Aratech Repulsor Company **MODEL** Biker Advanced Recon Commando speeder
TYPE Speeder bike

A swift reconnaissance vehicle, the BARC speeder is named for the specialized clone drivers who operate it. Most BARC speeders are painted in the traditional red and white colors of the Republic Army, though some bear brown or green camouflage markings. Each is equipped with a forward-facing blaster cannon and a repulsorlift engine capable of reaching speeds up to 520 kilometers (323 miles) per hour. On Saleucami, Jedi General Stass Allie pilots a BARC speeder when her escorts suddenly receive Order 66. The pursuing clone troopers blast her vehicle, killing her.

In formation
Clone troopers and their Jedi generals tend to use BARC speeders when scouting unfamiliar terrain *(above)*, but the vehicles can also be customized for other missions with optional sidecars *(top)*, or even detachable stretchers.

ALL TERRAIN RECON TRANSPORT (AT-RT)

APPEARANCES CW, III **MANUFACTURER** Kuat Drive Yards **MODEL** All Terrain Recon Transport **TYPE** Scout walker

The AT-RT, or All Terrain Recon Transport, is a bipedal walker built for a single operator. The open cockpit offers little protection to its clone trooper driver, but the AT-RT is speedy and sure-footed as a reconnaissance vehicle. Its chin-mounted laser cannon is useful against battle droids, but too weak to damage heavy vehicles. Communications antennas allow the AT-RT to transmit battlefield intelligence. The Republic uses AT-RTs throughout the Clone Wars, including at the Battle of Ryloth and during the hunt for Master Yoda on Kashyyyk following Order 66.

Two-legged mobility
AT-RTs are able to handle many types of planetary surfaces, ideal for Republic troopers during the galaxy-spanning Clone Wars.

TRIDENT DRILL ASSAULT CRAFT

APPEARANCES CW **MANUFACTURER** Colicoid Creation Nest **MODEL** *Trident*-class assault ship **TYPE** Gunship

The Trident drill assault craft is a Separatist gunship built for underwater operation, capable of drilling through the hulls of enemy vessels and installations. In the Battles of Kamino and Mon Cala during the Clone Wars, Tridents attack with their drills and laser cannons while releasing squads of aqua droids from their holds.

Armored tentacles
Mechanical limbs are equipped with magnetic grapples.

KHETANNA

APPEARANCES CW, VI **MANUFACTURER** Ubrikkian Industries **MODEL** Customized luxury sail barge **TYPE** Sail barge

Jabba's luxury sail barge, the *Khetanna*, is used by the Hutt crime lord whenever he leaves his palace to visit other parts of Tatooine. The vessel is driven by a repulsorlift engine in conjunction with two huge sails on the upper deck. Jabba never suffers the slightest discomfort inside the sail barge's vast interior, which is always packed with musicians, dancers, and staff serving refreshments. The *Khetanna* is protected by a large blaster cannon and several smaller blasters mounted on the side railings.

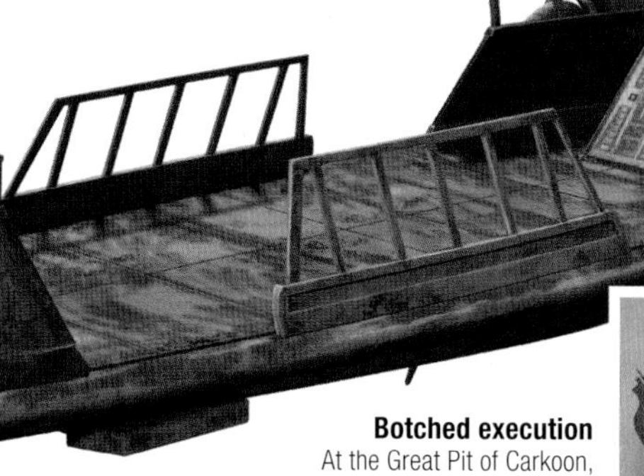

Service vehicle
From his sail barge, Jabba the Hutt watches the executions of prisoners in shaded comfort *(above)*. Jabba's sail barge has been in use since the Clone Wars and is always accompanied by armed guards on desert skiffs *(left)*.

DESERT SKIFF

APPEARANCES CW, VI **MANUFACTURER** Ubrikkian Industries **MODEL** Bantha-II cargo skiff **TYPE** Repulsorlift skiff

Skiffs are common modes of transportation that operate using anti-gravity repulsorlifts. Most are used for moving cargo, but they can easily carry passengers. Jabba the Hutt uses a number of rugged skiffs equipped to survive the heat and sandstorms of the Tatooine deserts. The Bantha-II cargo skiffs have an elongated deck with a safety railing designed to protect passengers or cargo. The skiffs are piloted from a rear control station, and at their maximum speed, they can exceed 250 kilometers (155 miles) per hour.

Smooth flying
Controls in the rear of the skiff are designed to be operated by a single pilot.

Reinforced bow
The armored nose is built to withstand head-on collisions.

Botched execution
At the Great Pit of Carkoon, Jabba's skiff guards make a big mistake when they try to force Luke to walk the plank.

Deployed
During flight, the V-19 makes a three-pointed silhouette *(right)*. Clone troopers receive orders from Anakin Skywalker, with their V-19s waiting on the hangar deck *(bottom)*.

V-19 TORRENT STARFIGHTER

APPEARANCES CW **MANUFACTURER** Slayn & Korpil **MODEL** V-19 Torrent starfighter **TYPE** Starfighter

The V-19 Torrent is one of the fastest and most maneuverable starfighters used by the Republic during the Clone Wars. Its folding S-foils provide stability and a wider area of fire for its two wing-mounted blaster cannons. The V-19 is also outfitted with concussion missile launchers that can home in on targets. Though primarily flown by Republic clone pilots, V-19s are also used by Jedi commanders. During the Battle of Ryloth, Ahsoka Tano leads a squadron against the Separatists.

CORPORATE ALLIANCE PERSUADER TANK DROID

APPEARANCES CW, III **MANUFACTURER** Techno Union **MODEL** NR-N99 *Persuader*-class droid enforcer **TYPE** Droid tank

The NR-N99 *Persuader*-class tank droid is a Separatist war vehicle primarily used by the Corporate Alliance. It is driven by a huge central tread and supported on either side by forward-mounted outriggers. The tank can reach speeds of up to 60 kilometers (37 miles) per hour, useful for ramming barricades. Controlled by a built-in droid intelligence, it is armed with ion cannons, heavy repeating blasters, and missile launchers. NR-N99s lead the assault against a Wookiee city during the Battle of Kashyyyk.

TWILIGHT

APPEARANCES CW **MANUFACTURER** Corellian Engineering Corp. **MODEL** G9 Rigger freighter **TYPE** Space freighter

The *Twilight* serves Anakin Skywalker and other Republic heroes as a faithful transport ship throughout the Clone Wars. Originally owned by Ziro the Hutt, the G9 Rigger space freighter is found by Anakin and his Padawan Ahsoka Tano on the planet Teth. The two Jedi steal the vessel and use it to ferry Jabba the Hutt's young son, Rotta, to Tatooine. When MagnaGuards attack, Anakin is forced to crash-land the *Twilight* into the desert sands. He later retrieves it, and the *Twilight* sees action in the Battle of the Kaliida Nebula and the raid on Skytop Station. The *Twilight* meets its final fate on Mandalore, when Obi-Wan Kenobi uses the vessel to try to escape a group of Death Watch soldiers. After the ship suffers critical hits from missile strikes, Obi-Wan and Duchess Satine evacuate the *Twilight* and it crashes into the surface below.

The *Twilight* is well armed for a freighter, featuring three heavy blaster cannons mounted on the wings and a rotating laser cannon operated from a periscope sight. Additionally, a concussion missile launcher provides explosive punch against large warships. The *Twilight*'s most distinctive feature is its long outrigger wing, which extends from the starboard side of the main cabin and contains two secondary engines. A lower wing can be folded up during landing and extended during flight. The ship is designed to haul cargo and consequently features a tow cable and a rear-opening cargo hatch. The hold is roomy enough to accommodate a Jedi starfighter.

Escape hatch
The rear cargo door can open while in flight to dump sensitive cargo.

Defensive fire
Forward-mounted blaster cannons keep pirates at a distance.

Aerodynamic
Large outrigger wing provides flight stability.

Old but fully armed
The *Twilight*'s engines don't always perform well in planetary atmospheres *(above right)*. With multiple cannons, the *Twilight* is able to hold its own in a fight against those who would raid its holds *(right)*.

"Grease bucket, you're my favorite ship ever!" **AHSOKA TANO**

TANTIVE IV

APPEARANCES CW, Reb, RO, IV **MANUFACTURER** Corellian Engineering Corp. **MODEL** CR90 corvette **TYPE** Corvette

The *Tantive IV* is an Alderaan cruiser of Corellian manufacture operated by the Royal House of Alderaan. Ships similar to the *Tantive IV* are sometimes called blockade runners due to their powerful engine banks and ability to race past slow-moving customs vessels. Like other corvettes of its type, the *Tantive IV* sports double turbolaser cannons on the top and bottom of the ship. The antenna dishes of the communications and sensor array are located just ahead of the drive system. Eleven ion turbine engines stacked on top of each other provide impressive sublight thrust. Within the confines of the *Tantive IV* are living quarters for the crew, dining rooms for hosting state dinners, and conference centers for sensitive negotiations with interstellar dignitaries. Escape pods give the passengers a chance to flee if the ship comes under attack.

The *Tantive IV* sees action during the Clone Wars and continues to serve Senator Bail Organa of Alderaan for nearly two decades. When Senator Organa's daughter Leia follows him into politics, the *Tantive IV* becomes her ship. Princess Leia becomes famous for her "mercy missions" to help populations in need, but the Empire suspects she is using the ship to carry out assignments on behalf of the Rebel Alliance. After the *Tantive IV* escapes the Battle of Scarif with the plans for the Death Star, Darth Vader chases the vessel and disables it above Tatooine. The *Tantive IV* is drawn into a Star Destroyer's docking bay and its passengers, including Princess Leia, are captured.

Firefight
The narrow hallways of the *Tantive IV* allow its crew to set up an ambush for a stormtrooper boarding party.

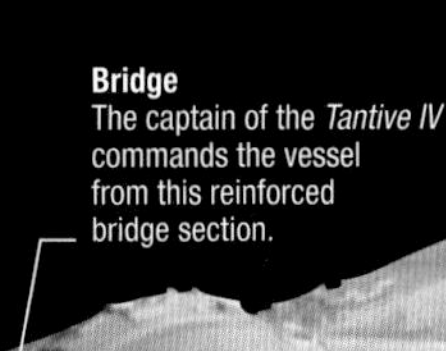

Bridge
The captain of the *Tantive IV* commands the vessel from this reinforced bridge section.

"Tear this ship apart until you've found those plans!" **DARTH VADER**

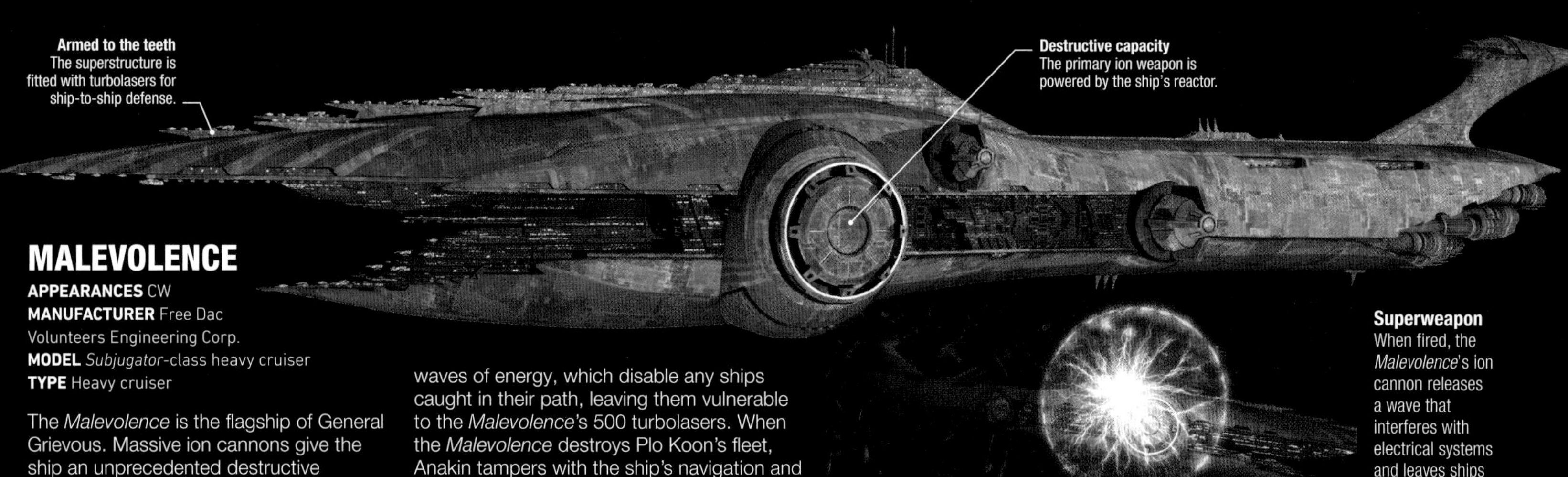

Armed to the teeth The superstructure is fitted with turbolasers for ship-to-ship defense.

Destructive capacity The primary ion weapon is powered by the ship's reactor.

Superweapon When fired, the *Malevolence*'s ion cannon releases a wave that interferes with electrical systems and leaves ships drifting in space.

MALEVOLENCE

APPEARANCES CW
MANUFACTURER Free Dac Volunteers Engineering Corp.
MODEL *Subjugator*-class heavy cruiser
TYPE Heavy cruiser

The *Malevolence* is the flagship of General Grievous. Massive ion cannons give the ship an unprecedented destructive capacity with the release of expanding waves of energy, which disable any ships caught in their path, leaving them vulnerable to the *Malevolence*'s 500 turbolasers. When the *Malevolence* destroys Plo Koon's fleet, Anakin tampers with the ship's navigation and the sabotaged vehicle crashes into a moon.

SOULLESS ONE

APPEARANCES CW, III **MANUFACTURER** Feethan Ottraw Scalable Assemblies **MODEL** Belbullab-22 starfighter **TYPE** Starfighter

The personal starfighter of General Grievous, the *Soulless One* is a customized Belbullab-22 starfighter designed for speed and agility when dogfighting. It is armed with two sets of triple rapid-fire laser cannons and features a state-of-the-art hyperdrive allowing it to reach any location in the galaxy. Near the end of the Clone Wars, General Grievous brings the *Soulless One* to Utapau. After Obi-Wan Kenobi kills him, he uses the late general's starfighter to escape Utapau and rendezvous with Yoda and Bail Organa.

Sleek profile The *Soulless One* is streamlined for maximum maneuverability in atmosphere.

TURBO TANK

APPEARANCES CW, III, RO
MANUFACTURER Kuat Drive Yards
MODEL HAVw A6 Juggernaut **TYPE** Tank

The HAVw A6 Juggernaut, known as the clone turbo tank, is a heavily armed and armored Republic military transport. A single Juggernaut can carry up to 300 clone troopers and is operated by a crew of 12. The tank's superconducting armor absorbs and disperses enemy fire, and the tank retaliates with a heavy laser turret, anti-personnel cannons, a repeating laser, and projectile launchers. A clone spotter occupies a pod above the vehicle's back. A later model of the turbo tank—the HCVw A9—is used by the Empire to move prisoners on the planet Wobani.

ARC-170 STARFIGHTER

APPEARANCES CW, III **MANUFACTURER** Incom Corp.
MODEL ARC-170 Aggressive Reconnaissance starfighter
TYPE Starfighter

The ARC-170 functions equally well as a fighter and a bomber. Its gigantic laser cannons are capable of punching holes in capital ship armor, while twin blaster cannons operated by a tail gunner cover the rear fire arc. Explosive ordnance comes in the form of proton torpedoes. Panels on the upper and lower surfaces of the wings can open during combat to bleed off excess heat. An ARC-170 is typically operated by a crew of three plus an astromech droid.

On patrol ARC-170s are equipped to deal with any threat they encounter.

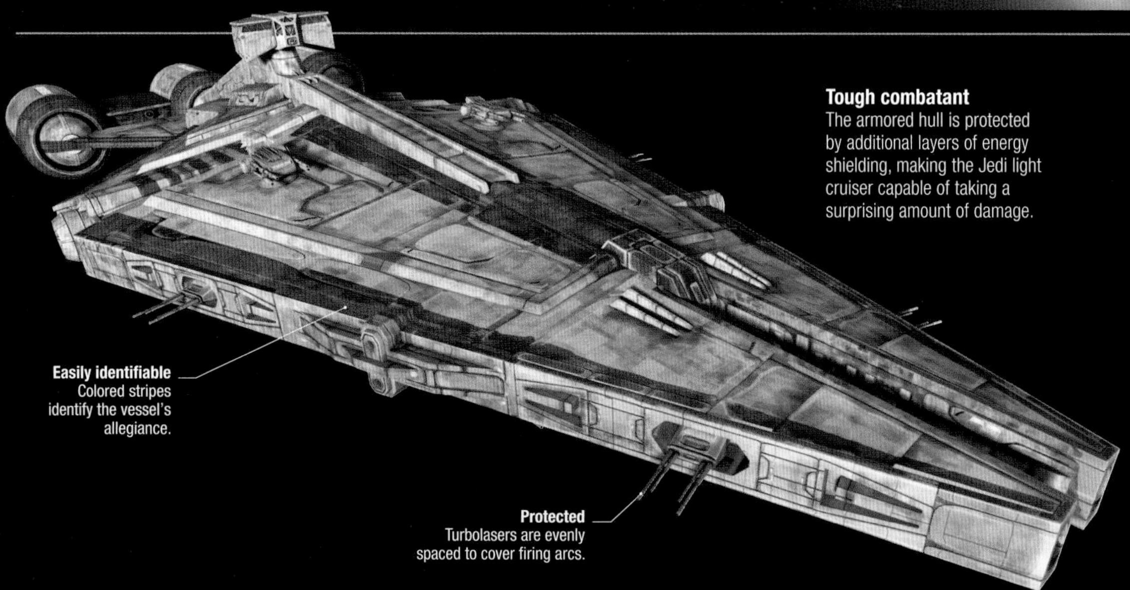

Tough combatant The armored hull is protected by additional layers of energy shielding, making the Jedi light cruiser capable of taking a surprising amount of damage.

Easily identifiable Colored stripes identify the vessel's allegiance.

Protected Turbolasers are evenly spaced to cover firing arcs.

JEDI LIGHT CRUISER

APPEARANCES CW, Reb **MANUFACTURER** Kuat Drive Yards **MODEL** *Arquitens*-class light cruiser
TYPE Light cruiser

This light warship is used by the Republic during the Clone Wars. Though not as large as other Republic ships such as the *Venator*-class Star Destroyer, the vessel is armed with four quad laser turrets and four double-barreled turbolaser batteries, as well as concussion missile launchers. Obi-Wan and other Jedi generals often take command of these ships, which results in their common name. After the Empire's formation, *Arquitens*-class cruisers continue to serve in the Imperial navy, seeing action against the Batonn rebels. A variant of the model, named the *Arquitens*-class command cruiser, is also introduced.

TRANDOSHAN FLYING HUNTING LODGE

APPEARANCES CW **MANUFACTURER** Ubrikkian Industries **MODEL** Ubrikkian Floating Fortress **TYPE** Armed hover platform

Trandoshan hunters use this platform as a mobile base when hunting live prey on the moon of Wasskah. It features a trophy room, living quarters, and a landing deck for airspeeders. In the Clone Wars, Ahsoka Tano and a few Wookiees attack the hunting lodge and the Trandoshans.

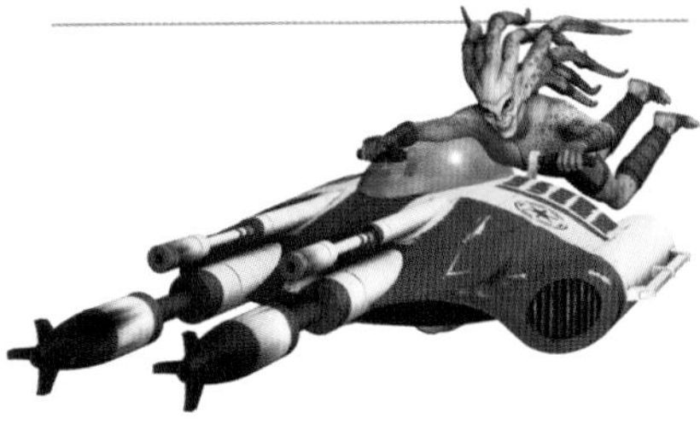

OMS DEVILFISH

APPEARANCES CW **MANUFACTURER** Kuat Drive Yards **MODEL** One-Man Submersible Devilfish **TYPE** Submersible

The Devilfish is a military craft designed for underwater use. It lacks armored protection, but features speedy propulsion jets and is armed with a forward-facing dual blaster cannon. During the Clone Wars, Republic troops use a swarm of Devilfish craft to fight off Separatist aqua droids on Mon Cala. When the planet later rebels against the Empire, Imperial seatroopers use Devilfish to quell the insurrection.

UMBARAN STARFIGHTER

APPEARANCES CW
MANUFACTURER Umbaran Militia
MODEL Zenuas 33 starfighter **TYPE** Starfighter

The Umbaran starfighter is operated by a single pilot, who sits in a command chair surrounded by a spherical energy shield and flies the ship using holographic controls. The command chair plugs into a spaceframe with loop-shaped wings. An Umbaran starfighter can defend itself with a single rapid-fire laser cannon and two electromagnetic pulse missile launchers.

HOUND'S TOOTH

APPEARANCES CW **MANUFACTURER** Corellian Engineering Corp. **MODEL** YV-666 light freighter **TYPE** Space freighter

The *Hound's Tooth* is the personal starship of the bounty hunter Bossk. This highly modified Corellian freighter contains holding cells for captured prisoners and an armory for stocking up on weapons. Many sensors allow Bossk to keep an eye on the integrity of the cages. The *Hound's Tooth* is armed with a quad-laser turret, an ion cannon, and a concussion missile launcher.

HMP DROID GUNSHIP

APPEARANCES CW, III **MANUFACTURER** Baktoid Fleet Ordnance **MODEL** Heavy Missile Platform droid gunship **TYPE** Gunship

The HMP droid gunship, a heavily armed repulsorlift airspeeder, is the Separatist counterpart to the Republic's LAAT/i. Operated by an advanced droid brain, the HMP's frame accommodates numerous weapons, which can easily be interchanged for different missions. A droid gunship boasts a chin-mounted cannon, two laser turrets, and two light laser cannons on the wingtips, but the ship's real power is its payload of 14 high-explosive missiles. During the Clone Wars, droid gunships are modified to serve as troop carriers for battle droids.

Showdown
Three droid gunships fly in a tight formation *(far left)*, while laser cannons assault ground troops *(left)*.

ANAKIN'S ETA-2 JEDI STARFIGHTER

APPEARANCES CW, III **MANUFACTURER** Kuat Systems Engineering **MODEL** Eta-2 *Actis*-class light interceptor **TYPE** Starfighter

Anakin Skywalker replaces his Delta-7B Jedi starfighter with a new Eta-2 interceptor model late in the Clone Wars. This smaller, more maneuverable ship is armed with twin laser cannons and twin ion cannons. Its forward windshield bubble features an octagonal shape that is later carried over into the Empire's TIE fighters. On the tip of each wing, S-foils can swing up and lock into a vertical position and are used during combat to safely bleed off excess heat. The ship's dual ion engines and narrow profile allow it to make tight turns while dogfighting, but it lacks sufficient engine space for a hyperdrive. Instead, the Eta-2 relies on an external hyperspace docking ring when traveling across the galaxy. A plug-in socket inside the port wing can accommodate an astromech droid for onboard repairs, and soon Anakin and R2-D2 are flying together on vital missions against the Separatists.

Anakin uses his starfighter to defend Cato Neimoidia from a Separatist attack. When a missile explodes near his ship, it releases a swarm of buzz droids, which cause extensive damage to the Eta-2. However, the ship is repaired in time for the Battle of Coruscant.

Droid swarm
Dozens of buzz droids latch onto the hull of Anakin's starfighter.

Accompanied by Obi-Wan Kenobi in a similar interceptor, Anakin fights his way through the Separatist navy and disables the hangar shields on General Grievous' flagship *Invisible Hand*. As soon as the Eta-2 is parked inside, Anakin and R2-D2 leave the craft behind to cause trouble for Grievous.

Racing colors
Anakin painted his starfighter in a custom design inspired by his podracing past.

Y-WING STARFIGHTER

APPEARANCES CW, Reb, RO, IV, V, VI
MANUFACTURER Koensayr Manufacturing
MODEL Y-wing **TYPE** Starfighter

The Y-wing line of starfighters has the dubious distinction of remaining in service long enough to fly under the command of Anakin Skywalker and to be shot down by Darth Vader. During the Clone Wars, Anakin leads Shadow Squadron's BTL-B Y-wings in an attack that disables the *Malevolence*, a heavy cruiser commanded by General Grievous and armed with a massive ion cannon. Decades later, at the Battle of Yavin, eight BTL-A4 Y-wings from the Rebel Alliance's Gold Squadron take part in the assault on the Death Star. Darth Vader leads a trio of TIE fighters to confront them, personally shooting down Gold Leader and six of his wingmates; only Gold Three, piloted by Evaan Verlaine, survives. Y-wings from Gray Squadron join the attack on the second Death Star.

The BTL-A4 Y-wing is a single-pilot starfighter, although additional support for the pilot is provided by the astromech droid positioned aft of the cockpit. Equipped with a hyperdrive for making lightspeed jumps, the ship has a pair of ion jet engines for primary propulsion. This makes the Y-wing slower and less maneuverable than other starfighters, such as the X-wing and A-wing, flying in the Rebel Alliance fleet. For defense, the pilot must count on the energy shields and the heavy armor plating around the cockpit. When dogfighting is unavoidable, the Y-wing relies on two fixed, front-mounted laser cannons and a rotating turret with anti-starfighter ion cannons. More commonly, the Y-wing operates as a bomber against capital ships in fleet battles or for ground targets in planetside action, making multiple bombing runs to deliver proton torpedoes and proton bombs from its arsenal.

"Stay on target." **GOLD FIVE**

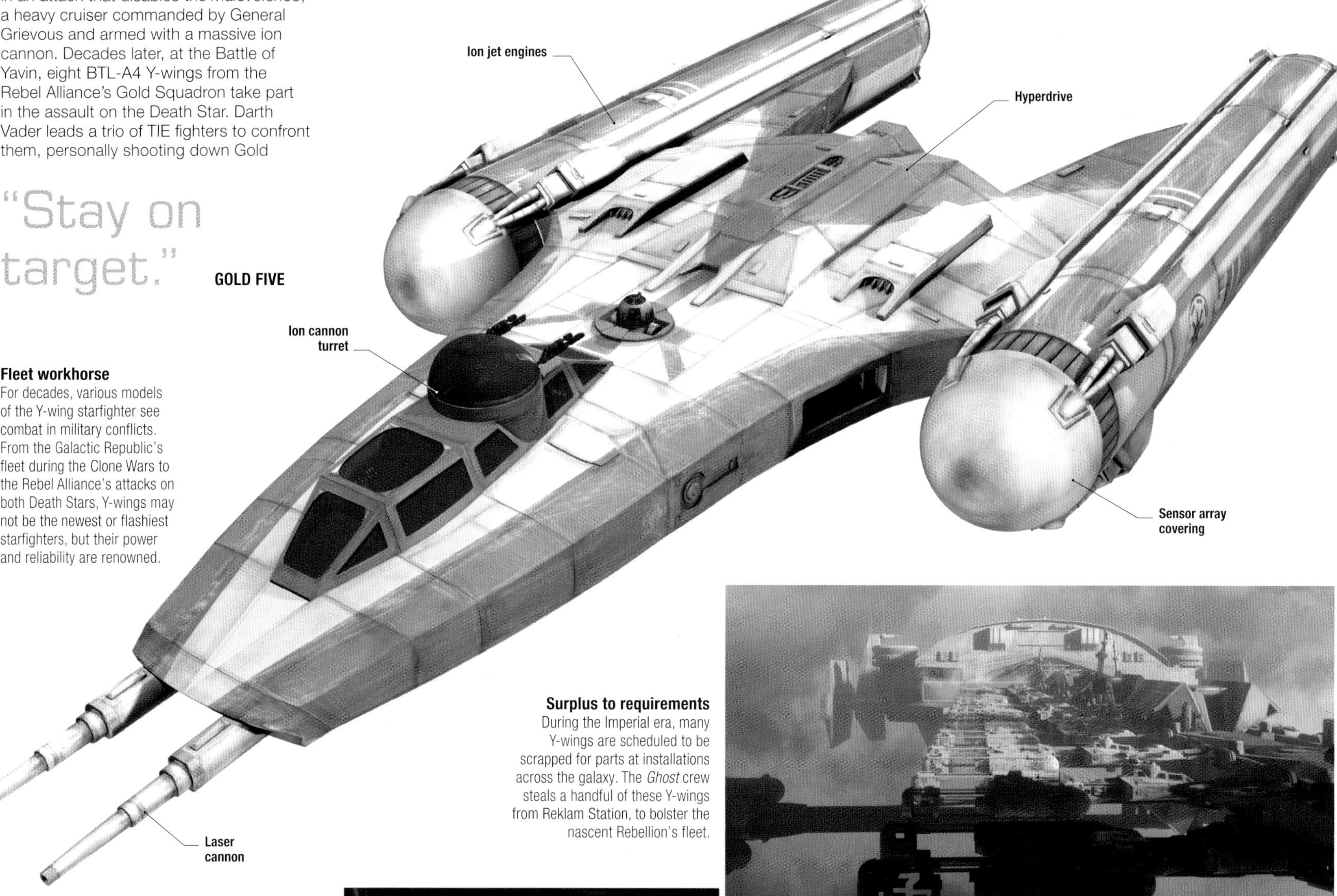

Fleet workhorse
For decades, various models of the Y-wing starfighter see combat in military conflicts. From the Galactic Republic's fleet during the Clone Wars to the Rebel Alliance's attacks on both Death Stars, Y-wings may not be the newest or flashiest starfighters, but their power and reliability are renowned.

Surplus to requirements
During the Imperial era, many Y-wings are scheduled to be scrapped for parts at installations across the galaxy. The *Ghost* crew steals a handful of these Y-wings from Reklam Station, to bolster the nascent Rebellion's fleet.

Fatal run
On the moon Yavin 4, a Y-wing is prepped for the upcoming battle with the Death Star *(below)*. Gold Leader leads a pair of Y-wings through the Death Star's narrow trench *(right)*.

Coward's retreat General Grievous attempts to flee from Obi-Wan Kenobi, but is caught in a fatal duel.

GENERAL GRIEVOUS' WHEEL BIKE

APPEARANCES III **MANUFACTURER** Z-Gomot Ternbuell Guppat Corp. **MODEL** Tsmeu-6 **TYPE** Personal wheel bike

General Grievous drives a Tsmeu-6 on Utapau during the Clone Wars. This line of vehicles is also popular in mining areas, where long-distance travel underground is necessary on a variety of terrains. The Tsmeu-6 is designed for a single passenger seated beside a large central wheel. The wheel bike has a maximum speed of 330 kilometers (205 miles) per hour rolling and 10 kilometers (6 miles) per hour running on its four retractable legs, and it carries enough fuel for approximately 500 kilometers (311 miles) of travel. With a wheel diameter of 2.5 meters (8 ft 2 in) and a length of 3.5 meters (11½ ft), the Tsmeu-6 also boasts a powerful double laser cannon.

Speeder chase Luke Skywalker and Leia Organa race to stop a biker scout from reporting their presence to the Imperials.

74-Z SPEEDER BIKE

APPEARANCES III, VI, FoD **MANUFACTURER** Aratech Repulsor Company **MODEL** 74-Z **TYPE** Scout speeder bike

The 74-Z is first used by the Republic during the Clone Wars, particularly on the planet of Saleucami. The speeder is used again by the Empire to patrol forests surrounding their shield generator on Endor. The speeder bike is ideally suited for patrols and scout missions over long distances in a variety of terrains, thanks to its exceptional maneuverability and self-charging battery system. Designed to carry one or two passengers, the 74-Z is controlled by four steering vanes, contains sensor and communications equipment between the handlebars, and includes a BlasTech Ax-20 blaster cannon for offensive strikes. The speeder measures approximately 3.2 meters (10½ ft) and can theoretically reach a maximum, but inadvisable, speed of 500 kilometers (311 miles) per hour.

V-WING STARFIGHTER

APPEARANCES III **MANUFACTURER** Kuat Systems Engineering **MODEL** Alpha-3 Nimbus **TYPE** Starfighter

In use during the last days of the Galactic Republic and the early years of the Galactic Empire, V-wings are compact support ships ideal in battle against large numbers of enemy fighters. V-wings are piloted by a single clone trooper backed by an astromech droid. The ship closely resembles various Jedi starfighter models (it is made by the same manufacturer) and, like those ships, lacks a hyperdrive. The most distinguishing feature of this craft is a pair of folding wings on either side of the hull, which extend above and below the ship. Dual rapid-fire laser cannons are situated on each of the two wing struts. The V-wing can also attain an impressive top speed of 52,000 kilometers (32,312 miles) per hour.

No mercy mission A trio of V-wing starfighters escorts Emperor Palpatine back to Coruscant with a critically wounded Darth Vader.

INVISIBLE HAND

APPEARANCES III **MANUFACTURER** Free Dac Volunteers Engineering Corps
MODEL *Providence*-class carrier/destroyer
TYPE Capital ship

"Get to the command ship! Get the chancellor!" **OBI-WAN KENOBI**

The Separatists employ a number of gargantuan warships during the Clone Wars, many of them falling under the command of the cyborg General Grievous. After Grievous loses the *Malevolence* in battle with the Republic, he claims the *Invisible Hand* as his flagship. This *Providence*-class vessel is 1 kilometer (1,094 yds) in length and is classified as both a destroyer and a carrier, a dual role that makes the Separatist dreadnought equipped for total planetary domination. It holds 20 squadrons of droid starfighters and more than 400 ground assault vehicles for use during invasions, while its numerous turbolaser turrets are capable of unleashing a surface bombardment from the safety of orbit. If threatened by Republic capital ships, the *Invisible Hand* can pummel the enemy with more than 100 proton torpedo launchers. An observation platform occupies a sensor pod high above the hull and allows commanders to get an unobstructed view of battle. The side of the ship bears the Separatist emblem of the Confederacy of Independent Systems. General Grievous uses the *Invisible Hand* during later Clone War skirmishes and soon receives orders to make a bold strike at the Republic's capital world of Coruscant. Accompanied by several Separatist warships, the *Invisible Hand* drops out of hyperspace and is soon embroiled in a space battle more intense than any conducted in the war to date. While the Republic responds to the naval threat, Grievous slips to the surface of Coruscant and kidnaps Supreme Chancellor Palpatine, bringing his captive back to the *Invisible Hand.* Anakin and Obi-Wan board the ship on a rescue mission. With the battle taking a terrible toll on his ship, Grievous blasts to safety in an escape pod. As the *Invisible Hand* breaks up around him, Anakin successfully pilots the forward section of the ship into a fiery crash landing on Coruscant.

Crash landing
As Anakin steers the wreckage of the *Invisible Hand* down to the surface, fire ships struggle to contain the damage.

Droid delegator
When General Grievous encounters Jedi Obi-Wan Kenobi and Anakin Skywalker on the bridge, he orders his IG-100 MagnaGuard to engage them.

Battle of Coruscant
The fierce space battle that rages above the Republic capital proves to be the end of the *Invisible Hand.*

DWARF SPIDER DROID

APPEARANCES II, CW, III **MANUFACTURER** Baktoid Armor Workshop
TYPE DSD1 dwarf spider droid **AFFILIATION** Separatists

The DSD1 dwarf spider droid is also known as the burrowing spider droid for its ability to invade narrow spaces. Frequently used by the Commerce Guild, it becomes a mainstay of Separatist ground forces during the Clone Wars. The dwarf spider droid's primary weapon is a long blaster cannon capable of both rapid-fire and high-intensity bursts. The legs of the dwarf spider droid are designed to affix securely to the sides of cliffs, and the droids are used by the Separatists during the Battle of Teth to fire at Republic AT-TE walkers trying to gain the high ground. In other engagements, dwarf spider droids provide heavy backup for squads of battle droids.

On the beach
Dwarf spider droids attack a coastal city on Kashyyyk, blasting the Wookiee defenders.

OCTUPTARRA DROID

APPEARANCES CW, III **MANUFACTURER** Techno Union
TYPE Octuptarra combat tri-droid **AFFILIATION** Separatists

Octuptarra droids are found among Separatist forces during the Clone Wars, often fielded by the Techno Union. These tall, three-legged automatons have large heads containing operational software and sensory equipment. Three laser turrets are mounted equidistantly beneath the droid's three photoreceptors. Because the octuptarra looks in every direction at once, it has virtually no blind spots. Despite its omnidirectional field of fire, the octuptarra droid is slow-moving and vulnerable to tripping. The Techno Union produces a number of different-sized droids during the war, some of them large enough to take on heavily armored Republic AT-TEs.

Three laser cannons
The rotating turrets deliver an offensive punch.

360-degree attack
The octuptarra can swivel its head to easily cover any angle.

Three spider-like legs

REPUBLIC ARTILLERY CANNON (AV-7)

APPEARANCES CW **MANUFACTURER** Taim & Bak **MODEL** AV-7 Anti-vehicle Artillery Cannon
TYPE Artillery cannon

The AV-7 is a self-propelled artillery unit that moves on anti-grav repulsorlifts. It can be operated by a single clone trooper who sits behind the gunnery controls located on the side of the central assembly. When an AV-7 is in position, it stabilizes itself with its four widely spaced legs. The blasts from an AV-7 can take out both tanks and battle droids.

"She may not look like much, but she's got it where it counts." HAN SOLO

MILLENNIUM FALCON

Agile and swift, the *Millennium Falcon* can easily slip from a Star Destroyer's grasp or fly into the bowels of the Death Star to destroy it.

APPEARANCES S, IV, V, VI, VII, VIII, IX, FoD **MANUFACTURER** Corellian Engineering Corp. **MODEL** Modified YT-1300f **TYPE** Light freighter

KESSEL RUN

Under the ownership of gambler Lando Calrissian, the *Millennium Falcon* is a pristine machine. The lure of profit tempts Calrissian to shuttle a crew of smugglers to Kessel. Among Lando's passengers is Han Solo, a talented pilot from Corellia who is familiar with the freighter design. Solo takes the controls of the *Falcon* when the mission goes awry. He uses the brain of destroyed droid L3-37 to plot a course through the dangerous space surrounding Kessel and makes the journey in a record time. Though the crew survives, the ship's interior and exterior are severely damaged. Despite no longer meeting Lando's high aesthetic standards, the light freighter loses none of its appeal to Han. He later wins the ship from Lando in a game of sabacc on Numidian Prime.

Flashy exterior
The *Falcon*'s durasteel hull has been painted in hue alabaster-7791 and has highlights in crys-anoblue-7255.

REBEL SERVICE

After safely transporting Leia, Luke, and the droids to Yavin 4, Han and Chewbacca set off in the *Falcon*. However, they soon return to help during the Battle of Yavin, ensuring that Luke can fire the critical shot that destroys the Death Star. Han and Chewbacca are handsomely rewarded for the rebel victory. During the next two years, Han and Chewbacca join the Rebel Alliance and fly the *Falcon* during many critical missions. They participate in the Dragon Void Run while rescuing rebel informants, and barely survive a dogfight with Darth Vader during the Assault on the Mako-Ta Space Docks. As Darth Vader's forces invade Echo Base on Hoth, the *Falcon* flees the planet with a fleet of Star Destroyers on its tail. Han boldly takes cover in an asteroid field.

Risky business
After a deadly chase through an asteroid field *(left)*, Han hides the *Falcon* in what he believes to be a cave. Leia and Han investigate the mysterious site, eventually realizing they are actually inside a space slug *(below)*.

Smuggler's ship
Aboard the *Falcon*, Luke practices with his lightsaber *(top)*. Hidden compartments under the deck plating *(above)* help Han hide contraband during inspections.

CAPTURED BY THE DEATH STAR

Years later, when Obi-Wan Kenobi and Luke Skywalker need swift, discreet passage to Alderaan, they choose the *Falcon*—the ship that made the Kessel Run in less than 12 parsecs, as its captain, Han Solo, likes to brag. Han has heavily modified the *Falcon* so it is optimized for smuggling. When the Death Star seizes the ship, the crew hide away to evade capture. While Obi-Wan sabotages the Death Star's tractor beam, Han, Chewbacca, and Luke mount a prison break to rescue the captured rebel leader, Leia Organa. Obi-Wan then duels Darth Vader as a distraction while the others escape aboard Han's ship. TIE fighters give chase, but powerful cannons in the *Falcon*'s upper and lower turrets dispatch them.

Looks are deceiving
The *Millennium Falcon* may not look like much, but special modifications give her exceptional speed, intelligence, and agility, making her ideal for a smuggler like Han.

Still going
After decades of service, the *Falcon* is still more than capable of holding its own in a dogfight.

SHARED OWNERSHIP

After Han is imprisoned in carbonite and delivered to Jabba the Hutt, Lando retakes his old position as the *Falcon*'s pilot, alongside Han's co-pilot, Chewbacca. Together, Lando and Chewbacca participate in Solo's rescue and reunite him with the *Falcon*. Faced with a new Death Star, Han offers his ship to Lando who leads the assault on the space station. This time, it is the *Falcon* that delivers the destructive shot to the Empire's newest superweapon. Lando returns the freighter to Han after the battle.

Death Star
The second Death Star is blown up in spectacular fashion by Lando Calrissian and his co-pilot Nien Nunb.

IN THE RESISTANCE

In the years following the fall of the Empire, Han Solo loses the *Falcon* to gunrunner Gannis Ducain. It then passes to the Irving Boys before ultimately being stolen by junk dealer Unkar Plutt. Plutt leaves the ship baking in the Jakku sun until it is used by Rey, a scavenger, and Finn, a First Order deserter, to escape the planet. The pair are discovered by Solo and Chewbacca, who have been searching the galaxy for their old ship. The *Falcon* and its former pilot take part in the mission to destroy yet another terrifying superweapon—Starkiller Base. When Han doesn't survive, the ship passes to Rey and Chewbacca who use it to save the Resistance at Crait. At that battle, the very sight of the ship draws Kylo Ren, Han's son and killer, into a rage. After the battle, Chewbacca takes the *Falcon* to Black Spire Outpost on Batuu for repairs, begrudgingly leaving it in the care of an old acquaintance—businessman and former pirate, Hondo Ohnaka.

STAR DESTROYER

APPEARANCES S, Reb, RO, IV, V, VI, VII **MANUFACTURER** Kuat Drive Yards
MODEL *Imperial I*–class **TYPE** Star Destroyer

Star Destroyers are the chief warships of the Imperial Navy and symbols of Imperial might. They enforce the Emperor's will by eliminating hindrances to commerce on Imperial worlds and bolstering their Imperial-backed governments. Admirals, Grand Moffs, ISB agents, and other senior Imperial commanders use Star Destroyers as their personal mobile headquarters. The ship's commanding officer can be just as intimidating as the approaching ship itself—and its shadow alone can bring results.

During the Clone Wars, *Venator*-class Star Destroyers (often called "Jedi cruisers" because they serve as flagships for Jedi generals) are utilized by the Republic. From this line of ships, the Empire develops the *Imperial I*–class Star Destroyers to wage war and maintain order across the galaxy.

Imperial I–class Star Destroyers measure 1,600 meters (5,250 ft) in length, nearly 460 meters (1,509 ft) longer than the *Venator*-class. They are propelled by Cygnus Spaceworks Gemnon-4 ion engines and a class 2 hyperdrive. Armaments include 60 Taim & Bak XX-9 heavy turbolaser batteries and 60 Borstel NK-7 ion cannons. Tractor beams pull captured vessels into the main hangar bay, where squadrons of armed stormtroopers wait to board. In addition to a contingent of 9,700 stormtroopers, Destroyers each carry a crew of 9,235 officers and 27,850 enlisted personnel. Star Destroyers are fully equipped to engage in protracted combat on planet surfaces. A maximum contingent of auxiliary vehicles includes 8 *Lambda*-class Imperial Shuttles, 20 AT-AT walkers, 30 AT-STs or AT-DPs, and 15 Imperial Troop Transports.

During the Galactic Civil War, the battleships hunt down high-priority targets, instill fear in civilian populations, and attack centers of rebel operations. At the Battle of Hoth, the Empire's fleet of Star Destroyers deploys a contingent of Imperial walkers that wages a successful ground war on the planet's surface. However, the Star Destroyers themselves exit hyperspace too close to Hoth and cost the Empire any advantage of surprise. During the rebel retreat, the Destroyers are too easily disabled, which allows rebel forces to escape. In the Battle of Endor, Star Destroyers deploy wings of 72 TIE starfighters, benefiting the war effort, but rebel fighters nonetheless exploit vulnerabilities in the Destroyers' shield generators and exposed bridges. *Imperial I*–class Star Destroyers prove far less effective against fleets of skilled rebel pilots than their *Venator*-class predecessors were against droid starfighters.

Overpowering the enemy
Darth Vader's Star Destroyer, *Devastator*, chases the rebel ship *Tantive IV*, which is in possession of the stolen Death Star plans. Vader orders a tractor beam to draw his quarry into *Devastator*'s docking bay, where it is boarded by stormtroopers.

Battle of Scarif
When the Alliance fleet travels to Scarif to support Rogue One, Admiral Raddus orders the *Lightmaker* to ram a Star Destroyer, causing it to crash into another. The resulting debris destroys the Scarif shield gate.

TIE/RB HEAVY STARFIGHTER

APPEARANCES S **MANUFACTURER** Sienar Fleet Systems
MODEL TIE/rb heavy starfighter **TYPE** Starfighter

Also known as the "TIE brute," the heavy TIE fighter is distinguished by a secondary outrigger pod with a powerful set of H-s9.3 twin laser cannons. The pilot is assisted by an MGK-300 integrated droid brain, which fulfills the role of an astromech. During his enrollment at the Carida Academy, Cadet Han Solo crashes a TIE brute in a hangar bay, leading to a tribunal and then his reassignment to the infantry on Mimban. While piloting the *Millennium Falcon*, Han is later pursued by a TIE brute through the Kessel Run.

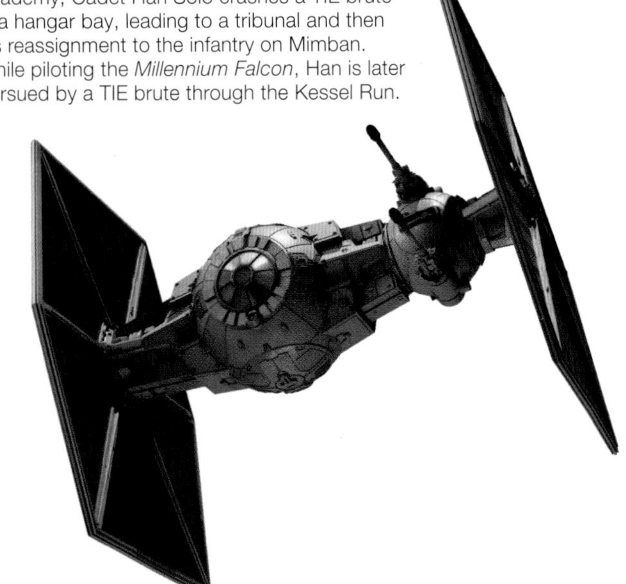

A-A4B TRUCKSPEEDER

APPEARANCES S **MANUFACTURER** Trast Heavy Transports **MODEL** A-A4B **TYPE** Landspeeder

Moloch of the White Worms gang drives a boxy A-A4B truckspeeder through the chaotic streets of Coronet City on Corellia. The vehicle's heavy, rugged design incorporates armored cages over the driver's seat and front grille, offering its occupants protection and making the vehicle a perfect battering ram in high-speed chases. The speeder also has a holding pen that often contains Corellian hounds. Moloch chases Han and Qi'ra in his speeder from the White Worms' hideout all the way to Coronet Spaceport.

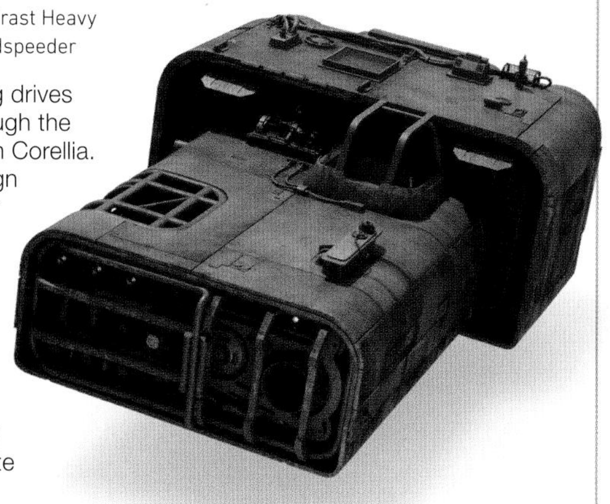

M-68 LANDSPEEDER

APPEARANCES S **MANUFACTURER** Mobquet Swoops and Speeders **MODEL** M-68 **TYPE** Landspeeder

Street-racing enthusiasts refer to the M-68 landspeeder as a "street blaster bolt." Available in both a hardtop and open-air version, this compact racer has air vents on its forward engine's front and dorsal surfaces to keep it cool. The rear sports a stylish spoiler above the two rear exhaust nozzles. The craft can attain speeds of 225 kph (140 mph). Han steals and hot-wires an M-68, using it as a getaway vehicle after acquiring some illicit coaxium. When Han and his girlfriend, Qi'ra, have to escape the White Worms, Han races the speeder to Coronet Spaceport with Moloch in pursuit.

AT-HAULER

APPEARANCES S **MANUFACTURER** Kuat Drive Yards **MODEL** Y-45 armored transport hauler **TYPE** Dropship

The Empire used their Y-45 haulers to transport walkers and other military equipment into active battlezones. The ship's engines can reach an in-atmosphere speed of 125 kph (77.7 mph). However, its hyperdrive only contains pre-set hyperspace jump destinations to specific Imperial outposts. The crane arms rotate upward during landing to conserve space in hangars. Owing to the long hours and muddy conditions crews work in on Mimban, local AT-haulers have an unusual feature: a shower stall. Tobias Beckett's crew steals an Imperial AT-hauler on Mimban for its conveyex train heist on Vandor.

CONVEYEX

APPEARANCES S **MANUFACTURER** Kuat Drive Yards **MODEL** 20-T Railcrawler conveyex transport **TYPE** Cargo train

On frontier worlds such as Vandor, the Empire uses Railcrawler conveyex transports to carry valuable cargo, such as coaxium, between high-security Imperial installations. The conveyex runs simultaneously above and below a central track with compartments on either side, and can reach a speed of 90 kph (56 mph). In case of attack, each conveyex is armed with two repeating laser cannons and an anti-aircraft laser turret. It is often guarded by a contingent of range troopers as well.

ENFYS NEST'S BIKE

APPEARANCES S **MANUFACTURER** Caelli-Merced **MODEL** Modified Skyblade-330 **TYPE** Swoop bike

Swoop bikes are essentially engines with seats, and are better suited for higher altitudes than most speeders. Enfys Nest and her Cloud-Riders launch their swoop bikes from a carrier ship named *Aerie* at an altitude of 400 km (249 miles), and fly down to the surface on their frequent raids. While Enfys' modified Skyblade-300 can accommodate a passenger, she normally flies alone and reaches a top speed of 600 kph (375 mph). Outriggers extend forward from her seat, with three steering vanes attached to them. Cloud-Rider bikes all feature a red-and-black color scheme to differentiate the vehicles from those belonging to other pirate swoop gangs.

ALL TERRAIN DEFENSE TURRET (AT-DT)

APPEARANCES S **MANUFACTURER** Kuat Drive Yards **MODEL** All Terrain Defense Turret **TYPE** Walker

The All Terrain Defense Turret, or AT-DT, is one of a number of walker models produced by Kuat Drive Yards for the Imperial Army. It has a powerful main cannon that can easily neutralize enemy emplacements and vehicles, while its smaller weapons are better suited to targeting opposing infantry. The AT-DT is undoubtedly a fearsome vehicle, but it possesses notable weaknesses that can be exploited. It is slow-moving; moreover its single pilot isn't fully protected in an enclosed cockpit, so is vulnerable to a flanking attack.

FIRST LIGHT

APPEARANCES S **MANUFACTURER** Kalevala Spaceworks **MODEL** Kalevalan star yacht **TYPE** Leisure ship

The striking *First Light* is the private yacht of Crimson Dawn leader Dryden Vos. The ship is constructed out of the finest materials and is adorned with Crimson Dawn iconography. Its amenities rival those of the best resorts and luxury liners in the galaxy. Visitors enter via the base of the ship, where security confiscates all weapons. The vast ship contains crew and guest quarters, state rooms, entertainment dens, and kitchens—where Master Chef Shrindi Meille prepares fine culinary delights. The main dining and party area is near the top of the ship, where live entertainment is in a continuous cycle. The largest of the six main decks is at the top of the ship and contains Vos' private residence, office, and meeting rooms. As the public face of Crimson Dawn, Vos acts as its leader, conducting much of his business from the ship. However, only a few trusted individuals know that Vos can contact the organization's actual leader, Maul, from his office.

Keen collector
In his private rooms, Vos keeps a collection of rare and highly valuable curiosities from around the galaxy, including a Sith holocron, ancient Mandalorian armor, and endangered species preserved in suspended animation.

"Get your hands off my craft! This fighter is property of the Empire!" BARON VALEN RUDOR

TIE FIGHTER

TIE fighters are the signature starfighter of the Imperial Navy. Their versatility and precision are a symbol of prestige for the Empire and a bane of the Rebel Alliance.

APPEARANCES S, Reb, RO, IV, V, VI, FoD **MANUFACTURER** Sienar Fleet Systems **MODEL** TIE/ln starfighter **TYPE** Twin ion engine starfighter

PRECISION AND SIMPLICITY

A TIE's twin ion engines provide thrust and its minute boosters are capable of quickly adjusting the ship's direction. To minimize power drain and maximize maneuverability, TIE fighters lack key systems such as deflector shields and hyperdrives. A TIE fighter's central cockpit is a tight fit, incorporating flight controls, viewscreens, targeting systems, tracking equipment, and room for a pilot, all in the central pod. The flight controls are so intuitive and easy to learn that rebel novices have been able to figure them out on the fly after stealing TIE fighters from Imperial landing fields.

Dogfights
High above Lothal, a TIE fighter fires on the rebel ship *Ghost*.

Lothal TIEs
Rebel artist and weapons expert Sabine Wren sneaks into an Imperial TIE airfield, looking to create a diversion for her friends aboard the *Ghost*.

Starfighters
A trio of TIE fighters returns to the Death Star after flying reconnaissance. Without a hyperdrive, TIEs are unable to travel far from base *(above)*. A TIE fighter pursues Luke's X-wing and is ambushed by Wedge's fighter *(right)*.

STRENGTH IN NUMBERS

During the Galactic Civil War, the Imperial Navy subjugates numerous planets and orchestrates large battles. TIE fighters are the primary Imperial starfighter at the Battles of Yavin and Endor. TIE fighter pilots are instructed that their own well-being is secondary to their mission's objectives. Since the fighters are so fragile and the pilots expendable, TIEs achieve best results attacking in large groups. So many features are sacrificed to facilitate rapid mass production by Sienar Fleet Systems factories that TIE fighters can be continuously refreshed as they are lost in conflict.

EVOLUTION OF THE TIE FIGHTER

TIE fighters display certain similarities with other, outmoded starfighter models from the old Republic era. While TIEs employ vertical wings similar in appearance to earlier V-wing starfighters, the old Jedi light interceptors are even more familiar, with a central cockpit pod, twin ion engines, common weapons technology, and vertical wings like a TIE. In their TIE fighter designs, Sienar Fleet Systems borrowed heavily from the designs of Kuat Systems Engineering ships, thanks to acquiring key assets and engineers employed by their competitor. A variety of other models have arisen from the TIE line, including TIE interceptors and TIE bombers. Sienar factories experiment with localized improvements, producing advanced models suited to local flying conditions and incorporating secret technological breakthroughs. The Grand Inquisitor uses a TIE Advanced x1 prototype, heavily based on Sienar's own *Scimitar* (Sith Infiltrator), while Darth Vader himself flies a TIE Advanced x1 model.

Solar power
A pair of TIE fighters engages the *Ghost* above Lothal. A TIE fighter's black wings contain an array of solar energy collectors that pool power and direct it to twin ion engines and two low-temperature lasers.

"This Corellian ship matches the description of the rebel craft we've been looking for."

IMPERIAL SCANNING TECHNICIAN

GHOST

Piloted by Hera Syndulla, the *Ghost* is named for its ability to evade Imperial sensors. The *Ghost* is not only a starfighter, but also a freighter and home to its misfit crew. A smaller auxiliary fighter, the *Phantom*, makes the *Ghost* particularly adaptable.

APPEARANCES Reb, RO, FoD **MANUFACTURER** Corellian Engineering Corp.
MODEL Modified VCX-100 light freighter **TYPE** Freighter

HERA'S SHIP

Hera is the owner of the *Ghost*, so she is naturally protective of her ship. When things get out of hand, or if other crew members—namely Ezra, Zeb, and Chopper—become too rambunctious, she sends them on novelty errands (like shopping for meiloorun fruit) to get them away from the ship. The *Ghost* is an old vessel with a few scars from battles with Imperial freighters and TIE fighters, but it still performs reliably. Nonetheless, Chopper makes a lot of unusual modifications himself, to the extent that he might be the only one who knows how to fully repair it. Although Hera owns the *Ghost*, and her co-pilot Kanan also knows his way around the ship, in an emergency, sometimes Chopper seems to have better control of the situation.

Team effort
Hera can manage a lot from the cockpit, but needs assistance from the crew to operate the lasers in the *Phantom* and dorsal turret.

Docking port
There are ports on each side of the ship.

Nose turret gunner station
Two forward laser cannons are located underneath the gunner station.

Curious cargo
The *Ghost* carries some interesting items in addition to its diverse crew. At various times the cargo includes T-7 disruptors and E-11 stormtrooper blasters, Kanan's Joben T-85 speeder bike, and puffer pigs.

MISSION READY

While the *Ghost* doesn't have a cloaking device, its countermeasure systems, such as jamming signals and transmitting false information, easily elude Imperial scanners. The *Ghost* is also a fast ship—it outruns Imperial starships, and not just *Gozanti*-class cruisers. Its hyperdrive helps the crew escape Imperial entanglements on more than one occasion. Though most of the crew's early missions are on Lothal, the *Ghost* takes members to far-flung worlds like Ryloth, Gorse, Garel, Kessel, and Stygeon Prime. When Jedi Kanan Jarrus is captured by the Empire, the *Ghost* takes part in his rescue and the destruction of Grand Moff Tarkin's Star Destroyer, *Sovereign*.

A BATTLESHIP

The *Ghost* has an advanced targeting system. The forward laser cannons can be controlled by Hera when a gunner is not available to manage the laser turrets below. TIE fighters are no match for the ship's 360-degree dorsal laser cannon turret, its most important weapon station.

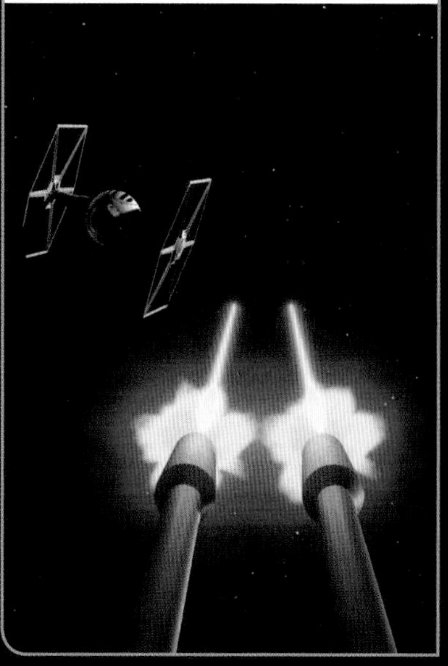

Early missions
The *Ghost* arrives at Kessel to rescue Wookiee prisoners from the Empire's spice mines *(above)*. Following the successful rescue of Kanan Jarrus, the *Ghost* and a small rebel fleet escape to hyperspace *(left)*.

Purrgil attack
Piloted by clone trooper Wolffe and rebel Mart Mattin, the *Ghost* leads a pod of purrgil into battle.

Historic proclamation
From the *Ghost*'s cockpit, Mon Mothma announces the creation of the Rebel Alliance. Chopper transmits her words across the galaxy.

REBEL ALLIANCE

The *Ghost* crew does not operate solo for long and joins up with a larger rebel cell named Phoenix Squadron. One of their most high-profile missions involves a rendezvous with Senator Mon Mothma. After an attempt to refuel Mothma's shuttle is interrupted by the Empire, the senator boards the *Ghost* to escape. From the ship's cockpit, Mothma later makes a declaration announcing the formation of the Rebel Alliance to the entire galaxy. During the Liberation of Lothal, the *Ghost* is key to Ezra Bridger's plan to break the Star Destroyer blockade surrounding the planet. From the ship, the rebels transmit a message on frequency zero that signals a pod of purrgil to join the battle and crash into the Imperial ships. While Hera continues to ascend the Alliance hierarchy (coming to command a Mon Calamari cruiser at one point), she still keeps her beloved freighter, and pilots the *Ghost* during the Battle of Endor.

Main cargo hold
The *Ghost* has four cargo holds with one in each corner of the ship.

PHANTOM

APPEARANCES Reb **MANUFACTURER** Corellian Engineering Corp. **MODEL** Modified *VCX*-series auxiliary starfighter **TYPE** Short-range Corellian shuttle fighter

The *Phantom* docks in the aft section of the *Ghost*, where it acts as the ship's third laser turret (when facing outward). A single-pilot cockpit is located at the front, with a small cargo section and fold-down seats situated in the rear. The *Phantom* is an ideal shuttle for making short-range supply runs and transporting members of the growing crew on secondary missions. Unfortunately, the *Phantom* is destroyed on a mission to Reklam Station on the planet Yarma. Ezra Bridger's miscalculation sends the ship crashing into the planet and leaves the crew of the *Ghost* without a secondary craft until they acquire a replacement, the *Phantom II*.

Stealth fighter
As a small ship, the *Phantom* can quietly maneuver through Imperial territory yet is capable of taking on TIEs and other small fighters in dogfights.

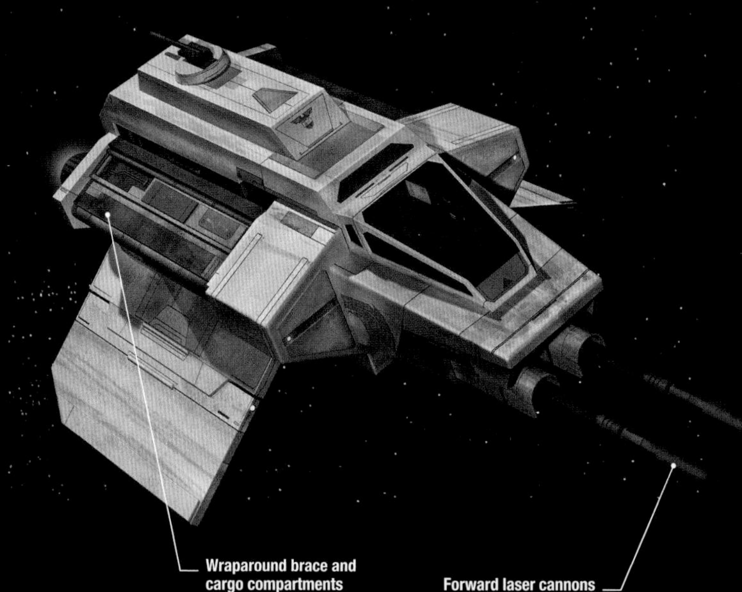

LAMBDA-CLASS IMPERIAL SHUTTLE

APPEARANCES Reb, RO, V, VI, VII, FoD
MANUFACTURER Sienar Fleet Systems
MODEL *Lambda*-class T-4a shuttle
TYPE Personnel shuttle

The *Lambda*-class Imperial shuttle transports high-ranking officers and dignitaries, from Captain Rae Sloane and Count Vidian to Darth Vader and Governor Tarkin. It can also be configured for sizable cargo shipments and troop deployments. The ship works well in both the vacuum of space and planetary atmospheres. Its heavy shielding and reinforced hull make it safe for important officials, and its cockpit can be jettisoned as a lifeboat and travel at sublight speed for short distances. The cockpit lacks room for the shuttle's full quota of 20 passengers, so priority is given to the highest ranks.

In the last days of the Empire, Emperor Palpatine travels to the second Death Star aboard his *Lambda*-class shuttle. The heavily modified ship also carries his Royal Guard and advisers such as Sim Aloo and Janus Greejatus. At about the same time, Leia and a team of rebels, including Nien Nunb, find themselves aboard a Star Destroyer called the *Shieldmaiden*. One of the team members sacrifices themself and Nunb's ship, the *Mellcrawler*, creating a path for Leia and her team to escape in a stolen Imperial shuttle, named the *Tydirium*. Using a stolen access code, Han Solo leads a strike team in this shuttle past an Imperial blockade and on to the moon of Endor, where they destroy the Death Star's shield generator.

The Emperor arrives
Darth Vader arrives on the Death Star to oversee its final construction and is greeted by Moff Jerjerrod.

Shuttle *Tydirium*
Han Solo and Chewbacca sit in the cockpit of their stolen Imperial shuttle, on their way to Endor.

At the end of the Battle of Endor, Luke Skywalker evacuates the Death Star on board Darth Vader's own Imperial shuttle. All three ships play vital roles in the final moments of the Galactic Civil War.

Imperial shuttles are 20 meters (65½ ft) long and can carry a maximum cargo of 80 metric tons (176,370 lbs). They are equipped with two sublight ion engines and a hyperdrive engine for long-distance travel. Forward armaments include two double blaster cannons and two double laser cannons. Aft, there is also a retractable double laser cannon. Military shuttles boast additional weaponry.

"An Imperial troop transport has been reported stolen from the Lower City." **AGENT KALLUS**

One of six troop/prisoner compartments

Forward transparisteel viewport

Putting on a show
Pilots and commanding officers sit in the front, while stormtroopers or prisoners are seated in the rear hold. On each side are three stalls to put prisoners on display, as a warning to others.

IMPERIAL TROOP TRANSPORT

APPEARANCES Reb **MANUFACTURER** Ubrikkian Industries **MODEL** K79-S80
TYPE Armored troop transport

Imperial Troop Transports (ITTs) are some of the army's most dependable vehicles. Their sturdy construction and heavy armaments make them an ideal mobile stronghold for soldiers in minor conflicts. As ITTs are designed to move stormtroopers between important locations, citizens of the Empire steer clear when they hear the transport's loudspeakers approaching their neighborhood. It always means one of two things: either stormtroopers are moving in or Imperials are moving locals out. Despite not being specifically designed for combat, the ITTs have protective laser guns. When the Empire seizes land from uncooperative farmers on Lothal, it uses ITTs to forcibly relocate them. When Ezra Bridger and Zeb Orrelios try to rescue Morad Sumar and other settlers with a stolen TIE fighter, they learn how tough ITTs are.

TIE BOMBER

APPEARANCES Reb, V, VI **MANUFACTURER** Sienar Fleet Systems **MODEL** Twin Ion Engine bomber **TYPE** Bomber

TIE bombers are robust Imperial crafts for planetary and ship bombardment. As with standard TIE fighters, solar panels supplement fuel tanks to power twin ion engines, but the ship lacks a hyperdrive, which limits its flight range. However, bombers are deployed for longer use than fighters, so they carry a two-day supply of air and rations. Bombers not only have a complete life-support system, but also cockpit ejector seats. Armaments include a pair of laser cannons and payloads of concussion missiles, orbital mines, and proton bombs.

Ordnance pod
A TIE bomber's secondary pod carries an assortment of mines, missiles, and bombs.

Surplus
Model 614-AvA speeders are used by Imperials. Older models are sold to civilians. Ezra has an orange-and-green speeder.

Load haulers
Ezra Bridger watches from above as officers prepare to deliver a shipment of E-11 blasters on their Imperial speeder bikes.

LOTHAL IMPERIAL SPEEDER BIKE

APPEARANCES Reb **MANUFACTURER** Aratech Repulsor Company **MODEL** 614-AvA speeder bike **TYPE** Speeder bike

The 614-AvA speeder bike is a popular Imperial model on Lothal. Fitted with twin BlasTech JB-37 blaster cannons, Imperial speeder bikes are indispensable to the military. Working in tandem with AT-DPs and TIE fighters, the bikes form a surgical strike team to take on rebel forces. They are more maneuverable than landspeeders, allowing stormtroopers to cover diverse terrain. Their ease of use for pilots and minimal fuel consumption make speeders the ideal vehicles for distant reconnaissance missions and patrolling large areas. Pilots steer their speeders using handlebars and foot pedals that control three steering vanes attached at the front of the bike.

The rebels on Lothal are often chased by Imperial speeders, but occasionally manage to steal one of the bikes. Novices like Ezra may require lessons, but Zeb and Kanan Jarrus find the 614-AvA easy to drive.

Cargo ship
Imperial freighters carry crucial supplies to Imperial bases throughout the Outer Rim. They are protected by a complement of TIE fighters and laser cannons, lest they are attacked along hyperspace routes like the Kessel Run.

IMPERIAL FREIGHTER

APPEARANCES Reb **MANUFACTURER** Corellian Engineering Corp. **MODEL** Imperial *Gozanti*-class cruiser **TYPE** Armored freighter

Gozanti-class cruisers are heavily armored to deter pirates and rebels (particularly the crew of the *Ghost*). The freighters have been used by a variety of factions, but the Imperial model employs heavier shielding, faster engines, and superior weaponry. Imperial freighters are used to carry important payloads, such as weapons and prisoners, or to transport AT-DPs. These transports carry their own TIE fighter escorts and a rotating crew of stormtroopers to defend their cargo. The ships are fitted with large brigs containing multiple cell blocks to transport their prisoners to Imperial prisons and labor camps, such as the spice mines of Kessel or the Spire on Stygeon Prime.

Heavy laser cannon
The weapon easily destroys speeders.

Terrain-sensing stabilizer pad
The walker's "feet" bear half of the AT-DP's 11,200-kg (24,692-lbs) weight.

ALL TERRAIN DEFENSE POD (AT-DP)

APPEARANCES Reb **MANUFACTURER** Kuat Drive Yards **MODEL** AT-DP **TYPE** Imperial walker

One of several walker models used by the Empire, AT-DPs are an improvement over the AT-RTs used by the Republic during the Clone Wars. AT-DPs are essentially high-speed tanks on legs that carry two officers: a pilot seated in front and a gunner behind, who controls the Kyuzo Maad-38 heavy laser cannon. The Lothal garrison finds them very effective when clearing out squatting farmers from land appropriated for mines and factories. AT-DPs patrolling the streets of Lothal are an intimidating sight, meant to discourage rebel uprisings, and they are also ideal for patrols and short scouting missions. Like speeders, they allow a limited number of troopers to patrol large areas. While AT-DPs can chase suspicious vehicles, they lack the firepower of AT-STs required for substantial combat, and as such are often relegated to defensive roles like sentry duty or policing.

C-ROC CARRIER SHIP

APPEARANCES Reb **MANUFACTURER** Corellian Engineering Corp.
MODEL Modified *Gozanti*-class cruiser **TYPE** Cruiser

The ore mined on Lothal is so valuable to the Empire that an Imperial Star Destroyer is permanently stationed above the planet. The ore is equally valuable to smugglers, who try to outrun the Imperial blockade. Modified from a Gozanti freighter frame, the C-ROC carrier ship has expanded open-bed cargo capacity to maximize the number of secured ore containers it can convey in one flight. The ship's five engine pods provide enough power to propel the C-ROC to high speeds quickly and evade the Imperial Navy's forces.

Engine pods

Ore containers

Blockade runner
The C-ROC's cargo capacity is modified to haul as much valuable Lothal ore as possible.

IMPERIAL LANDING CRAFT

APPEARANCES Reb, IV
MANUFACTURER Sienar Fleet Systems
MODEL *Sentinel*-class landing craft
TYPE Shuttle

The primary function of the Imperial landing craft is to shuttle the Empire's military forces from a Star Destroyer in orbit to planetside operations. These heavily armored landing craft come equipped with laser cannons and concussion missiles and can undertake missions such as short-range scouting, transporting cargo, and providing air support for ground troops. When Darth Vader dispatches sandtroopers to track down the missing escape pod discharged by Princess Leia Organa's *Tantive IV* during its capture over Tatooine, these landing craft ferry them down to the planet's surface.

TIE ADVANCED V1 PROTOTYPE

APPEARANCES Reb **MANUFACTURER** Sienar Fleet Systems
MODEL TIE Advanced v1 (prototype) **TYPE** Starfighter

Compared to standard TIE fighters, the prototype TIE Advanced v1 starfighters used by members of the Inquisitorius have faster engines, stronger laser cannons, and projectile launchers, which can fire tracking devices at ships. The ship's foldable S-foils have solar panels for keeping the starfighter fully charged in most field conditions. Even the swift freighter *Ghost* has difficulty evading a TIE Advanced v1 prototype.

Cockpit canopy

Blasting rebels
The prototype TIE Advanced has two powerful laser cannons for eliminating traitorous ships.

Latest tech
The Inquisitorius have access to the Empire's very best technological developments, including ships like the TIE Advanced prototype.

STAR COMMUTER 2000

APPEARANCES Reb, Res **MANUFACTURER** Sacul Industries **TYPE** Passenger shuttle

Star Commuters ferry passengers between nearby worlds, running regular commuter lines for tourists, businesspeople, low-level government officials, and dignitaries. Each is piloted by an RX-series droid and can carry up to 24 passengers. With the exception of the pilot, droids are required to remain in the back of the ship during flights as per Imperial regulations. The shuttles are commonly flown between Lothal and Garel, and also Castilon and its closest neighbors. However, Star Commuters are used throughout the galaxy and are common during the Republic, Imperial, and New Republic eras.

EZRA'S SPEEDER BIKE

APPEARANCES Reb **MANUFACTURER** Aratech Repulsor Company **MODEL** 614-AvA speeder bike
TYPE Speeder bike

Ezra Bridger steals an Imperial military speeder bike on Lothal and repaints it. This isn't the first time Ezra has stolen an Imperial speeder—though the young driver usually crashes them soon after. The 614-AvA speeder is rugged and versatile. It can even telescope to compact for easier storage. The speeder can attain speeds of 375 kilometers per hour (233 miles per hour) and is armed with a BlasTech JB-37 blaster cannon. Ezra uses Loth-rats for target practice while riding across the plains of Lothal.

POLICE LOW ALTITUDE ASSAULT TRANSPORT

APPEARANCES CW, Reb **MANUFACTURER** Rothana Heavy Engineering **MODEL** Low Altitude Assault Transport (LAAT/le) **TYPE** Gunship

The police variant of the Low Altitude Assault Transport (LAAT/le) is well armed, with two turret laser cannons, one tail laser cannon, and two missile launchers. During the Republic era, the LAAT/le is initially used for law enforcement efforts on Coruscant, and is used in a similar fashion on other planets after the Empire's formation. The ships usually carry police officers or stormtroopers and become synonymous with Imperial subjugation of indigenous populations. Their searchlights are often seen shining into city neighborhoods at night, looking for rebels or criminals.

PHOENIX HOME

APPEARANCES Reb **MANUFACTURER** Kuat Drive Yards **MODEL** *Pelta*-class **TYPE** Frigate

During the Clone Wars, the Republic uses *Pelta*-class frigates as medical vessels. They deliver medical supplies and transport injured clone troopers to military hospitals. Prior to the Battle of Yavin, Jun Sato—leader of the rebel cell named Phoenix Squadron—commands the *Pelta*-class frigate *Phoenix Home*. The ship can defend itself thanks to onboard turbolasers and laser cannons, as well as the cell's small complement of A-wing starfighters. However, *Phoenix Home* cannot survive an attack by Darth Vader himself. The ship is destroyed along with six A-wings.

REX'S AT-TE

APPEARANCES Reb **MANUFACTURER** Rothana Heavy Engineering **MODEL** Custom All Terrain Tactical Enforcer (AT-TE) **TYPE** Mobile residence

After the Clone Wars, clone troopers Rex, Wolffe, and Gregor retire to the planet Seelos, where they live in a modified AT-TE and spend their days relaxing. The AT-TE interior is emptied of military hardware to make room for bunk beds and a kitchen. Outside, handrails and ladders have been installed to make balconies, walkways, and decks. The main cannon is converted into a rod and reel for catching joopas—large, wormlike creatures native to Seelos. The AT-TE is still otherwise functional, until the clones and their rebel visitors are forced to do battle with Imperial AT-ATs. Afterward, Gregor and Wolffe move into an AT-AT.

BLADE WING

APPEARANCES Reb **MANUFACTURER** Quarrie **MODEL** B-wing Prototype **TYPE** Starfighter

The Mon Calamari shipwright Quarrie builds the *Blade Wing* at his secret workshop on Shantipole. The ship features a rotating pilot's cockpit and a ball turret gunner station on the tail end. The *Blade Wing* is armed with 3 Armek ion cannons, 2 high intensity Gyrhil blasters, and Rhed SNAPR proton torpedoes. Rebel Captain Hera Syndulla desperately needs the ship to break an Imperial blockade over the planet Ibaar. After proving her piloting skills to Quarrie, she is allowed to take the ship. Quarrie later works with the manufacturer Slayn & Korpil to turn his prototype into the B-wing starfighter line.

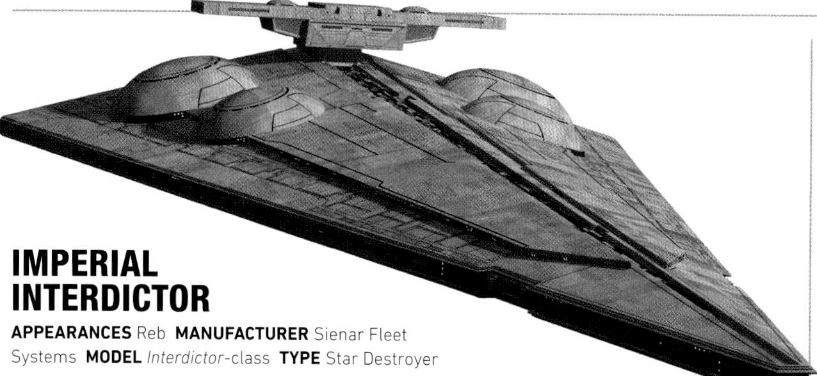

IMPERIAL INTERDICTOR

APPEARANCES Reb **MANUFACTURER** Sienar Fleet Systems **MODEL** *Interdictor*-class **TYPE** Star Destroyer

The Imperial *Interdictor* is an experimental vessel equipped with four dome-shaped gravity wells capable of pulling enemy ships out of hyperspace. The ship is 1,129 meters (3,704 feet) long, armed with 20 quad laser cannons, and can carry up to 20 TIE fighters. Admiral Brom Titus uses his ship to pull the rebel vessel *Liberator* from hyperspace, capturing Ezra Bridger and Commander Sato. The rebels' allies mount a rescue mission and manage to destroy the *Interdictor*. The prototype leads to a line of Star Destroyers named the *Interdictor*-class with the same specifications and capabilities. Two of these ships are used by the Empire to battle the rebels over Atollon, but both are likewise destroyed and the surviving rebels flee. One of the last Imperial Interdictors is destroyed at the Battle of Jakku.

Chain reaction
Thanks to rebel sabotage, the *Interdictor* malfunctions, drawing in other Imperial ships, which crash into the *Interdictor* and destroy it.

TAYLANDER SHUTTLE

APPEARANCES II, CW, Reb **MANUFACTURER** Gallofree Yards, Inc. **TYPE** Shuttle

Common throughout the galaxy, Taylander shuttles are popular civilian craft used to transport passengers and cargo. They are frequently seen on worlds like Coruscant, where levels of commerce and tourism are high. They are relatively small transport shuttles, measuring only 43.5 meters (143 feet) long. Their engines reach a maximum speed of 950 kilometers per hour (590 miles per hour), and they possess a Class 2 hyperdrive. Taylanders are also commonly used by rebels for covert missions, making them a target for Imperial searches over time. For a time, rebel leader Mon Mothma travels in a Taylander named the *Chandrila Mistress*.

SHADOW CASTER

APPEARANCES Reb **MANUFACTURER** MandalMotors **MODEL** *Lancer*-class **TYPE** Black Sun pursuit craft

Belonging to Black Sun bounty hunter Ketsu Onyo, the *Shadow Caster* is a *Lancer*-class vessel that is originally designed to chase down cargo vessels and raid them. The ship model is a favorite of the underworld because it requires very little maintenance or upkeep due to its sturdy construction and redundant systems. After rekindling her friendship with Sabine Wren, Ketsu uses the *Shadow Caster* to help her rebel friends escape an Imperial fleet and flee to safety.

HAMMERHEAD CORVETTE

APPEARANCES Reb, RO **MANUFACTURER** Corellian Engineering Corp. **MODEL** *Sphyrna*-class **TYPE** Corvette

The *Sphyrna*-class corvette, also known as the Hammerhead corvette, is an ancient line of ships. Hammerhead corvettes are 315 meters (1033 feet) long and can attain a speed of 900 kilometers per hour (559 miles per hour). They are armed with 2 forward dual laser cannons and one rear dual laser cannon. During the Imperial era, Hammerhead corvettes are commonly used by rebel cells and later by the Rebel Alliance. The vessels serve many roles—as scout ships, transports, tugs for inoperative craft, and even as battleships. During the Battle of Scarif, the Hammerhead corvette *Lightmaker* (under the command of Kado Oquoné) rams the Imperial Star Destroyer *Persecutor*, which crashes into the Star Destroyer *Intimidator*, and then smashes into the Scarif Shield Gate. The *Lightmaker*'s sacrifice changes the course of the battle in favor of the Rebel Alliance.

Reinforcements
Following Phoenix Squadron's losses fleeing Garel, Princess Leia Organa covertly ensures that a number of Hammerhead corvettes can reinforce their fleet.

FANG FIGHTER

APPEARANCES Reb **MANUFACTURER** SoroSuub Corp. and MandalMotors
MODEL *Fang*-class **TYPE** Starfighter

Designed for space and aerial battles, Fang fighters are fast, maneuverable, and deadly. Each ship is piloted by a member of the Mandalorian Protectors of Concord Dawn who has been personally trained by their leader, Fenn Rau. Fang Fighters are armed with powerful weapons, including two wing-mounted laser cannons and one ventral proton torpedo launcher. The ships' small profiles make them difficult for the opposition to target, and they prove deadly adversaries for A-wing fighters when the rebels first attempt to traverse the Concord Dawn system.

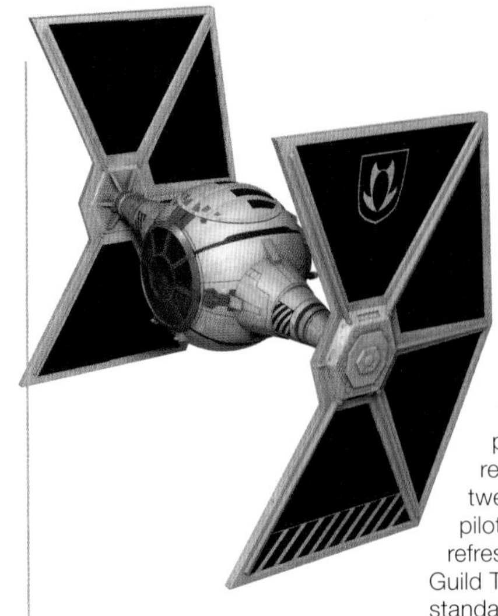

MINING GUILD TIE FIGHTER

APPEARANCES Reb
MANUFACTURER Sienar Fleet Systems
MODEL Modified TIE/Ln starfighter
TYPE Starfighter

The Empire supplies the Mining Guild with modified TIE fighters as recompense for the critical resources they provide. The Mining Guild TIE fighter is painted yellow to distinguish it from Imperial TIE fighters. It also has two solar collector panels removed on each stabilizer wing, reducing the total number of panels from twelve to eight. While this alteration improves pilot visibility, it comes at the cost of power refresh rate and maneuverability. Mining Guild TIE fighters are armed with two standard L-s1 laser cannons.

NU-CLASS SHUTTLE

APPEARANCES CW, Reb **MANUFACTURER** Cygnus Spaceworks
MODEL *Nu*-class transport **TYPE** Transport shuttle

Republic attack shuttles, otherwise known as *Nu*-class shuttles, are used during the Clone Wars. They are forerunners to later models, such as the *Lambda*-class, *Sentinel*-class, and *Theta*-class shuttles. *Nu*-class shuttles can carry up to thirty passengers or two tons of cargo, and are equipped with one escape pod and six laser cannons. They are less common during the Imperial era, however one such shuttle falls into the hands of the Free Ryloth Movement.

Custom job The Free Ryloth Movement have adorned their shuttle with rebel markings.

PHOENIX NEST

APPEARANCES Reb **MANUFACTURER** SoroSuub Corp.
MODEL *Quasar Fire*-class **TYPE** Cruiser-carrier

Quasar Fire-class cruiser-carriers, also known as Imperial light carriers, orbit occupied worlds and deploy squadrons of TIE bombers to quell local rebellions. The ship's strength is its four open bays, allowing multiple fighters to launch simultaneously. Its weakness is its minimal firepower—just two light turbolaser batteries. Hera Syndulla's rebel cell works with her father, Cham Syndulla, to steal a *Quasar Fire*-class cruiser-carrier. Re-christened *Phoenix Nest* (*Phoenix Home 2*), it then becomes the new flagship for rebel Commander Sato and his Phoenix Squadron. During the Battle of Atollon, Sato sacrifices himself and *Phoenix Nest* so that Ezra Bridger can get help.

TRAINING A-WING

APPEARANCES Reb **MANUFACTURER** Kuat Systems Engineering **MODEL** RZ-1T
TYPE Starfighter trainer

The RZ-1T is a modified A-wing starfighter used by rebel cells to train new pilots. The ship is fitted with an extra seat for an instructor in the rear of the cockpit. In most other ways the RZ-1T is a conventional A-wing, though some systems, such as the missile launchers, may be disabled until the student is ready to handle them. Ezra Bridger takes the Phoenix Cell's RZ-1T from Chopper Base on Atollon to Tatooine in search of Maul. Once he lands, the ship is quickly destroyed by Tusken Raiders.

GAUNTLET STARFIGHTER

APPEARANCES CW, Reb **MANUFACTURER** MandalMotors
MODEL *Kom'rk*-Class Fighter **TYPE** Starfighter

The violent Mandalorian splinter group known as Deathwatch flies in Gauntlet starfighters. These ships are similar to the Fang Fighters of the Mandalorian Protectors, but they are far more powerful, possessing four laser canons, and they are even faster. Gauntlet starfighters also have a large hold for 24 soldiers, thus they can act as troop transports. Maul owns a modified Gauntlet starfighter named the *Nightbrother*, which passes to Ezra Bridger after Maul's death.

PHANTOM II

APPEARANCES Reb **MANUFACTURER** Haor Chall Engineering
MODEL Modified *Sheathipede*-class transport shuttle
TYPE Transport shuttle

After the first *Phantom* is destroyed, the *Ghost* crew soon find a suitable replacement. While scavenging on Agamar, the team acquire a former Separatist shuttle. Renamed the *Phantom II* for its service in the rebellion, the ship is heavily modified by the *Ghost* crew. They add blaster cannons and turrets to the previously unarmed vessel, give it a new paint job, and add an astromech socket for Chopper. Much like its predecessor, the *Phantom II* docks in the aft section of the *Ghost*.

SATO'S HAMMER

APPEARANCES Reb **MANUFACTURER** Corellian Engineering Corp. **MODEL** YT-2400
TYPE Light freighter

Sato's Hammer belongs to a tiny and innovative rebel cell called Iron Squadron, which is comprised of Mykapo natives Jonner Jin, Gooti Terez, Mart Mattin, and their droid, R3-A3. Their freighter shares many design similarities with the *Millennium Falcon* and is a popular ship model among pirates and cargo haulers alike. It features two double laser turrets (one each on the dorsal and ventral sides) and concussion missile launchers. It is also a fast and highly maneuverable ship. The Iron Squadron use *Sato's Hammer* to conduct attacks on the Imperial forces occupying Mykapo.

TIE DEFENDER

APPEARANCES Reb **MANUFACTURER** Sienar Fleet Systems
MODEL Twin Ion Engine/d defender **TYPE** Starfighter

The TIE defender is a pet project of the Empire's Grand Admiral Thrawn, developed at the Sienar Fleet Systems factories on Lothal. In comparison to the majority of the TIE fighter line (which is manufactured to be easily replaceable), the TIE defender is superior and designed to outclass any rebel ships in battle. As well as being exceptionally fast, the TIE defender includes a hyperdrive (Class 2), deflector shields, and six wing-tip laser cannons. Thrawn deploys his TIE defenders against Hera Syndulla and her crew, attempting unsuccessfully to capture Senator Mon Mothma in the Archeon Nebula. Officially, the TIE defender program never makes it past the prototype stage, as the destruction of the fuel depot in Lothal's capital city seems to bring the TIE defender program to an end.

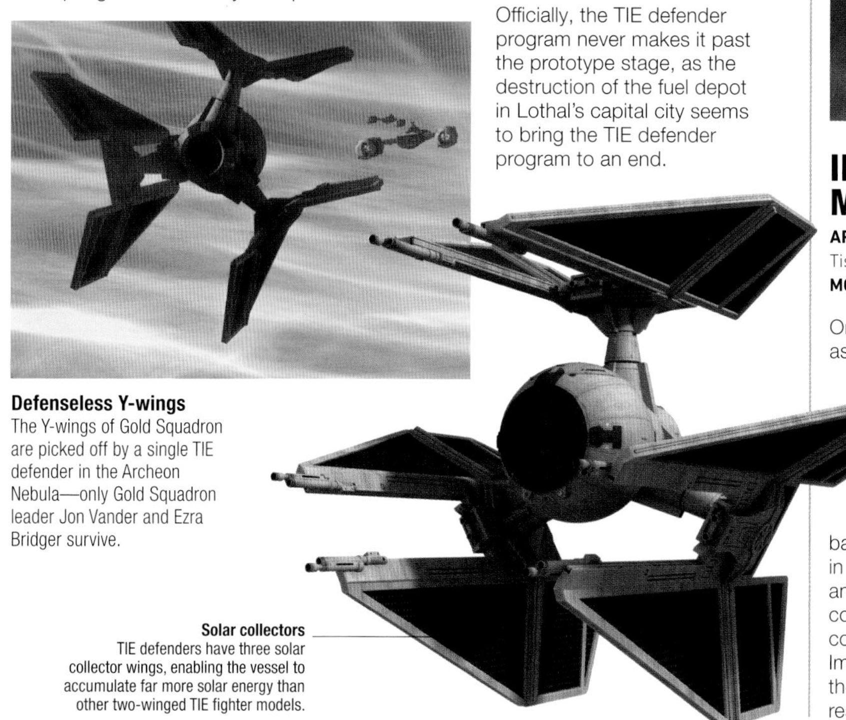

Defenseless Y-wings
The Y-wings of Gold Squadron are picked off by a single TIE defender in the Archeon Nebula—only Gold Squadron leader Jon Vander and Ezra Bridger survive.

Solar collectors
TIE defenders have three solar collector wings, enabling the vessel to accumulate far more solar energy than other two-winged TIE fighter models.

Reklam Station
A modified Imperial Construction Module named Reklam Station is based in the atmosphere of the planet Yarna. The Empire uses the station to scrap outdated starfighters, until the *Ghost* crew steal a number of fighters from the base and then cause it to crash toward Yarna's surface.

IMPERIAL CONSTRUCTION MODULE

APPEARANCES Reb **MANUFACTURER** Huppla Pasa Tisc Shipwrights Collective
MODEL ICM-092792 **TYPE** Space station

Orbital command habitats, also known as Imperial construction modules, are mobile space stations designed to oversee large construction projects. They house all the data concerning the projects and serve as a base of operations for personnel involved in them. The modules also contain cranes and mechanical arms, so can act as giant construction droids, of sorts. The Imperial command center in Lothal's capital city is an Imperial construction module, positioned to oversee the local Imperial factories, harvesting of local resources, and the subjugation of the Lothal population.

IGV-55 SURVEILLANCE VESSEL

APPEARANCES Reb **MANUFACTURER** Corellian Engineering Corp.
MODEL Modified *Gozanti*-class cruiser **TYPE** Espionage ship

The Empire uses IGV-55 surveillance vessels to uncover subversive activities. The ships are modified *Gozanti*-class cruisers with a wide array of sensors and communications dishes installed. They use this equipment to monitor civilian and government communications, as well as to sift through other forms of data. While they are often stationed far away from hyperspace lanes, the vessels are equipped with two heavy laser cannons in case they are found and attacked. The crew are equipped with Lobot-Tech headgear to make them more efficient.

BRAHA'TOK-CLASS GUNSHIP

APPEARANCES Reb, RO, VI **MANUFACTURER** Braha'ket Fleetworks Conglomerate **TYPE** Gunship

Also known as Dornean gunships, *Braha'tok*-class gunships are designed to protect Dornea from the Empire, and later serve in the Rebel Alliance during the Galactic Civil War. The ships excel at combating great numbers of enemy starfighters due to their eight double turbolaser cannons and eight concussion missile launchers. They can also carry two starfighters into battle. *Braha'tok*-class gunships see action during the Battle of Atollon, the Battle of Scarif, and the Battle of Endor. Years after the Galactic Civil War, the vessels are still used by the Dorneans to protect their homeworld.

IMPERIAL SUPPORT VESSEL

APPEARANCES Reb **MANUFACTURER** Rendili StarDrive
MODEL *Dreadnought*-class **TYPE** Heavy cruiser

Imperial support vessels are mid-sized capital ships that have twelve sublight engines and a Class 2 hyperdrive. They are versatile vessels designed to support multiple weapon configurations. Prior to the Battle of Yavin, insurgents from Batonn use a contingent of Imperial support vessels in an attack against Grand Admiral Thrawn's forces, but they are defeated. Thrawn later employs the vessels in his blockade of Lothal, but many are destroyed when they crash into a pod of purrgil that unexpectedly arrives out of hyperspace. The blockade is destroyed and Lothal is liberated.

Ejector seats
If necessary for safety, the seats (and their occupants) can be ejected from the cockpit

T-6 SHUTTLE

APPEARANCES CW, Reb, FoD **MANUFACTURER** Slayn & Korpil **TYPE** Shuttle

Designed to be ambassadorial craft for the Jedi, T-6 shuttles do not have any weapons. They are manufactured by Slayn & Korpil of the Verpine Hives. Unusually, when in flight, the T-6's wing blades rotate around the cockpit, passenger hold, and engines, which remain in a level position. This innovative feature inspires the later Rebel Alliance B-wing starfighter. T-6s become a rarer sight following the Jedi Order's destruction. However, Ahsoka Tano and Sabine Wren depart Lothal in one such shuttle after the Battle of Endor.

U-WING

APPEARANCES Reb, RO **MANUFACTURER** Incom Corp.
MODEL UT-60D U-wing starfighter/support craft **TYPE** Troop transport

U-wings are dropships with large interior holds, used by the Rebel Alliance to transport soldiers into battle. The vehicles can also function as starfighters, should the need arise. Their weaponry includes two Taim & Bak KX7 laser canons and two optional heavy weapon installation points behind the main doors, for greater versatility in battle. U-wings are fitted with an Incom 4J.7 fusial thrust engines capable of reaching 950 kph (590 mph), and impressive Class 1 hyperdrives. Their wings have two configurations: they can face backward to prioritize shield strength and engine heat dissipation or face forward to lessen atmospheric friction. The vehicles are notably flown by Saw Gerrera, as well as Cassian Andor during the search for Galen Erso. They also provide support for Rebel Alliance fighters at the Battle of Scarif.

Rare ships
The Alliance owns a small number of U-wings sourced by Bail Organa, who ensured a consignment is lost in transit.

Imposing passengers
Wherever Director Krennic travels in his shuttle, he is always accompanied by a contingent of death troopers. These troops instil fear in whoever Krennic is visiting.

DELTA-CLASS T-3C SHUTTLE

APPEARANCES RO
MANUFACTURER Sienar Fleet Systems
TYPE Personnel transport shuttle

The *Delta*-class T-3c shuttle is part of the Abecederian line of executive shuttles first manufactured by Cygnus Spaceworks and later by Sienar Fleet Systems. Imperial Director Orson Krennic commissions production of the craft and acquires ship ST 149 (nicknamed the *Pteradon*) as his personal shuttle. The craft has a minimalist interior with very basic seating. It is armed with twin KX9 laser cannons and three wingtip KX3 laser cannons. Captain Magna Tolvan also commands a *Delta*-class T-3c shuttle that she uses to travel to Skako Minor in pursuit of Doctor Aphra.

TX-225 COMBAT ASSAULT TANK

APPEARANCES Reb, RO **MANUFACTURER** Rothana Heavy Engineering
MODEL TX-225 GAVw "Occupier" combat assault tank **TYPE** Ground assault vehicle

The Empire deploys combat assault tanks to patrol the streets of the Holy City of Jedha and to transport any valuable kyber crystals that they've commandeered from the city and its inhabitants. These tanks are highly maneuverable, easily navigating the Old City's alleys. They are armed with three Dymek MK 2e/w medium laser cannons. Each tank typically requires a crew of three: a commander, driver, and gunner. They can reach speeds of up to 72 kph (45 mph) on open roads. The Empire also possesses a hovering variant of the tank, the TX-225 GAVr, that sees action during Lothal's occupation.

AT-ACT

APPEARANCES RO **MANUFACTURER** Kuat Drive Yards **MODEL** All Terrain Armored Cargo Transport
TYPE Imperial walker

The AT-ACT is a much taller version of the Empire's AT-AT walker. However, instead of being deployed on the battlefield, it is designed to haul cargo at Imperial construction projects and research facilities. The AT-ACT's central containers hold 550 cubic meters (19,423 cubic ft) of cargo; stevedore droids load and unload the freight. Despite its ostensible non-combat purpose, the AT-ACT is heavily armored and fitted with advanced weaponry to combat rebel attackers and pirates. The imposing vehicle's twin Taim & Bak MS-2 heavy laser cannons pose a significant threat to Rebel Alliance fighters during the Battle of Scarif.

TIE STRIKER

APPEARANCES RO **MANUFACTURER** Sienar Fleet Systems
MODEL TIE/sk x1 experimental air superiority fighter **TYPE** Starfighter

TIE strikers are utilized by both the Imperial Army and Navy. They are primarily designed for in-atmosphere flight, although they are also capable of space flight. TIE strikers are heavily armed with four fire-linked L-s9.3 laser cannons, two H-s1 heavy laser cannons, and a payload of proton bombs. The cockpit typically carries a pilot and gunner, but may be enlarged to carry extra passengers and cargo. TIE strikers form the dominant air support on Scarif, and are key players in the battle against the Rebel Alliance.

TIE REAPER

APPEARANCES RO **MANUFACTURER** Sienar Fleet Systems
MODEL TIE/rp reaper attack lander **TYPE** Troop transport

Similar in design to the TIE striker, the TIE reaper is a dropship used to ferry troops into the center of active battlefields. The transports can reach a maximum speed of 950 kph (590 mph) and are armed with two laser cannons. During the Battle of Scarif, a TIE reaper transports Director Orson Krennic's squad of death troopers. In the years following the fall of the Empire, the ships fall into the hands of criminal organizations, including the Ranc gang.

PROFUNDITY

APPEARANCES RO
MANUFACTURER Mon Calamari Shipyards **MODEL** Modified MC75 star cruiser **TYPE** Star cruiser

The *Profundity* is a large ship, 1,204 meters (3,951 ft) in length. It is the former Civic Governance tower of the city of Nystullum and is flown under the command of the city's Mayor Raddus during the Mon Calamari exodus. Raddus continues to command the ship as an admiral in the Rebel Alliance. After being modified into a warship, the *Profundity* operates with a crew of 3,225 and is heavily armed, with 20 point-defense laser cannons, 12 turbolaser cannons, four ion cannons, 12 proton torpedo launchers, and six tractor beam projectors. Raddus leads the Alliance fleet during the Battle of Scarif, and his ship receives the Death Star plans from Jyn Erso on the planet's surface below. The plans are then transferred to Princess Leia aboard the *Tantive IV*, which has docked inside the *Profundity*. While the *Tantive IV* escapes Scarif, the *Profundity*'s hyperdrive isn't operational, and it is destroyed.

Headquarters
Up to the Battle of Scarif, the *Profundity* serves as the Alliance's flagship. It is eventually replaced by Admiral Ackbar's *Home One*.

ZETA-CLASS SHUTTLE

APPEARANCES RO **MANUFACTURER** Felgorn Corp. **TYPE** Cargo shuttle

The Empire uses *Zeta*-class shuttles to transport kyber crystals and other materials between Jedha, Eadu, and Scarif for the Death Star's construction. The pilot and co-pilot fly the ship from the cockpit, located in the upper deck's bow. The central deck carries the bulk of the cargo and may be detached at the delivery point. The ship is powered by a Class 3 hyperdrive with a very slow Class 12 as backup and armed with two wing-mounted KV22 heavy laser cannons and three hull-mounted KX7 laser cannons. Rogue One uses a *Zeta*-class shuttle to infiltrate Scarif and steal the Death Star plans.

LUKE SKYWALKER'S X-34 LANDSPEEDER

APPEARANCES IV **MANUFACTURER** SoroSuub Corp.
MODEL X-34 **TYPE** Landspeeder

A civilian vehicle of mundane design, the X-34 landspeeder has neither weapon mounts, nor armor, nor any other combat capability. Levitating no higher than 1 meter (3 ft 3 in) above the ground on its repulsorlifts and propelled by three turbine engines, a landspeeder can travel smoothly over even the roughest terrain. With either an open-air or sealed cockpit to choose from, the landspeeder is perfect for Tatooine's harsh desert climate. In the years before he leaves his homeworld and joins the Rebel Alliance, Luke puts his landspeeder to extensive use.

Low trade-in value
After discovering his aunt and uncle murdered *(above right)*, Luke brings Obi-Wan Kenobi, C-3PO, and R2-D2 to Mos Eisley *(right)*. He sells his landspeeder to help fund the cost of passage to Alderaan.

Fond memories
Holding a T-16 model, Luke remembers his many adventures in his skyhopper.

T-16 SKYHOPPER

APPEARANCES II, IV, VI **MANUFACTURER** Incom Corp.
MODEL T-16 **TYPE** Airspeeder

Recognizable by its distinctive tri-wing design, the T-16 skyhopper airspeeder is a popular civilian vehicle across the galaxy, providing stable and reliable transportation on almost any world. Reaching speeds of up to 1,200 kph (745 mph) from its ion drive and altitudes of 300 meters (984 feet) from its repulsors, the T-16 provides many youngsters with their first flight-training opportunity. On Tatooine, Luke flies his T-16 through the dangerous twists of Beggar's Canyon, taking potshots at womp rats with the craft's pneumatic cannon. On one occasion, Luke in in his T-16 saves his falling Uncle Lars by catching him on one of the ship's wings. When he joins the Rebel Alliance, Luke benefits from the similarities between the controls of the T-16 and the X-wing starfighter, which is also manufactured by Incom.

"This is Red Five; I'm going in."

LUKE SKYWALKER

Faithful co-pilot

Even though Luke is a starfighter rookie at the Battle of Yavin, seasoned astromech R2-D2 is ready to back him up. During the attack run on the Death Star, R2-D2 keeps Red Five functional by making on-the-fly repairs until he is disabled by Darth Vader's laser blast. Rebel technicians are able to repair the droid, and he continues his legendary partnership with Luke.

RED FIVE

Red Five is Luke Skywalker's pilot designation when he destroys the first Death Star. The name becomes synonymous with the actual X-wing fighter he flies.

APPEARANCES IV, V, VI, VIII **MANUFACTURER** Incom Corp. **MODEL** T-65B **TYPE** X-wing starfighter

Blaster cannon
When firing synchronized blasts, the X-wing's guns easily vaporize TIE fighters.

Fusial thrust engines
These powerful and efficient engines provide top-notch speed and acceleration.

Cockpit
Luke flies his single-pilot starfighter with assistance from R2-D2.

Attack position
The X-wing's S-foils remain closed for swifter flight, then spread open for combat.

Perfect shot
Red Five careens down the Death Star trench, heading for the exhaust port.

BATTLE OF YAVIN

Luke's experience on Tatooine flying T-16 skyhoppers, made by the same manufacturer as the X-wing, gives him enough familiarity with Incom flight controls to be assigned pilot duties in Red Squadron as the Death Star approaches the Rebel Alliance base on Yavin 4. Red Leader Garven Dreis assigns Luke the position of Red Five, with more experienced pilots Wedge Antilles and Biggs Darklighter rounding out the trio as Red Two and Red Three, respectively. During their run down the trench, Luke hears the ethereal voice of Obi-Wan Kenobi telling him to "use the Force." He turns off Red Five's targeting computer and fires his torpedoes into the Death Star's exhaust port, sealing the Rebel Alliance victory.

Switching off
During his attack on the Death Star Luke shuts off his targeting computer. He later does the same thing when he pilots Red Five into the *Harbinger*.

DARING MANEUVER

Luke participates in a bold rebel plan to capture an Imperial Star Destroyer called *Harbinger*. Thanks to a hull breach made by the *Millennium Falcon*, Luke flies directly into the *Harbinger* and through its primary reactor, causing it to start overloading. The stunt causes the Imperial crew to abandon ship, allowing it to be commandeered and then repaired by a rebel crew. The mission is one of the first major victories after the Battle of Yavin for the rising Rebel Alliance.

JOURNEY TO DAGOBAH

When a dangerous patrol around Echo Base on the ice planet Hoth puts Luke near death, a ghostly apparition of Obi-Wan appears and directs the rebel hero to seek out Yoda on the planet Dagobah. After a timely rescue by Han Solo, Luke joins Rogue Squadron to defend the base from an Imperial invasion. With the Rebel Alliance forced into a retreat from the doomed base, Luke hops in his X-wing and makes his escape. Although R2-D2 is ready to take over piloting duties on the way to the rendezvous point, Luke insists upon a detour to further his Jedi training. Despite Luke's formidable skills as a pilot, Dagobah's atmosphere proves sufficiently challenging that he crashes his X-wing into a boggy swamp.

Controlled crash
Only a pilot as skilled as Luke could avoid the numerous trees rising out of the Dagobah swamp *(right)*. Despite surviving the crash, he is still wary of the many unseen perils waiting for him *(far right)*.

Proving a point
For Jedi apprentice Luke, Yoda's chief admonishment, "do or do not, there is no try," can be a difficult concept to grasp. After Luke gives up on levitating his crashed X-wing, Jedi Master Yoda proves to Luke it is possible.

SIZE MATTERS NOT

Faced with the task of shooting an impossibly small mark without a targeting computer during the attack on the Death Star, Luke confidently believes he can make that feat a reality. Yet, when it comes time for an important lesson in using the Force during his training with Yoda—levitating his X-wing from the bog into which it crashed—Luke's inexperience with the mystical Force creates a seemingly insurmountable obstacle. Yoda tackles this inhibition by revealing the amazing power within all Jedi. With a furrowed brow and a slight swipe of his tiny hand, Yoda frees Luke's starfighter. Ironically, this gesture enables Luke to leave Dagobah after he has visions of his friends in danger, even though Yoda pleads with him to stay and complete his training.

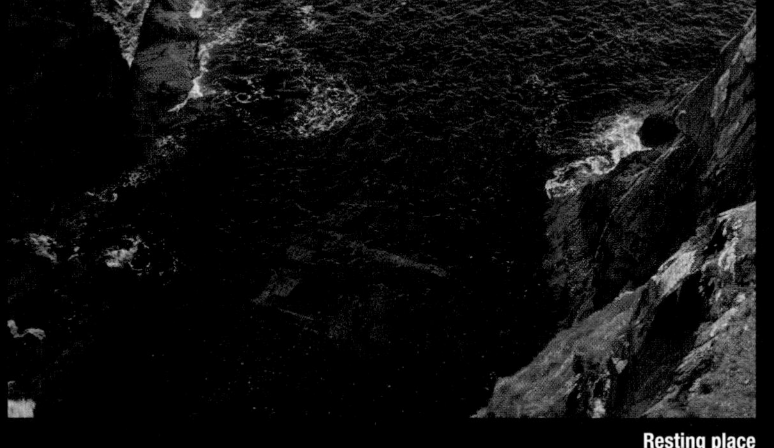

Resting place
While it isn't the first time Red Five has been submerged under the water, this time seems more final.

ULTIMATE FATE

When Luke's attempt to train another generation of Jedi fails, he pilots his X-wing to its final destination. He arrives at Ahch-To, one of the most remote parts of the galaxy. His ship rots away in the shallow seawater around the ancient village Luke calls home, largely out of his sight as he seeks to live out his final days alone. A piece of the fighter's wing—once used to fly in epic battles to save the galaxy—now serves as a makeshift front door to Luke's simple hut.

TIE ADVANCED FIGHTER X1

APPEARANCES Reb, IV **MANUFACTURER** Sienar Fleet Systems
MODEL Twin Ion Engine Advanced x1 **TYPE** Starfighter

Darth Vader only flies the best. His starfighter is a modified early prototype of the TIE Advanced x1 line. Unlike most TIE models, the Advanced x1 has a hyperdrive and deflector shield generator. Vader's fighter is fast and heavily armed, featuring fixed-mounted twin blaster cannons and cluster missiles. The custom cockpit matches Vader's exacting specifications and accommodates the unique features of his suit. Vader displays his prowess at the controls of his starfighter at many points, including single-handedly laying waste to the rebel A-wing pilots of Phoenix Squadron several years before the Battle of Yavin. At the Battle of Vrogas Vas, he successfully defeats two squadrons of rebel X-wings before he is stopped by a head-on collision with Luke Skywalker.

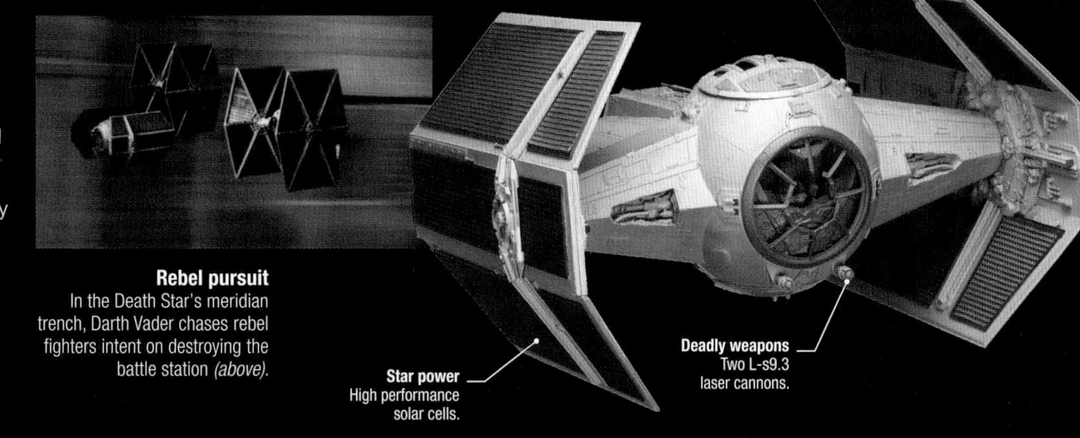

Rebel pursuit
In the Death Star's meridian trench, Darth Vader chases rebel fighters intent on destroying the battle station *(above)*.

REBEL SNOWSPEEDER

APPEARANCES V **MANUFACTURER** Incom Corp. **MODEL** T-47 **TYPE** Airspeeder (modified)

Rebel ingenuity
Former farm boy Luke Skywalker devises a way to take down the massive AT-ATs by using tow cables to lasso their legs.

While on Hoth, the extreme cold creates a unique set of operational issues that threaten to permanently ground the Rebel Alliance's force of airspeeders. Ingenuity overcomes the bitter Hoth elements: the rebels modify their T-47 airspeeders to become snowspeeders. The craft is a wedge-shaped, two-man vessel armed with two forward laser cannons and a rear harpoon gun. It is designed to be flown by a single pilot, backed up by a rear-facing tail gunner.

The Imperial assault force that lands on Hoth is led by AT-AT walkers, which are tasked with destroying Echo Base's main power generator. Spearheading the defense of the generator is the elite Rogue Squadron, piloting the newly operational snowspeeders. As Rogue Squadron does not possess the necessary firepower to bring down the walkers, its commander, Luke Skywalker, suggests an alternative tactic: trip up the massive assault vehicles using their ships' harpoons and tow cables. Dak Ralter, Luke's gunner, is killed before he can take a shot, and a short time later their snowspeeder crashes into the snow after absorbing an explosive blast from an attacking AT-AT. Luke is nearly crushed by the walker's foot while retrieving the speeder's unused harpoon gun.

Wedge Antilles and Wes Janson have better luck, harpooning a walker and tripping it up, per Luke's recommendation. Precision firing from Antilles finishes the job, as he hits the downed AT-AT's vulnerable neck. Nonetheless, the rebels' power generator is destroyed, leaving the base vulnerable to invasion.

Rogue pilot
A snowspeeder from Rogue Squadron barely evades enemy fire as it rapidly closes in on the invading Imperial AT-AT walkers.

EXECUTOR (SUPER STAR DESTROYER)

APPEARANCES V, VI **MANUFACTURER** Kuat Drive Yards **MODEL** *Executor*-class Star Dreadnought **TYPE** Super Star Destroyer

The Super Star Destroyer is one of the largest, most powerful Imperial vessels in the galaxy and signifies the might of the Empire. Viewed from above, it presents an arrowhead-shaped profile, and boasts more than 1,000 weapons, including turbolasers, ion cannons, and concussion missile tubes. The main hangar bay is situated ventrally and forward and houses a mix of TIE fighters, TIE bombers, and TIE interceptors. The gargantuan craft is propelled through space by 13 colossal engine thrusters. The command tower rises from the aft of the central habitable island and is capped with two geodesic communication and deflection domes.

The first Super Star Destroyer, the *Executor*, is given to Darth Vader as his personal flagship after he successfully stops an attempt by a rogue Imperial scientist, Doctor Cylo, to commandeer the ship. The *Executor* is then specifically modified to Vader's needs, including a meditation chamber much like the one in his castle on Mustafar. While Vader has control over the entire Imperial fleet, he often leads the Death Squadron from the *Executor*, for example during the Imperial assaults on the Rebel Alliance's Mako-Ta Space Docks and Echo Base on Hoth. During the attack on Echo Base, Vader is displeased when Admiral Ozzel brings the fleet out of hyperspace near Hoth rather than stealthfully using a wider approach from the system's outskirts. The tactical blunder buys the Alliance time to raise their base's energy shield. Having tired of Ozzel's incompetence, Vader telekinetically executes the admiral, but cannot prevent much of the rebel fleet from escaping. Serving as the Imperial command ship during the Battle of Endor, the *Executor* is finally destroyed when a rebel A-wing starfighter crashes into its command bridge, causing it to lose control and smash into the second Death Star.

REBEL TRANSPORT

APPEARANCES Reb, RO, V, VI **MANUFACTURER** Gallofree Yards, Inc. **MODEL** GR-75 **TYPE** Medium transport

The GR-75 is a sister design to the civilian GR-45, which is used by shipping firms to haul cargo. The transport's outer hull is a thick shell with the interior entirely open for cargo pods. To maximize space, the GR-75 is minimally armed with four twin laser cannons and a deflector shield. Inexpensive to produce, the GR-75 is known for keeping maintenance personnel on their toes. Some of these transports are used as shuttles for high-ranking rebel personnel when the Alliance flees its base on Hoth. GR-75s are also used by the Alliance in the battles of Atollon, Scarif, and Endor.

Fleeing Hoth
GR-75 transports play a crucial role in the Rebel Alliance *(above)*. The last transport, *Bright Hope*, leaves Echo Base during the Battle of Hoth with the help of starfighter pilots Wedge, Hobbie, and Janson *(right)*.

ALL TERRAIN ARMORED TRANSPORT (AT-AT)

APPEARANCES Reb, V, VI, VII, VIII, FoD **MANUFACTURER** Kuat Drive Yards **MODEL** All Terrain Armored Transport **TYPE** Assault walker

The All Terrain Armored Transport, commonly known as the AT-AT, is a four-legged combat vehicle used by Imperial ground forces. The cockpit is located in the "head," while dual fire-linked, medium-repeating blasters protrude from the "temples," and two heavier Taim & Bak MS-1 fire-linked laser cannons are mounted under the "chin." The armor plating is impervious to blaster bolts, rendering the AT-AT nearly unstoppable.

At over 22 meters (72 feet), the AT-AT's size gives it a powerful psychological advantage, creating fear in its opponents as it marches forward like an armored behemoth. However, the AT-AT is not without its weaknesses. Its neck, especially, is vulnerable to blaster barrages. Unstable legs and the AT-AT's high center of gravity also make it susceptible to tripping. This tactic is employed by Rogue Squadron snowspeeders defending Echo Base on Hoth as key personnel flee the planet. When pilot Wedge Antilles makes a close pass on an AT-AT, his gunner Wes Janson fires an ace shot, harpooning the AT-AT with the tow cable. Antilles loops the speeder around the walker's legs until it tumbles to the snow. With the machine's neck better exposed, Antilles' next shot destroys the fallen AT-AT.

The walker also lacks armor covering on its underbelly, leaving the area open to mounted guns or portable missile launchers. For this reason, AT-STs are usually stationed around the flanks of the walker to protect the AT-AT's weak underside. The Empire never anticipates an attack as bold as Luke's—he uses a harpoon gun to reach an AT-AT's underbelly and then drops a grenade through the walker's floor.

Target eliminated
On Hoth, the AT-AT succeeds in destroying the shield generator, allowing Imperial forces to attack Echo Base.

Sneak attack
After his snowspeeder is downed by an Imperial AT-AT and his gunner Dak Ralter is killed, Luke attempts to disable the walker another way. He ascends to the belly section, where he leaves behind a concussion grenade, destroying the walker's interior.

Walking death
Rebel ground troops on Hoth do not stand a chance against the Imperial invasion forces led by AT-ATs under the command of General Maximilian Veers. The walkers advance on the shield generator, decimating rebel troops in their trenches.

Improved model
Decades after the Galactic Civil War, Kuat-Entralla Drive Yards constructs a new AT-AT model for the First Order that sees action on Crait. This later version has minimized the stability issues and addressed the weak points in the armor found in the Imperial AT-AT.

ALL TERRAIN SCOUT TRANSPORT (AT-ST/ SCOUT WALKER)

APPEARANCES RO, V, VI **MANUFACTURER** Kuat Drive Yards **MODEL** All Terrain Scout Transport **TYPE** Walker

A quick-strike companion to the larger and more formidable AT-AT walker, the AT-ST's lightweight bipedal design enables swift movement across most types of terrain. Its speed and agility make the AT-ST well suited for patrol and reconnaissance duties supporting Imperial ground operations, and lead to its moniker "scout walker." The Empire deploys AT-STs in vastly different environments. AT-STs are used against Saw Gerrera's Partisans in the crowded streets of Jedha, but also take on the Rebel Alliance in remote ground battles. While the scout walkers help defeat the rebel forces at Hoth, the AT-STs are soundly defeated at Endor.

For all its advantages in speed and size over the AT-AT, the AT-ST's offensive and defensive power is significantly compromised. The pair of chin-mounted medium blaster cannons offer a range of just 2 kilometers (1 mile 427 yds), while the concussion grenade launcher and light blaster cannon fitted on either side of the head are effective only at close range against infantry. Similarly, its much lighter armor can repel attacks from blasters and other small arms, but cannot withstand laser cannons, missiles, or other heavy weapons. The AT-ST is also vulnerable to a variety of other short-range attacks, exploited to great effect by the Ewoks in the Battle of Endor. Thick ropes slung across its lower legs like a tripwire can topple the walker, while rocks or other debris dropped from hang gliders can destabilize its footing. The Ewoks also discover that ramming logs that are suspended from trees into the sides of the walker's head will strike with enough force to smash through the light armor, destroying the cockpit.

Perhaps the scout walker's greatest weakness, though, is its susceptibility to hijacking. After swinging on a rope to land on top of an AT-ST, Chewbacca uses his mighty arms to rip open the roof hatch, and then reach inside to grab the pilots and hurl them out of the cockpit. The Wookiee then uses the commandeered walker's cannons to destroy other AT-STs in the battle, as well as wreak havoc on the unsuspecting stormtrooper infantry.

Forest failure
The Imperial AT-STs *(left)* struggle against Ewok ingenuity during the Battle of Endor. Chewbacca uses his commandeered AT-ST to turn the tide in favor of the Rebel Alliance at the shield generator complex *(above)*.

First Order AT-ST
Recognizing the value of the Imperial AT-STs, the First Order develops its own model to complement its assortment of ground vehicles. BB-8 uses a First Order AT-ST to create a distraction and save his Resistance allies, Finn and Rose, from execution aboard the *Supremacy*.

Clean-up duty

Scout walkers are often deployed alongside the larger assault walkers for major ground operations. While the bigger cannons on the AT-AT devastate the opposing force's emplacements and vehicles, the AT-ST moves quickly to eliminate any infantry or other smaller threats that manage to evade the barrage. When Imperial ground troops invade the Rebel Alliance hideout on Hoth, the AT-ATs must trudge slowly across the snowfields toward Echo Base, making them open to aerial attacks by the rebels' snowspeeders. The nimbler AT-STs, by contrast, are able to advance much faster across the frozen terrain to launch attacks against the trenches and laser cannons defending the Base.

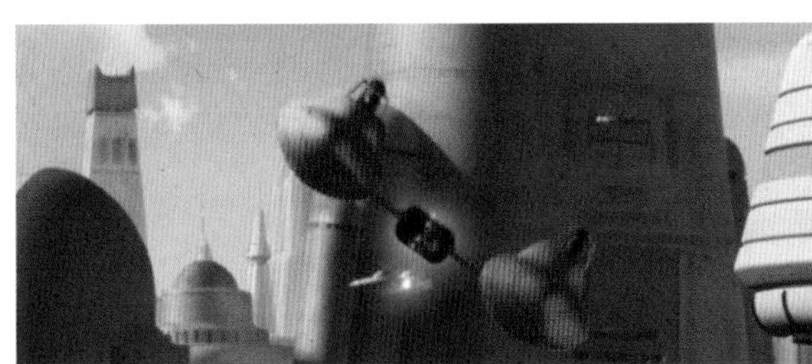

TWIN-POD CLOUD CAR

APPEARANCES V, VI **MANUFACTURER** Bespin Motors **MODEL** Storm IV Twin-Pod **TYPE** Atmospheric repulsorcraft

A familiar sight over the skies of Cloud City, the bright orange twin-pod cloud car polices the surrounding airspace. Specifically designed for patrol purposes, the pod is powered by an ion engine and a repulsorlift drive. The port-side pod houses the pilot, while the gunner in the starboard pod controls a pair of blaster cannons. When the *Millennium Falcon* seeks refuge in Cloud City for repairs, Han Solo nearly provokes a confrontation with a cloud car before receiving landing clearance from his old friend Lando Calrissian.

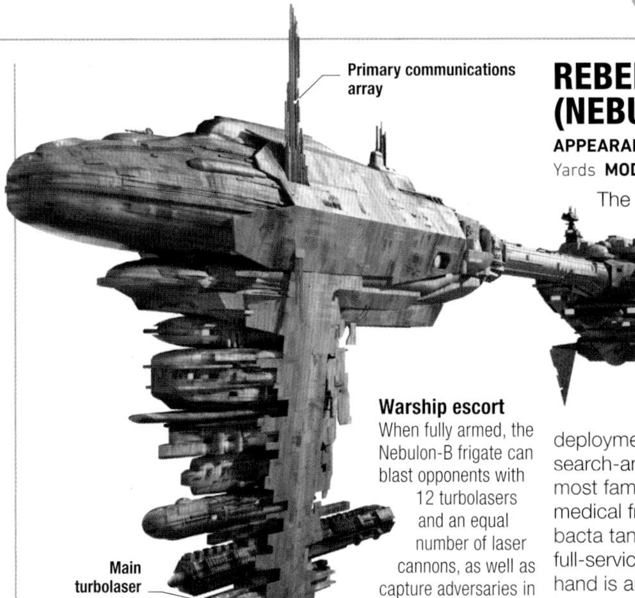

Warship escort
When fully armed, the Nebulon-B frigate can blast opponents with 12 turbolasers and an equal number of laser cannons, as well as capture adversaries in its dual tractor beams.

REBEL CRUISER (NEBULON-B FRIGATE)

APPEARANCES Reb, RO, V, VI **MANUFACTURER** Kuat Drive Yards **MODEL** EF76 Nebulon-B **TYPE** Escort frigate

The Rebel Alliance deploys Nebulon-B frigates, with their highly versatile design platform, in several different capacities across its fleet. Equipped with heavy armament and powerful tractor beams, they escort convoys to protect transport ships against Imperial attacks and pirate raids. While some frigates are modified for deployment on long-range scouting missions or search-and-rescue operations, Nebulon-Bs become most famous for their use by the Rebel Alliance as medical frigates. These ships are equipped with bacta tanks to promote healing, medical droids, and full-service hospital facilities. When Luke Skywalker's hand is amputated in a lightsaber duel with Darth Vader, a surgical droid attaches the cybernetic replacement in a Nebulon-B medical frigate.

TIE INTERCEPTOR

APPEARANCES Reb, VI, VIII **MANUFACTURER** Sienar Fleet Systems **MODEL** Twin Ion Engine Interceptor **TYPE** Starfighter

Easily recognized by its sharply pointed solar panels, the TIE interceptor is a far deadlier opponent than a standard TIE fighter. Although it also lacks shields and a hyperdrive, the interceptor has four laser cannons mounted on its wingtips, as well as upgraded engines providing considerably improved maneuverability and speed. The Empire places its elite pilots in interceptor cockpits to maximize the craft's effectiveness. With these advantages, interceptors are ideally suited for their main function: chasing down and eliminating rebel starfighters.

MON CALAMARI MC80 STAR CRUISER

APPEARANCES Reb, VI **MANUFACTURER** Mon Calamari Shipyards **MODEL** MC80 **TYPE** Star cruiser

The MC80 star cruisers in the Rebel Alliance fleet operate as command ships or battleships capable of direct engagement with an Imperial Star Destroyer. Each MC80 has a unique design, though common features include a tapered bow, bulbous hulls, hangar bays, heavy armor and shielding, and 10 sublight thrusters. With over 5,000 crew at full strength, it can deploy as many as 10 squadrons of starfighters into a space battle. The MC80's own powerful weapons include dozens of turbolasers and ion cannons.

HOME ONE

APPEARANCES Reb, VI **MANUFACTURER** Mon Calamari Shipyards **MODEL** MC80 **TYPE** Star cruiser

Originally a civilian Mon Calamari vessel intended for long missions exploring deep space, *Home One* is retrofitted for military service and can function as a flagship, battleship, or carrier. With heavy hull plating and triple-strength shields, the ship carries extensive offensive weaponry and boasts 20 hangars for bearing other warships or starfighter squadrons. It is sometimes called the Headquarters Frigate because it houses the command and control center for Admiral Ackbar. At the Battle of Endor, *Home One* is the most celebrated of the MC80 star cruisers in the Rebel Alliance fleet. Decades later, this legendary vessel becomes part of the Resistance fleet.

Admiral's flagship
The largest, most advanced capital ship in the fleet, *Home One* brings pride to the Rebel Alliance whenever it joins the battle *(top)*. From the bridge, Admiral Ackbar leads the Rebel Alliance fleet at the Battle of Endor *(above)*.

Spy craft
Using its full suite of sensor, tracking, and imaging systems, the A-wing exploits its speed and maneuverability on highly effective intelligence-gathering missions.

A-WING STARFIGHTER

APPEARANCES Reb, VI **MANUFACTURER** Kuat Systems Engineering **MODEL** RZ-1 A-wing interceptor **TYPE** Starfighter

The A-wing is one of the fastest starfighter models in the galaxy. Essentially a cockpit attached to two large engines, it requires precision manipulation of the dorsal and ventral stabilizers without assistance from an astromech. As a result, only the best pilots can fly an A-wing without losing control. The A-wing possesses superior speed, defensive shields, and a hyperdrive, and is armed with two laser cannons and 12 concussion missiles. During the Battle of Endor, an A-wing crashes into and demolishes the bridge of the Imperial flagship *Executor*.

Quick strikes
Powered by an ionization reactor that fuels four high-performance engines *(above)*, the B-wing races swiftly across the battlefield to engage enemy capital ships *(right)*.

B-WING STARFIGHTER

APPEARANCES Reb, VI **MANUFACTURER** Slayn & Korpil **MODEL** A/SF-01 B-wing starfighter **TYPE** Starfighter

The B-wing starfighter is designed by Mon Calamari engineer Quarrie, and is among the most heavily armed assault starfighters in the Rebel Alliance fleet. The cockpit's gyroscopic mounting, with full 360-degree rotation, ensures the pilot remains sitting upright regardless of the fighter's orientation. The center of the primary airfoil houses the engines, while the fighter's far end holds the heavy weapons pod, which includes ion cannons and proton torpedoes. When extended, the smaller S-foils broaden the firing arc of the B-wing's twin laser cannons. Specializing in attacking Imperial capital ships, squadrons of B-wings play a major role in the Battle of Endor.

T-85 X-WING

APPEARANCES Res **MANUFACTURER** Incom-FreiTek **TYPE** X-wing

In the last years before the destruction of Hosnian Prime, the New Republic Defense Fleet flies T-85 X-wings; among the most innovative X-wing starfighters created by Incom-FreiTek. The ships are more advanced than the T-70s flown by the Resistance and the Rebel Alliance's T-65B and T-65C X-wings. Flown by New Republic pilot Kazuda Xiono on his first encounter with Captain Poe Dameron, the blue-and-silver New Republic T-85s have the words "Republic Navy" written in Aurebesh across the ships' bow.

RESISTANCE BLOCKADE RUNNER

APPEARANCES Res **MANUFACTURER** Corellian Engineering Corp. **MODEL** CR90 **TYPE** Corvette

The Resistance flies old but trusty ships that are both familiar and comfortable to its former Rebel Alliance members, especially its leader, General Organa. Much like the *Tantive IV*, this CR90 corvette participates in the Battle of Scarif. It later serves as Leia's mobile operations center for the Resistance prior to the destruction of Hosnian Prime. After their dogfight with Major Elrik Vonreg, Poe Dameron and Kazuda Xiono dock with the ship to contact her via hologram. Later, they return to the ship and are briefed by Leia in person regarding a new mission.

TIE BARON

All-red
The fact that Vonreg flies in an all-red TIE suggests that his skills far surpass those of the Special Forces TIE pilots, who fly in ships adorned with a red stripe only.

APPEARANCES Res **MANUFACTURER** Sienar-Jaemus Fleet Systems **MODEL** TIE/in **TYPE** Starfighter

Major Elrik Vonreg is one of the First Order's most skilled pilots, and flies a crimson First Order TIE interceptor. The starfighter's twin ion engines are powered by two ion reactors with pre-charged deuterium power cells which are capable of achieving an atmospheric speed of 1,250 kilometers per hour (777 miles per hour). The ship's weaponry includes four wingtip L-s9.7 laser cannons and projectile launchers capable of firing ST7 concussion missiles and mag-pulse warheads. The TIE interceptor is well-protected with shielding and it contains an ejection seat if all else fails. The ship is also managed by an experimental Torplex flight computer and is equipped with a class 2 hyperdrive. In his advanced ship, Vonreg is can easily annihilate most enemy starfighters.

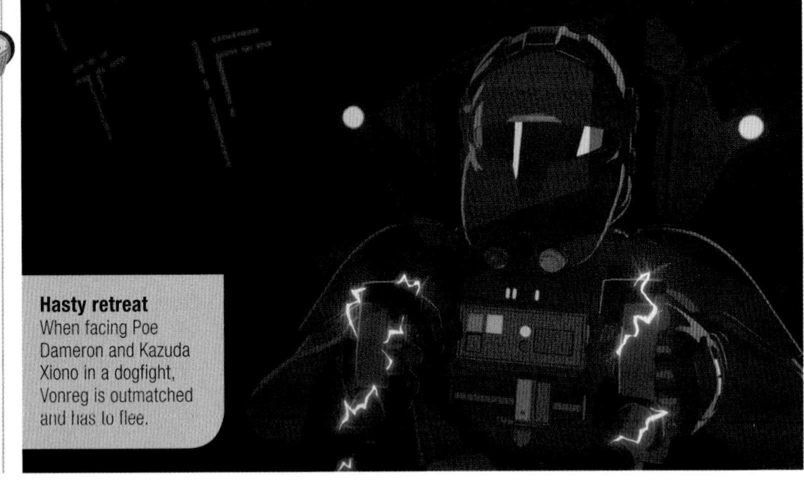

Hasty retreat
When facing Poe Dameron and Kazuda Xiono in a dogfight, Vonreg is outmatched and has to flee.

BLACK ONE

APPEARANCES VII, VIII **MANUFACTURER** Incom-FreiTek **MODEL** T-70 **TYPE** X-wing

Poe Dameron flies a customized T-70 X-wing for the Resistance, code-named *Black One*. Poe leads Black Squadron but is also in command of Red and Blue Squadrons. He flies *Black One* during many skirmishes and battles—including the mission to Ovanis, the Battle of Takodana, and the assault on Starkiller Base.

The orange and black ferrosphere paint covering Poe's X-wing differentiates it from the other Resistance X-wings and scatters First Order sensors, allowing Poe to run covert missions undetected. The astromech slot behind Poe's cockpit is specially fitted for BB-8, allowing for his unique shape and internal toolset.

Unlike the Rebel Alliance, which historically manufactures its T-65 X-wings in secret, the New Republic can build its X-wings openly. The Resistance lacks such resources, so relies on donations of surplus assets from powerful people and governments. The organization must ration supplies and conserve finances in order to maintain its humble fleet.

The T-70 X-wings are faster and carry better weapons than the older T-65s of the Rebel Alliance. T-70s owe their sleeker, slighter design to new technological breakthroughs in miniaturization of ship components. They are, however, a downgrade from the New Republic's cutting-edge T-85s.

Though these X-wings are more expensive to buy and maintain than the First Order's TIE fighters, they are more versatile and can perform in a range of combat situations. The wingtip laser cannons can fire in single, dual, and quad modes. Interchangeable magazines allow pilots to swap payloads of eight proton torpedoes with mag-pulse warheads, concussion missiles, and other ordnances.

During the evacuation of D'Qar, *Black One* is outfitted with an experimental accelerator pod that greatly increases its speed, allowing Poe to launch an assault on the First Order fleet preparing to attack the Resistance base. After fleeing the planet, *Black One* is in the *Raddus*' main hangar when it is destroyed during an attack by Kylo Ren's TIE fighter squadron. The resulting carnage is devastating to the Resistance's already depleted starfighter corps.

Poe to the rescue
When C-3PO's droid contact alerts the Resistance to BB-8's location, Poe races to retrieve him.

Local support
The *Fireball*'s first sponsor is local Gorg seller Bolza Grool.

FIREBALL

APPEARANCES Res **MANUFACTURER** Unknown **MODEL** Unknown **TYPE** Racing starfighter

The *Fireball* is an aging starfighter that belongs to Jarek Yeager, who runs a repair shop on the *Colossus* refueling station. It's called *Fireball* because of its unfortunate tendency to erupt in flames during flight. Yeager promises the ship to his employee Tam Ryvora if she can get it fixed up. Tam is not happy at all when the Resistance spy Kazuda Xiono arrives on the *Colossus* and Yeager lets Kaz fly it in a race against Torra Doza. Nonetheless, Team Fireball (which is named after the ship itself) work together to acquire parts and get the ship in working order. Most of the used parts come from Flix and Orca at the *Colossus* Office of Acquisitions. Kaz must do several favors for them in exchange for the parts he needs. Kaz does well in the race—nearly finishing—but pushes the ship too far and crashes into the sea toward the end of the race.

Afterward, Team Fireball spends a lot of time and work repairing and improving the ship. Though Kaz and Tam grow to be friends, they experience occasional friction over the *Fireball*. Clumsy Kaz breaks the ship's newly repaired acceleration compensator at one point, so Tam makes him fix it. He accomplishes this with the help of some new Chelidae friends. Kaz also learns a valuable lesson when he tries to sneak away with the ship to meet Poe Dameron without telling Tam. It is not until he is far from the *Colossus* that he realizes she was in the middle of fixing the ship's stabilizers, and the ship is once again in danger of crashing.

During the First Order's occupation of the *Colossus*, Tam feels betrayed by her friends and joins the group, leaving them and the *Fireball* on the platform. When the station's residents rise up to free their home for the occupiers, Kaz pilots the *Fireball* alongside the Aces and Yeager, and shoots down Major Vonreg.

Rumor has it that Jarek Yeager used to race it himself, and that he cobbled it together from an old rebel X-wing and a Z-75 Headhunter he inherited from some family members. It has impressive weaponry and is heavily armed with two wingtip Taim & Bak KX11C laser cannons and a pair of missile launchers capable of firing miniaturized Krupx MG7-A proton torpedoes and concussion missiles.

Racing against the best
While Kaz comes close to beating Torra Doza in their first race, Torra still wins.

Mission to Dassal
Alongside Poe Dameron in *Black One*, Kaz travels in the *Fireball* to the Dassal system. They discover the space system's sun is gone, and its planets have been mysteriously cored.

BLUE ACE

APPEARANCES Res **MANUFACTURER** Joben and Sons **MODEL** Custom made **TYPE** Racing starfighter

Torra Doza, daughter of the administrator of *Colossus*, flies a luxurious custom racer. Torra spares no expense to create an aerodynamic, state-of-the-art ship to suit her unique flying style and aesthetic tastes. A lavish racer that would have fit right in among Coruscant's airspeeders during the golden age of the Old Republic, the *Blue Ace* is a stylish starfighter with more than a few tricks up its sleeves. It's much faster and sleeker than most of the old Resistance ships and has enough firepower to take on First Order TIE fighters.

RED ACE

APPEARANCES Res **MANUFACTURERS** Kuat Systems Engineering and Freya Fenris **MODEL** Custom made **TYPE** Racing starfighter

Taking inspiration from Kuat Systems' legendary line of A-wings, Freya Fenris comes up with a starfighter design incorporating added wings with laser canons for additional stability and extra firepower. Her *Red Ace* is an achievement in precision design, technological advancement, and speed. Her ship is propelled by a pair of Novaldex K-99 Event Horizon sublight engines. Weaponry includes a pair of wingtip Zija Valkyr-2 laser cannons, and at the bow are a pair of Zija Asgar-4 lasers. In her *Red Ace,* Fenris often leads the other Aces from the front when they must defend the *Colossus* from attack.

GREEN ACE

APPEARANCES Res **MANUFACTURER** Incom-FreiTek **MODEL** Modified G30 **TYPE** Racing starfighter

Bearing some similarities to Incom-FreiTek's classic X-wings, Hype Fazon's flashy *Green Ace* is covered in sponsor names and logos, many of them from businesses that have been around since the Clone Wars. The ship's S-foil wing positions can be adjusted for speed and maneuverability as well as for aiming the ship's two wingtip Taim & Bak KX10B laser cannons. The left wing carries an advertisement for "Outer Rim Supply Co.," while the right advertises "Craft Repair and Maintenance." The ship is also equipped with missile launchers.

YELLOW ACE

APPEARANCES Res **MANUFACTURER** Ravager Mechanics **MODEL** Customized "Changeling" Mark 71NB **TYPE** Racing starfighter

Colossus Ace pilot Bo Keevil's ship is customized for speed and agility. The *Yellow Ace*'s wings change configurations to facilitate his many dangerous flight acrobatics. This maneuverability comes at a price—the ship is exceptionally difficult to handle and the controls are highly sensitive. Bo installs extra countermeasures for likely crash-landings. The "Primeval" Keevil has flown his ship in countless significant races, including the Platform Classic and the All Aces Battle Royale on the *Colossus*, and the Cloud City Grand Prix.

BLACK ACE

APPEARANCES Res **MANUFACTURER** Sienar Fleet Systems and Griff Halloran **MODEL** Custom **TYPE** Racing starfighter

Griff Halloran builds his own custom starfighter from an old TIE fighter, but tricks it out with many customizations. It is barely recognizable as a former Imperial craft, apart from the signature TIE forward viewport. Some believe that the fighter resembles an old Eta-2 *Actis*-class interceptor more than a TIE. Not only is his ship sleek and fast, its Imperial style intimidates Griff's competitors. The *Black Ace* is heavily damaged during the Platform Classic race, but Halloran has it up and running in time to help with the giant rokkna attack on *Colossus* station. During the *Colossus*' battle against the First Order, Griff's ship is hit but Kaz saves both Griff and *Black Ace* from destruction.

THE GALLEON

APPEARANCES Res **MANUFACTURER** Warbirds **MODEL** Self-made **TYPE** Pirate ship

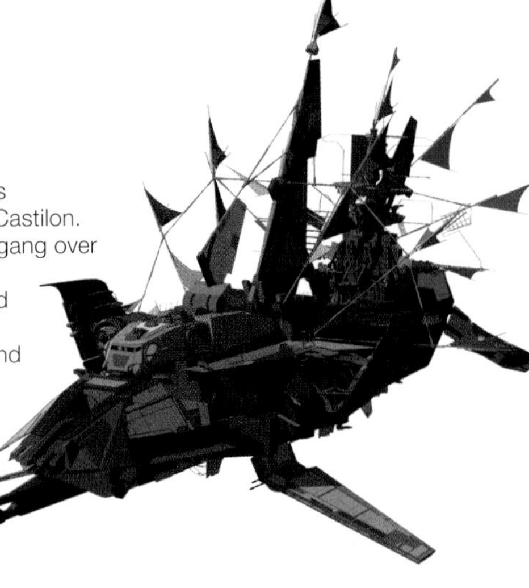

The *Galleon* is the flagship of Kragan Gorr's Warbirds—a gang of pirates operating on Castilon. The ship is built and modified by Kragan's gang over decades, gradually incorporating Imperial ship components and scavenged parts and cannons onto the original Ubrikkian barge hull. An AT-AT makes up the main cabin, and an upside-down AT-AT foot and leg forms the crow's nest. *Lambda*-class shuttle wings stabilize the vessel. The stern hosts a landing platform for large ships. When the *Colossus* needs help against the First Order, the Warbirds assist them, joining the battle in the *Galleon* and docking with the station before it escapes to hyperspace.

WARBIRD SKIFF

APPEARANCES Res **MANUFACTURER** Warbirds **MODEL** Self-made **TYPE** Skiff

Kragan Gorr's Warbirds gang uses a number of heavily modified repulsorlift skiffs as mobile platforms on Castilon. The custom-built skiffs are ramshackle combinations of Imperial parts and other scavenged pieces. When the Warbird pirates sneak aboard the *Colossus* and kidnap Ace pilot Torra Doza, they initially escape on a pair of swoop bikes. Then they rendezvous with a pirate skiff. Pilot Kazuda Xiono tries to follow them from his ship, the *Fireball*, as the pirates fire at him from a cannon turret at the stern of the skiff. He is forced to fall back however, lest he hurt Torra aboard the tiny skiff.

KRAGAN GORR'S SHUTTLE

APPEARANCES Res **MANUFACTURER** Warbirds **MODEL** Self-made **TYPE** Shuttle-fighter

The Warbird leader Kragon Gorr's personal shuttle is a unique vessel that clearly derives some of its parts from scavenged Imperial *Lambda*-class shuttles. The ship is covered in lasers and ion cannons which are taxing on the ship's power reserve, putting the weapons in danger of failing during heavy use. Though the ship is fast and maneuverable in-atmosphere, the shields are minimal and the hyperdrive is unreliable. Still, the shuttle has ample cargo space for stolen loot—a quality necessary for any true pirate ship.

WARBIRD STARFIGHTER

APPEARANCES Res **MANUFACTURER** Warbirds **MODEL** Self-made **TYPE** Starfighter

The Warbirds' starfighters are a hodgepodge of several different ships—including parts from A-wings, Eta-2 *Actis*-class interceptors, and Imperial TIE interceptors. Although they look like they could fall apart or explode at any moment, these ships are actually highly maneuverable, and well armed with precision targeting systems. Kragan Gorr's pirate gang uses the ships to raid the *Colossus* station and other vulnerable targets on Castilon. While the pirates' piloting skills may not be as celebrated as the Aces, they are experts at operating their deadly and speedy ships.

GALAXY'S GLORY

APPEARANCES Res **MANUFACTURER** Unknown **MODEL** Unknown **TYPE** Racing starfighter

Famous across the galaxy, Marcus Speedstar is a renowned racing pilot who arrogantly names his custom racer *Galaxy's Glory*. Speedstar's ship is designed to win races rather than fight in big space battles. His racer has a pair of laser cannons, but they are more for aesthetics than heavy combat. The ship has a distinctive black, purple, and silver color scheme that matches both Speedstar's flight suit and his droid co-pilot R4-D12.

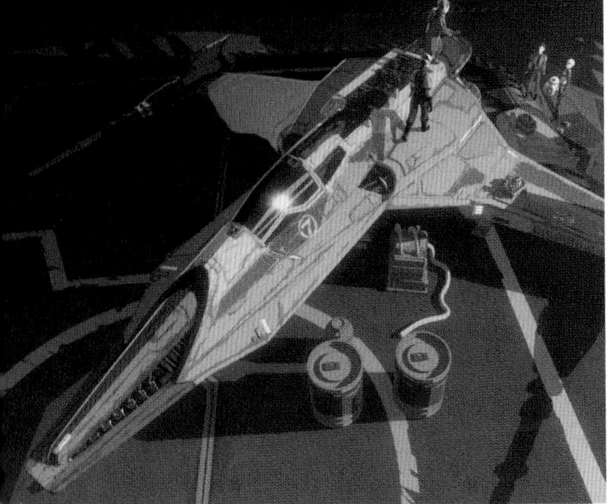

RUCKLIN'S RACER

APPEARANCES Res **MANUFACTURER** Unknown **MODEL** Unknown **TYPE** Racing starfighter

Racing fanatic Jace Rucklin spends his life savings and countless hours working on his ship in an effort to make it as light and fast as possible. He removes everything from the ship that he considers to be unnecessary weight, including the ejection seat parachute. Rucklin steals hyperfuel from Jarek Yeager's garage to get an edge on his upcoming race, but as a result, he unknowingly turns his ship into a flying bomb. Rucklin is nearly killed, but Kazuda Xiono saves him just before the ship explodes. Nonetheless, the ungrateful wretch blames everything on Kaz.

JAREK YEAGER'S RACER

APPEARANCES Res **MANUFACTURER** Unknown **MODEL** Unknown **TYPE** Racing starfighter

Jarek Yeager's personal starfighter is a fast and powerful racer. Yeager competes in and wins many races during his career. When he first arrives on the *Colossus*, he continues to race in the ship, but soon gives up and opens a garage instead. His ship remains grounded for years until his brother, Marcus Speedstar, arrives. Yeager agrees to race against Speedstar in the Platform Classic. At first, Yeager is intent on beating his brother, but in the end, he realizes that Marcus needs to win to save his friend's life, so lets his brother win instead. Yeager flies in the ship during the *Colossus*' fight with the First Order, wishing that he could by piloting under friendlier circumstances. Kaz saves Yeager from death by shooting down Major Vonreg, allowing Yeager and Kaz to board the *Colossus* before it jumps to hyperspace.

DARIUS G-CLASS FREIGHTER

APPEARANCES Res **MANUFACTURER** Darius **MODEL** G-Class **TYPE** Freighter

Common across the galaxy, Darius G-class freighters are a spacious line of cargo ships with chin-mounted loading ramps. They are often equipped with eighteen single-occupant escape pods which launch from the ventral surface of the hull. The First Order's Major Elrik Vonreg delivers a fuel shipment to *Colossus* station aboard one such freighter. Kazuda Xiono and Poe Dameron later rescue pirate Synara San aboard a derelict Darius freighter overrun by Kowakian monkey-lizards. Another Darius freighter is owned by a Keteerian named Teroj Kee, who claims to work for the Mining Guild but is actually a secret agent for the First Order. After Teroj steals a phase connector from the *Colossus* Department of Acquisitions, Kazuda sabotages his ship, forcing Teroj and his crew to abandon it. Meanwhile, the stowaway Kazuda (with the pet gorg Bitey) returns to the *Colossus* in an escape pod.

FIRST ORDER TIE FIGHTER

APPEARANCES Res, VII, VIII **MANUFACTURER** Sienar-Jaemus Fleet Systems **MODEL** TIE/fo space superiority fighter **TYPE** Starfighter

While the Empire considered its pilots expendable, the First Order values its pilots. First Order TIE fighters may resemble their Imperial predecessors, but its engineers have made many technological advances on the original design. These TIE fighters have more robust weaponry, more efficient solar energy collector arrays in their wing panels, and the crucial addition of shield generators. Standard First Order TIEs still lack hyperdrives however, limiting them to short-range missions. The TIE is the First Order's standard starfighter, and squadrons are stationed aboard all Star Destroyers in addition to Starkiller Base.

FIRST ORDER SF TIE FIGHTER

APPEARANCES VII, VIII **MANUFACTURER** Sienar-Jaemus Fleet Systems **MODEL** TIE/sf space superiority fighter **TYPE** Starfighter

Unlike standard TIEs, the Special Forces model has the capacity for an additional crew member—a gunner. Designed for long-range missions, it is equipped with a hyperdrive. Thanks to banks of high-yield deuterium cells, each fighter has additional power devoted to engines, shields, and weapons systems. The TIE/sf is equipped with forward-facing laser cannons as well as 360-degree coverage via a heavy weapon turret and warhead launcher. The rear-facing gunner is best suited to control the turret, though the pilot can manage if required. The extra systems mean that the ship has a tendency to overheat.

Sensors Upper wings contain hyperwave scanners and sub-space communications.

Designed to intimidate The threatening look of the *Upsilon*-class ship contrasts with the unassuming Lambda and Sentinel shuttles used by Imperial dignitaries.

Protection Lower wings are protected by durasteel armor and deflector shields.

Firepower Twin laser cannons easily cut through Resistance X-wings.

KYLO REN'S SHUTTLE

APPEARANCES VII, VIII **MANUFACTURER** Sienar-Jaemus Army Systems **MODEL** *Upsilon*-class shuttle **TYPE** Transport

Kylo Ren commands First Order military forces from aboard the *Finalizer*, but he requires smaller craft to shuttle down to planet surfaces. Like other high-level First Order officers and dignitaries, Kylo Ren terrorizes approaching worlds from an elite *Upsilon*-class shuttle. The ship's features are developed in part thanks to secret Imperial research and continued in top secret labs by the First Order within the Unknown Regions of the galaxy.

During flight, the craft's bat-like wings tilt outward and nearly double in length, exposing long-range sensor arrays in the upper extensions. When landing, the 37.2-meter (122.04-foot) wings retract and the sensitive technology is protected by the wing bases' armor. Shield generators located also protect the passenger cabin and its very important occupants.

While it is are normally accompanied by a TIE fighter escort, each shuttle possesses two twin heavy laser cannons (a pair on each wing). A countermeasures system at each wingtip is capable of deflecting incoming projectiles with ghost signals that confuse warhead sensors. The upper wings carry long-range scanners to detect approaching ships, while the lower wings contain jammers to wipe out enemy communications. *Upsilon*-class shuttles are capable of sweeping star systems for errant communications and pinpointing Resistance spies' transmissions. Kylo Ren's command shuttle can easily isolate a lone ship and eliminate it before it even detects the shuttle's imminent approach—let alone gets out a distress call.

Kylo's shuttle accommodates five crew with space for 10 additional passengers. A pilot and co-pilot remain ready on board at all times, awaiting Kylo's return. Upon landing, Kylo descends a ramp underneath the main cabin as stormtroopers stand guard to bar any unauthorized access to the vessel and defend it from any enemy assault.

Supreme leader After killing Snoke, Kylo Ren becomes the First Order's Supreme Leader. Flying above the battleground in his shuttle, Kylo personally oversees the attack on the Resistance base on Crait.

FINALIZER

APPEARANCES VII, VIII **MANUFACTURER** Kuat-Entralla Engineering **MODEL** *Resurgent*-class Star Destroyer **TYPE** Capital ship

The *Finalizer* is a flagship of the First Order's fleet and the command seat of both Kylo Ren and General Hux. The First Order has far fewer Star Destroyers than the Empire, not because of a lack of desire on the part of its Supreme Leader Snoke, but simply due to limited resources. The *Resurgent*-class Star Destroyers are a symbol of the First Order's power and are well staffed. The *Finalizer* maintains an entire legion of more than 8,000 stormtroopers, 55,000 enlisted crew, 19,000 officers, and pilots of all levels. The stormtroopers aboard have been trained since birth to be loyal to Snoke and the First Order. They consider the *Finalizer* their only true home.

As a military carrier, the *Finalizer* hosts two wings of TIE fighters and more than a hundred assault vehicles, including walkers. A refined design means that starfighters are more easily launched from the dorsal flight decks and side hangars than from Imperial Star Destroyers. Approaching enemy ships find themselves surrounded by squadrons of TIE fighters before they've even detected that the starfighters have left the *Finalizer*'s bays. The command bridge is much more efficiently defended than those on the older Imperial warships as it is no longer set so far apart from the rest of the vessel, and its deflector shield generators are not the large, obvious, and relatively undefended targets they once were.

As a mobile weapons platform, the *Finalizer* is fitted with more than 3,000 turbolasers and ion canons, as well as tractor beams and projectile launchers situated in multiple locations. These provide more than adequate munitions for ship-to-ship combat and planetary bombardment. Smaller defensive missile launchers and laser turrets are located at key areas of strategic importance.

The *Finalizer*'s weapons capabilities and size violate the treaties between the First Order and the New Republic. For a time, *Resurgent*-class Star Destroyer development is kept secret by the First Order, yet General Leia Organa is well aware of the ships' existence. The Resistance does its best to track sightings and the movements of these ships. Nonetheless, reports made to senators in the New Republic have largely fallen on deaf ears. Branding Leia as a warmonger, few in the Senate heed her warnings until it is much too late.

FIRST ORDER SNOW SPEEDER

APPEARANCES VII, FoD **MANUFACTURER** Aratech-Loratus Corp. **MODEL** Light Infantry Utility Vehicle (LIUV) **TYPE** Speeder

The First Order relies on repulsorlift snow speeders as its primary mode of ground transportation on Starkiller Base. The craft has capacity for two seated occupants, but an additional passenger can crouch in the front. A FWMB-10 repeating blaster turret is mounted in the bow, with wide firing arcs to spray enemy fortifications with horizontal blaster fire or aim for the skies above to take out incoming fighters. The blaster can be easily disassembled to make room for large cargo loads at the front of the speeder. Compared to civilian models, the First Order snow speeder has a bigger power source and upgraded power converters. The driver and gunner are both exposed to the elements and rely on heated seats to stay warm. Without any protective barriers, they must also take care at high speeds not to be dislodged should the vehicle hit a snow bank.

ERAVANA

APPEARANCES VII **MANUFACTURER** Corellian Engineering Corp. **MODEL** *Baleen*-class heavy freighter **TYPE** Bulk freighter

After Han Solo and Chewbacca lose their beloved *Millennium Falcon*, they are forced to find a new ship. The legendary pair end up with the *Eravana*—a giant, slow, and sluggish vessel that is quite a contrast to the small, fast, and agile *Falcon*. Bulk freighters like the *Eravana* are often manufactured in space. They rarely enter planetary atmospheres, and instead they tend to dock at space stations and orbital platforms to load and unload cargo. Few of these expensive ships are owned by private individuals, and most belong to guilds, corporations, or governments. The *Eravana* possesses a labyrinth of shipping containers that are attached externally between the docking bay and the engines. This large docking bay is used for more delicate cargo, requiring special attention. At 426 meters (1,398 feet) long, this *Baleen*-class ship can carry a large amount of cargo. Indeed, Han and Chewie typically carry diverse loads—from Kiirium ingots to Aldo Spachian comet dust—bound for different buyers. When Rey and Finn encounter the *Eravana*, the ship's current cargo includes a shipment of three dangerous rathtars for King Prana. The ship's size makes it difficult for Han and Chewie to monitor, so they are not immediately aware that a couple of gangs have boarded the ship and that Rey has accidentally released the rathtars.

STORMTROOPER TRANSPORT

APPEARANCES Res, VII **MANUFACTURER** Sienar-Jaemus Army Systems **MODEL** Atmospheric Assault Lander (AAL) **TYPE** Troop transport

The stormtrooper transport is a mainstay of the First Order's arsenal. Each transport can transfer two squads of stormtroopers quickly and directly into battle from orbiting command ships. When landing, each ship uses searchlights to dazzle the enemy and a dorsal gunner covers the soldiers with a 240-degree range of fire. An AAL may leave its soldiers on the ground for the operation, return with reinforcements, or wait back at its base until the battle is over and return to pick up surviving troops later. Shields and heavy armor protect the AAL from danger as it moves in and out of combat. The isolated cockpit is a key weakness. It is conceivable that a well-targeted weapon could take out the pilot mid-flight. While the lander possesses a secondary set of controls, these are far less precise than the primary system.

QUADJUMPER

APPEARANCES VII, FoD **MANUFACTURER** Subpro
MODEL Quadrijet transfer spacetug **TYPE** Spacetug

Rey's first choice for a ride off Jakku is a quadjumper belonging to a team of junk haulers. It would have provided a fast escape, if it had not been destroyed by a TIE fighter first. A quadjumper pilot uses magnetic clamps to attach the ship to heavy cargo containers, then uses the ship's four powerful and oversized thrusters to move the loads across shipping yards. Around the pilot's seat are 180-degree viewports in all directions, allowing the pilot to keep track of the other spacetugs, loader droids, and personnel working alongside them in busy ports. While designed for planetary cargo transport, the craft can also operate in space. The vessel's versatility makes it desirable to smugglers, prospectors, and pirates.

REY'S SPEEDER

APPEARANCES VII, FoD
MANUFACTURER None **MODEL** Custom vehicle
TYPE Repulsorlift bike

Rey's speeder is a custom repulsorlift vehicle made from a range of parts. Part speeder, part swoop, it does not quite fit into either category—technically it is something in between. Rey is incredibly proud of her treasured vehicle that is uniquely suited to her abilities. Her Jedi-like piloting skills and reflexes make it easy for Rey to drive her speeder at near podracing speeds when other drivers would surely crash into the dunes.

The speeder's propulsion comes from twin turbojet engines from a wrecked cargo-hauler, customized with racing-swoop afterburners and repulsorlifts from crashed X-wing starfighters for lift. A primary heat exchanger keeps the powerful engines from overheating, and a strategically-positioned heat sink keeps Rey from burning herself on the rear afterburner assembly. Vertical stabilizers help keep the speeder upright, and a tractor web holds Rey to the seat. With these modifications, Rey can attain the elevations of a typical airspeeder—and when nobody is looking, she takes flight.

While her speeder can carry large loads, Rey knows that this will attract unwanted attention. She tends to carry a small load of salvaged scrap that hangs on each of the speeder's sides in nets and make more frequent trips at higher speeds on her way to Niima Outpost.

Rey's speeder is not equipped with any weapons, but has other defenses. If someone tries to steal her salvage or speeder, Rey can electrify the chassis to incapacitate the prospective thief, and the engine will not start without her fingerprint. The speeder simply is not worth the trouble for most thugs to tamper with.

RESISTANCE TRANSPORTER

APPEARANCES VII **MANUFACTURER** Slayn & Korpil
MODEL Customized Resistance Transport **TYPE** Transport

Resistance transporters are a hodgepodge of components assembled from a variety of vessels—most notably the B-wing series first developed by the former Rebel Alliance, but also from Republic-era *Montura*-class shuttles. The transporters are difficult to maneuver and their cockpits have poor visibility, so they are normally accompanied by X-wing escorts for defense. If the transporter is caught without an escort, it can utilize a full array of weapons adapted from B-wing fighters. Two seating compartments in the middle of the ship provide space for up to 20 passengers, droids, and equipment. The transporters are subject to frequent malfunctions due to the nature of their custom construction with used parts. Astromechs are usually stationed on board to make repairs on the fly and restore backups of ship computer systems.

B/SF-17 HEAVY BOMBER

APPEARANCES VIII
MANUFACTURER Slayn & Korpil
MODEL MG-100 Starfortress SF-17
TYPE Bomber

The Resistance's potent heavy bombers require significant hands-on management from their crew, which includes one pilot, two gunners, one flight engineer, and one bombardier. The ships are armed with three Merr-Sonn Munitions EM-1919 paired repeating laser cannons and six medium laser cannons, but the truly important payload is composed of a modular bombing magazine containing up to a total of 1,048 proton bombs. During the evacuation of D'Qar, the Resistance sends their entire fleet of heavy bombers to attack the First Order's Dreadnought *Fulminatrix*. Though Paige Tico's bomber successfully destroys its target, all of the Resistance's bombers are lost in the effort.

FULMINATRIX

APPEARANCES VIII **MANUFACTURER** Kuat-Entralla Engineering **MODEL** *Mandator IV*-class
TYPE Siege Dreadnought

When Iden Versio steals Imperial data about Project Resurrection, she also acquires the blueprints for the First Order's *Mandator IV*-class Siege Dreadnought. The massive warship is armed with two devastating orbital autocannons, 26 dorsal point-defense turrets to take out enemy ships, a myriad of TIE fighters, and six tractor beams. Iden Versio's information is passed on to Captain Poe Dameron, who uses it to destroy the Dreadnought *Fulminatrix,* which is bombarding the Resistance base on D'Qar. The destruction of the *Fulminatrix* is a major blow to the First Order, but comes at great cost to the Resistance as well.

RZ-2 A-WING

APPEARANCES VIII
MANUFACTURER Kuat Systems Engineering
MODEL RZ-2 A-wing interceptor **TYPE** Starfighter

Capitalizing on the popularity of the original A-wing starfighter flown by the Rebel Alliance during the Galactic Civil War, Kuat Systems creates a new version soon after the war's end. The RZ-2 A-wing incorporates the best upgrades made by rebel cells in the field while also elongating the bow of the ship for increased speed. These second-generation A-wings are armed with two Zija GO-4 laser cannons and two concussion missile launchers. A number of A-wings accompany the Resistance fleet during the evacuation of D'Qar, including one piloted by Blue Leader Tallissan Lintra. When Kylo Ren attacks the Resistance flagship, Tallissan is killed and her A-wing is destroyed.

U-55 ORBITAL LOADLIFTER

APPEARANCES VIII **MANUFACTURER** Sienar Fleet Systems **MODEL** U-55 **TYPE** Personnel transport

The U-55 is a basic shuttle craft found throughout the galaxy. The Resistance versions lack weapons or hyperdrives but are equipped with simple cloaking systems devised by technician Rose Tico. They are capable of transporting an average of 60 passengers and are normally used to transport dignitaries and Resistance members to and from secret meetings. When the Resistance is forced to leave the *Raddus*, its personnel escape aboard 30 U-55 "lifeboats" docked inside the flagship. Sadly, they are betrayed, and 24 U-55s are destroyed by the First Order before they can reach Crait.

NINKA

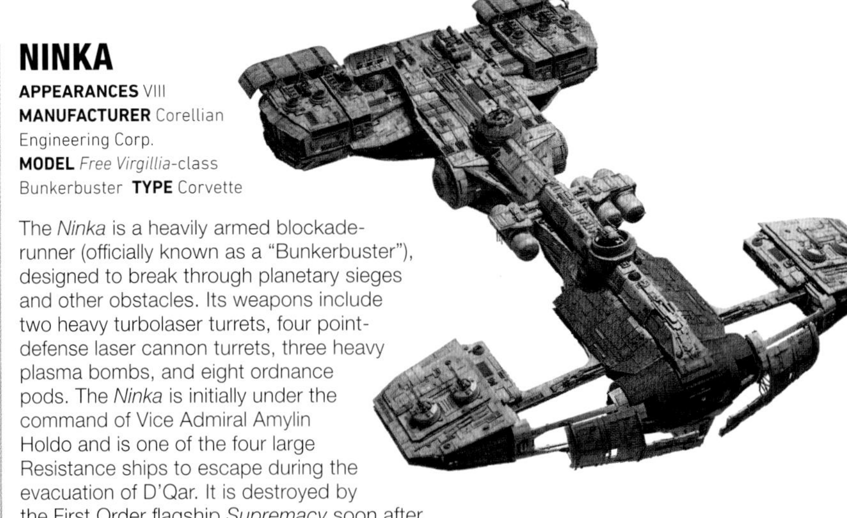

APPEARANCES VIII
MANUFACTURER Corellian Engineering Corp.
MODEL *Free Virgillia*-class Bunkerbuster **TYPE** Corvette

The *Ninka* is a heavily armed blockade-runner (officially known as a "Bunkerbuster"), designed to break through planetary sieges and other obstacles. Its weapons include two heavy turbolaser turrets, four point-defense laser cannon turrets, three heavy plasma bombs, and eight ordnance pods. The *Ninka* is initially under the command of Vice Admiral Amylin Holdo and is one of the four large Resistance ships to escape during the evacuation of D'Qar. It is destroyed by the First Order flagship *Supremacy* soon after.

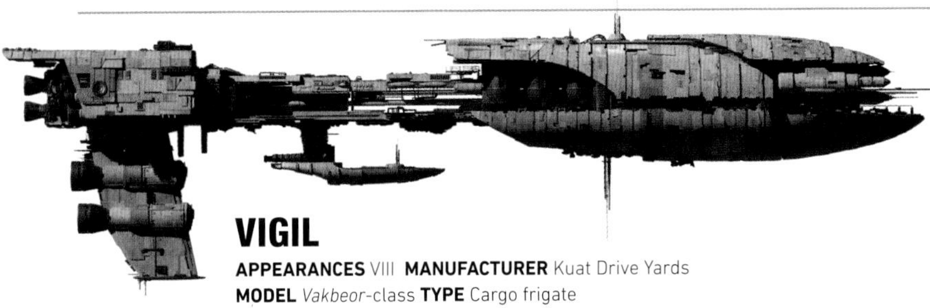

VIGIL

APPEARANCES VIII **MANUFACTURER** Kuat Drive Yards
MODEL *Vakbeor*-class **TYPE** Cargo frigate

The *Vigil* is captured by the Resistance from pirates during the Battle at the Chasidron Shoals. It has only light weapons systems, with four laser cannons and two tractor beam projectors, and it is supported by a crew of twenty-six. The *Vigil* falls under the command of Resistance Vice Admiral Joris and is one of four large ships that evacuate from D'Qar following the destruction of Starkiller Base. It is carrying vital Resistance supplies but is soon destroyed by the *Supremacy*.

LIBERTINE

APPEARANCES VIII
MANUFACTURER Guild d'Lanseaux
MODEL Custom **TYPE** Star Yacht

The *Libertine* is a star yacht stolen by the droid BB-8 and slicer DJ, who use it to rescue Resistance fighters Finn and Rose. They then fly from Canto Bight to the First Order Flagship *Supremacy*. The *Libertine* is formerly owned by Sienar-Jaemus Corporation manager, Korfé Bennux-Ai, a weapons dealer who sells his products to all sides in the fight between the First Order, and the New Republic and Resistance. The luxury craft is used by Bennux-Ai to host guests and strike business deals.

RADDUS

APPEARANCES VIII
MANUFACTURER Mon Calamari Shipyards and Corellian Engineering Corp. **MODEL** MC85
TYPE Star Cruiser

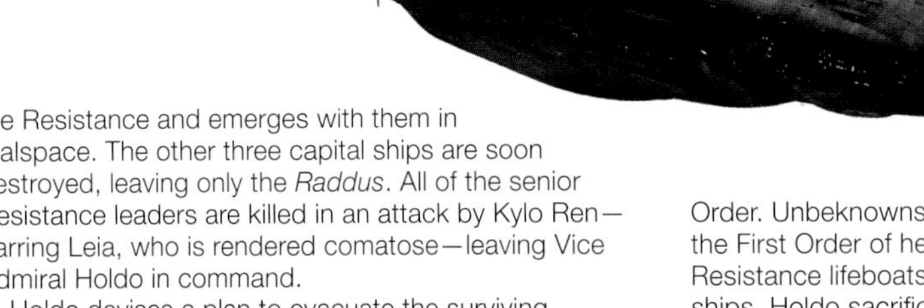

Destruction
Vice Admiral Holdo's final attack with the *Raddus* devastates the First Order fleet.

The *Raddus* is the flagship of the Resistance and the mobile command center of General Organa. Originally named the *Dawn of Tranquility*, it was decommissioned by the New Republic and then acquired by the Resistance. Admiral Ackbar successfully petitioned to have the ship renamed after the valiant Admiral Raddus, who gave his life at the Battle of Scarif to secure the Death Star plans.

The immense ship measures 3,438 meters (11,280 feet) in length, with a width of 707 meters (2,319 feet) and a height of 462 meters (1,515 feet). Its durasteel hull is heavily armored and it is protected by experimental deflector shields. The *Raddus* is a speedy ship for its size, with 11 sublight ion drives and a Class 1 hyperdrive. It is also powerfully armed, with 18 heavy turbolasers, 18 heavy ion cannons, 12 point-defense laser cannons and six proton torpedo launchers.

Following the destruction of the First Order's Starkiller Base, the Resistance is forced to evacuate their base on D'Qar. Four capital ships escape and successfully jump to hyperspace. However the First Order continues to track the Resistance and emerges with them in realspace. The other three capital ships are soon destroyed, leaving only the *Raddus*. All of the senior Resistance leaders are killed in an attack by Kylo Ren—barring Leia, who is rendered comatose—leaving Vice Admiral Holdo in command.

Holdo devises a plan to evacuate the surviving Resistance to the nearby planet Crait, fleeing aboard a small fleet of U-55 lifeboats. She elects to remain behind to pilot the *Raddus* alone, as a distraction to the First Order. Unbeknownst to Holdo, the traitor DJ informs the First Order of her plans, and they begin destroying the Resistance lifeboats. In an effort to save the remaining ships, Holdo sacrifices herself. She turns the *Raddus* toward the First Order's pursuing flagship *Supremacy* and jumps to hyperspace. The resulting collision tears the *Supremacy* in half, but also destroys the *Raddus*.

TIE SILENCER

APPEARANCES VIII **MANUFACTURER** Sienar-Jaemus Fleet Systems
MODEL TIE/vn space superiority fighter **TYPE** Starfighters

The TIE silencer is Kylo Ren's personal starfighter. It is exceptionally agile, making it a difficult craft to fly for even the most skilled pilots, however Kylo's connection to the Force makes him a natural pilot. The TIE silencer is 10.7 meters (35 feet) longer than a standard First Order TIE fighter. It is potently armed, with SJFS heavy laser cannons and missile launchers equipped with Arakyd ST7 concussion missiles, mag-pulse warheads, and proton torpedoes. This makes it ideally suited for attacking capital ships—something Kylo demonstrates when his attack on the *Raddus* destroys the ship's main hanger and wipes out the entire Resistance starfighter corps.

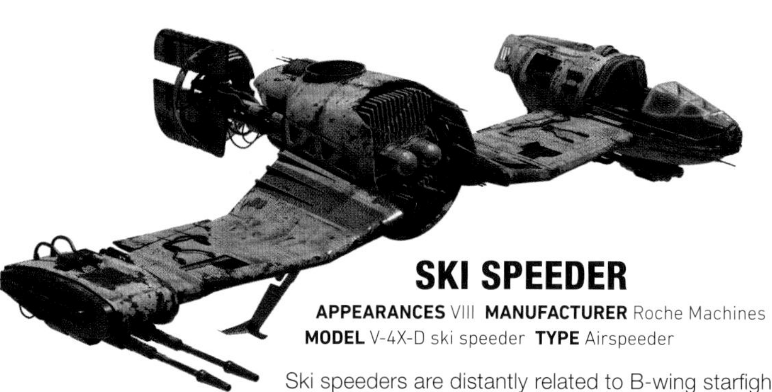

SKI SPEEDER

APPEARANCES VIII **MANUFACTURER** Roche Machines **MODEL** V-4X-D ski speeder **TYPE** Airspeeder

Ski speeders are distantly related to B-wing starfighters, as both ship types are inspired by Verpine designs. The V-4 series is originally created for asteroid slalom racing, but after the sport loses popularity, the design becomes a favorite craft of explorers. The Rebel Alliance brings a small contingent of ski speeders to Crait but abandons them there. When the Resistance flees to Crait decades later, they use the decrepit old ships to face the First Order. Led by Poe Dameron, they charge at the enemy's siege cannon, but are forced to turn back by the overwhelming firepower of the enemy walkers.

AT-M6

APPEARANCES VIII **MANUFACTURER** Kuat-Entralla Drive Yards **MODEL** All Terrain MegaCaliber Six **TYPE** Walker

The AT-M6 is the First Order's most powerful combat walker. A contingent of them is deployed to the surface of Crait to pursue the Resistance remnant. The AT-M6s are each armed with two heavy fire-linked dual laser cannons, two medium anti-ship laser cannons, and one MegaCaliber Six turbolaser cannon—the source of the vehicle's name—which is mounted on its back. The cannon is powerful enough to penetrate shields rated to resist orbital bombardment. The front legs are modified to support the immense additional weight of the cannon, as well as stabilize the walker to withstand the cannon's considerable recoil.

SUPREMACY

APPEARANCES VIII **MANUFACTURER** Kuat-Entralla Engineering **MODEL** *Mega*-class **TYPE** Star Dreadnought

The *Supremacy* is the flagship of the First Order and effectively its capital, serving as the mobile headquarters of Supreme Leader Snoke. The vast ship is more than 60 km (37 miles) wide, with a crew of 2,225,000 First Order personnel. The majority of the crew are adolescents still in training to become officers and stormtroopers. The *Supremacy* is protected by heavy turbolasers and ion cannons, anti-ship missile batteries, and multiple tractor beam projectors. The ship is also a gigantic weapons factory, able to produce AT-M6s, AT-ATs, AT-STs, and TIE fighters. Two *Resurgent*-class Star Destroyers can be docked internally and six more externally.

After the *Supremacy* joins the vessels commanded by General Hux, Snoke directs the attack on the Resistance fleet. Though the Resistance escapes, a tracker aboard the *Supremacy* traces them as they flee through hyperspace. The *Supremacy* emerges back into realspace in front of the Resistance and commences its attack, quickly destroying three of the four Resistance capital ships.

A short while later, Rey arrives aboard the ship, and is brought before Snoke. Kylo Ren suddenly turns on and kills his master, and both Rey and Kylo team up to defeat Snoke's Praetorian Guard—before Rey escapes alone. At the same time, Finn, Rose, and DJ board the ship. Finn and Rose believe DJ is helping them deactivate the First Order's hyperspace tracker, however he betrays them for a large sum of money. DJ informs the First Order of the Resistance's plans to flee to nearby Crait, and the First Order begin shooting down the defenseless Resistance U-55s.

With no other options left, Resistance Vice Admiral Holdo turns the Resistance flagship *Raddus* on the *Supremacy* and splits it apart in a cataclysmic collision. The Resistance remnant escapes to Crait, but are followed by Kylo Ren and the First Order, who depart the *Supremacy's* wreckage and continue their pursuit of the Resistance to the planet's surface below.

War machine
Huge hangars serve as assembly areas for legions of stormtroopers, as ground vehicles are loaded onto dropships in readiness for a planetary invasion.

KYLO REN'S TIE FIGHTER

APPEARANCES IX
MANUFACTURER Sienar-Jaemus Fleet Systems
MODEL TIE/wi modified interceptor
AFFILIATION First Order

Supreme Leader Kylo Ren speeds into battle aboard a TIE whisper modified to his exacting specifications, boasting increased range, speed, and firepower than the standard model. The whisper carries sensor-confusing technology that allows Ren to avoid enemy detection.

SITH TIE FIGHTER

APPEARANCES IX
MANUFACTURER Sienar-Jaemus Fleet Systems
MODEL TIE/dg starfighter
AFFILIATION Sith

Forged in secret by sinister forces, this new generation of TIE fighter swoops into action, with triangular wings that give the sleek Sith vessel a menacing profile.

Y-WING

APPEARANCES IX
MANUFACTURER Koensayr
MODEL BTA-NR2
AFFILIATION Resistance

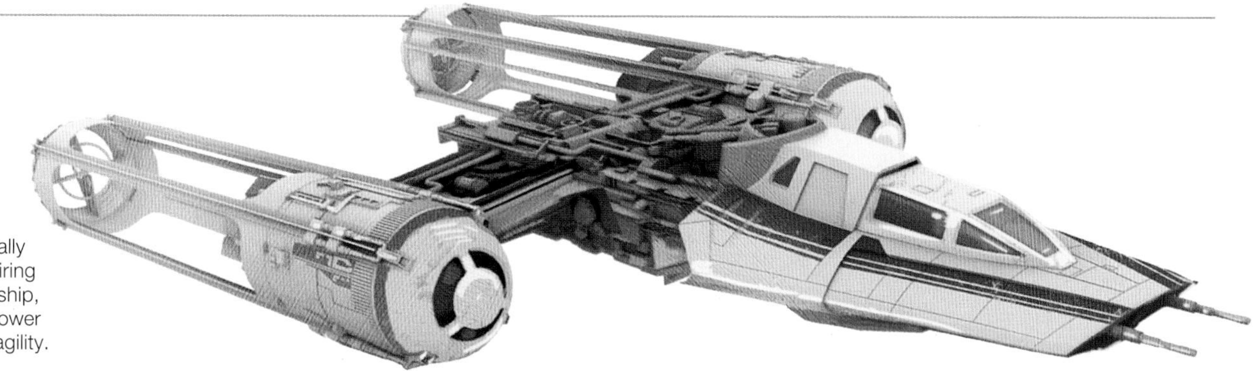

The BTA-NR2 is the latest version of a venerable starfighter design dating all the way back to the Clone Wars. Its unusually large ordnance bay and powerful forward-firing laser cannons make it a formidable attack ship, but as with all Y-wing variants, that hitting power comes at the price of reduced speed and agility.

BEHIND THE SCENES

"I've always been fascinated by speed, because of my interest in cars... because of that it has always been an element in the films." George Lucas

It is an overused term, but *Star Wars* vehicles truly are iconic. The *Millennium Falcon*, X-wing, and AT-AT are universal symbols not just of *Star Wars*, but also of the wider genre. When the saga's vehicles were designed, they were made to look real and lived in—as though they could exist and work in the way they are shown on screen. *Star Wars* is ultimately about characters, but the extraordinary diversity of its vehicles gives the series a richness that remains unparalleled in movie history.

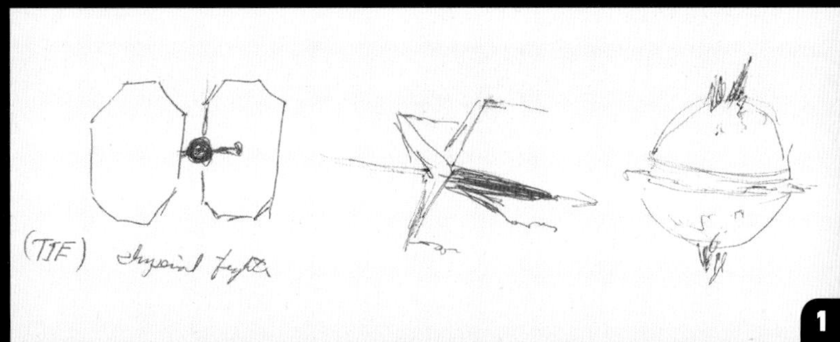

1

2

George Lucas gave these sketches of a TIE fighter, X-wing, and Death Star to concept artist Ralph McQuarrie when he started work on *Star Wars* **(1)** (he gave similar sketches to concept model maker Colin Cantwell). McQuarrie's concept artwork titled "Battle for the Death Star (fighters dive on sphere)" shows a preliminary concept for a Y-wing based on Colin Cantwell's design **(2)**.

3

4

This life-sized T-65 X-wing starfighter from *Star Wars*: Episode IV *A New Hope* is being lifted by a cable hooked to a crane outside "H" stage at Shepperton Studios, UK, so that it can be filmed from below to simulate takeoff **(3)**. The AT-AT walkers were based on Joe Johnston's vehicle designs. Models of various sizes were made and filmed using stop-motion and other techniques at ILM **(4)**.

5

6

The *Millennium Falcon* under construction at Elstree Studios, UK, for *Star Wars:* Episode V *The Empire Strikes Back* **(5)**. An AT-ST chicken walker model is painstakingly moved on a miniature Endor forest set by ILM model makers Paul Huston and Larry Tan for *Star Wars:* Episode VI *Return of the Jedi* **(6)**.

The digital animatic stage of Gasgano's podracer by David Dozoretz, one of the many spectacular vehicles to feature in the Boonta Eve Classic in *Star Wars:* Episode I *The Phantom Menace* **(7)**. Anakin Skywalker (Hayden Christensen) leaps aboard a swoop bike to rescue his mother in *Star Wars:* Episode II *Attack of the Clones*. The bluescreen will later be replaced by the arid landscape of Tatooine **(8)**.

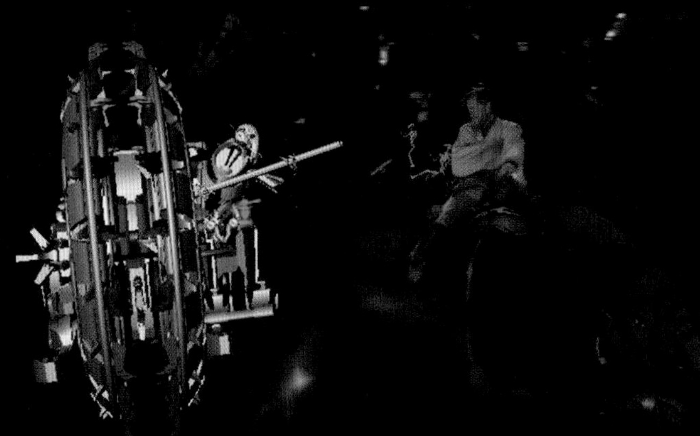

An early digital stage of the high-speed duel between General Grievous, aboard his wheel bike (an initial CGI rendering), and Obi-Wan Kenobi, riding a varactyl named Boga **(9)**. Many concept artworks are created before a design is finally chosen—this art of Jedi starfighters for *Star Wars:* Episode III *Revenge of the Sith* is by concept design supervisor Ryan Church **(10)**.

Cast and crew shoot a scene including the *Millennium Falcon* on the planet Ahch-To at Longcross Studios for *Star Wars*: Episode VIII *The Last Jedi* **(11)**. An early maquette for the *Fireball* starfighter, the primary vehicle seen in the animated TV series *Star Wars: Resistance* **(12)**.

INDEX

Page numbers in **bold** refer to main entries.

D

E

K

L

M

N

O

P

Q

R

S

T

U

V

W

Z

Senior Editor Emma Grange
Editor Matt Jones
Senior Designers Anne Sharples and Rob Perry
Project Art Editor Jon Hall
Designer Chris Gould
Pre-Production Producer Marc Staples
Senior Producer Mary Slater
Managing Editor Sadie Smith
Managing Art Editor Vicky Short
Publisher Julie Ferris
Art Director Lisa Lanzarini
Publishing Director Simon Beecroft

Design by Simon Murrell

For Lucasfilm
Senior Editor Brett Rector
Creative Director of Publishing Michael Siglain
Art Director Troy Alders
Story Group James Waugh, Pablo Hidalgo, Leland Chee, Matt Martin and Emily Shkoukani
Asset Management Steve Newman, Gabrielle Levenson, Tim Mapp, Bryce Pinkos, Erik Sanchez, Nicole LaCoursiere, Kelly Jensen and Shahana Alam

Dorling Kindersley would like to thank: Chelsea Alon at Disney; Lisa Lanzarini for cover design; David Fentiman and Emma Grange for additional text; Ruth Amos, Beth Davies, Alastair Dougall, David Fentiman, Shari Last, Lisa Stock, Nicole Reynolds and Cefn Ridout for editorial assistance; Lynne Moulding, Lisa Robb, Clive Savage and Jess Tapolcai for design assistance; Cameron + Company, Anna Formanek, Toby Truphet and Lauren Nesworthy for their work on the original edition; Maxine Pedliham for initial design concept; Helen Peters for the index and Julia March for proofreading.

This edition published in 2019
First published in Great Britain in 2015 by
Dorling Kindersley Limited
One Embassy Gardens, 8 Viaduct
Gardens, London, SW11 7BW

10 9 8 7 6 5 4 3
014-311512-Oct/2019

The authorised representative in the EEA
is Dorling Kindersley Verlag GmbH.
Arnulfstr. 124, 80636 Munich, Germany.

A CIP catalogue record for this book
is available from the British Library.
ISBN: 978-0-24135-766-8

Printed in China

For the curious

www.dk.com

www.starwars.com

This book was made with Forest Stewardship Council ™ certified paper– one small step in DK's commitment to a sustainable future. For more information go to www.dk.com/our-green-pledge

Carrie Fisher (Priness Leia) relaxes on set during a break in filming trash compactor scenes in *Star Wars*: Episode IV *A New Hope*

Joonas Suotamo (Chewbacca) sits down with an umbrella on location in Italy during a pause in filming for *Solo: A Star Wars Story*